THE OXFORD HISTORY OF
THE CHRISTIAN CHURCH

Edited by
Henry and Owen Chadwick

The Church in Africa
1450–1950

═══

ADRIAN HASTINGS

CLARENDON PRESS · OXFORD
1994

Oxford University Press, Walton Street, Oxford OX2 6DP
Oxford New York
Athens Auckland Bangkok Bombay
Calcutta Capte Town Dar es Salaam Delhi
Florence Hong Kong Istanbul Karachi
Kuala Lumpur Madras Madrid Melbourne
Mexico City Nairobi Paris Singapore
Taipei Tokyo Toronto
and associated companies in
Berlin Ibadan

Oxford is a trade mark of Oxford University Press

Published in the United States
by Oxford University Press In., New York

British Library Cataloguing in Publication Data
Data available.

Library of Congress Cataloging in Publication Data
The Church in Africa: 1450–1950/Adrian Hastings.
(The Oxford history of the Christian Church)
1. Christianity—Africa—History. 2. Christians, Black—Africa
—History. 3. Church and state—Africa. 4. Missions—
Africa—History I. Title. II. Series.
BR1360.H364 1994 276—dc20 94–5677
ISBN 0–19–826921–8: £60

1 3 5 7 9 10 8 6 4 2

Typeset by J&L Composition Ltd., Filey, North Yorkshire
Printed in Great Britain
on acid-free paper by
Biddles Ltd., Guildford and King's Lynn

PREFACE

Limitations are inevitable. A work of history must have its frontiers and yet it is often impossible to adhere to them very rigidly without cutting into a flow of interacting developments unduly. This book is about the Churches within black Africa. The history of Churches on the Mediterranean coast or in the south when composed principally of white people is excluded except in so far as it forms part of the story of a black Church. I have also, with regret, excluded Madagascar. Its Church history is exceptionally interesting but it stands essentially on its own and to do it justice would have required more space than I could afford.

The frontiers in time have been more elastic: 1450–1950 provides a clean 500 years but it is inevitably rather arbitrary and I have not forced myself to feel constrained by these dates. Medieval Ethiopia is the right place to start but it seemed sensible to review, at least briefly, the earlier history of Christianity in Africa. Moreover, fifteenth-century Ethiopia cannot make sense without quite detailed discussion of developments, monastic and royal, of a century earlier. At the other end, 1950 is no less unsatisfactory, as a sharp point of conclusion: 1960, 'the Year of Africa', is a better cutting-off point, beyond which I have not gone. Nevertheless, I have kept to 1950 in the title for two reasons beyond that of neatness. The first is that a very great deal was happening in the 1950s, a time when the Churches were growing very rapidly in societies conscious that their political future was about to see great changes. I have not had the space to focus on these developments in adequate detail. In many ways they can, anyway, be better studied with the 1960s. My second reason is that I have already done this in *A History of African Christianity 1950-1975*, published in 1979. Having had more space to deal with these decades there, I did not think it sensible to repeat it, except rather briefly, here. The intention of the book is to end with some account of where the Churches had reached on the eve of colonialism's collapse, but not to chart in detail the way they were beginning to respond to a new predicament. A history of African

Christianity 1960–90 could be of exceptional interest but at present the material is not available.

My indebtedness is, above all, to a small army of scholars who, over the last forty years, have made this book possible. It rests wholly on their shoulders, its special contribution being the attempt to make of so many different stories something of a single whole. Writing it has made me see clearly what very big gaps remain. On topic after topic, from sixteenth-century Ethiopia to the nineteenth-century missionary movement, there is not a single, wide-ranging, reliable modern work.

I have to thank the British Academy for a grant in 1990 to support study at Yale, and Yale Divinity School for a research fellowship both then and in 1988. The Overseas Ministries Study Center at Yale provided me on both occasions with hospitality and assistance of every sort for which I am particularly grateful. The librarians at the Divinity School and the Sterling Library at Yale were always immensely helpful, as have been those at Rhodes House, Oxford, and in the Brotherton here in Leeds. My wife has throughout supported and encouraged me in a work which has often seemed too dauntingly vast, since I agreed to undertake it in 1980. She has also improved its English at many points. I must also thank the Department of Theology and Religious Studies at Leeds not only for a generous grant towards the preparation of this book but also for providing a community of friendship, pleasure, and shared learning of a sort not these days so easily found in our harassed and over-competitive university world. Last, but first in the debt I owe, Ingrid Lawrie, whose commitment to the book has been throughout no less determined than my own. She has typed and revised every line, checked it for inconsistencies, struggled to meet deadlines by working late at night. For such professionalism, joined to affection, there is no adequate way of saying thanks.

ADRIAN HASTINGS

Leeds
August 1993

CONTENTS

A Note on Names   xi
List of Abbreviations   xiii

PART I. 1450–1780: A MEDIEVAL ENVIRONMENT

1. The Ethiopian Church in the Age of Zara Ya'iqob   3
    i. Introduction: The Council of Dabra Mitmaq   3
    ii. Coptic and Aksumite Origins   5
    iii. Ethiopia's Hebraic Character   11
    iv. Monasticism and Monarchy in the Fourteenth Century   17
    v. The 'House of Ewostatewos' and Sabbath Observance   28
    vi. The Policies of Zara Ya'iqob   34
    vii. The Age of Baida Maryam   42

2. Africa in 1500 and its Christian Past   46
    i. Society, States, Statelessness, and Religion   46
    ii. African Islam   54
    iii. The Christian Past of North Africa and Survival in Egypt   62
    iv. Nubia   67

3. The Kongo, Warri, Mutapa, and the Portuguese   71

   The Fifteenth and Sixteenth Centuries   71
    i. Portugal Overseas   71
    ii. Kongo and its Initial Evangelization   73
    iii. Benin and Mutapa   77
    iv. Kongolese Catholicism under Afonso I and his Immediate
       Successors   79

   The Seventeenth and Eighteenth Centuries   87
    v. The Diocese of São Salvador and the Jesuits   87
    vi. The Mission of the Capuchins   94
    vii. The Battle of Ambuila, Kimpa Vita, and the Antonian
       Movement   102
    viii. The Kongo Church in the Eighteenth Century   109
    ix. Angola, Sierra Leone, Warri, and Mutapa   118
    x. The Slave Trade and its Implications   123
    xi. An Evaluation   126

4. Riches to Rags: Ethiopia 1500–1800   130
      i. The Church of Lebna Dengel   130
     ii. The Jihad of Gran   136
    iii. Galawdewos, the Jesuits, and Enbaqom   139
    iv. Paez and Susenyos   148
      v. Mendes and Fasiladas   154
    vi. The Eighteenth Century   162

PART II. 1780–1890: FROM THE ANTI-SLAVERY TO TOTAL
SUBJUGATION

5. Equiano to Ntsikana: From the 1780s to the 1820s   173
      i. London, Africa, and Protestantism   173
     ii. West African Protestant Beginnings and the Foundation of
        Freetown   177
    iii. The Advance of Islam   188
    iv. Kongo Christianity under Garcia V   194
      v. South Africa: Genadendal, Bethelsdorp, and Kuruman   197
    vi. The Mission Village: A Discussion   209
   vii. Khoi Leadership and Ntsikana   215

6. The Lion Revived: Ethiopia in the Nineteenth Century   222
      i. The Age of the Princes   222
     ii. Tewodros 1855–68   229
    iii. Yohannes IV and Menelik   234

7. The Victorian Missionary   242

   The Evolution of a Movement   242
      i. Where Protestant Mission had Arrived by the 1840s   242
     ii. The Catholic Revival   248
    iii. David Livingstone and his Influence   250
    iv. Verona Fathers and White Fathers   253
      v. The State of Missionary Complexity by 1880   255

   Style, Priorities, and Mind   258
    vi. Missionary Characteristics and Life-Style   258
   vii. Missionary Teaching   270
  viii. The Uses of Medicine   275
    ix. Language and Translation   278
     x. Christianity, Civilization, and Commerce   282
    xi. The Three Selves and the Pursuit of Adaptation   293
   xii. What Missionaries Thought of Africa   298

8. Kings, Marriage, Ancestors, and God   306
      i. Monarchies and Christianization   306

ii.	Rain	313
iii.	Social Structure: Marriage, Circumcision, and Secret Societies	317
iv.	Ancestors, Deities, and God	325

9. Christian Life in the Age of Bishop Crowther — 338
  i. 'Black Europeans' — 338
  ii. Crowther and the Niger Diocese — 343
  iii. Yoruba Christianity — 349
  iv. The South African Predicament — 358
  v. Buganda: Conversion, Martyrdom, and Civil War in the 1880s — 371
  vi. Revival in the Kongo — 385
  vii. The Niger Purge — 388

PART III. 1890–1960: THE CHRISTIANIZING OF
HALF A CONTINENT

10. A Variety of Scrambles: 1890-1920 — 397
  The Context of Conversion — 397
  i. The Why and How of the Scramble — 397
  ii. Islam within the Scramble — 405
  iii. Missionaries and the Politics of Partition — 408
  iv. The Changing Shape of Missionary Endeavour — 417
  v. The Ownership of Land — 424
  vi. Missionaries as Critics of Colonialism — 428

  The Shaping of Conversion — 437
  vii. Black Evangelism: Some Southern Examples — 437
  viii. West African Conversion Movements in the Age of Harris — 443
  ix. The Catechist and his Tools — 453
  x. Logics of Conversion — 461
  xi. Buganda: mass Conversion in the 1890s — 464
  xii. Buganda as a Model for its Neighbours — 468
  xiii. A Comparison between Conversions — 475
  xiv. Varieties of Ethiopianism — 478
  xv. The Impact of World War — 487

11. From Agbebi to Diangienda: Independency and Prophetism — 493
  i. 'African Churches' in Nigeria and South Africa 1888-1917 — 493
  ii. The Rise of Zionism — 499
  iii. Elliot Kamwana — 504
  iv. Harrists and Kimbanguists — 505

   v. Aladura   513
  vi. East and Central Africa: From Kunyiha to Lenshina   519
 vii. Independency in the 1950s   525
viii. Causes and Motivations   527
  ix. The Character of Prophetic Christianity   533

12. **Church, School, and State in the Age of Bishop Kiwanuka**   540

   The State and the Missionary   540
    i The 1920s and Education   540
   ii The Second World War and the Triumph of Nationalisms   546
  iii Protestant Missionary Priorities in the Oldham Era   550
  iv The Catholic Breakthrough   559
   v The Missionary of the 1950s   567

   The Character of Christian Community   571
  vi Catholic Masaka   571
 vii Conversion, Community, and Catechist   575
viii Dreams   584
  ix Church and Society   586
   x Associational Religion: From Welfare Group and
    Manyano to Balokole and Jamaa   592
  xi A Modern Leadership   604

Appendix 1. Kings of Ethiopia and Kongo Referred
        to in the Text   611

Appendix 2. Maps   613
  1. Ethiopia, fifteenth to seventeenth centuries   613
  2. Christian Nubia   614
  3. The Kingdom of Kongo, fifteenth to seventeenth centuries   615
  4. Islam in West Africa and the nineteenth-century Fulani
     empires   616
  5. The West Africa coast in the late nineteenth century   617
  6. Protestant missions in South and East Africa established
     by 1885   618
  7. The principal Catholic missionary societies at work in
     Africa between 1850 and 1890   619
  8. Buganda and its neighbours   620

Bibliography   621

Index   686

A NOTE ON NAMES

I have tried to follow as uncomplicated an approach to names as I could, but any approach is bound to be somewhat arbitrary. The rendering of Ethiopian names is particularly varied. Thus, the name of the province I have called Shoa (following the *Cambridge History of Africa*) is also written in recent English works as Säwa, Shäwa, Shawā, and Shewa. I have followed modern standard practice in not anglicizing the names of Ethiopian kings: Galawdewos not Claudius.

I have used Kongo when referring to the ancient kingdom but Congo for the far larger Belgian colony, now the independent state of Zaïre, as also the French colony which has, in independence, retained the name of Congo. The river I have called either Zaïre or Congo. There is a comparable distinction between Buganda and Uganda.

I have not been fully consistent in the use of prefixes for the names of Bantu peoples. Normally I have dropped them, which is fairly standard practice. Thus I have spoken of the Shona or the Bemba, not the Mashona or the Babemba, but I have not done this in the case of the Baganda because much writing, following local insistence, retains the use of prefixes in their case. Thus any Shona, speaking English, will call the language Shona, while a Muganda in the same position will speak of Luganda. However, I see no reasonable alternative to employing 'Ganda' without a prefix adjectivally. For simplicity's sake, I have also omitted the use of dots in Yoruba names, again following the example of the *Cambridge History*.

It is hardly possible to be consistent in rendering the Christian names of Africans. The general practice is to call people as they called themselves in their primary language. However, this rule is more difficult to follow when the language someone spoke is not the language of the only accessible literature. In regard to people who spoke English well and are widely known by the English forms of their names, such as Samuel Crowther, John Chilembwe, or Joseph Kiwanuka, I have used the English form. For those, however, who always used a vernacular form of the name and are known by it, I

have retained it when possible, thus Gabrieli Kintu or Yohane
Masowe. Unfortunately there are many cases where the vernacular
form has not been used in the secondary, or even available primary,
literature. There is here no alternative to using the English form of a
name even though one may question whether the people concerned
ever spoke of themselves in this way.

As this history comes to an end in 1960, I have not used the names
of independent states adopted subsequently to that date to refer to
colonial states in the period 1890–1960. Thus I speak of Southern
Rhodesia, or just Rhodesia, not Zimbabwe; Nyasaland, not Malawi;
and Tanganyika not Tanzania. The same is true for towns: thus
normally Salisbury, not Harare; Élisabethville not Lubumbashi;
Leopoldville, not Kinshasa. However, in some cases, towns or their
black-inhabited parts were long known to Africans by the name
subsequently adopted. Leopoldville was always Kinshasa for Africans
(and even identified by that name on the railway station). Hence it is
appropriate to speak of Kinshasa already in 1920 in regard to its black
inhabitants.

ABBREVIATIONS

AA	*African Affairs* (London)
AAPS	Anglican Adam's Preaching Society
ABCFM	American Board of Commissioners for Foreign Missions
AFER	*African Ecclesiastical Review* (Kisubi and Eldoret)
AIM	African Inland Mission
AIPC	African Independent Pentecostal Church
AME	African Methodist Episcopal Church
Beccari	C. Beccari, *Rerum Aethiopicarum Scriptores Occidentales*, 15 vols. (Rome, 1903–17)
BIHB	*Bulletin de l'Institut historique belge de Rome* (Brussels)
BMS	Baptist Missionary Society
BSACH	*Bulletin of the Society of African Church History* (Aberdeen)
CAC	Christ Apostolic Church
CBMS	Conference of British Missionary Societies
CHA	R.D. Fage and Roland Oliver (eds.), *Cambridge History of Africa*, 8 vols. (Cambridge, 1977–86)
CIA	E. Fasholé-Luke, Richard Gray, Adrian Hastings, and Godwin Tasie (eds.), *Christianity in Independent Africa* (London, 1978)
CICCU	Cambridge Inter-Collegiate Christian Union
CMS	Church Missionary Society
CSCO	*Corpus Scriptorum Christianorum Orientalium* (Paris and Louvain)
CSM	Church of Scotland Mission
DTC	*Dictionnaire de théologie catholique* (Paris, 1899–1972)
EHA	*Études d'histoire africaine* (Kinshasa and Louvain)
GHA	*Unesco General History of Africa*, 8 vols. (1981–)
HIA	*History in Africa* (Atlanta, Ga.)
IBEA	Imperial British East African Company
IBMR	*International Bulletin of Missionary Research* (New Haven, Conn.)
IJA	*International Journal of African Historical Studies* (Boston, Mass.)

IMC	International Missionary Council
JAH	*Journal of African History* (Cambridge)
JES	*Journal of Ethiopian Studies* (Addis Ababa)
JHN	*Journal of the Historical Society of Nigeria* (Ibadan)
JRA	*Journal of Religion in Africa* (Leiden)
JSS	*Journal of Semitic Studies* (Manchester)
KISA	Kikuyu Independent Schools Association
KTWA	Kavirondo Taxpayers' Welfare Association
LIM	Livingstone Inland Mission
LMS	London Missionary Society
MMA	Antonio Brasio (ed.), *Monumenta Missionaria Africana*, 20 vols. (Lisbon, 1952–88)
MMS	Methodist Missionary Society
NGK	Nederduitse Gereformeerde Kerk
PFMR	Joseph Metzler (ed.), *Sacrae Congregationis de Propaganda Fidei Memoria Rerum* (Rome, 1971–6)
RHM	*Revue d'histoire des missions* (Paris)
RSE	*Rassegna di studi etiopici* (Rome)
SCH	*Studies in Church History* (Cambridge)
SIM	Sudan Interior Mission
SLB	*Sierra Leone Bulletin of Religion* (Freetown)
SMA	Society of African Missions (Cork and Lyons)
SPG	Society for the Propagation of the Gospel
UJ	*Uganda Journal* (Kampala)
UMCA	Universities' Mission to Central Africa
UN	United Nations
UNESCO	United Nations Educational, Scientific, and Cultural Organization
USPG	United Society for the Propagation of the Gospel

PART I

1450–1780
A MEDIEVAL ENVIRONMENT

1

THE ETHIOPIAN CHURCH IN THE AGE OF ZARA YA'IQOB

i. *Introduction: The Council of Dabra Mitmaq*

At the feast of Mary in the middle of August in the year 1449,[1] the Emperor of Ethiopia, Zara Ya'iqob, assembled a Church council in the monastery at Dabra Mitmaq in Shoa. It was called to resolve matters of great moment. Here were gathered in large numbers the Church's principal leaders, the two Egyptian metropolitans, the Abunas Mika'el and Gabri'el, the Abbots of Dabra Hayk, Dabra Libanos, Dabra Bizan, Dabra Maryam, Dabra Damo, and many other monasteries, together with the chief clerics of the royal and episcopal courts. But it was Zara Ya'iqob, who had significantly taken the regnal name of Constantine, who presided and it was, most certainly, his policies that were agreed upon. He had become emperor sixteen years before, in 1434, to rule over an Ethiopia larger, wealthier, richer in religion and culture than it had been in any previous age. Nor was Dabra Mitmaq chosen accidentally for an event which he intended to be of great significance in the enhancement of Ethiopia's ecclesiastical polity. It was in Tagulat, a favourite haunt of his mobile court, that he had himself founded the monastery of Dabra Mitmaq and given it the name of Mitmaq upon hearing of the demolition of an Egyptian monastery of the same name by the Muslims. That was the defiant action of a ruler whose sense of religious responsibility was profound, but it represented too a confident, almost aggressive, imperial Christianity.

Shoa, in the central highlands of Ethiopia, had only relatively recently become a firmly Christian province, but it was now the heart of the kingdom, the home of many of its most influential

---

[1] An alternative dating is 14 Feb. 1450 or 1451. For Aug. 1449 see G. Haile, 'The Letter of Archbishops Mika'el and Gabre'el Concerning the Observance of Saturday', *JSS* 26 (1981), 73–8, for a Feb. date see C. Conti Rossini, 'Il "Gadla Filpos" e il "Gadla Yohannes" di Dabra Bizan', *Atti della Reale Accademia dei Lincei*, 1900 5/8 (1903), 163.

monasteries, yet it was also strategically close to its most exposed eastern frontier, over which there was almost continuous warfare with the Muslim sultanate of Adal, centred upon Harar. In Shoa the heart of the kingdom had moved far south of its original fourth-century location at Aksum in Tigre or the later twelfth- or thirteenth-century capital of Lalibela. These holy places had by no means been abandoned. Aksum, only 100 miles from the Red Sea, remained the symbolic focus of the kingdom's identity, its single cathedral, home of the Ark of the Covenant, Ethiopia's original New Jerusalem. Here Zara Ya'iqob's own solemn coronation had taken place in scenes ritually reminiscent of Jesus' entry into the holy city. In Tigre too Dabra Damo and the other monasteries of ancient times retained a position of particular prestige as providing the link in monastic succession of all later Ethiopian monks back to Pachomius and Anthony, and the monastic succession in Ethiopian eyes was as precise and significant a chain as the episcopal. One hundred and fifty miles to the south of Aksum in the early thirteenth century the Emperor Lalibela, greatest of the Zagwe kings, had chiselled out the eleven subterranean churches named after him, the new capital modelled once more upon Jerusalem. It was intended, presumably, to outdo Aksum as the Ethiopic reincarnation of Zion. This was already a considerable move away from the coast into the Zagwe heartland of Lasta, but the political, military, and religious thrust of the Christian kingdom had advanced well south of Lasta by the fifteenth century. The kings of the revived 'Solomonic' line after 1270 continued to be crowned in Aksum, whose primacy they did not challenge by founding any new symbolic capital up-country. None the less they lived, for the most part, in Shoa. Dabra Mitmaq was a good 400 miles from Aksum, over 500 from the sea. Here in 1449 the Emperor, surrounded by his wives, his bishops, his abbots, his generals, was resolved to settle once and for all the problem of the Sabbath.

The status of the Jewish Sabbath had proved, religiously and politically, an awkward and divisive issue within the Ethiopian Church for centuries. Of late it had been the cause of schism. To understand why, we need to look back a good deal and to consider the way Ethiopia's self-consciousness had developed. The Church began in the fourth century with the Christian conversion of King Ezana of the small Semitic or Semiticized kingdom of Aksum upon the Red Sea coast, a kingdom already well established by that date, and spreading inland to absorb the Cushitic peoples of the highlands behind them. The first bishop, Frumentius—the first Abba Salama to the Ethiopians—was a Greek, consecrated and mandated by Athanasius, Patriarch of Alexandria, and it was one of the enduring peculiarities (and problems) of Ethiopian Church life that it was never accorded a metropolitan of its own race nor even—until the reign of Zara Ya'iqob, and then only exceptionally—more than one single bishop. When an abuna died an embassy had each time to make the difficult journey to Alexandria (and later to Cairo), laden with suitable gifts, to beseech his replacement. That explains why, in 1449, two Egyptian prelates, Mika'el and Gabri'el, were present at the Council of Dabra Mitmaq. But to understand the full significance of their presence and what they stood for, it is necessary to turn first to the history of the Church of Egypt itself from which they, Frumentius, and therefore the Ethiopian Church tradition as a whole, derived.

ii. *Coptic and Aksumite Origins*

The first beginnings of African Christianity are to be found in Alexandria, though they remain obscure enough. Alexandria was by far the most important centre of the Jewish diaspora in the Mediterranean world, both in terms of numbers and of intellectual vitality. It had become, *par excellence*, the spiritual and literary centre of Hellenistic Judaism and we could naturally expect early Christian history to be formed here more than anywhere. But it was not so. In point of fact we know next to nothing about the Church in Egypt during the first century and a half of its existence. Eusebius in the fourth century records the tradition that Mark established the Church of Alexandria. It may be true but no New Testament writing is connected with that city. There is no name of weight identified with the Church of Alexandria to have made its mark in Christian tradition in the sub-apostolic period: the contrast with Rome, or Antioch, or Corinth is exceedingly clear and somewhat strange. What would seem to have happened is this: while Christianity did develop to some extent in Alexandria from a very early date, it did so within a highly Jewish context which in fact inhibited its growth. For rapid expansion, one may surmise that the most favourable circumstances were those in which, while the Jewish diaspora did exist, it consisted of relatively small communities which functioned less as a source of large numbers of converts than as a stepping-stone to the Gentile world. Christianity needed that stepping-stone but it also needed to be able to get rather easily beyond it. In Alexandria the very size of the Jewish population and the definitely poor relations which had developed between Jew and Gentile would seem to have inhibited rather than contributed to Christian expansion. It was, presumably, from these early days that the practice of circumcision became established as a characteristic of Egyptian Christianity just as it must have remained a characteristic of the Christian Church of Jerusalem in the first century.

In the second century, in the reign of Trajan, the Jews of Cyrenaica and Egypt rose in a disastrous revolt as a result of which the Alexandrian Jewish community was reduced to a shadow of its former self. Only at this point, it would appear, did the Christian Church really begin to spread out into the Greek-speaking community of lower Egypt. In the particularly liberal and intellectual atmosphere of Jewish Alexandria it had developed not only a somewhat Judaeo-Christian character but an unusually philosophic and questioning one. The fact is that the only two second-century Christians of Egypt we know almost anything about are the Gnostic teachers Valentinus and Basilides; yet it was not the case (though some have claimed it to be) that second-century Egyptian Christianity was more or less entirely Gnostic. On the contrary, despite the overall paucity of evidence, what does exist suggests a central body of essentially orthodox Christians, from which increasingly the Gnostics were forced to separate.

It was probably only in the third century that the Christian Church effectively penetrated the native Coptic-speaking population. Yet, before the close of that century, most, if not all, the books of the Bible had been translated into Coptic, and even into the different varieties of Coptic, Sahidic, and Bohairic. Anthony, who knew no Greek, could follow the lessons read in church and he and his followers were reciting the psalms together in Coptic in the 290s. The *Rule* of Pachom, or Pachomius, drawn up about 321, assumes that the Psalter and Gospels were readily available in Coptic and there was, undoubtedly, much more than that. The monastic movement is inconceivable without a previous evangelization of Coptic communities and the translation of the Scriptures into several Coptic dialects, languages which hitherto had had next to no literature.

In undeniable fashion, fourth-century Egyptian Christianity was to be paradigmatic for the Africa of the future. Starting as a religion of the urban imperial civilization with its Greek language drawn from outside Africa, it had crossed the culture and language gap to appeal to the native African. It had done so by taking his language seriously. Biblical translation into Coptic seems both to have helped generate a new sense of cultural identity and to have triggered off, in monasticism, a new religious movement of amazing vitality which was soon to flood back across the universal Church, Greek- and Latin-speaking. Senior civil servants and subtle professors of rhetoric would, mysteriously enough, be swept off their feet by the life of Anthony.[2] The history of African Christianity—rather than the history of Christianity upon the continent of Africa—really begins with things like a third-century land register on the back of which has been written by a single hand a Graeco-Coptic glossary of words and phrases to Hosea and Amos; each column deals with twenty verses of text, the Greek first (in part abbreviated), then Coptic, always in full: the notes, quite probably, of a Greek-speaking evangelist for his class of Coptic catechumens.[3] It begins with Anthony, a Copt hermit, in the desert, yet marching down to Alexandria in support of the Greek-speaking Athanasius. It begins with Pachom, a pagan boy from far up the Nile who had been forcibly recruited, probably in 312, for the imperial army of Maximus Daia and was being transported, bewildered, down the river with a gang of other conscripts when one night at Luxor a group of Christians came on board with food and drink to minister to the conscripts. 'What would a Christian be?', he asked, and was converted by the reply, 'They bear the name of Christ, the only-begotten son of God, and do good to all men, hoping in him who made heaven and earth and us men.'[4] A few months later the war ended, the conscripts were released, and Pachom was back in upper Egypt. His Coptic-speaking coenobium founded at Tabennisi about 320 was the first recognizable monastery in Christian history. A movement begun by Anthony and Pachom, Coptic speakers caught up in a wave of mass conversion in the African countryside, was to prove one of the most truly decisive spiritual and institutional developments not only for the Egyptian Church, but for the world Church, and the Ethiopian Church too.

[2] Augustine, *Confessions*, book 8, 14-15.
[3] H. I. Bell and H. Thompson, 'A Greek–Coptic Glossary to Hosea and Amos', *Journal of Egyptian Archaeology*, 11 (1925), 241-6.
[4] The *Vita Prima*, see L. T. Lefort (ed.), *Les Vies coptes de S. Pachôme et de ses premiers successeurs* (Louvain, 1943), 82, cf D. Chitty, *The Desert a City* (1966) 7-8.

The impressive richness and strength of Egyptian Christianity in its greatest age from Anthony to Cyril derived very largely from its ability to cross the language and culture divide easily and unself-consciously. Most of the translating was from Greek to Coptic,[5] but it is clear that the amount of Christian literature available in Coptic was now considerable and its Gnostic side should not be exaggerated. The important thing was that the liturgy was in both languages, the Bible was in both languages, there were monasteries functioning in both languages and much toing and froing between them. Doubtless most of the academic theology was written in Greek, while most of the monks spoke Coptic, but what comes across is a sense of a united rather than a segregated experience. Athanasius had considerable personal responsibility for the way things developed.[6] He could, without doubt, be a tough, even ruthless, fighter and ecclesiastical administrator, the Cardinal Manning of the fourth century, but he was also a churchman of exceptional vision and wide experience as well as being a theologian of outstanding coherence and depth. It was the combination of the speculative and the practical in his character which made him so influential. There had been a wide cultural and linguistic gap between Alexandria and the Coptic countryside and it was by no means self-evident that the bishop of the one would have the full support of the other. Undoubtedly Dionysius the Great, the Bishop of Alexandria in the mid-third century, had already done something in church terms to bridge that gap and establish the Bishop of Alexandria's wider Egyptian role, but it seems to have been Athanasius, in his own person Greek theologian and Egyptian ascetic, who really united the two: author of the *De Incarnatione* but also of the *Life of Anthony*. It was his working knowledge of Coptic, his friendship with Anthony, Pachom, and Theodore, which forged the characteristic shape of Egyptian Christianity.

And it was Athanasius who, about 340, consecrated Frumentius as bishop for Aksum and so mysteriously laid down the ground lines of Ethiopian Christianity as in very significant ways an extension of that of Egypt. When one sees the use of Coptic in the fourth-century Egyptian Church and the anonymous translation of the Scriptures

---

[5] There was, however, also translation from Coptic to Greek. See e.g., R. Draguet, 'Notre Édition des recensions syriaques de L' "Asceticon" d'Abba Isaie', *Revue d'histoire ecclésiastique*, 63 (1968), 843-57.
[6] See, in particular, W. H. C. Frend, 'Athanasius as an Egyptian Christian Leader in the Fourth Century', in *Religion Popular and Unpopular in the Early Christian Centuries* (1976).

into it, one naturally expects an extension of the Egyptian Church to do the same. Which is what happened. The Ethiopian Bible is a remarkable achievement, but its production was clearly taken for granted in the missionary practice of the time. Again, we do not know just how or when or by whom the Scriptures were translated into Ethiopic—probably it was done bit by bit and by more than one hand—but we can be certain that the New Testament was translated from Greek at a quite early stage in the history of the Church of Aksum, certainly before the end of the fifth century. The Old Testament was at least no later and may well have been initially translated, at least in parts, direct from Hebrew.[7] The mission of Frumentius was only a start. We know very little of its immediate consequences but two of them seem certain enough. It established a permanent relationship of dependence upon the Patriarchate of Alexandria and it gave Ethiopia what was essentially the Egyptian liturgy and the Egyptian theological tradition: an intense commitment to the Council of Nicaea and to the teaching of the great Alexandrians Athanasius and Cyril. But Ethiopian tradition also attaches much importance to the arrival of the 'Nine Saints', nine monks, probably from Syria, rather over a century later. They have often been characterized as 'anti-Chalcedonians', the source of Ethiopia's alleged monophysitism. They have also been claimed as Chalcedonians. Again, the fact is that we know very little about them, but the evidence suggests that for long after this the beliefs of the Ethiopian Church were pre-Chalcedonian rather than anti-Chalcedonian. If Monophysite, it was only verbally so, rather firmly following the essentially orthodox teaching of Cyril of Alexandria. Ethiopia's Christological faith, expressed again and again with great firmness and subtlety, was and remained substantially no different from that of Rome or Constantinople.[8]

What the Nine Saints most definitely did do was to establish a number of monasteries around Aksum in Tigre, among them Dabra Damo, which would remain for more than a millennium the most decisive institutions for the passing-on of the tradition and ministry of the Church, the copying of manuscripts, the cultivation of a minimum core of theological learning. The *Rule* of Pachom and the

[7] See R. H. Charles, 'Ethiopic Version', in J. Hastings (ed.), *Dictionary of the Bible*, i (1902), 791–3.
[8] B. M. Weischer, 'Historical and Philological Problems of the Axumitic Literature (especially in the Qerellos)', *JES* 9/1 (1971), 83–93.

Life of Anthony were now, if not earlier, translated into Ethiopic. At much the same time a number of other books were to be translated which would be profoundly influential in the long and lonely course of Ethiopian Christian history. One example is the *Shepherd* of Hermas, which Athanasius used as a textbook for catechumens and Clement of Alexandria had regarded as part of the canon. Here in fact, in Ethiopia, it did become an additional canonical book. On the Old Testament side there were more—the Book of Enoch,[9] the Book of Jubilees, and others. In general these additions to the canon either reflected or easily contributed to a somewhat Judaizing form of Christianity, something in its way not surprising in a child of Alexandria. The Ethiopian Christian library remained a small one, at least until the fourteenth century, but it included the decrees of the first three councils together with its fundamental work of theology, the *Qerellos*, an anthology consisting principally of the writings of Cyril of Alexandria. Whatever survived from this early period seems in later ages to have merged, in terms of category, into one large canonical whole. To understand the subsequent Christianity of Ethiopia, one needs to envisage a process of continual redigestion across centuries of a very limited range of texts, a process carried out with no more than the most minimal contact with the rest of the Church.

In its early days, the Christian kingdom of Aksum had been a not too remote or special part of the Christian world of the eastern Mediterranean. In the sixth century in the reign of King Caleb it had become a power of some importance, the principal Monophysite kingdom, a state to which Coptic Monophysites could look for patronage and with which Justinian could need to negotiate. It is the period in which the Kebra Nagast, the supreme myth of Ethiopia's Solomonic origins, was probably first written. It was only with the coming of Islam in the seventh century that regional power was replaced by isolation. The Red Sea soon fell under Islamic control; the Church of Alexandria lost much of its authority and wider significance. The kingdom of Ethiopia withdrew little by little away

---

[9] It is certainly odd that the Jewish Book of Enoch, a work actually quoted in the New Testament (Jude 14–15) and written for the most part in the 1st or 2nd cent. BC, should have disappeared from the whole of the rest of the world, except in Aramaic, Greek, and Latin fragments, while more than thirty manuscripts of it exist in Ethiopic, cf. M. A. Knibb, *The Ethiopic Book of Enoch*, 2 vols. (1978); Matthew Black, *The Book of Enoch or I Enoch* (Leiden, 1985).

from the Red Sea inland into the highlands. While never wholly shorn of wider contacts, these very nearly withered away. There were decades in which there was no abuna sent from Egypt and the shortage of priests could become perilous. It is noteworthy that the kings of Aksum minted coins from the third century to the eighth, after which there were no more. In these circumstances of quite extraordinary religious and political isolation, while the Christian identity of the kingdom was continuously reaffirmed, its form developed in ways significantly distinct from those of the central Christian traditions, Greek and Latin, from which initially it may have been little different—no more than that of other outlying areas.

iii. *Ethiopia's Hebraic Character*

There are no Ethiopic manuscripts of any sort extant in date prior to the thirteenth century, and inevitably there must be a considerable measure of surmise as to how to explain the way the Church had developed by the later Middle Ages (when we first know much about it) and especially its strikingly Hebraic character. Besides the keeping of the Sabbath, this includes the acceptance of dietary prescriptions about clean and unclean animals, the concept of ritual pollution and cleansing, circumcision, the threefold arrangement of churches (divided into areas for priests, males, and females), forms of music, and the central liturgical importance for the Ethiopian Church of the Ark of the Covenant.

Theoretically there would seem to be four distinct ways of explaining all this. The first accords with Ethiopia's traditional self-interpretation and is one accepted by some of the best modern scholarship: the people of Aksum, or some of them, had been converted to Judaism prior to their conversion to Christianity and retained many Judaic practices after their second conversion. The second explanation is that Ethiopia's pagan, Cushitic, and Semitic customs had a lot in common with early Israelite religion, that much of this survived Christian conversion and was subsequently justified in terms of Old Testament parallels. The third is that the Egyptian Christian tradition was, for whatever reason, far more 'Judaic' than either the Antiochene or the Latin and that this quality was passed across to Ethiopia, though subsequently, little by little, reduced in its homeland. The fourth is that, isolated for centuries from the rest of the Christian world, but in possession of the Old Testament and not so much else, the Ethiopian Church felt the latter's impact far more than did other Churches and slowly remoulded itself along Old Testament lines.

The truth may well lie in a combination of several, possibly all four, of these hypotheses. Thus circumcision had long been part of the culture of the peoples of this part of Africa, though this included female circumcision, something never practised by Israel. Ethiopian Christians practise both.[10] It is highly improbable that they learnt either through Jewish conversion. Nevertheless, circumcision became in time part of their 'Hebraic' identity. While male circumcision is always performed on the eighth day and, among all the peoples who practise circumcision, only Jews and Ethiopians tie it to this particular point, this does not of itself demonstrate direct Jewish influence upon Ethiopia. It is as likely that it was when already Christian that the Ethiopians revised their existing male circumcision rites in accordance with Old Testament rules.

There are, however, two pieces of evidence—neither decisive but both of considerable weight—which have been taken to point to a direct, pre-Christian, Jewish influence, an influence in no way inherently implausible given the certain fact that there were very considerable Jewish colonies in the South Arabian peninsula in the first centuries of the Christian era.

The first piece of evidence for an original Judaic contribution to Ethiopian religious history is, of course, the Ethiopian tradition itself, both Christian and Falasha, that their religious (and physical) descent goes back to no less than the Queen of Sheba and Solomon. The importance of this myth is that it shows that Ethiopian Christians have for centuries believed that they had been Jews before they were Christians. While the classic account of this ancestry is to be found in the Kebra Nagast, whose present form and translation from Arabic dates from the fourteenth century, it is certain that the tradition far pre-dates that period and is witnessed to by the Armenian writer Abu Salih, living in Egypt in the late twelfth century.[11] It seems most probable that the substantial core of the Kebra Nagast dates from no later than the sixth century and the age of Caleb and was originally composed in Coptic to glorify the Ethiopian monarchy of the

[10] So do Coptic Christians. For female circumcision in the Coptic Church, see Otto Meinardus, *Christian Egypt, Faith and Life* (Cairo, 1970), 318–41.

[11] Abu Salih, *The Churches and the Monasteries of Egypt and Some Neighbouring Countries*, ed. B. T. A. Evetts (Oxford, 1895), 284–91.

period, as heir to Solomon, superior in authority to the emperors of Byzantium and destined protector for the whole Monophysite world.[12] If so, it is improbable that the tradition of Jewish descent simply began then; in which case it is very close indeed to the Christian conversion of King Ezana in the fourth century.

It is, however, certain from inscriptions that Ezana himself moved to Christianity not from Judaism but from belief in a polytheist pantheon. Hence it remains possible to regard the Kebra Nagast tradition as devoid of any historical foundation whatsoever, a mere matter of Ethiopian musings upon Acts 8: 26–39, 1 Kings 10, and Matthew 12: 42. If Philip the Evangelist could convert to Christian faith an Ethiopian eunuch, the treasurer of Candace, Queen of the Ethiopians, who had been to Jerusalem to worship, was not the implication of this strange story that the Ethiopians were believing Jews already? Were not the two 'Queens of the south' to be linked together? While we know that scholars tend to place Candace far away from modern Ethiopia, Ethiopians did not. The myth of the Kebra Nagast could be woven from such threads. Yet it seems at least tenable to argue that there is rather more to it historically than this: the story in Acts could reflect the existence at the time of 'black Jews' on the Red Sea coast south of Egypt, and the Kebra Nagast could be correct in claiming that the people of Aksum had in part been Jews before they were Christians. If the people of Aksum, to whom Frumentius preached, retained as Christians elements of their previous customs and beliefs, but the latter had already in part been Judaized, then they could in terms of religious inheritance be seen as Jewish Christians as well as African Christians. That is indeed how they have long regarded themselves.

The second piece of evidence has been the existence of the Falasha, a small group of people in north-west Ethiopia accepting the Old Testament and living according to it as faithfully as they can, but who are not Christians. The Falasha must surely be one of the most mysterious of Africa's peoples, 'black Jews'. They were not Jews, being no different ethnically and linguistically from their Ethiopian neighbours. They knew themselves as 'the House of Israel', Beta Israel, yet in identifying themselves with Israel, and using its name, they were not as such doing anything very different from Christian

[12] I. Shahid, 'The Kebra Nagast in the Light of Recent Research', *Le Muséon*, 89 (1976), 133–78.

Ethiopians who thought of themselves in the same way. Their literature, in so far as it exists, is Judaic, but quite pre-Talmudic. Their lives have in practice been dominated by rites of purification and an especially high view of the Sabbath, but their customs include non-Jewish practices such as female circumcision, and monasticism was central to their religious life.

When did they begin? From the fourteenth century Ethiopian records speak of groups of *áyhud*, 'Jews', but the term was widely used for unorthodox Christians of any sort. The medieval records seem mostly to regard these 'Jews' as renegade Christians and it is at least plausible to accept that judgement as largely true.[13] If there was a strong Hebraizing movement at work within later medieval Ethiopian Christianity (and there was), a movement insisting upon taking more and more parts of the Old Testament *au pied de la lettre*, then it is not at all impossible to imagine a comparable movement in the earlier and still more uncontrolled period going still further and coming to reject anything of the New. It has in fact happened in the twentieth century in Uganda,[14] a parallel which needs to be pondered. If the origins of the Uganda Bayudaya were not known and they were only discovered a century or two hence, direct Jewish influence might well be claimed for their beginning. Christians may consider a reversion to the Old Testament as the primary or unique sacred Scripture as perverse or inexplicable but in fact it fits the needs of an African people more obviously than the New. It has to be remembered that the Ethiopian Church, especially prior to the thirteenth century, was wholly decentralized and different groups of people in the mountains might well develop in very different ways, especially if in one area the Christian priesthood actually disappeared for a while, due to a prolonged absence of ordinations, which was only too likely. Remember too that in Ethiopian manuscripts the Bible (Old and New Testaments) was never all in one piece. Separate manuscripts were needed for several different parts. It is even reasonable to imagine a place where only some of the Old Testament books remained available.

---

[13] The hagiographer of the Ewostathian monk Gabra-Iyasus, who worked among them, did, however, accept the view that they descended from Jewish immigrants of the 1st cent. See C. Conti Rossini, 'Note di agiografia etiopica, Abiya-Egzi', 'Arkaledes e Gabra Iyasus', *Rivista degli studi orientali*, 17 (1938), 446.

[14] See Arye Oded, 'The Bayudaya of Uganda', *JRA* 6 (1974), 167–86; also the odd Italian example of a village converting to Judaism, without apparently knowing that there were still any Jews in the world, E. Cassin, *San Nicandro* (Paris, 1957).

If such a development could almost have been accidental, it is more likely that it depended too on conscious choice. If the early Ethiopian Church carried an especially heavy Judaic element, it is very understandable that this element would—as in Egypt—come later under attack from a more 'Christianizing' viewpoint but, equally, that it should in such circumstances be adhered to at whatever cost by others. It looks rather as if, between the ninth and the twelfth century, this is what may have happened. While the Christian Church of the Zagwe period as a whole moved somewhat away from its Hebraism, a minority developed instead into a segregated and consciously non-Christian Beta Israel. The Zagwe glorification of Sunday by the one side, of the Sabbath by the other, would seem to represent already by the thirteenth century both the symbolic differentiation and, perhaps, the actual grounds for separation. While one is suggesting that the Falasha should almost certainly not be seen as the survival across a thousand years of a distinct group of Judaized Ethiopians never affected by the Christian conversion of the country, their existence does witness to a Judaic tradition which is embedded as deeply as the Christian within Ethiopian religion.

The earliest evidence we actually have of them, from the later Middle Ages, shows the Falasha as still not too sharply separated from Christians in terms of experience. Both sides held to Judaic usages like circumcision and food taboos, both sides were open to Christian developments like monasticism. Above all there is no single element of Falasha religious practice which requires explanation in non-Ethiopian terms. We know of Christians who continued to become Falasha, indeed Beta Israel sources attribute the major elements of their religion to former Christian monks, Abba Sabra and Sagga Amlak; we are told too that other Falasha became Christians (not only under royal pressure, but also through the preaching of saints).

Without any possible doubt, however, the Beta Israel had come to exist as a distinguishable group of Ethiopians prior to the late medieval monastic and royal influences which so largely reshaped their community life. They possessed both the Old Testament in a common translation with the Church and the national mythology of descent from Solomon and the Queen of Sheba. They glorified the Sabbath and practised Judaic dietary prescriptions and the laws of ritual pollution more rigorously than the Christians. They were not followers of Christ nor even theoretically monogamous, but it is in their relationship with Christianity, rather than their separation from it, that they throw light upon the deep Judaism of the Ethiopian religious tradition as a whole.

It would certainly be mistaken to imagine that the amalgam of Christian and Jewish elements as encountered in the medieval and post-medieval Ethiopian Church dates as such from the beginning of the Church. Rather was there a continuous process across many centuries of adoption, rejection, and reinterpretation. The missionaries—Frumentius and the Nine Saints—who established the Church in Aksum were not Jewish Christians and the Christianity they initiated will not have had the character it later developed. Instead, what seems to have happened is that the Ethiopian Church, almost wholly isolated from the rest of the Christian world for five centuries, from the seventh to the twelfth, but possessing both a conscious tradition of Jewish origin and the full text of the Old Testament, little by little shaped its practice in conformity, not only with its central Christian faith, but also with its sense of Israelite identity. This was not achieved in one harmonious and timeless way. It was a backwards, forwards movement, challenged from time to time both from the inside and the outside of the Church. Elements of a specifically Judaic character, the Queen of Sheba story especially, came to be fastened upon more and more deliberately as the characterizing marks of Ethiopian identity and pride, yet this was not done for the most part within a diminishing sense of Christian identity. A minority may indeed, deliberately or inadvertently, have taken this path and so found themselves Falasha. The very temptation to do so could help explain the deep rage of the majority with those for whom Jewishness came to exclude Christianity, a rage very clearly present in the medieval Ethiopian Church. But certainly the detailed practice of the Ethiopian Church in, say, the sixteenth century (when it came under such heavy fire from the Jesuits) is not to be explained in simple terms either of 'survivals' from pre-Christian times or of a long process of medieval 'corruption' of a Church initially no different from that of Egypt or Syria. It was rather the product of a complex historical, religious, and cultural process lasting more than 1,000 years, most details of which it is now quite impossible to unravel.

In regard to this question it should, finally, be emphatically asserted that a recognition of the highly Judaic character of much Ethiopian Church practice, whatever its source, is in no way equivalent to a denial of its authentically Christian character. There is no single Christian way of relating New Covenant to Old. That constitutes one of the great ambiguities of the Christian tradition. The relationship between the two did, indeed, become the first major theological and practical issue to face the Church, setting a fairly radical Pauline position squarely in opposition to that of James and, still more, 'Judaizers' more conservative than James. Did 'fulfilment' imply displacement or did it imply continuity? In practice almost every answer includes a bit of both but can still lean heavily one way or the other. Certain guide-lines were laid down at the Council of Jerusalem but they could be, and were, interpreted and applied in a variety of ways. The Pauline position was never the only acceptable one. While the early Church of Jerusalem had cherished a Jewish Christian tradition which did not survive as such, neither was it condemned. But elements of it did live on in Alexandria and elsewhere. The Ethiopian Church is important theologically just because, over long years and with doubtless inadequate self-interrogation, it became more than any other surviving Church the heir and continuer of the original tradition of Jewish Christianity. Without recognition of this inheritance its medieval history is inexplicable.

iv. *Monasticism and Monarchy in the Fourteenth Century*

Ethiopian Hebraism did, however, often worry the Egyptian abunas sent from Alexandria (and later from Cairo) to rule and teach the Christians of this remote and mountainous land. An abuna spoke Coptic, or, later, Arabic. The learning of Ethiopic, at least for more than liturgical purposes, will often have been beyond him. He was immensely dependent upon the Ethiopian clergy who surrounded him and interpreted for him. He often arrived, an elderly monk from the monastery of St Anthony in the desert, after long years in which there had been no abuna. He was, especially in the earlier period, a bit of a queen bee (bishops in early Christian Ireland seem to have had somewhat the same function), his chief duties being to crown the king and ordain priests and deacons. No one else was able to ordain. He had as well to consecrate *tabots*, and to excommunicate heretics and rebels. He could, all the same, become politically a very powerful figure, especially after the death of a king and during a period of minority. He was, above all, the symbol of the catholicity of the

Church, one and universal. He was the proof that, however isolated Ethiopia might be in practice, in principle its Church and its State as well were not merely national entities but parts of the one great Christian world. Inevitably, however, his teaching role was a limited one. Yet it was not non-existent and, understandably enough, an abuna was likely to be worried by much that he saw around him in Ethiopia: not only the strange Judaic practices, but the theological ignorance, and the manifest prevalence of paganism within so much of the Christian kingdom. If the keeping of the Sabbath over and above Sunday was worrying to a medieval Egyptian monk, it was not, by any means, his only worry.

Even the matter of circumcision could cause tension. The Christian populace of Ethiopia was so very firmly committed to circumcision before baptism. There seems no particular theological pressure behind this, but doubtless in the common mind, however much circumcision was basically there because it was part of age-old Ethiopian custom, it could be perceived as the way whereby the whole nation retained its corporate identity as Israel. Pauline remarks on the subject were ignored. As the Copts of Egypt also practised circumcision, this custom was not as such a worry for the Abuna. In so far as there was tension over this, it would seem to have been the other way: a theologically minded abuna might occasionally, under a bit of Pauline inspiration, suggest that circumcision did not actually matter all that much. To suggest even so much could, however, worry his hearers exceedingly and in one case the rumour got around in consequence that the abuna in question (Bishop Yohannis) was in fact uncircumcized. It seemed scandalous, and a petition was submitted to the king that the matter be remedied. Fortunately the Abuna was able to show that he was in point of fact circumcized already. The incident illustrates how easily misunderstandings could arise between Christian theology and national tradition and how limited was the abuna's authority when the fundamental character of Ethiopian tradition was in question.

From the fourteenth century, however, that authority did undoubtedly grow. The arrival of the Abuna Ya'iqob in 1337 marks, perhaps, the beginning of a new era. Upon one side circumstances called for greater ecclesiastical leadership. It was the zenith of the power of the Emperor Amda Seyon. State and Church had expanded. New monasteries were opening in many parts. There was, clearly enough, both a great need and considerable desire for improvement in ecclesiastical administration, theological knowledge, moral standards, and missionary enterprise. Ya'iqob was a man of both vision and determination, an active pastoral archbishop rather than a mere dispenser of sacraments, and, as we shall see in due course, he would in consequence finally be dismissed from the country. Nevertheless, from now on the abuna was increasingly important. Indeed, Ya'iqob's successor, Salama, abuna from 1348 to 1388, was in Ethiopian eyes the greatest of all metropolitans and seen as responsible for a great increase in Ethiopic Christian literature translated from the Arabic. Furthermore, he extensively revised the Ethiopic Bible itself. In the words of the Synaxarium, 'From your lips sweeter than the scent of myrrh . . . came forth books from Arabic to Ge'ez.'[15]

Important symbolically, and even at times effectively, as the abuna was, the emperor was undoubtedly very much more so. The Ethiopian Church and the monarchy had been as one from the beginning, the conversion of Ezana. Christianity here had come down from above rather than up from below. The identity and spread of the kingdom were inevitably closely bound to the identity and spread of Christianity. The latter might flourish within its borders but seems never to have gone far beyond them, though doubtless Christian migrants to the highlands in the ninth or tenth century were very much on, at times even over, the border, and fourteenth-century monks were not afraid to evangelize areas ruled by pagan chiefs. Again, there were many non-Christians within the kingdom and the kings prior to Zara Ya'iqob recognized this, even by giving high position to Muslims in Muslim areas and (in earlier years at least) Falashas in Falasha areas. Amda Seyon had incorporated so many non-Christians into his realm, and he was, moreover, at times so irritated with the behaviour of the monks, that he in fact seems to have adopted a policy of general religious tolerance. 'Go and live according to the rules and customs of your ancestors,' he is said to have remarked to a group of prospective converts who had declared themselves willing to respond to monastic preaching.[16] Nevertheless, the character of the kingdom was indisputably Christian and the loyalty of non-Christians was almost always questionable. No king could fail to recognize that the strengthening of the State would be

[15] A. Van Lantschoot, 'Abba Salama metropolite d'Éthiopie (1348–1388) et son rôle de traducteur', *Atti del convegno di studi etiopici* (Rome, 1960), 397–401.
[16] C. Conti Rossini (ed.), *Acta S. Basalota Mika'el et S. Anorewos*, CSCO 28 (1905), 27.

achieved most securely by the spread of Christian belief. Many of the kings of the Zagwe dynasty had actually been priests and many of the kings of every dynasty were afterwards venerated as saints.

The new Amharic dynasty took power with Yikunno-Amlak in and after 1270, but it was his grandson Amda Seyon ('the Pillar of Zion') who was, more than anyone else, creator of the new Ethiopia. He ruled 'Zion', as his chronicles regularly described the country, from 1314 to 1344. In this period he effectively incorporated the central and southern provinces around Shoa into the kingdom. This seems to have been achieved above all by the reorganization of the army and the court, which provided him with a powerful professional military force far beyond the resources of anyone else in the horn of Africa and made possible a long series of military victories over his neighbours, Muslim, pagan, and Falasha. As his soldiers sang triumphantly in popular Amharic,[17]

> Who is left for you at the frontier?
> Whose face have you not disfigured?
> Whose wife and children have you not captured?
> Hero Amda Seyon
> To and from the frontier.

Ethiopia was to be from this time on a military state and it is not surprising that by far its most popular saint from outside the country was St George, a military man, the soldier's saint. For the authority of the king had to be upheld and validated not just by spears and arrows but by saints and theology. It was, fittingly enough, in the reign of Amda Seyon that there was translated into Ge'ez from Arabic (and perhaps in part rewritten at the same time) what was to become the most important of all works of Ethiopian political and religious ideology, the Kebra Nagast, the 'Book of the Glory of Kings'. In it is described how the Ark of the Covenant (the true meaning of 'Zion') was the first of all things in creation, and how it came to earth containing the Mosaic law. Transported to Jerusalem, the latter became Zion in consequence. Then, in due course, came the Queen of Sheba (Ethiopia) to hear the wisdom of Solomon and be converted to his faith in the God of Israel. She returned to Ethiopia bearing Solomon's son, Menelik. When Menelik grew up he visited his father and was presented with the first-born of the leaders of Israel

---

[17] G. W. B. Huntingford (ed.), *The Glorious Victories of Amda Seyon, King of Ethiopia* (1965), 'Soldiers' Songs in Honour of King Amda Seyon', 129–30.

to return with him to Ethiopia. In order not to be separated from Zion these young Israelites stole the Ark of the Covenant and bore it to Ethiopia which, henceforth, became in consequence Israel. The Ark was installed at Aksum, from now on the true Jerusalem.

The Kebra Nagast provides at one and the same time the justification for the religious identity of Ethiopia as Israel, with all its Judaic practices, for the supreme authority of its kings as heirs of Solomon, and for the sacredness of the wooden *tabot*, central to the Ethiopian liturgy, whose original was in Aksum and sacramental replicas in every church throughout the country. Zion is the Ark of the Covenant installed securely in Aksum. It is, by extension, the *tabot* upon which everywhere mass is celebrated. It is, by another extension, the Cathedral of Aksum itself. Again, it is another name for Mary, whose equivalence with the Ark of the Covenant goes back to the Gospel of Luke. It is, by the politically most important extension, Ethiopia. Ark, mass, Mary, Ethiopia, the king—'Pillar of Zion'—have been united by a single mystique of divine selection at work both in the Israel of the past and Christ's Church of the present and guaranteed to continue until the end of time. When the king marched forth at the head of his armies, the *tabot* carried by monks in their midst, their confidence rested in the certainty of divine protection, in the frequently quoted line of Psalm 68, 'Ethiopia shall stretch forth her hands to God'.

The Kebra Nagast is a literary and spiritual expression of the ecclesiastical and monastic revival of the age, a revival which—while very much part and parcel of the national revival—could also come into quite sharp confrontation with the less pious realities of Ethiopian monarchy. Amda Seyon's view of his kingdom may have been a great deal more secular than that of the monk who rewrote the Kebra Nagast. The new monastic movement had begun independently in the central highlands well before the 'Solomonic' dynasty had come to power. Until the mid-thirteenth century no new monasteries had been founded outside the old Christian area of Tigre around Aksum. What churches existed elsewhere were served by secular priests, married and mostly very little educated, though a few major churches were staffed by a far larger number of 'canons', also married, but whose collective level of knowledge was doubtless rather better. There were dynasties of priestly families, claiming descent from the Levitical families of Israel, and these dynasties really constituted the crucial core that enabled Ethiopian Christianity to survive. Every church required at least three priests and the number of those ordained when an abuna was present in Ethiopia could be enormous. The ordination of huge crowds went on day after day to the amazement of foreign observers. While an abuna might explain that he needed to do this because he was old and did not know when another would arrive to ordain once more, the real point of it went deeper than that. The liturgy was a complex ritual requiring plenty of participants and the Ethiopian Church really had no other pastoral weapon but this. The more people were ordained to the priesthood, the more people were committed to the work of the Church, the priesthood being associational rather than hierarchical. They were, moreover, also committed—as the laity in practice were not—to monogamy and to a minimal literacy as well. The mass ordinations of the Ethiopian Church were more crucial to its survival than outsiders could have realized.

It was mostly from such families that the first of the new wave of monks probably originated. They were men who, growing up in the Christian migrant minority of the southern highlands, felt called to learn more of religion than they could gain from their fathers, went north to join the monastic community at Dabra Damo or some other in Tigre, but then desired to return to the mountains of Amhara or Shoa.

It was about 1248 that a monk named Iyasus-Mo'a left Dabra Damo and established a monastery and school on the island in Lake Hayq. It was a date and an initiative of exceptional importance, the start of a great forward movement of the Church which would continue for 250 years. Iyasus-Mo'a is remembered as a man of outstanding learning. Certainly there was no such school before his in all these parts, and soon young men were flocking to join his community, among them his most famous disciple, Takla Haymanot. It is not surprising in these early years of the new monasticism that a man like Takla Haymanot, after some years at the young community of Hayq, felt the need to go on to one of the ancient monasteries. And this is what he did, moving for a while to Dabra Damo, before returning to Shoa to found a series of small houses, among them that of Dabra Asbo, which would grow steadily in importance and be renamed in the mid-fifteenth century Dabra Libanos. By the early fourteenth century from these communities a wave of monks was flowing outward in all directions, committed to the evangelization of Amhara, Shoa, Gojjam, and the lands around.

The monasteries of this early period were remote and simple places, maybe no more than a cave divided into two, one part chapel, one part living quarters. The monks practised the greatest asceticism, following in this the example and spirit of fourth- and fifth-century Egypt. The leaders may, at the start of a new venture, have lived more or less as hermits, but a community seems to have been taken for granted as the model—a community of prayer and manual work (both farming, at least in the early days, and the copying of manuscripts), of teaching the young (including boys who would not afterwards stay in the monastery) and evangelistic activities outside the monastery, including the service of distant churches. Monastic buildings always remained small and informal in comparison with those of Western Europe and the round form frequently prevailed as it did in village churches. Male communities seem normally to have had female communities close beside them, but we know very little of the latter. While the nuns seem generally to have governed themselves, they certainly took part at times in the wider activities of the monks. The normal monk was likely to be a priest, though his ordination might be delayed for quite a few years. The monasteries were very much places of books, as well as of prayer and of pastoral ministry, and neither the liturgy nor the wider teaching would have been possible without the books. The growth in monasteries produced in consequence a sudden large increase in both the demand for, and the production of, literature. But the evangelism is what is most in evidence in the written *Gadla*, the lives of the saints, which is the source from which we know about them. Every great monk had his life written in the monastery which cherished his memory, hoping for miracles at his tomb and in response to the invocation of his name.

All the monasteries of the central highlands were initially established in largely pagan areas, often—as at Dabra Libanos itself—on a site till then sacralized by pagan religion. The monastery was the advance guard of the Church. Monks took it for granted that they would preach to the unbeliever, argue with pagan priests, battle with devils, the spirits that the pagans worshipped and the monks diabolized, persuade local rulers to turn to God, baptize their converts with next to no catechumenate, and then celebrate the mysteries of the Eucharist in whatever church was built in the vicinity. In the fourteenth century, at least, they were not in all this acting as agents of the king. They did not see themselves in that light.

Nor did Amda Seyon, his predecessors, and immediate successors much encourage their activities. Certainly the king needed a relationship to one or another monastery where he could find a reliable confessor and be assured of prayer in time of war. For many years kings mostly found this at Dabra Hayq, which, more or less from the start of the new dynasty in the late thirteenth century, functioned as a royal monastery with duties (including that of acting as gaoler to prisoners of distinction) quite different from that of other houses. Amda Seyon turned to the Aqabe-Sa'at, the Abbot of Hayq, as 'my father'. More than a century later Zara Ya'iqob would do quite the same. But, for Amda Seyon, missionary activity among his pagan or Muslim subjects was quite another thing and one in which he saw no particular point, especially if conducted by headstrong people given to criticizing him and his personal life. The monks themselves, it would appear, wanted independence. They were exhilarated by Christian faith and the monastic inheritance, and the monarchy did not appear to have so much to do with either. When Amda Seyon tried to make gifts to Dabra Libanos, its abbot, Filpos, Takla Haymanot's immediate successor, turned them down and was flogged for doing so.

In their missionary activities, the monks went well beyond any effective protection the Christian king could offer them. They challenged pagan chiefs on their own ground and often received a not unfavourable reception. Certainly they could be hard on the priests and diviners of traditional religion. They denounced their belief in the spirits of trees, snakes, and the like as devil worship, and either cut down the sacred groves or built a Christian church on the site. No wonder their lives were at times in danger. But they could be warmly welcoming once their religious opponents accepted the Christian God. In more than one instance the conversion of a diviner was followed by almost immediate admission into the monastic life. It was a battle with devils rather than with men, devils very emphatically believed in. When the devils were driven out of Shoa they took refuge in Gojjam. When, little by little, they were driven out of eastern Gojjam too, the demons were believed to have retreated for a last stand to Ajawmeder, which was held to explain why, in the wars of the sixteenth century, the people there did so much harm to local Christians. The advance of Christianity across the central Ethiopian highlands was, then, a slow affair taking many generations and largely dependent on the somewhat random presence in a given area of a holy man and his monastery.

This movement was certainly well under way by the second quarter of the fourteenth century. Then, in 1337, a new metropolitan arrived, the Abuna Ya'iqob. He seems to have excelled most of his predecessors both in zeal and in ability, but above all the circumstances were different: the Church was expanding and needed a new kind of leadership. Ya'iqob grasped the situation and resolved to respond to it. Hitherto the abuna had been closely attached to the royal court, surrounded by the royal chaplains, almost unrelated to monks, except when they arrived at his tent for ordination. Ya'iqob reversed this. He saw that only the monks could reform the Church or convert the country. He sought their confidence and gave them his. The Shoan monks of that generation found this quite natural: he was, after all, a monk himself and had come from Egypt, the fountain-head of monasticism. It seems that he devised an ambitious division of the central Shoan highlands into twelve parts and appointed an apostle for each. The area involved was a circle with a radius of some 120 miles with its centre roughly at Dabra Libanos. Filpos, its abbot, was given the central area of Shoa immediately around his monastery, Anorewas the Elder was given Warab, Qawestos Mahagel, and so on. While we know a little more about what was happening in Shoa, it looks as if Ya'iqob may actually have been making similar arrangements in Amhara and even Tigre. Partly as a consequence of this most of these areas were nominally Christian by the early fifteenth century in a way that had not at all been the case 150 years earlier when Iyasus-Mo'a first settled at Hayq. There were now many monasteries and, around them, many more village churches. Across a quite large area of the highlands Christianity had appeared to conquer. This was, however, to a considerable extent, delusory. Petty kings and their followers might, relatively easily, accept baptism at the hands of these enthusiastic holy men, but the instruction given to them was limited indeed. The Amharic-speaking priests in the village churches could barely read. They had had no theological education whatsoever.

The deepest obstacle to the Christianization of the common man was probably one of language. There were a great many languages spoken and they were not Semitic. Ordinary people did not learn Ethiopic but the Scriptures and the liturgy were not, so far as one can tell, translated into any other tongue. It was almost impossible for

Christianity to grow deeply into any non-Ethiopic-speaking community and, even among the Ethiopics, the increasing gap between the literary Ge'ez, the language of Scripture and liturgy, and popular Amharic will certainly not have assisted the understanding of true religion even among the village clergy, let alone among the laity. The celebration of mass even in a small village church required three priests, and all priests were required to have a smattering of literacy. It was taken for granted that their sons would be ordained. Effectively the Christian community may mostly have consisted of small groups of Ethiopic-speaking priestly families, protected by nominally Christian local chiefs, out of deference to the Christian king, but surrounded by a multitude of people for whom Christian formulas and public rituals, especially the baptismal rituals in January, were absorbed within a religious mix predominantly traditional. The spirit possession of the past continued much as ever, even if at times it now took an overtly Christian form. Marha Krestos in the later fifteenth century was confronted by more than one such case. The three persons of the Trinity had taken possession of some people in one instance; in another a woman 'spoke through the spirit of Satan and said "Mary speaks to me, Mika'el and Gabra'el speak to me." She said to the priests of that village, "Mary says to you serve the Eucharist at noon on Wednesday and Friday." And they did so.'[18] Perhaps in this rather interesting case an attempt was being made in the only way the locals knew to adapt Christian ritual to local need, but inevitably to Marha Krestos it was unacceptable.

Weak as it inevitably was in effective implementation, Bishop Ya'iqob's plan for pastoral and missionary administration was the nearest thing the Ethiopian Church would get for a long time to a pattern of episcope remotely comparable with what even a pre-Tridentine Church took for granted in other countries. Even so, it was not to last. Amda Seyon, so far as can be judged, had no particular enthusiasm for any of this, but lack of support was soon to be turned to positive discrimination. The Abuna and the monks wished to Christianize Ethiopia. They did not see that task as only an outgoing exercise. Christians themselves needed to reform and that included the emperor. Ecclesiastics have often felt called to take a stand on the marital morals of kings, seldom successfully. The basic problem was that it was customary for Ethiopian kings to have three

---

[18] S. Kur (ed.), *Actes de Marha Krestos, CSCO* 331 (1972), 77.

official wives, plus, most probably, additional concubines. The nobility was little different. Divorce too was easy and much practised. This could hardly not worry a conscientious Egyptian metropolitan. In the past he had been without allies, powerless to fight his case, though one twelfth-century Zagwe king, Yimrha-Krestos, himself a priest, had decreed monogamy but ineffectually. The new 'Solomonic' line of Yikunno Amlak was more polygamous. But now the metropolitan had at last enthusiastic clerical allies. Indeed some among the monks, led by Basalota-Mika'el, had mounted something of an attack upon the King, even before Ya'iqob's arrival. His hagiographer has him declare uncompromisingly in the royal presence: 'God has ordered us, Christians, not to marry two wives nor buy concubines, nor sleep with the wives of others. But you have broken all (these) orders of God. And worst of all, you married the wife of your father.'[19] Hardly surprisingly, Basalota Mika'el was flogged and exiled, and when Bishop Ya'iqob and, maybe, Filpos of Dabra Libanos attempted to revive the issue, the royal anger was vented once more and further monks were sent into exile in remote parts of the kingdom. While this disrupted parts of Bishop Ya'iqob's plan, it also provided the monks with new fields to evangelize.

When Amda Seyon died his successor, Sayfa-Ar'ad, recalled the exiles and even promised the Bishop to keep to one wife, though he soon went back on that word. Bishop and monks protested once more, at which point the Bishop was sent back to Egypt and his monastic allies again exiled to the frontier areas. The reform movement had, to some extent, failed. The kings of Ethiopia would continue to have three wives for a long time to come and the Church would no longer publicly protest. However, at least from this time the Church's standard practice was to exclude the polygamous from Communion (whether this always applied to fifteenth-century kings may be questioned) and the clergy at least were committed to monogamy. As the state clearly accepted polygamous marriage for Christians, this may even have helped to ensure a measure of differentiation between the two.[20]

Royal polygamy might well be seen as one more example, like circumcision, of the 'Hebraic' character of Christian Ethiopia. It could even be that a theologically minded polygamist like Zara

---

[19] Conti Rossini (ed.), *Acta*, 26.
[20] See Francisco Alvares, *The Prester John of the Indies*, ed. E. F. Beckingham and G. W. B. Huntingford (Cambridge, 1961), i. 105.

Ya'iqob would maintain that there was no New Testament injunction to outlaw the practice of his forefathers David and Solomon. Yet it is noticeable that the writer of the Kebra Nagast, despite his glorification of the Solomonic monarchy, is careful to declare that while Solomon is not to be blamed for his plurality of wives, 'to those after Christ, it was given to live with one woman under the law of marriage'.[21] The kings of the Zagwe dynasty had tried to establish monogamy, just as they promoted the cult of Sunday. Polygamy, like circumcision, had, nevertheless, remained the custom of Ethiopia. While all informed Churchmen accepted the latter and rejected the former, neither—it seems—was seen as a theological issue. In regard to the Sabbath it was different. Here was a matter upon which two schools of theological and monastic thought had come to clash.

v. *The 'House of Ewostatewos' and Sabbath Observance*

In the early fourteenth century, a generation or so later than the monastic movement which sprang from Iyasus-Mo'a and the island monastery of Hayq and which came to be seen essentially as the 'House of Takla Haymanot', a second movement got under way in the north of the country. We know less about its early days, partly perhaps because its monasteries were mostly situated in areas where there had already been monks for many centuries. It was not, geographically, innovative, but it seems from the start to have carried on ancient Aksumite traditions to a greater extent than did the southern houses. The major figure here was that of Ewostatewos, born in the 1270s. Nephew of Abba Daniel of Gar'alta, an ancient house of one of the Nine Saints, he was professed by his uncle but soon left to establish a community of his own in which the keeping of the Sabbath became a marked characteristic. Conflict arose over this and in about 1337 Ewostatewos left for Egypt with many of his monks. Whether he had hoped to find support abroad is not clear. In fact in Cairo he was accused by fellow Ethiopians of observing the Sabbath and refusing to communicate with those who broke it. The Patriarch was not sympathetic. Ewostatewos moved on to Jerusalem, to Cyprus, and then to Armenia where he died in 1352 (presumably 'Little Armenia', north of Antioch in Cilicia). His disciples then

[21] E. A. Wallis Budge (ed.), *The Queen of Sheba and her Only Son, Menyelek, being the 'Book of the Glory of Kings' (Kebra Nagast)* (1932), ch. 28.

returned to Ethiopia, joining the rather dispirited group who had always remained there, to found the community of Dabra Maryam. It and Dabra Bizan, founded a little later by Filpos, who became the true leader of the 'House of Ewostatewos', were the principal centres of the movement. By the end of the fourteenth century it would seem to have outshone the old monasteries of Tigre in terms of spiritual and apostolic zeal. Its monks were now advancing the Christian frontiers of the north, preaching in Muslim and Falasha areas, just as were those of the House of Takla Haymanot in the south. What distinguished them as a group was the close commitment to the memory of Ewostatewos, the explicit linking of their houses within a wider organization, and the keeping of the Sabbath rest. They had more of the character of a religious order than the earlier communities, and this included a more developed convent life for nuns. Ewostathian abbesses apparently had the right to give absolution to their nuns for lesser faults.[22] The vitality of the movement was shown too by the number of new foundations their three principal houses were making. But it was the Sabbath which divided them, in an almost inevitably bitter manner, from other monks—at least southern monks—and from the metropolitan, and made of them a movement bordering on the heretical and the schismatic.

In 1388 the Abuna Salama died after an Ethiopian ministry of forty years in which he had concentrated upon improving the biblical and theological knowledge of the Church entrusted to him. He was not replaced for ten years until the arrival of the Abuna Bartalomewos in 1398. We can imagine that Salama in his last years may have been reluctant to face up to what was becoming a major problem. In the ten-year interim the Ewostathians had grown greatly in numbers and confidence and Bartalomewos was quickly convinced that firm action needed to be taken. His anti-Sabbath views were shared, so far as is known, by all the monastic leaders of the south and in particular by those of the major monasteries of Dabra Hayq and Dabra Libanos. Nor was the King of a different mind. Dawit had come to the throne in 1380. As with many of the kings, his closest spiritual adviser was the Aqabe-Sa'at of Hayq, at that time Saraqa-Birhan, and Saraqa-Birhan was adamantly opposed to the keeping of the Sabbath. A Council was called in 1400 by royal authority. Messengers were sent

[22] Conti Rossini, 'Il "Gadla Filpos"', 162.

to ensure the attendance of the Ewostathians, led by the aged Filpos, but it was the Abuna not the Emperor who presided. The upshot was predictable. They were forbidden to continue observing the Sabbath, but refused to obey and were imprisoned until they conformed. Filpos was himself detained at Dabra Hayq.[23]

At this point it is convenient to consider the evidence in a larger way. How and why had this dispute arisen? How did it relate to the Ethiopian Christian tradition and to wider Church practice? The degree of Sabbath observance of the very early Church is not entirely clear, nor could it have been uniform. The Sabbath was nowhere immediately abandoned even though Christian worship was quickly focused upon Sunday as the day of the Resurrection. As the Jewish element within the Church proportionately decreased, Sabbath observance doubtless declined. In some sort of way, if not quite explicitly, Sunday was seen to replace Saturday as the day of rest decreed in the Pentateuch. To have two such days could be judged inconvenient and unnecessary. Nevertheless, Saturday as well as Sunday continued to be observed to some extent in some places, notably Egypt, and St Gregory of Nyssa, among others, commended the practice. The Coptic Church subsequently rejected Sabbath observance as a Jewish practice but this was at a quite late date.

We have no evidence in regard to either Ethiopian practice or disputes on the subject in Ethiopia prior to the fourteenth century. The original conflicts which Ewostatewos was himself embroiled in seem to have been within the Tigrean Church. This suggests that the practice he was advocating was not simply the current usage of northern Ethiopia and its more ancient, Aksumitic, Church. Moreover, there is no suggestion that the ancient monasteries of Tigre, like Dabra Damo, were involved in the dispute or fell under the censure of Bartolomewos. Indeed, if the practice of Dabra Damo had been strongly sabbatarian, it is hard to believe that Iyasus-Mo'a and Takla Haymanot would not have carried it, at least to some extent, across to their new monasteries or that, two or three generations later, the monks of the south, led by the communities of Hayq and Dabra Libanos, should have been so firmly in opposition. It would then be greatly mistaken to regard the Ewostathian

---

[23] For four years. However, his memorial in the synaxarium of the Ewostathian monastery of Dabra Worq says that while he was kept for years in Amhara he was only six months at Hayq (R. Schneider, 'Notes sur Filpos de Dabra Bizen et ses successeurs', *Annales d'Éthiopie*, 11 (1978), 135-9).

observance of the Sabbath as simply reflecting Ethiopian tradition, challenged by an Egyptian abuna anxious to enforce the Cairo line.

On the other hand, it is hard to believe that the Ewostathians were wholly innovating either. The amount of local support they seem to have received in the north, the ease with which their cause eventually triumphed, and the congruity between this and other Ethiopian characteristics (such as retention of the Mosaic dietary laws, which are, however, witnessed to in the Kebra Nagast as Sabbath observance is not) do all suggest that the Ewostathians were reflecting or resurrecting an ancient Ethiopian tradition, still held to some extent among the people, but which had fallen into considerable desuetude and was no longer regarded by most churchmen as a necessary part of Christian life. Certainly hostility to it among the monks of Dabra Libanos seems as clear as the commitment to it among those of Dabra Bizan. One other piece of evidence, enigmatic as it is, may be considered.[24] At Lalibela there are a number of Ethiopic texts carved in wood which claim to be the work of King Lalibela. As such they are about the earliest surviving religious texts we have in the language. Now by far the longest is a piece in praise of the Christian Sunday, a mystical personification comparable to the Falasha personification of the Sabbath. Should we see this as evidence that the Zagwe dynasty in abandoning Aksum also abandoned, or played down, the Sabbath, while stressing the holiness of the first day of the week? If this was royal orthodoxy in the mid-thirteenth century, it might help to explain how Iyasus-Mo'a, founding Dabra Hayq while the Zagwe were still ruling, never included Sabbath observance as part of its practices, and how an absence of sabbatarianism became so decided a mark of the whole southern monastic movement springing from Hayq.

The Council of 1400 proved ineffectual. The persecution of monks as holy as Filpos was distressing, while support for them in the north appeared to be considerable. The King of Ethiopia now lived in Shoa, but it was crucial that he retain the loyalty of Aksum and the north, and not too easy to do so. There were already signs of an incipient Eritrean separatism, a political movement needing and at times obtaining local religious support. If the Ewostathians had revived the traditional practice of Aksum in regard to the Sabbath and were now to be persecuted for it, the effect on the unity of the

[24] Gigar Tesfaye, 'Inscriptions sur bois de trois Églises de Lalibala', *JES* 17 (1984), 107-26.

kingdom might well be perilous. But the unity of the Church was threatened no less, even, conceivably, the future of Christianity.

The Ewostathians had been excommunicated by the Abuna for years and this had prevented them from being ordained. As a result, while elsewhere monks were priests, here they were not. Now it is true that in this they were no different from the early monks of Egypt and the West. Nevertheless, the custom for monks, and especially their abbots, to be ordained priest had long been established in Ethiopia as elsewhere, and this was really needed for their wider pastoral responsibilities outside the monastery. It is true that the Ewostathians were not, apparently, entirely priestless. From time to time they received priests into their ranks who, after undergoing penance for lapsing from Sabbath observance, were then able to celebrate mass. Nevertheless, it seems clear that there was a danger of an almost priestless, even mass-less religion emerging, a religion whose most striking characteristic was Sabbath observance. The Ewostathians were only too clearly moving in a direction that the Beta Israel may have taken a few centuries earlier: the giving of precedence to Hebrew institutions over Christian ones, and the closeness of their ideals to the religion of the 'Falasha' (probably not yet regularly called by that name) may not have escaped notice, particularly as some of the Ewostathian communities were actually in Falasha territory. They had, it seems, been evangelizing there not unsuccessfully. Gabra-Iyasus had been one of Ewostatewos's early disciples and had accompanied him abroad. On his return he was sent to the country around Lake Tana, and, his hagiographer tells us, 'Even the sons of the Jews believed, received baptism and entered into his teaching.'[25] This could well be so, the very sabbatarianism of the Ewostathians proving a bridge to the Falasha. In point of fact King Dawit did not only have the Ewostathians on his hands. He also had the Falasha, who had been involved in a major revolt during his reign. It is not implausible to see the possibility of a Falasha–Ewostathian *entente* if the monks were effectively driven out of the Church on account of their commitment to the Sabbath. Such an alliance might have endangered the whole royal position in the north, if it could claim the blessing of Aksumitic tradition itself.

About 1404 the old Aqabe-Sa'at, Saraqa-Birhan, died. Almost at

[25] C. Conti Rossini, 'Note de agiografia etiopica: Gabra-Iyasus', *Rivista degli studi orientali*, 17 (1938), 409–52.

once Dawit ordered Filpos to be released from Hayq. Furthermore, the king commanded that in future the disciples of Ewostatewos should observe both Sabbaths. The speed of this volte-face was remarkable. In itself it was a compromise. No one else was commanded or advised to observe the Sabbath. A serious division of practice was, for the time, thus admitted within the Church. Moreover, as the Metropolitan had no intention of ordaining Ewostathians, nor they of seeking ordination from a Sabbath-breaker, the semi-priestless state of their monasteries with its inherent threat to the whole sacramental structure of the Church remained unhealed. But the sabbatarians felt vindicated and enthusiastic. Their houses and their influence spread.

Even non-Ewostathians were moving towards Sabbath observance. The most significant case is that of Giyorgis of Gascha (or Sagla), probably the greatest Ethiopian theologian for many centuries, author of the 'Book of the Mystery', *Mashafa Mistir* (completed in 1424). His father had been a chaplain at the royal court and sent his son to school at Hayq, which seems to have been for the Ethiopia of the time a cross between a monastic seminary for the élite and a detention centre. It was during the last years of Abbot Saraqa-Birhan, and young Giyorgis may well have met and got to know Abbot Filpos, there under house arrest. After some years the father of Giyorgis decided to retire to a monastery and his bright and well-educated young son took his place as a court priest. Recognized as a man of exceptional learning, he was entrusted with the education of Dawit's sons. He had, however, been fully converted, perhaps through conversation with Filpos, to the rightness of Sabbath observance, which he firmly defends in the *Mashafa Mistir*.

The long reign of Dawit would seem to have been a time of maturation for Ethiopian Christianity. He had continued Amda Seyon's military successes against the Muslim sultanate to the east. Central Ethiopia was, for a period, a moderately secure land in which the victories of a century had brought increasing prosperity. Conflict between monarchy and Church seemed a thing of the past. Dabra Libanos and the monasteries derived from it had fallen in with the line of Hayq in receiving gifts and co-operating with the king. The years of Abuna Salama had seen many new books translated from the Arabic. There must have been a noticeable growth in the number and size of monastic libraries. Dawit himself was a man of piety who particularly favoured the two devotions which were advancing in these years: veneration of Mary and veneration of the Cross, a piece of the true Cross having recently been brought from Jerusalem, as also most probably one or more of the Byzantine 'Luke' icons of the Virgin.

No book seems to have been more popular in fifteenth-century Ethiopia than the *Miracles of Mary*. The origins of this book lie in twelfth-century France. It was put together at Marian shrines responding to the plagues of the time. Numerous expanded versions are to be found in almost every medieval vernacular including Icelandic. Sometime in the fourteenth century it was translated into Arabic and then, probably in the reign of Dawit, from Arabic into Ethiopic. Thus twelfth-century French devotions had reached fifteenth-century Ethiopia, and Zara Ya'iqob imposed it as compulsory clerical reading for the thirty-two Marian feasts (following in this an Egyptian regulation of a little earlier). What in the West was really only a piece of popular piety became in Ethiopia part of orthodoxy itself.

vi. *The Policies of Zara Ya'iqob*

Zara Ya'iqob was brought up in the pieties and new learning of the court of Dawit, his father. A boy of outstanding intelligence, he was probably taught at court by Abba Giyorgis and all his life maintained theological positions remarkably close to those of the latter. Subsequently, it seems, he may have been sent to a monastery. However, on Dawit's death, when his brothers Tewodros and Yishaq became king in turn, Zara Ya'iqob was confined (in accordance with Ethiopian practice) in the mountain prison of Amba-Gishan reserved for all princes of the blood. There he remained for twenty years until, on the death of his brother, he was called to the throne in 1434.

'God made us king on this orthodox throne of the kingdom so that we may root out all worshippers of idols,'[26] Zara Ya'iqob later wrote in his *Mashafa Milad*, one of several works of political theology he was to compose. He had clearly had plenty of time to think, and he possessed an education and a knowledge of theology far beyond that of his predecessors. He combined these qualifications with fierce determination and an ability to plan in large terms. He set himself to

---

[26] *Das Mashafa Milad und Mashafa Sellase* ii, (text) 95–6, qv. T. Tamrat *Church and State in Ethiopia* (1972) 242–3.

unify and reform both Church and State, applying to Cairo for two
bishops, whom he set to work in separate parts of the country. He
changed the name of Dabra Asbo to Dabra Libanos, enriched it with
possessions, and entrusted its abbot, the eccage, with wide pastoral
responsibilities for the control of other monasteries, at least in Shoa
and maybe more widely. In particular he handed over to it direct
responsibility for his new royal foundations at Dabra Mitmaq, Dabra
Berhan, and elsewhere. In receiving these duties the eccage did not,
as is often suggested, replace the aqabe-sa'at of Hayq, for their two
roles remained very different. The new function of the abbot of
Dabra Libanos was one of oversight over a multitude of monasteries.
There is no evidence that the abbot of Hayq had ever had such a role.
His was instead one of being the king's principal spiritual adviser, and
this certainly continued well beyond the death of Zara Ya'iqob.

The active presence of two bishops and the advancement of the
eccage were not, however, intended to establish any sort of
independent ecclesiastical administration but, rather, to make royal
control of the Church effective. In the previous reign even the Abuna
Bartholemewos had been accused of heresy, and a royal commission,
including Giyorgis of Sagla and the Abbot of Hayq, had been
appointed to investigate. The Abuna was acquitted, but royal control
of both doctrine and pastoral practice was now to be applied
effectively. As Zara Ya'iqob saw it, he was faced with a Church which
had grown greatly in size and learning but was failing to get to grips
with its principal problem, the paganism in its midst, or its secondary
problem, the appeal to an irremediably Hebraist Church of the full
Falasha option. There was in point of fact no other authority able
either to direct the pastoral ministry or to control the increasing
diversity of belief and teaching consequent upon the growth of
essentially unco-ordinated monasteries. In these circumstances, Zara
Ya'iqob took upon himself the duties of bishop as much as of king.

Central to his programme was the matter of the Sabbath. It had still
not been resolved. The House of Ewostatewos received no
ordination, while the rest of the kingdom ignored Sabbath
observance. Zara Ya'iqob seems to have been a convinced
sabbatarian from his youth. Perhaps he learned it from Abba
Giyorgis: the 'two Sabbaths', the Jewish and the Christian, must both
be faithfully observed, and essentially as one. He claimed to be
convinced of this from the instructions of the Apostles themselves (as
in chapter 38 of the Apostolic *Didascalia*, a work which may have

been translated into Ethiopic from Arabic during the fourteenth century), but perhaps still more decisive was his meditation upon Matthew 5: 17–19. 'Do not think that I have come to abolish the Law or the Prophets . . . not an Iota will disappear from the Law.' Was the Law of Sabbath Observance (one of the Ten Commandments, after all) not an iota? Was not Jesus himself the Iota (the identity was established by the numerical value of the letters of the word)? Fidelity to Jesus required observance of the Sabbath. All this Zara Ya'iqob went over again and again in his most influential work the *Mashafa Berhan*, or 'Book of the Light', a collection of readings for the two Sabbaths.

Politically, full reconciliation with the Ewostathians was no less important. Disagreement over the celebration of the Sabbath in fifteenth-century Ethiopia was as damaging politically as disagreement over the celebration of Easter in seventh-century Northumbria. In regard to each, royal authority had to prevail over monastic infighting. Everywhere Zara Ya'iqob was concerned to unify the kingdom, reinforce his control of it, and to strengthen the frontiers. But in the early years of his reign, at least, he showed a particular concern for the north. Crowned at Aksum in 1436, he spent the next three years entirely in those parts. He was clearly determined to regain, and extend, Ethiopian control over Eritrea and the Red Sea coast. Later, in 1449–50, precisely the time of the Council of Mitmaq, he began to build a sea-port at Girar. Dabra Bizan, the greatest of Ewostathian monasteries, lies on the eastern edge of the plateau of Eritrea, only ten miles from the sea and overlooking the coast. The political value of supporting Sabbath observance within Zara Ya'iqob's strategy is obvious enough. Without Ewostathian loyalty Eritrea, the coast, and even wider areas of the north might hardly be secured. Yet he waited pretty patiently before calling the Council. It was essential that it should fully succeed and for that he had to carry the Egyptian bishops with him as well as the monks of the south. Persuading the bishops to sanction the abandonment of the Alexandrian position within Ethiopia must have been exceptionally difficult, but finally it was achieved.

Hence it was that in August 1449 some hundreds of senior abbots and clerics assembled in the church at Dabra Mitmaq under the presidency of the Emperor and resolved that, in accordance with apostolic injunction, both Sabbaths must henceforth be observed. It looks as if Abba Nob of Dabra Damo was influential in the final reconciliation. As, earlier, Giyorgis of Sagla had been for a time abbot of Dabra Damo, it may be from his time that the most respected and ancient of Ethiopian monasteries had veered towards the Ewostathian position. The Zagwe glorification of Sunday and the Falasha– Ewostathian glorification of Saturday were now both to be central to the orthodoxy of Ethiopia, as we see it developed in the writings of Zara Ya'iqob himself. It was also agreed, and this was no less important, that the House of Ewostatewos would no longer refuse to accept ordination from the metropolitan. Thus the Sabbath practice of the Ethiopian Church was established and its unity re-established. Henceforward all serious labour (though not basic cooking) was forbidden on Saturday as well as upon Sunday. Ewostatewos had passed the word to Filpos of Dabra Bizan, Filpos passed it to Giyorgis of Sagla, and Giyorgis passed it to Zara Ya'iqob. We cannot be totally sure of that genealogy, but it looks distinctly probable. Thus the idiosyncrasy of an early fourteenth-century monk who died in consequence in exile in Armenia became in little more than a hundred years the orthodoxy of Ethiopia's greatest emperor and the practice of his country ever since. If one asks how even the power of the emperor could suffice to enforce what was really rather an inconvenient restriction in daily life and render it permanently normative, the answer may lie in a religious and social system's internal need for coherence. Sabbath observance triumphed because it cohered so well with the Solomonic myth, circumcision, the dietary laws, and much else which had long characterized Ethiopian Christianity.

Many observers and scholars have subsequently seen the practice as something itself dating back to the Judaic origin of the Church. Others have seen it, on the contrary, as a Judaizing innovation of Zara Ya'iqob. In fact both are largely mistaken. If one had visited the Ethiopian Church a hundred years before Mitmaq one would have discovered very few signs of Sabbath observance. Yet it was not in origin, though it was in legitimization, the work of Zara Ya'iqob, and in so far as it was, it was not a matter of Judaizing. Indeed no king was more anti-Jewish than he. It was essentially to New Testament and Christian authorities that he appealed. Again it would be simplistic to see it as a mere piece of politics or nationalism, or traditionalism, though all three did indeed enter into the issue. At its heart it was truly a matter of both theology and religious practice, yet it was also very much a matter of politics: the securing of northern loyalty, the isolating of Falasha dissidence.

Zara Ya'iqob was highly tolerant of the Ewostathians. He treated other monastic deviants very differently. Essentially he was looking for conformity like many another political leader in matters religious. The viewpoint of Ewostatewos was not to be tolerated as a distinct viewpoint, it was to be imposed nationally. But fifteenth-century Ethiopia was witnessing a proliferation of monastic viewpoints. Among them that of Estifanos probably seemed to the King the most obnoxious. Estifanos was born in Tigre in the reign of Dawit. About 1430 he left the monastery of Qoyera with a group of disciples to found his own. They were the new radicals. Just as the house of Takla Haymanot had been unwilling to compromise with royal authority in the early fourteenth century and the House of Ewostatewos in the late fourteenth century, so now, when these were being more or less successfully absorbed into the web of royal religion, it was the turn of Estifanos.

Estifanos, in so far as we can reconstruct his character from particularly fragmentary sources, appears as one quite remarkably critical of the whole way the Church was going, above all in regard to the royal ideology and the mixing of Church and State. He said he respected the King far less for being an Israelite than for being a Christian king of Christians but that, as a Christian, the King counted for less than the Church. He also declared that he did not reject 'Mount Zion' (which he was accused of doing), but added at once a shift in meaning from the territorial to the moral: 'for those who purify their heart and bear the yoke of Christ's gospel will find it'.[27] Everything we know of this monk, who became in subsequent orthodox tradition a heretical bogy, suggests a remarkable sense of spiritual freedom, a refusal to conform to nationalist religion. On being called to the court he rather ostentatiously declined to do what other priests were doing and take part in secular decision-making.

The standpoint of Estifanos appears quite revolutionary in relation to the royal ideology, but it seems to have been in regard to new devotions that he was ostensibly condemned. For Zara Ya'iqob the cult of the Cross and of Mary, precisely in their latest form, were of enormous importance. They were the devotions of his father and

[27] R. Beylot, 'Estifanos hétérodoxe éthiopien du xve siècle', *Revue de l'histoire des religions*, 198 (1981), 279–84.

mother. 'During his days the Cross of the Lamb came,' he declares in one of his hymns to his father.[28] Of course the devotion to the Mother of Jesus was always present in the Ethiopian Church and there is no reason to believe that Estifanos rejected it, but one senses in the fifteenth century and particularly in the work of Zara Ya'iqob (reflecting without doubt a much wider movement fuelled by many of the new translations from Arabic) a fiercer concentration upon it. Estifanos did not care for this and judged it unbalanced: 'I worship the Father, the Son and the Holy Ghost and I prostrate before this. I shall not add to this . . . for the love of the rulers of the world.'[29] Essentially he appears as challenging the royal supremacy to impose new devotions and it was for rejecting the latter that he was flogged and sent into exile where he died. His followers were soon subjected to out-and-out persecution but somehow managed to survive as a community and in due course established the monastery of Gunde Gunde, famous for its exceptional inaccessibility. The Stefanites never became as numerous as the earlier houses and long remained under suspicion. They matter as evidence of the continuing diversity, religious vitality, and openness to independent theological thinking of mid-fifteenth century Ethiopian Christianity.[30]

These, however, were not the virtues to appeal to Zara Ya'iqob. As he grew older, he grew more and more worried by the weakness in faith of his people, the superstition, the ignorance, the pagan practices, the appeal of Judaism, the pastoral laziness of the clergy, the theological deviations of monks, the sins of all and sundry. His *Mashafa Berhan* consists of readings for Saturdays and Sundays of the month, two for each day, in which he preaches, appeals, denounces, and threatens. Christians were even ordered to be branded with a mark of their faith, that they might not abandon it, while priests who failed in any way in their duty were to have their homes sacked by the military. The details of Saturday and Sunday observances, an onslaught upon pagan beliefs and practices, preoccupation with the unity and Trinity of God, these are the themes which recur again and again. His references are to the New Testament far more than to the Old, but it is an extraordinarily rigid and detailed religion which he is

[28] G. Haile, 'Documents on the History of Ase Dawit 1380–1413', *JES* 16 (1983), 25–35.
[29] T. Tamrat, 'Some Notes on the Fifteenth Century Stephanite "Heresy"', *RSE* 22 (1966), 103–15.
[30] For a very interesting reference of Alvares to the Stefanites and their attitude to the cross two generations later see Alvares, *The Prester John of the Indies*, i. 170.

expounding and woe to those of his subjects who in any way deviated from it, monks, priests, laity, but non-Christians still more. His chronicle declares him 'the exterminator of the Jews' and if that was in point of fact exaggerated, his hostility to the Falasha, just as to his pagan subjects, was clearly unbounded. His compromise on the Sabbath was not intended to open the door to further movement in their direction, but instead to close it.

'Whoever kills pagans has committed no sin,' pronounced Zara Ya'iqob.[31] Clearly his approach to a multi-religious empire was very different from that of Amda Seyon. The Church had, of course, advanced a great deal in the meantime, and the policy of Zara Ya'iqob did not appear quite as unrealistic in his day as it would have done in that of Amda Seyon, and it was probably no more ruthless than that of his elder brother, Yeshaq. It remained, nevertheless, deeply impractical. The syncretism and surface Christianity inevitably characteristic of the Church of his empire could not be overcome by such means.

An ultimately more plausible approach may have been the liturgical. In 1521 Zara Ya'iqob's great-grandson, Lebna Dengel, had an interesting conversation with a Portuguese visitor to his country, Francisco Alvares. Alvares had just been witnessing the annual ceremony of rebaptism, performed at Temqat, the Feast of Christ's Baptism, 6 January. After the Emperor himself had been rebaptized by the Abuna, he sat and watched as his subjects were immersed one by one in a tank of water before him. While the line went on and on, the Emperor called to ask Alvares what he thought of it. Alvares was a quiet and diplomatic person, but he replied that in his Church there was no such rite and that, indeed, it was forbidden to give baptism more than once. To this the Emperor replied that their books too were against rebaptism, but what was one to do? So many people became Muslims, Jews, or whatever and then repented. Endless souls would be lost if there was not some convenient way of sweeping the slate clean from time to time. Alvares' solution was to write to the Pope and obtain additional powers of absolution, but that, too, would have required a more informed clergy than the Church of Ethiopia could dispose of. In practice neither that nor Zara Ya'iqob's desperate measures could work, so the annual

---

[31] His *Mashafa Milad* is full of such teaching, as also the *Mashafa Berhan*.

rebaptism of Temqat would continue to perform an almost essential function of purification.

Zara Ya'iqob's preoccupations drove him, physically and mentally, into an extraordinary isolation in his later years. The court of his predecessors, as his own for more than twenty years, had been a migratory one, a capital of tents. In the last fourteen years of his life this quite changed. Instead he built at Dabra Berhan a church and a palace, inside which he lived, almost invisibly. The two buildings were linked by a covered passage; when he went through it to the church, everyone else had to leave except for his personal confidant, the Aqabe-Sa'at, Amha Scyon, and four other priests. Zara Ya'iqob was gripped by an acute terror of bewitchment. Priests had ceaselessly to patrol the palace, spraying holy water upon its inner walls. Every Ethiopian court was a perilously bloody place, but the tragedies of those years seemed exceptional as accusations of pagan practices mounted into a sort of witch-hunt in which the King showed no mercy. It is striking how more than one person had his name changed to that of the devil: thus Amda Masqal was renamed on conviction Amda Saytan. One of the King's wives and several of his sons and daughters were flogged to death on the accusation of taking part in pagan practices. Upon the ecclesiastical side among the victims of his latter years were Indiryas, the Abbot of Dabra Libanos, St Takla Hawaryat, Estifanos, and Gyorgis, a monk who taught the unknowability of God and gave rise to the group known as the Mikaelites.

The figure of Zara Ya'iqob, emperor of Ethiopia for thirty-five years, remains a mysterious one. About his extensive reform of the administration of the country we know much less than we do of his ecclesiastical policy, and even of that we know far too little. But his own writings, the lives of the saints, even the royal chronicles are concerned far more with one than with the other. At once scholar and tyrant, he imposed a unified model for Church and State upon his country, in some ways significantly different from that of its former tradition. Much of this could not and did not endure beyond his death; it nevertheless became a sort of baseline for future development. No king before him had had either the power or the will to reorganize religion systematically, and the increasing terror which this produced may have deterred his successors from attempting quite the same. Yet if feared and hated by many on account of the ruthlessness with which he attempted to enforce his form of religion, the record of his long reign, when Ethiopia was at the height of its power and prosperity, coupled with his writings and mysterious existence within the palace of Dabra Berhan ensured for Zara Ya'iqob a unique place within the national and ecclesiastical mythology. He was of course canonized.

vii. *The Age of Baida Maryam*

The chronicle of Baida Maryam, Zara Ya'iqob's son and successor (son too of the queen who had been beaten to death), gives us a more pleasant impression of the life of the court in the 1470s. It had at once resumed its peregrinatory character. The people rejoiced actually to see the King, who rode around, went hunting, led his soldiers to war. Yet, as seen through the eyes of a monastic chronicler, his concerns appear largely religious: the building of new churches, almost invariably dedicated to Mary, the richer endowment of existing monasteries, the giving of alms to the poor, the conversion of his subjects if necessary by force, the reburial of former kings in suitable shrines, supervision of the annual rebaptism of the nation in river or tank, the celebration of feasts. Almost every day in Ethiopia was either a fast day or a feast day, and both had to be observed religiously. There is one charming, more unexpected moment in the chronicle when it records how, beside the reburial of his father and other kings, he also reburied the body of his much-loved old teacher, Takla Iyasus, who had taught him to read the psalms, and how he reclothed his corpse in white vestments. The characteristics of African monarchy and monastic spirituality were being merged at the Ethiopian court, unhindered in their inculturation by powers from without.

Yet one noticeable development in fifteenth-century Ethiopia, all the same, was its declining isolation. The rulers of Egypt feared to be cornered between the Christian kingdom and the countries of Europe, so they did their best to prevent contact. All the same the revival of links is very clear. Jerusalem was the principal point of meeting, 'the clearing house of the Eastern Christian cultures'.[32] We do not know just when an Ethiopian monastery was first established in Jerusalem, but it must have been there well before 1290 when the Emperor Yagbe'a Seyon wrote it a letter. The attraction of Jerusalem

---

[32] E. Cerulli, *Tiberius and Pontius Pilate in Ethiopian Tradition and Poetry* (1973), 19.

for Ethiopia was always enormous and, dangerous as the journey was, the number of pilgrims was steadily growing. There was too an Ethiopian community in Cairo at the church of St George in the Harat Zuwaila and others elsewhere in Egypt. In Cairo, and still more in Jerusalem, Ethiopian monks came into considerable contact with the wider Christian world, and some of them—probably a small minority, for the hazards of the road were enormous—returned to Ethiopia with new books and new ideas. A few others by the fourteenth century were visiting western Europe. By the reign of Zara Ya'iqob they were travelling still more widely, and two of them attended the Council of Florence, delegated not by the emperor but by the Abbot of Jerusalem, Nicodemus. On 2 September 1441 one of them, Peter, spoke before the Council, declaring at the close of his address that the Emperor desired nothing so much as 'to be united with the Roman Church and to cast himself at your most holy feet'. It is unlikely that Zara Ya'iqob shared those sentiments or was aware of their expression, and in the letter Peter presented from his abbot it was stressed that 'without our king we can do nothing'.[33] The Ethiopian Church was not included within the reunions of Florence, but the two monks made a great impression and can still be seen portrayed upon the doors of St Peter's.

A number of European sovereigns beginning with Henry IV of England in 1400 attempted to send letters to the Emperor of Ethiopia, the idea of an alliance with a powerful Christian state on the other side of Muslim Egypt being naturally attractive. It was, however, extremely difficult actually to arrive in Ethiopia and still more difficult to leave again. The Emperor almost always insisted upon outsiders settling down for good with an Ethiopian wife at the court. From the mid-fifteenth century there were probably always ten or more Europeans in Ethiopia but only one or two ever returned to Europe. In consequence this did little to improve relationships. Nor do they seem to have contributed much to Ethiopian life, with the one exception of the painter Nicolas Brancaleone, an artist who spent some forty years in the country and some of whose works survive. His own paintings, together with other Western imports, had a considerable effect upon Ethiopian art, which was for a while markedly open to Byzantine and Italian influences.

All this did not transform the conscious relationship of Ethiopia

---

[33] Joseph Gill, *The Council of Florence* (Cambridge, 1959), 322-7.

and the rest of the Christian Church. It was more of a pregnant new start than an achievement. Nevertheless, in Christian terms the almost total isolation of Ethiopia which had lasted since the seventh century, apart from a very narrow lifeline to Alexandria, had come to an end. Theological, devotional, and artistic contacts were multiplying. The new links were met with both suspicion and eagerness. Ethiopians were anxious for allies against Islam and very much aware that they were part of a wider Christian world. What religious differences they had with even a Western Christian like Alvares were really quite small in comparison with what they held in common. At the same time, after so long an isolation and so national a tradition, they could not easily relate to ideas from abroad which challenged that tradition in any significant way.

Indeed, even the link with the Patriarchate of Alexandria was now in question. Zara Ya'iqob died in 1468. His two bishops, Mika'el and Gabri'el, had died some ten years earlier, and, it seems, he never requested their replacement. Perhaps he feared lest any new bishop might disagree with him. Nor did his successor, Baida Maryam, at first make such a move. There seems to have been mounting opposition to the connection with Alexandria itself. The Copts did not observe the Sabbath. They also ate what was forbidden by the Law. The Council of Dabra Mitmaq had, for the first time, committed the Church of Ethiopia explicitly to an orthodoxy recognizably different from that of Alexandria, and—one can surmise—those who had most strongly backed the Sabbath decision, the House of Ewostatewos and its allies, now questioned the request for any further bishop from Egypt.

Yet the shortage of priests was inevitably becoming acute and in 1477 Baida Maryam summoned a council to decide on what was to be done. Upon one side was the 'nationalist' party, opposed to further dependence upon a foreign see and one now actually unorthodox in their eyes. It seems that, at the council, this group was actually a majority. Upon the other side stood the eccage, Marha Krestos. The abbots of Dabra Libanos had long maintained a tradition of co-operation with the Egyptian abuna, yet in the prolonged absence of the latter, the eccage must have been behaving increasingly like a substitute. In these circumstances Marha Krestos might have been tempted to argue against the need for further Egyptian metropolitans, though that would have been to abandon the tradition of his house. In fact he did the opposite. In the fourteenth century the house of Takla Haymanot had lost the battle over royal polygamy, and in the early fifteenth century it lost that over the Sabbath. This time, however, it did not lose, Marha Krestos persuading the king not to abandon so ancient a custom. Baida Maryam died the following year, but a delegation was subsequently sent to Cairo and in 1480–1 returned with two senior bishops, Yishaq and Marqos, two junior bishops, Mika'el and Yohannis, and one *qomos*, Yosef. Perhaps the Patriarchate recognized how perilous the situation had become and how important it was to reinforce the abuna's authority. The Ethiopian link was, after all, important to the Patriarchate too. Faced with his Muslim rulers it helped to be able to demonstrate that he could exercise some influence over a powerful Christian neighbour, whose periodic gifts to both the sultan and the Patriarch were no doubt welcome enough. As a result of all this the chronicler of Eskendir's reign was able to record: 'In his reign came bishops from Holy Jerusalem. The priests became many, the churches were restored, happiness filled the land.'[34] There can be little doubt that a decision to break with Alexandria could have been suicidal for Ethiopian Christianity. The issue of the Sabbath had precipitated a more basic confrontation between catholicity and nationalism. The links with the world Church were very limited, yet both their theoretical significance and their recognizable effects were clear enough. Presumably the monks of the House of Takla Haymanot saw something of this. It may not have escaped them that the proponents of the 'nationalist' case were communities who had, a little earlier, been willing to give up ordination altogether for more than half a century. If the Council of 1477 had decided otherwise there might have resulted a major shift in both Ethiopian theology and Church order. This course appeared altogether too perilous. The undoubted nationalism and particularism of the Ethiopian Church was to remain, but it would be held just a little in check by the continued authority of Alexandria.

[34] J. Perruchon (ed.), 'Histoire D'Eskender, de Amda-Seyon II et de Na'od, rois d'Éthiopie', *Journal asiatique,* 9/3 (1894), 340.

2

AFRICA IN 1500 AND ITS CHRISTIAN PAST

i. *Society, States, Statelessness, and Religion*

In 1520 a Portuguese embassy, led by Dom Rodrigo de Lima, landed on the Ethiopian coast and made its way to the court of the Emperor Lebna Dengel. Of its experiences there we have a most detailed account written by the chaplain, Francesco Alvares, after his return to Portugal six years later. It was the first embassy from the West to Ethiopia ever to arrive back. The new factor which really made this possible was the circumnavigation of Africa by Vasco da Gama in 1498, an event preceded by numerous Portuguese expeditions down the west coast. Portugal, entering its imperial phase, had established a first permanent base in Africa at Ceuta on the north coast in 1415, to be followed in the west by the building of Elmina Castle on the Gold Coast in 1481, and in the east by forts at Sofala and on Mozambique Island in 1505 and 1507. But Portugal was not the only new power to be entering Africa on a large scale in these years. In 1517 a far more powerful empire did so when the Ottoman Turkish army of the Sultan Selim I conquered Egypt. From being an independent but, latterly, relatively weak state under the Mamluks, Egypt became part of a vast, aggressive, and very potent empire centred upon Istanbul, which was soon to take over Algeria as well.

Now it was quite possible for Lebna Dengel in the 1520s to be informed of these various events affecting the different parts of Africa, just as it was possible for the king of Portugal, the Pope, and the sultan on the Golden Horn to know of them. There is a genuine sense in which a common continental history of Africa, perceivable as such not only by us but by contemporaries, began around 1500, which makes of it a moderately convenient date from which to assess, very roughly, the state of the continent as a whole.[1] It is, moreover,

---

[1] It is also true that the encyclopedic historians in 14th- and 15th-cent. Egypt, especially Ibn Khaldun and al-Maqrizi, were already demonstrating a nearly continent-wide knowledge of Africa, assisted both by Arab travellers like Ibn Battuta and by people from north, west, and east on pilgrimage to Mecca, a century before the Portuguese rounded the Cape.

about the last moment at which the state of Africa is no more than marginally affected by the rise and expansion of western Europe, a factor which will be increasingly decisive for the central part of our history. Of course, in so far as it was possible in the first quarter of the sixteenth century to look at Africa in some way as a whole, that was an opportunity vouchsafed to only a tiny handful of people and it applied only to the continent's coastal territories. Almost everyone within Africa was entirely unaware that a new age and a new conscious interlocking of local histories within a wider story was at the point of beginning.

The typical experience of early sixteenth-century humankind in most of Africa was utterly different. Not only was there no sense of a confrontation of superstates, there was no sense of a state at all. It is with that experience that an African overview can best begin, the world of the large majority of people who lived in stateless societies. Even in the late nineteenth century many tens of millions of Africans still lived in such societies, and it is certain that the proportion within them had been steadily falling over the centuries. They may well be said to represent, in one form or another, Africa's principal contribution to social polity. It is true that with the outsider they have seldom been popular: the colonial official, the trader, the missionary, and the historian have all concentrated their attention upon kingdoms. The stateless society is easily judged as only a backward survival of a primitive past. It is a one-sided and misleading evaluation. The ingenuity with which some peoples have carried on their affairs very efficiently and on a quite considerable scale without formal rulers is impressive. Rulers in all parts of the world and in all ages have far too frequently burdened their subjects very heavily while providing quite limited benefits. One suspects that many people in medieval Europe or elsewhere would have been only too happy to live in a stateless society had they been given the chance. Indeed, the effective maintenance of communal identity, the regular functioning of public life for quite large groups of people, through a combination of lineage obligation, age grades, and 'secret' societies entrusted with particular functions of education, good order, and defence may be claimed as a genuine contribution to human civilization far beyond that of most monarchies.

Such societies were of various kinds, depending upon the density of population and the geographical extent of a shared sense of community as well as many other factors relating to kinship and economic system. Some were no more than tiny lineage groups or a small cluster of villages; others, of much larger territorial spread, were linked less by lineage or immediate neighbourhood than by language, initiation into age groups, and secret societies. In smaller groups it may be hard to distinguish between the gerontocracy of eldership and the sacred kingship of the head of a small lineage community, and the one may at times have developed into the other. Sacred kingship was not incompatible with a basically democratic authority of elders. A leadership confined to emergencies rather than the institutionalization of power in a few identifiable functionaries was the characteristic of the stateless society, but there is no precise frontier dividing it from the mini-state or, perhaps, even the maxi-state: their components were very much the same. Villages might be compact or scattered, and to a greater or lesser degree constructed on the basis of lineage, but their almost shapeless spread by the million across the length and breadth of Africa was the continent's most characteristic social feature.

In the period around 1500 in a good many areas, west and east, stateless units were being slowly integrated into kingdoms of a certain size, with a capital and a royal dynasty of which the members had names and tombs which would be remembered and sacralized in perpetuity. One reason for this would appear to be an increase in the density of population. It is possible—though increasingly difficult—to maintain a stateless society with a relatively dense rural population, but it is almost impossible to have a kingdom without a central area of some density. The thicker population stimulates trade, the diversification of economic functions and social classes, the development of permanent trading centres or even towns, and it makes the control of power by a few both practicable and (for them at least) apparently desirable. Africa is so vast that the natural response to an increase in density of population was simply to move away. That may also have been the response of many to the attempt of others to impose the authority of monarchy upon them with all its attendant claims to tribute and obedience and the threat of rather arbitrary punishment if the monarch's displeasure be incurred. This continued to be the situation in much of East and southern Africa but in the west, especially in the coastal areas, the rising density of population made migration less feasible and it prompted instead the development of recognizable states with increasingly firm borders.

This could be considerably assisted by lines of trade, as across the Sahara, focusing at certain points.

Nevertheless, the ability of a king to control his subjects was limited by many things, communications especially. He had little that they did not. The horse, the mule, and the camel were of considerable importance in making the development of larger states practicable both in the horn of Africa and south of the Sahara. Elsewhere there was no real substitute. Where a monarchy came to exist it consisted almost invariably of a large central court surrounded by an area of relatively high population able to claim and to exercise a limited suzerainty over the mini-kingdoms and villages of more remote areas. The real life and structure of such villages remained barely touched and there was next to no intermediate level of provincial town, though as a monarchy grew so did the secondary courts of provincial and client chiefs. The problem of this pattern in any of the drier areas of the continent was how to provide adequate permanent provisioning of food and fuel for the large population required by the court. The most extraordinary early example of a monarchy in central Africa is undoubtedly that of Great Zimbabwe, which flourished in the fourteenth century in the climatically fairly favourable plateau area between Zambezi and Limpopo. But it is clear that Great Zimbabwe was all the same economically impractical. The scale and skill of its buildings reflect a powerful king surrounded by quite a large population. Yet it was impossible for long to maintain such a court. Without wheeled transport, water transport, or even a supply of horses and mules, such as those upon which the king of Ethiopia depended, Zimbabwe had to be abandoned in the fifteenth century because the area around it was simply exhausted. Two successor states developed, one to the west at Khami, where a small but somewhat similar stone capital was constructed, the other (Mutapa) to the north. Neither flourished for very long. The basic reason for the peregrinatory nature of the capital of Ethiopia was probably the same: no area of the country could tolerate so many additional mouths to feed for very long.

Only if there was considerable trade requiring a concentrated focal point or if there was a grave military threat from neighbours, or—again—if the population in a given area had become fairly dense and could no longer easily move anywhere else, were the conditions present to encourage (though not to compel) the establishment of some form of monarchical state. Apart from the empires of the

Sudanic belt this had, by 1500, quite clearly taken place in several areas along the west coast, where climate and vegetation were anyway unusually propitious, and one or two elsewhere. Ife, Ijebu, and still more Benin were recognizable states of considerable power, size, wealth, and reputation. So was Kongo, if weaker on the side of material wealth because unhelped by Saharan trade connections. So, though smaller and more recent, was Ndongo further down the coast. So were Khami and Mutapa, assisted a little by trade with the east coast Arab port of Sofala. So, in the exceptionally favourable climatic area of the great lakes (principally north and west of what has since been named Lake Victoria), were the kingdoms of Buganda, Bunyoro, and Rwanda, though at this time these were only just achieving a fairly stable shape and could certainly not be compared in scale with Benin or Kongo. Earlier kingdoms had existed here and there, but their relatively small scale and the attractions of migration, operating in a continent of vast and thinly occupied areas, had ensured their disappearance as much as their appearance.

It would seem to be the case that by the early sixteenth century a rise in population almost everywhere was, on the whole, discouraging large-scale migration (or ensuring that, when it did take place as with the Galla in the horn, it brought with it massive disruption of existing stable societies) and making for a greater stability and continuity in such states as did exist. It seems clear that a fair number of states all over Africa, existing in a recognizable form in modern times, claim origins about the sixteenth century, but for the most part they were at that time very much smaller than they subsequently became in the eighteenth and nineteenth centuries. Adding all these kingdoms together, as they then were, they still come only to a small proportion of the Africa of that time. All around them, and even within their claimed borders, were the stateless societies of immemorial tradition, self-sufficient villages and groups of villages. The outsider coming to Africa would quickly focus upon Benin and Kongo, Mutapa and Ethiopia. The historians mostly continue to do so, and not without reason. The development of urban complexity, the accumulation of material wealth and artefacts of a fairly permanent kind, together with patronage of technicians able to produce such things, the formation of standing or semi-professional armies, the construction and servicing of public temples and shrines, the creation and handing-on of history and literature through chroniclers and poets: all such activities depended almost entirely upon, or at least progressed almost inseparably from, the formation of monarchies of a certain size and organizational complexity. Of course some of these activities might in other cultural circumstances (such as those grounded in a literate world religion) be advanced otherwise as through monasteries. But in the non-literate world of sub-Saharan Africa they seem to have required, and understandably, the closest connection with state formation of a monarchical sort.

These were societies relatively intelligible to the sixteenth-century European trader or priest and they will in consequence capture most of our attention in the ensuing period, but if they were abnormal in being at least to some extent in contact with Christianity, this was largely due to the fact that they were in basic African terms still themselves abnormal in existing as recognizable states in a largely (and, on the whole, perhaps blessedly) stateless continent.

The religion of these societies was no more homogeneous than their political structures, yet there was an underlying pattern which, if not universal, we may still regard as normative.[2] There is enough evidence to suggest that belief in a single creator god was normally foundational in their world-view. God was generally associated particularly with the sky, or with the sun in the sky, yet sometimes too with the earth, and the existence of these alternative and symbolically contrasting possibilities could itself engender a certain divine dualism between earth and sky, the female and the male. This was the more so as the beliefs and practices of one society could easily be carried by migration and intermarriage into those of another, so that gods and symbolic systems could be multiplied and overlie one another, only partially integrated. Belief was shaped by the particularity and variety of experience, and no society should be presumed to have had a single static or necessarily consistent theology (perhaps no society in the world ever has had one, at least for long). Words and symbols for deity multiplied and overlapped—some having a far more anthropomorphic connotation than others—but

---

[2] To a large extent we can infer that African religion as observed in the 19th and 20th cents. was present in its main lines in the 16th and 17th, but we also have many interesting accounts of African religion at that time from the hands of missionaries in such works as João dos Santos, *Etiopia oriental* (Evora, 1609), Manuel Alvares, *Etiopia menor e descricão geografica da provincia Serra Leoa* (1615), A. Donelha, *Descricão da Serra Leoa e dos Rios de Guiné do Cabo Verde* (1652), Giovanni Cavazzi, *Istorica descrizione de tre regni, Congo, Matamba ed Angola* (Bologna, 1687), and the Abbé Proyart, *Histoire de Loango, Kakongo et autres royaumes d'Afrique* (Paris, 1776).

the power and presence of God tended to be seen above all in a range of natural phenomena (the sun, rain, thunder) whose names might well be no different from the names of God.

However, between God and the living was a vast world of spirits, far nearer to humankind and therefore on the whole in daily life more important to approach and propitiate. Their images, symbols, or impersonations—the 'idols' or 'fetishes' visible almost everywhere in western Africa especially—provided the principal expression of religion for the eye of the outsider. These spirits were mostly of two kinds: spirits of the village and spirits of the wild. The former were one's ancestors, inherently friendly and supportive at least so long as one followed the customary norms of right living, but also tiresomely demanding; behind and above them often stood the hero figure or proto-ancestor, who first established the people or led them to their present home and whose miraculous power seemed little less, though more ambiguous, than that of divinity itself. The latter were not necessarily evil, but could be frightening, unpredictable, and dangerous like the forest in which they dwelt. Divinity and the original creation might be perceived and named in terms, and across the experience, of either the one or the other. And both expressed their will through possession. Spirit possession was an almost universal phenomenon of African religion, an ongoing revelatory experience. There was nothing seen as evil about it, it was simply as such a primary way (though there were important other ways too, mostly manual) for communication between the visible and invisible worlds. Yet clearly possession by a spirit of the wild was a more dangerous experience, and some such spirits (as also those of the evil dead) might be close to being seen as evil. As the forest was tamed and the village expanded, the spirits of the forest tended to grow in scale (but effectively to be reduced in number), becoming the nature deities of a pantheon above the ancestors but below the creator. Within a monarchical theology many of them might merge with powerful kings of the past and might so grow in majesty and worship as effectively, or wholly, to exclude any more ultimate power. Religion was, however, much less a matter of theology than of ritual, rituals intended to control the present and safeguard the future in both the social and the physical orders: rituals of initiation and kingship, of fertility and rain, of sickness and death. They were all performed in the hope of securing the fullness of life by appealing to, or even attempting to control, whatever spiritual powers there be beyond yet within the visible world. While this appeal was sometimes to God in the most ultimate sense, it was far more often to other spirits around whom the ritual, sacrificial, and invocatory life of *Homo religiosus Africanus* mostly revolved.

The balance of life, physical, social, spiritual, was well constructed in principle but easily disturbed in practice. It was not a golden world in which generations passed without undue pain, crisis, or history. The rains failed. Children died unexpectedly. Men fought over women and murdered one another in anger. More powerful neighbours seized one's cattle or invaded one's ancestral holding. But most such tragedies, millions of times as they occurred, left no trace whatever beyond the memory of one or two generations in the story of humankind. They were small-scale. They were never recorded in writing. Life went on. People forgave, moved their dwellings, bore other children, recognized new lords and new gods. The knowledge and technology available even to the more powerful could have next to no effect upon the ecology (except, perhaps, in the over-use of some limited terrain around a royal capital) and relatively little upon the majority of their neighbours. Then as now the human heart had more than enough to endure, but upon all sides it was—from the viewpoint of our modern eyes—endurance within a context of micro-concern but macro-powerlessness.

Benin we may take as something already rather different. The 'Great city of Beny', as Pacheco Pereira called it in his *Esmeraldo de Situ Orbis*, written about 1506,[3] was in 1500 ruled by the Oba Ozulua, son of the Oba Ewuare, who about the middle of the fifteenth century had established Benin as the most powerful state in Africa south of the Sudanic belt. While extending the power of the monarchy over the nobles, he had reformed the constitution, built an inner wall and ditch around Benin City, and extended the frontiers of the state both east and west. Benin benefited, it would seem, from being a centre of long-distance trade as well as being a home of crafts, in brass and bronze and terracotta, of extraordinary skill. Some of this the Ede of Benin had learnt from their neighbours, the Yoruba to the west, or, perhaps, the mysterious people who had some centuries earlier made the artefacts recently discovered a little east of the Niger at Igbo-Ukwu. In a smaller and less distinguished form Benin went

---

[3] Duarte Pacheco Pereira, *Esmeraldo de Situ Orbis*, Eng. trans. G. H. T. Kimble (1937), 125.

back with its dynasty at least a couple of centuries, while the city and kingdom of Ife, to which Benin continued to pay a ritual deference, went back to probably the tenth century. By the end of the fifteenth, in this exceptional area, there was a small cluster of monarchies developing, each centred upon a city, of which Ife was the oldest and Benin currently the most powerful. They were the sort of state the king of Portugal could do business with.

ii. *African Islam*

To the north of Benin and Ife, in the Sudanic savannah, were empires larger still or rather, in 1500, there was one principal and immensely extensive empire, that of Songhay, which had been built up around its capital at Gao on the middle Niger and was, at this time, ruled by Askia Al-hajj Mohammed Ture. A century and a half earlier the principal Sudanic state had been Mali, considerably to the west, and still earlier it had been Ghana. The Sudanic story of the rather rapid rise and fall of states, immensely much vaster in extent than anything to the south of them, and documented in the writings of Arabic-speaking travellers, seems in sharp contrast with anything we have yet encountered other than Ethiopia. In part that is indeed the case, but in part it is deceptive. There seems little reason to believe that the process of indigenous state formation was here so greatly different or, even, so greatly in advance of what was going on among the Yoruba or Ede peoples. In the tenth and eleventh centuries small kingdoms were being consolidated here and there at focal points of trade and where the population had grown denser. What altered that so sharply to provide in central west Africa a new sort of history was the fusion of this indigenous process of slow state formation with the arrival in increasing numbers of white foreigners—Arab and Berber merchants, crossing the 'sea' of the Sahara in great caravans in search of gold and slaves, and bringing with them a new religion, Islam.

By 1500, when the ruler of the Songhay empire had made his pilgrimage to Mecca and returned, many other kings and notables of the Sudanic belt had already done so, the pilgrimage of King Mansa Musa of Mali in 1324 being an especially famous example due to the impression he had made in Cairo. In 1500 Islam was already the official religion of the kings of most of these parts as far south as Hausaland, but to understand how this had come about and what it really signified, it is necessary to turn back a little at this point to consider briefly but as a whole the long forward movement of Islam in Africa.

In 642, only ten years after the death of Muhammad, Alexandria was surrendered to the Islamic Arab army, and the province of Egypt, which for centuries had been one of the most important parts of the Roman–Byzantine Empire as of the Christian Church, became from then on a central pillar of Islam. The whole religious and cultural history of Africa, as of the Mediterranean, was decisively changed by this act of military conquest, to be followed over the next fifty years by further advances all along the North African coast. The large majority of the population of these provinces remained for long both Christian and non-Arabic speaking, but in terms of military and political control by the early years of the eighth century Islam, that is to say the armies and governors of the Caliph of Baghdad, was unchallenged in North Africa from the Red Sea to Morocco. The Roman Empire had been in the same position for centuries but had never attempted to advance militarily across the desert. Whether its traders did so, we simply do not know. For the most part, despite occasional forays south, the Arab–Islamic military advance also ended with the desert. However, within the next century or so the knowledge that there was much gold to be had south of the Sahara had stimulated an organized trade, controlled from its northern end, which made of the Sahara for almost a millennium Africa's principal trade frontier. It is essential to realize that especially for the long medieval period, while the coast of West Africa had no significance whatsoever for trade or communication or the growth of knowledge, the Sahara was crucial for all such things. The world to the south of it was increasingly being reshaped under its influence. Strange as it may appear to modern minds, the Sahara was the hard but open road to civilization—the civilization of the Mediterranean coast and, above all, Cairo. For the West Africa of that long age Cairo was what, in later centuries, London became: the great urban heart of wealth, sophistication, learning, and power, a model for every little state drawn within the margins of this great world of commerce, literacy, and religious confidence, the place where kings from afar longed to visit and to strut briefly about on the way to fulfil their religious duties at Mecca.

The Saharan trade did not merely link areas south of the desert with those to the north, it partially transformed the former in doing do. It was of the nature of the trade, of the large caravan in foreign country, to select and thereby aggrandize a limited number of markets. Once some quite petty state had become a regular trading centre for the whites (Berbers and Arabs) from the north, it inevitably grew by leaps and bounds in relation to its neighbours. It did so because it had first choice of imported goods and could levy customs dues on all that went through. It did so, further, because of the prestige brought by the permanent settlement of foreigners and the skills of literacy (in Arabic) and wider knowledge which they brought with them and were willing to put, to some extent, at the service of a local, friendly king. Finally, it did so, very particularly, because of the nature of much of the trade. In the earlier years of the great age of Saharan trade when Ghana and then Mali were its principal beneficiaries, a large part of it was gold. Gold for salt was an early core exchange. Undoubtedly the northerners brought a far wider range of goods than they took back with them, but as the principal long-distance entrepreneurs in the exercise, it was they who called its central tune. To gold was added slaves. By the fifteenth century slaves had replaced gold as the staple commodity. The supply of gold was in itself quite limited, the supply of slaves was not. Hence the shift eastwards, to the middle Niger, of the heart of the trade and in consequence of the heart of Sudanic political power. Here gold was unavailable, but slaves were nearer the Sahara crossing than they were in Mali.

The Islamic world flourished upon slavery, female slaves very specially. Slaves were integral to its domestic, military, naval, and even sexual system (a Muslim was allowed only four wives, but any number of slave concubines, over and above that, was permissible: when a Sudanic king became a Muslim, the number of his wives went down, but that of his concubines went up. The wives had been 'free', the concubines were slaves. Whether the women noted much difference, one does not know). In some parts of the Middle East— and it is important to remember that African slaves were exported well beyond Africa—they were also important for agricultural work on large plantations, but in terms of the trade this was probably of secondary, rather than primary, importance. Females were valued more on the Saharan line, on the transatlantic they would be valued less. For over a thousand years the large-scale need for fresh slaves was incessant, and was met by a highly organized, and still far too little understood, slave trade focusing upon the Upper Nile, the coasts of eastern Africa, West Africa, and central Asia. In late medieval Europe, the role of the slave was marginal, though in Portugal and Spain in the fifteenth century it was increasing, but these were lands which had for long been Arab-ruled anyway. They were in many ways still uncharacteristic of Europe. In medieval Islam it was crucial: concubines, eunuchs, soldiers. While in subsequent centuries the imports of the Atlantic slave trade were settled together and allowed to breed among themselves, thus producing in time a permanent enslaved labour force (though here the birth-rate only caught up with the death-rate in the late eighteenth century or after), the imports of the Arab slave trade never were. They could not become a distinct society. While the conditions of the long trek across the Sahara were appalling and the wastage rate very high, once arrived the condition of the slave greatly improved. Most became Muslims. Many were freed when their period of utility was over, and if not their children were likely to be free. In so far as they bred at all, their offspring were most often mixed. They darkened the skin colour of the whole community but did not produce a society of their own. This system did, of course, necessitate a regular and rather rapid replacement of slaves. They aged fast. Herein lies the incessant logic of the Saharan trade, which was, most probably, not overtaken quantitatively by the Atlantic trade until well into the seventeenth century. A sub-Saharan spin-off was the retention of a great many slaves in the more fortunate Sudanic societies. The more they were into the Islamic system, the more slaves people possessed. Thus the Islamic 'capital' of Timbuktu was a great slave-owning city, and well into the nineteenth century the principal Hausa towns seem to have had a majority of slaves among their population.

What was the principal object offered in exchange? Undoubtedly merchants had much to offer; however, from the fourteenth to the sixteenth century, politically and socially, the most important object can be singled out as the horse. Horses, of very small breeds, had been present in most parts of West Africa north of the tropical forest for centuries. They had relatively little political or economic significance. The larger horse, brought by the thousand across the desert in these centuries, had a very different role. Just as slaves could only be sold by people with power, so horses were only bought by such people. For a time the new breed was probably almost a royal monopoly and it gave the king a quite new power, the ability to terrorize larger areas than previously, and it enhanced prestige.

Without the imported horse the extremely extended empires of the medieval Sudan are not really explicable, nor are the rapid rise and fall of these empires explicable without this controlling factor of foreign trade, which, by shifting its interests and favoured centres, could effectively strangle one empire and establish another. Furthermore, the horses were needed to round up the slaves, just as the slaves were needed to exchange for more horses. The going rate seems to have been between ten and twenty slaves per horse (the terms of north–south trade were quantitatively disadvantageous to the south, then as now). It seems that there was for long little breeding of the new type of horse south of the desert. For that they needed to be far more of a rural than—as was the case—urban phenomenon. Hence, just as the Mediterranean world needed to renew its slaves each generation from outside, so did Sudanese kings need to renew their horses from outside still more frequently. Once you were in this game, you could not stop. Probably, however, by the mid-sixteenth century the Sudanese breeding of horses was expanding, initially under royal control, yet this was likely to decrease the centralized control of horses so important for royal power. However, with the Battle of Tondibi in 1591 and the collapse of the Songhay empire, a loss of royal control over horses hardly mattered, in Songhay at least. To some extent guns would anyway replace horses as the new instrument of power which the powerful needed to monopolize. Kings were, even in the early sixteenth century, already very much on the look-out for guns. However, in reality for a couple of centuries more the effectiveness of the gun would remain very limited. For the Saharan slave-trade, as for the later Atlantic trade, a multiplicity of goods in exchange was always on offer. If the horse trade declined, it was not hard to replace it.

In North Africa Islam spread originally through military conquest. In West Africa, prior to the nineteenth century with few and relatively ineffectual exceptions, it did not do so. It spread through trade. Commerce (of the sort described), civilization, and Islam went together. Islam remained, in consequence, a very urban and royal affair. The merchants were, indeed, followed by imams whose original function, however, was probably more to chaplain the merchant communities settled south of the desert than a missionary one. But kings were encouraged to convert and already in the eleventh century they had begun to do so. From then on we hear, through Arabic records, of kings of an increasing number of areas who became Muslims. Some made the hajj. Some built mosques and attended them. Some, to a very limited extent, attempted to impose wider Islamic law and practice upon their subjects. Mansa Musa, ruler of Mali from 1307 to 1332, was the model of the new Islamic ruler. He was, declared Ibn Battuta, who visited Mali a few years later, 'a generous and virtuous king who loved whites and gave gifts to them'.[4] He built mosques, ensured at his capital the regularity of Friday prayer, imported Islamic lawyers, and went on the hajj with such a large entourage and so much gold that it was long remembered. He even attempted a jihad against the non-Muslim inhabitants of his empire.

Askia al-Hajj Muhammad Ture, ruler of Songhay from 1493 to 1528, was of much the same vintage, a man of Islamic piety, wide experience, and immense power. The thousands of his horsemen were a menace to any of his neighbours unwilling to recognize his superior authority. It is said that one of his successors even had a cavalry regiment consisting of 4,000 eunuchs. Islam had indeed been present within his realms for some 500 years, and to the west of his capital there stood the principal Islamic city of West Africa, Timbuktu, then at the height of its glory. Here was a town ruled by its cadi, a city of mosques, schools and learned men, dynasties of imams. But they were mostly white, though when the city was smaller and less important they had been Sudanese. Here, as in the lesser centre of Jenne further up the Niger, or earlier at Walata in Mali and Awdaghust in the Ghanaian days, there was a genuinely Muslim society. Among these immigrant religious scholars, resident from birth to death in Timbuktu, the most distinguished in 1500 was probably al-Hajj Ahmad. His grandson thus describes him:

A man of goodness, virtuous and pious, mindful of the *Sunna*, a very upright and distinguished man, full of love for the Prophet and devoting himself unceasingly to the reading of poems in honour of Muhammad . . . Lawyer, lexicographer, grammarian, prosodist and scholar, he occupied himself with the sciences all his life. He possessed numerous books, copied in his own hand with copious annotations. At his death he left about 700 volumes.[5]

---

[4] H. A. R. Gibb (ed.), *Ibn Battuta: Travels in Asia and Africa 1325–1354* (1929), 329.
[5] Ahmad Baba, in the late 16th cent., thus describes his grandfather, as quoted by al-Sa'di, the 17th-cent. Timbuktu historian; cf. T. Hodgkin, *Nigerian Perspectives*, 2nd edn. (1975), 117–18.

Al-Hajj Ahmad was not Sudanese and was in no way characteristic of Sudanic religion in 1500, but it mattered a great deal that men of this sort were living and working in Timbuktu in the fifteenth and sixteenth centuries.

As a devout king Askia Muhammad paid considerable attention to such teachers, but outside the walls of Timbuktu and the royal capital things were very different. It is true that one can detect something of a wider surge forward of Islam in this period when the Hausa states of Kano and Katsina were also setting out on the Islamic path; moreover, there were a few areas of the Sudan, such as the Senegal river valley, where many more ordinary people might genuinely be called Muslims, but it seems that such areas were in all fairly inconsiderable. Muslim scholars writing at the time but at great geographical distance, or Muslim scholars writing on the spot but several centuries later, both understandably tended to give an exaggerated impression of the degree of Islamicization achieved by the end of the fifteenth century. In stateless societies the appeal of Islam was nil, but even within the principal kingdoms it had left people outside the towns almost wholly unaffected. Indeed, if it had not been so, the slave trade—which was not meant to operate on Muslims—would have been in trouble. In so far as Islam existed outside Timbuktu and one or two other similar places, it was, moreover, a religion of ritual rather than of law, while in principle Islam is far more a religion of law than of ritual. Its most widespread contact with ordinary people was through the protection afforded by Qur'anic amulets. If kings were mostly Muslims, they remained for the most part hardly less participants within the web of traditional religion, and Muslim visitors could often be scandalized by the quick transition from one form of discourse to the other. In international and intertribal terms, their status lay in their Islamic identity, but in terms of local support at the heart of their kingdom, it lay within the rituals of traditional religion, and only the greatest king could afford to dispense with the latter. When his power dwindled and the merchants moved away, the warm embrace of traditional religion, its rituals, and its own monarchical mystique would remain the one safe option.

In the years just before and after 1500 the distinguished North African theologian al-Maghili was travelling around West Africa. In Kano in 1492 he wrote a treatise for its ruler Muhammad Rumfa upon the art of kingship. He was a rigorist and advised the imposition of full Islamic law. Rumfa was deferential and, at al-Maghili's request, built a Friday mosque, but it does not look as if he did much more. A few years later al-Maghili wrote a further set of *Replies* to Askia Muhammad upon much the same matters. Al-Maghili was unwilling to countenance even such compromises as the Ulema at Timbuktu had learnt to allow. Again, it is unlikely that at the time these *Replies* had much practical consequence. The gap between Islamic ideal and social and religious reality was simply too wide. A prudent king could not see his way to overcome it. But the replies had been written. They remained: a call written upon the spot to normative, uncompromising Islam, and in the nature of Islam some time in the future that call would be sure to be heard. In less than a hundred years Islam conquered the north of Africa by force of arms; in six or seven hundred years it had made a very wide but very shallow impression upon the west. Its long march in the Sudan was not without reverses, brought on most likely by the withdrawal for one reason or another of Arabs from an area. Almost everywhere the effect was superficial. Nevertheless, it was now in the ascendant everywhere from the Red Sea to the Atlantic as far south as latitude 15—and in some areas such as the horn, the isles of the east coast, and Hausaland well to the south of that—and it provided the one and only form of intellectual validation and conceptualization of the world of a more than local, non-literary, and traditional kind. It had the authority of the written word, the authority of high civilization as encountered by pilgrims in Egypt, the authority of technology and the control of manufactured articles, the authority of some quite learned and devout men who were not traders but teachers. Islam had then a lot going for it and faced, at its own level, no challenge whatsoever.

In 1494 a king from the Sudan, most probably Ali Ghaji of Bornu, arrived in Cairo on pilgrimage with his entourage including the cadi and a group of students. While there they called on the great scholar al-Suyuti, listened to his teaching, and took away with them more than twenty of his books on quite a range of subjects including grammar, law, and the history of the caliphs. The cadi presented al-Suyuti with a slave, a eunuch, one of the many they had brought with them to sell in the Cairo market. The King meanwhile asked his help in obtaining some sort of statement of official legitimization of his government, something in writing to help strengthen his authority at home. Scholarship, a new mystique of kingship, the slave-trade, and all the varied experiences of the hajj were here, as again and again, merged into one. All together they do something to explain, in its strength and its weakness, what the Islamization of West Africa really signified.

iii. *The Christian Past of North Africa and Survival in Egypt*

When one considers that long march of Islam penetrating not only West Africa but up the Nile too, almost encircling Ethiopia in the horn and spreading down the east coast of the continent, one realizes just how much the Christian kingdom of Ethiopia had become by 1500 an anomaly, a left-over from a far earlier religious movement which had in its time, 1,000 years before, seemed little less promising but had then slowly evaporated under the pressures of Islam.

We must therefore once more look back a little in order to interpret aright the religious scene as it existed at the start of our period. We will begin with the 'North Africa' of tradition, excluding Egypt, the area which is today Algeria, Tunisia, and, to a lesser extent, Morocco. Here was the old Latin-speaking African Church, presided over by the Archbishop of Carthage because Carthage was the principal city of this province of the Roman Empire, just as, in still earlier centuries, it had been the principal city of the ancient Punic state, Rome's greatest rival for hegemony in the western Mediterranean. The special hero of African Christianity was Cyprian, Bishop of Carthage in the third century, martyred in 258. Sixty years after his death, at the beginning of the reign of Constantine, his Church split disastrously between 'Donatists' and Catholics, ostensibly over the issue of how Christians who had succumbed during the great persecution should now be treated. The Donatists were rigorists while the Catholics favoured a more lenient approach to the large numbers of Church people who had compromised their faith under persecution but now wished to return to Christian practice. Almost everywhere in the Empire this problem had arisen, but nowhere else was the group of the uncompromising so large or so determined. In origin the Donatists were not an anti-Roman movement, they were not predominantly rural, and they could not without anachronism be described as an expression of African nationalism. Nevertheless, while both Catholics and Donatists appealed at first to the emperor and to the authority of Cyprian too, there developed an increasing polarization between

'Roman' and 'African'. The Catholics had the backing of the bishop of Rome and, mostly, of the emperor; they retained their strength in Carthage and in circles linked with imperial government and the Church outside Africa, while the Donatists multiplied in rural Numidia among the least Romanized of people. By the later fourth century in most parts of the country the Donatists appeared to have the upper hand and they were supported by wandering bands of militant religious fanatics called the Circumcelliones.

The Catholics, on the other hand, appear as a rather weak and demoralized group until the arrival back from Italy of the brilliant young academic convert Augustine, whom the Catholic diocese of Hippo quickly chose as its bishop. Augustine and his friends reinvigorated Catholicism and easily out-argued the Donatists, but they did it by an appeal to values and powers which were universalist rather than local. Catholicism and Africanism were here falling apart. After a debate at Carthage in 411 Donatism was proscribed by imperial authority and, to some extent, driven underground. Its roots, however, had sunk deep and the country people of Numidia were unlikely to feel very affectionate towards either an extortionate and inefficient imperial government or its protégés. Less than twenty years later, furthermore, imperial authority itself collapsed beneath the Vandal invasion. Augustine himself died in a Hippo besieged by the Vandal army. The Vandals were Arians and treated the Catholics as badly as the imperial government had treated the Donatists. A century later they were driven out and Roman authority restored to a devastated province under Justinian. At the end of the sixth century the Donatists were still there and the Catholics were still appealing to the emperor to suppress them. There can be no doubt but that this long and bitter schism had much to do with the failure of the North African Church to push vigorously south among the Berber tribes. Some progress had, undoubtedly, been made in this direction but no diocese existed beyond the imperial frontier and, so far as we know, the Scriptures had not been translated into any local language. Latin had been the lingua franca of the province, of Catholic and Donatist alike. No sign has survived of an ecclesiastical effort to get beyond its increasingly shrunken boundaries, yet it has to be said as well that we really know exceedingly little of the condition of this very extensive Church upon the eve of the Arab invasion.

The Arab conquest of Egypt in 642 was neither inevitably nor immediately followed by that of North Africa. The first attack came seven years later, but it proved little more than a destructive raid. For fifty years the future of the province remained in doubt and its defence by an alliance of imperial troops and Berber auxiliaries was by no means wholly unsuccessful. Carthage did not fall to the forces of Islam until 694 and was then recaptured by a Byzantine fleet the following year. Only in 698 was it finally lost and the Berber Christian forces too overwhelmed. A rapid decline in the number of Christians followed, leaving what soon became a minority and largely urban Church to struggle on for five more centuries. By the latter part of the eleventh century it was reduced to no more than a single bishop. At that time a Muslim prince, al-Nasir, in a move which was as charming as it was unusual, actually appealed to Pope Gregory VII to consecrate another bishop, named Servandus, which Gregory did, replying to al-Nasir with equal and genuinely ecumenical graciousness. That was in 1076. A century later the end came. The Almohads, a more ruthless dynasty, while reconquering Tunis and other coastal towns which had been temporarily captured by the Normans of Sicily, offered to the Jews and Christians in the area the stark choice between conversion and death. In the words of the Arab commentator, 'Some became Muslim and the rest were put to death' (Ibn al-Athir).[6]

It is a little odd how frequently modern Christian writers have moralized rather judgementally upon the disappearance of the Church of North Africa and sought out its weaknesses to explain its fall. As we have seen, weaknesses there were—everywhere there are—linked in this case very particularly with the long-drawn-out and frequently bitter struggle between Catholic and Donatist. Nevertheless, it might also be appropriate to ask what were the strengths of the Church which enabled it to survive for five hundred years under Muslim domination. Sicily was ruled by Muslims for just 250 years from 827. At the close of that period only one of its sixteen dioceses remained. Sicilian Christianity would soon have disappeared entirely had it not been for the Norman Conquest. If a contrast is drawn between the survival of Coptic Christianity in Egypt and the fate of the province of Carthage, one reason may well lie in the immediate circumstances of the two conquests and the geographical situation of North Africa. There was no long struggle to conquer Egypt, which fell almost at a blow. In consequence of the imperial

[6] J. Cuoq, *L'Église d'Afrique du Nord, du deuxième au douzième siècle* (Paris, 1984), 171.

collapse and the inevitable acquiescence of Egyptian Christians in the *fait accompli* (partly to be explained by the great unpopularity of Byzantine government in Egypt at that time), there was a rather easy beginning to the Christian–Muslim relationship. There was no way in which the many millions of Egypt's largely Christian population could be other than tolerated more or less benignly by the couple of hundred thousand of its conquerors. While some Christians will have emigrated, they were probably few. Where, after all, could they go? In North Africa things were very different. Some eight campaigns extending over nearly fifty years were needed before the province was subdued. The effect of that long resistance was both to stimulate Christians to leave (and emigration to Italy, Sicily, or Spain was relatively easy) and to help foster a more noticeably intolerant tradition within North African Islam, particularly within its teaching city of Kairowan, although its rulers could at times be tolerant enough. Yet, whether more or less accommodating, the basic status of Christians in a Muslim state was everywhere one of permanent discrimination and marginalization. New churches could never be built, the public expression of religion was almost always prohibited. Everywhere such a condition has tended over the generations to the annihilation of minorities.

It may also be the case that the general system of Church ministry existing in Egypt was very much better suited to survival in hard times than that of the Latin Church of North Africa. The strength of the Coptic Church lay in the combination of monasteries, many of them in rather remote places, and a numerous married clergy. Both were needed. The latter enabled the ritual and pastoral life of the Church to continue close to the people, the former provided symbolic strongholds of learning and spirituality. The Western discipline, as favoured already by Augustine, in attempting to impose a more celibate and segregated model upon the pastoral clergy in fact weakened their ability to survive, both numerous and close, to their flock. At the same time while there were monasteries in North Africa they do not appear to have had as much importance as those of Egypt. While Augustine's model of the slightly gentlemanly monastic cathedral community was valuable enough, it was almost certainly not one to thrive in crippling circumstances.

Thus, when our history begins in the fifteenth century, the great Church of North Africa survived only in the writings of Cyprian and Augustine, which had been carried across the sea to become truly foundational for the theological and religious development of the West in both its Catholic and its Protestant traditions. In Egypt the story was different. For some two centuries after the Arab conquest there remained a Christian majority, which Arab rulers at the time simply had to take for granted. The rather pacific start to the new regime helped to create a relationship of tolerance which endured to some extent through several subsequent periods. Doubtless Egyptians, who had so often been ruled by foreigners and, only a little before, for a dozen years by Persians, saw this at first as just one more interlude in their long history. Its finality could not have been foreseen, nor even, maybe, the essentially non-Christian character of Islam: Christians were inclined to regard it as something a bit like Arianism and no more destined to last. Its increasingly oppressive rule stimulated a major Christian uprising in the ninth century, and its merciless repression was probably the moment from which Egypt had a Muslim majority. At all times the Christians had to suffer special taxes, and frequently they were abused by much more discriminatory laws. However, the Fatimids (967–1171), perhaps because they were themselves not orthodox Muslims, were extraordinarily tolerant (with the one ghastly exception of al-Hakim) and some even attended public Christian ceremonies. The brief Ayyubid dynasty (1171–1250) was rather less so, but it was in the long period of Mamluk rule (1250–1517) that repression became more persistent, and the resources of the Copts to withstand it steadily diminished.

In the thirteenth century the Coptic Church was still both vigorous and numerous. It had had to abandon Coptic, the traditional language of Egypt, but it had adapted itself to the use of Arabic (except within the liturgy itself), just as the Patriarch of Alexandria had moved to the Arab city of Cairo. In Abul Barakat Ibn Kabar (died about 1320) it even had a writer and theologian of some power. Yet at the time that Ibn Kabar was dying new onslaughts were being directed at his Church. Thus in 1320 some fifty-four churches were destroyed throughout Egypt, while no church was ever permitted to be built. John XIII was Patriarch from 1484 to 1524. He witnessed the end of Mamluk rule and a return under the Ottomans to government from the very city, Constantinople, which had ruled Egypt 900 years earlier, before the arrival of Islam. But this change would not assist the Coptic Church, which was approaching its lowest ebb. It had survived in the past by the sheer strength of numbers, the maintenance of the monastic citadels from which it drew its bishops, and its profound sense of identity as representative of the true Egypt, but the pressure of so many centuries of discrimination had worn it down pathetically. In desperate need of help from somewhere, it entered after the Council of Florence for a few years into union with Rome. Yet Rome had neither a true sympathy for its tradition nor any real power to help, while any link with the West was politically dangerous in raising the suspicions of its Muslim rulers. From the fifteenth to the eighteenth century the Coptic Church went through a long dark tunnel about which we know rather little. Yet it survived.

iv. *Nubia*

The Church in Nubia to its south did not survive. Yet, when we begin this history, Nubian Christianity did still just exist. The territory along the Upper Nile, south of the border of the Roman Empire, had doubtless in part been evangelized in an informal way at quite an early period—no later than the fourth century and quite possibly earlier—as a natural extension to the Church of Upper Egypt. Sahidic Coptic was used in the Nubian Church, as was Greek. By the late sixth century there were several Christian kingdoms in Nubia, a northern state called Makuria with its capital at Dongola, and a southern state of Alwa centred upon Soba close to the modern Khartoum. We do not know whether the Scriptures were translated into Nubian, though in later centuries Nubian did come to be used for formal documents such as ecclesiastical land charters as well as for lives of the saints. This was a period when Coptic was ceasing, or had ceased, to be a spoken language even in Egypt. Maybe in an earlier age a knowledge of Coptic and use of the Coptic Scriptures were quite widespread; it is hard to believe that knowledge of Greek ever was. Following the Arab conquest of Egypt, Nubia too was attacked, but put up such a spirited resistance, while at the same time appearing to have relatively little to offer in the way of economic inducement, that the Baqt treaty was concluded in 652 whereby it was agreed that no Muslim should enter the country, but that Nubia should make an annual payment of slaves to Egypt (probably in return for other goods). It would seem that the treaty was kept for several centuries, and between the eighth and the twelfth centuries Christian Nubia flourished. Monasteries and cathedrals like those of Faras, Qasr Ibrim, Soba, Sai, and Dongola were built and decorated with splendid paintings. Here as in Ethiopia Christianity was a royal religion, greatly dependent upon the king, but unlike Ethiopia Nubia had several bishoprics and they were held by local Nubians rather than Egyptians, though consecrated by the Patriarch of Alexandria. The experience of increasing isolation from the rest of Christendom was the same.

Being quite limited in its area of settlement each side of the Nile, Nubia was far more vulnerable to invasion than Ethiopia became, and it was from time to time raided and weakened by Muslim armies, but it would seem that its slow collapse was peaceful rather than violent. It lacked adequate internal resources to survive on its own and the decline of the Coptic Church after the thirteenth century is likely to have had its effect upon Nubia. After some centuries, despite the Baqt, Muslims did inevitably encroach upon the country through trade and the migration of less settled desert peoples, added to which in the thirteenth century a Muslim inherited the northern throne, apparently peacefully. At that point the majority was still Christian, but with a Muslim king the balance slowly changed, though it looks as if this was accompanied by a disintegration of royal power to be replaced by a multiplicity of tiny feudal lordships. Without a strong and supportive monarchy the Church too declined. In the far south, in the kingdom of Alwa, about which we know particularly little, Christian rule remained for rather longer, but in the north too there was for a time a Christian breakaway state called Dotawo, with its capital at Qasr Ibrim, a strongly defensible site. We now possess the splendid consecration and enthronement certificates of Timotheos, a Nubian bishop of Qasr Ibrim, signed by Patriarch Gabriel IV of Alexandria in 1372.[7] He was consecrated in Cairo and enthroned not in his own cathedral but at Qamula in Egypt three months later. He then brought back with him to Qasr Ibrim these scrolls, duplicate in Bohairic and Arabic, and when he died they were placed beneath his body in the cathedral. Even a century later, in 1484, there was still in Dotawo a Christian king, named Joel, and a bishop of Ibrim named Merki. Thus a Christian kingdom in Nubia lasted well beyond the reign of Zara Ya'iqob in Ethiopia. We do not know when the line of either ended, here or in Alwa, but certainly not much later than the beginning of the sixteenth century and the Turkish conquest of Egypt, yet some Christian villages and smaller communities lasted a

---

[7] J. M. Plumley, *The Scrolls of Bishop Timotheos* (1975).

good deal longer, even it seems into the eighteenth century. Here as elsewhere grass-roots Christianity was abandoned to its fate, yet did not easily expire. Nevertheless, it could hardly endure indefinitely without priests, and priests depended upon bishops, and the survival of a line of bishops depended upon either the patronage of kings or that of some external ecclesiastical authority. The Patriarchate of Alexandria was self-confident enough to survive on its own momentum, a line of bishops in a frontier territory was not.

In January 1742 Fr. Giacomo Rzimarz, a Franciscan in Upper Egypt, wrote to Cardinal Belluga to tell him that his servant, a Berberine, came from a village called Tangos, an island of the Nile near Dongola, where there were still Christians. 'How', asked Fr. Rzimarz in a subsequent letter, 'did Nubia go astray from the Christian faith? ex solo defectu pastorum, only because of a lack of pastors.'[8]

That was to some extent a simplification. One could, perhaps, add the lack of indigenous Scriptures too, though that is questionable. In the sixteenth century Enbaqom in Ethiopia, who read both Coptic and Arabic, affirmed the existence of the Scriptures in Nubian. A war may finally have ended the Christian monarchy and imposed Muslim rule, but there was, so far as one knows, no final persecution. The churches were little by little abandoned, not turned into mosques. Without a king to protect it the episcopate was too fragile to endure. Traditional Christianity is not, unlike Islam, a lay religion. It has very limited powers of survival without an ordained priesthood, but the priesthood cannot last more than a generation without the renewing activity of a bishop, and the episcopate has been so hedged around and limited in number (new consecrations requiring the presence of three bishops) that in frontier situations it very easily disappears.

We have by chance an account of, perhaps, the last appeal of a handful of Nubia's abandoned laity for clerical help. Francisco Alvares, while in Ethiopia in the 1520s, tells us of it. He had picked up information about Nubia from a travelling Syrian named John, now also in Ethiopia, who had been there and had found 150 churches still containing crucifixes and paintings of Our Lady. The people of this country, he reported, were now neither Christians, Muslims, nor Jews, yet still 'lived in the desire of being Christians'. Then, while Alvares was still in Ethiopia, less than forty years from

---

[8] J. Vantini, *The Excavations at Faras* (Bologna, 1970), 141–3.

the time of Bishop Merki, and just about when the last priests ordained by Merki would have died, six Nubians arrived in Ethiopia. They had come on a mission to beg the Emperor Lebna Dengel to send them priests and monks, but he refused. He did, he said, himself receive his abuna from Alexandria: 'How then could he give priests and monks since another gave them to him? And so they returned.'[9] And so they returned. Thus at times violently but more often quietly enough, did Islam advance while Christianity, like an ill-adapted dinosaur, declined and expired in place after place, crushed essentially by its own limitations, its fossilized traditions, and the lack of a truly viable, self-renewing structure.

[9] Francisco Alvares, *The Prester John of the Indies*, ed. E. F. Beckingham and G. W. B. Huntingford, ii (Cambridge, 1961), 461.

3

THE KONGO, WARRI, MUTAPA, AND THE PORTUGUESE

i. *Portugal Overseas*

The Portuguese state had arisen in a crusading spirit after the twelfth century when the far west of the Iberian peninsula was reconquered by Christians following several centuries of Muslim rule. It prospered and wished to expand. By the fifteenth century it was natural to carry the war across the sea to Africa just as Muslims had earlier carried it across the sea to Spain. But as the Portuguese, who were little more than a million in number, were unable to dent Islamic power in northern Africa, despite the capture of a few coastal bases, it was natural too to proceed southwards, hoping thereby to outflank Islam, gain control of the source of the gold which came north across the Sahara, and even establish links with 'Prester John', the Christian priest-king fabled to exist somewhere in the east, in Asia or Africa. An immediate economic benefit was slaves. The underpopulated economies of Spain and Portugal were developing plantation farming on an east Mediterranean model, alien to the past tradition of Europe. A few black slaves had already been brought to Europe from north Africa; from the mid-fifteenth century a rather more considerable stream began to arrive in Portugal, brought up from the West African coast. From the beginning there was a very substantial degree of royal control over this enterprise, which had been for a while masterminded by Prince Henry the Navigator.

Trade required the establishment of forts, but it was also seen as a religious, and even missionary, activity. It was part of an anti-Islamic crusade. It seemed then, once more, natural enough to obtain from the papacy documents of ecclesiastical authorization. Throughout the fifteenth century some seventy papal bulls sanctioned the imperial enterprise both bit by bit and as a whole and granted both civil and ecclesiastical authority over the lands Portugal was about to discover. However, the target of these early bulls remained the conquest of Morocco, a further piece of local *reconquista*, rather than the formation of an intercontinental empire. It was the journey of Vasco da Gama around Africa to Asia, following on that of Columbus to America, which created a new situation and led to the hasty establishment of the ecclesiastical 'patronage' of the kings of Spain and Portugal over a newly discovered world. The Portuguese *Padroado Real* was effectively granted by Pope Leo X in his 1514 brief *Praecelsae Devotionis*, a control over the Church overseas almost greater than that exercised by the king at home.

At the time of these grants there was next to no organized Catholic missionary activity anywhere in the world and, in the atmosphere of the Renaissance papacy and the general level of monarchical control of the Church almost everywhere in western Europe, they may have appeared almost uncontroversial. Even if Rome had not given them, the effective control of the Portuguese and Spanish monarchies over the extension of the Church in areas reached by their fleets and armies might have been hardly affected. However, it would not be very long before many people involved with the missionary apostolate in Rome and elsewhere would come to regret deeply the granting of these powers. Rome is always intensely reluctant to admit a mistake or to go back upon anything it has done. In consequence it lived with the *Padroado*, of a diminished sort, far into the twentieth century; nevertheless, from the decline of Portuguese power in the late sixteenth century on, it tried little by little to curtail its significance.

In 1482 the Portuguese, having reached the coast of gold, built there a fort at Elmina, their first tropical possession. A local chief begged the Portuguese to go elsewhere; they, in their turn, begged him to be baptized and so save his soul. Both requests were declined. The hitherto unpopulated island of São Tomé was settled by the Portuguese the next year, 1483, initially with an odd collection of whites from Lisbon, but it soon began to import slaves in large numbers from the mainland. Indeed for the next twenty-five years it was the principal recipient of the Portuguese slave-trade. It also became the advanced base for Portugal's West African empire and hence, inevitably, an ecclesiastical base too, even if for many years the population of the island was distinctly piratical and little amenable to directions from Lisbon. In 1534 a diocese of São Tomé was established to include the whole southern half of West Africa. While its bishops were often non-resident, they came, nevertheless, to fill an important role as ecclesiastical entrepreneurs between Portugal and the African mainland.

ii. *Kongo and its Initial Evangelization*

The very year that São Tomé was colonized an expedition reached the mouth of the River Zaïre under Diego Cao and took home to Portugal some hostages after making initial contact with its inhabitants, who were found to belong to a kingdom named Kongo. There were further expeditions in 1485 and 1487, more gifts, more hostages, and the growing realization on the Portuguese part that here was a monarchy of some size, unusually open and friendly, seemingly an ideal place to do business and make Christians. The fourth expedition of 1491 was the decisive one. It had been prepared upon both sides. There had been a few Portuguese in the Kongo (including, probably, a priest in Soyo) and Kongolese in Lisbon for some years. Priests, stonemasons, carpenters, horses, and a few women were all unloaded, together with plenty of cloth and other useful objects. The Mani Soyo, the chief of the coastal province of Soyo, was at once baptized with his son while a large symbolic bonfire was made of the implements of traditional religion. Two months later the Portuguese reached the capital, Mbanza Kongo, where the king himself, Nzinga Nkuvu, the Mani Kongo, welcomed them and was baptized, receiving the name João I, in honour of the reigning king of Portugal, João II. Thus did the Christian history of Kongo, and indeed of black and central Africa, begin.

It was a meeting between two societies and even two religions rather less different from one another than we are inclined to believe. Perhaps the Christianity and monarchy of Ethiopia can be used as providing a bridge in understanding the relationship. Francisco Alvares, the thoughtful Portuguese priest who spent six years observing Ethiopia in the 1520s, seemed to find there little too surprising. Beneath a surface of dissimilarity the structure and ideology of the two monarchies, and the Church which served each, had much in common. Certainly, he had his worries about annual rebaptism, mass ordinations of children, and the quality of the wine used at mass, but he recognized, correctly enough, that here was a Christianity very like that of Portugal, a religion of rituals and monks, of sacred images, and royal power. Portuguese and Ethiopians shared intense devotion to the Mother of Jesus and to the Cross, together with a huge loathing for Muslims and Jews. They shared religious attitudes in which violence and tenderness interplayed without apparent contradiction in ways often strange and repulsive to us. The Ethiopians recognized some degree of final authority in the Patriarch of Alexandria, and Alvares thought they would do much better to exchange it for that of the Pope, but in practice both the religion of Ethiopia and that of Portugal was a royal religion in which almost everything that happened in the Church was dependent upon the king.

While such a comparison may be at first surprising, it is not hard to recognize as apt. It is when one extends the parallel to the African religion of Kongo or Benin that complaint is more likely to arise, yet, deep down, the Catholicism of fifteenth- or sixteenth-century Portugal or Spain had far more in common with African religion than might be imagined. The popular Christianity of late medieval Europe had absorbed into itself a great deal of the pre-Christian religion of its peoples. In Europe as in Africa physical and social happenings of a disastrous sort were to be explained by a spiritual causality. Missionaries might come to complain that Africans worshipped the devil because he would otherwise harm them (though certainly they did not), but in Iberian popular religion at the time there was indeed a continual sense both of the power of the devil and of the anger of God. It was the latter, mostly, which explained disasters, and it needed to be placated both by penances— fastings and flagellations—and through the protection of lesser but still potent and more practically benevolent spiritual forces. There was a vast multiplicity of local saints and protective relics and holy places to turn to, but especially and increasingly Mary, mostly a very localized Mary, Mary of somewhere. Mary alone was always kind, never associated with punishment. Evil too was often highly localized in witch or diabolical possession. The physical and the spiritual were inextricably woven together so that miracles and prodigies of all sorts could be expected and revered. There was a profound 'sense of divine participation in the landscape', whereby nature was invested with a kind of innate sensitivity to the sacred[1]—a sort of animism, if one dare use the word, as much Iberian as African.

[1] William Christian, *Local Religion in Sixteenth-Century Spain*, (Princeton, NJ, 1981), 208; cf. George Brooks, 'The Observance of All Souls' Day in the Guinea-Bissau Region: A Christian Holy Day, an African Harvest Festival, an African New Year's Celebration or All of the Above?', *HIA* 11 (1984), 1–34.

The religious sensibilities, then, of sixteenth-century Iberians as much as of pagan Africans were absolutely pre-Enlightenment, and close cousins to one another. Africans would not be too conscious of moving into a different intellectual world by going from one to the other. You were, at least at first, doing no more than embracing a new name and source of superior power, almost as a village in Spain embraced a new saint, a new relic from Rome. In both the sacred object, a cross or some ju-ju figure, was not just a symbolization of the spiritual but itself a localized protective power. It is of course true that the European and Christian attitude to the diversity of spiritual powers now limited the acceptable range of inclusiveness to the specifically 'Christian' while all non-Christian powers were on the contrary labelled demonic. The Christian spiritual world of the time had become a highly dualistic one in which the devil was an almost omnipresent reality which non-Christian cults were seen as necessarily serving. Here indeed there was a large contrast, for the African spiritual world, more like the Hindu, set no such limits and had in reality little dualism to it. Christian cults and rites could be incorporated as welcome additions rather than alternatives. The metaphysical and moral dualism of the late medieval mind imposed itself, often disastrously, upon the sixteenth- and seventeenth-century missionary. Despite that, the missionary and the African often understood each other better than most of us can understand either. They shared a conviction about the importance of the fetish, and if, at times, missionaries risked death from angry crowds as they tried to destroy these symbols of life, yet enthusiastic crowds could at other times participate in the bonfires themselves.

Again, a decisive and intimate relationship between the religious and the political was common to both. The king dominated the Portuguese Church, just as the king dominated the religion of Benin or Ife. The tombs of dead kings were of the greatest symbolic importance in all these places. In the mind of the Portuguese and in the mind of the people of Kongo religious conversion was dependent upon a royal decision—as it had been, again and again, in Dark-Age Europe—and its consequences were largely a matter to be arranged between two monarchies—the sending and the receiving.

Nzinga Nkuvu was the king of a large and remarkable society divided into at least six major provinces extending in all some 250 miles south along the coast from the River Zaïre and much the same inland. Its monarchy was partially elective with very little of a military character to it but a very sound economic base. Among the king's sons one, Mvemba Nzinga, was in 1491 governor of the northern province of Nsundi. He was baptized together with his mother, a month after his father, on 4 June, and given the name Afonso; a month later the first church of Mbanza Kongo was blessed. But within three years most of this was reversed. Nzinga Nkuvu tired of the Christian insistence upon burning fetishes and restricting oneself to a single wife. Both insistences were socially and politically disruptive and he returned to the ways of his fathers. The function of the fetishes present in every village was to secure rain and health, to protect against witchcraft; the function of the king's many wives was to link him with different sections of his people. A few Portuguese priests performing their rituals in an incomprehensible language and hastily constructed building in the capital might add a novel prestige to the court, but it in no way substituted for what was lost in the experience of the people and the authority of the king. Like many another African ruler hurriedly baptized, he returned to 'paganism' as soon as he began to detect the implications of Christian conversion. That is to be expected.

What is less to be expected is that young Mvemba Nzinga, away in Nsundi, refused to do so, so that for the next twelve years the latter provided the surviving focus of Kongolese Christianity. In 1506 the king died. He was said to have nominated Afonso to succeed him, but the great chiefs at Mbanza Kongo chose a different, and pagan, son. Afonso marched on the capital, defeated his enemies—assisted in correct Iberian fashion, it was quickly claimed, by a heavenly vision of St James—and became king. He certainly was assisted by the Portuguese, who had been with him in Nsundi. He was, undoubtedly, and to an extraordinary degree, a modernizer, someone open to every aspect of life as promoted by the Portuguese. He was not a warrior king; his reign is not a record of war and territorial aggrandizement, but of a persistent concern for educational, social, religious, and even medical advancement. The Portuguese monarchy recognized this. Mvemba Nzinga was an independent Christian king, to be assisted to Christianize his kingdom and be trained in the behaviour suitable to Christian kings, even—if possible—to live in a two-storeyed house, as Christian kings should do. The very detailed instructions sent by King Manuel of Portugal in 1512 together with priests and artisans of every sort are extremely enlightening as to the model behind the exercise. It was certainly not a racialist model. And with a king as intelligent, as forceful, and co-operative as Mvemba Nzinga, Afonso I, success for a time seemed assured.

iii. *Benin and Mutapa*

Let us compare this with two other, much less successful, examples of the same missionary method. Benin was a greater prize than even the Kongo and in 1514 its oba, Ozolua, sent an embassy to Lisbon to indicate an interest in Christian conversion while asking for firearms, including cannon. In reply the King of Portugal promised missionaries but declined to provide arms prior to conversion. On the other hand, he urged the Oba to open his country freely to trade, that is to say the slave trade:

With a very good will we send you the clergy that you have asked for . . . when we see that you have embraced the teachings of Christianity like a good and faithful Christian, there will be nothing in our realms which we shall not be glad to favour you, whether it be arms or cannon and all other weapons of war . . . these things we are not sending now because the law of God forbids it . . . we earnestly recommend that you order your markets to be opened and trade to be carried on freely . . .[2]

The Oba wanted guns, the Portuguese slaves. Christian conversion was the cement to ensure each side got what it wanted. But it did not work. As a matter of fact, the Portuguese did not sell guns even to convinced Christian rulers like the King of Kongo. Benin, on its side, did not want to sell slaves. Ozolua was much interested in war. When his missionaries arrived in 1515 he had little time for them and, soon enough, was assassinated by his own troops, who had had enough fighting. Moreover, guns were of rather little use to a sixteenth-century African king and only a ruler as militant as Ozolua greatly wanted them. When the missionaries saw there was no royal conversion in the offing they left in a huff. Yet in point of fact Benin does not appear to have been entirely stony ground. There was at least one quite persevering Edo Christian named Gregorio Lourenço. He had been in São Tomé, learned Portuguese and become a Christian there. Returning to Benin, he acted as an interpreter when his services were needed as in 1515. In 1526 he showed his continued

[2] A. F. C. Ryder, *Benin and the Europeans 1485–1897* (1969), 47–8.

Christian commitment by presenting a female slave in alms to the church of São Tomé, and in 1538, when a second group of priests arrived in Benin, he was still there offering his services and anxious to have his children and wives baptized, but the Oba forbade it. Lourenço illustrates rather well the sort of frontier person who was so often the bridge whereby Christianity entered a new society, not only at this period but in many later ones. For the time being, however, missionaries were set upon a royal conversion or nothing, so the humbler fare of a Lourenço and his wives was effectively disregarded.

In 1559 the Captain of Mozambique thought that some of the inland rulers, including the King of Mutapa, might be ready for conversion and a Jesuit mission, led by Gonçalo da Silveira, was sent from Goa to undertake the task, the whole east coast of Africa lying within the Goa diocese. A young Portuguese aristocrat with the most self-sacrificing missionary zeal and a thirst for martyrdom, Silveira set off inland from Sofala, stopping first at a Tonga chief, whom he baptized with the name of Constantino after seven weeks, together with his family and some 400 other people. He then journeyed up the River Zambezi via Sena and Tete to Mutapa reaching the court on Christmas Eve, 1560. Twenty-five days later he baptized the young Mwene Mutapa and his mother, giving him the name of Dom Sebastiano, in honour of the reigning king of Portugal. Less than two months later, after receiving a warning from a Portuguese trader and interpreter, Caiado, that his life was in danger, but refusing to flee, Silveira was strangled in his hut at night on the king's orders. The Mwene Mutapa had apparently been advised by rival Muslim traders that the Jesuit was a sorcerer; however, when Caiado pointed out that Silveira was a nobleman whose death would be avenged, the Mwene Mutapa regretted his decision and had some Muslims killed too.

Eight years later the Portuguese, increasingly interested in the African interior, did indeed equip a large expedition under Francisco Barreto to avenge Silveira's death, and have the Muslims expelled from Mutapa and Portuguese trading rights guaranteed. King Sebastian of Portugal was an exceedingly devout young man and deeply attached to the Jesuits, so concern for Silveira's death was not insignificant in his mind, and Barreto was given as his principal adviser and confessor a very hawkish Jesuit named Monclaro. The expedition took several years and was largely disastrous as most of its members perished from fever in the Zambezi valley, the route

Monclaro had insisted should be followed (despite much sound advice to the contrary) in order to follow as closely as possible in Silveira's footsteps. There was a massacre of Muslims at Sena, apparently under Jesuit encouragement. They achieved little else.

Silveira was unusual among sixteenth-century Portuguese missionaries in Africa in the quality of his zeal and even in the amount we know of him. Most of the sixteenth-century clergy are almost anonymous and some may well have been sent out to Africa as a punishment for misbehaviour at home. But, though a Jesuit, Silveira does not seem different in much else. It was only well after 1570, and the decline in power of Portugal brought on by over-expansion and repeated losses in expeditions as futile as Barreto's, that missionary methodology began to change. In Benin, Kongo, and Mutapa we have a common pattern. Missionaries are sent from king to king. Baptism is a matter of high policy. Accepted by the king, it is then offered to his subjects, more or less *en masse*. Christian mores will subsequently be imposed over the years with royal authority. Why should a king be willing to be baptized after twenty-five days and how did an intelligent man like Silveira imagine that he could be suitably baptized? Presumably he believed that God would grant some special enlightenment to achieve this obviously providential development. The king for his part might well be willing to undergo a ritual which was apparently closely connected with the power and wisdom of these strange foreigners. But he could, too, easily see it as something dangerous, either in religious terms as a matter of witchcraft, or in political terms as a matter of surrender to a threatening foreign power, or in social terms as acceptance of disruptive new behavioural norms. It is not surprising that the Oba Ozolua or the Mwene Mutapa turned away quickly enough from the Christian proposal.

iv. *Kongolese Catholicism under Afonso I and his Immediate Successors*

What is surprising is that Afonso I should persevere. He is very much the odd man out among sixteenth-century royal converts, and it is to him that we must now return. He remains an enigma, the one African figure of the sixteenth century who continues to bestride his age as a colossus. He was already Prince of Nsundi when he was baptized in 1491. He became King of Kongo in 1506 and only died in 1543. The sheer length of his rule is quite exceptional, but what is more remarkable is that in over fifty years he appears unfaltering both in his Christian commitment and in the general lines of his policy. Few rulers in human history have lasted so long or followed so consistent a course. He is the one African of his age of whom we actually possess a publishable, and interesting, correspondence. It has been facilely suggested that his letters were written by Portuguese and can throw little light upon his character or intentions.[3] That is untrue. The greater part of his letters across many years were written by a Kongolese, João Texeira, and there is no reason to doubt that they represent the mind of Mvemba Nzinga. The best guarantee of their reliability as evidence is that they extend over such a long period. There is a striking contrast between the changing moods of most of his relatively short-lived successors and his own undeviating line of policy. That consistency and the sincerity which went with it were quite clearly recognized by people in the Kongo and by both Lisbon and Rome.

The basic pillars of Kongolese Catholicism as it developed in the reign of Afonso and continued into the early seventeenth century would seem to have been four. The first, and most important, was the adherence of the monarchy. From the moment that Afonso defeated and killed his pagan brother, at no point did the monarchy, whatever the political and religious problems facing the country, quite go back upon that public commitment for over 300 years. Afonso established a new sacral legitimacy which was from then on an essential element in Kongo identity.

Second to this, and essential to its continuance, was the parallel commitment of a large core of the Kongolese ruling class, the Mwissikongo. The monarchy was essentially elective and the rule of the king, the Mani Kongo, was always balanced by that of another and more ancient religious dignitary, the Mani Vunda, whose authority sanctioned that of the king himself. In 1506 Afonso immediately entrusted the Mani Vunda, who had actually supported his brother in the war, with a Christian religious role. A hundred years later it would be another Mani Vunda, Antonio Manuel ne

---

[3] 'The correspondence of Afonso I . . . is of no help . . . The letters are the work of royal secretaries, all Portuguese, save one . . . their style is conventional' (G. Balandier, *Daily Life in the Kingdom of Kongo* (New York, 1968), 53). It is hard to believe that Balandier could have read the great letter of 5 October 1514, for instance, and penned such a misleading comment. The 'save one' ignores the fact that the secretary in question wrote all the more important letters which survive.

Vunda, whom Alvaro II sent as his first black ambassador to Rome where he died in 1608 and where his bust can still be seen in the church of Santa Maria Maggiore. But a basic continuing Christian attachment of other nobles is no less clear. What may have begun as the brief and opportunistic conversion of Nzinga Nkuvu and the persevering but idiosyncratic Christian commitment of Afonso became within the latter's lifetime the common will of the ruling class of a quite large country, a common will manifested by their extraordinarily consistent use of baptism, Portuguese family names, titles, chivalrous orders, and Church confraternities: together these constituted a kind of new collective identity for the nobility.

The third pillar consisted in the churches of the capital, its rituals and priests, its new symbolic identity. Poor as the stone building of the cathedral of São Salvador may seem in comparison with a European cathedral of the period (and it was never roofed other than with grass) it was certainly the most striking edifice in all that part of Africa. It had a bell—so that Kongo dia Ngunga, Kongo of the Bell, became one of the names of the capital—and its priests celebrated the office more or less regularly. The principal Christian feasts became part of the national and royal life cycle. Mbanza Kongo truly became at the same time São Salvador, a sacred city of churches, the heart and symbol of Kongolese Catholicism. The principal rituals of the cathedral, at which the king would always be present, were important to the enhancement of the monarchy and its mystique. They were performed by Christian *nganga* (the Catholic priest was called an nganga just as a pagan priest was: the function was not seen as identical, but it was seen within a continuity, verbal and ontological, without which the role of the Christian priest could hardly have been understood). Henceforth the monarchy and the Church of São Salvador supported each other—all the more so as throughout the sixteenth century there was often elsewhere, except in Mbanza Soyo, hardly another priest in the country. It was, pre-eminently, a ritual support.

The fourth pillar was that of the immigrant Portuguese community. The artisans sent by the King of Portugal to build a new Kongo were not a great success. The churches and palaces of Mbanza Kongo made slow progress. Nevertheless, a permanent Portuguese community was established in the capital and, to a lesser extent, in other places up and down the country. It was almost wholly concerned with slave-trading. By the end of Afonso's reign there were probably up to 100 Portuguese living in the country, some with white wives, but mostly with black ones or concubines. Twenty-five years later, when a small Portuguese army entered the country from São Tomé at Alvaro I's request, to rescue the Kongo from the Jaga invasion of 1568, most of its members subsequently settled there. These immigrants with their guns, their larger range of skills, and their mestiço children, became an important class within the country, but they did not gain entry into the traditional ruling class or appointment to chieftaincies. Their religion was Catholicism, their occupation slave-trading. They were not strong or numerous enough to control the country and they were, on the whole, loyal to the king, though they were also—at least in the first generation—an element which the king could not wholly control, as Afonso I was painfully aware almost from the start. As their children grew up this group of people became increasingly Kongo-based and fluent in Kikongo at least as much as in Portuguese. Because of their linguistic and technical skills, they could be of great service to the king, but they also provided an ongoing core to the Church from which in time a number of white and mestiço priests would come (which does not mean that they did not quickly adopt recourse also to traditional rituals for the control of witchcraft and sickness). Thus already in 1546, only three years after Afonso's death, the Bishop of São Tomé ordained at São Salvador a young white (or mestiço), Diogo Gomes, who had been born at São Salvador and became an excellent priest and, later, a Jesuit. He composed the first Kikongo catechism, printed in Lisbon, which does not, however, seem to have survived long for use in the Kongo.

The shortage of priests was acute almost from the beginning. In the earlier years of Afonso's rule quite a few were sent out from Portugal, but the conditions of life, the high mortality, and—perhaps most of all—the absence of an even moderately workable pastoral model for a few, wholly unprepared, priests to cope with a huge, profoundly pagan yet now nominally Christian society, ensured discouragement, withdrawal, or—alternatively—transference to a life of concubinage and slave-trading. Portugal believed from the start in training native priests and Afonso was enthusiastic to do so. In consequence a considerable number of young men were sent to Lisbon to be educated and ordained. For the most part this simply did not work—perhaps for reasons of celibacy and marriage as much as anything else, but health, inability to learn Latin, and the attractions of alternative careers were equally factors. Nevertheless, one, the King's own son, Henry, proved different. He was sent already by 1508 when hardly twelve years old and resided with the canons of Saint John the Evangelist in Lisbon. He apparently studied well and made an excellent impression so that the King of Portugal proposed he be made a bishop. This was done, with Roman permission, in 1521, when he was about 25. He returned to the Kongo, to the delight of his father. A few years later he disappeared from sight. In August 1526 his father refers to his continual illnesses, and what he did as a bishop (he was nominally an auxiliary of the diocese of Funchal) we simply do not know. By 1530 he was dead.

Again and again King Afonso appealed for priests, as for teachers, craftsmen, doctors, and ships. In the truly extraordinary letter of 5 October 1514 to King Manuel he even suggests that he be given the Isle of São Tomé to use as a sort of vast school to which he could send boys and girls to study more easily than in Lisbon. There is frequently a riveting intensity in Afonso's appeals for help, protests about the growing slave-trade and bad behaviour of the Portuguese, a fierce fusion of Christian faith, modernizing intentions, regal shrewdness, and a bitterness with the reality in which neither his secular nor his religious hopes were being realized.

We know of his death from a letter written by his brother Manuel, then in Lisbon, to the Queen of Portugal, 15 July 1543. Afonso had sent his brother in 1539 on a mission to the Pope, but the Portuguese had never allowed him to proceed beyond Lisbon. Now, the King dead, Manuel wished only to return to Kongo. By 1543 Afonso may well have been in his eighties. Maybe the account of him written in 1516 by the Portuguese priest Rui d'Aguiar is much exaggerated:

His Christian life is such that he appears to me not as a man but as an angel sent by the Lord to this kingdom to convert it, especially when he speaks and when he preaches . . . better than we, he knows the prophets and the Gospel of our Lord Jesus Christ and all the lives of the saints and all things regarding our Mother the Holy Church . . . He does nothing but study and many times he falls asleep over his books; he forgets when it is time to dine when he is speaking of the things of God. So delighted is he with the reading of the Scripture that he is beside himself . . . He studies the Holy Gospel and when the priest finishes the mass he asks for benediction. When he has received it he begins to preach to the people with great skill and great charity . . . he punishes with rigour those who worship idols and he has them burned along with these idols.[4]

If there was absolutely no truth behind such a picture, one wonders why a Portuguese should want so to depict a barbaric black king. In fact d'Aguiar's picture does in essentials cohere extremely well with what survives from his correspondence extending over many years. Certainly we have no other evidence that he burnt idol-worshippers, but we know he preached, we know he rejoiced in his son's return as a bishop, and when the latter fell ill suggested that his nephew be made a bishop. We know that he appealed again and again for priests but also—faced with an almost complete absence of priests—endeavoured to send out lay teachers. It is argued that he must have remained a polygamist, but there is really no evidence to prove it. The question is whether the sceptical modern historian has a right to dismiss so considerable and consistent a body of surviving evidence as somehow all a pious fraud, a mere pretence *vis-à-vis* the Portuguese. It seems more appropriate historically, and less racialist, to accept that the words his young black secretary used in a language the Kongolese were quick to master meant substantially what they said. Awkward as the outstanding particularities in history always are, Afonso should be recognized as rather extraordinary both as a man and as a ruler and, moreover—what the Kongolese tradition itself hailed him—'the apostle of the Kongo'.

The character of Afonso becomes the clearer when contrasted with that of all his successors. No Portuguese priest ever suggested that they were angels. Diogo I (1545–61), Bernardo I (1561–7), and Alvaro I (1568–87) quarrelled bitterly with their missionaries, in so far as they had any, but for the most part the kingdom of the Kongo was almost priestless through the second half of the sixteenth century. This was all the more serious in that the form of Christianity introduced was so predominantly a clerically ritualistic one. Little attempt was made to instruct in Kikongo, to develop lay ministries, or to establish a vernacular presence of the Scriptures or any other religious literature either, such as could be a substitute for the absence of priests. The late medieval Church had had little interest in translating the Scriptures into any vernacular in Europe—the

---

[4] *MMA* i. 361–3, *Correspondence de Dom Afonso, roi du Congo 1506–1543*, ed. L. Jadin and M. Dicorato (Brussels, 1974), 116–17, English translation from Balandier, *Daily Life in the Kingdom of Kongo*, 52–3.

Lollards were not commended but rather condemned for producing in the fourteenth century an English Bible. So it is not surprising if it hardly occurred to only slightly post-medieval missionaries in Africa that they needed to do quite otherwise. Nevertheless, already in the 1550s the Jesuit Fr. Gomes had produced a catechism in Kikongo, of which, however, no copy has survived. He was, perhaps, the only sixteenth-century missionary to begin to understand what its Church most needed.

What in general was brought was what Portuguese priests were accustomed to—a Church of liturgy and sacraments, all performed in Latin. The laity participated objectively through attending mass and the 'valid' reception of the sacraments, rather than intelligibly. Of course that sort of model of religiosity had been changing in northern Europe among Catholics as well as Protestants with the growth of a more individualistic lay and vernacular piety, but this had little affected early or mid-sixteenth-century Portugal. The model it provided did, more than any other, presuppose the presence of priests, not particularly well-educated priests, but many of them. Southern Europe at the time was filled with priests. But here were next to none, despite the arrival of various orders from time to time. There were some Franciscans and Augustinians in the early years, Jesuits in the 1550s, further Franciscans, a few Dominicans, and, in the 1580s, a brief venture by Spanish Carmelites. But no order in the sixteenth century maintained any long-standing commitment to the Kongo. It is hardly surprising. The material conditions were extremely hard, the political conditions highly unstable, the pastoral task seemingly almost impossible, the mortality rate very high.

From the 1570s, however, there was a change. The Portuguese had begun the conquest of Angola, the area directly south of Kongo, and with the establishment of a European-controlled port in Loanda, the Jesuits relocated their mission there. From here they would later revive their Kongo enterprise. At much the same time, in 1571, the Bishop of São Tomé opened a seminary on the island for the training of local priests. Though closed in the 1580s, it was reopened in the 1590s by Bishop de Vilanova. The intention, at least, was a sound one, and it may be that a few seculars from here actually did get through to work in the Kongo. Almost invariably the kings of Kongo quarrelled with what priests they got, yet wanted more. The kingdom had been committed by Afonso to Christianity and Portugalization and, in theory, his successors never went back on that commitment. In reality what the package amounted to by the later sixteenth century was little more than a few half-ruined church buildings, the absurd importation of titles—dukes, counts, marquises, and whatever—a taste among the upper classes for Western finery to wear on ceremonial occasions, and, principally, a host of unruly and uncontrollable slave-traders. It is not surprising that the kings believed there must be something better than this. If Portugal had failed them, could not Rome help?

It is clear that for much of his reign Afonso had been trying to get a direct line to Rome and even as late as 1539 had dispatched his brother on a mission to Rome which never got beyond Lisbon. Portugal, appealing to what it was beginning to call its 'historic rights', wanted no direct Kongo–Rome link. But the kings from time to time kept on trying and with Philip II of Spain's take-over of the Portuguese crown in 1580 the likelihood of success grew a little greater. In 1579 a Portuguese named Duarte Lopes had arrived in Mbanza Kongo. Four years later he left it as Alvaro I's ambassador to the Pope, having first been created a *fidalgo*, a gentleman of the royal house. Lopes carried precise instructions with him, which almost certainly included the obtaining for the Kongo of its own bishopric entirely freed from Portuguese control. Unfortunately Lopes had many problems. His ship was blown across the Atlantic and wrecked in the West Indies. Though he managed to swim to land, it was a year before he could cross the Atlantic once more and go in due course via Spain, to Rome. By then Alvaro I was dead. However, in Rome Lopes met Filippo Pigafetta, a writer, who composed a book about the Kongo based on Lopes' notes. The *Relatione del reame di Congo*, published in Italian in 1591, and quickly translated into English, Dutch, and Latin, proved for our story a work of immense importance. Until its publication the Kongo was essentially unknown to Europe, even to Rome. Only the Portuguese knew anything about it. From now on the rest of Europe was aware that there existed a strange Christian kingdom, commonly called Western Ethiopia, and that it was in the greatest need of priests.

THE SEVENTEENTH AND EIGHTEENTH CENTURIES

v. *The Diocese of São Salvador and the Jesuits*

It was undoubtedly due in large part to the publication of Pigafetta's book that in 1596 the Pope was willing to make of the Kongo a diocese with its cathedral at São Salvador in response to yet another appeal.[5] But it also meant that from this time on there was a lively interest in Italy, Spain, and elsewhere to do with the Kongo. The immense missionary effort of the seventeenth century to serve there could hardly otherwise be explained. The first bishop arrived in São Salvador in 1601, only to die a year later. In 1604 Alvaro II sent a new ambassador to Rome, one of the most important people in the land, Antonio Nsaku ne Vunda, who actually reached Rome after long delays in Spain but died immediately upon arrival. After that, more realistically, Alvaro appointed Mgr. Vives, a Roman ecclesiastic with missionary sympathies, to be his ambassador to the Pope and so gain the assistance he sought.

Certainly the Kongo needed help. Furthermore, the Catholic Church was a good deal more capable of providing it in the seventeenth than it had been in the sixteenth century. In the days of Mvemba Nzinga the Council of Trent was yet to take place. For better or worse there was at that time really no one to turn to, and no sense of missionary purpose, beyond the medieval and crusading spirit of the Portuguese kingdom. By the end of the sixteenth century, Portugal was indeed in decline, exhausted by too many overseas projects, many of them as futile and wasteful of manpower as the Zambezi expedition of Barreto. For centuries it would continue to cling bitterly and persistently to what it possessed, but any sense of dynamism, even occasional generosity, such as did exist in the reign of John II or Manuel, had faded. But the Catholic Church elsewhere was now awake and aware of its missionary responsibilities in a quite new way. The Council of Trent (1545–63) had set in process a steady reformation of the Church's pastoral and missionary structures. The establishment of diocesan seminaries for the training of the clergy was one point now widely insisted upon both at home and abroad.

At the same time missionary experience, especially in Asia, was

[5] The official documentation concerning the foundation of the diocese is printed in A. Brasio, *Historia e missiologia* (Loanda, 1973), 354–72.

bringing about a far more mature sense of what mission ought to involve. On one side the disadvantages of Portuguese control were ever more manifest; upon the other the necessity of language-learning and at least some adaptation to foreign culture was being realized. Doubtless Matteo Ricci, in China from 1583 until his death in Peking in 1610, and Roberto de Nobili, who worked in India for fifty years from 1605 to 1656, were exceptional in the degree of adaptation—to Chinese and Tamil culture—they pioneered. Nevertheless, as Jesuits they were part of what was essentially a world-wide team operation of astonishing dynamism. In the same years Alexander de Rhodes was establishing the Church in Vietnam and rewriting its language in Western script, 'reductions' were being organized to protect from enslavement the people of Paraguay, Jean de Brébeuf was at work among the Huron of Quebec. It was a movement in which other orders too were increasingly being caught up—if generally less imaginatively and often in painful rivalry. A typical Jesuit missionary in the early decades of the seventeenth century came to his work with a concept of the task distinctly different from that which had seemed sufficient for Silveira sixty years previously.

There was also in Rome itself an increasing determination to recover some measure of control over mission from the governments of Portugal and Spain or even from the largely independent initiatives of the great orders. All this development culminated in 1622 in the foundation of the Sacred Congregation of Propaganda Fide by Pope Gregory XV as the Church of Rome's own missionary department. Juan Baptist Vives, who took his responsibilities for the Kongo seriously, was one of the main protagonists in the establishment of Propaganda and he himself bought a palace in the Piazza di Spagna to serve both it and the missionary college which was opened to train the new missionaries who could help realize its purposes. The establishment of Propaganda was a very important step in the long process of wresting control of the missions from Spain and Portugal, and the Kongo was almost Propaganda's favourite child, perceived through the benevolent eyes of Vives as a far-away but loyal Christian kingdom desperately in need of priests. The order closest to Propaganda in those early days was the Capuchins, and an appeal to Spanish Capuchins to volunteer for the Kongo had already been made by Vives in 1618. The response was immense: over 400 offered to go. When Propaganda was founded it at once supported this plan, but the resistance of Lisbon to any Spanish entry into a Portuguese preserve meant that no Spanish Capuchin went forth and it would be another twenty-five years before the first Italian Capuchins were able to set foot in the Kongo.

In the meantime Propaganda Fide, under the guidance especially of its first secretary, Francesco Ingoli, was developing its classic missionary norms: avoidance of politics, stress upon the early formation of a local clergy, upon language-learning, and even upon the printing of works in the vernacular. It almost at once set up a remarkable printing-press, the most polyglot in the world of the seventeenth century. Ingoli explicitly included in his guide-lines the translation of the Bible into the vernacular and the Arabic Bible was one of the greatest achievements of his press in the seventeenth century. However, apart from that, the press seems to have printed next to nothing of Scripture and became subject to increasingly restrictive control. In this, as in much else, Ingoli was far ahead of both the typical seventeenth-century Roman curial official and the typical missionary.

Ever since the Portuguese conquest of Angola in the 1570s, there had been Portuguese Jesuits in Loanda and it was they—perhaps in part as a way of justifying the refusal to allow the Spanish Capuchins to come—who would now resume a care for the Kongo mission, despite their own rather limited numbers.

In 1619 the Bishop of São Salvador, Manuel Baptista Soares, after spending several years in the Kongo—the only bishop ever to do so—presented his *ad limina* report to the Holy See.[6] It is only too clear how profoundly the good man hated his diocese: the cathedral was roofed with grass, there was only one small bell in the tower, the king came to mass with all his wives, Christians practised pagan rites. One cannot speak of it all without tears. There were in all twenty-four priests for Kongo and Angola combined and the only hope was a large increase of clergy. For years for his part Alvaro III had been writing to Rome to complain of the bishop and his behaviour. If the kings wanted bishops they had no idea of canonical norms and a bishop's authority became in practice as intolerable to them as were the practices of the Kongolese to the bishops. The king wanted to expel one kind of priest, the bishop—and Soares seems to have been

---

[6] The full text is to be found in T. Filesi, *Roma e Congo all'inizio del 1600: Nuove testimonianze* (Como, 1970), 79–83.

quite a zealous bishop—another kind. Yet both at least were committed to the great need for more priests.

In point of fact the state of the Church was probably rather less hopeless in 1619 than it had been thirty years earlier. When the Carmelites visited the Kongo in 1584, they had found only four priests in the entire country. If there were now rather more than this it was chiefly due to the seminary established by the Bishop of São Tomé, which had produced a score or more of priests, white, mestiço, and black, to serve the diocese of São Salvador from its existence in 1596. In the early seventeenth century, besides a group of half a dozen canons attached to the cathedral at São Salvador, there were also priests in the main provinces of the kingdom—Mbata, Nsundi, Mbamba, Soyo, and elsewhere.

One man in particular seems to have provided a measure of continuity and clerical leadership in this period, Bras Correa. Born in Salamanca about 1577, he is one of the few Spaniards to appear in Kongo history. He came to the country in his youth to earn a living, studied with one or another priest, and was ordained at São Salvador by the first bishop around 1601. For some years he was the pastor at Nsundi, became a cathedral canon about 1606, and from then on was for many years the real leader of the Kongolese Church, royal chaplain, president of the royal council, archdeacon, Vicar-General. He spoke Kikongo perfectly, arranged the royal succession in the 1620s more than once, and assisted in the coronation service. Alvaro III wanted the Pope to make him a bishop, but this the Portuguese authorities, whose control of the diocese as falling within the *Padroado* remained officially unquestioned, would not allow. Clearly Bras Correa must have gone along with a degree of Kongolization of Christianity far beyond what Bishop Soares could find tolerable, yet Correa had by no means become just a local big man—a white trader who had found the Church a good way to the possession of power— and in due course he joined the Jesuits. He was the first of a number of seventeenth-century priests who came some way to the making of Kongolese Catholicism a viable reality.

If there were to be more Kongolese priests there had to be a college in São Salvador to educate and prepare them. King Afonso had already tried to establish such a college a century before, but he lacked a group of permanently committed and competent priests to run it. Now the Jesuits, already staffing a not unsuccessful one in

Loanda, were prepared to open another in São Salvador and this took place in 1624.

From a Church point of view the early 1620s were a hopeful time for the Kongo. Pedro II, a great-grandson of Afonso I, elected king in 1622 under the influence of Bras Correa, seemed a very considerable improvement upon his predecessor, Alvaro III. Alvaro was a polygamist: 29 years old when he died, he had had one son by his Church wife, thirty-one by other women. Pedro was a monogamist. Alvaro was continually conducting war-dances, though he seldom followed them up. Pedro was more cautious. Both wanted missionaries. Both attended daily mass. Both were probably only too well aware that the kingdom was cracking around them under increasing pressure from the Portuguese in Angola upon the one hand, forces of decentralization upon the other. But no king could do much and in the early seventeenth century no king of Kongo lasted long. From the death of Alvaro II in 1614 eight kings reigned before Garcia II began to rule in 1641. The kings lacked the resources to maintain an adequate central authority and more and more the principal provinces—Soyo especially but also Mbata, Mbamba, and Nsundi—were beginning to go their own way. The Church, with its ritual and organizational concentration upon São Salvador, was one of the few real assets the monarchy and a unified Kongo still retained.

Certainly the Jesuits and their quickly constructed college must have seemed very good news indeed. Fr. Cardoso, the first rector, was clearly an outstanding person. In an earlier visit to the country he had learned the language, had then imitated Fr. Gomes in translating the standard Portuguese catechism into Kikongo, and on returning to Portugal had arranged for a printed edition in Kikongo and Portuguese. At the same time he had written a history of the Kongo, which remained unprinted until modern times. Both as linguist and as historian and recorder of culture he was characteristic of the very best sort of seventeenth-century missionary. When he arrived in São Salvador in August 1625, it was with hundreds of copies of his quite considerable catechism to dispose of, and among his presents to the king (by now young Garcia I, Pedro's son) were twelve copies of the book. He had already been distributing them to literate chiefs along his route. The importance of this one book can hardly be overstated. Even simple prayers were often learnt in Latin by the Kongolese. It seems only to have been the Jesuits who began a systematic teaching of prayers in Kikongo. That was followed up by the catechism. There was probably no other printed book in Kikongo, though there may have been a few briefer works, and there would be none other for centuries. Its authority was inevitably immense and, as many of the Kongolese élite could read, it is not difficult to imagine that through reading or class memorization they will have known this one piece of vernacular literature by heart.

Effectively, from the sixteenth to the eighteenth and even the nineteenth century, Kongolese Christianity survived through the work of the *maestri*, lay interpreter-catechists and Portuguese speakers. They remain the least studied but by far the most important factor within the Church. From their beginnings in the sixteenth century and the better training they received in the seventeenth from Jesuits and Capuchins, they developed a role, the handing-on of teaching from generation to generation which continued almost regardless of any clerical presence. Without them the degree of persistent Christian commitment which undoubtedly long existed would be quite inexplicable. It was the catechism which provided both *maestri* and priests with a tool without which they could have done little. Its question-and-answer form was easy to use. Its content may well seem to us in many ways deeply unsuitable, as it had certainly not been adapted to Africa: a set of doctrinal texts without any sort of story. It is sad that not a single Gospel was translated. That might well have made still more difference, though it would too have introduced a vastly much greater opportunity for diverse interpretation. Nevertheless, the vocabulary at least which Cardoso employed was to a considerable extent, even for more theological terms, traditionally Kongolese. Here was the teaching of God, Nzambi mpungu, by his nganga, his priests. It was centred sacramentally upon one great visible sign, the Cross, the Santa Cruz (theoretically left in Portuguese, but in practice it became Kongolese, 'kuluzu'). Kongo Christianity never had its village priest or eucharist, but it did have its Santa Cruz, the Christian symbol standing in the middle of the village in place of the fetish which had been torn down, and many a village had too its *maestro* treasuring and passing on across the generations his single tool of trade, Cardoso's catechism.

There were a few more rural priests by the end of the 1620s. Francisco de Soveral was Bishop of Saõ Salvador from 1626 to 1642. While he never visited the Kongo, spending all his time in Angola— which showed how far Loanda had already become the real administrative centre of the diocese, though its only cathedral was as yet in São Salvador—he did exercise a greater pastoral care over it than had some of his predecessors. Probably he feared to go: white mortality was high in São Salvador at this period and accusations of poisoning were rife. De Soveral's immediate predecessor died five days after arrival and no bishop since the establishment of the see had had a very happy time there. But the college in Loanda was making possible a fairly regular flow of local ordinations, mostly of mestiços. In his *ad limina* report of 1631 he was able to list ten parishes within the Kongo kingdom, each staffed by a single priest, besides the considerable number of canons and a few Jesuits now in the capital. There was a priest each for Pangu, Pemba, Chiuva, Soyo, Oanda, and Motemo, as well as the duchies of Mbamba, Nsundi, and Mbata. These areas were very large and the priests probably not very zealous; nevertheless, a permanent sacramental presence in all the principal centres of the country outside the capital was something of an advance. It meant at least that the leading dukes, marquises, and so forth had chaplains of their own: a mass to attend in ritual state, a priest to confess to.

The college in São Salvador would soon add still further to the ranks of the ordained with a number of Kongolese, black or mestiço. Among them by far the most notable was Manuel Roboredo, a mestiço cousin of the King, ordained in 1637. Canon of the cathedral and confessor to the King, he played in the 1640s and 1950s something of the role that Bras Correa had filled twenty years earlier, but he was black where Correa had been white. Just as Correa decided to join the Jesuits, Roboredo would in 1653 join the Capuchins, becoming in religion Francisco de São Salvador or—as his Italian brethren liked to call him—Francesco Conghese. By this time Antonio do Couto, another mestiço born in São Salvador, who had joined the Jesuit novitiate in 1631, was rector of the college. A further group of Kongolese mulattos, also of royal blood, including the brothers Miguel de Castro and Simao de Medeiros, were canons running the cathedral.

In the sixteenth century the core of the Church in the Kongo would seem to have been Portuguese settlers, most of them slave-traders; by the mid-seventeenth this group was very clearly mulatto. They remained of some importance for the Church of São Salvador, especially in maintaining the confraternities on account of which there were various churches in the capital besides the cathedral and the royal churches (that of St James, which was the principal royal mausoleum, and that of St Joseph, which was the palace chapel). But the ongoing core of the Church was now constituted less by anything looking like an immigrant community than by the clergy, the *maestri* and a wider circle of devout Kongolese aristocrats who frequented the liturgy, including a group of royally connected old ladies, almost the sort that might be found in any small European capital, the widow of one king, the sister of another. With a functioning Jesuit college educating large numbers of Mwissikongo youth in literacy, Portuguese, and Christian doctrine, a functioning cathedral with its clergy and regular offices, the city of São Salvador from the 1620s to the 1650s could give the authentic impression of a Christian capital. There were even plans afoot in Europe to set up convents of Carmelite and Ursuline nuns, plans which Vives derided as 'manifest idiocy'.[7] While the secular clergy now residing in the countryside will have made a slight difference there too, the religious contrast between capital and country was nevertheless profound. Bras Correa wrote to a well-wisher in Europe that, while the capital was more or less Christian, 'the rest of the great kingdom is still plunged in paganism'.[8] He was not exaggerating. Bishops and missionaries, fed on somewhat glamorized accounts of São Salvador and its aristocracy, could imagine that the Kongo really was a Christian society until they experienced the countryside. A zealous Jesuit, Fr. Tavares, had been trying desperately hard to Christianize one bit of country around Bengo on the southern borders of the Kongo for a few years in the 1630s. He did it with the help of a number of *maestri* and Fr. Cardoso's catechism. But he was clearly quite exceptional. No one else before the arrival of the Capuchins tried so seriously to tackle the glaring contrast between São Salvador and the countryside.

vi. The Mission of the Capuchins

It was the task of the Capuchins to Christianize the Kongolese countryside. Throughout the seventeenth century the Portuguese Empire was shrinking as the Dutch, the English, the French, and the Spanish all encroached upon its vast extent, or—as in East Africa—the local powers simply rose up and drove them out. Up to this point

---

[7] P. Sérouet, *Jean de Brétigny (1556–1634): Aux origines du Carmel de France, de Belgique et du Congo* (Louvain, 1974), 329–30.   [8] Ibid. 322.

Lisbon had consistently prevented any non-Portuguese missionary from reaching the Kongo. But in 1640 the Dutch conquered Angola as they had conquered Elmina in 1637, Cochin in 1633, and Malacca in 1641. In 1652 they settled at the Cape. For a moment a Dutch Protestant empire appeared to be replacing the Portuguese. This freed the Kongo from Portuguese pressure and (together with the Spanish–Portuguese conflict going on simultaneously) made it just a little less difficult for non-Portuguese missionaries to get there. That very year, 1640, Rome established an Apostolic Prefecture for the Kongo and confided it to the Italian Capuchins. It was a new kind of missionary structure recently devised by Propaganda Fide. The Prefect to whom it was encharged was not a bishop but had almost episcopal jurisdiction and he was appointed directly by Rome. It was a way of escaping the royal stranglehold over missions through control of episcopal appointments.

For several decades Capuchins, Italian, Spanish, and French, had been trying to worm their way into the African mission despite the stonewalling tactics of the Portuguese government. In the 1630s a number of French Capuchins had begun to do so along the west coast in areas where any Portuguese control had disappeared; but the climate was almost as effective a bar to mission as the *Padroado* and most quickly died. Moreover, the Dutch were as anxious to keep out all Catholic missionaries as were the Portuguese to keep out all non-Portuguese ones, so the general position was little improved. Missionaries had no ships of their own. They were dependent for getting to Africa at all upon co-operative traders and European port authorities.

Nevertheless, in 1644 Propaganda Fide added to the Apostolic Prefecture for the Kongo another for the Guinea Coast and Sierra Leone, confided this time to the Spanish Capuchins of the province of Andalusia; in 1647 it created a third—for a mission to Benin—and gave it to the Capuchins of Aragon. In the second half of the century the Portuguese attitude also changed to some extent. There were very few Portuguese priests now able and willing to go abroad, and Lisbon revised its position to allow missionaries of other nationalities, so long as they were not Spanish, to work within the *Padroado*, provided that they travelled via Lisbon. Before the end of the century even the island of São Tomé had become an area of Capuchin ministration: they had come to see it as a convenient base from which to succour the Christians of Warri and Sierra Leone, areas in which no missionary seemed able to survive for long.

It was within this context at once of a change in the wider European and colonial political situation, of a new missionary structure devised by Propaganda Fide of apostolic prefectures, and of a very considerable missionary enthusiasm within the Capuchins of many lands, that the arrival of twelve Italian and Spanish missionaries in Soyo in May 1645, led by their prefect Bonaventura d'Alessano, must be seen. It was to be the start of almost 200 years of Capuchin involvement in the Kongo. They were received in Mbanza Soyo by its Count and people with much enthusiasm as 'priests of the great God', nganga za Nzambi mpungu,[9] but their mission was to the Kongo as a whole and its king, so naturally the prefect wished to proceed as soon as possible to the capital, Mbanza Kongo, São Salvador. But there at once was a problem. Soyo and Kongo were at war. The Count in consequence did his best to keep them in Soyo whereupon the Prefect began to threaten to make use of the quite special papal excommunication incurred by those impeding missionaries from attaining their objectives. The Count weakened, providing the porters without whom the missionaries were unable to proceed, and the Prefect and three companions then set out.

The welcome they experienced from King Garcia II when they reached São Salvador was no less enthusiastic. Nevertheless, the fact of first entering the land at Soyo and establishing a base there always marked the Capuchin mission, so that it continued to have two sides to it—Soyo upon the one hand, the rest of the kingdom on the other. Soyo, benefiting from a certain amount of direct overseas trade, had been growing increasingly powerful and had in fact defeated the Kongolese army in the recent war, but it had had no priest for several years. Mbanza Kongo, on the other hand, had both Jesuits and secular canons, and the Capuchins would always relate somewhat uneasily to both. The King welcomed them as not being Portuguese, not coming from Loanda, and as representing a direct line to Rome—the achievement, it might be felt, of fifty years of diplomacy. Yet in Soyo the Capuchins were in undisputed ecclesiastical control as they never could quite be in São Salvador. Moreover, when, three years later, the Portuguese drove the Dutch

---

[9] F. Bontinck (ed.), *Brève relation de la fondation de la mission des Frères Mineurs au royaume de Congo par Jean-François de Rome* (Louvain, 1964), 30.

from Loanda, the Kongo was in trouble as a Dutch ally and the very attractions of the Capuchins became an added embarrassment: they were a group of Italians and Spaniards without a Portuguese among them. Their very language was wrong and they had never embarked from Lisbon in the first place. The presence of Spaniards in particular much increased the Portuguese case against Garcia, for Spain was now Portugal's enemy almost more than Holland. In the complex and unstable politics of the next years the Capuchin mission was under frequent suspicion from both Kongolese and Portuguese. The Capuchins, who were deeply committed to an intensely religious mission and very little interested in politics, were time and again disillusioned by the realities of their situation.

What kept many of them going in face of almost overwhelming difficulties was an immense commitment to a specifically missionary calling, a great sense of Capuchin *esprit de corps*, but also a lasting feeling that—in spite of everything—they really were wanted and respected in the Kongo. They started, in São Salvador, by learning the language from Manuel Roboredo, and some of the early missionaries learnt it well. The Spaniard Antonio de Teruel actually composed seven books in Kikongo and in neighbouring languages, and the first prefect requested Rome to send out a small printing-press, but in practice the authorities in Rome and elsewhere now appeared little interested in furthering such crucially important work. Some of the later missionaries failed to learn Kikongo well and always heard confessions through an interpreter—a practice which Bernardo da Gallo in the early eighteenth century was by then clearly unusual in finding both unnecessary and undesirable. But in the early days that does not seem to have been so. Manuel Roboredo himself soon became a Capuchin, and his ministry in São Salvador in the 1650s was one of exceptional influence. Antonio do Couto was by then the only Jesuit priest left in the Kongo, and a school run by the Capuchins became probably more important than that of the Jesuits. Indeed there were at times more than a dozen Capuchins in the capital, though they tended to be those who were ill.

The primary Capuchin task, as they saw it, was all the same to evangelize the countryside and, having learned Kikongo (which was less needed for São Salvador where Portuguese was widely understood), they were distributed through the principal provinces, especially Nsundi, Mbamba, and Mbata. While houses were also opened elsewhere, they were seldom maintained for long. At least a third of the friars died within a couple of years of arrival; others were invalided home. Despite the scores of Capuchins sent to the Kongo, there were seldom even in the early years more than about a dozen active at any one time. Men like Jerome de Montesarchio and Antonio de Teruel, who were at work for some twenty years in the kingdom, were quite exceptional. What is more surprising is that anyone survived at all, wearing a hair shirt, taking the discipline, fasting in Advent and Lent—all that over and above the most difficult conditions of lodging and food, constant travelling, very hard work, and plenty of tropical disease.

The ministry of the seventeenth-century 'apostolic missionary' was one of the sacraments and a measure of basic teaching. Here was a 'Christian kingdom' whose people were largely unbaptized or, if baptized, not married canonically. It was that which had first to be rectified. The number of baptisms and marriages claimed is often surprising—Jerome de Montesarchio once baptized more than 1,000 people in one day—but the figures are by no means incredible, and, as the fathers seem normally to have recorded on paper the names of those they baptized and married, it is unlikely that the figures are much exaggerated. Again and again they were visiting places where there had been no priest for many years, if ever. Why should the people in such places want to be baptized or married canonically? It seems clear enough that they did want to be. The common consciousness of the people of the Kongo, following their king, was that they were Christians. It was their tribal religion. This meant going through the recognized rites of incorporation which related them to Nzambi mpungu, the great God, through 'taking the salt', the way the rite was called. What baptism could possibly mean to the rural population beyond this, it would be hard to say. But it was still an occasion of communal delight. Witness an occasion in 1668, the baptism of a young country girl who came stark naked to a travelling Capuchin to be baptized. Before instructing her in 'the Principles of Christianity', he arranged for her to be covered with some leaves, and, as it was the feast of St Joachim, he baptized her Anne. Men, women, and children then made a ring, placed her in the middle, and danced around, playing on their instruments and crying 'Long live Anne, long live Anne'.[10]

[10] Denis de Carli, *A Curious and Exact Account of a Voyage to Congo*, in A. and J. Churchill (eds.), *A Collection of Voyages* (1704), i. 627.

Local governors, who had mostly lived for considerable periods in Mbanza Kongo and attended school and services there, were no less anxious that the people should be baptized. It was the class of the Mwissikongo, formed in Mbanza Kongo but ruling the provinces, who really made the sacramental work of the Capuchins on a large scale possible. What the people did not want was to give up their existing rites. Addition was one thing, subtraction quite another. In 1697 Luca da Caltanisetta commented on this in Nsundi quite perceptively: 'Some men and women told the interpreter that I behaved badly in being an enemy of the fetishists and burning their idols because they could not abandon the custom of their country and that as Christians they did first have recourse to God for the health of the sick person but, not obtaining it, turned to the fetishists.'[11] This, he commented, is the view held universally in this miserable kingdom. He saw the traditional rites as being a sort of devil-worship, and that indeed was the general missionary view; yet even so unsympathetic a missionary as Luca could admit that fetishists 'do not make a pact with the devil and do not aim at their neighbour's destruction but to do him good'.[12]

This second side of the ministry of the 'apostolic missionary'—the war upon *nkisi*, idols, 'devil-worship', secret cults like Kimpassi and Atombola—was a far more difficult and dangerous one. Georges de Geel, a Flemish Capuchin, came upon one such cult in the 'Christian' village of Ulolo, broke it up, and flung the *nkisi* into a fire. The infuriated villagers attacked him so fiercely that he died of the effects ten days later. It is surprising that this did not happen more often. It was not only the Capuchins who dealt so high-handedly with the instruments and sacred objects of local religion. Fr. Tavares had done quite the same around Bengo a few decades earlier, though he did at least respect enough the great idol of Golungu to carry it off and send it home to the university of Evora. One cannot quite imagine the Capuchins doing anything so academic. Lonely and exposed as they were when faced with uncomprehending crowds of resentful people who saw their symbols of life, rain, and health being smashed before their eyes, the Capuchins frequently triumphed in the immediate situation, not only through an appeal to secular authority, but by the sheer force of their own spiritual power. A man

[11] R. Rainero, *Il Congo agli inizi del settecento nella relazione di P. Luca da Caltanisetta OFM Cap.* (Florence, 1974), 210.   [12] Ibid. 123.

like Jerome de Montesarchio was an extraordinary thaumaturgic figure (even the locusts fled before him!) and the missionary's sense of divine compulsion, the evident willingness to die for God's cause, must have had a lot to do with his success. The fact that these white men were wholly unconnected with the slave-trade, refused the offer of women, and sought nothing for themselves was recognized by the people and set them quite apart.

The fatal weakness in the strategy was not so much the burning of *nkisi*: that might be ruthless enough, but it was in its way understood. It was the way fourteenth-century Ethiopian monks had behaved and the way twentieth-century prophets would behave. It at least took the *nkisi* seriously. It shared with them a sort of common logic. The weakness was their non-replacement. Of course there was the cross and the rosary: the cross standing at the centre of a village, the rosary hanging around the necks of the faithful. The services which, here and there, the *maestri* led in village churches appear to have consisted in little but saying the rosary and singing the Salve Regina and other canticles. The discipline was taken on Fridays in Lent. There were processions for St Anthony or at great feasts, but such things will have happened only where there were *maestri* and a tradition of devotion, in villages for the most part rather close to Mbanza Kongo, Soyo, or the capital of Mbamba. It is amazing that the *maestri* were never authorized even to baptize. The attack on the *nkisi* was pointless, not so much because of its violence and sense of stark confrontation, but because it simply left a ritual void in local life which could only be filled by carving new *nkisi* once the missionary had passed on.

For the twenty-five years following 1645 a good deal of this sort of apostolate was carried on, but it affected some parts of the country more than others: the east always less than the west. It was everywhere intermittent and its scale soon declined in every province other than Soyo. There just were not the priests available. Moreover, within ten years the centre of the prefecture—the residence of the prefect himself—had been moved from São Salvador to Loanda (just as had happened to the diocese) and the Capuchins were beginning to turn their attention to the spiritual needs of the white colonial population surrounding it: the re-established colony of Angola had decided that, in the near absence of Portuguese priests, it could well tolerate the ministry of zealous Italian friars.

At the same time the core of the Kongolese Church which had seemed to be improving just a little from the 1620s to the 1640s and which the Capuchin offensive was intended to enlarge appeared, on the contrary, to be disintegrating. The diocese had no bishop from 1642 to 1673 on account of the Portuguese–Spanish conflict and Roman support for the Spanish side. This meant that there were no local ordinations (though one or two people were still sent by the Capuchins for training and ordination to Lisbon or Rome) and also that there was no real diocesan leadership or planning. After the Portuguese recapture of Loanda, the few Portuguese priests who had survived moved there. Mbanza Kongo was left with no more than five mestiços: the one surviving Jesuit, do Couto, now acted as Portuguese Ambassador, and the Jesuit impact on São Salvador had virtually come to an end. For the rest the surviving canons lived openly with their concubines and exercised a ministry which gives the impression of having consisted to a large extent in closing the churches when their dues were not paid. A hundred and fifty years earlier Afonso I was already complaining of Portuguese priests who lived with their concubines, and in 1534 the Nuncio in Lisbon had sensibly suggested in a letter to the Papal Secretary of State that the clergy in the Kongo should be given permission to marry 'as one has done for the Maronites'.[13] It was not done. Now that a local clergy had developed, the consequence was only too clear. Their training was quite inadequate and all the circumstances of their life militated against the practice of celibacy. Marriage being forbidden, their lives generated a continuous public scandal at the heart of the Church which inevitably undermined the almost impossible struggle to persuade the laity to adopt the basics of Catholic marital teaching— monogamy and lifelong fidelity. Inevitably too this generated a continual conflict between religious and seculars. In some cases the latter were also deeply involved in slave-trading. When local ordinations were resumed late in the century, it would be largely of the illegitimate sons of the Angolan clergy, black, white, or mestiço. A correct insistence upon the necessity of developing a local clergy, but tied by a wholly inappropriate system, had generated a pattern of clerical life profoundly disastrous for the development of an authentic Christian community.

The only hope for the Kongolese Church probably lay in separating it firmly from Angola and placing it in the hands of the

---

[13] *Correspondence de Dom Afonso*, 83, 97, and 195; cf. also F. Bontinck, 'Du nouveau sur Dom Afonso, roi de Congo', *African Historical Studies*, 3 (1970), 151–62.

Capuchins. At the end of the 1640s this was probably the Roman intention, but the Portuguese restoration in Angola and the apparent impossibility of relating to the Kongo on a regular basis except through Lisbon deterred *Propaganda* from carrying it out. Inevitably from then on, as the centre of diocese and prefecture ceased to be in São Salvador and became the Portuguese colonial, slave-trading, port of Loanda, ecclesiastical concern for the Kongo steadily declined. That decline was, however, much precipitated by political events. Everywhere else east of the Atlantic the Portuguese Empire was fading, but in Angola it was not. On the contrary, its grip was extending as the colonized area expanded and around it the far larger area of persistent slave-raiding. The expansion of Angola meant the contraction of Kongo. In most of the sixteenth century Portugal could affect a friendly relationship to the kingdom because it had developed no territorial aspirations in this part of Africa, but in the seventeenth century the requirements of Angola were inherently destructive of a strong independent kingdom immediately to its north. Moreover, as the Portuguese Empire declined, Angola and its economy became more and more important to what remained of it, and Angola's economy consisted of just one thing—the traffic in slaves. Brazil was beginning to flourish, but Brazil's prosperity depended upon a ceaseless importation of African slaves to cultivate its estates. Angola had become effectively no more than a subsidiary to the Brazilian economy, and the Kongo, with its well-populated provinces, was an obvious target for the trade.

vii. *The Battle of Ambuila, Kimpa Vita, and the Antonian Movement*

Throughout the later years of Garcia II (1641–61) Portuguese pressure was mounting, but it was in the reign of his successor, Antonio I, that it came to a head, and, faced with Loanda's territorial demands, Antonio mobilized the whole kingdom on an almost unprecedented scale for a major war. In general the missionary accounts of Garcia II and Antonio are distinctly unfavourable. The Capuchins disliked the slave-trade, but they did not at all perceive its larger implications and their basic loyalty was shifting in these years Loandawards. Whether Garcia and Antonio were more cruel or less reliable Christians than some of their predecessors, it is hard to say. Garcia, at least, would seem to have had for much of the time a fairly strong pro-Church policy: the whole initial Capuchin advance had taken place under his patronage. What altered the situation in his later years was less anything happening in the Kongo than the development of Loanda's policy subsequent to the ejection of the Dutch. The Kongo monarchy was forced to respond to a new Portuguese expansionism. Hitherto the policy of Kongo kings had never been diametrically anti-Portuguese. With Antonio at least it became so, but basically because Portuguese policy left him little alternative. Not unnaturally rejection of the Portuguese alliance brought with it hints of a rejection of Christianity too, but not more than hints.

On 30 October 1665 the army of the Kongo engaged in battle with that of the Portuguese of Loanda at Ambuila, and the Kongo was wholly defeated. Among the dead[14] was the King and his son, the Duke of Mbamba, the Duke of Mbata, the Duke of Nsundi, the Duke of Gorimba, the Marquess of Mpemba, ninety-five title-holders in all, as also the Capuchin Francesco de São Salvador, who had accompanied his king against the orders of his prefect. Effectively the kingdom of Kongo as it had existed since the time of Afonso I, together with its Christianized ruling class as it had developed in the course of the seventeenth century, was so shattered that it never recovered. Gone was the confident framework which had supported the growth of Kongolese Christianity. Antonio had brought with him to war his crown and sceptre, even the royal archives. All was lost. The monarchy was so vastly weakened, it no longer possessed the resources, effective or symbolic, to withstand the pressures of disintegration operating within the Kongo, or the pressures from Loanda to annex its southern provinces.

The royal succession had always been a difficult and bitter matter. Now succession disputes and rival kings multiplied, especially between the claimants of two rival clans, the Naza and Mpanzu. In 1678 one of the rival armies sacked Mbanza Kongo itself, the churches and royal palace were left in ruins, the inhabitants fled, and for twenty-five years no one lived in São Salvador. At times in this period there were no fewer than four contending kings. Portuguese settlers, never numerous outside São Salvador, had almost all moved to Angola. The basic pillars of the Church had disappeared. The Jesuits had gone. New canons, while nominally still appointed to the cathedral of São Salvador, had in fact since the 1650s been residing in

---

[14] See e.g. *MMA* xii. 589–90.

Loanda. Miguel de Castro, last of the old canons, died in 1685. The remaining Capuchins were no longer extending an existing Church from town to country. They were simply conducting strange one-man itinerant missions, dispensing baptism and marriage rites to a people who had grown accustomed to expect to receive these basic Christian rituals as part of their traditional identity.

Kongo suffered in these years a profound social and psychological dislocation. Its identifying and unifying character, national mythology, and political organization had for two centuries possessed a rather stable, functioning, almost self-conscious character. Now it lay in ruins. And the symbolic expression of that dislocation became the movement of St Anthony. It began in 1703. Pedro IV, the Pacific, the nearest the Kongo had at the time to a recognized king, was living in a fortified camp on Mount Kimbangu, but there was increasingly insistent popular pressure that he return to São Salvador. He had in fact dispatched some of his supporters, led by his uncle-in-law and Captain-General, Dom Pedro Constantino da Sylva, the Chibenga (the Valorous), to resume agricultural cultivation nearer the town. He had, however, come subsequently to distrust the Chibenga. With the King was a single Capuchin, Bernardo da Gallo, a man who at least knew Kikongo well. The Mani Vunda, Dom Manuel, now appealed to Bernardo to return to São Salvador himself and so draw the King back there, the true centre of Church and state. But just at this time various religious developments were going on among the people around Mount Kimbangu. Outside the church after evening devotions the practice developed of saying the Ave Maria three times, followed by a triple cry of 'Sari' (Mercy). It was reported that Christ was indignant that the King had not returned to São Salvador and that only Mary was holding back his anger. An old woman named Apollonia or Mattuta, a prophetess, declared that the mountain would go up in fire if the King did not descend. She then began to burn *nkisi* and to perform miraculous healings. Everything added to an atmosphere of acute political and religious expectation.

It was some time after Easter in 1704 that St Anthony appeared upon the scene. A young woman whose Kongo name was written as Kimpa Vita and whose baptismal name was Beatrice attached herself to the old woman in burning both *nkisi* and the cross in the villages around the mountain. She was reported to die every Friday and rise to new life every Sunday. When she visited Mount Kimbangu and its church she knelt before the statue of the Blessed Virgin, striking her head three times on the ground. She walked on her toes with her neck extended and spoke in a delirious way. Da Gallo thought her certainly possessed. When interrogated by him she said she was St Anthony come from heaven, and when he asked her, crudely enough, 'What news do you bring from there? Tell us, are there any Kongolese blacks in heaven and are they there with their black colour?', she replied, with sound theological accuracy, 'There are both Kongolese children there and adults, those who have observed God's law, but they don't have a black or white colour, because in heaven there is no colour.'[15] Reproached for her false teaching, she denied it and began to weep. She had, she said, spoken in favour both of the Pope and of Fr. da Gallo. The interpreter, a *maestro*, endeavoured to calm her, called her 'daughter', and assured her that she was under their protection. At this da Gallo denounced him as a heretic. As a *maestro* he should be on the priest's side. How could he call a fetishist his daughter? Because she was of his clan, the interpreter replied, to the Capuchin's fury. Had she not burned crosses as well as *nkisi*? Yes, replied Beatrice, but the crosses are equally mixed with superstition. How could a woman possibly be St Anthony? he demanded. God sent St Anthony, she replied, into various people but he had been rejected each time, until he entered her head when she was ill and St Anthony dressed in a Capuchin habit had appeared to her. She was now dead because St Anthony had taken the place of her soul. She had given away all she possessed, just as Capuchin missionaries did, and was preaching the word of God and teaching the people to prepare for the return to São Salvador.

Why St Anthony? Firstly, because St Anthony was one of the best-known saints in the Kongo, at least by name. The original Franciscan missionaries had called the church at Mbanza Soyo Sant Antonio and the Capuchins had fostered this devotion. One of the four pious congregations of the faithful was named after him. But there was more to it than that. Beatrice had heard a sermon on St Anthony read from the Portuguese book of a friend.[16] This sermon was most probably that preached in 1638 by Fr. Antonio Vieira, SJ, at São

---

[15] L. Jadin, 'Le Congo et la secte des Antoniens: Restauration du royaume sous Pedro IV et la "Sainte-Antoine Congolais" 1664–1718', *BIHB* 33 (1961), 499.

[16] See ibid. 515 and W. Randles, *L'Ancient Royaume du Congo, des origines à la fin du XIX siècle* (Paris, 1968), 157–9.

Salvador de Bahia in Brazil after the Dutch had raised the siege of the town. Vieira had taken as his text 2 Kings 19: 34, 'I will protect this town and I will save it on account of me and my servant David'. He then compared São Salvador de Bahia with Jerusalem, and St Anthony with David. To save São Salvador God has 'delegated his power to St Anthony'. Vieira's sermons enjoyed a widespread popularity. For Beatrice this Brazilian Portuguese text was to be recontextualized at São Salvador of the Kongo.

After she had left Mount Kimbangu, the King and his servants came to mass, each wearing a cross. The day was passed, they declared, in which St Anthony had prophesied that all those upon the mountain would be destroyed. However, having left the King's court, Beatrice's confidence seemed to grow. People should now pray to no other saint than Anthony, she now claimed as she led a group of commoners back to São Salvador. It was just what da Gallo had been urged to do but had not done. After establishing her own abode beside the cathedral on the spot where the bishop once lived, she sent out messengers, 'little Anthonies', all round the Kongo, calling people back to the capital. These messengers were summarily rejected by authorities in more stable areas like Soyo and Nsundi, but in many parts the new movement was afoot and Lorenzo da Lucca, another Capuchin, encountered it close to the sea at Musseto in mid-1705. Soon the capital was being repopulated and Beatrice hailed as the true nganga, a restorer and ruler of the Kongo, while da Gallo was denounced as 'little Bernardo', a cowardly nganga who had not had the courage to lead the people back and so restore the kingdom. The Chibenga now moved into the capital, ostensibly to protect her, and when the Mani Vunda went there on behalf of the King to find out what was happening, he was very nearly killed. On return he continued to press on Pedro the importance of returning, so in February 1705 the King left the mountain armed with the crucifix taken from the altar of the local church: he would return, but as an orthodox Catholic monarch. However, the Chibenga continued to control the capital and Pedro set up temporary camps, first at Mulumbi, then on Mount Evululu, a day's journey from Mbanza Kongo. He remained anxious not to precipitate a battle, declaring that continual wars had simply destroyed the kingdom, and for the next three years unsuccessfully negotiated for the Chibenga's submission.

Meanwhile, at São Salvador the Antonian movement was reaching its climax, an extended religious doctrine and practice. Jesus Christ had been born, declared Beatrice, at São Salvador, the true Bethlehem, just as he had been baptized at Nsundi, in the River Zaïre.[17] The Salve Regina had become a Salve Antoniana with quite a theology attached. 'You say *Salve* and you do not know why. God takes the intention. Marriage matters not at all. God considers the intention. Baptism matters nothing. God considers the intention. Confessions serve for nothing. God considers the intention. Prayers serve nothing. God considers the intention. . . . St Anthony is our remedy. . .'.[18] While the missionaries considered all this blasphemous nonsense, much of it might well be regarded as a remarkably acute judgement upon the externalism of Kongolese Christianity. Of her final interrogation Lorenzo da Lucca remarked that she spoke with gravity, giving the impression of weighing her words with care.

Beatrice had a male assistant or 'guardian angel' who called himself St John. She became pregnant by him. As she had herself stressed her own chastity—on the Capuchin model—this presented a problem. It clearly did not fit with the St Anthony identity. She disappeared from the capital while awaiting childbirth, but, soon after the child was born, she was arrested and taken for trial to Evululu. It would appear to have been Dom Manuel, the Mani Vunda, who took the lead in the trial as Kongolese custom would suggest as appropriate, but Bernardo da Gallo and Lorenzo da Lucca, who was visiting his colleague (after several years in which Bernardo had seen no other Capuchin), interrogated both Beatrice and old Apollonia. At the petition of the missionaries Apollonia (on account of apparent senility) and the baby were spared. Beatrice (aged about 22) and John were flung live upon the flames on 2 July 1706.

The Antonian movement did not at once collapse with the death of Beatrice. The population of São Salvador remained committed to it, so far as can be seen, at least until the recapture of the city by Pedro IV in February 1709. In the final battle, in which the Chibenga fell and Pedro triumphed, the solders of the former cried 'Salve Antoniana' and 'Sari, Sari' while the King went into battle carrying

[17] St Francis, it was asserted, had been a member of the Vunda clan, the source of Kongo religious legitimacy. The male leaders of the Antonians wore crowns made from the musenda tree, of women Beatrice alone wore one. They called them 'Ne Yari' (or 'Sari'), 'mercy'.

[18] Jadin, 'Le Congo et la secte des Antoniens', 516, T. Filesi, *Nationalismo e religione nel Congo all'inizio del 1700: La setta degli Antoniani* (Rome, 1972), 77.

a crucifix. Thus was restored the unity of monarchy, capital, cross, and Catholic Church which was to continue—despite the ever more prolonged absence of priests and the gradual diminution of the kingdom—for another century and more. Appallingly heretical as the Capuchins found Beatrice, there is perhaps less of her teaching that orthodoxy need finally fault than one might have imagined. We do, of course, only know it across a few outside and hostile observers. There is no need to think that everything reported of it is fully accurate, or that everything Antonians did corresponded to what Beatrice said. Again, it is unlikely that she was always consistent. Nevertheless, a deeply Christian, and even Catholic, character to the movement does come across through the surviving evidence. The very attack on the cross was probably a justifiable indictment of the way it had been turned into just another *nkisi*. That the movement also drew deeply upon traditional religion (very likely including Kimpa Vita's own experience of the Bisimbi cult) will be no less true.

In her political intuition of the absolute need for the Kongo to restore São Salvador, Beatrice was absolutely right. Her 'prophecy' was socially accurate. While her ability to dream dreams and see visions may well have derived from cult experiences in early life unconnected with Christianity, her teaching and sense of mission were expressed in decidedly Christian terms and in regard to a society which could no longer make sense, even to itself, except in such terms. Yet it was inevitable that the Capuchins were unable to sympathize with what she said. They were lost in the political and religious maelstrom around them: even a functioning Kongolese society was largely incomprehensible to the foreigner, much more so one as damaged as the kingdom in the long aftermath of the Battle of Ambuila.

In the years following the death of Beatrice, Pedro IV slowly re-established the unity and viability of the kingdom. He reoccupied São Salvador and stabilized a political order balancing the capital and the provinces which was to endure for 150 years. Undoubtedly the power of the king and the prestige of the capital were much diminished. Soyo had become effectively independent in the seventeenth century, Nsundi and Mbamba followed in the eighteenth. By the early nineteenth century, while a nominal sovereignty was recognized very much more widely, the king actually controlled nothing more than the villages around São Salvador. None the less, there remained a genuine continuity of religious, cultural, and institutional identity from the time of Afonso I in the early sixteenth century to Garcia V and Henrique II in the nineteenth. The Christian kingdom did then survive its traumatic crisis in the late seventeenth century, but henceforth there would be no regular priestly presence in the capital. The twelve ruined churches would remain the burial grounds of the nobility, but they would never be rebuilt.

viii. *The Kongo Church in the Eighteenth Century*

Greatly reduced in number, increasingly committed to the European-based ministry of Angola, the Capuchins would henceforth limit their presence in Kongo to two or three priests at the most in order to maintain a minimum sacramental continuity. For the first decades of the century there might be two in Soyo; elsewhere, in the Kongo proper, probably no more than a single peregrinatory missionary. What Christian life did remain—indeed, if the very desire for it remained among the common people—it would depend upon the *maestri* chosen originally more as interpreters but becoming little by little a succession of catechist Church leaders. They were in two classes: a lower one which taught and interpreted, a senior one which also heard confessions. It is a great pity that the Capuchins tell us so little about them and it suggests that they undervalued both the importance of the *maestri* and their own role in training the *maestri*. The latter, already in the seventeenth century and still more in the eighteenth, nevertheless constituted the ministry, to us almost invisible, of a Church determined not to die.

Soyo followed a very different road from the rest of the Kongo in the latter part of the seventeenth century. Already by the 1640s, when the Capuchins first arrived, it was functioning as an almost independent entity. More than any other part of the country it had profited, through the port of Pinda, from the slave trade and wider European contacts, not only with the Portuguese, but with the Dutch and the French. Being far more accessible to outsiders than anywhere else, it had always enjoyed a more considerable missionary presence. In the late seventeenth century all this was accentuated. After the battle of Ambuila (in which Soyo was not represented) the Portuguese endeavoured to crush it too. A Portuguese army in 1670 defeated the Soyo army and killed its prince, but Soyo rallied and wiped out their enemies in an unexpected attack on 18 October, the feast of St Luke. Soyo was never again thus threatened and St Luke's Day became a national festival of deliverance, with its processions and war-dances, in which the Church fully participated. Soyo was also the only place in the whole of the Kongo in which there was an almost unbroken Capuchin presence from the 1640s until well into the eighteenth century. Hence, while their impact on the rest of the kingdom became more and more erratic and ill supported after Ambuila, in Soyo one finds instead, not exactly a golden age, but a Christianity relatively stable and sure of itself, operating within a society which for a while enjoyed the same characteristics.

The four pillars of Soyo Christianity were the prince, the *maestri*, the confraternities, and the Capuchins. The Capuchins had, from their first arrival in 1645, felt particularly at home in Mbanza Soyo, or Sant Antonio as it had been named by its first Franciscan missionaries in the early sixteenth century. In São Salvador, on the contrary, the Capuchins were never quite at home: the Jesuits and the cathedral canons had established a priority and maintained a degree of Portuguese identity which left the Capuchins (with not a Portuguese among them) a bit out of it. And then, of course, from the 1660s and—still more—1678 São Salvador was in ruins. In Soyo there were no Jesuits and almost no seculars, the Capuchins had the field to themselves, and Soyo Catholicism came to express their specific religiosity with its strengths and weaknesses far better than anywhere else. As Soyo's own political power grew under the da Sylva dynasty, Mbanza Soyo took on the characteristics of São Salvador, if in a less grandiose way. It too had now some eight churches—one for the tombs of the counts, one for the royal chapel, others for pious confraternities which the Capuchins established here for the first time and membership of which became almost a *sine qua non* for high political office. The prince was normally chosen from among the Confraternity of St Francis. The group of *maestri* too became particularly stable in Mbanza Soyo, and more than one of them was later chosen to be prince. The princely rituals which were developed, again reflecting those of Mbanza Kongo, must have done much to sacralize the status and strengthen the hand of the ruler of Soyo as it developed as an effectively independent state, encroaching upon the lands of Mbamba to the south and negotiating with more than one European power. Both literacy and fluency in Portuguese were probably taken for granted by the upper class at this period.

Soyo's relatively limited extent and defined borders made it more feasible for the religion of Mbanza Soyo to be carried to the countryside both by the Capuchins themselves in reasonably regular itinerant missions and through the appointment of both *maestri* and Christian chiefs at the local level. A village Christian community with its own chapel and *maestro* would seem to have existed in consequence in at least some parts of Soyo, those nearer the capital, especially the peninsula between the sea and the River Zaïre, in a way that it surely never did in Nsundi, Mbata, or even Mbamba. But the extent of this should not be exaggerated. In the 1680s, the time of Merolla, there were some eighteen churches in all in the country, a third of which were in Mbanza Soyo. Lorenzo da Lucca could find in 1704 villages hardly thirty miles from Mbanza Soyo suffering from 'inconceivable ignorance' which had never been visited by a priest before.[19] The high point of Soyo's Christianity would seem to have been the 1690s and the ministry there of Andrea da Pavia. Yet move on thirty years, to the second or third decade of the eighteenth century, and one gains the same impression of religious disintegration at work here as elsewhere in the Kongo. Capuchin vigour and Soyo political stability would seem to have made a noticeable difference, but it was not a very long-term difference. Why was this? One cannot here mainly blame Portuguese colonialism or the slave-trade: their immediate effects upon Soyo were not considerable. More significant was the nature of Capuchin, and indeed late seventeenth-century Catholic, religiosity. Effectively the system depended upon the patronage of the prince, the activity of the Capuchins, and their harmonious relationship. Time and again the relationship was not harmonious. Undoubtedly, that was at times due to the erratic and violent behaviour of the prince, but it was also at times due to the unimaginative and rather bullying attitude of the Capuchins—as, for instance, the refusal of Lorenzo da Lucca in 1714 to allow the Prince any more the privilege of kissing the Gospel at mass, a refusal which did enormous damage to the Church at a time when things were anyway not going well: by then relations appear different indeed from 1702 when a visiting Capuchin preached for an hour in Portuguese and the Prince himself (a former *maestro*) interpreted it for another hour in Kikongo, or when the Prince sang the epistle in Latin to the amazement of a visiting French ambassador!

[19] J. Cuvelier (ed.), *Relations sur le Congo du Père Laurent de Lucques 1700–1717* (Brussels, 1953), 101.

The fathers in this period do not appear an outstandingly able group. Their linguistic knowledge was mostly poor—very different from that of two generations back. The Capuchin sense of mission and collective commitment to the task given them was not easily eroded, but their understanding of its problems was disastrously limited. Their very fidelity to the instructions of *Propaganda* not to alter culture, and their consequent overwhelming preoccupation with 'religious' things in a rather narrow sense, meant that their impact was in some ways far less than that of the Jesuits. One of their brothers, Leonardo da Nando, who worked in Soyo from 1654 to his death in 1687, did for many years run a quite influential school in Mbanza Soyo, but such work had not the priority it had for the Jesuits.

Most disastrous was the absence of any policy in regard to a local clergy. In fact the Capuchins criticized and disapproved so strongly of the behaviour of local priests elsewhere, they could hardly wish to extend them. But what alternative was there if the Church was to continue? Underlying failure to grapple with this question was the absence of authority. The Capuchins in the Kongo did not constitute a diocese of their own; they and their prefecture were now centred upon Loanda. For both bishop and prefect Soyo had become an outlying area of marginal importance, rather than the one possible viable centre for the development of a genuinely African Catholic Church. Equally Propaganda Fide, which in the time of Vives and Ingoli had demonstrated such an outstanding concern for the Kongo as well as a remarkable wider missionary imaginativeness, seems to have lost heart over the Kongo, just as it lost confidence in the kind of adaptation which Ricci pioneered in China. In 1615 Pope Paul V had given permission for Chinese priests to celebrate mass in Chinese. In 1656 Rome approved, a little vaguely, the adaptationist Chinese 'rites' recommended by the Jesuits. In 1704 the rites were condemned and the use of Latin was being insisted upon for all Chinese priests. The effective Roman and missionary abandonment of the Kongo has to be seen within this far wider shift, and decline, in missionary commitment and vision characteristic of the eighteenth-century Church.

While the diocese of São Salvador was established in 1596, no bishop had lived there or visited it since the 1620s. Ecclesiastically, as Loanda—essentially a colonial city grew—São Salvador was abandoned. There were still appeals in the 1680s and later for this to be reversed, for São Salvador to be detached ecclesiastically from Loanda.[20] Very late in the day indeed, in 1711, a Capuchin, Eustachio da Ravenna, wrote to *Propaganda* begging that a bishop, and a young one, be appointed for the Kongo and a seminary established. As he rightly pointed out, there was absolutely no way in which his fellow Capuchins in the Kongo could effectively evangelize it—there were never more than six or eight in all, and they quickly fell ill or died. He even charmingly drew pictures of the bishop's house and vegetable garden and of an African-style seminary for *Propaganda*'s benefit.[21] He was quite right, but by then it was far too late. His whole proposal was naïvely sensible in an ecclesiastical world where sense almost never prevailed. It was anyway too late because such plans required both missionary imaginativeness and considerable numerical missionary support to get going, while in fact missionary numbers and enthusiasm were fast diminishing by 1711. There were no longer many volunteers. The eighteenth century was different from the seventeenth in the African mission field largely because the European Church had changed. Both the missionary enlightenment which one finds in a few quarters in the earlier seventeenth century and the enthusiasm one finds a great deal more widely had faded in a Rome both more rigid and less zealous.

Eustachio da Ravenna's plan also remained intrinsically impractical because it continued to imply a post-Tridentine model of the secular priest. And this model simply did not work in Africa. At the time Fr. Eustachio wrote there was in fact once more a secular mestiço priest living at São Salvador, Estavao Botelho. He was the only priest to live there for any length of time after Pedro IV's return. He was a slave-trader and open concubinist, and the only other 'Portuguese' who now lived in the capital were his children. He was accused of many other faults too, including the poisoning of a Capuchin, yet the Bishop—who never visited the Kongo—had appointed him Vicar-General. Botelho became the centre-piece of a considerable conflict which boiled up between the Capuchins and the Bishop in the 1720s and was taken to both Lisbon and Rome.[22] The Capuchins declared

---

[20] See e.g. the appeal of a secular priest, Manuel de Saa, to *Propaganda*, 2 Nov. 1687, L. Jadin, 'Le Clergé seculier et les Capuchins du Congo et d'Angola aux XVIIᵉ et XVIIIᵉ siècles: Conflits de jurisdiction 1600–1726', *BIHB* 36 (1964), 432–6, and that of Fr. Domingos de São Jose (a former secular in Kongo), 2 Apr. 1702, 438–42.

[21] Jadin, 'Le Clergé seculier et les Capuchins du Congo et d'Angola', 443–5 and pictures opposite 260.   [22] For the very considerable dossier, see ibid.

that not only Botelho but most of the priests of the Angola diocese lived in open concubinage, that they did next to no missionary work and only impeded such work both through the scandal they caused and through requiring the sacraments to be paid for. There can be little doubt that the charges were substantially true, but the Capuchin case was hardly strengthened when one of the younger new brooms, Agostino dalle Pieve, could request that the bishop of Angola should be ordered in future only to ordain whites. What a contrast between Fr. Eustachio in 1711 looking idealistically at the situation from the viewpoint of Kongolese need and Fr. Agostino in 1725 looking at the situation from the viewpoint of Angolan reality!

The more the *Padroado* crumbled as an even moderately viable ecclesiastical system, the more the Portuguese authorities—both the bishops in Africa and the government in Lisbon—were only able to look on Capuchin complaints, or whatever, as further proof of the maliciousness of Italians and Propaganda Fide in regard to Portugal. Roman–Portuguese relations in the 1720s were already bad, and the last thing Rome actually wanted was to get embroiled, inevitably ineffectually, in upholding the cause of Italian missionaries within or near a Portuguese colony and against a Portuguese bishop. Effectively, neither side now offered a viable Catholic future to the Kongo. Fr. Eustachio's appeal for a fresh start was—given the continued requirement of celibacy—deeply unrealistic. Yet in an area like Soyo the Capuchins could, even within their own line of vision and the parameters of canon law, have devised a better strategy: the *maestri* could have been empowered to baptize while the Capuchins themselves could have administered the sacrament of Confirmation (the power of confirming had been available to missionaries from much earlier, but it was only at the very end of it all that Fr. Cherubino da Savona in 1776 requested Propaganda that this power be included in their faculties) a sacrament more or less never offered in the Kongo. They could also have done something more about a local Christian literature. But Capuchin zeal was seldom matched by intelligence.

From the 1740s there was no longer a priest living even in Soyo and seldom more than one anywhere in Kongo. Twenty years later a fresh difficulty would arise when in 1763 the anticlerical Marquis de Pombal prohibited Italian Capuchins from embarking at Lisbon. In the period of his power, from 1750 to 1777, the only missionary in the Kongo for most of the time was a single Capuchin, Fr.

Cherubino da Savona. Because he was a rather wonderful man who spent fourteen unbroken years in the Kongo and when he finally left there was, for a while, no one at all, it is worth considering the situation in the second half of the eighteenth century through his eyes.[23] A century and a half of continuity of priestly apostolate within the Kongo comes to an end with Cherubino. He traversed almost every part of the country, and—given the demand for infant baptism of a whole nation—it is not surprising that he claimed to have baptized over 700,000 people in these years. He appears to have been on excellent terms with everyone and almost never has anything but good to say of people. Even of an old polygamist like Dom Pedro Manicongo Ambamba de Quimulaza, duke and effectively independent ruler of one of the provinces into which the Kongo was now divided, he remarked that he loved missionaries, could never get himself to make a canonical marriage or abandon his concubines, but would much like to receive all the other sacraments.

It is the respective Christian state of the three great provinces of Soyo, Mbamba, and Nsundi which it is most useful to consider as he reports on them in 1774. Of Soyo he can still say 'the inhabitants are almost all Christians . . . the prince holds his court with more pomp than the King of Kongo himself. He is at present named Dom Miguel Castro da Sylva, a married man and a good Christian. He can read and write in Portuguese. His people are strongly attached to missionaries and anxious to receive the sacraments.'[24] The churches were now almost all in ruins, but their sites were kept clean, their crosses stood, and the inhabitants made processions on the feast days of the saints to which they were dedicated. If we turn to Mbamba, its duke, Fr. Cherubino insisted, was 'perhaps the best prince I have known'.[25] Married to Dona Christina, he maintained the local church in good order and every Saturday and on feast days gathered his nearest vassals to recite the Catechism and the rosary. He paid three *maestri* to teach the Catechism. Of Mbamba and this same duke, Fr. Rosario dal Parco, the Capuchin Prefect in Angola, had written fifteen years earlier in 1760: 'I cannot express with what sentiments

---

[23] L. Jadin, 'Aperçu de la situation du Congo et rite d'election des rois en 1775, d'après Le P. Cherubino da Savona, missionnaire au Congo de 1759 à 1774', *BIHB* 35 (1963), 343–419; for the situation twenty-five years earlier one can turn to the often enlightening pages of *La Pratique missionnaire des PP. Capucins italiens dans les royaumes de Congo, Angola et contrées adjacentes* (Louvain, 1931) written about 1747 by a returned Capuchin, probably Hyacinto da Bologna, who was in the Kongo from 1741, including four years in Soyo.

[24] Jadin, 'Aperçu de la situation du Congo', 380.   [25] Ibid. 382.

its Duke wrote to me continually, for the love of God, to send him a missionary.'[26]

The picture of Nsundi, as Fr. Cherubino described it, was far worse:

The population is almost entirely pagan on account of lack of missionaries. The Duke, Dom Alvaro Brandone, wrote me twice in 1765 letters which made me weep in presenting the situation of the souls in his grand duchy . . . these letters, I say, would have moved a rock. Nevertheless, I found myself for more than two years without wine and without hosts, unable to celebrate the holy sacrifice of the mass and not knowing how to procure any, the roads to Loanda being closed on account of war . . . Nevertheless I wrote him letters of comfort, exhorting him to maintain one or another church . . . I sent him two *maestri* of catechism to encourage him.[27]

The contrasts here are enlightening. Nsundi was the oldest of Christian provinces but one of the least accessible. It had had almost no regular ministry since the late seventeenth century. By 1775 the situation seems beyond recall. Soyo, on the other hand, was the best. It had only been deprived of a permanent priestly presence thirty years earlier and had received some visits since. The contrast between the two is clear. Yet, clearly too, Soyo itself had slipped a long way, its churches desolate. Mbamba stands between the two. A vast area, it was never much favoured, yet because it lay between São Salvador and Loanda it was visited far more frequently than Nsundi and still had a resident priest during periods of the eighteenth century. It also happened to have an outstandingly zealous duke. Here too the situation had not been wholly lost even by the 1770s. From these accounts and those of almost every other province of the Kongo referred to in Fr. Cherubino's report, what strikes one is the tenacious collective resolve of the Kongolese ruling class to retain their Christian identity. Kings came and went with generally disastrous rapidity, but the Christian commitment of the Mwissikongo remained almost unchanged. The other thing that strikes one is the continuance of a group of literate *maestri* in several parts of the country. It was the patronage of *maestri* by a local lord together with maintenance of a church building, in which he himself regularly attended services, which could still provide some sort of a core to what may be claimed as a genuine Church. Nevertheless, without the power even to baptize themselves and without even a single priest

[26] Ibid. 375.   [27] Ibid. 386.

remaining within the country after Cherubino's departure, the slide away from the consciousness of Christian identity and any sort of surviving core community which had already taken place almost irreparably in Nsundi was more than likely to happen increasingly in most other parts of the country.

We happen, however, to have contemporary with the last period of Cherubino's ministry some remarkable independent evidence of the persistence of Soyo Christianity and its limitations. For nine years from 1766 to 1775 there was a mission of French priests to the two kingdoms of Loango and Kakongo north of the River Zaïre. The Capuchins had never penetrated these societies, which had remained entirely non-Christian. Nevertheless, more than once the missionaries encountered individual Christians, slaves or traders, hailing from Soyo and always intensely pleased to meet a priest. As soon as the Count of Soyo heard of their presence he sent messengers begging them to come. Unfortunately Soyo was not within the territory confided to them! Then in 1773 a man named Pedro turned up to say that there was a whole group of Soyo Christians who had migrated some years before across the River Zaïre and were now living within the kingdom of Kakongo under their own head, Dom Iouan.[28] The prefect of the mission set off with Pedro, and his arrival at Manguenzo, the centre of this community, must surely be one of the more extraordinary episodes in African Church history. They were met by Dom Iouan and his people, saw the great cross in the middle of the village, and entered the chapel to pray before its altar and crucifix while the people chanted canticles. Over the next week, before leaving, they baptized several hundred children. However, when they later returned to reside in Manguenzo they were bitterly disappointed. The Christian identity of the people, of which they had at first been so enthusiastic, seemed now to have no effect whatever in terms of moral behaviour or personal belief. Deeply distressed and struggling with illness and the loss of several among them, they soon withdrew.[29] On the one hand the community of Manguenzo had demonstrated an extraordinary perseverance of Kongo Christians in their communal Christian identity. The missionaries had no difficulty in recognizing outwardly that they

[28] Abbé Proyart, *Histoire de Loango, Kakongo et autres royaumes d'Afrique* (Paris, 1776), esp. pt. 2, ch. 17, 315–51, also 226 and 257.

[29] J. Cuvelier, *Documents sur une mission française au Kakongo 1766–1775* (Brussels, 1953), 126–9.

were Christians, surprising as they found it. But the limitations of this sort of Christianity, of which the Capuchins had mostly been only too well aware, had now triumphed unchecked. In the Kongo Christian heartlands rather more remained to this identity, if only among an increasingly small group of people. In the almost entire absence of missionaries it was still to some extent self-sustaining through the *maestri* and a certain ritual tradition to which the ruling class at least continued to conform.

ix. *Angola, Sierra Leone, Warri, and Mutapa*

Almost nowhere outside the Kongo did Christianity in this period escape being a mere appendage of colonial presence. The history of the Church in Angola is depressingly lifeless, even though with time it became relatively considerable in size, because it remained so emphatically a colonial religion, present as part of a foreign establishment without almost any of the signs of indigenous vitality one can detect in the Kongo. Nevertheless, the Church in Angola did survive and it did so largely because of a small stream of local priests, mostly mulattos, which continued through the eighteenth and nineteenth centuries.

Even Lisbon had regarded Kongo as in its way the one special case: the king of Kongo was recognized as an independent sovereign and his country as an independent Christian state. This seems to have happened before the principles of the *Padroado* were really worked out after 1512. The basic principle elsewhere was that the Church did not extend beyond the conquista and, if an area seemed suitable for evangelization, then it needed to be absorbed within the *conquista*.

In 1514 the diocese of Funchal in Madeira was established for the whole overseas Portuguese Empire. Somewhat later this became an archbishopric with, beneath it, new dioceses of Santiago in the Cape Verde Islands and São Tomé, as well as Goa and the Azores. For West Africa the islands—hitherto uninhabited—of Cape Verde, São Tomé, and Principe were the safe core for the Empire and, therefore, for the Church. Settled compulsorily by white convicts from Portugal and black slaves brought from the mainland, they were hardly an ideal base for the Church. 'The dung heap of the Portuguese Empire', a disillusioned governor described the Cape Verde Islands in 1627, and São Tomé was often more like a pirate's lair than a royal colony and diocese. When the diocese of São

Salvador was established for the Kongo in 1596 within the province of Funchal, it was a Roman rather than a Portuguese decision and very much the odd man out: a diocese not based in the Empire. It is hardly surprising that within twenty-five years its bishops had effectively moved it to Loanda, again a colonial fortress. In principle all evangelization of the mainland was meant to depend on these places; in practice this was inevitably disastrous, particularly as these were the focal points for the organization of the slave-trade. Economically they had no other function, and in many cases the same people, including priests, were intimately involved both in slaving and evangelization.

Occasionally there were temporary apparent breakthroughs, as in Sierra Leone between 1604 and 1617. A Wolof priest, João Pinto, now a canon of São Tomé, had asked the King of Portugal for a Jesuit mission to be sent there. Two Jesuits, Baltasar Barreira and Manuel Alvares, worked for some ten years along the coast until the latter's death in 1617. They baptized various petty kings and wrote a good many reports, mostly unpublished, about the country and their attempts to convert it. But at once there arose the issue of establishing the area as a Portuguese *conquista* including a Portuguese monopoly of the local slave trade. Neither was a very practical proposition in the seventeenth century with ever increasing Dutch and English pressure all along the coast, and the 'mission' quickly died out.

Only in one place was there, almost by accident, a sort of mini Kongo and that was Warri, a small state consisting of Itsekiri people on the coast near Benin. In the late sixteenth century a mission of Augustinian monks from São Tomé, at that time ruled by a rather good Augustinian bishop, Gaspar Cao, undertook a mission to Warri presumably because—given the non-collaboration of Benin—the Portuguese were attempting to make of it an alternative base for trade in the Bight. The ruler's son was converted and, as was usual for the period of Sebastian of Portugal, he was named Sebastian. Unlike the Sebastian Mwene Mutapa, however, he persevered with his new faith, became Olu of Warri, and ruled for many years. The poverty and climate of Warri discouraged any permanent white presence, clerical or lay. The Augustinians did not last, nor did a group of Franciscans sent there by the next bishop. It was then proposed that the ships trading from São Tomé to Warri be compelled to carry a priest to minister each year for a few months to the Warri Christians. Moreover, the bishop, Francisco de Villanova, persuaded the Olu

Sebastian to send a son of his named Domingos to Lisbon to study so that he might 'afterwards serve Almighty God in the priestly office'.[30] Domingos arrived in Portugal in 1600 and stayed there eight years, but, instead of returning a priest or even a bishop, he arrived back in Warri ten years later with a white wife. Meanwhile, de Villanova had secured a priest to live in Warri, but when he died the problem of priestlessness recurred yet again and Sebastian was reported in his old age to be himself instructing the people and arranging processions.

In the next century and a half Christianity hobbled along in Warri, never quite disappearing. There were missions from Capuchins based in São Tomé for several years in the 1650s, again in the 1690s, around 1709, and then from 1715 to 1717. There was a final mission in 1770. It is clear that most, though not all, of the rulers of Warri were baptized from the late sixteenth to the end of the eighteenth century, that a Church was more or less maintained there under the patronage of the Olu, that the court saw itself as Christian, but that there was very little wider penetration. It is unlikely that any missionary learnt much of the language or that there was any real continuous Christian life beyond certain minimal ritual practices. Warri was a poor place anxious for foreign trade and willing to trade in slaves as Benin was not, but it lacked a good port, and slavers hardly favoured it. Warri wanted priests, but white ones did not survive and the only black one to be sent, from São Tomé in 1770, a man of Itsekiri origin, is reported to have 'indulged in such licentiousness, libertinism and strange business that even the inhabitants were scandalized, and to such a degree that they declared the Almighty had never intended negroes to be priests'. So, for the most part, Warri Catholicism survived for 200 years priestless but, as a zealous Capuchin prefect wrote to *Propaganda* in 1694, 'The morals of Rome are bad enough; can you imagine what they would be like if left for ten years without a single priest?'[31]

In the Zambezi valley and the kingdom of Mutapa in the seventeenth century missionary priests, here mostly Dominicans, lived longer in the rather more temperate climate. The kingdom of Mutapa was being drawn into a relationship of dependence upon the Portuguese in the Zambezi valley not unlike that of the kingdom of Kongo upon Angola. While the great Mutapa Gatsi (*c.*1585–1623)

[30] A. F. C. Ryder, 'Missionary Activity in the Kingdom of Warri to the Early Nineteenth Century', *JHN* 2 (1960), 5.   [31] Ibid. 21 and 3.

was anything but a Christian, several of his sons had been baptized and one had studied in Goa. The Jesuit Julio Cesar for a while acted as his secretary and a number of churches were erected in the next few years in places where Portuguese traders were active, such as Ruhanje, Dambarare, and Masapa. By the end of the 1620s the reigning Mutapa, Mavura, was baptized together with his queen. There is, however, nothing to suggest the growth of what could possibly be called a Church beyond small groups of Portuguese traders and settlers, their mestiço children, and the slaves that obeyed them. At various times the Mutapa himself was baptized by Dominicans: not only Mavura (Dom Felipe) in 1629, when he began to rule with Portuguese support, acknowledging at the same time the suzerainty of Portugal, but also his son and successor, Siti Kazurukumusapa (Dom Domingos), in 1652, and then his brother, Dom Afonso. These were not far short of being puppet kings of the Portuguese, sustained by a Portuguese bodyguard, yet the Augustinian ecclesiastical administrator Antonio de Conceiçao was unlikely to have been far wrong when, in a report at the end of the century, he declared that all the Mwene Mutapa had lived and died as heathen. Perhaps Mavura was an exception, and there were further Christian Mutapa in the eighteenth century, but the baptism of such kings was never much more than ritual recognition of Portuguese power and a symbolic expression of their acquiescence in the presence of Dominicans within the realm. The son of one Mwene (Mavura's rival, Kapavaridze) was taken to Goa where he became a Dominican and a Master of Theology, spending many years there at the convent of Santa Barbara where he eventually died. He at least had moved fully into Christian history, but he had also moved quite out of Zimbabwean history.[32]

The Dominicans in mid-seventeenth-century Zimbabwe can be compared with their Capuchin contemporaries in Kongo, but while the Italian Capuchins were basically detached from Portuguese imperialism and served what was, in rudimentary terms, a genuine African Church, the Portuguese Dominicans in Zimbabwe remained only too clearly an appendage of colonial power. The Christian presence within Zimbabwe was little different from what it was on a rather larger scale in Sena (the lower Zambezi headquarters of both the Portuguese colonial authority on the mainland and of the

---

[32] S. Mudenge, *Christian Education at the Mutapa Court* (Harare, 1986), 16–18.

Church), Sofala, or even Mombasa. The Dominican João dos Santos in his detailed, highly reliable account of East Africa in the 1590s, *Etiopia oriental*, gives one a very clear impression of such Christian communities, a core of Portuguese, a larger number of mestiços and Africans, a few hundred in all, ignorant and isolated, huddled around a Portuguese fort. That was a little before the Dominicans advanced into Mutapa, but they did so as chaplains to Portuguese traders and soldiers, not as missionaries to African society. Not a single missionary, declared Antonio da Conceiçao angrily in 1696, had ever worked among the Africans or taught them Christianity. Of all these tiny communities, essentially Portuguese, wherever in Africa they were to be found, it is that of Mombasa we know far the best because of the massacre of the Christians there in 1631 by the King of Mombasa and the evidence collected to assist their possible canonization for martyrdom. It included a number of Africans, some of whom were not slaves, but it remained predominantly a group of expatriates.

Inland, in the small communities surrounding Portuguese forts and churches, this was still more the case. In Zimbabwe the largest was probably at the 'fair' of Dambarare in the Mazoe valley some thirty miles north-west of modern Harare. Here was a fort, a church, one or more Dominican priests. Its church has been excavated, a brick building with clay floors and massed graves beneath and around it.[33] Here, through most of the seventeenth century, the Christian community worshipped and was buried. Beneath the floor, and outside the church, the bodies were crowded together without coffins. Within the church were only males, mostly white and young, some with gold rings. Outside there were no caucasoid females and no negro males, but some negro females and some of mixed race of both sexes, the females with copper and bronze bangles. A bronze medallion was unearthed, with St Elizabeth of Portugal (canonized in 1625) upon one side, St Anthony with the infant Jesus in his arms upon the other. A negro woman had a tiny worn bronze medallion of the Virgin standing on a moon. Such was the membership of this tiny Christian community subsisting for a couple of generations deep in the interior of the continent: a membership of white males and their black wives and concubines. In November 1693 it ceased to

[33] P. S. Garlake, 'Excavations at the Seventeenth-Century Portuguese Site of Dambarare, Rhodesia', *Proceedings and Transactions of the Rhodesia Scientific Association*, 54/1 (1969), 23–61.

exist, wiped out by a sudden attack from Changamire Dombo. Its inhabitants were killed before they could reach the refuge of their fort, the church desecrated, the priest flayed alive.

The priests sent to this part of Africa were almost all Portuguese, little influenced by the norms of *Propaganda*, and one detects little advance in method over the sixteenth century. Certainly an individual priest might occasionally come to identify more in sympathy with the people he was endeavouring to convert. Such a one was the Dominican Manuel da Purificaçao, who in 1645 was Mavura's secretary for a letter to the Viceroy of India in which he complained how the Portuguese merchants 'greatly interfere with the native inhabitants of this country, massacre and maim them and seize their children and cattle'.[34] The Viceroy was not pleased by such accusations.

The mission survived in the Zambezi valley where and so far as Portuguese colonial control, of a sort, prevailed. It consisted of a number of estates or 'prazos' held by Dominicans and Jesuits. Some of the inhabitants were simply tenants, others were seen as slaves— those, doubtless, in the direct employment of the priests. The fathers would seem to have treated them well and some were baptized, acquiring Christian names, but there is little evidence of any significant Christian community developing in any of these places. Among the eighteenth-century slaves at Caia, a Jesuit *prazo* east of Sena, there were some described as 'Isabella's group with ten African schoolgirls',[35] but even such small signs of missionary vitality other than in trade are few. In 1759 under the orders of Pombal the Jesuits in Mozambique and Angola were arrested and deported, their property sold—the slaves, the animals, a few knives and plates. Africans were undoubtedly angry and dismayed at the removal of the Jesuits. The number of missionaries and the institutions of the Church declined considerably in consequence, but it would be hard to claim that it made a significant difference to the life of an African Church.

x. *The Slave Trade and its Implications*

The flutter of renewed Portuguese activity around the Zambezi in the mid-seventeenth century was partly due to the persistent belief

[34] W. Randles, *The Empire of Monomotapa from the Fifteenth to the Nineteenth Century* (Gwelo, 1981), 35.
[35] W. Rea, *The Economics of the Zambezi Missions 1580–1759* (Rome, 1976), 151.

that somewhere in the region were gold-mines just waiting to be seized, partly to a need to supplement the slave supplies of the west coast with others from the east. Brazil's expanding economy could at this period never have slaves enough. The organized slave trade from the Zambezi Valley across the Atlantic began at this time and continued until far into the nineteenth century. The Portuguese African Empire had as its original function to act as a controlled passage between Lisbon and Asia; from the mid-seventeenth century its basic purpose changed and it became instead a source of labour supply for Brazil, the only economically thriving part of the Empire. Nowhere could the Church within the Empire escape this overriding interest. Even Loanda, a city of some size, had little point to it other than as the principal point of embarkation for slaves, and the Church of Loanda in consequence had as a principal public religious function to make sure that the slaves were baptized before embarkation.

There can be no doubt that many ecclesiastics owned slaves and that some participated actively in the slave trade in Angola as elsewhere. Almost all Portuguese clergy were effectively dependent upon it for their financial support. Again, the only way to or from Angola might be a passage on a slave-ship. Already in 1636 the Jesuit Jeronimo Lobo, returning from Ethiopia to Portugal, travelled from Loanda across the Atlantic on a slaver as the quickest way of getting home. There was, however, also a considerable protest against its injustices, especially on the part of the Capuchins. As the trade grew in the seventeenth century, so did their protests increase. They culminated in the 1680s when they succeeded in producing a very wide-ranging condemnation of the slave trade from the Holy Office.[36] It is, then, not true that Rome entirely failed to speak out against the slave trade in this period, nor that Catholic missionaries were simply indifferent to it or mostly participated in it. But it is true that these protests were entirely ineffective, blocked by the governments of Portugal and Spain and by an ecclesiastical system profoundly dependent on those governments. As the Nuncio in Lisbon frankly replied, without slaves one could not cultivate Brazil.

[36] Richard Gray, 'The Papacy and the Atlantic Slave Trade: Lourenço da Silva, the Capuchins and the Decisions of the Holy Office', *Past and Present*, 115 (May 1987), 52–68 (repr. in Gray, *Black Christians and White Missionaries* (1990), 11–27). See also 'La schiavitu e i Cappuccini', in P. G. Saccardo, *Congo e Angola* (Venice, 1983), iii. 263–305, C. Verlinden, *L'Esclavage dans l'Europe médiévale*, 2 vols. (Bruges, 1955; Ghent, 1977), J. F. Maxwell, *Slavery and the Catholic Church* (Chichester, 1975), and L. M. Bermejo, SJ, *Church, Conciliarity and Communion* (Anand Gujarat, 1990), 278–88.

Moreover, as the popes themselves made use of slaves in their galleys all through the eighteenth century, and some of them had been bought, they were in no position to mount an effective moral crusade against the Atlantic trade. The almost consistent Capuchin opposition was no less honourable, but, caught within an ecclesiastical system both in Rome and overseas, which they could neither escape from nor criticize in its underlying principles, it was bound to remain ineffectual.

It was not only Capuchin missionaries who protested in Rome. Black Catholics did so too. There was in Brazil and in Portugal, as well as in Angola and the Kongo, a considerable black Catholic community by the mid-seventeenth century, a few of whom were grouped in their own lay confraternities, organized for prayer and mutual help. A leader of one of them in Lisbon named Lourenço da Silva claimed to be 'procurator-general of the congregation of the Blacks and Mulattos of Our Lady of the Rosary'. Probably born in Brazil, he also claimed to be 'of the royal blood of the kings of Kongo and Angola'.[37] In 1684 Lourenço managed to get to Rome to protest to the Pope against slavery, particularly the perpetual slavery of black Christians and the appalling cruelties inflicted upon them. His protest united with that of the Capuchins to convince Propaganda Fide and led to the 1686 condemnation by the Holy Office. Lourenço is important, not just for his courage and determination in going to Rome to become the spokesman of his people against slavery, but in symbolizing the very considerable black Christian community which existed outside Africa on both sides of the Atlantic by the late seventeenth century.

Not only the injustice of the trade but its social destructiveness was most manifest in the Angola area. Elsewhere in West Africa the effects of the slave trade were sufficiently controlled that local populations and the coastal states continued to flourish. Not here. One big reason for this was that only here had Europeans themselves gone inland in the search for slaves, seizing them directly and forcibly instead of buying them from African traders and local authorities on the coast. Far more people were killed in consequence in the course of the violence and disruption this method produced, though by the height of the trade in the eighteenth century black entrepreneurs were controlling the inland process. It is estimated that some 40 per

[37] Gray, *Black Christians and White Missionaries*, 12, 14–15.

cent of the total of all slaves crossing the Atlantic came from the Angola–Kongo area, such a figure being quite out of proportion to its population. Africa south of the River Zaïre went backward socially and politically for several centuries, and the large thriving African polities of the early sixteenth-century coast were replaced by smaller, less significant, deeply cowed units.

Europeans have liked to think of Africans as cannibals. In some few cases they doubtless were. Africans too came to think of Europeans as cannibals as they watched helplessly or even collaborated, generation after generation, in the arbitrary, ruthless, unexplained carrying off of tens of thousands of their fellows for some unknown purpose and destination.[38] Perhaps they were more profoundly right.

xi. *An Evaluation*

In the early seventeenth century, when the full impact of the slave-trade was still to come, and the wave of post-Tridentine missionary enthusiasm was rising to a peak, there seemed a great and not entirely illusory hope for the conversion of Africa. It was well, if ambiguously, symbolized by that strangest of events in our history, the arrival in Rome of the Kongolese Ambassador to the Pope in January 1608: Dom Manuel, the Mani Vunda, bearer of the most ancient religious authority in his country. Sent by his king, as many kings of Kongo previously had endeavoured to send ambassadors direct to the Pope, he had finally arrived despite every obstacle raised by the Spanish and Portuguese. The Pope, Paul V, was awaiting him. But when he arrived, landing at Civita Vecchia, assisted by a few servants and a Spanish Carmelite priest who had visited the Kongo in his youth, he was mortally ill. On 5 January, the eve of the Church's principal missionary feast, the Epiphany, in which is traditionally celebrated the coming to Christ with their gifts of the kings of the world (including, in Western mythology, a black king) Dom Manuel reached Rome. Pope Paul visited him in his apartment; the Mani Vunda recommended to the Pope the king and Church of the Kongo and

---

[38] See S. Axelson, *Culture Confrontation in the Lower Congo* (Uppsala, 1970), 240–1, 264–5, 290–1; also W. Holman Bentley, *Pioneering on the Congo* (1900), i. 252, for the late 19th-cent. common opinion of the people: 'In the early days, when a native saw us open a tin of preserved meat, he would watch with curiosity until he saw the meat inside, then he would turn away with a shudder, and an expression of disgust on his face: "Poor things! That is what becomes of them, is it?" '. Cf. also J. Miller, *Way of Death* (Wis., 1988), 4–5.

then immediately passed away. Undoubtedly this extraordinary event, depicted in the frescoes of the Vatican Library, made a very considerable impact upon the Pope and those about him.

Move on ten years or so to the 1620s, that exciting time for the missionary movement when the Sacred Congregation of Propaganda Fide and its college were being established and men like Ingoli and Vives were planning a deeply renewed strategy for the effective evangelization of the non-Western world. In those same years at the court of the Kongo, Fr. Cardoso was arriving with his catechism, at the court of Zimbabwe the Mutapa Mavura had been baptized, and at the court of the Emperor Susenyos of Ethiopia, Fr. Pedro Paez was achieving the most remarkable conversion of all. In Warri, the Olu Sebastian was doing his very best to advance Christianity, while in Mombasa a young Christian king, Dom Jeronimo Chingulia, had just been installed with his Portuguese queen after baptism and years of education by the Augustinians in Goa. Here was a network of Catholic rulers spread all across Africa and they were being assisted by a number of remarkable priests. Behind these advance guards waited many hundreds of Capuchins, Jesuits, and others anxious to serve in the conversion of Africa. Such was the brief climax of the enterprise. But look again, eighty years later, the end of the century. The Changamire had expelled the Portuguese, missionaries included, from the lands of Zimbabwe; the Emperor of Ethiopia had expelled Catholic missionaries from his territories; and in 1698 Fort Jesus at Mombasa was captured by Oman. Even the kingdom of the Kongo lay in ruins and the Capuchins after fifty years of intense work and the dispatch of several hundred missionaries were near to desperation. Only Soyo would continue, moderately hopeful, a little longer. The likelihood of any enduring Catholic presence in black Africa of more than minuscule size had become by 1700 extremely slight. Why had this quite rapid reversal taken place? We have encountered various causes. Basically it might be claimed that the sixteenth-century pattern of mission, subjugated to the *Padroado*, had continued sufficiently to strangle the seventeenth-century model; moreover, the earlier pattern was now still further deformed by the steady expansion of the slave-trade as well as the drying-up of whatever element of religious idealism had formerly existed within the Portuguese sense of their imperial destiny.

The continued dominance of a 'Portugalization' model of Christian advance may be shown most precisely by a look at what happened in Mombasa in 1631. The Augustinian mission here was probably the nearest the Church came on the east coast to a very minor breakthrough. With the establishment as King of Malindi and Mombasa of Dom Jeronimo Chingulia, a Knight of Christ, educated by the Augustinians in Goa and married to a Portuguese woman, there could seem some possibility of a local Church taking root, if not among Muslim converts, at least among many local Africans who were not Muslim. There were a number of Portuguese priests based in Mombasa, and it had even been requested that a suffragan bishop be appointed. Beside the white Christian community were a rather larger number of native Christians already baptized. While most of these were women and children, they included, besides the King, his cousin, Dom Antonio of Malindi, who had also been educated abroad and served for some years in the Portuguese navy. When the King apostatized and carried out a massacre of all the Christians who refused to apostatize with him, Dom Antonio was one of those who refused and was killed.

The sworn evidence collected for a possible canonization of the martyrs certainly suggests that there were few native males among the Christians. But what is really more profoundly significant is that the list of those 'crowned with martyrdom' sent to Rome included the names only of Portuguese—4 priests, 47 men, 39 women, 59 children. The hundred and fifty or so Africans who died with them were not included, not even Dom Antonio, whose faith and leadership in the crisis was attested by more than one witness. The conclusion intended is clear enough: God was 'determined to honour the Portuguese nation by demonstrating the constancy and firmness of the faith that exists among the Portuguese'.[39] Black Christians, living or martyred, were only rather incidentally part of the story of the Mombasa Church.

Yet it was not only that the *damnosa hereditas* of the sixteenth century shackled more thoughtful initiatives of the seventeenth. The missionary practice of the latter remained gravely at fault as well. Few of the Capuchins, Augustinians, Dominicans, or Jesuits of the time came anywhere near fulfilling the ideals of Ingoli. Nor indeed did Propaganda itself really stick at all to his range of vision. And even that vision was inadequate. Northern and eastern Europe would

---

[39] Fr. João of Jesus, OSA, in G. S. P. Freeman-Grenville, *The Mombasa Rising against the Portuguese 1631* (1980), 79.

never have been converted if the missionary monks who undertook it had not very quickly been supplemented by a local married clergy, an indigenous ministry adapted to the economic and cultural conditions of the country. This was as true of England as of Russia. And in both a vernacular religious literature soon developed.

When one considers the long history of the Kongolese Church, its very considerable geographical dimensions, the disinterested zeal of the Capuchins, and the tenacity of Kongolese Christians themselves, one is constrained to ask (as so often in history) if it needed to end as it did. The answer must here, as always, be: it was not predetermined. The climate, the distances from Europe, the inevitable problems arising from African society, all created formidable difficulties, yet all were sufficiently overcome for it to be clear that they were not insuperable. The mission was not killed by them but by four other and extrinsic things: the systematic Portuguese opposition to missions of other nations (the Italian Capuchins only got in originally thanks to the temporary Dutch conquest of Angola and the coinciding Spanish–Portuguese conflict), the profound social and political dislocation produced by the slave-trade from the early seventeenth century onward, the general decline of missionary enthusiasm in eighteenth-century Catholic Europe, and the rigidities of canon law and current missionary practice. If Propaganda Fide had been able to send missionaries more freely and to establish dioceses uncontrolled by Lisbon (as did happen in parts of Asia), if the Portuguese had lost Angola and the slave-trade had functioned here at least no more or no differently from how it had functioned on other coasts, if the missionaries had printed more books in the vernacular and allowed the *maestri* to baptize, if Rome had listened to the early advice of the Nuncio in Lisbon and agreed to a married clergy for Africa (as it had done for the Lebanon and the Ukraine), then by the eighteenth century a large and expanding section of central Africa might well have been Christian. The 'antica missio', as it came later to be called, was not a futility, only a strangled opportunity.

4

RICHES TO RAGS: ETHIOPIA 1500–1800

i. *The Church of Lebna Dengel*

'The Ambassador replied . . . that they gave great thanks to God for having fulfilled their desires in bringing Christians together with Christians.'[1] Such was the principal theme of the meeting between the Portuguese Ambassador, Dom Rodrigo de Lima, and the Emperor Lebna Dengel at the latter's camp in October 1520. It certainly summarized what the Portuguese had been looking for and what the Ethiopians now greatly needed—another Christian state with which to enter into an alliance, commercial and military. As the Portuguese advanced by slow stages into Ethiopia, they had had plenty of opportunity to recognize that this was indeed, in terms they could well appreciate, a Christian country. The principal test applied upon either side would seem to have been a ritual one—the celebration of mass. The quite exceptionally detailed description of its Ethiopian form which Alvares provides (principally in chapter 11 of his account of the embassy), just as the insistence by Lebna Dengel that he see the Portuguese vestments and that his representatives attend the Portuguese mass (and then ask questions about any apparent ritual divergence of significance from the Ethiopian norm), all suggest that here lay the crucial test of whether Christians were meeting Christians. Both sides were satisfied, their rituals proving indeed to be remarkably close to one another.

As the embassy remained in Ethiopia for six years before leaving for Portugal, its members certainly had the opportunity to get to know the country very well. We have, as a result, Francisco Alvares' *True Relation of the Lands of Prester John*, the sole description by an outsider of Ethiopia in the age of its glory. As it is remarkably detailed and also remarkably unbiased, it is worth looking for a while at Christian Ethiopia in the 1520s through the eyes of Alvares, though

[1] Francisco Alvares, *The Prester John of the Indies*, ed. E. F. Beckingham and G. W. B. Huntingford (Cambridge, 1961).

we can fairly supplement this where appropriate with information from the more numerous accounts of the seventeenth century.

Ethiopia appeared a land of churches: indeed there were really no other buildings of any scale and permanence. The churches were mostly of stone, if often grass-roofed, and of varying size, function, and magnificence. Most were round, humble village churches, but some—among them the most ancient and the most impressive— were rectangular and elaborately decorated. Included in the latter were both a considerable number of monastic churches and the royal churches, enclosing the tombs of the kings. The rectangular basilican form would seem to have been Ethiopia's original model, one taken over from Egypt and Syria, while the round church may be seen instead as an adaptation to the African village in the interior. The shape of churches was, then, one of the ways through which the partial transformation of a coastal Semitic church into a more characteristically African, inland, one had been expressed.

Soon after landing, the Portuguese visited the Ewostathian monastery of Dabra Bizan and Alvares' description of Bizan (to which he returned more than once) and of another house close by provide a quite detailed picture of monastic life in late medieval Ethiopia: the celebration of mass, the chalices, the manner of making altar bread and altar wine, the recital of the psalms at Matins, the frequent processions, the thuribles, crosses, bells, cloths, and pictures carried in procession, the books in the sacristy, the feast days and the long fasts, the ownership of lands and the tribute the peasantry brought to the monastery, the relationship between the main abbey and the daughter houses, the number of the monks and the way they were distributed between the main house and the countryside. Containing as it did the tomb of Filpos, the fourteenth-century Ewostathian leader, Dabra Bizan remained one of the most influential monasteries of Ethiopia, but most of its monks, like those of other monasteries, lived outside its walls, at least until they grew old. Monasteries themselves, apart from the church, consisted of little more than an aggregation of huts. Their living quarters were not significantly different from those of the villages. Monasticism appears as a highly unregulated popular movement consisting of thousands of monks and nuns, of doubtless very varying degrees of religious fervour, living on their own or in small groups or simply sharing in village life but possessing an affiliation with one or another of the great monasteries.

By the sixteenth century monasticism seems, nevertheless, to have lost much of the dynamism, moral influence, and missionary élan of earlier periods. Not only were there areas of the country remaining without monasteries, but, by the age of Lebna Dengel, when a king or queen mother endowed a new church, it seems to have been no longer, as in earlier ages, entrusted to monks but to secular priests and lay clerks, the *dabtara*, whose skill in singing and general performance of the liturgy were probably superior. If the monks, or some among them, were the principal copyists of manuscripts, it was the *dabtara* who were the professional carriers of Ethiopia's unique musical religious tradition, enshrined in its own musical script. They themselves were trained to compose hymns, so the corpus of sacred music was not only maintained but continually enlarged. The survival of Ethiopia's specific form of Christianity across much more than a thousand years, often in very adverse circumstances, appears to have depended above all upon its two greatest possessions—the Ge'ez Bible and the Ge'ez musical repertoire, an essentially lay tradition, popular yet professional. The round church, the lay *dabtara* and highly complex and diversified sacred music, a monasticism which remained largely village-based and institutionally uncontrolled, these together created a form of public religion which was absolutely Ethiopian—only rather distantly related to its Mediterranean roots, while decidedly recognizable as African.

What the Ethiopian Church most lacked, in comparison with any other Christian Church, was any real hierarchy or system of wider pastoral care. Attempts to develop one in the fourteenth century had been defeated. There were no dioceses and, apart from the Egyptian abuna, no bishops. It remained the most monist of Churches, that is to say it was fused into one being with the State to an extent that is hardly possible where the episcopal order exists in a less minimalist way.

The Abuna Marqos was, in the 1520s, a very aged man, devout, revered, one of the finer abunas. He had been many years in the country—ever since the reign of Eskender. His authority had combined with that of the Queen Mother, Eleni, to ensure the selection of Lebna Dengel as emperor when still a child, but he exercised no pastoral control whatever over the Church beyond the conducting of thousands of ordinations. Responsibility for the Church lay with the king, just as responsibility for everything else in Ethiopia lay with the king, but in reality the religious life of the country simply flowed on, with little theology and less planning, in a river of rituals and of music.

When in 1520 the Portuguese embassy, after some considerable delay, was admitted to the presence of the Emperor, they saw that which in Ethiopian tradition ordinary people were rarely permitted to gaze upon, the embodiment of the entire life, spiritual and political, of the nation. It was a memorable experience, as they passed through a series of enclosures and curtains, each more gorgeous than the one before, walked through massed crowds of guards holding arms and lighted candles, until at last they came before a large dais covered with the richest of carpets and shielded by a final curtain. The curtain was pulled back and there was the King, sitting at the top of six steps, dressed in gold brocade, upon his head a crown of gold and silver, a silver cross in his hand, a piece of blue cloth covering his mouth and beard. On each side of him stood pages, the nearest holding another silver cross, then two with drawn swords, then four upon each side with lighted candles. Thus enthroned between cross and sword, was Lebna Dengel, at the time a young man 23 years of age,

King David (his regnal name), the head of his kingdoms, the beloved of God, pillar of the faith, descendant of the lineage of Judah, son of David, son of Solomon, son of the Column of Zion, son of the Seed of Jacob, son of the Hand of Mary, son of Nahum in the flesh (all references to Lebna Dengel's ancestors by their regnal names), emperor of the high Ethiopia and of great kingdoms, lordships and lands, King of Shoa, of Cafate, of Fatiguar, of Angote, of Baruu, of Balinganje, of Adea and of Vangue, King of Gojjam, of Amara . . .

The titles, as listed in his letter to the King of Portugal, would go on and on.[2] In the mystique surrounding the Emperor biblical and African threads had all but merged. As he processed continually through the countryside, he had by tradition to do so unseen by common eyes, around his horse being carried red curtains while inside the curtains six pages walked. In front of the King four chained lions were led, and in the vast procession which followed were the many thousand people of the court with all their possessions borne along as the King moved back and forth from the wet season camping-ground to the dry or to hunt or to war or to attend some monastery for a great feast. When firewood was exhausted in one

[2] Ibid. 495.

place he had of necessity to move to another. In the procession went the *tabots* of the thirteen churches of the court, each carried by four priests on a stretcher on their shoulders, covered with rich cloths, with four more priests to relieve them by and by. Thus the Emperor passed through his country, a sacred king hedged in by customs very similar to those of many a pagan African monarch.

In the traditional rituals of enthronement at Aksum, prior to coronation by the abuna in the cathedral, the king-to-be, riding a great horse, would find his way barred by a crimson cord. When asked 'Who are you?' he would reply, 'I am your king, the King of Ethiopia', to which the people would reply with one voice, 'You shall not pass, you are not our king.' Only at the third attempt, after replying, 'I am your king, the King of Zion,' would he cut the thread with his sword and the people cry, 'Truly you are the king of Zion.'[3] It was a ritual which at one and the same time emphatically asserted the biblical identity of Ethiopian monarchy and yet possessed resonances of a different, African, identity and parentage with rituals like the mock battle in the enthronement of the king of the Shilluk at Fashoda. The Ethiopian monarchy appears as a Christian form of the divine kingship long prevalent around the Nile valley.

Yet the sacredness of the Ethiopian monarchy did not entail political ineffectiveness. The country would never have survived without the forcefulness of many of its kings, and whenever they ceased to be forceful it was quickly in deep trouble. Furthermore, in the late fifteenth and early sixteenth centuries the monarchy was also undergoing what may well be described as a process of bureaucratic modernization, little as we know of its details. Thrice a year the young Lebna Dengel now showed himself to his people unveiled, a thing his predecessors did not do, and a symbolic sign of the diminution of the sacred. Already two generations earlier, Zara Ya'iqob and Baida Maryam had greatly reorganized the bureaucracy of government. This involved both the responsibilities of high officials and the development of the secretarial corps at the court. It has been suggested that the regular writing of land charters begins at this time. Writing was now being put to secular as well as to religious use.

Ethiopian society flourished in many ways, but it remained

---

[3] Beccari, xi. 259; see also the account in the *Historia Regis Sarsa Dengel* (Malak Dengel), ed. C. Conti Rossini, *CSCO* 20 (1907; repr. 1955), 90.

extraordinarily primitive in its economic formation and technology for a state of such size and stability. It was quite excessively dependent upon Arab traders for the provision of much of what it needed. There was a complete absence of indigenous urban life and of many of the more elementary skills of craftsmanship. Doubtless almost every cloth and ornament which gave the emperor's court its characteristic appearance had come from abroad, and Ethiopia had little to offer in exchange—principally gold, hides, and slaves. It needed to raid its neighbours for slaves to sell to the Arabs in exchange for luxury goods and for this reason it could hardly afford to convert them, as it might not enslave Christians. Failure to evangelize the Agaw of western Gojjam over several centuries is noticeable. The missionary advance of Ethiopian Christianity had not entirely ceased,[4] but it was, then, impeded by its primitive economy and dependence upon supplying the insatiable demand of the Arab world for slaves, much as in West Africa the advance of Islam was impeded for quite the same reason.

Military prowess, bureaucratic organization, a literary cultural tradition unique in Africa, and a highly confident religious orthodoxy had, nevertheless, combined to establish a major state, considerable and confident enough to be on the look-out for further progress. Lebna Dengel continued to promote the translation of Greek and Arabic works into Ge'ez. The Europeans who occasionally found their way within its borders were politely detained and put to work. Thus for forty years the Italian Nicholas Brancaleone seems to have been ceaselessly busy painting churches and icons.[5] An ingenious monk, Ezra the Stefanite, returned from abroad, when questioned at court offered to construct a watermill or a windmill, a hydraulic saw, an oil-press, or a hayrick worked by an ass. In fact he made the watermill to general amazement.[6] The Empress Eleni had brought artisans from Egypt to construct her new church at Martula Maryam.[7] In his letter to the King of Portugal

[4] At times of strength the monarch could still bring about the conversion of neighbouring societies. See the account of the conversion and mass baptism of Enarya in the 1580s in the *Historia Regis Sarsa Dengel*, 136–44. Sarsa Dengel stood godfather to its king, Badanco.

[5] Diana Spencer, 'Travels in Gojjam: St Luke, Ikons and Brancaleon Rediscovered', *JES* 12 (1974), 201–20.

[6] It was in the early years of the 16th cent., in the reign of Lebna Dengel's father, Na'od. A. Caquot (ed.), 'Les Actes d'Ezra de Gunde Gunde', *Annales d'Éthiopie*, 4 (1961), 110–13.

[7] See the account of it in E. F. Beckingham and G. W. B. Huntingford (eds.), *Some Records of Ethiopia 1593–1646* (1954), 103–7.

Lebna Dengel appealed for craftsmen of all sorts just as did his contemporary, Afonso King of Kongo, though he was appealing from a far higher base than that of Afonso. His appointment of the Arab convert Enbaqom to be abbot of Dabra Libanos, even if it was not a success, was still remarkable. None of this suggests fear of outside influences, so long as they could be made to tally with the intrinsic orthodoxy of Ethiopia. We know far too little to reconstruct a wholly reliable picture of the state of Ethiopian consciousness in the earlier years of Lebna Dengel, but the things we have referred to suggest a prosperous, basically confident, and forward-looking mood. Yet it was a deeply fragile condition. The always potentially hostile Muslim world around it was growing more than was Ethiopia and had of late been invigorated by the rise of Turkish power in the Red Sea. Innovations in firearms also benefited Muslims, who were in easy touch with world trade, far more than Ethiopians, who could obtain nothing beyond what Arab traders were willing to bring them. The prospect of an alliance with the Christian kingdom of Portugal might not be very realistic, but, in such circumstances, it was bound to seem attractive.

ii. *The Jihad of Gran*

All through the early years of the reign of Lebna Dengel war on the eastern frontier was endemic. When Christians were weakened by the Lenten fast Muslim armies annually raided the eastern marches. Yet the Christian–Muslim relationship was not an entirely straightforward one. On the surface, Muslims appear simply as the enemy. The Emperor's letter to the King of Portugal called down peace on King Manuel because, being strong in the faith, he was 'assisted by Our Lord Jesus Christ to kill the Moors'. But that was largely rhetoric. In Ethiopia Muslims were a very real threat both to Christianity and to the monarchy and, certainly, the former was highly unlikely to survive without the latter. There were no Christians in the lands of Adel or of Sennar. Nevertheless, there were plenty of Muslims within the Ethiopian state, and not only Arab traders. Parts of the kingdom were largely inhabited by Muslims and, so long as they were loyal, they were as safe as anyone else. There was much intermarrying. Thus the Empress Eleni's own father had been Muhammad, the Muslim governor of Hadya.

It is hard to know quite why in 1529 a jihad of unprecedented proportions was suddenly let loose upon the country. Perhaps the presence of a Portuguese mission for six years in Ethiopia had alerted its neighbours to a possible new danger. Perhaps Turkish influence underlay a new aggressiveness. But the chief cause does appear to have lain in the personality of one man, Ahmed Gran, leader of the armies of Adel. At once fearless military leader and religious fanatic, undeviating in his determination to wage a holy war for the destruction of the Christian kingdom and the establishment of a Muslim state, Gran was of a type which would appear several times in the religious history of Africa as in the wider history of Islam. He combined professional efficiency with religious single-mindedness to a high degree. He was, in all this, very different from generations of his predecessors. He equipped his armies with the latest weapons and, once begun, he continued his campaigns methodically from year to year. He came extremely near to achieving his aim.

In March 1529 Ahmed Gran defeated the army of Ethiopia with very great slaughter in the battle of Chembra Kouré, following which he set about the systematic destruction of the country and in particular the ravaging of churches and monasteries. He began with Shoa in the east and steadily moved north and west. On 14 July 1532 Dabra Libanos went up in flames, many of its monks throwing themselves into the fire in their despair. The invaders pushed on through Tigre and Gojjam until they arrived at the ancient heartlands of the north-west. The great cathedral of St Mary of Zion at Aksum, dating probably from the sixth century, was reduced to ruins. Early in 1540 the formidable royal fortress of Amba Geshen was captured with all its treasure and the archives of the State. As the chronicler sadly noted, 'They were conquerors in all the battles to the east, to the west, to the north and to the south.'[8] Everything of significance was destroyed or carried away. Few are the manuscripts which survive from before 1530. Tens of thousands of people adopted Islam, many others were marched off into slavery. What was happening in those twelve years was a systematic campaign of cultural and national genocide.

By 1540 Gran regarded himself as the unassailable king of Ethiopia. He was accepted as such by many of its people, who now obeyed his orders and served in his armies, while his original soldiers had

---

[8] *Chronique de Galawdewos (Claudius) roi d'Éthiopie*, ed. W. E. Conzelman (Paris, 1895), 123.

brought their wives from Adel to settle in their new kingdom. Lebna Dengel carried on what had become little more than a guerrilla war, rallying resistance where he could, until his death late that year at Dabra Damo, a monastery which had proved inaccessible even to Gran, as one could only reach its plateau by being pulled up from above in a basket by rope. He left his 18-year-old son Galawdewos to continue the struggle. He had, however, succeeded in 1535 in smuggling a Portuguese, John Bermudez, out of the country on a mission to Portugal to implore help. In 1541 the help at last arrived. A Portuguese force of 400 men with a number of cannon was landed at Massawa under Cristovao da Gama. They marched slowly inland and were joined by the Queen Mother, Sabla Wangel, who had remained in Dabra Damo. Despite the small numbers at his command, da Gama achieved some initial successes, but his lack of horses and the limited number of Ethiopians who had joined him rendered them indecisive. Gran, however, was thoroughly alarmed. Retreating into a hill camp for the winter, he called in 800 Turks to his assistance. Once they had arrived with a number of cannon he took the offensive and the Portuguese, still largely unsupported by Ethiopians, were overwhelmed. Da Gama, wounded and captured, was dragged before Gran to behold the heads of 160 Portuguese displayed in front of him before he too was decapitated by Gran himself.

Over-confident in the finality of his victory, Gran at once dismissed his Turkish allies and returned to what had become his capital near Lake Tana. Meanwhile, Sabla Wangel, who had played a remarkably active role throughout the campaign and had personally bound up the wounded in battle, managed to escape with the surviving remnant of the Portuguese and to link up with her son Galawdewos, who had been campaigning in the south of the country. The Portuguese rearmed themselves from a store which da Gama had wisely left at Dabra Damo. Some thousands of Ethiopians rallied around the King and together they marched once more to attack the unsuspecting Gran. On 21 February 1543 at the Battle of Woguera Gran was slain by a ball fired from a Portuguese matlock and his troops turned and fled. Without its leader the jihad and the incipient Muslim kingdom of Ethiopia simply dissolved and Galawdewos was left to restore a shattered state. Tens of thousands of apostates had to be reconciled, churches and monasteries rebuilt, books recopied. The cultural and institutional wealth of medieval

Ethiopia could never be recovered, and it is clear that even in the seventeenth century the condition of the country had by no means returned to that of the age before Lebna Dengel. The very cathedral of Aksum was only rebuilt under Fasiladas, and then in a manner by no means comparable with the great five-aisled church it replaced. Nevertheless, the remarkable moral and intellectual qualities of Galawdewos contributed greatly in the sixteen years of rule which were left to him to re-create the basic fabric of Ethiopian society and a sense of national confidence.

iii. *Galawdewos, the Jesuits, and Enbaqom*

There can be little reasonable doubt that without Portuguese help the Christian kingdom of Ethiopia would have ceased to exist in the 1540s. It would have gone the way of Nubia. Christians had rallied to help Christians in the hour of their greatest need and Galawdewos was very genuinely grateful. That did not make the Portuguese any easier to live with afterwards. The immediate problem was John Bermudez. He returned to the country with da Gama announcing that he had been appointed Patriarch both by the dying Abuna Marqos and by the Pope while he was in Europe. So far as one can tell both claims were lies.[9] It remains very doubtful whether he was ever ordained even a priest. Nevertheless, the Portuguese tended to believe him and to back his repeated demand to Galawdewos to recognize his authority and accept the Latin rite. To quarrel with the surviving Portuguese soldiers at this point would have been disastrous and Galawdewos managed to relegate him to a remote part of the country, writing meanwhile to Alexandria to send a new abuna as quickly as possible. Bermudez escaped once more from Ethiopia and returned to Portugal to write his memoirs, which did much ever after to confuse both Roman–Ethiopian relations and the wider history of sixteenth-century Ethiopia.

[9] João Bermudez's *Short Account*, first published in 1565, was translated into English and included by Whiteway with his edition of Castanhoso, *The Portuguese Expedition to Abyssinia in 1541–1543* (1902). It is highly unreliable. Some writers continue to accept his claim to have been appointed by Marqos, even though they admit that his further claim to have been confirmed by the Pope was bogus (see e.g. J.-B. Coulbeaux, *DTC* 5. 1. 950, and P. Caraman, *The Lost Empire* (1985), 8) but there is no good reason to accept either, cf. Whiteway's introduction, pp. lxxxii–ci, M. Chaine, 'Le Patriarche Jean Bermudez d'Éthiopie 1540–1570', *Revue de l'Orient chrétien*, 14 (1909), 321–9, and S. E. Guringer, 'Der Pseudopatriarch Johannes Bermudes', *Theologie und Glaube*, 17 (1925), 226–56.

Lebna Dengel had sent the Pope a letter with Alvares expressing reverent submission in terms which were taken to mean a great deal more in Europe than they meant in Ethiopia. It now entered the minds of the King of Portugal and the Pope that they might do well to send out a genuine Latin Patriarch. The rejection of Bermudez did not appear to them to indicate a going-back on Lebna Dengel's apparently unsolicited act of submission, especially as Galawdewos expressed himself exceptionally diplomatically. Pope Paul III's first idea, a wise one, seems to have been to ask the Emperor of Ethiopia himself to choose a Patriarch but the King of Portugal objected. They then turned to the Jesuits to provide someone, and Ignatius Loyola, though old and unwell, actually offered to go himself. That was, of course, unthinkable, but an experienced priest was chosen, John Nuñez Barreto, and two other Jesuits—Melchior Carneiro, also Portuguese, and Andrew Oviedo, a Spaniard—were consecrated as bishops to accompany and, if necessary, succeed him. That was in 1555.

It is well to note that Rome was not acting in ignorance in its dealings with Ethiopia at this time. For quite some while, probably since the 1480s, there had been a small community of Ethiopian monks near the Vatican at the chapel of St Stephen. As a consequence of their presence, the Ethiopian Psalter was printed in Rome in 1513. Then, about 1537, a most remarkable Ethiopian monk from Dabra Libanos arrived in Rome via Jerusalem with two companions to join the community. His name was Tasfa Seyon, but he was known in Rome as Petrus Ethiops. He stayed in Rome until his death in 1552, patronized by Paul III. He was an outstanding scholar and personally responsible for the printing in 1548 of the Ge'ez New Testament and eucharistic liturgy. Moreover, Alvares' *True Relation* was printed in Lisbon in 1540 and soon translated into Italian. It had certainly been read by Ignatius among others and he knew Tasfa Seyon well.

People in Rome could, then, be quite well informed in regard to the character of the Church of Ethiopia. The lengthy instructions Loyola drew up for the guidance of his men are, in consequence, of special interest. He stressed several times that in their exceptionally delicate mission they should proceed *con dolcezza*, with sweetness and gentleness. He was almost willing to tolerate circumcision but then thought better of it and deleted that line; he felt that the excessive fasts which the Christians of Ethiopia were accustomed to practise really ought to be mitigated.[10] Nevertheless, the aim he outlined to reduce the Ethiopian Church to eventual uniformity with Rome was deeply unrealistic. In the substance of his advice there was very little to suggest that its implementation could prove other than disastrous. While waiting for the Patriarch to arrive, the Portuguese Viceroy of India thoughtfully sent off a couple of Jesuits to Ethiopia to inform the Emperor that he was on his way. The mission was led by Gonçalo Rodrigues and arrived at the imperial camp in May 1555. Galawdewos received him politely but was profoundly disturbed by his message. Fully committed to the tradition of Ethiopia, the Emperor had no wish to quarrel with his Western friends but equally no wish to be saddled with a Latin patriarch. He already had his Egyptian one. In these circumstances he went off for a month to consult his mother, Sabla Wangel, who combined affectionate experience of the Portuguese with firm adherence to Ethiopian custom. While with her he seems to have composed his famous *Confession of Faith*, dated 23 June 1555. He informed Fr. Rodrigues and presented him with a copy to take to the Viceroy. Deeply disappointed, the Jesuit returned to Goa. A natural diplomatist, Galawdewos had affirmed his willingness to meet the Patriarch and seems to have thought in terms of his remaining in charge of the Portuguese, all 200 of them.

It was decided in Goa that, in these circumstances, it would be unfitting for the Patriarch to proceed, and Oviedo was sent instead. He arrived in 1557. Like many another sovereign, Galawdewos enjoyed theological disputation and proved well able to cope with the ecumenical dialogue Oviedo's presence initiated in his court. The good Jesuit then produced in Ethiopian a very combatively phrased work entitled *The Primacy of Rome and the Errors of the Ethiopians*. There was very little *dolcezza* about that. Tempers were rising on both sides. The King forbade the Jesuits to preach to Ethiopians, and Oviedo declared the King excommunicate. Shortly afterwards Galawdewos was killed in a war with Adel and canonized in Ethiopian tradition as St Claudius. He was succeeded by his brother Minas, a rather less courteous ruler. Ethiopia degenerated into a period of civil war, in which the Turks intervened against Minas while Oviedo, backing the rebels, found himself to his embarrassment on the same side as the Turks. Little by little, however, in the

---

[10] Beccari, i. 237–54; for Ignatius' hesitations over circumcision, see 79–80 as well as 242.

reign of Sarsa Dengel (1563–97), nephew of Galawdewos, order was restored once more, the Turks soundly defeated, and the Jesuits confined to serving the small Portuguese community centred at Fremona not far from Aksum.

By this time Barreto had died and Oviedo automatically succeeded him as Patriarch. In practice he remained as parish priest of the Portuguese community, its Ethiopian wives and children, until his death in 1577. He was recognized as a holy man but was not, intellectually, a very supple one. One of his companions, Francisco Lopez, formerly a lay brother but ordained by Oviedo, lived on at Fremona another twenty years, dying in 1597. He was replaced by an Indian secular priest, Belchior da Silva, who had managed to get through from Goa to minister to what had become a tiny, and only barely surviving, Latin community of some 2,000 people formed by forty years of Jesuit presence out of Portuguese immigrant origins. Few could any more speak Portuguese. Da Silva found that many, while still claiming to be Catholics, were already circumcizing their children and observing the Sabbath.[11]

Several young men of mixed blood born and educated at Fremona later became priests and died for their faith. Consider two of them: they tell us a little about the community. Abba Jacobo was the son of a Spaniard, João d'Alessandro, who had escaped from the Turks and joined the Portuguese settlement a generation after its beginnings. His mother was an Ethiopian, Wela Dahna. Baptized by Francisco Lopez in the 1580s he became a lay missionary sent by Fr. Paez around 1612 to the non-Christian Agaw in Gojjam where he was said to have baptized many. He was later ordained by the Patriarch Mendes and murdered in 1628 in one of the earlier risings against the Catholic policy of Susenyos. Antonio d'Andrade belonged to a younger generation but had a similar Fremona background. Ordained by Mendes and exiled with him, he was, years later, made a bishop by Propaganda Fide in 1668 and sent back to Ethiopia, only to be murdered at Massawa in 1670. The Catholic community at Fremona which nourished these two men was a group not at all

---

[11] Ibid. 413–39, there is a long letter from Belchior da Silva to the Archbishop of Goa from Ethiopia dated 5 Aug. 1695. Beccari accepts the date and regards it as evidence of the survival of the Catholic community at Fremona at the close of the 17th cent., which is improbable. Moreover, it means accepting that a second Goan priest, of identical name, was sent to Ethiopia exactly a century after the first, which is extremely improbable. There is internal evidence, including a reference to Francisco Lopez, to make it clear that the date of the letter must be late 16th, not 17th, cent.

unlike other small settlements of Portuguese in the Kongo, in Mombasa, or elsewhere. In colour they were, by the seventeenth century, little different from Ethiopians, and not much different even in language, but they retained a strong consciousness of difference and special skills with firearms and other things. They were half a help to a local ruler, half a continuing threat. This enduring, rather tough, but very small-scale presence of Catholics in the country was a good part of the reason for the continuing Jesuit interest in Ethiopia, but it would not really be of service to the wider cause of reunification sought by Rome because, by theoretically existing as a Latin Church within the country, it encouraged the wholly foolish and impossible endeavour of latinizing Ethiopia. On the contrary, if there was any chance at all of union with the Church of the West, it could only be through a very thoroughgoing acceptance of the Ethiopian rite and its related customs.

An important early consequence of the Jesuit mission was to stimulate the writing of Galawdewos's *Confession of Faith*, one of two remarkable works of Ethiopian religious literature produced in his reign.[12] It is divided into two parts. In the first the King declares his faith in the Trinity and the Incarnation. In the second he deals with the three matters over which the Jesuits were currently accusing the Ethiopian Church of Judaizing, that is the celebration of the Sabbath, the rite of circumcision, and the avoidance of pork. Unlike the writings of the Jesuits, the *Confession* does not contain a trace of controversialism. It is neither one-sided nor aggressive, nor in any way bigoted in tone. Quite the contrary. Galawdewos undoubtedly intended it to confirm his adherence to the faith of Alexandria and his rejection of the accusations the Jesuits were making that the Church of Ethiopia was gravely at fault and needed to be reformed in faith and practice, but he makes no contrary accusations, no attacks upon the faith of Chalcedon (in this being rather uncharacteristic of Ethiopian theological writing). There is in fact nothing in what he

---

[12] English translation in J. M. Harden, *An Introduction to Ethiopic Christian Literature* (1926), 104–7, and S. Pankhurst, *Ethiopia: A Cultural History* (1955), 334–7; the Confession was first published by Hiob Ludolf in Ge'ez and Latin in 1661 with his *Grammatica Aethiopica*; for Ludolf's discussion of it see his *Ad suam Historiam Aethiopicam Commentarius* (Frankfurt, 1691), 237–41, 278–9; for a modern commentary and discussion see L. Lozza, *La confessione di Claudio re d'Etiopia* (Palermo, 1947), also *RSE* 5 (1946), 67–78; for another Ethiopian response to Jesuit teaching at exactly the same time, see the work entitled 'The History of the Four Councils' or 'The Treasure of the Faith', in E. Cerulli (ed.), *Scritti teologici etiopici dei secoli* XVI–XVII (Rome, 1960), ii. 1–101.

wrote that the Jesuits and Rome should not have been able to accept. Its theological orthodoxy is incontestable.

What is particularly interesting is that he defended the customs of Ethiopia in remarkably secular terms. There is, undoubtedly, a firm insistence that Ethiopians possess true apostolic doctrine and 'turn aside neither to the right hand nor to the left' but there is also a sense of freedom and of rather restrained claims, especially in regard to the Sabbath, altogether different from the intolerant dogmatism of Zara Ya'iqob. As regards the Sabbath, circumcision, and the avoidance of pork, he points out that in each case Ethiopian Christian practice is significantly different from that of the Jews. Circumcision is performed simply because it is a local custom, while as for the eating of pork he blandly observes that everyone is at liberty to refrain from eating meat if he so wishes. 'There are some who love to eat fish, and there are some who like to eat the flesh of cocks, and there are some who abstain from eating the flesh of lambs; let every man, according as it pleases him, follow his own desire. There is no law about the eating of flesh.' Galawdewos began his *Confession* as follows: 'This is my Faith and the Faith of my fathers, the Israelitish kings, and the faith of my flock which is in the fold of my kingdom.' In these words he expressed simply but rather movingly the Ethiopian conception of the kingdom at its highest and most Christian, the sense of pastoral responsibility for this 'flock' committed to him and for the maintenance of its faith. It is, as so often in Ethiopian theological documents, grounded on explicit reference to the first three councils of Nicaea, Constantinople, and Ephesus. It may be that Galawdewos was considerably understating the common Ethiopian view of the customs in question and that many an Ewostathian monk would have grounded them quite explicitly in an interpretation of the New Testament of the sort he noticeably avoided. Strange as it may seem, Galawdewos wrote far more like a modern man than did his Jesuit opponents, gripped as they were by the mood of intellectual intransigence characteristic of the Counter-Reformation. He, on the contrary, was able to play down controversial issues by an appeal to the divergence of cultures. Everyone, even the Jesuits, agreed that he was an extraordinarily attractive as well as able person, someone of profound moral and intellectual qualities, yet he and his *Confession* remain something of an enigma. One wonders how he obtained his very considerable education during the devastating ten years in which he grew to manhood.

One answer to that question may lie in the character of his dear friend and mentor Enbaqom, the author of a no less remarkable work, the *Anqasa Amin*, the 'Door of the Faith'. Enbaqom was an Arab, perhaps from Iraq, who was converted to Christianity as a young man and had settled in Ethiopia in the reign of Eskender, probably about 1490. He became a monk at Dabra Libanos but was much at court and the close friend of the Abuna Marqos. He became a friend too of Alvares, who helped him with his Portuguese and also taught him a little Latin. Enbaqom was a linguist, fluent in Arabic, Copt, and Ethiopian, and—as was inevitable in the context of Ethiopia and monastic life—a translator. He was working in the 1520s, when Alvares met him at the court of Lebna Dengel and visited him too at Dabra Libanos, on John Chrysostom's Commentary on the Epistles of St Paul and, most probably, a little later, on St John's Apocalypse. About this time he was selected as the new Eccage, abbot of Dabra Libanos, the senior ecclesiastical post in the country after that of the abuna. The choice must certainly have been the King's, but it is a surprising one as it meant that both the top figures in the Church were in consequence non-Ethiopians. Enbaqom was in fact the only foreigner ever to be eccage and the resultant dissatisfaction—perhaps in part because his relations with Marqos were too intimate—brought about his deposition. He was exiled to Gunei and, though after a year the King recalled him, Enbaqom was distressed by his treatment and remained in solitude in Warab. Meanwhile, the country was devastated by Gran. When Dabra Libanos went up in flames in 1532, it was being ruled by another abbot. Enbaqom fled from place to place to avoid the soldiers of Gran until, in 1540, he addressed Gran directly, first by letter and then by this book.

It was a time when it must have seemed that Gran was indeed destined to rule Ethiopia for good, and it may have been with that in mind that Enbaqom first appealed to him to cease burning churches and killing monks and other innocent people, and then, when Gran apparently agreed only to kill those who resisted him, set about the hard task of demonstrating to Gran the truth of Christianity. It was a bold endeavour. The *Anqasa Amin* is an apologetic work based almost entirely upon Enbaqom's memory of the Qur'an. He did not, he said, have a copy with him as he wrote, which is very understandable in the circumstances. He may hardly have read it for many years, having been living in Ethiopia for fifty. This easily accounts for the slips and inaccuracies in his text. He appears to have written first in Arabic, specifically for Gran, and then to have translated it into Ge'ez. It remains the only book in Ethiopian Christian literature to include considerable texts of the Qur'an. Enbaqom's arguments may not convince a modern scholar any more than they were likely to convince many of his Muslim contemporaries. They seem mostly drawn from the standard Arab Christian responses to Islam, with some personal additions. His insistence that the Qur'an affirms things, for instance that Jesus is the Spirit of God, which really mean more than Muslims admit them to mean, is not, to say the least, an absurd or insignificant argument. But probably his most interesting proofs are two of a more general nature, one linguistic, the other moral, neither dependent upon a precise reading of the Qur'anic text. In the linguistic argument he insists that the Qur'an is the book of a single language, Arabic, while the 'book of the Jews' is also in a single language, Hebrew, but the gospel is in all languages. It is not language-bound. There are, he says, twenty written languages in the world divided into three groups. There are Hebrew, Syriac, Arabic, and others of the people of Shem; there are Frankish, Latin, Greek, and others of the people of Japheth; and there are Coptic, Ethiopian, Nubian, and others of the people of Ham. The gospel is written in them all. The very vastness of difference in culture and language between them he sees as a sort of guarantee of the truth of a gospel which can be at home in all of them. It is an interesting argument and as relevant for modern Africa as for sixteenth-century Ethiopia.[13]

Enbaqom's second argument is a moral one. In the laws both of the Jews and of the Muslims there are legal prescriptions about the conduct of wars and of other such things, but in the law of Christ you find nothing similar. It is a law of the poor and for the poor, and is thereby morally superior. This too represents a remarkable insight and one far outlasting the often dubious ways in which he endeavours to interpret individual Qur'anic texts.

Enbaqom was extremely untypical of Ethiopia and his book never became a popular one. Perhaps it even seemed somewhat pointless

[13] It is not unlike the recent thesis of another convert from Islam to Christianity, Lamin Sanneh, cf. *Translating the Message* (1989). Sanneh was not, however, familiar with the work of Enbaqom.

once the Imam he addressed was overthrown and the Christian monarchy restored. Yet he was a man of quite outstanding breadth of culture for the society he lived in and it is no wonder he was admired. Ethiopians are generous in their recognition of foreign talent. Once Galawdewos became king, we are informed, he recalled Enbaqom to his court and kept him there as his councillor for many years. The monk resumed his work of translation, rendering into Ethiopian at Galawdewos's command the ancient (originally Buddhist) romance of Baralam and Yewusaf. It is pleasant to think of one very aged member of the community of Dabra Libanos translating this novel into Ge'ez at just the time that another, younger, member of the same community was in Rome, 'working day and night', as Tasfa Seyon himself wrote, at printing in Ge'ez the New Testament. They were both endeavouring to counter the great shortage of Ge'ez books produced by the destruction of Gran. Enbaqom completed his in May 1553. Just two years later the first Jesuits arrived with their seemingly ceaseless determination to refute the 'errors' of the Ethiopians. Seyon in Rome acknowledged papal authority without hesitation but defended the orthodoxy of the Ethiopian Church no less emphatically. What his writings most suggest, however, is a lively sense of Christian unity and friendly co-operation able both to give and to receive. The Counter-Reformation mind of Rodrigues or Oviedo lacked the more medieval tolerance discernible in Enbaqom and Tasfa Seyon.

When Galawdewos fell in battle and was succeeded by his brother Minas, the eccage, Yohannes, died with him. Minas, who shared his brother's childhood devotion to Enbaqom, then insisted on his becoming once more abbot of Dabra Libanos. There he died at the ripe age—his *gadl* tell us—of 137 years, rather more likely about 95. Enbaqom may well have had something to do with the tone of Galawdewos's *Confession*. Whether he did or not, he was certainly doing what Galawdewos would have liked the Jesuits to do—to provide spiritual and intellectual leadership for the Ethiopian Church, and translate works and ideas from the rest of Christendom, thus bringing in a richer theology from abroad and higher standards of clerical education, but not attacking head-on the basic traditions of Ethiopic religion and, above all, not setting up a rival and divisive Church of their own.

iv. *Paez and Susenyos*

On 26 April 1603 Pedro Paez, a 39-year-old Spanish Jesuit, landed at Massawa and made his way to Fremona. There had been no Jesuit in the country for six years and none of consequence for over a quarter of a century. Paez had been endeavouring to enter since 1589. In the meantime he had spent six years in slavery in the Yemen, but this had not deterred him and, after being freed in 1596, he had begun again. Now he had arrived, and for the next twenty years Ethiopia would experience the presence and activity of one of the most remarkable missionaries in history.

Paez was one of a great generation—top university men for the most part who had streamed into the Society of Jesus from Spain, Italy, and France during the last quarter of the sixteenth century and volunteered for missionary work. They came with the confidence of Counter-Reformation theology at its most powerful, armed with lecture notes derived from Suarez and Bellarmine, but also in some cases with a missionary adaptability largely learnt in the field and distinctly different in spirit from the undeviating rigidities of post-Tridentine orthodoxy.

The Asian strategist who guided forward the Jesuit missions at this time to approaches which have never ceased to amaze subsequent generations of observers was Alessandro Valignano, for years Provincial of India and Visitor for both India and Japan. Paez certainly knew him from his Goan days and while he was in Ethiopia, Ricci was in China, de Nobili in India, Valignano himself in Japan. All were concerned to tackle issues of language and culture at a new depth of understanding and adaptation, and while they still sought the conversion of rulers, as an earlier generation had done, it was no longer to be a hasty conversion. Jesuit attitudes to mission had here moved far in sophistication beyond those of a half-century earlier. They had indeed become some of the most sophisticated the world has ever known and yet they remained bound to, and finally controlled by, a very inflexible home theology which in every case left the mission with, in the last resort, too little room to manoeuvre. Moreover, only a small minority of the Jesuits on the mission had really entered into such approaches, and they were mostly Italian, never Portuguese.

Ethiopia was once more going through a phase of political instability, resulting from a weak succession. Sarsa Dengel had died, after a long and effective reign, in 1597. His son and successor, Jakob, was overthrown in 1603 while still a child by his uncle, Za Dengel, and it was the latter whom Paez first met on arrival at court in 1604. Za Dengel made him immediately welcome and quickly entered into theological discussion. One feels that he was simply resuming things where they had been left off in the 1550s between Galawdewos and Oviedo, but with a priest who showed himself at once far more sensitive and understanding. Everyone was struck by Paez's endearing personality, full of warmth and humour and never judgemental. In a year or two he would become a master of both written Ge'ez and spoken Amharic, but at this early stage he was still partly dependent upon an interpreter. There can be no doubt that he was alarmed by the Emperor's quick announcement that he intended to become a Catholic, but his recommendations of caution were disregarded. Za Dengel wrote at once to the Pope and the King of Spain acknowledging papal authority and asking for missionaries, soldiers, and artisans. Most unwisely he issued a proclamation upgrading Sunday and downgrading Saturday. The Abuna Peter excommunicated him, and he was killed in a rebellion only a few months later. Jakob was restored to the throne but then challenged by a new claimant, Susenyos, a nephew of Sarsa Dengel. Early in 1607 both Jakob and the Abuna were killed, and the next year Susenyos rode into Aksum for his coronation.

These events are important for us, not just because they bring Susenyos to the throne, but because the brief history of Za Dengel reveals a good deal. Attractive as Paez undoubtedly was, it is not possible to believe that in those few days he had converted Za Dengel in a religious or intellectual sense. Za Dengel's conversion was political, though doubtless he was much encouraged in his plans to find that the Jesuit who arrived at his court was so exceptionally helpful. The grounds for the Emperor's decision appear sensible enough, but, again, they cannot reasonably be seen as just a sudden personal initiative. The Roman option was far less emphatically rejected by Galawdewos than the Jesuits had imagined. They had simply misplayed their cards by rudeness. The live-and-let-live policy of Sarsa Dengel whereby a small Latin Church had been allowed to remain in the country and even to grow a little was not due to absent-mindedness, but rather to a resolve to keep options open and the Portuguese happy. The Ethiopian monarchy desperately needed allies. Everyone remembered how helpful Portuguese intervention had been in the 1540s. If things had never since been quite so desperate, they were also seldom very good. Turkish intervention on the one side but, still more, ceaseless Galla raids on the other kept the country in a permanently unsettled state. Susenyos, wrote Paez, never had a quiet day in his life. He was always at war. The curious little 'autobiography' of the monk Pawlos covering the later years of the sixteenth century suggests just the same, a country annually at war. In a world which had moved forward some way in technology since the age of Zara Ya'iqob or Lebna Dengel, Ethiopia had not moved forward at all, economically or militarily. It had little but the willpower of its emperors to hold it together and was saved more by the collapse of Adel under pressure from the Galla, the decline of Turkey, and the lack of any centralized direction among the Galla themselves than by its own resources.

In such circumstances religion remained its great resource, but the historic allegiance to Alexandria brought little benefit at a time when the Church in Egypt had declined to a condition of great insignificance. Not one of the abunas of this period was a man of stature. Several were morally scandalous. With Turkish control of Egypt, even the old political relationship between the Ethiopian emperor and the sultan in Cairo had more or less disappeared. The Alexandrian connection was no longer genuinely linking Ethiopia with anything much outside it. Yet it was obvious enough that Christianity could be a most helpful link with the outside world. Europe seemed just waiting to enter into alliance. While some of its apparent attractions were a chimera, others were real enough. It did not seem impractical to emperor or missionary to ask for a small Spanish or Portuguese army to cope with the Turks and the Galla, but, of course, it was. The effective power of the Spanish–Portuguese Empire was steadily receding, and the likelihood of its being able or willing to land a permanent army of occupation on the southern shore of the Red Sea was next to nil, though no one in Rome, Lisbon, or Madrid would have been willing to admit it. But the value of religion and educational links was not chimerical. If a score of Jesuits had been able to work in Ethiopia throughout the seventeenth century, patronized by the State, it could have been of immense profit to the country, encouraging political stability, providing an élite with the elements of a rational and scientific education, stimulating craftsmanship, trade with the outside world, and a steady modernization of culture and society as a whole. Something of all this circles at the Ethiopian court would seem to have surmised. Za Dengel's submission to Rome, followed by the quick return of Susenyos to the same tack (and even Jakob had put out feelers), cannot be sensibly explained as the sudden, idiosyncratic decision of individuals overwhelmed by the personality of Paez.

Court and country, however, were not the same thing. Nor was the court undivided. It never was, especially at a time when alternative possible claimants to the throne were no longer banished to a mountain fortress. The influence of even an insignificant abuna and of the large number of other ecclesiastics at court was always considerable. But, beyond the court, rejection of the authority of Alexandria was sure to stir up the anger of ten thousand monks because it entailed so many ramifications: acceptance of the mysterious authority of the Council of Chalcedon and—in the eyes of its opponents—a sell-out to a Nestorianism which denied the unity and divinity of Christ; abandonment of the Sabbath; abandonment of circumcision. The entire religious culture of Ethiopia was bound to seem threatened, even—the Western observer can hardly not be amused to notice—its Marian piety: Roman Catholics were regarded as being distinctly cool so far as devotion to the Mother of God was concerned. When all this was at stake in the minds of countless religious people of great theological ignorance, the needs of long-term state policy were not likely to prevail. The intense reaction provoked by Rodriguez and Oviedo in the 1550s should have been warning enough. Za Dengel chose to ignore it and quickly lost both his throne and his life. Paez did not. In its way Za Dengel's fate was an invaluable message to him, reinforcing St Ignatius' stress upon *dolcezza* in instructions which Paez had certainly meditated. The history of the next twenty years would be one of the interplay of all these factors working throughout the reign of Susenyos in his relationship with his people on the one hand, with the Jesuits on the other. It was an interplay of which, so far as one can judge, the outcome was not determined. Heavy as the odds seem against any other long-term conclusion than the rejection of Rome, it remains the supreme achievement of Paez to make an alternative outcome appear an imaginable one.

Susenyos was a person of immense physical and moral vigour, a certain balance of mind and character, very considerable intelligence, a statesman of imaginative determination, ruthless enough but not foolhardy. He seemed fortunate in having a brother of high ability and greater education who was wholly trustworthy. Cela Krestos, governor of Tigre and then of Gojjam, was a more out-and-out Catholicizer than Susenyos himself, he was in truth a religious fanatic, but it was the close friendship and trust holding together the trio of Susenyos, Cela Krestos, and Paez which really provided their enterprise with its underlying credibility. While the personal relationship of Paez and Susenyos may remain unique in our history in its intensity of confidence and co-operation, it would be paralleled in after times by a number of strikingly close friendships between missionaries and kings. In this case, as in some others, the personal charm of Paez was so powerful because it was grounded both in the highest standards of personal morality and in great practical serviceableness. It was the sheer spiritual and intellectual quality of the Jesuits as a group, when compared with the rather dubious personalities coming of late from Cairo, which was so convincing in the eyes of the Ethiopian élite.

There were never more than six Jesuits in Ethiopia during the life of Paez. Roughly speaking, two looked after the 'Portuguese', the small Latin community centred round Fremona; two were at or near the court, based in their new centre at Gorgora on Lake Tana; two were with Cela Krestos in Gojjam and were chiefly at work on translation. Cela Krestos was received into the Catholic Church in 1612 and a handful of distinguished people followed him, but Paez regularly urged Susenyos to put off doing the same and he made no attempt to encourage any large movement of individual conversions. Numerically there were in fact very few. He engaged in as much discussion with monks as he could, while avoiding sharp disputation. He pushed ahead with a programme of translation. He wrote a lengthy *History of Ethiopia*, very carefully noting his sources, and he constructed for the Emperor a small but elegant stone palace, including an upper storey, at Dancaz, near Lake Tana.

As the years passed and Susenyos established himself through many victories as one of Ethiopia's most powerful kings, he could afford to take risks over religion. Pushed on by Cela Krestos and the Catholic party at court, he almost certainly misjudged both the immediate military advantages which might accrue from submission to Rome and the depth of popular resistance with which he would be faced. In March 1622 he put aside all his wives but the first, made profession of the Roman faith, and received the sacraments from the hands of Paez. Six weeks later, 3 May, the Jesuit died of a fever. Susenyos wrote to the Provincial in Goa comparing the grief of Ethiopia with that 'in Alexandria on the death of St Mark, a mourning like that in Rome on the death of St Peter and St Paul'.[14]

Had he lived, might Paez have squared the circle? The Jesuits already felt a growing hostility in many parts of the country. The Abuna Simon had declared excommunicate all those who held that there were two natures in Christ and had died in a subsequent rebellion in 1617. The Jesuits with some of their Ethiopian friends, including Bella Krestos, a very scholarly half-brother of the Emperor, had endeavoured to show that in the past the Ethiopian Church was not Monophysite but, basically, there was no way without a philosophical tradition of the Greek sort and without a wider system of formal theology of formulating in any meaningful way the Chalcedonian distinction of nature and person. It remains possible that Latin doctrine could have been accepted over this by royal command, if offered diplomatically in terms of the rediscovery of Ethiopian tradition, and that an abuna from Rome could have been welcomed in place of an abuna from Alexandria. On the other side, it seems reasonably likely that both the Jesuits and Rome could have accepted Ethiopian baptisms and ordinations as they stood together with the liturgy substantially unaltered including the calendar. Indeed, even after Paez's death the quiet work of amending texts and updating the clergy continued to go forward fairly untraumatically in some places. Jesuits had recently reconciled the Maronite Church in the Lebanon to Rome on this sort of basis. The most awkward points remained circumcision and the keeping of the Sabbath. An attempt to end either compulsorily at any time seems sure to have produced such popular opposition that no emperor could long have survived such a policy. In August 1637 the Congregation of Propaganda Fide, after consulting the Holy Office, confirmed that circumcision was a superstition which could not be tolerated.[15] It is conceivable that Paez and a group of like-minded missionaries might have found it possible to tolerate circumcision and to adapt the Sabbath. It seems inconceivable that Rome in the seventeenth century would have gone along with them any more than in the end it would go along with the methods of Ricci in China.

[14] Beccari, xi. 518.
[15] It is, of course, tolerated by all modern Catholic missionaries.

v. *Mendes and Fasiladas*

In 1624 Antonio Fernandes, one of Paez's closest collaborators and now superior of the mission, wrote to the Jesuit Provincial insisting that 'Priests sent to Ethiopia should be persons of great prudence selected with the utmost care, for any display of immoderate zeal would cause the collapse of the edifice so painstakingly constructed.'[16] Instead, Alphonsus Mendes was sent as Patriarch, arriving in the country in 1625. He was selected only by the King of Spain. He had no missionary experience. Physically a giant and academically quite distinguished as a Professor of Scripture at the University of Evora, he was filled with a great confidence in himself, and his office, and his theology, wholly lacking the sensitivities necessary for a mission of such exceptional delicacy. His choice was, clearly, disastrous, yet it has to be said that his attitudes were really much closer to the convictions of seventeenth-century Rome than were those of Paez. In February 1626 he arrived at court. Dressed in cope and mitre, met by a vast army, six governors of provinces carrying a canopy over his head, he processed to the church which Paez had completed only just before his death. He entered it to the roar of cannon to meet the Emperor awaiting him in his crown of gold. Four days later, Susenyos, followed by the leading clergy and laity, knelt publicly before Mendes to take an oath of allegiance to the Pope.

Mendes then issued his first proclamation, an irreparable blunder. No one in future was to offer mass or do anything else of an ecclesiastical kind until he had received faculties from the Patriarch. He had decided that all Ethiopian sacraments were of dubious validity and decreed that the faithful were to be rebaptized, the clergy reordained. This wholly undermined the basis of the Ethiopia–West relationship, for it impugned the very Christianity of the Ethiopians. Feasts and fasts were to be rearranged according to the Roman calendar. The mass, while it might be said in Ge'ez, must be according to the Roman rite. Saturday would become a fast day. Circumcision was prohibited. His only concessions were to allow the priests he reordained to remain married and to say their Roman mass in Ge'ez.

The total folly of such a declaration should have been obvious to

---

[16] Ibid. xii. 56.

the more experienced of the Jesuits, but most of it lay well within the inevitable logic of Tridentine Catholicism,[17] whose theology they shared and whose more awkward conclusions could be staved off only so long as reconciliation was performed quietly, piecemeal, and wholly without compulsion. The almost inescapable consequence of the arrival of the Patriarch and the public submission of the sovereign was to proceed henceforth by means of public ceremonial, legal proclamation, and a general latinization of the Church. It was, all in all, only a little more ruthless than the Synod of Diamper of 1599 whereby Aleixo da Menezes, the Archbishop of Goa, had latinized the St Thomas Christians of South India at the very time Paez was endeavouring to find his way from Goa to Ethiopia.

What is striking is that any of this was implemented at all, but Susenyos was at the height of his power and twenty years of Jesuit presence had built up a Catholic party of some significance within imperial circles, including a number of the clergy. Men like Cela Krestos were now deeply committed by conviction, not by any mere opportunism. Rebaptisms and reordinations went on apace in certain areas. For a short while the liturgy of the court was that of the Ge'ez form of the Roman rite and circumcision disappeared from view. A new marriage law excluding divorce was administered by the Patriarch himself. If the monks were infuriated by the attack on the Sabbath and festivals, the ruling class was still more alienated by the attempt to ban their marriage customs and the circumcizing of their many children. Inevitably, rebellions multiplied, led by members of the royal family, and even some who had become Catholics reverted, seeing how fiercely unpopular the Church of the Europeans now was, but Susenyos crushed them mercilessly, one by one. The final and most threatening rebellion was a peasant uprising. It was only too clear that the overwhelming majority of ordinary people felt themselves threatened in their entire spiritual existence by what the Jesuits were now seen to be doing and that any leader who rose up against the King would at once gain a following.

In 1629 Susenyos had already insisted that Mendes revoke his decrees on the calendar, days of fasting, and the liturgy, but this was

[17] But it fitted far less with the logic of pre-Tridentine Catholicism. The comments of Alvares upon Ethiopian ecclesiastical culture were remarkably unjudgemental. Note Paul III's original proposal simply to authorize the Emperor to choose a Patriarch of his own. Rome's natural willingness to tolerate oriental diversity declined considerably in the course of the 16th cent.

wholly inadequate. Any chance of a quiet process of transformation from one ecclesiastical regime to the other had been destroyed by the uncompromising arrogance of the Patriarch's initial actions, and in June 1632, after overcoming the latest rebellion, the Emperor sadly declared a return to freedom of worship as practised since the time of Galawdewos: let Ethiopians and Romans each have their own altars and their own liturgy. Tired and disillusioned, but not himself abandoning the Roman Church, Susenyos handed over power to his son Fasiladas. Less than three months later he died, attended to the end by a Jesuit. He was buried in state as one of the greatest of emperors, but already his religious heritage had been overwhelmingly abandoned by his people. Men and women danced together, smashed their rosaries and chanted in joy:

> At length the sheep of Ethiopia freed
> From the bad lions of the West
> Securely in their pastures feed.
> St Mark and Cyril's doctrine have overcome
> The follies of the Church of Rome.[18]

Catholicism, one may conclude, was expressed at its most universalist and sympathetic in Paez, Romanism at its most legalistic and unadaptable in Mendes. It seems the perennial tragedy of Roman Catholicism that, while again and again stimulating the sensitivities of the one sort, it then relapses into the rigidities of the other. We should, nevertheless, not put all the blame on Mendes nor underestimate his qualities. He certainly lacked the diplomacy of Paez and any sort of flexibility of mind to temper his mastery of Tridentine theology. He appears in the pages of the book he subsequently wrote, *Expeditio Aethiopica*, as a pompous ass of a university professor in love with the sound of the theological lectures he delivered to the Ethiopians. He brought clothes to dazzle them with, but also a large academic library (including the complete works of Suarez!). Rome thought subsequently that the débâcle was caused by Jesuit mishandling and Portuguese bellicosity and handed the job over to less well-educated French and Italian Capuchins. It was basically mistaken. The cause of the débâcle was less Portuguese arrogance than an inflexible ecclesiology, and the Capuchins were at least as subject to that as the Jesuits.

---

[18] Mendes reports such chants (Beccari, viii. 374), as does Almeida (ibid. vii, 176). The quotation comes from Ludolf's *New History of Ethiopia* (1682), 357–8.

Such a mission needed, above all, subtlety of mind and a maximum of theological discretion. It had temporarily flourished at the hands of a number of men of exceptional sensitivity. Ironically, it was sunk irremediably by the hand of a professor. However, the sensitivity had been one of initial method and of tone of voice. There is little sign that it ever extended to the ecclesiological goal. One may ask whether Paez was not fortunate in the moment of his death. In 1640, when it was too late to matter, Propaganda Fide forbade the Ethiopian Rite to be altered. Why was Mendes appointed as Patriarch without, it seems, any instructions on the subject of rite? The Ethiopian liturgy had, after all, been printed in Rome in the previous century. Neither the papacy nor the Society of Jesus seems to have adverted to the problem at all. Nor, so far as one can see, had Paez. Perhaps he had simply taken it for granted that the Ethiopian Rite and calendar would continue, but he seems never to have said so and he had many years in which to think about it and write to the authorities. He and his fellow Jesuits said mass according to the Latin Rite and the few Ethiopians he received into Communion then worshipped in that rite too, so Mendes was not obviously overturning the practice of Paez and was never subsequently blamed by his fellow Jesuits for so doing. Antonio Fernandez became Mendes' Vicar-General and never seemed to detect any great change in strategy. He certainly never criticized the Patriarch.

Within less than fifty years the Society of Jesus had been involved in the reconciliation of three Eastern Churches—the Maronites in Lebanon at synods in 1580 and 1596, the Syrian Christians of St Thomas in South India at the Synod of Diamper in 1599, and then Ethiopia. All three were heavily latinizing, that of the Maronites the least, that of Ethiopia the most. Yet the Ethiopian was the largest Church of the three and the most different in its practices, but also the most difficult effectively to coerce. It seems extraordinary that the Society and Rome had learnt so little from Lebanon and Malabar to apply to Ethiopia.

Paez shines in personal terms but there seems no evidence that he had during nearly twenty years in the country thought out a constructive strategy to cope with the liturgy or anything else once the process of Catholicization moved from winning over the minds of a handful of the élite to reshaping public religion. It is fashionable to praise Paez and damn Mendes, but it could be claimed that Paez let Mendes down quite as much as Mendes betrayed the legacy of

Paez. Could Paez, any more than Mendes, once Susenyos had publicly proclaimed his Catholicism, have put up with a court full of divorcing and polygamous noblemen set on circumcizing their children? And could such noblemen long have put up with a Church which damned so many of their ancestral customs? A pre-Reformation Catholic Church might have been reconciled with Ethiopia a great deal more easily than could a post-Tridentine one.

Fasiladas was by no means prepared to return to the way things had been under Sarsa Dengel. Unity of Church had become once more a national necessity. Sela Krestos and a number of Ethiopian Catholics who held loyally to their faith were banished or executed. The Jesuits were ordered to leave and the Patriarch hardly improved things by appealing to the Portuguese for military intervention to depose Fasiladas. Portugal had, in fact, just succeeded in reconquering Mombasa from its Muslim king. That was quite sufficient to alarm Fasiladas. A few of the Jesuits went into hiding and survived in Ethiopia for several years. It may well have been the foolish attempt of two Capuchins, sent by *Propaganda*, to enter the country in 1638 which brought about not only their own deaths but also that of the surviving Jesuits, the last of whom were executed in 1640. There were, however, a number of Ethiopian secular priests who survived, ministering in secret, for another thirteen years. Their leader was Fr. Nogueira, another Fremona priest and a descendant of one of Cristovao da Gama's companions of 1541. If he and his colleagues were able to continue so long, it was because they had the support of a very loyal lay community to shelter them. Fr. Nogueira was killed himself in 1653. It was the end of any established Catholic clerical presence for a century and a half. Various Capuchins who continued to try and enter the country, some in the reign of Fasiladas, others later, were in most cases quickly murdered.

For two centuries Ethiopia cut itself off from the outside world or, at least, from Latin Christianity. The isolation was not complete. The tiny Ethiopian monastic community in Rome soon ceased to exist, but the much larger ones in Jerusalem and Egypt continued to flourish. The learned Abba Gregorio, whom Paez converted and Mendes ordained, had gone into exile with the latter to Goa in the 1630s. He was in Rome by the late 1640s, helping the German scholar Ludolf with his Ethiopian studies, and was entertained at the court of the Duke of Saxony in the 1650s. Several of the emperors would willingly have resumed relations with the West, but popular hostility to any Roman priest remained for long quite overwhelming. Greeks, Syrians, and Armenians were still welcome. To some extent, they replaced the Portuguese and must have helped to build Gondar, but the chief effect of the Jesuit mission was to stimulate a paranoid sense of isolationism which lasted for 200 years and deeply damaged Ethiopia's social and mental development.

The quantity of high-quality Jesuit writing about Ethiopia for the first forty years of the seventeenth century (much of it unpublished until the twentieth century) is remarkable. It includes the lengthy accounts of five different authors together with hundreds of letters. Inevitably, once the Jesuits are gone we know a good deal less about what happened next. Yet their mission may have helped to stimulate a new literary wave, principally translations from the Arabic such as a first book of ecclesiastical law, the *Fetha Nagast*, or the thirty-five chapters of the book entitled *Spiritual Medicine*, translated for Sabla Wangel, the wife of Yohannes I. Then there was the writing or revision of various rites including penance and marriage, further lives of the Saints, but, above all, an explosion of Christology.

One piece of hagiography deserves special attention. It is the Life of Walatta Pietros, perhaps the first biography of an African woman. Whether the details are wholly accurate matters little. The hagiographical genre had to set an individual's life within a suitable context, combining secular history and religious ideal. If written little after the death of its subject, as this was, it would certainly be basically faithful to the way things were and it presents a picture of very considerable interest. An upper-class lady, extremely self-confident, indeed both headstrong and outspoken, she has at the same time to be shown to demonstrate the necessary qualities of humility and deference. While able to kill people at a distance, possessing in this the qualities more usually associated with a witch than a saint, it is clearly seen to be for the good of their souls, or at least someone's soul. Married to a devoted husband, she saw her three children die in succession, in response—it is suggested—to her own prayers to ensure their eternal salvation. That could well have been sufficient to ensure divorce and her withdrawal to a monastery, but this decision is put instead in the context of her husband's contamination by Romanism. As a married lady, Walatta was a model of the virtues, a patron of the clergy, whom she provided with dinner on Sundays. On becoming a nun, she founded her own monasteries for both men and women, exercised full authority (woe betide the priest who did not obey her commands), gave the lead in the building of churches, and suffered from the Romanizing persecution of Sela Krestos. She converted a princess, sent to her by Fasiladas, who had fallen into Roman beliefs, she spent time in pious reading, she performed various miracles, and in due course died, but not before a final vision in which she was constituted by Christ 'Head of the Deacons' (even though in Ethiopia women did not become deacons). So Walatta Pietros may be seen as something of an ecclesiastical feminist, as well as saint, nationalist hero, witch, and miracle-worker. The hagiographic conventions do not make it easy to see through to the real person, but a sense of the principal concerns of the time and of the degree of initiative possible for a devout woman of the upper class comes across clearly enough.

We have few such glimpses into the interior of seventeenth-century Ethiopian Christian life, but one other still more extraordinary is that of the movement of za-Krestos and his followers in Amhara.[19] He proclaimed himself the new Christ, born again for the Gentiles in Ethiopia, about 1604. Though he was executed by the Emperor Za Dengel, his followers multiplied, developing a Church complete with hierarchy, rituals, and a Communion service in which the faithful received 'the body of za Krestos, our God, which he took from Amata Wangel, the Lady of us all'. The movement was effectively wiped out by orders of Susenyos, many of its members flinging themselves to death over a precipice. It remains, in the little we know of it, not too dissimilar to that of Kimpa Vita in the Kongo just one century later.

The post-Jesuit age is dominated by Gondar. Fasiladas was as strong and single-minded a ruler as his father, and he ruled for well over thirty years. Having rejected Rome, he set about the reconstruction of Ethiopian orthodoxy in a new and yet traditional way. Ever since the jihad of Gran, the cathedral at Aksum had been in a very poor condition indeed. Fasiladas built a new one, not nearly as impressive as that of antiquity but still as fine as he could make it. It is the

---

[19] G. Haile, 'A Christ for the Gentiles', *JRA* 15 (1985), 86–95. We would have a third, very different but no less fascinating, glimpse into 17th-cent. Ethiopian religious life if we could accept the *Hatata* of the philosopher Zara Ya'iqob as genuine as, for instance, Pankhurst, *Ethiopia*, 359–65, still does. For its full text in Ge'ez and Latin translation see *Philosophi Abessini*, ed. E. Littmann, *CSCO* 18–19 (1904, repr. 1955). Unfortunately it appears to have been composed by a 19th-cent. Italian Franciscan, see C. Conti Rossini, 'Lo Hatata Zara Ya'qob e il Padre Guisto da Urbino', *Rendiconti della Reale Accademia dei Lincei*, 5/29 (Rome, 1920), 213–23.

cathedral that has been there ever since. The establishment of a capital at Gondar may have been inspired by the building at Dancaz by Paez of a stone palace for Susenyos, though Zara Ya'iqob had done the same two centuries earlier at Dabra Berhan. His successors had at once abandoned it. But perhaps Aksum itself or even Lalibela may have been at the back of the mind of Fasiladas, or simply the consciousness that in other countries kings lived in castles and capitals. The great stone castle of Fasiladas still looks impressive enough. It seemed progressive. It provided protection, a centre for administration, an appearance of power. Almost certainly it contributed, nevertheless, to the decay of the Ethiopian monarchy and of Ethiopia itself. Gondar had little to offer beyond its palaces. It neither presupposed nor generated any sort of middle class or wider urban life other than the Arab town a mile away, so similar to the towns which grew up next to the transient courts of the kings of West African medieval empires. Economically Gondar generated nothing. It merely isolated the Emperor from his provinces. Only the ceaseless imperial itinerations of the past could hold the country together, while maintaining his apartness from provincial loyalties— the power of Solomonic isolation. The more the Emperor remained at Gondar, immersed within the mirrors and ivory of the latest palace, the more Shoa, Tigre, Amhara, and Gojjam would go their independent ways.

Gondar had, however, a more intrinsic significance. At least in the original conception of Fasiladas, it was to be a religious as much as a royal city, a revitalization of Ethiopian Orthodoxy, a symbol to outshine the buildings of the Jesuits. Gondar was not in purpose a secular power-centre, but a mysterious combination of the divine and the royal, a kremlin in which, surrounded by high walls and great gates, a mass of churches would be as important as the palaces: St Mary of Zion, St Mary of Sihor, St Mary of the Gondar people, St Michael of Aira, St Simon of Tzaamdi, St George of Damot, St George of Ueerangueb, St John of Guara, the Church of the Apostles of Deva, the Church of the Four Saints; a little later came the Church of God the Father, the Church of St Anthony, and many more, over forty in all (Poncet claimed over a hundred). In Gondar lived only the royal family, its ministers, servants, and soldiers, the Abuna, the Eccage, the Aqabe-Sa'at, and numerous other priests and monks. It was a city shared between prayer and political intrigue.

vi. *The Eighteenth Century*

For some seventy-five years, through the reigns of Fasiladas, his son Yohannes I, and his grandson Iyasu I, the Ethiopian monarchy retained a certain strength and seeming vitality within the new shape that Gondar had given to it. The French doctor Charles Jacques Poncet, visiting the country in 1699–1700, provides a description of prosperity and good order not too unlike that of Alvares 180 years earlier. The art of the period, both in manuscripts and in wall paintings, was remarkable, more naturalistic than that of previous centuries and not at all averse to European influences. Again it was a great age for music, the period in which the Ethiopian musical tradition developed its standard annotation. Unfortunately music, art, even theology are only a small part of life. The kingdom was declining in size and centralized control as waves of Galla (more attracted to Islam than to an Amharic-dominated Christianity) infiltrated many parts of it. From the deposition of Iyasu in 1706 Ethiopian political history degenerated into a chronicle of palace revolutions, the rise and fall of emperors who controlled little more than Dembea, the province immediately around Gondar. Shoa became effectively independent, kings slaughtered their subjects and one another or were deposed by the Ras of Tigre, Begemdir, or Gojjam. Yet within the walls and soon half-ruined palaces, a ritual but no longer creative semblance of the ancient Solomonic kingship retained its high claims and continued to preside over the fanatical rivalries of monastic orthodoxy while averting its eyes from the reality of social and political disintegration.

Ecclesiastical history became dominated by a struggle between two Christologies, one championed by the House of Takla Haymanot, the other by that of Ewostatewos. It seems to have been set off by a monastic sense of the need to respond theologically to the arguments of the Jesuits about the two natures of Christ. Fasiladas denied to Mendes (probably correctly) that there was any substantive doctrinal difference between the two Churches.[20] Mendes, unbending Counter-Reformation theologian that he was, could not agree. Certainly, while kings tried regularly to play down theological disagreement, clerics equally regularly accentuated it.

---

[20] The decisive 1632 letter of Fasiladas to Mendes, which the latter reproduced in full in his *Expeditio Aethiopica* (Beccari, ix. 29–32) rather reminds one of the *Confession of Faith* of Galawdewos in the tolerance of its theological judgement.

For the Ethiopian theologians the problem came to be focused on the verse in Acts 10: 38 where Peter is reported as declaring that 'God anointed Jesus of Nazareth with the Holy Spirit and with power'. If, as in Western doctrine, two natures—divine and human—are admitted to exist in Christ, then it seems easy to explain that God anointed the human nature. But if the doctrine of the two natures is rejected, as is required by monophysitism, then there arises the problem: what was anointed? A German Lutheran named Heyling, who came to Ethiopia with the new abuna, Marqos, in 1637 may actually have set off the form of the resultant controversy by focusing attention upon the meaning of the word 'anointed' (which underlies, of course, the meaning of 'Christ'). Two schools developed, reflecting the traditional division of monastic orders. The Ewostathians held that the anointing was the divinization of the humanity, identical with the union of the two natures into one. This was known as the Kebat. The House of Takla Haymanot, on the other hand, held that the anointing had nothing to do with the union itself, which it presupposed, but instead made Jesus into the Messiah or second Adam. This became known as the Tewahdo. The Kebat was more rigorously Monophysite, the Tewahdo approximating more to Western views. In this the Houses of Takla Haymanot and Ewostatewos were more or less replaying their roles from earlier Sabbath controversies. It is noticeable, nevertheless, that whereas in the fifteen century the Ewostathians were led by coastal monasteries, like Dabra Bizan, in the far north, by the eighteenth century these areas had been so Islamicized as to matter a great deal less. The kingdom had withdrawn from the sea. Just as the truly ancient monasteries around Aksum, like Dabra Damo, were already taking second place by the fifteenth century because the heart of the kingdom had moved away from Aksum, so by the Gondarine period even Dabra Bizan had effectively yielded leadership to the Ewostathians of Gojjam.

Two synods were held in the 1650s under Fasiladas to decide between the opposing views. The first supported the Kebat, the second the Tewahdo. From then on the Tewahdo, the orthodoxy of Dabra Libanos, was upheld by the emperors through a series of synods for some fifty years. Yohannes I (1667–83), Iyasu the Great (1683–1706), and Takla Haymanot (1706–8) all maintained the doctrine of the Tewahdo. After that, however, things changed. Theophilus, Justus, and David III veered round to the monks of

Gojjam and under David there was, furthermore, a considerable massacre in 1720 of the leading monastic supporters of the Tewahdo in the palace of the Eccage at Gondar. Other monastic strongholds of the doctrine in Dembea were also stormed by the army. From then on the Ewostathians were for long the dominant party. The explanation for the shift in imperial favour may have been a geopolitical one. Up to the early eighteenth century the emperors were still seriously trying to maintain a real unity for Ethiopia. For that it was absolutely required to retain the loyalty of Shoa and of its principal religious tradition upheld by Dabra Libanos. From about the fall of Takla Haymanot, the son of Iyasu the Great, in 1708 this policy fell by the wayside. Shoa could no longer be controlled and so there was less point in placating its monks. There was much more to be said for ensuring the loyalty of Gojjam, a province far closer to Gondar. Geography prevailed over theology. The palace of the Eccage was stormed, and Shoa effectively withdrew for more than an hundred years into autonomous existence, an existence about which we know exceedingly little.

Rome never gave up hope of reviving its Ethiopian mission. It was occasionally encouraged by emperors clutching at straws, for they too had never quite abandoned the miasmic hope that somehow Rome might once more provide the sort of help which, in the legend of the past, Cristovao da Gama had brought to Galawdewos in the country's supreme hour of need.[21] Given popular opposition at home, the political state of Europe, and the missionary rigidity of Rome, it was a singularly ill-founded hope. It produced a joint Jesuit–Franciscan mission around 1700 and another Franciscan mission in the 1750s, but they were entirely ineffectual. However, two Bohemian members of the 1750s mission, Remedius Prutcky and Martinus Lang, were permitted to remain in Gondar for seven months and acquired considerable influence over the royal family, despite showing no sympathy at all for Ethiopian orthodoxy. When they returned to Rome, they recommended the appointment of an Ethiopian bishop. This may have encouraged Propaganda Fide to have another try of a different sort toward the end of the century. Tobia Ghebragzier, an Ethiopian who had studied at its college, was

---

[21] One claimed imperial submission to the Pope, that of Iyasu I, sent via the Franciscan Joseph of Jerusalem in 1702, is probably entirely fraudulent, though M. C. da Nembro appears to regard it as genuine ('Martirio ed espulsione in Etiopia', *PFMR* i/1 (1971), 646–70), see Beccari, i. 441–54.

consecrated bishop in June 1788 and dispatched via Egypt to his home country with another Ethiopian priest also trained at *Propaganda*. They worked for some months around Adwa but were bitterly attacked once their character became clear. The ancient and hospitable monastery of Dabra Damo provided refuge for a time, but, after spending many miserable years wandering from place to place, Bishop Tobia finally arrived back in Egypt in 1797. Before consecration, which had been appropriately performed by a bishop of oriental rite, he had been required to take an oath to use only the Ethiopian Rite. Had Rome then learnt its lesson? The Patriarch of Alexandria was particularly bitter at this move, declaring that 'from the time of St Mark until now there has not been a single Ethiopian bishop'.[22] The Patriarch therefore requested the princes of Ethiopia to imprison, torture, and execute the bishop. Tobia's mission did indeed threaten the Egyptian monopoly and Ethiopia's total dependence upon Egypt. It is not to be condemned for that, but it may be remarked that the very need to exact an oath about the use of the Ethiopian Rite is revealing. It was only necessary because Tobia had been trained, not within the Ethiopian tradition, but in the Latin environment of Propaganda Fide and had for years shared regularly in the Latin Rite. The Ethiopian Rite he was now required to use was not a rounded Christian tradition but simply a certain liturgical form to which, hitherto, he may have been too little accustomed. If Rome was to respect Ethiopian Christianity it would have to go a great deal further than that.

James Bruce visited Gondar in 1770–1 and gives us a lively picture of a much diminished kingdom, almost impotent emperors, the dominance of Ras Mika'el of Tigre—a dominance never for long uncontested by alternative warlords. Less than twenty years later things had fallen completely apart and there began what came to be known as 'Zamana Masafent', the 'age of the Judges'—a reference to the post-Mosaic period when 'there was no king in Israel'. The last king to rule at all effectively was Takla Giyorgis and his reign was appropriately nicknamed 'Fasame Mangest', the end of government. It is worth pausing a little at this point and we are fortunate in possessing a chronicle that tells us a great deal about the uncertain years of his reign (1779–84 plus various brief restorations as far as

[22] C. Conti Rossini, *Documenta ad Illustrandum Historiam: 1 Liber Axumae*, CSCO 54 (1909), 99–102.

1800). His secretary could still describe him with the rhetoric of an earlier age, now almost mockingly unreal: 'King of Kings, the new Alexander . . . whose eyes are as the morning star and whose countenance is shining and beneficent, whose stature is like an exalted angel, and his valour like the terrible Samson, his mind pure as the heart of the Creator, his wisdom great as the wisdom of Solomon, his dominion extensive like that of Alexander.'[23] He seems to have tried hard to do the things an emperor should do, to process around the country, pitching his crimson tent here and there, adjudicating cases, marching against rebellious governors, battling with the Galla, guarding and governing the Church. There is a rather touching moment when the bones of Zara Ya'iqob are brought to him, dug up for some reason after 330 years, the remains of the greatest (but also one of the cruellest) of the emperors shown to the last diminished ruler of his dynasty, and Takla Giyorgis proclaims mercy on all who take sanctuary with the bones of 'great Zara Ya'iqob, the just king'.[24]

Care for the Church remained central to the role of the emperor. When he was not marching here or there to outmanœuvre his over-mighty subjects, he was keeping the fasts and feasts of the Christian year, giving banquets on the occasion of the latter, making ecclesiastical appointments, feeding the 'children of the priests of the establishment of Mary' and listening to the concert they performed for him, presenting new sacerdotal vestments to a church, presiding over the baptism of groups of Galla, or endeavouring to moderate the fate of Christians carried into captivity. In all this nothing remained more important, especially to the eyes of the chronicler, than the reconciliation of monastic controversy. It was in fact only just before his first deposition that a new piece of bickering had broken out between the two monastic houses and some of their number had refused to sit down together at a meal in the house of the Aqabe Sa'at. The Emperor had then to take the best part of two weeks peace making. Finally it was done:

On the 10th [*Maskaram*, September] there were great rejoicings in the town of the Negus because Azaj Gabru and Tserag Masare Fequr Egzie (Beloved of God) had reconciled, by order of the Negus, the men of the House of Ewostatewos with the Aqabe Sa'at Kabte from their hearts and on oath, as

[23] H. Weld Blundell (ed.), *The Royal Chronicle of Abyssinia 1769–1840* (Cambridge, 1922), 230.   [24] Ibid. 266.

the Book says, 'And they came to the place of contention, and settled it by taking oaths'. On the 11th the men of Dabra Libanos stayed with the men of the house of Ewostatewos singing hymns of love in the Church of the Holy Fasiladas, for previously they sang the music of discord. And they came out of there and spent the time in festivity at the royal palace, eating and drinking, and the next day the Negus again feasted the priests mentioned above. And the Aqabe Sa'at Kabte also serenaded the Negus with songs of peace-making.[25]

On 22 *Maskaram*, we are told, Takla Giyorgis stayed at the house of the Abuna Yosab for a banquet with his generals.

Monks at this stage were more easily reconciled than generals, though hardly more lastingly. Four months later Takla Giyorgis was deposed. Bonds of loyalty, despite a multiplication of oaths, had ceased to hold. The next fifty years were a time of near anarchy in which various local rulers jostled for some sort of primacy while more and more areas of the country were forcibly taken over by groups of Galla, some nominally Christian, some of their ancestral religion, many confirmed Muslim. Galla conquest frequently meant the massacre of monks, the desecration of churches, and even their conversion into mosques. Never since the jihad of Gran had the state of the Ethiopian Church been so depressed.

During the first part of this period the Church was served by an unusually courageous and sensible abuna. Yosab was abuna from 1770 to 1803. Again and again the royal chronicler refers to how Abuna and Eccage had exerted themselves in support of the King or of peace, if generally to little avail. 'Wherefore hast thou come here, thou who art nothing but a heathen?', the aged Abuna demanded fiercely of one particularly anti-Christian Galla warlord who had made his way into Gondar.[26] In 1802 he even laid the whole country under an interdict forbidding the celebration of the Eucharist in a vain endeavour to draw the nation back to 'serve the king and do justice to the widows and the children', but after two months 'seeing that nothing was done, he removed the interdict'.[27] A few months later he died: 'There was mourning in the land, first our Negus vanished from us and now our Patriarch. "Who will protect us, body and soul?" is what all the world said weeping.'

Christianity in Africa did, then, enter the nineteenth century weaker and more imperilled in its one traditional area of strength

[25] Ibid. 302.   [26] Ibid. 464.   [27] Ibid. 473.

than it had been for centuries. With Yosab dead some monks took the lead in sending to Cairo for a new abuna. They saw the need and could no longer leave the matter to the Emperor. A measure of ecclesiastical initiative was returning. Perhaps political disintegration did something to induce the Church to turn back towards both moral unity and episcopal leadership, difficult as it was in the context of its own tradition to achieve much of either.

Among the many interwoven tensions within Ethiopian Church history—over Judaic observances, Ethiopianism versus a wider Catholicism, the divergent traditions of Ewostatewos and Takla Haymanot—that between king and abuna is by no means the least significant, weak as an Egyptian abuna was bound to be when the king was strong. It was fortunate if, when the monarchy could offer least to the Church or to society, the abuna was still able to offer at least something.

By Ethiopianism is meant here the primacy of the national religious tradition, by Catholicism the primacy of a wider international orthodoxy whether conceived in terms of Alexandria or of Rome. The monastic House of Ewostatewos had consistently veered towards the former, that of Takla Haymanot towards the latter. In general the interests and sympathies of the abuna were inevitably with Dabra Libanos. However, whenever the monarch's sympathies were wandering Romeward, even possibly encouraged by individual monks of the Shoan tradition, the abuna had instead to range himself with the Ewostathians. The normative orthodoxy of Ethiopia was constructed by a triangular accord of emperor, abuna, and eccage, with the Ewostathians tolerated but not dominant. The triangle could be overturned by the king turning towards Rome, but also for reasons of a geopolitical kind. When the monarchy was mobile it had spent much time in Shoa. When it settled at Gondar the political power of Dabra Libanos was weakened and that of the Gojjam supporters of the Kebat strengthened. Just as the emperor's need for international support could push him in one direction, towards a Catholicism beyond that of Dabra Libanos, so his need, at a time of great weakness, for internal local support could push him toward a more nationalist theology than that of Dabra Libanos. Thus both Zara Ya'iqob in the fifteenth century and the emperors of the eighteenth, though for very different reasons, judged Ewostathian backing indispensable. Yet too large an injection of Ewostathian national deviationism could also prove in the longer run dangerously narrowing both theologically and politically: it upset the abuna and alienated Shoa. Imperial and ecclesiastical order alike required that the men of Dabra Libanos should retain the primacy which they had traditionally been accorded, but should at the same time sing 'hymns of love' with those of the House of Ewostatewos. When Takla Giyorgis and Yosab achieved a reconciliation in the Church of the Holy Fasiladas, they were struggling as best they could to save for Ethiopia one of its few remaining assets in an era of disastrous disintegration—the unity of the Church and of its principal religious traditions.

PART II

1780–1890
FROM ANTI-SLAVERY TO TOTAL SUBJUGATION

5

EQUIANO TO NTSIKANA: FROM THE 1780s TO THE 1820s

i. *London, Africa, Protestantism*

On 19 March 1783 a young Christian Igbo in his late thirties called on Granville Sharp, the anti-slavery agitator, at his London home, to bring to his attention a report of how 130 Africans had been thrown into the sea off a slave-ship for the sake of the insurance money. The Igbo was Olaudah Equiano, and Sharp in consequence began another of his campaigns to bring the perpetrators to justice. He was not successful. It was the first recorded appearance of Equiano upon the public stage.

Captured by African traders from his home village at the age of 10 and sold to British traders, he was carried across the Atlantic, first to Barbados and then to Virginia. Here a British captain took a liking to the boy, bought him, and took him to England, renaming him Gustavus Vassa. He received some education, sailed in many ships, and acquired a good deal of experience of both the West Indies and North America. He was baptized while still a boy in 1759 and later had an experience of conviction of salvation by faith in Christ alone while on a ship in Cadiz harbour in 1774. His pocket Bible, he could write, 'was my only companion and comfort'. In 1779 he had applied to the Bishop of London to be ordained and sent as a missionary to Africa, but this petition was not accepted. In the following years he emerged as a leader of London Africans, a considerable little community, and active in the struggle against slavery. It was as such that he approached Sharp in the spring of 1783.

One of Equiano's friends, Ottobah Cugoano, a Fanti with the English name of John Stuart, published in 1787 a book entitled *Thoughts and Sentiments on the Evils of Slavery*. It included the fiercest of denunciations of 'abominable, mean, beastly, cruel, bloody slavery carried on by the inhuman, barbarous Europeans against the poor unfortunate Black Africans', 'an injury and robbery contrary to all law, civilization, reason, justice, equity and charity'. Writing in a Protestant country, the author appropriately insisted that 'Protestants, as they are called, are the most barbarous slave-holders, there are none can equal the Scottish floggers and negroe-drivers, and the barbarous Dutch cruelties'.[1] This book was rapidly translated into French and appeared in Paris the following year.

Equiano and Cugoano were at once the intellectuals and the campaigners within the new African diaspora. It is true that there is some evidence that Cugoano's book may be the product in part of hands other than his own. One of them, indeed, may have been Equiano's. Two years later Equiano published a further book of his own which, while still being very much a piece of anti-slavery literature, was more naturally enthralling in being first and foremost an account of his life and adventures, including a quite lengthy description of his African childhood. There is no reason to think that Equiano did not write it. He was clearly a man of remarkable intelligence, versatility, and forcefulness, and his mastery of English is shown by letters surviving in his own hand. *The Interesting Narrative of the Life of Olaudah Equiano, or Gustavus Vassa*, as he entitled it, was indeed a very interesting book and it is not surprising that it went into eight British editions in his lifetime and ten posthumously. But Equiano's considerable contribution to the anti-slavery battle was not confined to his books and discreet interventions with Granville Sharp. He was a campaigner all over Britain, for some years travelling almost incessantly to speak and sell his book in the principal towns of the United Kingdom. Thus in 1791 he spent eight and a half months in Ireland, selling 1,900 copies of his narrative and being particularly well received in Belfast. The thought of this Igbo carrying on his campaign for the hearts and minds of the citizens of Birmingham, Manchester, and Sheffield in the late eighteenth century in favour (as he put it in a petition of 1788 addressed to the Queen) of 'millions of my fellow African countrymen, who groan under the lash of tyranny' is as impressive as the book itself. Two points may especially be noted. The first is that it was not ineffective. Equiano died before Parliament declared the trade illegal in 1807 but it only did so because opinion in the country against the trade had steadily hardened, and Equiano would appear to have been one of the abolition lobby's most persistent and convincing public speakers. It is

[1] O. Cugoano, *Thoughts and Sentiments on the Evils of Slavery* (1787), 42–3, 62, 146.

odd that his name does not appear in most accounts of the movement. The second is that Equiano represented at its most articulate a new social reality: a black, Protestant, English-speaking world which had grown up in the course of the eighteenth century on both sides of the Atlantic in the wake of the slave trade. A dozen of its leaders, 'Sons of Africa', including Equiano and Cugoano, addressed a special memorial of thanks to Granville Sharp in December 1787. They had all been given, and willingly employed, European names, but it is noticeable that both Equiano and Cugoano chose to stress their African names on the title-pages of their published works, and Cugoano remarked insistently that 'Christianity does not require that we should be deprived of our own personal name, or the name of our ancestors.'[2] They had no problem in using both. Equiano, the Igbo, could sign himself 'Gustavus Vassa, the Oppressed Ethiopian, No 53 Baldwin's Gardens', London. They appear already conscious of constituting something of a cultural, linguistic, and religious bridge. Equiano in London appears as a more articulate equivalent to Lourenço da Silva, active in Lisbon and Rome a hundred years earlier.

There were at this time far more African Protestants west of the Atlantic than east of it, but it was appropriate that Equiano and Cugoano, the most vocal among them, should be based in London. London, one may well say, was not only the capital of the empire in which most of them lived (including, until the 1780s, the North American colonies), it was just at this point becoming a sort of capital of Africa itself. And so it would remain for 150 years. Just a year after Equiano's book appeared, people in London would be avidly reading an account of the east of the continent, James Bruce's description of Ethiopia in his *Travels to Discover the Source of the Nile*. Britain was about to take control of Cape Town and its hinterland, the decisive entry point into the southern half of the continent. No European state possessed more forts along the African coast; no nation carried in its ships more African slaves across the Atlantic; nowhere else in the world was there such knowledge or such concern for Africa, a concern demonstrated by the formal establishment in 1787 of the Committee for the abolition of the slave trade. It was essentially a British, and a London-centred movement. Eight years later the London Missionary Society was founded—not precisely for Africa,

[2] Ibid. 147.

but its interests would be very considerably African and no other society would send such influential missionaries to Africa over the next half-century. Other missionary societies too, founded at this time, like the hardly less influential Church Missionary Society, were based in London.

By no means the majority of Africans carried overseas into slavery were, by the late eighteenth century, even nominal Christians. In the West Indies very few were, but in North America Christianity had been spreading fast, especially among those who had escaped from slavery, legally or illegally. The men who joined the British Forces in the war of American Independence to fight for their freedom against white colonists, who had asserted the equality of all men in their opposition to His Majesty's government in London but were not willing to extend that equality as far as black slaves, found Christianity a unifying and strengthening force. When the war was over and some of them were resettled in Nova Scotia, Christian congregations led by their own preachers were their strongest institution. Men like David George, who had been a slave in Virginia, become a Christian there, joined the British Army, and was evacuated to Nova Scotia in 1782 to become a Baptist preacher, or the blind Moses Wilkinson, also from Virginia, who became in Nova Scotia a notable Methodist preacher, were the local leaders of a new black society. Legally free, basically literate, it was a society whose Christianity was that of a tolerant Protestant sectarianism—a religion of much preaching, much hymn-singing, and a certain amount of spirit-filled enthusiasm. It was a religion which, sharing in the essentials of late eighteenth-century Evangelicalism, took the authority of the Bible wholly for granted. Equiano's portrait on the frontispiece of *An Interesting Narrative* shows him holding open the New Testament at the verse in the Acts of the Apostles by which he was vouchsafed his second conversion. The Bible had become, far more than any deed of manumission, the charter to which one could appeal for freedom and dignity. It constituted little less than the foundation document of this new society as it shaped itself the other side of slavery. The underlying sense of African unity was wholly pervasive. The experience of the middle passage was a great unifier. Some of its leaders, like Equiano and Cugoano, had been born in Africa and still knew at least something of an African language. Many others were sons of those who had been. In the late eighteenth century little distancing had been achieved from their continent of origin. The continued scale of the trade, the tens of thousands of annual new arrivals, ensured that. Yet the diversity of their origins and their languages necessitated the adoption of English as the language of this new Africa, an Africa in diaspora, a Christian and biblical Africa, an expanded Ethiopia.

ii. *West African Protestant Beginnings and the Foundation of Freetown*

African Protestant Christianity was then, by the 1780s, very much a reality. The one place it did not exist was in Africa, though even that statement requires a slight qualification. The Dutch, English, and Danish forts along the slave coast had had chaplains since the late seventeenth century, though not all of them all the time, because white mortality was exceedingly high on the coast and the job hardly an attractive one. The forts were there chiefly as depots for the slave-trade, though some had started with other kinds of trade in mind and continued to function when the slave-trade ceased. Their garrisons could in some cases include well over 100 white men but extremely few white women. Inevitably the white males had their black mistresses or common-law wives, hence a mulatto population had grown up around every fort. The function of a chaplain was to take services on a Sunday, to baptize babies (mostly mulattos), to take the frequent funeral services, and to run a small school for the children of the garrison. Occasionally the sons of a local king might join the mulatto children to learn Dutch or English at the fort school.

In all this the Protestant chaplains of the eighteenth century fulfilled a role almost exactly the same as that of their Portuguese Catholic predecessors, and they were caught within the same ambiguous situation, though doubtless many hardly noticed it. They were, indeed, chaplains not missionaries, but chaplains of institutions whose *raison d'être* was no more and no less than the wholesale buying of their fellow men and their forcible detention in loathsome circumstances in the castle's cellars before being forced on board a ship for transport in chains to America. Some of the people engaged in the trade managed to square it with their Christian consciences. They did not, they insisted, enslave people themselves. They bought slaves from other blacks in free exchange. African legal authority was most anxious that it should continue. The prosperity of a kingdom like Dahomey depended upon it. It was not the trader's business to find out why each had been enslaved, but, doubtless, in most cases for a good reason: the merciful alternative, it was claimed, to capital punishment. They had, according to most European law and opinion, a fair title to this human property. John Newton, we are assured, wrote the hymn 'How sweet the name of Jesus sounds' while captain of a slaving-ship waiting to take aboard his cargo. He was already a fervent Christian; only years later would he be converted to an equally fervent advocacy of abolition of the trade.

The first Anglican missionary to Africa, Thomas Thompson, sent out by the SPG in 1752 to live and work at Cape Coast Castle, reported an early service on the voyage out: 'Being Sunday, Captain Wilson invited several Masters of vessels which were slaving off there to come on board of him, and some English traders belonging to those parts, and I read prayers and preached to them.'[3] Thompson had personally asked to be sent to Africa, after working with black slaves in North America, yet when he got back to Britain and became a vicar in Kent he published a book entitled *The African Trade for Negro Slaves Shown to be Consistent with the Principles of Humanity and with the Laws of Revealed Religion*. His black successor at Cape Coast, Philip Quaque, who survived as a respected chaplain of the fort for fifty years, wrote that his congregation never came to Communion: 'the only plea they offer is that while they are here acting against light and conscience, they dare not come to that holy table'.[4] Whether their sexual or their commercial sins most weighed upon the conscience, we cannot, however, be certain.

Quaque was not the first black chaplain. The first African to be ordained to a Protestant ministry was Jacobus Capitein, a Fante, who was taken to Holland as a boy, entered the University of Leiden in 1737, and, after five years of study there, delivered a *Dissertatio Politico-Theologica*, denying that slavery was opposed to the gospel. He was ordained in Amsterdam and returned to a ministry in Africa where he translated into Fante the Lord's Prayer, the Articles of Belief, and the Ten Commandments, which were printed in Holland in 1744, but he died there three years later. Two others we know of were educated in Denmark and worked for a time at the Danish fort of Christenborg—Pederson Svane and Christian Protten. The latter produced a Fante grammar in 1764 and some Bible translation. It is

[3] T. Thompson, *An Account of Two Missionary Voyages by the Appointment of the Society for the Propagation of the Faith in Foreign Parts* (1758; repr. 1937), 29.
[4] M. Priestley, 'Philip Quaque of Cape Coast', in P. D. Curtin (ed.), *Africa Remembered* (1968), 116.

clear that the Protestant concern for vernacular translation was already present with these Gold Coast Fante—it was the very spearhead of their work—but it is clear too that in missionary terms they were all failures. They all had white wives and, in Capitein's case, his suggestion that he might marry a black was rejected in Holland as dangerous. They were gifted individuals, blossoming in Europe but tied in Africa to a tiny white slaving community and only serving beyond it a rather nominally Christian fringe of mulattos living in the shadow of a fort.

Even in the case of Quaque, whose ministry lasted far longer, this hardly changed. Ordained in London in 1765, his position at Cape Coast Castle was defined as that of 'Missionary, School Master, and Catechist to the Negroes on the Gold Coast' as well as 'Chaplain' to the castle. He survived for fifty years, so witnessed in old age the end of slaving within the castle. His white wife died and he married a black woman. She died and he married another. He died in 1816, a highly respected figure who had persevered in the ideal of priestly ministry he had learnt in London as a young man. As a missionary he had had little success. Nevertheless, there did come from his small school men who a generation later would be among the leaders of a struggling coastal Church. Two of them, John Martin and Joseph Smith, wrote in 1834 to the Wesleyan Missionary Society to invite it to the Gold Coast, an invitation which led to the arrival in 1838 of Thomas Birch Freeman, the father of Ghanaian Methodism. There is, then, a genuine black continuity between Quaque and the Church of a century later.

From the late 1780s Protestant Christianity would impinge upon Africa in a new and far more dynamic way. Granville Sharp, the charming, determined, but slightly eccentric protagonist of African freedom in London, was persuaded that it would be a real step forward if some of the black people in London, many of whom were penniless and in trouble, could be resettled on the coast of Africa. The 'Black Poor' of London could be transformed into a flourishing, free agricultural community, an example of the way things could be without the slave trade. There was, in Sharp's vision, to be no governor. They would rule themselves according to the ancient Anglo-Saxon principles of the Frankpledge, as understood in eighteenth-century England. The government agreed to ship them out, and a first settlement was made in this 'Province of Freedom', as Sharp liked to describe it, in 1787. The settlers were, for the most part, from among the dregs of London society with seventy white prostitutes thrown in, while the problems even a very well-managed enterprise was bound to encounter were huge. Unsurprisingly, it was not a success. Some of the settlers were quickly re-enslaved; some turned slavers; many died; quarrels with the local inhabitants mounted until in December 1789 a neighbouring ruler burnt the settlement down. Reinforcements, indeed a new start and a governor, were imperative if the whole exercise was not to be dramatically counter-productive: apparent proof of the inability of freed blacks to make good. A Sierra Leone Company was established and new settlers sought. At that point Sharp seems to have received a letter from Cugoano suggesting that there were plenty of suitable blacks in Canada, formerly British servicemen, who would like to go to Sierra Leone and might even pay their way: 'They are consisting of Different Macanicks such as Carpenters, Smiths, Masons and farmers, this are the people that we have immediate use for in the Province of freedom.'[5] Cugoano had been visited by Thomas Peters, a millwright, formerly a slave in North Carolina, then a sergeant in the Guides and Pioneers, now settled in Nova Scotia. Sharp met Peters, the directors of the Company accepted the plan, and the Treasury agreed to cover the expenses of shipping. Thomas Clarkson, a leading abolitionist and a director of the Company, had a younger brother John, a naval lieutenant, who was willing to superintend the operation and did so very well. Fifteen ships were chartered to carry 1,100 emigrants from Halifax to Sierra Leone. In January 1792 they sailed; six weeks later they arrived in Freetown and the real history of Sierra Leone began.

In Halifax, awaiting embarkation, they had been divided into companies, each with its captain, and in many cases the captains were the preachers of the Christian congregations which had formed themselves in Nova Scotia. David George, the Baptist, was one; Luke Jordan, the Methodist, another; so too were William Ash and Cato Perkins, preachers in the Countess of Huntingdon's Connection. Doubtless not all the Nova Scotian emigrants were committed Christians, but a large core of them were, so that Freetown became from its start an emphatically Christian town. It was not Christian because of its English Evangelical sponsors or on account of any missionary (at the early stage there was none), but because its African

---

[5] Cugoano, *Thoughts and Sentiments on the Evils of Slavery*, p. xxii.

leaders were already boisterously Christian on arrival. Thus in 1792 the already existing African, English-speaking, Protestant society which had come into existence in diaspora over the preceding half-century established a foothold in Africa. As the members of the Countess of Huntingdon's Connection marched ashore, they sang together one of their favourite hymns, 'Awake and sing the song of Moses and the Lamb':[6] Exodus, from the slavery of Egypt into the promised land of one's ancestors, was being renewed.

'I never met with, heard, or read of, any sort of people observing the same appearance of godliness,' wrote Mrs Falconbridge, a none-too-sympathetic observer.[7] Services, sermons, and hymns were the core element whereby the cultural identity of the new colony was to be established through a multitude of congregations and preachers which provided from the start a viable minimum of social structure which the 1787 settlers had so completely lacked. Few of the governors cared for such sectarianism, but they had little power to alter it in a land in which freedom of religion had been firmly proclaimed. Inevitably there were tensions between the Nova Scotians and the Company, the governors, and the native Temne inhabitants. In 1794 the French, at war with Britain, ransacked the tiny colony, destroying everything destroyable. In 1800 there was a small insurrection. But it survived. In 1796 a 'Remonstrance' to the Governor, signed by 128 Methodists, declared 'we cannot persuade ourselves that politics and religion have any connection, and therefore think it not for a Governor of the one to be meddling with the other'.[8] Twenty years later, when a British Methodist missionary, William Davies, had quarrelled irrevocably with the Nova Scotian Methodists he had come out to serve, he complained, 'As far as I can judge, most of our leaders are of the American Republican spirit and are strongly averse to Government. I am a loyal subject to my King, and wish to do the little I can for the support of that Government especially in a foreign part.'[9] Here we have expressed in early colonial Sierra Leone two contrary views of the relationship between Christianity and colonial power which would come back again and again in one form or another over the next 150 years: the

[6] A. F. Walls, 'A Christian Experiment: The Early Sierra Leone Colony', in G. J. Cuming (ed.), *The Mission of the Church and the Propagation of the Faith*, *SCH* vi (1970), 108.
[7] A. M. Falconbridge, *Narrative of Two Voyages to the River Sierra Leone* (1793), 201.
[8] M. Knutsford, *Life and Letters of Zachary Macaulay* (1901), 145.
[9] June 1817. Walls, 'A Christian Experiment', 126.

separation of Church and State, the missionary desire to support and be supported by government 'especially in a foreign part'. In this case both were Methodist expressions. In practice, however, they were divergent tendencies rather than contradictory polities. Almost no one could quite disconnect politics and religion for long; almost no one sought for an established Church. The Nova Scotians for the most part knew perfectly well that they needed and benefited from British rule and a general British patronage for Christianity, however little establishmentarian was the temper of their religion. They fought against the American Republicans under the British flag precisely because they shared with the Republicans a concern for freedom which now they were able to express most emphatically in the sphere of religion. And in Sierra Leone they were constitutionally free to do so, however much their governors might personally prefer a more Anglican face for the Church.

Their power to build upon and develop this highly congregational form of Christianity was limited. They lacked resources, educational and academic, and the deeper sense of a religious tradition to pass on, and, as the years went by and the original leadership who had benefited from a wide North American experience aged, they could not but feel the need for qualified assistance. Thus in 1807 a Methodist preacher, Joseph Brown, wrote most earnestly to his brethren in England requesting 'a pious person who could assist in preaching to the people, and taking the charge of our small flock . . . as I am old, my assistant, Mr Gordon, is likewise advanced in years, and there is not any suitable person being raised up here'.[10] It proved, however, too difficult to reconcile this early Freetown tradition of African independency with the authoritativeness almost inherent in the leadership of a white British minister sent from abroad, and the Methodist congregation at Rawdon Street which had appealed for help in 1807 reconstituted itself in 1821 as a Church independent of the mission which had been provided for it.

In 1807, however, a far more important development took place, the passing by the British Parliament of the bill for the abolition of the slave-trade, just twenty years after the Abolition Committee was first constituted in London and Cugoano's *Thoughts and Sentiments on the Evil of Slavery* had been published there. It was, despite the delay (in large part due to the counter-effect of the French Revolution and

---

[10] *Methodist Magazine* (1807), 203–4.

the war), an impressive achievement, going as it did against the undoubted economic interests of Britain and a powerful interested lobby of planters and merchants. It legally placed the interests of public morality above profit and market forces. It was in no way at the time a necessary achievement. It was managed by the combination of an efficient 'moderate' leadership, at once religious and political, with a nation-wide public opinion produced by a great deal of campaigning. The sustained parliamentary spokesmanship of the morally impeccable Tory Wilberforce, personal friend for so many years of the Prime Minister, was invaluable, though the true architects of abolition were Granville Sharp and Thomas Clarkson, not Wilberforce. A cause which in the early 1780s still seemed eccentric was rendered respectable by the underlying support of the two greatest parliamentarians of the age—Pitt and Fox—and by its coherence with the best in contemporary thought, philosophical and religious. It would certainly not have been carried through without very powerful religious convictions at work which, starting from the Quakers, took hold of an exceptionally able group of upper-class Anglican Evangelicals, but it was by no means an inevitable consequence of the Evangelical Movement, and indeed its movers, Sharp and Clarkson, were far from typical Evangelicals. In America Evangelicalism brought no comparable conclusion. In Holland and France religion remained little affected by such concerns. Only in England did things take this course at the start of the nineteenth century, and it seems hard to deny that it was due to the persevering commitment to the abolitionist cause of a quite small group of men whose separate abilities and positions were knitted together to form a lobby of exceptional effectiveness.

Its effects upon Sierra Leone were to be momentous. The Act of Parliament sanctioned the stationing off the West African coast of ships of the Royal Navy charged with the interception of slavers. It was agreed that the cargo should be landed at Freetown, thus giving the tiny colony a new *raison d'être*. It badly needed one. The Sierra Leone Company's original aim of establishing a thriving settlement on the shores of Africa which would demonstrate by the success of legitimate commerce the economic pointlessness of the trade in slaves had wholly failed. The Company had never made any profits and its resources were exhausted. The British government had needed to subsidize it increasingly heavily just to keep Sierra Leone going at all. The unanticipated circumstances of a long war with France had destroyed any chance of realizing the original commercial aim, but there was, and long remained, only one really profitable trade on the West African coast and that was the slave trade, though a worthwhile timber trade was beginning to develop at this time. Inhabitants of Freetown, black as well as white, often abandoned the town, whose economy was negligible, to set up elsewhere along the coast as profit-making slavers.

From 1 January 1808 Sierra Leone became a Crown Colony, the authority of the Company being taken over by Parliament. It had a mere 2,000 inhabitants, the survivors and offspring of various groups of settlers brought there from Britain, Canada, or the West Indies. Reformers and parliamentarians in England had thought little about the consequences of intercepting slave ships or what to do with their liberated cargo. They will not have imagined how many they soon would be. Certainly the blockade was far from fully effective; indeed the majority of slavers—in southern waters the vast majority— evaded capture, and the total number of slaves reaching the Americas in the first half of the nineteenth century was not so much less than the total number in the second half of the eighteenth. Not until the middle of the century was the trade effectively crippled, and only in 1864 was the last load of a captured ship landed in Freetown. Nevertheless, if many still got through, many were captured, and Sierra Leone was transformed as a result. By 1814 there were 10,000 'recaptives', Liberated Africans, in the colony, more than three-fifths of the total population. With the ending of the Napoleonic War the trade increased and recaptives reaching Sierra Leone could number 3,000 a year. The original idea that they be apprenticed to existing citizens or enlisted in the army could never work with many of the people arriving, women above all, but the numbers were anyway far too great. Subsidized for years by the British government, most inevitably settled, officially or unofficially, in villages beyond the town. Naturally they tended to do so by language group.

The Liberated Africans, unlike the Nova Scotians, had no previous experience of anything western, no knowledge of the English language or Christianity. A few were Muslim. The rest possessed the traditional religion, the culture, the language, the technology of their ancestors. But, dragged away from their homes and unable to return there, dropped instead into a strange but fairly friendly world, they were extremely docile. If they had simply been left to their own resources, Sierra Leone would have returned quickly enough to being almost indistinguishable from any other society up and down the coast. That was far from the intention of those who had first set up the colony and who still remained highly influential in its development. Britain had at this time no desire to extend its rule in Africa and there was certainly little profit to be had in doing so, but it was not willing either to renege upon the original intention of establishing Freetown or upon its responsibilities, as it saw them, to the captives its Navy had freed. Good intentions, however, were seldom matched by the provision of enough money for the government of Sierra Leone to embark on and adhere to a workable policy. Moreover, the very heavy death-rate among whites on the coast in this period—prior to the fairly regular use of quinine, which began about the mid-1840s—made it almost impossible, quite apart from money, to remain there long enough to adhere to any policy and make something of it.

The one great exception was Sir Charles MacCarthy, Governor (at first Lieutenant-Governor) from 1814 until 1824. His governorship ended when he was beheaded in an unsuccessful war with the Ashanti, having had the British Gold Coast forts added to his jurisdiction. It was he who faced the problem of the Liberated Africans and even persuaded Whitehall for a few years to provide him with adequate finance to do so. A series of officially recognized villages were established in the peninsula behind Freetown from Leicester, Wilberforce, and Regent to Wellington, Hastings, and Waterloo. Each, as he envisaged it, would be a 'parish', an administrative unit centred upon church and school. Divided into parishes the newly arrived would be civilized, Anglicized, Christianized. Correctly he recognized that this sort of a task was wholly beyond the Christian congregations of Freetown. But he did not care for their sort of Christianity anyway. Despite his French, Irish, and Roman Catholic background, MacCarthy was wholly a 'Church and State' man and it was to the established Church of England and its latest missionary society that he turned for collaborators.

There had already been missionaries in Sierra Leone, if not very successful ones, sent by the London Missionary Society and the Church Missionary Society. But their principal aim had been to get beyond the colony to convert the heathen. The CMS had been recruiting a stream of Germans to evangelize the Susu, but no field was proving less profitable: semi-Muslim societies ridden with the slave-trade and malaria. MacCarthy was insistent that the CMS give up its pointless mission to the Susu and concentrate instead on civilizing and Christianizing the recaptives so as to turn Sierra Leone into an orderly Anglican society. The CMS sent out Edward Bickersteth in 1816 to inspect, and he agreed with MacCarthy. They would take over the management of the villages. In England at that time many a vicar was also a JP. MacCarthy's plan to unify religious and civil functions was not so extraordinary for the age. Nor indeed for Africa. 'It is nearly impossible', he wrote, 'for a clergyman residing in the mountains with Captured Negroes to do much good, unless to that character he unites that of Magistrate and Superintendent:—by the authority of the two latter offices he can keep the uncivilized in due order and reward the industry of the well behaved.'[11]

It was an imaginative scheme, perhaps the best possible in the circumstances, and he received a few missionaries who for a few years made it more or less work. William Johnson at Regent and Henry During at Gloucester were particularly successful in achieving, in MacCarthy's judgement, 'progress in civilization'. Regent under Johnson became a model of 'neatness, regularity, order and industry'. While the sects in Freetown divided the people religiously (though seldom acrimoniously), MacCarthy's ideal for the Liberated Africans was to be a unified Church most closely linked to the State. It worked and it did not work. It set the first generation of recaptives in a certain direction and helped ensure that their appropriate culture, as much as that of the Nova Scotians, should be Christian and anglophone. The bewildered boatloads of freed Africans drawn from all along the coast and now discharged here certainly needed to receive some sort of leadership. So close a linking of the civil with the religious, if it was incongruous to early nineteenth-century liberals or to Nova Scotians nourished on Evangelical sectarianism, was natural enough to Africans themselves. But it could hardly last. Some missionaries were quite unable to carry such responsibilities; the CMS simply did not have enough men to send, and neither it nor the government was willing to go on for long spending the money required. Johnson wrote home in 1822 that the colony needed at least twenty-seven more missionaries and teachers. Two years later MacCarthy was dead and the CMS withdrew from its agreement. Henceforth the recaptives would be left far more to make their own

[11] 1819. J. Peterson, *Province of Freedom* (1969), 97.

arrangements, and they would, doubtless, prefer it. Johnson's Regent, repeated in various forms again and again in nineteenth-century missionary Africa, with or without the backing of colonial authority, would be a model: the village or plantation centred on church and school in which the missionary endeavoured to Christianize and civilize more or less benignly, more or less compulsorily, not only spiritual guide but mini-chief, not only instructing but punishing the inhabitants of his little world. Africans often had much to gain in the short run from inhabiting such places—security, food, and instruction. But they seldom put up with it for very long unless conditions outside the mission village were very unattractive indeed, while missionaries sooner or later came to realize that the Christianity of such enclaves mostly left too much to be desired in the matter of conviction.

In Sierra Leone it hardly outlasted MacCarthy, but the importance of the CMS presence did. If the Nova Scotians were characteristically sectarian, the Liberated Africans were largely Anglican, benefiting especially from the educational facilities, culminating in Fourah Bay College, which the CMS came to provide. But if recaptive Christianity was distinguishable from that of the Nova Scotians— just as their society remained somewhat apart—they did none the less owe a great deal to the first settlers, into whose inheritance they had entered. They took over and made their own the experience of a confident, internally free society, predominantly Christian and English-speaking, while ensuring that Freetown would not remain—as it otherwise would have done—a post-American ghetto isolated from the rest of Africa.

A young Yoruba boy named Adjai was among the slaves landed in 1822. He was settled in Bathurst village. Baptized and renamed Samuel Crowther, he would soon become a teacher at Bathurst and then at Regent, a priest in 1843, a bishop in 1864. Others became Methodists. As Anglican or as Methodist, they would carry the Afro-Christian confidence of the first Freetown settlers into a rather more structured, more educated, more mission-connected form of religion. In white eyes, Sierra Leone was not proving a great success. Economically and politically it remained a mess, neither profitable nor very well governed. But in black eyes it was very much a success, a land in which there was a lot of black freedom and some relative black prosperity. It was a land to which missionaries had made a rather limited contribution but which, all the more, was beginning

by the 1820s to look like a possible Christian bridgehead within
Africa. After only thirty years it was really surprisingly secure but also
increasingly open, through the annual intake of recaptives, to the
total stretch of the west coast.

iii. *The Advance of Islam*

It would be gravely mistaken to think of the little Christian colony of
Sierra Leone, interesting as it was proving to be by the 1820s, as the
most important religious development in West Africa in this period.
It is entirely overshadowed by what was going on in the great Muslim
communities of the interior to the north and east of it. To these
developments we must now turn briefly, because a history of
Christianity in Africa can be but part of the wider religious history
upon which it is in many ways dependent. Christian developments in
the nineteenth century and the shaping of a Christian geography of
Africa were greatly controlled by the presence or absence in any area
of Islam. In some places the prior presence of Islam was such as either
to exclude Christianity entirely or to restrain it within very modest
dimensions. In many others Islam was present in a minority role and
the arrival of Christianity in the same area could both restrict the
advance of Islam and generate competition and conflict. It could,
again, even make conversion to Christianity actually easier, in that it
had prepared the way both socially and linguistically for the
acceptance of a book monotheism. While the relationship of Islam
to traditional religion and custom was not identical with that of
Christianity, they did have a good deal in common. The relationship
of the one can most certainly throw light, through both similarities
and dissimilarities, upon that of the other. Above all it is necessary to
insist that Christian history did not develop within an otherwise static
religious context. This is true of traditional religion itself, which
could change in ways significant for the shaping of Christian history,
but it is far truer of Islam, which was in Africa in the nineteenth
century a religion in movement, both externally expansive and
internally reformist.

While the centre of Islam did not lie within Africa, it did not lie far
outside it either. The cult and pilgrimage centre of Mecca, the
academic centre of Cairo, were both accessible to many Africans in
the eighteenth and early nineteenth centuries far more than were the
Christian centres of western Europe. You could, and did, go to them

under your own steam. There was a worthwhile degree of continuity in language and culture between the Arab world and the heart of West Africa, a continuity which had been forged by many centuries of contact. There were plenty of black Muslim scholars who could read and write Arabic, who had made the hajj and were anxious as recognized participants within the Islamic community both to apply its traditional norms more firmly and to introduce its more recent Sufi devotional practice within their homeland.

The eighteenth and early nineteenth century was a period in which Islam as a whole was in deep trouble. For a thousand years it had advanced largely through its political and military cohesiveness, conquering land after land in the Middle East, Europe, Asia, and Africa, but spreading also through trade and a certain civilizing mission, carrying with it literacy and a sense of universalism. All of this was now under massive challenge. For the very first time Christian Europe was undeniably its master in terms of worldly power—military might, industrial productivity, commercial expansion, and cultural self-confidence. The Turkish Empire, still a huge threat to the Christian heartlands of central Europe in the middle of the seventeenth century, now survived in large part because Europe could see no acceptable alternative. Egypt was conquered for a while by France. India was falling to the control of Britain, North Africa would soon be falling to that of France. The impact of all this upon Muslim consciousness stimulated the upsurge of various movements of religious and spiritual reform—in Arabia the fundamentalism of the Wahhabis, elsewhere a resurgence of old Sufi orders and the beginning of a new one, the Tijaniyya, which spread rapidly through Africa. In political terms religious revivalism could not affect the decay of Islamic power around the Mediterranean or in the Indian subcontinent when caught within the grip of the new European commercial and military supremacy. It can happen, nevertheless, that when a religious regime is in some way decaying at its centre, unable to cope with contemporary secular circumstances or an alternative spiritual system, it may all the more expand aggressively at some points on its circumference in areas of little resistance, almost as a reaction to its central impotence. Such could be in part the explanation for the manifest and vigorous expansion of Islam in Africa in the first half of the nineteenth century, particularly through the zeal of the Sufi brotherhoods.

This expansion owed most to a single people, the Fulani, a group of erstwhile pastoralists who had derived centuries before from the middle Senegal valley but had since spread across much of the interior of West Africa to settle in the midst of other peoples. A large part of the Fulani early embraced Islam, one of the first black peoples of Africa to do so, and subsequently they had come to stand as a group for a purer and more literate form of Islam than that of most of the peoples and kingdoms amongst whom they dwelt. By the eighteenth century the majority, but not all, of the kingdoms of the sub-Saharan interior were nominally Islamic, but it was an Islam of a very mixed kind, coalescing tolerantly with a great deal of African religion and custom. After the collapse of the empire of Songhay at the close of the sixteenth century, there was no major state, only a multitude of small ones whose kings had no desire to alter the status quo, enforce the *shari'a*, or put any pressure upon their pagan subjects to convert. This appears the same situation as al-Maghili had already protested against at the start of the sixteenth century. The kings of the time, the Hausa kings above all, had not cared to act upon his protests. Nor were their successors any keener to do so when faced with similar protests three centuries later. Nevertheless, in the meantime much had changed beneath the surface: the proportion of Muslims of one sort or another within the population had increased, as had the size of the minority anxious to enforce a purer form of Islam. What had been unrealistic in the time of al-Maghili was now achievable.

Again and again, in one little state or another, there had been attempts, jihads, forcibly to replace 'mixed Islam' by 'the whole Sunna', to set up the truth by both the sword and education. In the eighteenth century jihads took place in the far west in Futa Jalon (north-east of Sierra Leone) around 1725 and in Futa Toro (north-east of Dakar) around 1775. Of only local importance, they were nevertheless significant signs of the consolidation in depth of Islam under Fulani leadership.

The Hausa kingdoms lay more than a thousand miles east of Futa Jalon and Futa Toro. Here in the kingdom of Gobir near where Sokoto now stands, the Shehu Usuman dan Fodio was born in 1754 of a scholarly Fulani family. Strangely, he never made the hajj. A scholar and a zealot, though not the most rigid of extremists, he was early convinced that he had a personal mission to reform Islam as the *mujaddid* of his age, 'the Renewer of Faith' whom God is expected to send once in every hundred years. He preached, he wrote in both

Arabic and Hausa, he called upon the King of Gobir to enforce the *shari'a*. In a series of visions beginning in 1789 his sense of destiny was continually reinforced until he was finally presented with 'the Sword of Truth', to 'unsheathe it against the enemies of God'.[12] That was 1794. But it was only ten years later, in 1804, when 50 years old, that the Shehu finally withdrew from Gobir, re-enacting the hegira, in order to begin the jihad of revolution. He was now at the head of a committed army of Fulani Muslim purists and in four years they overthrew, not only the kingdom of Gobir, but all the neighbouring Hausa states such as Kano, Zaria, and Nupe, creating a Fulani-ruled society of emirates unified under Usuman dan Fodio as Caliph of the newly created city of Sokoto.

While the jihad of dan Fodio was directed primarily against the complacent 'mixed Islam' of the Hausa kings to impose at long last the rulings of al-Maghili, who had much influenced the thinking of the Shehu as to the necessity for the enforcement of the *shari'a*, it did in fact extend the frontiers of Muslim hegemony, creating further areas of 'mixed Islam' around it. This was still more the case with the later jihads of Ahmad bin Muhammad (beginning after 1810) in Masina and al-Hajj Umar bin Said (or Umar Tal) on the upper Niger after 1853. Umar Tal carried the war against the still-pagan Bambara. Both were influenced by the tradition of dan Fodio, carried on by his son and successor the Sultan Muhammad Bello, but al-Hajj Umar had been years abroad and was deeply influenced too by his time in Mecca and Cairo, where he had joined the Tijaniyya. There were considerable differences both of spirituality and of method between Usuman dan Fodio and Umar Tal, and the wars of the latter were far longer and bloodier than those of the former. Despite the violence, in both men a life of scholarship and sense of special personal calling to be a divinely appointed *mujaddid* came first. But in each too it led on to 'the struggle of the sword' and a ruthless disregard of the rights of any but the fully faithful. Umar Tal's well-known work the *Rimah* was entitled in full 'The Lance of the Party of the Compassionate (God) at the Throats of the Satanic Party'. For each of these men visions during prayer and fasts and the expectation that the Mahdi would not be long in coming led to a fierce determination to overthrow the satanic party, worldly half-Muslim rulers especially, so

[12] M. Hiskett, *The Sword of Truth: The Life and Times of the Shehu Usuman Dan Fodio* (1973).

as to replace it with some form of purer theocracy committed to the enforcement of the *shari'a*.

Undoubtedly, the strength of Islam in West Africa was much enhanced by these movements, the consequence of which was also to extend the Muslim presence southwards towards the coast. Thus Ilorin, south of the Niger and formerly a dependency of Oyo, became a Fulani emirate after a jihad in 1817. Yorubaland had been entered by force in Ilorin but already through commerce elsewhere. Of course, the literature of each jihad affirmed its effectiveness. Such is the nature of most religiously committed literature. Yet Africa is a perennial witness of religious reform movements, as much as political reform movements, which flow across a tolerant continent and slowly die of their own inability to change human nature. Futa Toro was converted into an Islamic state from paganism in a jihad in the late seventeenth century. It was reconverted by another jihad in the late eighteenth century. In 1853 Umar Tal's jihad began with a hegira, a withdrawal to Dinguiray from 'the territory of unbelief', and that territory was once more Futa Toro. Mixed Islam is not easily annihilated. Nevertheless, the importance of the early nineteenth-century jihads for the consolidation of Islam over wide areas by both the enforcement of law and the strengthening of the Sufi orders was very great.

The story was always written in purely religious terms and the modern historian cannot easily, without seeming tendentious, transform it into another idiom. Yet it is no less clear that the effect of the jihads, especially that of Usuman dan Fodio, was to establish the rule of a Fulani minority over the native inhabitants, Hausa or otherwise, and to create the most powerful state in sub-Saharan Africa. The pattern of a 'pastoralist' minority ruling over an agricultural majority is frequently to be found in Africa in circumstances quite unconnected with jihad or Islam, and the religious dimension of the Fulani conquest should not be allowed to obscure, as it often does, the alternative side of what really happened. It was the unity of the Fulani people, their sense of purpose heightened by Islamic righteousness, which enabled them to triumph so strikingly over the many petty kings of Hausadom and establish the hegemony of their own race. The Fulani order which resulted proved remarkably stable. It was a society with more slaves than freemen in its cities, a society whose chiefs were models of Islamic polygamy, just as their predecessors had mostly been models of traditional polygamy: dan Fodio had thirty-seven children, his son Bello seventy-three. While their wives were mostly Fulani, their concubines were not. But the status of the children was not different. The Fulani–Hausa divide was thus not accentuated, while the remarkable development of an Islamic Fulfulde and Hausa literature, something rather unusual in African Islam, contributed greatly to strengthen its popular character. Those who could understand Arabic would remain the leisured few, yet the presence of an ongoing local tradition of Arabic scholarship was no less important.

There could seem little reason in 1820 to question that the religion of Sokoto and Ilorin, Harar and Zanzibar was destined to become the religion of almost the whole of black Africa in the course of the next century or so. In the west it was beginning to enter Ashanti and Dahomey as well as the Yoruba states. The roots now went very deep south of the Sahara as well as on the east coast, while the outward growth was gathering momentum. In the east a Swahili Muslim literature was developing, comparable to that of the Hausa, while in the wake of the slave-trade, managed in the east from Zanzibar and servicing Arabia, Islam was penetrating the interior. Even in Cape Town in 1820 there were 1,326 Muslim slaves counted, probably ten times the number of Christian slaves. Overwhelmingly the impression that a careful observer would have gained of the Africa of 1820 was that Islam was substantially a missionary religion, and an effective one, while Christianity was not. The white Protestant presence in Cape Town for a century and a half had led to no significant advance beyond the ranks of the settlers. The ancient Christianity of Ethiopia had never been communicated to anyone well beyond its own borders and it had allowed its Christian neighbour, Nubia, to fade away unassisted. The Catholic missionary effort from the sixteenth to the eighteenth century had been considerable in scale and often personally heroic, but it had been remarkably ineffectual. It had now, anyway, almost entirely disappeared. A handful of Protestant missionaries was beginning to make its impact in south and west, but there was no large-scale missionary *élan* in Africa in 1820 and, still more, no response in depth of its inhabitants to compare with the onward march of Islam on almost every side of the continent. It was a march assisted by the sword but not confined to the sword, a march in education, learning, and devotion, a march which was above all one of Africans themselves: it might be inspired by what was seen in Cairo or Mecca, but it was in no way controlled from anywhere outside black Africa.

iv. *Kongo Christianity under Garcia V*

In one place at least Christian missionaries were almost desperately wanted. After the departure of Cherubino da Savona in 1774 no Capuchin ever again exercised a settled ministry in the Kongo. From time to time priests from Angola continued to visit the kingdom for fairly extensive periods, but the continuity of missionary experience and language skills, in so far as it had existed, was lost. A black secular priest from Brazil, Fr. Godinho, lived in the country together, at least initially, with three Portuguese Franciscans for seven years between 1781 and 1788. Like many of their predecessors they were struck by the initial fervour of their popular reception, the processions of children chanting their prayers, the continued work of the *maestri*. What they were chiefly called upon to do, however, was to baptize, which they did 380,000 times, so the total size of the intentionally Christian community was still considerable and stretched far beyond São Salvador, where hardly more than 1,000 people can have lived. Five years later another Capuchin, Raimondo da Dicomano, was at São Salvador for two and a half years around 1793, and a few years after that Serafino d'Acqui visited Soyo, the last Capuchin to do so.

None of this is surprising, neither Kongolese tenacity in their kind of Christianity nor the missionary collapse. There were 100 priests in the diocese of Angola in 1760, hardly thirty by the beginning of the nineteenth century, and just five by the 1850s. The expulsion of the Jesuits in 1761 by the Marquis de Pombal, Portugal's anticlerical chief minister, and the dissolution of the entire Society of Jesus by Pope Clement XIV in 1773 were the first blows to the Catholic missionary effort. Still more serious was the French Revolution and its ecclesiastical consequences. Religious houses were closed in France and then in other parts of Europe, such as Italy and the Low Countries, overrun by the revolutionary armies. The Papal States were abolished, Pius VI died a prisoner in France in 1799 and his successor Pius VII was also in prison and exile for many years. The Congregation of Propaganda Fide for a time ceased to function, dissolved by Napoleon in 1809. The Napoleonic invasion of Spain and Portugal and the long Peninsular War disrupted that side of the Church too and the King of Portugal retreated to Brazil. In such circumstances, with much of Europe involved in war for nearly a quarter of a century, it is not surprising if the already tenuous Catholic missionary presence in Kongo, Angola, and elsewhere deteriorated into next to nothing. The vast pool of European religious almost disappeared while the structures of ecclesiastical command lay in fragments. After the peace of Vienna in 1815 it would take years before the Catholic Church returned to institutional normality.

Garcia V was King of the Kongo from 1803 to 1830. Few Kongolese kings lasted as long and Garcia was throughout as anxious as any of his predecessors for a missionary presence, first and foremost, to authenticate his own authority by carrying out the rituals of coronation and the blessing of his marriage. Sacerdotal sanctioning of royalty remained as desirable as ever, but he had to wait for it a long time. Only in 1814 was the Prefect of the Capuchins in Loanda, Luigi–Maria d'Assisi, able to spend eight months in the Kongo: 25,000 people were baptized, 5,000 came to confession, while King Garcia and Queen Isabella were solemnly married and crowned on 17 March. The delighted King wrote a letter to 'his brother, the King of Portugal', just as Afonso I had learned to do, to express his gratitude and suggest that he ask the Pope to make Luigi–Maria a cardinal. There had been no priest at São Salvador for twenty years since the departure of Fr. Raimondo, so there was cause for rejoicing. Luigi–Maria's visit was followed by another, by Pietro da Bene, five years later. He was welcomed as warmly.

In 1803 the King had sent his nephew, Afonso, to be educated in Loanda. In 1809 he also sent a son, Dom Pedro. The Portuguese Governor looked after them and sent reports on their progress in learning and behaviour. Afonso's reports were not favourable, and, as there was anyway at the time no bishop in Loanda able to take responsibility for their clerical advancement, the Governor returned them to São Salvador in 1813. Garcia, however, insisted that he must have a priest in the family, at least one Kongolese to maintain the Church of the kingdom, so Pedro returned to Loanda in 1818 and was ordained a priest in 1824. Thus the nineteenth century starts, like the sixteenth, with a devout and long-lived king of the Kongo in regular correspondence with the Portuguese authorities and with his son a priest. The persevering determination of Kongolese Catholicism to adhere to the original model appears extraordinary.

Yet in reality Garcia was king of a tiny area in comparison with Afonso. He had still a few trappings of the ancient tradition, a couple of secretaries to write his letters, and a considerable sense of history, but the power and customs of the kingdom as described in the reports of the missionaries were now hardly different from those of thousands of other African mini-states. Little really was expected of the occasional priest visitor other than baptism and coronation, and, as the Capuchins themselves no longer knew Kikongo nor were able to draw on the experience of the past, there was little more they could provide in their occasional visitations.

Garcia V died in 1830 and, one last time, a Capuchin went to São Salvador to conduct the funeral ceremonies. In the anarchy which ensued he was unable to crown a successor. Even that seems symbolic. The mission ended with the funeral of a king not wholly unlike the one who had established the whole tradition. The Capuchin, Bernardo da Burgio, returned to Loanda accompanied by a Kongolese lay brother to find his last European colleague dead. Both the kingdom and the Capuchins were passing away. Dom Pedro, Garcia's priest son, himself abandoned the Kongo for employment in Angola. Here too there was now no bishop (from 1826 to 1852) and fewer than a score of priests. Both Italian diocesan priests from Milan and a group of Swiss Benedictines offered in this period to serve in the Kongo to resurrect its Church. The image of a Catholic Kongo, an independent African Christian kingdom, had not been forgotten in Europe, and it could still stir an outburst of missionary fervour, but in each case the plans came to nothing, due to Capuchin and Portuguese intransigence. Then in 1834 a new anticlerical government came to power in Lisbon and all convents were ordered to be closed. The goods of the Capuchins were promptly sold and Bernardo da Burgio left Angola in May 1835, taking with him to a convent in Palermo the archives of the mission and the Kongolese lay brother, now his sole companion, Bernardo of São Salvador. As Brother Bernardo stepped on to the boat and sailed away to Europe, a tiny rump of Christianity was still obstinately struggling to survive around his birthplace, but a long missionary era, which had already run out of steam at least sixty years earlier, had come at last to its formal term.

v. *South Africa: Genadendal, Bethelsdorp, and Kuruman*

The year 1792 was something of an 'annus mirabilis' for Protestant missionary history. It was the year in which William Carey, a Northamptonshire cobbler, published *An Enquiry into the Obligation of Christians to Use Means for the Conversion of the Heathen* and in which, in consequence, the Baptist Missionary Society was founded, first of the modern missionary societies. Some nine months after the Nova Scotians had landed at Freetown another cobbler, a tailor, and a cutler landed at Cape Town and on Christmas Eve of 1792 they arrived at a place called Baviaanskloof to begin a mission to the native peoples of southern Africa. The tailor was Dutch, his companions German. They were by denomination Moravian and they chose this particular place for their work because in fact they had had a predecessor.

Fifty years earlier a lone Moravian named Georg Schmidt had attempted for a few years to found a mission at this spot to the Khoikhoi or 'Hottentots' as they were generally called by Europeans. He had received financial help from no one. He helped the Khoikhoi with their farming, planting vegetables and fruit trees. He even baptized a few of the people who had listened to his teaching, in a nearby stream. That caused trouble. He had no authority to baptize, protested the Dutch Predikants, who were still more shocked to learn that, though he arrived at Cape Town a layman, he had since been ordained by post. Schmidt was not expelled, but he felt too painfully the suspicions of the white community and, lonely and depressed, returned to Europe in 1744. Only in 1792 were the Moravians permitted to replace him. To their astonishment our three friends found at Baviaanskloof, still alive, the last of Schmidt's converts, old Lena, treasuring the Dutch New Testament, wrapped in a sheepskin, that Schmidt had given her. She had cooked for him, but a Christian memory had been preserved by others too, as memories are preserved in Africa, in its way as remarkably by this unstructured group as over long priestless years in the Kongo. Among those soon baptized by Marsveld, Schwinn, and Kühnel were a number of descendants of men and women baptized by Schmidt a half-century earlier.

The Moravians were themselves a tiny group of continental pietists, influential out of all proportion to their numbers. In the eighteenth century they constituted something of an avant-garde for a new Protestant spiritual and missionary consciousness. John Wesley experienced his 'conversion' in Aldersgate Street when his heart was 'strangely warmed' after encountering the Moravians and visiting their centre at Herrnhut. It was just five years before Lena's conversion. The Moravian spirit was very different from that of the rather rigid and legalistic Dutch Reformed Church, which was not only the Cape's State Church but (until in 1780 a Lutheran presence was tolerated) the only Church. Yet here too things were changing a little, and the Moravians of 1792 received more of a welcome and ongoing support in their missionary endeavour than had Schmidt. Nevertheless, they also faced white opposition, especially from local farmers, who saw the men they wanted to work for them decamp to Baviaanskloof.

The Moravian trio were devout but practical men. In 1798 they were joined by a hatter and his wife, and the other three received wives from Europe as well, so there was quite a little white colony to order and teach their black brethren. Soon there were over 1,200 people living around the mission, which, a little later, was renamed Genadendal. It was a happy community, brotherly, rectangular in its layout, a place for spiritual ministration and regular praying in their steadily enlarged church, but also for 'paternal order' and efficient work. At 5.30 every morning a bell called the inhabitants to church, school, and industry. There was a monastic note about it. Besides the farm work the missionary artisans had each their apprentices, while their wives were also busy teaching skills to the women and girls. It was a voluntary community with an unworldly gospel which only those could join who seriously intended to become Christians. For 'Hottentots' and Coloured, mostly by this time landless and frequently ill-used by the white farmers, who treated them little differently from slaves, Genadendal had obvious worldly attractions too: dignity, stability, a modest degree of prosperity, the opportunity to learn.

The Moravians were not unaware of the injustices which non-whites suffered throughout the Cape, but being of a Lutheran and quietist temperament they did not see it as their task to make public protest or to concern themselves with anyone other than the inhabitants of Genadendal. Their mission was with the maintenance of a small enclave of Christian faith and spiritual freedom rather than with the conversion of the many or the redress of social ills. Very different was another Dutch missionary who arrived at the Cape in 1799. Johannes Van der Kemp was not only one of the pioneers in the Protestant missionary movement, he might also be claimed as the most remarkable ever to set out. When young he had been a fashionable dragoon officer and a womanizer, but after marriage he left the army and studied philosophy and medicine at Edinburgh, publishing works of originality in both fields. In 1791 he lost his wife and daughter in a sailing disaster on the Meuse and this led to a conversion back to the Christianity he had abandoned years before. Shortly afterwards, in 1792, he visited a Moravian community and his mind began to move in a missionary direction.

From the Moravians he heard of the founding of the London Missionary Society and resolved to offer himself to it for service abroad. So distinguished a recruit was warmly welcomed. Britain had occupied the Cape in 1795 when France conquered Holland. The British authorities were rather more open to missionary activities than had been the Dutch. Moreover, there was some local missionary interest among Cape people. Van der Kemp, as a Dutchman in the service of the London Missionary Society, could seem an ideal choice to pioneer a new mission in these circumstances. However, his eccentric life-style, his habitual outspokenness, his horror to find that in Cape Town there were thousands of slaves (in fact over two-thirds of the whole population), his quick conviction that both the slaves (who had been imported) and the local 'Hottentots' or Khoikhoi were gravely ill-treated meant that, while he was often revered, he was also increasingly disliked by both the colonial authorities and up-country farmers as a religious fanatic and intolerable nuisance.

His initial mission, however, was not to the inhabitants of the colony but to the Xhosa who lived beyond its eastern frontier, while two of his colleagues went north to evangelize the Bushmen. Neither mission lasted long or appeared successful. In this they were like a number of others to uncolonized people in this period when the missionaries had no books on African languages to turn to, no advance knowledge of the customs and religion of the people, and little of any recognizable worldly value to offer to prospective converts. As Mrs Falconbridge scathingly remarked of one LMS man preaching to a congregation of natives near Freetown: 'How preposterous! Is it possible a sensible man, like Mr Horne, can suppose it in his power to imprint notions of Christianity, or any sort of instruction, upon the minds of people, through the bare medium of a language they do not understand?'[13]

A mission to the peregrinatory Bushmen, hunters and gatherers for

---

[13] Falconbridge, *Narrative of Two Voyages to the River Sierra Leone*, (1793) 199–200.

the most part, could only conceivably be successful with a quite extraordinary degree of imaginativeness, a quality Van der Kemp's colleagues certainly lacked. Van der Kemp himself was by no means short of that quality, but he came to the Xhosa in a state of war and grave unsettlement. Many Khoikhoi, and even a few disgruntled whites, had taken up residence at the Great Place of King Ngqika, increasing the threat to the colonial government. In his fifteen months among the Xhosa, Van der Kemp's only baptized convert was a Hottentot woman, a wife of one of the temporary refugees. He could instruct her in Dutch. It is striking how his approach to one person of quite low social status was as serious and as lasting as if her conversion might be the key to a whole community. But he set himself at once to master the Xhosa language and put together both an elementary grammar and a word list, *Specimen and Vocabulary of the Caffree Language*, divided into twenty-one classes. He did his best, not wholly unsuccessfully, to gain Ngqika's confidence, and he developed a reputation as a rainmaker. His companion, Edmonds, abandoned him after just three months: the conditions were too hard and Edmonds decided that his mission lay, instead, in Bengal. After fifteen months Van der Kemp left too. The refugees from the colony were leaving and they constituted the only congregation he had. In their condition of acute unsettlement it seemed hopeless to expect the Xhosa to pay him much attention.

Was his mission to the Xhosa, then, a failure? Sixteen years later, after Van der Kemp's death, when two LMS missionaries again visited Ngqika, he confessed that he still thought of Van der Kemp a lot and now felt ashamed that he had scorned the word of God as preached by him. Maybe that was just diplomacy, but there is no doubt that 'Jank'hanna' (or Nyengana)—as the Xhosa called him—had made an irremovable impression. The tradition is that both Nxele and Ntsikana, prophetic leaders of the next generation, had listened to Jank'hanna in their youth. Three generations later Eugene Casalis, one of the pioneer French missionaries in Basutoland, would write 'up to this hour, in all parts occupied by the Caffres and their immediate neighbours, the many natives who have embraced Christianity are frequently called 'Ma-Yankana'—the 'people of Van der Kemp'.[14] What an impact does that suggest!

In missionary, as in all religious history, the impact of the saint, the

[14] E. M. Casalis, *My Life in Basutoland* (1889), 105.

truly charismatic individual, the prophet, is something of primary rather than marginal weight. That should perhaps be self-evidently the case in any examination of the tradition of Jesus of Nazareth. What made Van der Kemp so different, not from all other missionaries, but from most of them? Four characteristics stand out. First he was seen as a man of God, of spiritual power, of prayer, a rainmaker. Secondly, he was a man of the most absolute poverty. Other Europeans might be seeking for land and cattle, he wanted nothing. He walked bareheaded and barefoot, he fed on what was put before him, he was satisfied with the poorest of huts. Thirdly, he was a man of high intelligence, struggling with the study of Xhosa, anxious to explain to Ngqika the role of electricity in lightning. Fourthly, and probably most important of all, he lived on a principle of the most absolute human equality, behaving in a friendly, familiar way in everyday matters. Colour, race, the material level of culture and of living conditions meant absolutely nothing to him relative to the human personality, the rights of humanity, and the gospel of God. With blacks as with whites what was striking, whether to fascinate or infuriate, was the way an extreme evangelicalism had given birth to a radical social and political egalitarianism. He was, indeed, an extraordinary personage and it is not surprising that he touched hearts more than was immediately evident. It is moving, and rather fitting, that Christians should for long have named themselves after so Christlike a missionary.

The colonial authorities had hoped to use Van der Kemp to control Ngqika. They now hoped to use him as a way of controlling the Khoikhoi. It was the depressed state of the Hottentots within the colony which had driven some of them into alliance with the Xhosa. If some could be found a home within the colony, supervised by missionaries, that might not please the farmers, who saw it as depriving them of labour, but it could ease pressure on the frontier and at the same time satisfy missionary and philanthropic aspirations. And there was, of course, a small measure of justice in providing such a home. So Van der Kemp was given Bethelsdorp in the eastern Cape in 1803. It was to be a 'missionary settlement' or 'institution', theoretically modelled upon Genadendal. In reality it turned out very differently. For one thing, the land was less good. For another, Van der Kemp, even joined by a British missionary, a carpenter named James Read, by no means formed a team comparable to the quiet artisans of Genadendal. Both of them soon married native wives—Van der Kemp a young Malagasy slave girl he had himself bought with her family. She was baptized three years after the marriage and bore him four children. The missionaries at Bethelsdorp were immersed within African life as the missionaries at Genadendal were not. Certainly the long services and a school were the centre of life at Bethelsdorp, but rather few of the Bethelsdorp inhabitants were baptized, and the impression given is that there was a degree of freedom, both to do nothing and to provide leadership in their own way, unimaginable at Genadendal. We know the names and something of the careers of the more prominent members of the community. 'Bethelsdorp is not Genadendal,' wrote a disappointed missionary observer in 1813. Bethelsdorp people appeared cheeky and lazy. Indeed there was a difference, and if Bethelsdorp people were so judged by whites, the underlying reason was that it was a freer place, far more of a genuine Khoikhoi home, and far less of a 'mission institution' than most white people cared to see.

When in 1807 the news of the abolition of the slave-trade reached Bethelsdorp, Van der Kemp wrote:

We held a day of public thanksgiving. We assembled all our people, old and young, and pressed on their minds the horrid iniquity of trading in human flesh, that our youth might remember it to their latest years . . . Being eye-witnesses of the horrid usage of the poor slaves still in bondage in this colony, so renouned for its mildness to them, we agreed to be urgent at the throne of grace, in public and private, that the Lord may be pleased wholly to do away with this great evil.[15]

If this service, a good piece of liturgical politicization, reflected Van der Kemp's continual concern with justice, it was not likely to endear him to government or to white people, almost all of whom owned slaves. It looks as if even Van der Kemp's dear friend and collaborator at Bethelsdorp, Mathilda Smith, deaconess and founder of the knitting school, who had sold her home to live and work at the mission, returned to Cape Town because the Bethelsdorp rule was to allow no one who kept slaves to reside there, but she could not bring herself to free her own slave. This 'second Phoebe', as Van der Kemp called her, had given herself for years to the evangelization of slaves. Their emancipation was another matter. Van der Kemp kept up a

---

[15] *Report of the Directors of the Missionary Society,* 1809, 302, in J. Sales, *Mission Stations and the Coloured Communities of the Eastern Cape 1800–1852* (Cape Town, 1975), 35.

continual barrage of attack upon social injustices suffered by non-whites. It would be continued in due course by the next LMS superintendent, John Philip, and would make each of them for generations the religious bogyman of white tradition: the priest interfering in politics.

Bethelsdorp was derided by whites, and their view of it was well reflected in the remarks of the German zoologist Martin Lichtenstein, who visited it during his African travels in 1803, when the settlement had scarcely begun. His book first appeared in German in 1811 and in English and Dutch translation shortly afterwards. Its account of a developed institution was thus fundamentally unfair and was anyway based on a very short visit, but it was no less influential for that. Van der Kemp, he wrote, 'had never turned his thoughts seriously to instilling habits of industry into his disciples; but all idea of their temporary welfare appears with him to be wholly lost in his anxiety for their eternal salvation . . . his total neglect of husbandry and of all mechanical employments . . .'.[16] Despite appearances, such criticism was unjustified and tendentious. Bethelsdorp had poor land, unsuited for the support of such a considerable population, but it is by no means true that its missionaries had no interest in inculcating industry. By 1809 mat- and basket-weaving, soap-boiling, lime-making, fishing, shoe-making, candle-making, and wood-cutting were included among its occupations. Mathilda Smith's school of knitting had been continued by Mrs Read. Read himself began a blacksmith's forge, Ullbricht (who joined them in 1805) a windmill and watermill.

Van der Kemp died in December 1811, aged 64. It is surprising he lasted so long, given the way he lived. He was a man of extremes both in behaviour and in language, an intensely other-worldly pietist in his gospel, yet the most intensely outspoken of all missionaries in his defence of the this-worldly rights of the downtrodden. Van der Kemp was an outstanding product of the intellectual civilization of his age, a linguist who began his work with the Hottentots by composing and printing a catechism in the Khoi language, but who could work at the same time on a Latin treatise on the Epistle to the Romans and a handbook in Dutch on midwifery for use at Bethelsdorp. He had a different species of mind from the artisans of

---

[16] Henry Lichtenstein, *Travels in Southern Africa in the Years 1803, 1804, 1805 and 1806* (1812; repr. Cape Town, 1928 and 1930), i. 294–5.

Genadendal or the often illiterate farmers with whom he had to deal.
He was an officer and a gentleman, a scholar contemptuous of the
narrow vision of the whites around him yet endlessly sensitive to the
needs and moods of his black dependants. Traditionally the Khoikhoi
worshipped under the moon, so it is intriguing to find a visitor
commenting on 'the simple and venerable appearance of the good
man in the midst of his family, leading their devotion, on a lawn
surrounded by shrubs and enlightened by the beams of the moon'.[17]
His ability to adapt radically, to 'be a Khoikhoi with the Khoikhoi'
was extraordinary. To most of his white contemporaries and, still
more, his Victorian successors, it was almost scandalous. The thought
of his stooping to wash his own laundry in the river, and, infinitely
more, to marry a young slave, was abhorrent. Van der Kemp's
approach to mission could seem flagrantly opposed to one focused on
the details of 'civilization'. In the words of the Revd John Campbell,
a senior LMS man inspecting the South African mission field a
couple of years later, 'Had the founder of Bethelsdorp, Doctor Van
der Kemp, been more aware of the importance of civilization, there
might at least have been more external appearance of it than there
now is. He seems to have judged it necessary, rather to imitate the
savage in appearance than to induce the savage to imitate him.'[18] In
reality Van der Kemp was not unconcerned with 'civilization', but he
saw it as more a matter of political freedom and equality before the
law than in the details of the exterior neatness of a mission
compound or in clothes.

The issue of clothes expresses the contrast between the two views
pretty clearly. For most missionaries, in common with most other
Europeans, the wearing of western-type clothes was decidedly
important. For Van der Kemp and Read it was not. Janssens,
Governor in the brief period of Dutch Restoration after the Peace of
Amiens from 1803 to 1805, criticizing Van der Kemp's viewpoint and
particularly his concern for writing, remarked that he could not see
the point of teaching Hottentots to write when they had no 'desire
to wear clothes nor the least share of civilization'.[19] At Bethelsdorp
European clothes were not discouraged and the Khoikhoi certainly
liked to wear them when they could, but they were not insisted
upon, even in church. Van der Kemp rather encouraged skin

[17] Sales, *Mission Stations and the Coloured Communities of the Eastern Cape*, 35–6.
[18] J. Campbell, *Travels in South Africa* (1815), 129.
[19] Sales, *Mission Stations and the Coloured Communities of the Eastern Cape*, 31.

clothing, which to other missionaries could appear shocking, at least in church. After his death, Read remained under attack over this but argued that many people, especially old women, had simply no money to obtain clothing of a more Western sort. Van der Kemp's own clothes were for him, as for his critics, part of the issue. Once he had decided to live as close as he could to his Bethelsdorp Khoikhoi it was important that his own clothing should not differentiate him too obviously from his congregation. With the Xhosa he went barefoot for eighteen months; with the Khoikhoi he wore 'leather sandals bound upon his feet, the same as worn by the Hottentots'.[20]

The issue of clothes would go on and on. Civilizers like Robert Moffat simply could not understand how Africans could refuse 'to adopt our plain and simple modes of dress' in place of theirs, which were, he judged, 'disgusting', especially in regard to the red ochre adornment. The Moffat view generally prevailed. 'Thus', he wrote,

by the slow but certain progress of Gospel principles, whole families became clothed and in their right mind . . . When opportunity was afforded by the visit of a trader, British manufactures were eagerly purchased. For a long period when a man was seen to make a pair of trousers for himself, or a woman a gown, it was a sure intimation that we might expect additions to our inquirers.[21]

Some time later a Norwegian missionary could remark that among the Zulus the wearing of trousers and a hat are 'the basic characteristics of a Christian'. All the photographs sent home by Swedish missionaries in the Kongo from the 1880s showed the pagans as naked, the Christians as clothed, evangelists and teachers as particularly well dressed. There were those who disagreed, in part at least, more occasionally in entirety. Mrs Guinness in the Kongo objected to 'Europeanized Africans' in clothing, and particularly to trousers, but she wanted some sort of dress for the women. Mary Slessor was liberated enough herself to travel around without shoes or a hat. Archdeacon Johnson on Lake Nyasa deprecated 'any change in outward dress, even of those with whom we live closely'.[22] The

---

[20] Lichtenstein, *Travels in Southern Africa*, i. 292.
[21] R. Moffat, *Missionary Labours and Scenes in Southern Africa* (1842), 348 and 505.
[22] T. Jorgensen, 'Contact and Conflict', Ph.D. thesis (Oslo, 1989), 165; S. Axelson, *Culture Confrontation in the Lower Congo* (Uppsala, 1970), 284; H. G. Guinness, *The New World of Central Africa* (1890), 433; J. Buchan, *The Expendable Mary Slessor* (1980), 167 and 169; E. H. Barnes, *Johnson of Nyasaland* (1935), 105–6; see also James Stewart, *Lovedale, South Africa* (1894), 14.

White Fathers would endeavour on principle to dress in a non-European way and would long struggle to prevent their seminarians from wearing shoes or clothes of a Western sort, to the increasing bitterness of their protégés. However, on the long view, Van der Kemp and Read, Slessor, Johnson, and the White Fathers would be the eccentrics, Moffat the norm. Western clothing would in most places become for white and black alike the sacrament of mission Christianity.

The Xhosa mission was renewed by Joseph Williams in 1816. On his death two years later it was once more temporarily suspended, after little apparent gain, and then opened up a third time by John Brownlee. By then, however, the number and variety of missionary societies and mission stations in southern Africa was rapidly growing. The decade following the battle of Waterloo and the Peace of Vienna was one of large expansion. In January 1817 four LMS missionaries arrived at the Cape, including Robert Moffat, a tall young gardener from Scotland, aged just 21. The same year an English-speaking Swedish theologian, Hans Peter Hallbeck, arrived as superintendent of the Moravians with the task of giving that somewhat in-turned group a new type of leadership and of opening up new stations, three of which were in existence by 1824. One year later came John Philip, a Congregationalist minister from Aberdeen, as Superintendent of the LMS, a man in his forties, a masterful and politically conscious Evangelical with a considerable sense of missionary strategy. He would take up the cause of the Khoikhoi where Van der Kemp had left it, lobby tirelessly both at Westminster and in Cape Town, but equally press upon Bethelsdorp the importance of physical improvement—stone or brick houses, straight streets, a central square. On such matters Philip was Moffat's man, not Van der Kemp's, but in the central lines of his strategy he was quite other. His two-volume *Researches in South Africa*, published in 1828, was a major assault on colonial oppression, and it was by far the most important book written by a missionary in this period. But others too were arriving, in particular English Methodists and Scots from the Glasgow Missionary Society. Some of the former were chaplains to the '1820 Settlers' whom Lord Charles Somerset established in the eastern Cape to strengthen the white colony and hold back the Xhosa rather than, primarily, missionaries. The pastorate of whites was a necessary role, already exercised by the Dutch Predikants, and there was a lot to be said for not separating the two functions too completely.

Nevertheless, it could contribute only too easily to an ambiguity of identity which undermined the relationship with the black community and made missionaries appear as the softening-up advance guard of a white colonial army.

In 1824 the Glasgow Society founded Lovedale, later to become probably the most influential of all Christian educational centres in the south. In 1829 two continental societies arrived, the Paris Missionary Society (shortly to begin work among the Sotho of Moshesh) and the Rhenish Mission (which went north to Namaqualand in what is now Namibia). Thus by the end of the 1820s one can begin to see the highly complex Protestant missionary army, so characteristic of modern African history, really taking shape—diverse in institute, nationality, and denomination; diverse too in attitude and often cantankerous: a few the religious wing of colonial power and white settlement, others persistent defenders of African rights, but between them a rather apolitical majority, resolved to adhere as closely as possible to its evangelical message and avoid the contamination of politics, but in reality forced to give a very large part of its time and attention to building, gardening, maintaining a viable existence, providing a little elementary schooling. Within this group a small but decisive minority struggled brilliantly with language and the long battle over biblical translation.

Such a one was Robert Moffat, who in many ways typifies the early Victorian missionary at both his best and his most simplistic. The mission of Kuruman had been established among the Bechuana by Read and a group of Khoikhoi from Bethelsdorp in 1816. Robert and his wife, Mary, arrived in the middle of 1821 and would stay there for the next fifty years. Kuruman has a special importance as the first thoroughly successful and enduring mission established quite beyond the colonial frontier. It lies over 600 miles inland from Cape Town. Let us pause, then, to consider Kuruman in the late 1820s, because it would in its way be the prototype African mission far more than Genadendal or Bethelsdorp.

The Moffats were at Kuruman as guests of the local chief, Mothibi of the Tlhaping, but Mothibi was not very powerful and the times were exceedingly unsettled with marauding bands devastating the country. They came either from the east, escaping Shaka's power in the *Mfecane* (enforced migration), or from the south-west, escaping the expansion of white power. Moffat was a cool man, confident, affable, well able to impress, a figure of authority of a kind which it is difficult quite to define. He was not a colonial agent. He was not an other-worldly saint. He was eminently a man who could be relied upon, pacific but not timorous. In circumstances of surrounding weakness he established himself for half a century with a semi-independent status of a kind which missionaries of the abler sort would not infrequently attain, both in the pre-colonial and the early colonial era, in areas where there was no clear hegemonic power. In 1824 he moved eight miles away from Mothibi to a better-watered spot where he would effectively be his own master. Here over the years he built up the mission of Kuruman with its canal, its irrigated gardens, its square stone houses standing in a straight line beside the canal, its fences, its fruit trees, its wheat, barley, grapes, and figs. By 1835 there were 500 acres under irrigation and a population of 700 souls.

That was a sizeable community and it consisted, not just of Tlhaping, but of a mixture of people, many of them refugees, who chose to benefit from the political protection, the economic and educational facilities, that the mission provided. Its inhabitants, Moffat wrote, 'know that they are living on the grounds of the missionary society and are required only to live honest and peaceable lives and attend to the means of instruction; dancing and other heathenish amusements are not allowed'. The first six candidates for baptism were admitted in 1829—the same year in which Moffat concluded his translation of St Luke, the first Gospel in Sechuana— so it was hardly a Christian community and it was certainly a voluntary one, but it was one in which European and missionary ideas of what was right prevailed over African custom, in which the 'gospel and plough' message was firmly applied and a 'superior civilization'—a phrase favoured by Moffat—emphatically demon- strated. Moffat had absolutely no doubts about that message, and the European visitor was as full of admiration of Kuruman as, earlier, he was distressed by Bethelsdorp. Here was European control, the missionary benevolently but firmly in charge, his authority accepted by Africans because it worked, brought local peace, and produced such wonders as the printing-press. At Kuruman the 'mission village' was proving viable beyond the colonial frontier where Africans had plenty of alternatives. Nevertheless, its attraction derived in part from the social dislocation which encouraged people to take refuge within it. It remained, of course, the home of the few, but it was not cut off from the rest of society. There was a continual to-ing and fro-ing between Kuruman and the wide Bechuana world. The message of Moffat, the message of the Sechuana books soon coming off his printing-press, found its way far beyond the huts of Kuruman. In many ways the minds of the Moffats remained excessively British, their understanding of African custom decidedly low. Yet in Kuruman by the end of the 1820s a bridge of one sort most certainly did exist, linking Christianity to the millions of the African interior.

vi. *The Mission Village: A Discussion*

'The mission village': Kuruman, Bethelsdorp, Theopolis, Genadendal, could all by the 1820s be so described, as might, in distant Sierra Leone, Regent and Gloucester under Johnson and During. All were large missionary-controlled African communities functioning in the first decades of the nineteenth century, and there would be many more of various sorts across the next hundred years. They should not be confounded though they do have many common characteristics. Among the early examples, only in Sierra Leone did the inhabitants have absolutely no immediate alternative to being there and did missionaries exercise civil jurisdiction. Legitimately or illegitimately, they would exercise it in a number of later examples, at times more or less inescapably when there was no other civil authority to turn to and some order had to be maintained within a large and none too homogeneous community. This apart, Regent and Bethelsdorp might not be so dissimilar. All our examples show the common purposes of evangelizing, educating, and civilizing, but the mix varies. Entry into the community was considerably more selective at Genadendal, and the standard of Christian commitment, as also the degree of missionary control over the details of life, far higher. Most of its members were baptized or clearly on the way to being so. In all cases the missionary had something of a captive community to mould, but this should not be overstressed: in the South African villages no one entered under compulsion other than that of the wretchedness of the state of things outside. In Sierra Leone there was indeed a basic compulsion, inevitable upon the release of captives in a strange land, but the short space of time during which in fact missionaries exercised a role of superintendency in the recaptive settlements prevented any real mission village, compulsory or voluntary, from developing. Moreover, the missionaries there as elsewhere, if Protestant, were themselves most reluctant to baptize a multitude. They represented Christianity at its most individualistic. It was Governor MacCarthy, not the missionaries, who envisaged some sort of mass compulsory Christianization of the recaptives. In all cases, however, there was undoubtedly a strong element of social compulsion, within the ethos of a mission village, to conform sooner or later to Christian standards.

From the missionary point of view it appeared a practical way to begin the Christianization of Africa, as some sort of natural extension to their own household and domestic life-style. The attempt to Christianize people within a completely traditional context, tried at the very beginning by LMS and CMS missionaries, outside the borders of Sierra Leone, seemed on the contrary almost impossibly difficult. But it was not only a matter of missionary practicalities, it could also be one of ecclesiology and spirituality. Yet here again the models are diverse. In the Moravian settlements the pattern in Africa simply responded to the Moravian norm elsewhere of spiritual village communities deliberately withdrawn from secular society. This could be to some extent true of most other Pietists, especially in the earlier part of the nineteenth century. One sees it very noticeably, for example, in the Christian villages of the Basel Mission in the Gold Coast. They wished to segregate themselves so far as could be from the secular world at home, so in Africa they naturally encouraged a similar way of life. This could not be the case for establishment Churches and it is noticeable that the CMS were too Anglican ever to feel very happy with this way of working. A national Church could not encourage a sharp division between the religious community and the rest of society. On the other hand, far more easily than Free Churchmen, the missionary from the Church of England or of Scotland could be willing to take on civil authority. Thus the mission village could reflect in reality two quite different ecclesiastical ideals: one, the withdrawal of the religious from the secular, the other the linking together of the two authorities. Genadendal symbolizes the one, the Church of Scotland mission at Blantyre from the 1870s the other. Theoretically their spiritual inspiration is diametrically opposed, but both were 'mission villages' and to the African they might not seem all that different.

One question requiring explicit recognition is why mostly non-

Christian Africans could want to enter the community of a mission village in the first place. In a few cases, undoubtedly, the personality of a missionary or the pleasantness of a community already functioning, like Genadendal, provided sufficient positive reason. But in the majority of cases, both at this time and later, the reason was largely a negative one: escape from far worse conditions outside. People were willing to live in a mission village not so much as an alternative to traditional life but as an alternative to the chaos which had followed upon the complete disruption of traditional life. It was only because the Khoikhoi had no way any more of living according to their custom and had been reduced to labouring on white farms or to landless wanderers that Genadendal and Bethelsdorp seemed— and were—distinctly attractive. It was because the 'recaptives' had been carried off from their homes and countries, families and culture, and could not go back to them that they settled down so docilely in Regent or Gloucester. This would always be true, though missionaries frequently failed quite to realize why Africans were prepared to live this sort of existence, so alien to their past, controlled by regulations devised by strangers.

The attraction of Kuruman was the attraction of employment, education, and protection. For the next 100 years, the missionary would very often favour the model of the mission village where he could remain sedentary, living and working beside his vegetable garden, his books, his printing-press, workshops, and whatever, while Africans settled around him or came on prolonged visits. Where African power was strong, the mission village was small or non-existent; where it was weak, but still existent, the mission village grew stronger, but its inhabitants were still there by their own option and essentially subject to African civil jurisdiction. Only where African power was non-existent did the mission village become almost a state of its own. The large east coast settlements of ex-slaves, particularly that of Bagamoyo, run by the Holy Ghost Fathers from 1868, and that of Freretown, run by the CMS from 1874, verged on this type, though nominally within the dominions of the Sultan of Zanzibar. So did many a 'chrétienté' in the Congo. They were like Regent, but continued under mission control for far longer. At Bagamoyo some twenty missionaries, priests, brothers, and sisters, were there to supervise and train the former slaves. The workshops and well-cultivated estates always impressed the European observer. 'I can recommend no change in the arrangements,' wrote Sir Bartle Frere in 1874.[23] 'I would recommend it as a model to be followed in any attempt to civilize and evangelize Africa.' Groups of Bagamoyo inhabitants were subsequently resettled inland to form the core of new mission villages as the basis of the missionary advance. Freretown was, with modifications, modelled upon Bagamoyo, as were settlements run by other missionary groups in East Africa, by the UMCA at Masasi, the White Fathers at Ushirombo and Kibanga. Despite the commendation of Sir Bartle, 'the arrangements' of Bagamoyo were basically dependent upon the slave market of Zanzibar, and the ability of British ships to intercept slavers and land their cargo at the door of the Holy Ghost Fathers. Once the slave markets were closed, such 'arrangements' were bound to be in trouble because the source of their converts had been closed as well.

The internal problems of such mission villages could, moreover, be formidable. Most people stayed there only because it was unsafe to go elsewhere. The absence of any shared traditional or tribal basis on which to run the society and the extreme violence to which many of their inhabitants had been earlier subjected could well induce a situation in which violence continued. In some cases the missionaries in control had no civil authority to which they could turn to deal with crime. In consequence they assumed it themselves or appointed Africans to do so in their name. In 1880 Britain was scandalized to learn that missionaries at the Blantyre mission of the Church of Scotland had ordered quite brutal floggings of people suspected of theft and even the execution by firing-squad of a man accused of murder. Those responsible were in this case dismissed. Yet it was almost impossible to run this sort of settlement without some degree of civil jurisdiction. Blantyre, like the early Livingstonia, a little to the north, did not consist only of freed slaves but of large numbers of local people coming to live around the mission. They chose to accept its protection in a world where local African authority was so minuscule or so upset by the disorders of the times that the mission seemed in comparison a considerable power whose patronage, regulations, and even punishments were well worth accepting. Both of these Scottish missions at first saw themselves as a kind of mini-

---

[23] Bartle Frere, *East Africa as a Field of Missionary Labours* (1874), 49. For the Congo *chrétienté* see R. Slade, *English-Speaking Missions in the Congo Independent State* (Brussels, 1959), 164–82.

state, a 'Christian Colony' somewhat comparable to Sierra Leone. Blantyre's first clergy were explicitly instructed to 'act as the General Director, and Christian Magistrate, of the settlement'.[24] Robert Laws of Livingstonia, always discriminating and somewhat uneasy about what was happening, put the problem clearly enough to his home committee in a letter of early 1880: 'Is the Livingstonia Mission to be regarded as a Mission, like the early ones to the South Sea Islands, trusting to God for protection, though outwardly at the mercy of the natives when they think fit to rob or murder its members or is the Livingstonia Mission to be regarded as a Christian Colony, having its foreign relationships and internal administration?'[25]

Livingstonia, after hesitations and unlike Blantyre, opted clearly for the former: it developed as an educational centre but not as a large Christian settlement. The Blantyre atrocities really demonstrated both how easily a mission village developed into a 'Christian colony' outside a territory firmly controlled by colonial authority, and how dangerous this could be in missionary terms. 'The exercise of Magisterial Functions by the head of the Mission', Laws continued, 'I think rather hinders than furthers his work as a minister of the Gospel.' That was just what the CMS had come to realize in regard to the recaptive villages of Sierra Leone sixty years earlier. Any such exercise of jurisdiction by missionaries quickly came to an end after the colonial period began in British and French Africa; effectively, in the Congo, at least in Catholic missions, it did not. But even where civil jurisdiction in major matters was not claimed, the regulation of minor issues could still be all-engrossing of a missionary's time.

Again, the degree of Christianization varied. In many of the White Father villages the slaves had been bought individually by them, selected in markets, their names written down in the local mission's *Régistre des rachats*. Thus the fathers at Ushirombo made an annual shopping expedition to the slave market of Ujiji. The ones they bought were children, and a fairly intense process of Christianization was part of the process of socialization in the mission village. Not more were bought than could conveniently be trained and converted. Nevertheless, they were often joined by adults who were not Christians but, once more, sought the mission's protection and were not turned away. For them little more than a rule of

---

[24] M. W. Waldman, 'The Church of Scotland Mission at Blantyre, Nyasaland: Its Political Implications', *BSACH* 2/4 (1968), 299–310.
[25] J. McCracken, *Politics and Christianity in Malawi 1875–1940* (1977), 64–5.

monogamy for the as yet unmarried might be insisted upon. In the larger land concessions, especially further south such as that of the White Fathers at Chilubula (in northern Zambia) or the huge Jesuit 'farms' at Empandeni and Chishawasha, even this might not be required. It would certainly be hard to enforce with people already living on a stretch of land now regarded as part of the mission territory because it had been arbitrarily bestowed upon the Church by an African king or by Cecil Rhodes.

Mission villages were thus enormously diverse in size, reasons of origin, and degree of discipline and Christian commitment, as well as in the social context in which they emerged. What was common was the sense that this was a place in which the European mind rather than African custom controlled the details of life—patterns of work and marriage, the shape of houses, the public practice of religion. Boundaries with the surrounding world might be harder or softer. At Masasi, established in 1876, W. P. Johnson wrote in retrospect, 'the local chiefs trained us very gently' to recognize their authority, but even there for most things they were their own authority. 'It has been said that we ruled in our own village simply by Church censure, but this is hardly correct. We were in the position of well-to-do squires. We had a fair amount of work to give out, and this was coveted. We were recognised as heads of the station by the headmen around.'[26] Chauncy Maples wrote already in 1883

Upon the whole I think the presence of the returned slave community retarded rather than assisted the work among the tribes . . . Our great difficulty . . . at Masasi . . . was this. We had to take care of a number of worthless people who not only were not Christians but whose conduct was so bad that there was scarcely any hope of their ever becoming Christians: meanwhile their misdoings, quarrels and excesses of all kinds took up an untold amount of time as day after day I had to listen to their disputes and mete out satisfaction to the partners injured by them.[27]

Johnson and Maples were both UMCA men and one feels that few missionary traditions in the late nineteenth century grew faster to maturity. By 1890 Bishop Smythies could say firmly, 'I think that we ought to dismiss altogether from our minds that rather fascinating idea of a Christian village,'[28] though there were other missionary

---

[26] W. P. Johnson, *My African Reminiscences 1875–1895* (1924), 126.
[27] Maples to Waller, 29 July 1883, R. Oliver, *The Missionary Factor in East Africa* (1952), 65.
[28] E. F. Russell (ed.), *The Life of Charles Alan Smythies* (1898), 170.

groups, Catholic ones especially, which would take another forty years to arrive so far.

We have travelled well beyond the 1820s in pursuit of a theme, but as the mission village was already so very much a fact of life by 1829 it seemed best at this point to look more widely at its growth and its limitations. It provided one of the most characteristic forms of Christian presence in nineteenth-century Africa, but never the only form. That it was attractive, in a variety of circumstances and for quite a range of reasons, to both missionaries and many Africans is clear and understandable enough. Yet Moffat in the 1840s already recognized its limitations, and in place after place disillusioned missionaries would turn away from what had appeared at first so very attractive. Basically it created a form of Christian society too artificially dependent upon the authority of the white missionary and unreal in regard to the problems of 99 per cent of the inhabitants of customary Africa. From being a bridgehead it came to seem a cul-de-sac, yet that may well have been more of a white judgement than a black one. Missionaries had seen the Christian village as final, where the converted would remain. For Africans it was far more a place which provided breathing-space. In due time they or their children would get up and go, but when they went they would take part of its ethos with them as well as a tattered copy of a vernacular Mark's Gospel or a book of hymns, and the Christian village would begin to reappear in the bush. The long-term influence of the mission village was in consequence far more considerable and extended than an immediate contrast between a few score well-ordered, European-style villages, straight, square, windowed, and officially monogamous, and the shapeless, apparently disorderly world of tens of thousands of traditional villages might lead one to conclude. The road from the one to the other was always open and many there were who took it.

vii. *Khoi Leadership and Ntsikana*

The Khoikhoi, or most of them, were, however, by 1820 quite unable to return to any customary world, much as they might wish to do so. It had been irrevocably taken from them by the expansion of the European colony, and they had themselves been transformed over several generations of contact with the colony into a semi-Westernized society, many of whose members could no longer speak their original languages. Some had European blood, many picked up a measure of Christianity, most spoke Dutch. They were united by a common folk memory, by their Dutch names, an ability to use guns and horses effectively, and a crushing experience of alienation. They seemed very Western in comparison with their Bantu neighbours, but the colony had little use for them except as labourers and house-servants. Just as the Sierra Leoneans were becoming a new English-speaking social entity, essentially upon the frontier of two worlds, so were the Hottentots, and the two may be usefully compared in their position within the Christian history of the early nineteenth century, even though the quite different political histories of south and west would mean that the former would have large opportunities both to flourish in new ways and even to regain old roots, while the latter would continue to be ground under foot generation after generation.

The Khoikhoi were split four ways. A few survived around the Orange River in the far north, speaking Gona or Nama and maintaining a traditional life in the most inhospitable of geographical surroundings. Some were absorbed by the Xhosa, their Bantu neighbours to the east. Many, as we have seen, became landless employees of white farmers or, when they could, entered missionary settlements at Bethelsdorp or Theopolis. A fourth group, retaining more social cohesion than the third but more Europeanized than the first or second, survived for a while as independent Dutch-speaking communities a little beyond the northern colonial frontier. Largest of these were the Griquas, but the group led by the much-feared chieftain Afrikaner more to the west was another example. Dutch-speaking Khoikhoi turned very willingly to sympathetic missionaries. Some were already Christians of a sort. All needed someone to speak out on their behalf against settler oppression. They venerated Van der Kemp. They accepted James Read as one of themselves. They took John Campbell's advice at Griquatown, changed their name from 'Bastards' to 'Griquas' and adopted a constitution. They were very convertible. Afrikaner was baptized and went to Cape Town with Moffat on a famous visit in 1819. 'The scourge of the country' charmed Governor and Cape Townsmen with 'the unexpected mildness and gentleness of his demeanour'.[29] He was, one might say, the first Christian ruler of the new dispensation.

At much the same time the Griquas elected Andries Waterboer, a mission school teacher, as their new leader. 'That brave Christian

[29] Moffat, *Missionary Labours and Scenes in Southern Africa*, 178.

man', Livingstone called him,[30] and it was certainly Waterboer's military skill and considerable courage which, in 1823, saved the Bakhatla and the mission of Kuruman from the invading force of 'Mantatees'. Waterboer continued to preach regularly in church and proved for more than thirty years a thoroughly able leader of his community, probably the ablest the 'Hottentots' ever had. He, again, is the earliest example in the modern period (for there were similar cases in Soyo in the seventeenth century) of a political leader with the background and education of a mission teacher.

A certain ease of movement and sharing of leadership between missionaries and 'Hottentots' was certainly assisted by James Read. With a Hottentot wife and family he had in a very real sense 'passed' from the white to the non-white community. It is asserted, though it is not certain, that Van der Kemp's wife was no help to him. That was not the case with Mrs Read or with their sons and daughters, who shared very actively in the common task. Indeed James Read Jr. appears as both thoroughly loyal to his father's ministry over many years of shared activity and as almost equally energetic in the struggle, both for the advancement of Christianity and for that of the community to which they belonged.

Andries Stoffels was outstanding among the Bethelsdorp folk. Born about 1776 on the Bushman River, he had worked on Dutch farms and fought on the Hottentot–Xhosa side in the war of 1799. When he first came to Bethelsdorp he wore skins and red clay, but there he learnt both literacy and such a wider range of European skills that he was asked to accompany several missionaries on crucial expeditions, including Read when he went to establish Kuruman in 1816. In 1836 he and Jan Tshatshu—the half-Khoi chief of the Ntinde, a Xhosa group, probably the first Xhosa to be baptized— accompanied John Philip to England to give evidence before the Select Committee on Aborigines. Bootsman Stuurman, on the other hand, remained illiterate. He was the youngest of three brothers. Klaas, the eldest, had led the Hottentots against the Dutch in the war of 1799 but died soon after. The second brother, David, was sent as a convict to Australia. The surviving Stuurmans went mostly to Bethelsdorp. Bootsman was converted to Christianity at Theopolis. When his wife died he became a full-time evangelist and spent his last years preaching to the Bushmen. He knew their language, shared

[30] D. Livingstone, *Missionary Travels and Researches in South Africa* (1857), 91.

their clothing, but held on to his Bible and his plough. He was not, in conventional terms and unlike Stoffels, a very 'civilized' man.

Waterboer, Afrikaner, Stoffels, Stuurman, as well as Jan Tshatshu, and even James Read Jr. stood for a range of Christian African leadership directly following upon the first missionary generation. It is not unimpressive. It would in coming years be ceaselessly squeezed both by the tighter missionary control of the second generation and by the pressure of white racialism as the settler community advanced inland and eastward. But it was already there quite clearly by the 1820s, and it is exceedingly important that preoccupation with the complexities of missionary history as it unfolded in the Livingstone era should not obscure the quality of Christian life and the genuine leadership of which the local Church was already at its best capable.

These men were clearly within the Church: baptized, instructed by missionaries, able to speak Dutch or English. But one man, a great deal stranger than any of them, was none of these things. Ntsikana was born about 1780. The son of a chief, circumcized like all the Xhosa and fond of smearing red ochre thickly on his body, he was never baptized, never knew a European language, and never went through any course of missionary catechesis, but his subsequent influence as prophet, poet, and pacifist has been incomparable. In a unique way Ntsikana represents a genuinely new birth of Christian insight within African society and culture.

Ntsikana was brought up to be a warrior and royal councillor like his father, Gaba. He became renowned as an orator, dancer, and singer of Xhosa songs. He had two wives, two sons, and three daughters. As a young man he probably heard Van der Kemp preach: later, he heard Read. Then, probably in 1815, he underwent a strange visionary experience, after which he plunged into the Ggorha River, washing from his body every trace of red ochre. 'My children, something has commanded me to wash off the red ochre, therefore do you also wash it off.' Again, a little later, he declared 'This thing which has entered me, it says "Let there be prayer! Let everything bow the knee".' Again, he called his two wives and said to them, 'It does not agree with the thing that has entered me that I have two wives' and he sent one away with a share of his property.[31] The vocabulary sounds like a form of spirit possession, but not its

[31] J. Hodgson, 'Ntsikana, History and Symbol: Studies in a Process of Religious Change among Xhosa-Speaking People', Ph.D. thesis (Cape Town, 1985), i. 135–6.

behavioural effects. Perhaps only slowly did he come to understand that 'the thing' was the teaching of Nyengana on the word of God. It was part of this original experience to reject the leadership of the Xhosa prophet Nxele, who had also come under Christian influence, but who was stirring up the nation to war against the British, promising that the ancestors would rise to assist them. He sent a message at once to Nxele, whom he had previously supported, to say that he was misleading the people.

Later Ntsikana met the LMS missionary Williams, and attended services at his mission, but he refused any further baptism, declaring that he had already been baptized in his own way and he took no additional Christian name. He gathered around him a group of disciples, including his own children, he composed for them a series of magnificent hymns, and he refused to participate in the war when it came. His followers named themselves 'the Poll-headed'—cattle without horns, pacifists. It is impossible to be certain how Ntsikana came first under Christian influence, but the tradition that he had listened to Van der Kemp is intrinsically probable, and he may well have watched Nyengana baptize his convert Sarah and her two daughters in the Keiskama river in October 1800. He seems too to have been aware of Read, but Christianity was in the air and, if Nxele heard and reinterpreted some elements of it, Ntsikana heard others: the sovereignty of God, the holiness of Sunday, river baptism, the rejection of red ochre, monogamy, prayer. These constituted the core elements of Ntsikana's message together with an urgent appeal not to heed Nxele:

Why does he say he will raise the dead? Can he open the heaven and close it again? And how did they die that they can be raised again by a man? . . . I am not like Nxele. I am sent by God, but am only like a candle. Those who are chiefs will remain chiefs because they were made such by Him, and only He can take it away; I have not added anything to myself.[32]

In the course of the services he held twice daily in his hut or under a tree Ntsikana composed the four hymns which were so soon taken over by the mission Churches and printed already during the 1820s, to become for ever the core of the Xhosa Christian worshipping tradition.

---

[32] Ibid. 152 and 164.

Ulin guba inkulu siambata tina
He who is our mantle of comfort,
The giver of life, ancient on high
He is the Creator of the heavens,
And the ever-burning stars:
God is mighty in the heavens,
And whirls the stars around in the sky.
We call on him in his dwelling-place.
That he may be our mighty leader,
For he maketh the blind to see;
We adore him as the only good,
For he alone is a sure defence.[33]

Soga, Ngqika's principal councillor and a relative of Ntsikana's wife, was among those who believed, but the disciples remained a small band of the committed. He died (probably) in the autumn of 1821, having predicted his death, chosen the place of his grave, turned the first sod himself, and supervised the digging. His burial was probably modelled upon that of Williams at Kat River two years previously. Like his ox, his washing in the river, and much else, Ntsikana's burial was for him deeply symbolic. His very commitment to it became a sign of his commitment to God. After his death his disciples moved, on his instructions, to settle at the mission, now directed by Brownlee, who wrote to John Philip: 'On the day when Sicana died, all the people of the Kraal met as usual for worship in the morning. He was present and addressed his audience in a very solemn manner . . .'. The African sources give that last address substantially as follows:

I am going home to my Father. Do not, after I die, go back to live by the customs of the Xhosa. I want you to go to Buleneli (Brownlee) at Gwali. Have nothing to do with the feasts, but keep a firm hold of the word of God. Always stick together . . . Should a rope be thrown round your neck, or a spear pierce your body, or be beaten with sticks, or struck with stones, whatever persecution comes upon you, on account of the word of God don't give way, keep it and stick to it and to each other.

   To my two sons I say, Kobe, you will be my backbone, and Dukwana, you will be my walking-stick. Do not allow the children to return to the red clay . . .

[33] J. Hodgson, *Ntsikana's Great Hymn* (Cape Town, 1980), 14.

And the message was sent to Ngqika, 'The man with the milk–bag of heaven . . . has gone home.'[34]

So far as one can judge, Ntsikana's gospel was in origin the message of Van der Kemp as heard by a Xhosa mind of exceptional sensitivity. It was a selective hearing but not a misrepresentation, and in due course it was reinforced after conversion by contact with Williams and Brownlee. It was a message primarily about God, creator and saviour, about moral holiness, prayer, and some simple ritual norms including the keeping of Sunday. Ntsikana is so important because this quite straightforward gospel worked for years through his mind, quite divorced from every accident of European culture and language, to take on a profoundly Xhosa symbolic form, a form which would survive. In the Wesleyan *Book of Songs* published in Grahamstown in 1835, Ntsikana's Great Hymn is number one. Music and song are at the heart of African culture. It was, perhaps, when the 22-year-old Moffat took his violin and in the stillness of the evening played and sang a hymn that he conquered the heart of Afrikaner, but to reach the heart of Africa the hymn and its tune needed to be authentically African. Hymnody is not only demonstrative of the indigenization of Christianity, it is also causative. That was especially so in the case of Ntsikana. With Equiano we considered the surprising phenomenon of a highly literate Christian African in the London of the 1780s. We were then carried back by evangelical enthusiasm via Freetown and Cape Town to the continent itself, but still to a Christianity expressed largely through the medium of English or Dutch and in decidedly Western dress. In the world of 1820, Ntsikana is no less surprising than was Equiano, for he erupts, wholly unexpectedly, as Christianity in an African idiom. Mission histories tend, unsurprisingly, not to mention him.

---

[34] Hodgson, 'Ntsikana, History and Symbol', i. 323, 325, and 327.

6

THE LION REVIVED: ETHIOPIA IN THE NINETEENTH CENTURY

i. *The Age of the Princes*

The state of Ethiopia in the 1830s was as wretched as could be. The Zamana Masafent, 'The era of the Judges (or princes)', had been an age of disintegration. There were still emperors in Gondar, chosen always from the old royal line. They retained a certain mystique but were virtually powerless and were frequently deposed by one or another warlord. Gondar functioned more as a city of monks, the seat of the eccage, than as a centre for even minimal political authority. Most of the time there were three principal local rulers: one in Tigre ruling the north, one in Shoa ruling the south-east, and one in Bagemdir ruling the central and western provinces, including Gojjam. But that is a simplification as the governors, mostly hereditary, of many other provinces were themselves in frequent rebellion against the Ras of Tigre or Bagemdir. The ruler of Shoa was alone in daring to adopt the title of negus, 'king'. His dynasty claimed to belong to the old Solomonic line and Shoa had effectively for a century been a separate state, the most clearly defined, stable, and well-governed part of Ethiopia. It was ruled from 1813 to 1847 by Sahela Sellase. Bagemdir now belonged to the Yajju, a Galla dynasty which had, at least superficially, adopted Christianity. Closest to Gondar its ras, ruling from his provincial capital of Dabra Tabor, effectively controlled the central rump of the country. He could appoint or depose emperors but his Galla origins and Muslim affinities set limits to his legitimacy. To the north Tigre stood as the third centre of power, benefiting from being nearer to the outside world of Egypt and Europe. In these years it was dominated first by Sabagadis and, from 1831, by an Amhara subordinate of the Yajju, Webe, who invaded the north and overthrew and killed Sabagadis. A little earlier, Gugsa, who had been Ras of Bagemdir for many years, died, to be succeeded first by his son and then by his 13-year-old grandson, Ali II. Ali's mother, Menem, became in consequence, for a time, the effective ruler, and installed her new husband, Yohannes, a son of Takla Giyorgis, as emperor. However, once Webe had consolidated his power over the north, he turned his mind to the overthrow of Ali and his own establishment as controller of Gondar. As the Yajju dynasty was suspected of being Muslims in disguise, it was useful for Webe to project himself as defender of the Church.

Throughout the 1830s and through most of the first forty years of the nineteenth century, there was no abuna in Ethiopia. The authority of Qerelos, who arrived in 1815 in succession to Yosab, who had died in 1803, was largely rejected within a Church now riven more than ever by Christological controversy. Whichever side an abuna countenanced, the two or three other parties were immediately alienated. After Qerelos there was again no one to ordain priests for more than a decade, but the collapse of any regular ordinations merely rendered more rapid an ecclesiastical falling-apart which had been going on for several generations. There never had been any real jurisdictional authority over the clergy other than that of the king, and the collapse of the monarchy, confined within the ruined palaces of Gondar, left the Church, already rent apart by theological disagreement, almost entirely without direction. The eccage might do his best but he was not a bishop and his moral authority seldom went beyond the party to which he adhered. Again, the weakness of the Patriarchate of Alexandria at this period meant that no great help could be looked for from that direction, and, without royal backing, an abuna—even when there was one—was unable to cope with the ceaseless conflicts over the intricacies of dogma.

Pagan or Muslim Galla had settled over considerable areas of what had once been strongly Christian territory. Thus there was a thick swathe of Galla-occupied land in Wallo, which now largely separated Shoa from Amhara, Bagemdir, and Gojjam. While the major monasteries survived, partly because they were mostly so inaccessible, they often now represented mere pockets of Christianity, survivals of a past religion, respected as sacred shrines by the new arrivals in the land, but isolated and quite ineffective evangelically. Thus the monastery of Lake Hayq, the first of all houses in the south, while still served by a Christian village on the shore, was otherwise surrounded by a predominantly Muslim population. Christianity had crumbled even more in the outlying areas of the old kingdom, though even here Christian villages or groups of villages survived in some places, particularly in the far south-west, in Enarya and Kafa, often in the more defensible areas. Their religion, nevertheless, had inevitably become increasingly syncretistic, and while the hereditary families of priests might continue to minister, in many cases they now did so without ordination.

While some Galla did become Christians, especially among the new nobility, who, in general, outwardly respected the principle that Ethiopia was a Christian state, Christianity had little wide appeal for them. The fasting required seemed excessive while the liturgy and holy books imprisoned within a now almost incomprehensible language offered neither sense nor attraction. For Christians too the language problem had steadily grown as Amharic and other regional forms of speech had diverged more and more from Ge'ez, leaving the Church without Scriptures or liturgy intelligible to anyone other than the more learned of the monks. And learning too had everywhere declined. Hundreds of churches had been destroyed or abandoned and, after a whole generation and more in which ordination had been exceedingly difficult to obtain, the very survival of the priesthood was seriously in question. Henry Salt, whose agent and informant, Nathaniel Pearce, was in the country for a long period during the first two decades of the century, concluded gloomily but not unreasonably, 'the nation, with its religion, is fast verging on ruin; the Galla and Mussulman tribes around are daily becoming more powerful; and there is reason to fear that, in a short time, the very name of Christ may be lost among them'.[1]

In February 1830 Samuel Gobat and Christian Kugler, two German missionaries employed by the CMS, arrived in Ethiopia at the court of Sabagadis at Addigrat. The modern missionary and colonial period had begun. Both Britain and France were soon to open consulates at Massawa, and an increasing number of Europeans of every sort were making their way into the country. For the next thirteen years some half-dozen CMS missionaries, all German, worked in Tigre, Gondar, and Shoa. They established an initial rapport with Sabagadis and, after his death, some degree of confidence with Webe in Tigre and Sahela Sellase in Shoa. Gobat, the most sympathetic to Ethiopian ways, managed to enter into dialogue quite positively with the Eccage Filpos in Gondar. The

---

[1] Henry Salt, in G. Annesley (ed.), *Voyages and Travels* (1809), iii. 256.

purpose of their mission was not to establish a Church separate from the Ethiopian but to purify and strengthen the latter by spreading printed copies of the Scriptures, especially in Amharic, and by convincing Ethiopians of the errors of their ways in praying to Mary and the saints, venerating images, kissing the cross, keeping fasts, cherishing monasteries, and all other un-Protestant practices. They were rather simple biblically minded Evangelicals, largely appalled by the Ethiopian Church, about which they were frequently very rude. It was certainly a gain to have for the first time an Amharic Bible; nevertheless, they came to recognize how reluctant Ethiopians could be to turn from Ge'ez to Amharic for their sacred texts, and sensibly suggested that it might be better to print both versions in parallel columns of a single volume. They also realized that Amharic was hardly acceptable in Tigre where its own vernacular needed to be used. All this was, or could have been, a help to the Ethiopian Church, but it was their continuous criticism of Ethiopian devotion to Mary which really brought about their ruin. Even Gobat, appealing as he was in personality, was advocating a religious revolution more radical and more offensive than that of Mendes.

It was inevitable that the initial welcome was changed into increasing hostility, even if that hostility was veiled for a while by the desire of the rulers to obtain help from abroad. 'He does not seem to feel the necessity of a reformation of their Church,' Charles Isenberg wrote sadly of Sahela Sellase.[2] As ever, rulers wanted guns, technicians, and foreign alliances, not another wave of religious controversy. The missionaries were unable to perceive the consequences of their own simple certainties and—like Evangelicals on many a later occasion—blamed on 'Romanist intrigues' or similar causes what was rather caused by their own lack of rapport with African reality. It was the enormous gap in religious ideal between a Protestant and an Ethiopian Christian at his best which rendered the CMS mission so essentially unrealistic. In failure Johann Krapf, in some ways the ablest among them, turned to advocate British political, and even military, intervention (from India) to ensure the survival and success of their mission—much as the Jesuits had done in the seventeenth century: 'Our spiritual embassy to these countries will be according to the success of the British Mission, with them we

---

[2] D. Crummey, *Priests and Politicians* (1972), 46.

fall and with them we stand,' he wrote in 1841.[3] The last thing
Britain could have wished to do in 1841 was to send an army into
Shoa to ensure its Protestantization, but it is interesting that at this
period a German missionary could so easily identify Britain and
Protestantism. Despite its absurdity, Krapf's suggestion is nevertheless
to be noted as forerunner to a missionary approach which would be
very much more common forty years later. A kind of evangelical
impatience could very easily turn the most other-worldly of
missionaries into aggressive imperialists.

Krapf was forbidden in 1842 by Sahela Sellase to return to Shoa,
and he and Isenberg were expelled from Tigre the following year,
their mission having achieved virtually nothing. Meanwhile, in the
late 1830s a new Catholic mission had opened in Tigre and in 1839
its principal architect, Justin de Jacobis, a Neapolitan Lazarist, arrived
in Adwa. He is one of the most attractive of nineteenth-century
missionaries, and by no means the least successful, despite being heir
to a long, mostly unhappy, history of Catholic attempts to 'reconcile'
the Ethiopian Church with Rome. None ever understood Ethiopia
better or identified more deeply with its religious tradition. Earlier
attempts had produced a profound and long-lasting anti-Roman
bitterness, but with the passing of time, the failure of Egyptian
bishops to help, and the depressed state of the country generally,
there was much greater willingness by the nineteenth century to give
a hearing to European Christians. We have seen it with the
Protestants, but they largely threw away their opportunity by lack of
sympathy with the basic devotional and ritual practices of popular
religion. Here Catholics had the advantage, sharing almost all the
practices which Evangelicals abhorred.

The great strengths of de Jacobis were his deep spirituality, his
genuine affection for Ethiopia and its religious traditions, his resolve
to work sincerely within the Ge'ez Rite, and his ability to gain the
loyalty and enduring friendship of individual Ethiopians, yet he
too—when things were going badly—could look for French
intervention to protect his mission. The Italian could at this stage
identify French interests and Catholicism as simplistically as could the
German Protestant identify British interests with his religion.

De Jacobis established himself in Tigre and soon made of Webe a
sincere protector. For the next fifteen years Webe's patronage, the

---

[3] Ibid. 51–2.

character of de Jacobis, and the almost leaderless, near desperate state of the Ethiopian Church were sufficient to ensure the coming into being of a Catholic Ethiopian community which would survive all subsequent storms, even if its larger national aspirations would never be realized. A number of monks, especially from the monastery of Gunde Gunde, joined de Jacobis, as did whole villages, but the greatest single conversion was that of Ghebra-Mika'el. One of the most learned and respected of Gondar monks, he felt the appeal of de Jacobis for several years before becoming a Catholic in 1845 (the same year as Newman's conversion) when he was already in his late fifties. His attraction to Catholicism was not an aberration for circles in Gondar, being shared by the Emperor, Yohannes III, the Eccage Mahsantu, and other clergy, but for few did it become a full commitment, in his case unto death. As in the past, the tendency towards Catholicism was mostly to be found among the House of Takla Haymanot, but Ethiopian Catholicism not only made converts among people of distinction, it also bred them. Fr. Takla Haymanot of Adwa, who was converted by de Jacobis in his teens and was the first priest to be ordained by him, would become one of the most remarkable religious and literary figures of nineteenth-century Ethiopia and the biographer of de Jacobis, 'Abuna Jacob'.

The Lazarists were joined in 1846 by a group of Capuchins led by Guglielmo Massaja, who went further south with a mission to the Galla. Massaja ordained de Jacobis a bishop, but the approach of the two groups was in some ways different. In theory Massaja was a Latiniser extending the Latin rite to non-Christians, not purifying the Ethiopian rite among those already Christian. In practice, however, he not only largely worked among people already at least partly Christianized, as in Kafa, but he did also adopt the Ethiopian calendar and other practices such as fasting. It is noticeable, too, how tolerant Catholic missionaries could be in the mid-nineteenth century over matters like circumcision which appeared so unacceptable in the sixteenth or seventeenth.

Both de Jacobis and Massaja went Ethiopian in one decisive way: they ordained Ethiopians, some who were married, and some of quite slight education, at least of a formal Western sort. There can be little doubt that one of the most decisive reasons for the survival of the Ethiopian Church across the centuries, often in highly unfavourable circumstances, was its ordination practice—particularly criticized all the same by Western observers—of ordaining men

of the slightest education in very large numbers. De Jacobis and
Massaja did not do quite the same, but they were both committed to
the ordination of Ethiopians and both actually fulfilled their
commitment despite the criticism of colleagues. The acceptance of
a married clergy is in striking contrast to Catholic missionary practice
elsewhere in Africa. De Jacobis opposed an increase in foreign
missionaries, holding that Ethiopian priests could very well by
themselves renew Ethiopian Christianity. Massaja was accused of
ordaining 'Children, scarcely 23 years old, who know neither how to
read nor write, not even having the knowledge of our Holy Religion
which one requires in Europe of a child taking its first communion
. . . how can these indigenous priests properly dispense the treasures
of the Church?'[4] In the latter half of the century when foreign
missionaries were largely excluded, some of these Ethiopian priests in
fact saved the Church.

It is conceivable that, if there had continued to be no Egyptian
abuna in Ethiopia or at least no authority to back him, then the
moral suasion of de Jacobis surrounded by an increasingly large group
of Ethiopian Catholic clergy might have shifted the Church as a
whole from Alexandrian to Roman loyalty. De Jacobis himself even
at one moment thought it would happen. In fact things were to
develop in a quite different direction. In 1841 a new bishop was
appointed in Cairo in response to a request from Webe. The Abuna
Salama was a very young man who had been educated in a CMS
school and seems in all traditional ways an astonishingly inappropriate
choice. He had none of the qualities of the customary monastic
abuna chosen from the community of St Anthony. He was proud,
forceful, and cruel, determined to vindicate his own authority but
also, increasingly, the traditional ecclesiology of the Ethiopian
Church. His sympathies for Protestantism and for Britain gave him
some slight protection but hardly affected his policies. Protestantism
was no threat to the Ethiopian Church and its dependence on
Alexandria, Catholicism in the form of de Jacobis, and the group of
Ethiopians developing around him, most certainly was. It was
inevitable that an Egyptian abuna of any vigour would endeavour to
fight the influence of the Catholic mission and exclude it, for
instance, from the use of Ethiopian Churches. De Jacobis as a bishop
in Ethiopia making use of the Ge'ez Rite was, in principle, a rival

---

[4] Des Aranchers to *Propaganda*, Mar. 1860, in Crummey, *Priests and Politicians*, 4–5.

abuna, but Salama's hostility was directed even more towards Ghebra-Mika'el, who had actually been one of the Ethiopian delegation to Cairo before he became a Catholic and the only one to oppose Salama's appointment publicly. Salama seems never to have forgiven this. With the missionaries Salama could at times be almost friendly; to the reverend Ethiopian theologian more than twice his age who had publicly rejected him, he could offer only imprisonment and torture.

For years, however, Salama was in almost no position to do anything. Caught between the clergy of Gondar, who suspected his theology, the Catholicizing sympathies of Webe, and the Islamizing reputation of Ras Ali, there was little scope for Salama either to strengthen his own authority or to weaken that of de Jacobis, until the arrival of a new political star, Kasa, Governor of Qwara, changed irrevocably the context of ecclesiastical conflict by restoring that central point of reference, royal power, which had always been so crucial to Ethiopian polity, but which had been so wholly absent since the late eighteenth century.

ii. *Tewodros 1855–68*

Kasa was an upstart, a poor relative, a rebel who had fought his way up, been made Governor of Qwara (the area to the west of Lake Tana), married the daughter of Ali, and then proceeded in a series of campaigns to advance his power until in 1853 he overthrew Ali to replace him as ruler of central Ethiopia. That, however, was not enough. The last of the 'judges' in the age of the Zamana Masafent, his ambition went far beyond that. In February 1855 he overthrew Webe, conquered Tigre, and immediately afterwards was anointed and crowned king of kings by Abuna Salama. He took as his throne name Tewodros. Only Shoa remained effectively independent, and within a few months it too had been subdued. After seventy years of effective kinglessness, the regal authority was thus restored and by a man of enormous energy, determination, piety, and sense of election. Plowden, the British Consul in Massawa, who had his ear very close to the ground, summed up his programme quite simply as to 'reform Abyssinia, restore the Christian faith, and become master of the world'.[5]

[5] 7 Apr. 1855, *Parliamentary Papers*, LXXII. *Accounts and Papers*, 33 *Correspondence respecting Abyssinia 1846–1868* (1867–8) 193.

In adopting the name of Tewodros, Kasa identified himself with a king whose coming had long been prophesied. The sixteenth-century apocryphal *Fakkare Iyasus* includes in the teaching of Jesus at the Last Supper the prophecy of a disastrous era to be ended by the coming of a king named Tewodros who would do Christ's will, restore the churches, and bring peace. Everything will go according to the word of the king and the abuna. Bruce in the late eighteenth century had recorded the prophecy, and from time to time unsuccessful claimants to power had proclaimed themselves by this name. Now, seemingly, he had arrived, and the immediate response was enormous.

The authority of Tewodros derived from many sources: from his own conviction of divine election demonstrated by success, from the country's desperate need for reunification and a forceful monarchy, from the Solomonic tradition and his own coronation, from the sheer quality of his character. The coronation was immensely important in transforming him from just another ras into negus, heir to the Solomonic tradition, and for it he needed Salama. It was inevitable that the triumph of Tewodros should be, at least initially, the triumph also of Salama. A well-established emperor might conceivably, like Susenyos, play with a Roman alliance. An emperor on the make could not conceivably do so. The Solomonic succession was not appealed to in the same way, at least not in the first years. He is the 'Elect of God'; only later would he assert his ancestry all the way back to Solomon. By 1866 'Son of David and of Solomon' had entered his official titles, but initially it was military success and ritual, not ancestry, which vindicated his authority. Observers recognized the sheer quality and conviction of the man. 'Without Christ I am nothing,' he would repeat, and his personal life was remarkably Christian, a monogamist who received communion with his queen at the coronation. He remained faithful to her even though she was childless, something extraordinary in an Ethiopian monarch. His concern for the poor, for destitute children especially, was well attested. At the same time he reorganized the army, ending the old system of indiscriminate pillage which was to be replaced by regular pay, improved the administration of justice, encouraged the Galla to convert to Christianity, rebuilt churches, and planned for the day when he would march out from Ethiopia to liberate Jerusalem.

The programme was fantastic. Unfortunately its sheer scale and the Emperor's ruthlessness in its implementation soon led to trouble:

with de Jacobis and the Catholics, with the provincial nobility who had not really accepted that their independence was at an end, even with the Church once he decided to tax the clergy to pay for his army.

De Jacobis had at first been immensely impressed by Kasa: 'As for Kasa, visible instrument of Providence, I cannot prophesy his intentions, and, if I have praised him to you, it is because virtue is such a rare thing here that merely its appearance immediately seduces us.'[6] That was in 1854. But the alliance of Tewodros and Salama could leave little room for the sort of ecclesiastical future de Jacobis had been working for. He was arrested and detained for five months before being sent into exile, but the full force of Salama's anger was now unleashed against the leading Catholic Ethiopian monks, Ghebra-Mika'el above all. While the others were eventually released as essentially insignificant, for Ghebra-Mika'el it was different. He was a man of national importance. He had publicly challenged Salama and he refused in any way to back down. Imprisoned, tortured again and again, brought before the Emperor, to whom he replied with almost contemptuous disregard, Ghebra-Mika'el represented the principle of the primacy of the spiritual judgement over against the power of the erastian state, in which he 'refused to recognize any authority'.[7] Ghebra-Mika'el alone, Tewodros complained to Plowden, had refused to obey the supreme authority which God had given him. After further tortures he finally expired in July 1855, sealing with his blood the integrity of the Ethiopian Catholic tradition. During the next few years the Catholic mission favoured Neguse, Webe's nephew, in his endeavours to re-establish the effective independence of Tigre, and tried to gain French support for him to balance British favour for Tewodros. Neguse, in the meantime, suggested that he would become a Catholic at the appropriate moment. If central Ethiopia was to be reconstituted as an Orthodox kingdom, could not the north become a Catholic one and an ally of France? It was all a chimera. Neguse had no power to stand up to Tewodros and France no desire to become so deeply involved in Ethiopian affairs. In 1860 de Jacobis died, Neguse was finally defeated, and the unity of the kingdom—for a time—assured.

Tewodros had no desire to eliminate a small provincial Catholic

---

[6] De Jacobis to Sturchi, 2 Jan. 1854, in Crummey, *Priests and Politicians*, 96.
[7] *Parliamentary Papers*, 152.

Church which henceforth offered no threat to royal power, the unity of the kingdom, or even the religious authority of Orthodoxy. De Jacobis had no real successor, and the European missionaries, few of whom had sympathized with his ideals, were soon in prolonged conflict with the Ethiopian Catholic clergy. Yet, almost leaderless, the Church survived. By 1885 it counted—apart from its Lazarist missionaries—some 30,000 Catholics, mostly in Tigre, 50 Ethiopian priests, and 15 sisters. Nowhere else in Africa was there anything comparable. Nor would there be until, thirty years later, ordinations began in Buganda.

In 1855, as the Catholic mission withdrew from Gondar, a Protestant team arrived once more, consisting of Krapf and Martin Flad and representing Gobat, now the Anglican-Lutheran Bishop in Jerusalem, and the CMS. Tewodros and Salama welcomed its arrival, but made clear that they wanted technicians to civilize the country, not Protestant evangelists. In particular the Emperor wanted a gun-maker, an architect, and a printer. Somewhat uncomfortably they agreed to his terms, without quite intending to abide by them, and the mission arrived in 1856 led by Flad. It was to stay in Ethiopia for twelve years. Its initial members were by no means the artisans Tewodros was looking for, but little by little a group of lay artisan missionaries trained at the St Chrischona Institute near Basle were recruited and put to work near the Emperor's working capital at Dabra Tabor. Belonging to the pietist tradition, they were as a group not unlike the Moravian community at Genadendal, committed to prayer and work rather than to evangelism. They had not, however, intended the sort of work Tewodros wanted them for: road-making was one thing, repairing thousands of broken muskets—which is what Waldmeier and Saalmüller actually found themselves doing—was rather another. The decision, however, had been taken to find a way in through imperial service and there was little alternative to complying with the requirements of Tewodros. It would end up with casting heavy artillery. Both the Emperor and Salama were pleased with the compliance and a considerable willingness on the part of the missionaries to go Ethiopian—to receive Communion, to take Ethiopian wives. A more evangelical group, led by Flad and Stern, were permitted in recompense to preach to the Falasha so long as converts were baptized into the Orthodox and not the Protestant Church. Evangelicals have mostly a great need to convert someone. So, if they were not permitted to convert Orthodox into Protestants, the conversion of Falasha into Orthodox seemed the next best thing, though it did not much please Flad, who thought the Falasha morally superior to Ethiopian Christians anyway. What seemed to justify everything was the increasing confidence of the King, who liked to discuss theology and seemed at least half-convinced by Protestant tenets: 'Do not believe I am an Abyssinian at heart; no, I am as one of you,' he told Kienzlen in a moment of confidence in 1859.[8] The missionaries were convinced he was 'a model prince'.

And for a time Tewodros saw them too as model missionaries, Waldmeier especially. They were providing him with things he wanted, and could, he hoped, obtain for him the help from Europe of which he felt increasing need. By 1859 things were not going well for him. Again and again he had to put down revolts in the provinces, not only among the Galla but almost everywhere else too. As the revolts multiplied, his violence in response to them grew, alienating people still further. There had always been a side to him which could not brook the slightest questioning of his authority and responded with a merciless cruelty. He was also at odds with the Church, which objected to assisting him financially, as with Tigre, Shawa, Gojjam, the Muslims of Wallo. Disaffection grew deeper not only among the nobility but amongst the common people, who had at first hailed him as a saviour. His turning towards the Protestant missionaries has to be seen in this context but, inevitably, they were unable to gain him the foreign help he sought or to escape his suspiciousness indefinitely.

From 1864 Tewodros was almost alone. Most of the missionaries and even the Abuna Salama were now imprisoned in Maqdala. Shoa was once more independent. The 'Slave of Christ' he had proclaimed himself to be disappeared more and more—though never completely—beneath megalomania, irrationality, and violence. Gondar was devastated by his own armies, almost all its churches pillaged and burnt, a thousand manuscripts carried away by the King. His very sympathy with Protestantism had, perhaps, helped to diminish his respect for his own Church, while bringing nothing of value to the missionaries' purpose. When the British government sent an expedition in 1867 to free his European hostages, it succeeded so easily because Ethiopia as a whole had abandoned its king, who by then ruled no more than his army and a small stretch of territory

---

[8] *Notes from the Journal of F. M. Flad*, ed. W. D. Veitch (1860), 81.

around Maqdala. His cannon, forged by the missionaries and transported at such cost from Dabra Tabor to Maqdala, proved useless, and his army was mown down by British rifles in the sole battle of the war on Good Friday 1868. Tewodros released the missionaries and all his other European prisoners and, as the British stormed Maqdala, shot himself. Salama had already died in captivity while the missionaries left the country with the British army, absolutely nothing achieved. Tewodros had wholly failed to establish the era of Tewodros, the prophesied era of peace. He had, on the contrary, still further increased the devastation of Ethiopia's central provinces.

ii. *Yohannes IV and Menelik*

The immediate aftermath to the battle of Maqdala and the death of Tewodros was an interregnum in which Shoa, Gojjam, and Tigre each once more became virtually independent. The historic and practical attraction of national unity was, however, too great for that to last uncontested and Kasa, the ruler of Tigre, had established himself as the new emperor within four years. He sent for a new abuna and in January 1872 was crowned at Aksum with all the ancient ceremonies as Yohannes IV, King of Zion of Ethiopia.

Yohannes IV, who ruled until his death in war with the Sudan Mahdists in 1889, may not unreasonably be compared with Yohannes II of the seventeenth century. He sought to rebuild the kingdom and maintain its unity by excluding, as far as possible, European influences. He was to some extent successful in an essentially traditional policy, forcing even the young king of Shoa, Menelik, to recognize his imperial authority but as the years went by, Ethiopia's perennial royal problem—how to hold the provinces together—was exacerbated by a new wave of foreign infiltration by the Egyptians in the north-west, the Mahdists in the west, and the Italians on the north coast. Menelik, meanwhile, in the south-east, had no comparably powerful enemies to withstand. He armed himself with a large increase of foreign guns, and, with their help, pushed the frontiers of Shoa far further to the south and east than they had ever been. As the north came under pressure and the south expanded, the national balance tipped once more towards Shoa as it had been in the late Middle Ages. In the meantime Yohannes did something to reunite the Church. In 1878 the Council of Borumeda, which

Yohannes called and Menelik and Ras Adal (later the Negus Takla Haymanot) of Gojjam both attended, settled once more the doctrinal issue of the dual nature of Christ and in a way satisfactory to Alexandria. Yohannes insisted upon the imposition of doctrinal orthodoxy and an end to controversy, much as many an emperor had insisted before him.

Three years later four Coptic bishops were brought from Egypt and divided across the country—a considerable step forward in pastoral organization. For Yohannes and his vassal kings the rebuilding of churches and the Christianization of the Galla (now known as the Oromo) by force or persuasion was central to their policy. When Yohannes died in 1889 and was succeeded as emperor by Menelik, despite the continued warring, famines, and even loss of some northern territory, Ethiopia was far more coherent, considerable, and Christian a state than would have been imaginable fifty years earlier.

To this recovery the Protestant and Catholic missionaries had in the end contributed quite little. The Abuna Salama, across twenty-seven years of ministry, had probably given a good deal more. With many enemies and few friends, he had nevertheless exerted the vast traditional authority of abuna with sensitivity and a very great sense of responsibility for the life of a Church. He was in a very real way the first modern archbishop, exercising the sort of jurisdictional responsibility required for a large Church. Still more important, however, was the surviving sense of a great and unique religious and national tradition, a sense shared by people in Tigre and Gojjam, Bagemdir and Shoa, and even by some further afield. There was nothing else like it in Africa and its nineteenth-century revival, first by Tewodros and Salama, then by Yohannes, is evidence not only of its depth of possession of the Amharic soul, but of its ability still to appeal to others, and to incorporate new membership.

The intrinsic force of a religious tradition with its own specific literacy, music, and rituals was, nevertheless, very much supported at this point by a superior political system and a larger number of guns. Just as those very factors ensured the loss of ground in the north either to Egypt or to Italy, so did the Ethiopian superiority in guns and organization over the peoples to the south ensure in the course of the nineteenth century a large measure of advance—admittedly, in many cases, over lands which had belonged to some degree to the Christian empire centuries earlier. In a way it was then the same factors which produced the Arab advance inland in eastern Africa or the Boer advance into the southern interior—in each case the triumph of quite simple local powers over less developed groups made possible by the mid-nineteenth century improvement in fire power—which ensured the growth southwards of the Ethiopian State and Church. Nevertheless, because these were so much more indigenous, they were able to integrate the new societies into their own system to a degree well beyond that of Arab or Boer but rather more comparable with that of a West African Fulani jihad, even though the Ethiopian recovery had little of the latter's sense of a pursuit of religious purity. By the death of Yohannes these processes were well under way, if masked by the high degree of inter-Ethiopian conflict which continued to divide south from north. For long the one thing Ethiopian Christianity had not been able to achieve was peace and the absence of peace had been particularly destructive in the lands around Gondar. Under Menelik this would slowly change and the revival of the Ethiopian Empire would reach its apogee.

Menelik was the son and grandson of kings of Shoa. His grandfather, Sahela Sellase, had ruled through most of the first half of the century and on his death in 1847 was succeeded by his son, Haile Malakot, who had died in 1856 just as Tewodros was conquering his country. His young son, Menelik, was handed over to the Emperor and spent the next ten years in detention. In 1865 he escaped from Maqdala when Shoa was already in revolt. As King of Shoa with very firm local support and a network of loyal cousins, Menelik was henceforth in a very strong position *vis-à-vis* the rest of Ethiopia, which had been far more devastated by war and famine. For the most part he recognized the suzerainty of Yohannes, but after the latter's death was quickly accepted as emperor everywhere except in Tigre. Shoa had expanded while Tigre was already threatened by Italian invasion, so it was natural enough that for the first time since the sixteenth century the centre of Ethiopia should be once more Shoa and the new capital of Addis Ababa, which Menelik had recently founded. He had then considerable natural and hereditary advantages. It was, however, still more his personal qualities—a consistent political astuteness in regard to issues, national and international, a great firmness in regard to the essentials of his policy, but also a moderation which Tewodros had so disastrously lacked, a gift for combining the traditional and the modernizing in the most effective way, an ability to retain the loyalty of his most powerful servants—which enabled him to preserve Ethiopia as the one African traditional state whose full sovereignty was recognized by Europeans.

It was not an inevitable development, and it was not what Italy had intended. In the scramble for Africa beginning in the late 1880s, Italy saw Ethiopia and the horn as its principal booty. At first Menelik, confronted not only by Italian colonization but by Tigrean dissidence, was prepared to give something away, including Massawa and Asmara. Continued Italian territorial aggression and the clear intention to establish a 'Protectorate' over the whole of Ethiopia forced him to make a stand. The country was mobilized, and in March 1896 a large Italian army was totally defeated at Adwa, a decisively important date for African history, religious as well as political. Ethiopia was to be preserved, not only as an independent political entity of considerable size but as a symbol for the whole continent of enormous power: independence from European control, Africanness, traditional culture, Christianity. Everywhere, in West and South Africa, Adwa was important and heartening news. The details of Ethiopian Christianity were understood no more than its secular polity. They did not matter. It was black. It was free. It was Christian. Even if Christianity elsewhere was brought by white missionaries linked with European colonialism, Christianity itself was not so linked. Ethiopia was proof of it and constituted both justification for being Christian despite white domination and a name to cover any African movement of protest within the Church against perceived missionary errors. The combination of politics and Christianity which was crucial to the identity and survival of Ethiopia was no less crucial to its message for Africans elsewhere, to the 'Ethiopianism' which Europeans would soon be suspecting in every corner of continent and Church.

The Italian invasion had particularly serious consequences for the little Catholic community, served by French Lazarists and its own priests, which had survived since the time of de Jacobis. As the Italian colony of Eritrea was enlarged through the later 1880s, it absorbed many of the places where the Ethiopian Catholic Church was established. In 1894 the whole of the Italian colony was handed over ecclesiastically to Italian Capuchins, and shortly afterwards the Lazarists were expelled. Even more seriously, Rome decided in July 1890 to substitute the Roman Rite, translated into Ge'ez, for the Ethiopic. It was a decision only too characteristic of the European and missionary mood of 1890 up and down the continent. The Ethiopian Catholic community, upon the one side suspected of disloyalty by the State and the nation because of the Catholicism of the Italian invaders and the Italian nationality of the Catholic missionaries, was upon the other side threatened by Rome itself with the loss of its liturgical identity. Nevertheless, it survived. A handful of the priests ordained by de Jacobis, such as Takla Haymanot of Adwa, lived through into the new century, buffeted by the fire-eating Ras Alula on the one hand, Latinizing missionaries on the other, but enduringly faithful to the tradition of 'Abuna Jacob'. The decree of 1890 was in fact never implemented. In due course, in 1913, it was reversed. The plan to Latinize the Ethiopian Catholic Church was recognized as particularly dangerous in regard to the calendar, the point at which a rite impinges most obviously on the laity, but without which a change of rite is quite impractical. After some years even the Italian Capuchins came to argue for the retention of the Ethiopian Missal. Thus in the age of high imperialism were the mistakes of Mendes very nearly, but not quite, repeated.

The years after Adwa were for Ethiopia years of exceptional peace. The authority of Menelik was almost unchallenged, the feudal independence of the great provinces was quietly diminished. His rule was far more a revival of the traditional royal system, the combination of a network of great lords, a loyal army, and the Church than the importation of a modern or Western one, yet it owed a lot to certain simple elements of European technology, not only a great many guns, obtained first from Italy then from France, but telegraph, telephone, and railway. The size of Menelik's state made communication and control extremely difficult. That had indeed always been the case in Ethiopian imperial history. If Menelik was able in the early years of the twentieth century to rule fairly peacefully and effectively over an Ethiopia larger than it had ever previously been, it was because of quite the same technical developments which elsewhere in Africa were making the European scramble so relatively easy.

The revival and expansion of the Ethiopian Church in the later nineteenth century depended upon the revival of the State. Immediately after the Council of Borumeda in 1878, Yohannes and Menelik called the Muslim leaders before them, some of whom had actually been at the Council, and declared to them 'we are your apostles. All this used to be Christian land until Gran ruined and misled it. Now let all, whether Muslim or Galla (pagan) believe on the name of Jesus Christ! Be baptized! If you wish to live in peace preserving your belongings, become Christians . . . Thereby, you will govern in this world and inherit the one to come.'[9] Soon afterwards, Muhammad Ali, Governor of Wallo, was baptized, becoming Ras Mika'el. There can be no doubt that the policy of Yohannes was at this point one of mass conversion and that, to some extent, it worked. It applied to Muslims, pagans, Falasha, and Catholics, at least in principle. Mayer, a Protestant missionary, described what was going on in Wallo as follows, in 1884:

The enforced conversion of the pagan Galla to Christianity is progressing steadily. They must let themselves be baptized when ordered and they do it so that they will not be deprived of their land and property. Where there are no churches they are built. The clergy assigned there must be paid the tithe by the Galla. They are instructed to fast and to make confession and to observe the holidays. But they are still wed to pagan rituals which nobody disturbs; even the Christians who live among them take part in them.[10]

The philosophy of Yohannes was simple: 'Different religions in one land only cause difficulties for the ruler.'[11] To some extent that had been the philosophy of many of his predecessors, but it could never be consistently applied because there were just too many non-Christians within the empire. That remained true. While Menelik co-operated with Yohannes's policy in Wallo, he made no attempt at all to impose forcible conversion on the Muslims of Harar or any other of the new areas he had subjugated. Wallo in fact appears as a special case—a province of the empire once entirely Christian, but lately quite overrun by Galla, it separated Shoa from Bagemdir and provided a permanent threat to the heartlands of the empire. A special determination to rechristianize the lands around Lake Hayq is understandable and in fact it was Galla leaders from this part who had almost taken over the empire at the beginning of the century. Wallo was the province which had resisted Tewodros most strongly and suffered from his reprisals most terribly. It was, then, seen as a political danger in a way that Muslim minorities in Bagemdir or majorities in the new conquests were not, and while Menelik was undoubtedly

---

[9] Gabra Sellase, *Chronique du règne de Menelik II, roi des rois d'Éthiopie* (Paris, 1930–1), 156.
[10] R. Caulk, 'Religion and the State in Nineteenth-Century Ethiopia', *JES* 10 (1972), 27.
[11] Ibid. 30.

more tolerant than Yohannes, even the latter did not really attempt to
impose throughout the empire the sort of campaign of conversion he
attempted, with some success—due in part to the loyal co-operation
of Ras Mika'el—in Wallo.

The pattern of Christian expansion which developed more widely,
particularly through the long years of the rule of Menelik, was rather
different. It still largely depended upon the support of the rulers. At
every level their influence was actively used in the cause of
Christianization, but it was never a matter of compulsion. Thus Takla
Haymanot, the Negus of Gojjam and at one time Menelik's enemy,
was no less a builder of churches, or the emperor's cousin,
Makonnen, or Dazazmac Balca, who had led the Ethiopian
vanguard at Adwa and was given the task of ruling the far
southern, and hardly at all Christian, province of Sidamo. Each saw
his religious task in the same way: to patronize priests, if necessary
bringing them from elsewhere, to build churches, to open a local
school, to put some pressure on the local aristocracy to convert.
Christianization began at the top of society and spread slowly down.
In remote areas like Sidamo and Qelem, near the Sudanese border,
the process of conversion with a multiplication of churches and
schools gathered momentum only after the death of Menelik and
through into the 1920s, but it was a process which had started well
before, and most clearly with the council of Borumeda.

Though so closely connected with the strength of the State, it was
not purely dependent upon the action of lay authorities. The arrival
of a group of bishops from Egypt, instead of only one, certainly made
a difference. Thus, for the first time, Shoa could have a bishop,
Matewos, to itself. The monasteries revived. There was an increase in
Christian literature, mostly in manuscript, a little in print. There were
also popular movements quite uncontrolled by the State, the most
remarkable being that of Sheikh Zakaryas, an Amhara Muslim of
Bagemdir. Born about 1845, the Sheikh began in the 1890s to have a
series of visions which led him to reconsider the figure of Jesus as it
appears in the Qur'an. His movement began as one of Muslim
reform, but slowly turned into one of Christian conversion. In the
age of Menelik there was certainly no attempt to convert Muslims by
force but it is understandable that in the context of the revival of the
Christian empire, Amhara who had been Muslims for generations
could feel drawn to return to the religion of their ancestors. Zakaryas
knew the Qur'an well and he argued from it much as Enbaqom had

done three and a half centuries earlier. A quite considerable number of Muslims were caught up in his movement, something which seemed actually to alarm rather than please civil authorities. Not until 1910 was Zakaryas baptized. The ceremony was performed at Easter at Dabra Tabor. He was given the name of Newaya Krestos and 3,000 of his followers were baptized with him. He died two years later, but the movement continued for some time as a largely autonomous group, not easily able to become wholly absorbed within orthodoxy.

Sheikh Zakaryas reminds us of the unexpectedness of religious history. He appears not wholly unlike prophets who were about to arise elsewhere in Africa, Harris in the west, Shembe in the south, but his mission was not, like theirs, on the interface between missionary Christianity and traditional religion, but, instead, on that between Islam and Christianity, both highly traditional, but both of which he approached as a literate person, student at once of gospel and Qur'an. In him as in the Catholic Fr. Takla Haymanot of Adwa in the north of Tigre, writing his life of Abuna Jacob, or simply in the priests who each day, far to the south in Sidamo, some 600 miles from Adwa, read to Dazazmac Balca from the Lives of the Saints, a tradition of literate Christianity rooted in a very far past was renewing itself and expanding all across the empire of Menelik.

7

THE VICTORIAN MISSIONARY

THE EVOLUTION OF A MOVEMENT

i. *Where Protestant Mission had Arrived by the 1840s*

On 7 January 1844 Johann Krapf arrived in Zanzibar, the first modern missionary in eastern Africa. A German from Württemberg, educated in the University of Basel, he was employed by the Anglican Church Missionary Society like a good number of other German missionaries. His five years in Ethiopia, hoping to develop in Shoa a base for a mission to the rest of Africa, especially the Galla, had ended in expulsion. He had shared the old dream of Ludolf in the seventeenth century—to Christianize Africa through Ethiopia. It was, however, as impractical in the nineteenth century as it had been in the seventeenth. Krapf's arrival at Zanzibar represents his extrication from participation in a very ancient history and insertion instead as East African pioneer within a new history which was just at that moment bursting into a first round of wide-scale achievement. For the next thirty years Krapf and his colleague and successor Rebmann would be based in Mombasa while patiently exploring both its hinterland and, still more important, East Africa's coastal languages. They completed a translation of the New Testament into Swahili while beginning work as well on Nyika, Kamba, and other tongues.

At just the same time, J. F. Schön, another Basel graduate and CMS employee and an equally able linguist, was doing the same on the West Coast for Hausa and Igbo, while Samuel Crowther, his African colleague, recently ordained by the Bishop of London, was at work on the Yoruba New Testament. Further along the coast in Cameroon, the Jamaican Baptist mission begun in 1843 produced four years later a translation of Matthew's Gospel into Isubu, made by the Jamaican Joseph Merrick, and, in 1848, another into Duala by the English missionary, Alfred Saker. South, in Kuruman, Moffat's

Sechuana New Testament had been completed by 1840. In 1847 David Livingstone settled at Kolobeng, several hundred miles to the north of Kuruman, the most forward point reached hitherto by what had now become a very extensive network of southern African missions. In Natal, the American Board of Missions was busy establishing a number of stations, while Norwegian Lutherans were just beginning to do the same in Zululand. Back in the west the first inland mission north of the Equator was established in 1846 by Henry Townshend and Crowther at Abeokuta.

The point demonstrated by these various facts is that the 1840s witnessed the penetration of the continent by an army of earnest Protestant missionaries to a degree hitherto unprecedented. Some were incompetent enough, some were cantankerous, many died. Nevertheless, there was already a smell of a breakthrough in the air, and, while a generation earlier the missionary had been at home an object of ridicule or mistrust, a low-class religious fanatic attempting the absurd if not the undesirable, now he was starting to be seen instead as the hero of both religious and secular achievement. That was true even before Livingstone arrived back in Britain in 1856 from his trans-African journey to take the nation by storm. 'Conversions' might be few, but the sharp edge of the work, and it would prove a sharper one than any could have guessed, was the linguistic edge. What was already beginning to make a decisive difference to Africa by 1850 was the diffusion of copies of the New Testament, of hymn-books, prayer-books, and what have you (including, quite soon, a series of versions of *Pilgrim's Progress*) in a number of important languages. In none of them had anything hitherto been printed, and in very few had anything ever been written. This beginning to a popular literature would provide not only a tool for each future wave of missionaries to use and extend, but also, far less predictably, an autonomous instrument of Christianization of immense authority, at once Western and native. Modernization would go with reading, and reading meant acculturation into the world of Christian literature and ideas. Alternative literature there was none. The 1840s saw established a novel form of influence which would, over the next 100 years, continually grow in quantity and remain almost unchallenged.

The missionary movement was, then, by 1850, becoming more than it realized a truly creative force within African history, the provider of much that was genuinely new and revolutionary, both mental and material, things that neither African societies themselves, nor the old Catholic missionaries, nor European traders and consuls had, or could, provide. It was already a more important, and less easily labelled, force than modern secular historians mostly admit. How had it come to develop and what were its characteristics? It is not too easy to answer either of those questions. Post-Reformation Protestantism had for centuries remained rather strangely uninterested in missionary or evangelical responsibility towards non-Christian peoples. There were a few exceptions, especially in North America, but even the SPG, the Society for the Propagation of the Gospel in foreign parts, founded in England in 1701, had in practice almost wholly limited its interest to the pastoral care of the English overseas. No organization or movement had in any way felt committed to a mission of evangelization of the non-Christian before the Moravians in Germany in the eighteenth century, and they were tiny in number, a group of communitarian pietists. From them, however, a missionary consciousness began to spread more widely in Germany and then also in England towards the close of the eighteenth century. The impact both of the Evangelical Movement and of ever wider contacts between Europe, Britain especially, and the non-Western world must have contributed to produce this change. Nevertheless, like so many spiritual and cultural movements, it remains far from clear why the Protestant missionary movement came just when it did and, then, so very fast.

The Baptist Missionary Society, founded in 1792, was the first of what soon would become a multitude. It had been stimulated by William Carey, a Northamptonshire cobbler, who at once set off for India. The inaugural meeting consisted of a dozen people gathered in a back parlour in Kettering. Other Free Churchmen picked up the enthusiasm from the Baptists and established the non-denominational London Missionary Society in 1795. This time the inaugural meeting was held at the Castle and Falcon public house in Aldersgate. The point to be noted is that the missionary movement began in Britain as a working-class initiative, far removed from universities, the wealthy, or the State Church. Both Edinburgh and Glasgow saw the founding of societies in 1796. Upper-class, evangelical Anglicans centred upon the Clapham group did not want to be outdone, so the Church Missionary Society was created in 1799. As important as anything, the British and Foreign Bible Society was formed in 1804 with the specific task of ensuring the translation and printing of the Scriptures. In 1810 a Board of Commissioners for Foreign Missions (the ABCFM) was set up in the United States. In England the Wesleyan Methodists founded their own society in 1813. Next year the first of the German societies was established at Basel. A little later came Berlin and Paris, Leipzig and Bremen. What in 1780 existed in the Protestant world as at most the rather idiosyncratic concern of a handful of Moravians was by 1840 central almost to the very *raison d'être* of all the mainline Churches as understood by their more lively and enthusiastic membership.

It is true that these were private societies set up mostly by lay people. Bishops were distinctly slow to share in the new enthusiasm, just as they had, for instance, been slow to share in any enthusiasm for the friars in the thirteenth century. It required all Wilberforce's tact over many months to secure a very moderate measure of non-disapproval of the CMS at its foundation from the Archbishop of Canterbury. It would be 1815 before a couple of bishops could be persuaded to join the Society's vice-presidents. Only in 1841 did the Archbishop of Canterbury accept an *ex officio* role in the Society and the bishops as a whole give it their patronage. A State Church found it hard to see the propriety of being a missionary Church. There could, nevertheless, be no going back on a phenomenon which not only sparked off a growing wave of populist spiritual enthusiasm but also reflected only too well the increasing sense of world hegemony and responsibility entrusted not just to Great Britain but to Anglo-Saxon Protestantism. A world missionary outlook suited a Britain which now ruled the best part of India, the West Indies, Australia, Canada, Cape Colony, and much else. London was becoming, every year more consciously, the world's imperial and intellectual capital. In an age of evangelical seriousness it could hardly avoid taking up the burden of a world-wide religious responsibility as well.

The early missionary movement, however, was not, at least consciously, an aspect of British imperial expansion. It spread without the slightest need for adaptation to quite un-British lands like Norway or anti-British lands like America. It is true that British governors, both in Sierra Leone and in Cape Colony, expected to use missionaries as their agents for various tasks both inside and outside the borders of the colony and that missionaries often accepted such responsibilities, but, at least at times, they did it somewhat reluctantly and awkwardly. If they were British, they came mostly from the Free Churches and in no way from the governing classes. If not British, they were even less likely to wish to be identified with the colonial government. At times, perhaps, they relished it somewhat naïvely just because in background they were so socially insignificant. Some mid-Victorian missionaries, British Methodists and German Lutherans as much as Anglicans, were naturally erastian and glad enough to have a colonial role, but their conception of Christianity was for the most part highly other-worldly in message and congregationalist in form.

While the upper-class Evangelicals who had founded the CMS were Anglicans of the political class, such people did not themselves contemplate for a moment becoming missionaries. Somewhat to their disappointment, they found that their reluctance was shared even by Anglicans of a humbler sort. Indeed for quite a while recruitment among the clergy seemed well-nigh impossible. It was therefore convenient to find that Germans were both more amenable and already being rather well prepared for mission in Basle and Berlin, and quite a few were recruited for CMS employment. After 1820 the CMS, sensitive to a certain awkwardness in an Anglican missionary society spreading Christianity by means of Lutherans, managed to increase the supply of English missionaries, but few were of the calibre of the Germans. A training institute was opened at Islington in 1825 to polish up the British candidates, but even here its most distinguished students were largely German. It is striking how, as late as the great CMS mission of 1876 to the interior of East Africa destined for Buganda and Karagwe, in some ways one of the sagas of Anglican missionary history, there was only one Englishman—a young naval officer—in the original party of seven, and the only Anglican clergyman available was a still-younger Australian. The mission's key figure was a lay Scottish Calvinist deeply distrustful of the Church of England. Only in the 1880s did this really change on the Evangelical side. On the more Anglo-Catholic wing it had altered twenty years earlier with the foundation of the Universities Mission to Central Africa. It was doubtless the needs of India and elsewhere which through the middle decades of the century drained off such English Evangelical clergy of better education as did apply, but in African terms the effect was clear.

All this mattered the less in that, until the middle of the century, the missionary movement was a singularly non-denominational function of international Protestantism of a rather lay and individualistic sort. Its most characteristic organ in the early period was undoubtedly the London Missionary Society, and nearly all the LMS's ablest men were Scots. If the LMS sent out a Dutchman as its pioneer to the Cape, or Philip, Moffat, and Livingstone, all Scotsmen, if the CMS sent out a succession of German Lutherans, it was all one. The political leadership of the movement could be English, its personnel German, Scottish, or, a little later, French, Scandinavian, or American. They were united in spreading a non-denominational Protestant gospel. There was much concern for Scripture, direct preaching, the personal experience of sin and of conversion; there was little concern for Church order or a liturgy other than the simplest. Effectively the missionaries became the clergy, African converts the laity, in a new kind of Presbyterianism, dependent for its existence on the control and financial support not of bishops but of a board in Europe. However, the high white mortality rate, the expense of supporting numerous missionaries, many of them married, and the obvious problem of language, all pointed to the need for something which soon came to be nominated, a trifle awkwardly, 'native agency'. It was more a matter of practical necessity than of theology or far-sighted strategy.

The 1840s, the first age in Africa of at least some signs of significant missionary success, was also the time when the first simple, almost undifferentiated character of the missionary movement began to alter and break apart. There were four factors making for this. One was the impact of theory, stress upon 'civilization' on the one side, on a more adaptive missiology upon the other. A second, connected both with the disastrous course of the 1841 Niger expedition, which reinforced recognition of the appallingly high missionary death-rate in West Africa, and with the increasing maturity of the Sierra Leone Church, was a sharp practical sense of the need for more, and properly trained, African agents, including ordained clergy. The third was the general multiplication, with overlapping and at times irritable friction, of missionary societies producing an inevitable denominationalism as a variety of Churches took root. The creation of Anglican bishoprics at Cape Town and Freetown towards the end of the decade (and others later) reflected the increasing acceptance of the missionary movement by the establishment in the Church of England and it provided a much needed authority for those concerned, but it also contributed to a larger division, creating an inevitable separation in ethos and Church order between Anglicans and others. Up to 1840 there is a sense of Protestant mission, anarchical but one. After the 1840s there is a sense rather of Anglican, Methodist, or Baptist missions, better disciplined but more divided.

ii. *The Catholic Revival*

The fourth factor producing change in the 1840s was the revival of Catholic mission. The old movement, which had begun in the sixteenth century, received new direction by the establishment in Rome of Propaganda Fide in the early seventeenth, and continued with little change, if declining momentum, into the late eighteenth, largely collapsed under the impact of the French Revolution and Napoleonic Wars. Religious houses and seminaries were closed in most parts of Europe. Even the Roman Curia was for years disrupted. Only after Waterloo could recovery begin. It did so almost at once, but a great deal of leeway needed to be made up. The Society of Jesus was officially reconstituted in 1814 and new congregations of a more or less missionary nature were soon being founded, such as the Oblates of Mary Immaculate at Marseilles in 1816. In 1822 at Lyons a young laywoman, Pauline Jaricot, began a pious lay association named the Work for the Propagation of the Faith, a fund-gathering body which would spread throughout the Catholic world while retaining its headquarters in Paris, and provide the financial undergirding for the new missionary movement which was about to develop. But the shortage of clergy was so considerable in some parts of Europe and the demand was also so pressing in new emigrant areas, above all the United States, that it was only in the 1840s in the pontificate of Gregory XIV that a real impetus was once again given to the African mission.

Gregory, Pope from 1831 to 1846, had previously been Prefect of the Congregation of Propaganda. An extreme conservative at home, his missionary commitment was outstanding and could lead even to seemingly radical actions such as the publication in December 1839 of the Apostolic Letter *In Supremo Apostolatus* condemning the slave-trade, something which too many Catholic countries were still very much abetting. While this was not a reversal of the previous papal position, it was a far more public and weighty statement of condemnation than anything that had gone before. It has to be said that it was, in part, a response to British pressure.

A Vicariate-Apostolic of the Cape of Good Hope was erected by Gregory in 1837, one for the 'Two Guineas' (effectively the whole west coast north of Angola) in 1842, another for Egypt in 1844, and a fourth for the Sudan or Central Africa in 1846. By 1850 the eastern Cape and Natal had become separate vicariates. Already de Jacobis had landed at Massawa in 1839 while a remarkably mixed group of Jesuits, led by a Pole, Maximilian Ryllo, ascended the Upper Nile in 1847. Irish secular priests were dispatched to the eastern Cape, French Oblates of Mary Immaculate to Natal. Already a new Catholic missionary assault upon Africa was, then, well under way, but while the Protestant assault was centrally unplanned and largely under the management of a multitude of lay boards, the Catholic was far more centralized beneath the control of Propaganda Fide.

Doubtless anxiety about Protestant missionary progress helped stimulate the Catholic revival but, basically, it was simply the natural renewal of an activity which the Catholic Church had always regarded as crucial and which had only been, in part, abandoned under pressure of extraneous circumstances. The most influential single development within the revival was the foundation in France by Francis Libermann, a convert Jew, of a new Congregation, the 'Missionaries of the Holy Heart of Mary', in 1840 and its merging a few years later with the far older, but almost defunct, Congregation of the Holy Ghost, based in Paris. The amalgamated group took the name and buildings of the older society but the leader and orientation of the new one. It was to be a missionary congregation explicitly directed to Africa. Libermann was an outstandingly perceptive and charismatic figure, able to inject a new dynamism and a more specifically missionary spirituality into his group, but he died in 1852 when it was still just beginning.

Only a few years later, in 1854, another new society was founded for Africa in France, this time in Lyons, where the Association for the Propagation of the Faith was already centred. The Society of African Missions (SMA) owed its existence to Melchior de Marion-Bresillac, who had formerly been a missionary bishop in India. It took over from the Holy Ghost Fathers responsibility for a large central section of the west coast. De Bresillac and his first missionary party were wiped out by yellow fever in Freetown in 1859 only a few weeks after arrival, but a second party established itself at Ouidah on the coast of Dahomey in 1861 led by an Italian, Francesco Borghero. They had chosen Dahomey in preference to Sierra Leone as 'virgin territory', but the kingdom itself was firmly closed to missionaries and their establishment on the coast at Ouidah proved anything but virgin. It represented instead almost total continuity with the least effective Catholic presence of the past. The home of a Portuguese-speaking community of mixed blood and slave-trading traditions,

Ouidah was Christian enough to want a Catholic ritual presence and to tolerate a school for its children. Language-learning took second place.

Jean-Remi Bessieux, the Holy Ghost Congregation's pioneer on the west coast and Vicar-Apostolic of the Two Guineas, had already had a Pongwe grammar and a Pongwe–French dictionary printed at Amiens in 1847, indicative of the way some Catholics, no less than Protestants, were developing a greatly increased concern for African languages, but both at Ouidah and in South Africa the impression is one of a primary concern for people already somehow nominally Catholic because of European origin or mixed blood, and of a pattern of mission in practice rather little affected by the half-century of hiatus since the close of the eighteenth century. It would take another twenty years for new approaches to develop sufficiently to alter the character of the movement as a whole. They would be associated above all with the name of the French Archbishop of Algiers, Charles Lavigerie.

iii. David Livingstone and his Influence

On 9 December 1856 David Livingstone arrived in England, after fifteen years working for the LMS in southern Africa. He had just completed a crossing of the heart of the continent on foot from Loanda to Quelimane. Within a week he had addressed a special meeting of the Royal Geographic Society, followed the next day by another of the LMS, chaired by Lord Shaftesbury. Oxford and Glasgow presented doctorates, the Royal Society elected him a Fellow. Livingstone, by the force of his character, his almost indestructible physical constitution, his meticulous observations, climatic, botanic, and anthropological, relating to so much of Africa hitherto wholly unreported, his enormous and infectious sense of high purpose both religious and humanitarian, so vastly reinvigorated the missionary scene that its post-1856 history takes, for a good quarter-century, a decidedly post-Livingstonean character.

The Livingstone agenda was now more complex and even contradictory than the apparent simple honesty of the man might suggest. As an LMS missionary tied to a single station in southern Africa he had grown increasingly frustrated. Not for him the somewhat complacent perfectionism within one small location of his father-in-law, Robert Moffat. As a conventional missionary,

Livingstone had not been a success, and the ambitions of his restless soul were stung by bitterness both towards his fellow missionaries and towards the brutal injustices carried out by Boer farmers of the Transvaal upon their African neighbours. He was early convinced that Christianity would advance better with fewer missionaries and more 'native agency', but his own use of the latter had not worked happily for him. From being a failed local practitioner he turned himself by travelling into a continent-wide strategist. The great central mass of Africa north of Kolobeng remained untouched by missionary influence. His great journey demonstrated, he believed, that it was far less inaccessible than had appeared, a field full of receptive peoples threatened only by the continuance of the slave-trade.

As a young man, Livingstone had been present in Exeter Hall in June 1840 when the Society for the Extinction of the Slave Trade and for the Civilization of Africa had celebrated its first anniversary in the presence of Prince Albert, Sir Robert Peel, Mr Gladstone, and a bevy of bishops. It was the meeting preparatory to the miscalculated and disastrous Niger Expedition of the following year, but its message of introducing Christianity and Civilization through Commerce had sunk deep into his mind, and now that he had returned to England seventeen years later it was flung forth again with all the authority of his unique experience, an authority which was, of course, wholly irrelevant to it.

Livingstone resigned from the London Missionary Society to become instead a British consul, a professional explorer, an anti-slave-trade propagandist, but, above all, a sort of honorary patron and guide to the missionary world generally, a world galvanized by his speeches and writings into a new frenzy of activity. 'Native agency' was henceforth less heard of in Livingstone circles than the advances of commerce, 'the preparation of the raw materials of European manufactures in Africa', as a better means to the 'larger diffusion of the blessings of civilization than efforts exclusively spiritual and educational'.[1] The Niger plan of 1841, he had come to believe, should somehow be resurrected on the Zambezi in 1860. His words of farewell in December 1857 in the Senate House in Cambridge remain the most memorable expression of mid-Victorian missionary zeal: 'I beg to direct your attention to Africa:—I know that in a few

[1] David Livingstone, *Missionary Travels and Researches in South Africa* (1857), 24.

years I shall be cut off in that country, which is now open; do not let it be shut again! I go back to Africa to make an open path for commerce and Christianity; do you carry out the work which I have begun. I leave it to you.'[2]

Livingstone excelled in the combination of rhetoric, ideology, and experience. Unfortunately he did not excel in realistic judgement and advice where other Europeans were concerned, yet his British achievement was extraordinary: the result of his year-long advocacy was not only a British government expedition up the Zambezi led by himself as Consul, not only two new LMS missions to be set up north and south of the Zambezi, but also the foundation of a wholly new missionary society—the Universities' Mission to Central Africa (UMCA). It was a lot for one year. The Zambezi expedition was nearly an early disaster owing to the total navigational block, unsuspected by Livingstone, of the Cabora Bassa rapids, but the discovery of the Shire River and its way through to the Shire highlands and Lake Nyasa postponed the failure and provided a new focus of attention which would be important for the future. The missions, however, both LMS and UMCA, had been gravely misled and all three ventures proved appalling disasters. At the end of six years the Zambezi expedition was withdrawn by the British government after considerable loss of life, including that of Mrs Livingstone, and no start at all to Livingstone's dream of a commercial settlement in central Africa.

The pull of the deep interior was, nevertheless, now irresistible even if the following years witnessed a lull in grandiose plans. Livingstone's impact had established it as never before within the agenda of the European mind. He had also done two other things. He had greatly stimulated missionary interest among the upper class and graduates. The UMCA team of Bishop Mackenzie may not have been immediately better missionaries than men fifty years earlier. Their academic sensitivities certainly helped them avoid some of the earlier naïveties, though they could also contribute to a profound impracticality. Not, of course, that they were the first graduates, even the first British graduates, to become missionaries in Africa. But UMCA's collective commitment pointed to a significant widening in those responding to the missionary call and not only within its own ranks. Livingstone's often repeated and somewhat sarcastic remark

[2] William Monk, _Dr Livingstone's Cambridge Lectures_ (Cambridge, 1858), 24.

that a missionary is not just a dumpy little man with a Bible under his arm was sinking in. As the first UMCA men sailed up the Shire River they read to themselves not only Moffat's *Missionary Labours* but also Darwin's *Origin of Species*. They were exceptional. Most missionaries, even Cambridge graduates from the University's Eight, remained rather little affected by the more secularizing and critical aspects of late Victorian culture. Livingstone's third lasting contribution was to revive the commitment both to anti-slavery and to commerce as being conjunctive with the missionary movement, more so in fact than they had ever been in the past. Missionaries seem much more personally affected by anti-slavery sentiment in this second wave, relating to the east of the continent, than they had been in the first, western, wave. While this may have been a good thing the stress on commerce was almost certainly misguided. It appealed particularly to Scots.

The manifest failure of all the Livingstone initiatives in the Zambezi years did, nevertheless, leave the movement in some confusion. It came to be recognized that in practical terms he was an unreliable guide. It would all the same be the emotion stirred by his death in 1873, the amazing story of the transportation of his body by his servants across half the continent to Bagamoyo on the coast, and his burial in Westminster Abbey, which set off a new wave of inland mission across east and central Africa, the wave which would establish in large part its definitive ecclesiastical geography.

iv. *Verona Fathers and White Fathers*

Well before the death of Livingstone, however, two other African missionary societies were founded within the Catholic Church. Daniel Comboni was an Italian priest from the seminary of Verona which had accepted responsibility for reinforcing the Jesuits and Franciscans in the Upper Nile mission where the casualty rate was particularly high. Thus of five Slovene recruits who arrived in 1851, four were dead within four months. Faced with the futility of pouring in Europeans who died off as fast, Comboni again thought harder than most about how to develop instead an African ministry. His 'New Plan' suddenly came to him as a blinding intuition on 15 September 1864 in St Peter's, Rome: 'It flashed before my mind,'[3] a

---

[3] Pietro Chiocchetta, *Daniel Comboni: Papers for the Evangelization of Africa* (Rome, 1982), 93.

plan for the 'Regeneration of Africa by Africans'. European missionaries in Africa died. Africans selected for training in Europe also, only too often, died. If they did not, their training still proved both costly and ineffective. They seldom wanted to return home. If they did return, they could fail to fit in. Comboni's 'New Plan' was essentially to leave the conversion of Africa to Africans who had been prepared for it within Africa but in the more temperate zones. It seemed a sensible idea; to him it was a revelation from God. Initially two institutions were opened in Cairo in 1867, one for boys, one for girls. Comboni appealed for their support in a moving petition to the first Vatican Council in 1870. Yet the Cairo schools were themselves not a great success, and what came out in due course from Comboni's 'New Plan' was simply the establishment of the two missionary societies of Verona, one for priests, the other for nuns. Their principal field of work would remain the Upper Nile, and their missionary approach would be no different from that of others, canon law proving more powerful than blinding intuition. What would alter Catholic missionary achievement between the middle and the late nineteenth century was less a revolutionary change of method—wonderful as that might have been, if genuinely applied—than quinine, railways, and European administration.

Further to the west, however, a somewhat more revolutionary initiative was developing. In 1867 Charles Lavigerie was appointed Archbishop of Algiers, hitherto a position of little importance and one concerned with not much more than the chaplaincy of French settlers. But Lavigerie was an exceptional person both in intelligence, at once learned and imaginative, and in an ambitious forcefulness. He was to prove the most outstanding Catholic missionary strategist of the nineteenth century, determined to turn his see of Algiers into something of continental significance. In 1868 he founded yet another society, the Missionaries of Our Lady of Africa, soon to become known as the White Fathers on account of the Arab dress they were given to wear. The White Sisters followed. More consistently than any one else Lavigerie insisted on a strategy of adaptation in clothes, language, food. It did not, however, include theological adaptation. The White Fathers, like all the new Catholic missionary societies of the nineteenth century, were theological ultramontanes. In the post-revolutionary era and the age of the first Vatican Council Catholic institutional renewal was carried out with a sense of dependence upon Rome and of the necessity for theological and liturgical conformity still greater than that of the Counter Reformation period.

The White Fathers were based quite deliberately not in France but in North Africa—in Algiers and in Carthage, outside Tunis. Lavigerie had added to his existing position that of Archbishop of Carthage and 'Primate of Africa', as well as Apostolic Delegate of the Sahara. He saw himself as the reviver of the ancient Christian Church of Africa, the Church of Cyprian of Carthage. He remained at the same time very much a French statesman for whom the French conquest of North Africa was a matter of high pride. Without it, of course, his job would not have existed. The White Fathers had their first mission to work with the Muslims in North Africa, but they soon received a second: the evangelization of the far interior of Africa, both west and east. The Holy Ghost Fathers and the SMA could take the coasts, Verona the Nile, Lavigerie would have the vast interior, which, in the age of Livingstone—and Lavigerie was something of a Livingstone fan—seemed a great deal more important. In January 1876 three White Fathers were murdered in the first party moving south across the Sahara. Two years later another party arrived on the coast of East Africa, led by Leon Livinhac. It was destined for both Buganda, north of Lake Victoria, and, to the south of it, Unyanyembe. From then on White Fathers would provide the vanguard of Catholic participation in the missionary scramble for the centre of the continent around the great lakes.

v. *The State of Missionary Complexity by 1880*

Lavigerie's White Fathers, Libermann's Holy Ghost Fathers, Comboni's Verona Fathers, and Bresillac's Missionaries of Africa were the most specialized of the new Catholic groups at work. It is noteworthy that not one among them ever ventured to South Africa. By instinct, perhaps more than by conscious decision, the missionary professional avoided settler society. But there were many other orders at work, including older groups like Capuchins and Jesuits and an increasing number of congregations of nuns. Propaganda Fide exercised some overall control more successfully in the nineteenth than in the seventeenth century. But none of the new congregations mentioned above placed its headquarters in Rome. The Catholic missionary movement remained, until after the First World War, a network of very distinct organizations, often none too sympathetic to one another.

Yet upon the Protestant side the picture was still more complex and disorganized. If the London Missionary Society and the Church Missionary Society retained a certain pre-eminence (at least in the literature), they were reinforced, or challenged, by more and more societies, coming from more and more nations. They overlapped and clashed. Without any central equivalent to Propaganda Fide, or, indeed, any really international society (the LMS and CMS became steadily less international as the century wore on), there was an unplanned multiplicity of organizations often overlapping on the ground, co-operative in part but also jealous of one another's influence, anxious that their own Church rather than another should prevail. British Methodists and Anglicans, Scottish Presbyterians, American Congregationalists, French Calvinists, and Norwegian Lutherans were, for instance, all at work in the area between the Transkei, the Drakensburgs, and Zululand.

Away from the south they were, admittedly, less numerous, less diverse, and far less overlapping. Nevertheless, by 1880 the advance into the great interior, north of the Limpopo and away from the coast, was already well under way, well in advance of the colonial scramble, a thing missionaries before the mid-1880s were certainly not expecting. A quick survey of their presence in East and central Africa—the Livingstone area—in what was to be the last phase of pre-colonial Africa may now be helpful.

They came from two directions: through Cape Town (or Durban) in the south and Zanzibar or the Zambezi–Shire River in the east. From the south there was the LMS mission with the Ngwato of Khama at Shoshong, just north of the Limpopo. Then came the further LMS station at Inyati among the Ndebele, established by Moffat himself by permission of Mzilikazi in 1859. They had been joined by the Jesuits at Bulawayo in 1879 while François Coillard of the Paris Evangelical Mission, who had been in Basutoland since 1858, had just received permission from Lewanika of the Barotse to open a mission among them, north-west of the Zambezi. But none of these missions, north of Shoshong, had any real clientele in 1880.

On the east coast there had been Anglican and Catholic stations on Zanzibar Island since the early 1860s. The Anglican UMCA had retreated there from Magomero, south of Lake Nyasa, after the death of Bishop Mackenzie. The Catholics had advanced from a far older presence in Mauritius. Each had begun with freed slaves. The slave market in Zanzibar was only closed in 1873. On the coast of the mainland was the CMS station at Rabai outside Mombasa where Rebmann, old and finally blind, maintained his solitary stance until 1875 when the mission was re-established on a different site as a refuge for slaves freed by the British naval patrol on the coast. Since 1862 there had also been a not very successful Methodist mission further to the north and, since 1868, a Catholic mission at Bagamoyo opposite Zanzibar. It was run by the Holy Ghost Fathers as the first large east coast freed-slave settlement. Inland the move was just beginning, cautiously, not venturing too far, as the Bagamoyo priests resettled some of their population at selected posts up-country. The UMCA was doing much the same, opening a station at Magila in 1868, Masasi in 1876, Newala 1878.

None of these were wildly ambitious moves involving major expeditions, but a number of the latter were taking place at the same time. James Stewart, who had been with Livingstone on the Zambezi and been somewhat disillusioned by the experience, had later gone to head the prestigious mission of Lovedale in South Africa. In 1874, the year after Livingstone's death, he proposed to the General Assembly of the Free Church of Scotland a new central African mission to be named Livingstonia and to develop as 'a great centre of commerce, civilization and Christianity':[4] the quintessence of all that Livingstone had stood for. It came into existence on the banks of Lake Nyasa the following year and was quickly joined by a comparable mission of the Church of Scotland in the highlands to the south, christened Blantyre after Livingstone's birthplace. Soon afterwards the CMS mission arrived in Buganda in response to Stanley's appeal, and, a few months later, the White Fathers too arrived not only in Buganda but also in the Lake Tanganyika area. In 1878 an LMS mission also made for Lake Tanganyika while, far to the west on the Kongo River, British and Jamaican Baptists from the Cameroon and the Livingstone Inland Mission were also beginning work that year.

The scale of the new missionary presence, much of it far inland, was now clearly considerable. Most of these ventures were far beyond the borders of any colony and undefended by colonial power. From

---

[4] J. McCracken, *Politics and Christianity in Malawi 1875–1940: The Impact of the Livingstonia Mission on the Northern Province* (1977), 27.

time to time missionaries were murdered, as was Bishop Hannington on Mwanga's orders in 1885, and no one suggested that anything could be done about it. Certainly this would soon change, but there is no evidence to suggest that the missionary growth in central or West Africa before the late 1880s was in expectation of a European political take-over. It was, on the contrary, very clearly to uncolonial Africa that they had gone. If we cut off the story at this point there is adequate evidence across more than three-quarters of a century for the interaction of missionaries with an Africa outside colonial control—from Kuruman and Ibadan to Livingstonia and Buganda. It can both be considered on its own and compared with that from within the settler areas of the south.

STYLE, PRIORITIES, AND MIND

vi. *Missionary Characteristics and Life-Style*

The normative early nineteenth-century missionary was a working man. To describe him as a member of the lower middle class would be to mislead. He was an artisan, a worker with a skill, and even such clergy as went were seldom of a very different background. Even the rather grand Dr Philip was the same. He had been well educated, no doubt, but he had been to no university and had acquired his honorary doctorate by kind arrangement of Princeton. Missionaries of Philip's generation were quintessentially Free Churchmen who received and expected from government at home little but an uneasy tolerance. Abroad some indeed would soon develop an establishmentarian quality—colonial life was always a way of acquiring airs—but they were not obvious colleagues for a colonial state. As missionaries, many had had little, if any, training and were even convinced that training, education, and theology were rather pointless. What was needed was a good knowledge of the Bible, a great deal of faith, and a strong voice. The job, as at first they saw it, was one emphatically of preaching. The truth of the biblical and Christian message would be all the clearer in a non-Christian world than it was when preached in the villages and slums of Britain. Send out your cobblers, tailors, carpenters, blacksmiths, weavers, and whatever. To found a Christian community, obviously, to teach trades, naturally, but the early nineteenth-century stress was neither upon the ordering of a Church nor upon industrial mission. It was upon evangelism, and it was assumed that such people could be excellent evangelists. It is, perhaps, amazing that in a number of cases they were. Some turned for home quickly enough, others to secular employment in the field: they were, after all, leaving Britain at a time when large numbers of their class were emigrating to seek a better life in America or elsewhere. The white Grahamstown settler and the missionary were of quite the same background and, in some cases at least, of not too dissimilar a motivation. Yet it was the cobbler Carey, the gardener Moffat, and Livingstone, the employee in a cotton factory working his way through medical school, who turned into outstanding linguists and missionary statesmen.

Without question the run-of-the-mill missionary could feel sadly lost with almost no useful instruction from his home committee, little sense of teamwork in the field, huge language problems, and—most often—total lack of interest among Africans in regard to the message he was forever trying to impart. The appointment of John Philip, a 40-year-old clergyman of superior intellect, as LMS Superintendent in South Africa in 1819 was recognition from home that there was a problem and that better education and on-the-spot supervision might help resolve it. The number of recruits of comparable background grew rather slowly until the middle of the century, but missionary training, while almost absent in some cases, was taken extremely seriously by some continentals long before that. Charles Isenberg spent nine years in preparation in Basle, Berlin, and London, and, even after setting off for Africa in 1833, he still spent another eighteen months in Cairo polishing up his Arabic and Amharic.

There was also a fairly steady alteration in the balance between the lay and the clerical. The societies at home sent out recruits who were overwhelmingly lay, but many of those who stuck it out were ordained in the field within a few years. A man as little educated as James Read was hardly ordainable at home, but, once his commitment was proven, the need for more ministers quickly prevailed even in Church traditions which regarded themselves as anything but clericalist. Only in the large institutions like Lovedale and Livingstonia was there really place for a considerable number of the unordained. Otherwise, on the smaller station, the layman remained unordained only if he really was intellectually not up to it or had some clear technical job to keep him fully occupied. But as the ordained man spent much of his time gardening, building, or printing, the need for the unordained to do such things was not so obvious. This was, again, true of medical mission, which was not seen as a distinct field until the end of the century. Until then the typical medical missionary was almost invariably ordained as well. The normative missionary was an all-rounder endeavouring to cope with bodies and souls, laying bricks, translating texts, and administering the sacraments. That was true alike of Protestant and Catholic.

In intention, nevertheless, and, to some extent, in practice, there remained a difference between 'Protestant' and 'Catholic' missionary patterns. Roman Catholic missionary societies were overwhelmingly of priests, supported by 'lay brothers' who were almost purely artisan, less numerous, and clearly subordinate. There were no genuinely lay missionaries. The high church UMCA looked rather more like a Catholic than a Protestant society; its staff was far more clerical than its Protestant predecessors and far more academic; its lay assistants were divided from the clergy more emphatically. Above all, its members were celibate. Women were essential to the Protestant approach. Men without wives would soon be in trouble and taking a native wife was seen as at least unfortunate (though the marriage of the black minister Tiyo Soga to a Scottish girl, Janet Burnside, in 1857 was quite accepted in mission circles at least, even if it caused a stir on the streets of Port Elizabeth). Men might be sent out unmarried, but once they were settled suitable women would be selected to go out to marry them, or they would find a wife on their first furlough. Single missionary men would quite often marry single missionary women on the station where both had been placed. In new and particularly risky missions, like the CMS East African venture of 1876, married men would go out leaving wife and children at home, with the idea that the latter would follow them when it was judged safe to do so. The men might be dead first. At times one gasps at the degree of apparent recklessness in the arrangements, the strain upon wives and children whether left at home or taken out. One has to remember that such arrangements were no less common at the time in the colonial service, the army, or in trade.

The single woman missionary appears quite early. Jane Waterston opened the girls' boarding school at Lovedale in 1867, Mary Slessor arrived in Calabar in 1876, but single women had been going out for many years before that. The CMS was averse to sending them out before the 1880s and it is only in the last twenty years of the century that they become very numerous—the huge total increase in missionary numbers after 1880 is made up to a quite considerable extent of unmarried women. Nevertheless, the unmarried woman was a notable part of the Victorian missionary team from a far earlier date, and in few other ways might European women of the middle and lower classes find so much freedom to work and to exercise responsibility, despite the undoubted male dominance of the missionary world as a whole. But the central model for Protestant mission was certainly that of the missionary couple in which husband and wife were seen as fellow workers. In the pleasant atmosphere of Kuruman and the home of Mary and Robert Moffat it worked well enough. They lived there fifty years and brought up a large and healthy family. Further north it was more often disastrous, and the death-rate was particularly high among children and pregnant wives. Anna Hinderer may well have survived— if at times only just—for seventeen years at Ibadan in the 1850s and 1860s precisely because she was childless. The strain on missionary wives in frequent childbirth in the most awkward of circumstances is clear enough. Emily Moffat wrote advisedly in 1860, 'I am almost an advocate, in such raw missions as this, so remote from help in times of need, for a bachelor *commencement*.'[5] Only a year later Roger Price of the ill-fated Makololo mission wrote to Emily's husband,

On the 7th (March) I found little Henry Helmore lying dead amongst the others on the bed, and his father and mother, lying on the ground like logs of wood, scarcely took any notice at all of it, his mother none whatever, though passionately fond of him. On the 9th my own little babe died in its mother's arms as she sat by my bedside, where I laid in a wet sheet . . . on the afternoon of the 11th, dear little Selma Helmore died . . . Next morning Mrs Helmore followed.[6]

Thirty years later the CMS had actually adopted Emily Moffat's advice and was refusing to send 'young married women' to Uganda while agreeing to send such unmarried as were 'willing to forgo any intention of marriage for some years'.[7] Yet being married could also be a help. The Baptist Grenfell, exploring the upper reaches of the Congo River in the 1880s, took his black Jamaican wife and child

---

[5] J. P. R. Wallis (ed.), *The Matabeleland Mission: A Selection from the Correspondence of John and Emily Moffat, David Livingstone and Others 1858–1878* (1945), p. xvi.
[6] Ibid. 143–4.
[7] E. Stock, *A History of the Church Missionary Society* (1896), iii. 736.

along with him to demonstrate his pacific intentions. The particularly disastrous Makololo experience was a little unusual for the southern hemisphere. On the west coast it had for long been nearer the norm. The picture of the mission house of the American Mendi Mission, the frontispiece of an 1851 publication, has beneath it the words: 'This house was built by Wm Reynold, the founder of Mendi mission: in it I lived two years, was sick and supposed to be dead. In it Misses Harnden and Allen, Mrs Tefft and Arnold, and Messrs Garnick and Carter died.'[8] All within a couple of years. That lists a high proportion of women. In the earlier period, women were most numerous at the more Protestant and American end of the missionary spectrum, but Mother Anne-Marie Javouhey and her French Catholic nuns were already at work on the west coast in the 1820s and she survived, though again only just. Undoubtedly, the regular use of quinine from the 1850s began to make quite a difference. If Anna Hinderer did survive in Ibadan for seventeen years, her husband lasted still longer. Henry Townsend went out to Sierra Leone in 1836, moved to Abeokuta in the 1840s, and returned to England in 1876. Alfred Saker left England in 1843 and returned from Cameroon in 1876. The American Presbyterian Robert Nassau went out to a particularly unhealthy bit of the coast, the estuary of the Gabon, in 1861. With a few furloughs he was still at work in Africa in 1906. But long before him Mgr. Bessieux, the Catholic pioneer in the same area, had first gone out in 1843 as a member of Mgr. Barron's otherwise disastrous expedition. The one priest survivor, he died in Libreville in 1876, still active to the end. Thus while there was a very real difference in health and life expectation between the south and the west, so that, for long, the majority of missionaries in the west died within the first two years while most in the south not only had no health problems but had their life expectancy actually improved, yet from the 1840s there was an increasing number of survivors in the west, and some of them, adequately acclimatized, survived for a very long time. To that small but powerful group—T. B. Freeman in the Gold Coast, Townsend and the Hinderers in Nigeria, Saker in Cameroon, Bessieux in Gabon, among others—the Church of the second half of the century would owe a great deal of its shape.

Missionaries not only turned back or died. Quite a few turned to

[8] George Thompson, *Thompson in Africa* (New York, 1852).

other occupations, some none too creditable. In early West African days, one or two became slave-traders. Stokes, a CMS man in East Africa, took a black wife and turned gun-runner and general trader. Many more, in South and central Africa, quietly turned into settlers, large landed proprietors, or colonial officials. Livingstone left the employ of the LMS and became a British consul instead. He indeed did not give up his missionary interest, but the change of employment was not seen as abnormal. His brother-in-law, John Moffat, did the same, but later changed back once more to the mission. For many missionaries who failed to master the language and to sympathize with Africans, the decision to leave missionary employment was clearly appropriate. For others, it went with sexual lapses, drink, or a complete inability to get on with missionary colleagues. The idea of returning to Europe was seldom an attractive one. Some, even as missionaries, had become partially integrated within the local settler community, and it was seen as natural to move across entirely. All this immensely increased, for Africans, the difficulty of discerning any significant difference between the missionary and colonial government or white settler.

A frequently recurring Protestant problem was the interrelationship of missionaries among themselves. They had not been trained for community or to share a common work; they tended to be individualistic and obstinate by temperament; they often quarrelled fearfully. The Catholics, on the other hand, were members of religious orders who had been through tough novitiates before profession and were expected to live and relate to one another much the same in Africa as in Europe. When faced with strange circumstances this did not always succeed in avoiding friction and it often inhibited initiative, but it did provide far more of a framework both for harmony and for survival than most Protestants (apart from the Moravians) were offered. Where Catholic mortality was high it was often among those who insisted on continuing to practise forms of bodily asceticism, including heavy fasting, designed for Europe. Catholics, because they were celibate and bound by the regulations of a religious order, did not fuse with other local white groups in the way the Protestants tended to do. Even in dress you could distinguish them from the trader. And if they abandoned the mission they went home. Before the mid-twentieth century you very rarely find former Catholic missionaries who have settled in Africa. Finally, the place of women was decidedly different. Catholic women missionaries were all nuns, even more tightly disciplined than the priests, and they were very few until near the end of the century. Widespread female participation was one of the novelties of the Protestant missionary movement. It was a dimension almost entirely absent on the Catholic side.

In the second half of the century, class background and education moved up quite considerably. Doubtless the upper-class English Jesuits in Matabeleland in the 1880s were socially exceptional: Alfred Weld had been Director of the Stonyhurst Observatory and English Provincial and had done diplomatic work for the Vatican in regard to India and Gibraltar before becoming Superintendent of the Zambezi Mission; Augustus Law, grandson of Lord Ellenborough, had been a naval officer; Henry Schomberg Kerr, second son of the sixth Marquis of Lothian, had been chaplain to Lord Ripon while Viceroy of India. Nowhere else did you find people of such exalted experience entering the African mission, but their calling had not been to Africa but to become Jesuits. They went to Africa in obedience. Their class, education, and relatively advanced age did not, however, improve their missionary skills. They appear as a devout, self-sacrificing, but rather rigid group, poor on language-learning.

Newton Adams, a well-qualified doctor and educationalist from New York sponsored by the American Board of Mission, had already arrived in South Africa in 1835, six years before Livingstone. He may well have pointed the way towards the mission of the future better than any of his contemporaries. Adams and Livingstone were followed from the 1860s by increasing numbers of graduates. We have seen the English UMCA group of university men, led by Bishop Mackenzie, going up the Zambezi in 1861 and then withdrawing to Zanzibar. Still more influential were Scottish graduates like James Stewart, Robert Laws, Alexander Hetherwick, and William Elmslie. Like Livingstone, Adams, and Henry Callaway, they all had degrees in medicine, though some had theological degrees as well, but other disciplines could also be attracted. Mackay was an engineer of distinction, Colenso a mathematician. Emily Moffat's complaint in 1860 'Home folk think anyone will do for Africa, however ignorant'[9] was ceasing to be true.

The change was clearest of all with the UMCA, an entire society of graduates. On the whole, the quality of mind they displayed and a

---

[9] Wallis, *The Matabeleland Mission*, 118.

more discriminating approach to tricky issues justified this initiative, though a certain Anglo-Catholic rigidity produced its own disadvantages. To opt for celibacy might be wise, but to insist— even into the twentieth century—that a doctor and nurse who decided to marry must leave the mission, even when they were practically irreplaceable, was surely not. But in no other group was there a larger number of good linguists.

William Percival Johnson, who worked in and around Lake Nyasa from 1876 to 1928, is, perhaps, an almost unfairly fine example, but he was not untypical. He represents the quality that the missionary movement was able to field at the point it had reached well before the colonial scramble, even if his exceptional longevity (despite living almost at native level) saw him through to a very different era. He had studied Sanskrit at Oxford before volunteering, and, indeed, tutors thought it crazy that this exceptional young orientalist should decide to go to Africa. As he travelled up country with his bishop from Zanzibar in 1876, he was reading *Two Gentlemen of Verona*. Certainly he and his bishop, Edward Steere, were gentlemen, as the missionaries of an earlier age, so cruelly derided by Sydney Smith, were not. Like some of their predecessors they were also scholars. Steere was largely responsible for the Swahili Bible, Johnson for the Chinyanja Bible.

Livingstone and Colenso remain the intellectual princes of the nineteenth-century missionary movement. Livingstone was the most remarkable of Victorian Free Churchmen, Colenso the most remarkable of Victorian Anglican bishops. But they were both rogue elephants, too independent in mind for the movement to contain them. Men like Adams, Stewart, Laws, Johnson, were less intellectually flamboyant and individualist, but they and many others were people of considerable education, intelligence, and imaginative judgement. It is important that the sheer human calibre of the missionary leadership be adequately recognized. It was not principally a group of cranks and zealots, even if it included both, but of men of exceptional and wide-ranging ability though, admittedly, even in the ablest a slightly cranky dimension is often discernible and in fact may add to the attraction.

Catholic missionaries also changed in this half-century, if somewhat differently. Classwise, the English Zambezi Jesuits were, of course, quite untypical. While Protestant missionaries had been recruited principally from the urban population and then from academia (though there were groups from a largely rural background such as the Württemberg missionaries of the Basle mission), Catholics came predominantly from the countryside, the farming families of the more devout areas of Europe. Their background was always much the same as that of the home clergy and many in fact began as French diocesan priests or—at least—students in a French or Italian diocesan seminary before transferring to a missionary society. What changed in the course of the nineteenth century was the degree of professionalism produced by the new missionary societies wholly devoted to Africa. It was also affected by imitation of the Protestant example—more conscious attempts to 'civilize' here, more insistence on language proficiency and the use of texts in translation there. That is not to deny that some Catholic missionaries of the earlier dispensation were already remarkably insistent upon the serious study of language as a necessary element in cultural adaptation. De Jacobis is one outstanding example from the first half of the century. No less remarkable was his contemporary Dr Ignaz Knoblecher, the Slovene Vicar-Apostolic on the Upper Nile from 1848 to his death in 1858. He was second to none of any age in his learning of languages and study of local custom, but several of his colleagues, men like the German Kirchner and the Italian Beltrame, a pioneer in Dinka studies, were of similar quality. It was one of the most interesting of missionary groups, its mix in national background being character-istic of the Austrian Empire from which it mostly came. Unfortunately the Sudanese climate had claimed by 1866 no fewer than forty-six missionary casualties, and the mission was closed with no local surviving Church of any sort. Nevertheless, the figure of Knoblecher, 'Abuna Suleiman' as he was known up and down the Nile, in his white turban, reddish-brown beard, and flowing purple robe, author of important manuscripts on the language and customs of the Bari and the Dinka, remains one of the most charming figures in nineteenth-century missionary history.

Knoblecher also represents quite recognizably the normative Catholic approach at its best as opposed to the normative Protestant: far less concern with 'civilizing', far closer cultural identification. Dressed as he was, he did not look European and clearly did not want to be taken for a European. In general the cassock and its variants distinguished the Catholic missionary from white trader or settler while the trousers of the Protestant were a mark of cultural identity. But the Sudan mission was affected less happily by clinging to ascetic practices, especially fasting, in circumstances in which the missionaries were already debilitated, just as had been the case with the Capuchins of the seventeenth century. Yet this too conveyed an intelligible religious message. The Catholic fathers looked and behaved altogether more recognizably to native eyes as spiritual figures, other-worldly gurus, and much less like an officious, moralizing wing of European power. If their language knowledge was often good, they lacked printing-presses, to which Protestants gave a high priority. It was Protestants, not Catholics, who effectively created a vernacular literature. In 1873 Bishop Steere remarked that the French Holy Ghost Fathers at Bagamoyo 'are beginning to use our words and to study our translations'. He had come upon Frère Marcellin sitting under a bush and 'working away at our St Matthew' while Père Étienne was 'most glad of a copy of our hymns'.[10] More than anything else it was the instruction of Lavigerie and the practice of the early White Fathers from the 1870s which put a considerable segment of the Catholic missionary force in the forefront of the struggle to understand both language and custom. It is noteworthy that when Pilkington, best of the early CMS linguists in Uganda, arrived in 1890 and began studying the language, he found the French, White Father, Luganda grammar far better than the English.

More use of quinine, the easier climate of many inland areas, and a general growth in geographical knowledge and experience were all factors enabling missionaries to live longer and be more effective by the 1870s. Basic problems of inland travel were still far from overcome, but they started fitter. In the past many had been so debilitated by the sea voyage that they were in no condition to withstand the first attacks of fever. Quicker voyages and, for the east coast, the opening of the Suez Canal in 1869 made a considerable difference. After that the difficulties remained almost unchanged. In South Africa there was no problem. The mission spread on the back of the horse and the ox wagon. The mid-nineteenth-century advance would have been a very different thing without their help, as would the Boer advance to the Transvaal. The ox cart could just about reach the Zambezi before the animals expired from the bite of the tsetse fly. North of that you walked, sat in a 'machila' or 'palanquin' carried by from four to ten Africans, or rode a donkey or

---

[10] R. M. Heanley, *A Memoir of Bishop Steere* (1888), 118.

horse. Everything was tried. Horses were used a certain amount even in Nigeria, and Coillard brought a horse from South Africa as far as Barotseland and rode it for years before it died—'that good old servant', he lamented in 1891, 'without whom I never went any excursion',[11] and Bishop Knight-Bruce regularly rode a salted horse in Rhodesia in 1892. But horses did not flourish in most parts of central Africa and donkeys were in commoner use. George Grenfell rode on an ox in the Congo. Many missionaries disliked being carried. Livingstone almost always walked. Occasionally he rode a donkey. Only in his very last days do we read in his Journal, 'carried in the Kitanda'.[12] Women were regularly carried longer distances, but at times carriers could not be found and even they had to walk a few hundred miles. Walking was exhausting, even more so if—like Bishop Mackenzie—you marched along with a crozier in one hand, a double-barrelled gun in the other, and a bag of seeds on your back.[13] Lavigerie blamed the superior of a missionary who had died worn out because he had allowed him to walk and not insisted on his riding a donkey or being carried.[14] It is surprising that they did not use donkeys more than they seem to have done. Mackay in 1877 was given a horse by the Sultan of Zanzibar. It soon died, but later he was given a donkey by the Sultan of Sadami and it kept going all the way to Buganda: 'It saved me many a mile on foot.'[15] In 1890 Bishop Tucker took two donkeys on his first journey to Buganda, but in 1892 on his second he took seventy. Protestant missionaries tended to carry far more equipment than Catholics in the big expeditions— boats, printing-presses, and the rest—requiring many hundreds or even thousands of porters, each with a load of 70 pounds. If they died or defected, so much the worse for your luggage. Again and again, equipment had to be discarded. In December 1877 Mackay, following CMS board instructions, set off from the coast for Lake Victoria with six large carts and eighty oxen to draw them. The oxen soon began to die and by February he had had to abandon the lot.

The idea of water transport was naturally appealing. Though Mgr. Knoblecher had a boat, the *Stella Matutina*, on the Nile in 1851, this was once more mostly a Protestant stratagem, encouraged by

---

[11] 14 Apr. 1891, François Coillard, *On the Threshold of Central Africa* (1897), 418–19.
[12] R. Coupland, *Livingstone's Last Journey* (1945), 243.
[13] Owen Chadwick, *Mackenzie's Grave* (1959), 44.
[14] Cardinal Lavigerie, *Instructions aux missionnaires* (Namur, 1950), 128–9.
[15] *The Story of Mackay of Uganda*, by his sister (1892), 59.

Livingstone and the 'commerce' school. Supporters at home much liked the idea of launching boats on the great lakes and rivers of Africa. In due course it made a difference on the River Congo and Lake Nyasa. Livingstonia's *Ilala* (from 1875), the UMCA's *Charles Janson* (1888), and the BMS *Plymouth* on the Congo (from 1881) were certainly of real use. Elsewhere the distances required for porterage were just too much and there were plenty of large canoes on Lake Victoria, for instance. Crossing a lake was the least of missionary problems. Getting there remained a formidable one. Inevitably, in consequence of all this, the missionary in the interior tended to be sedentary. Surviving the inland journey was already a feat. Establishing a mission station with its house and church, reliable water supply, and gardens was a second. The station itself then required continuous servicing while the survival of the missionaries depended above all upon its amenities. Where health and life were always so much at risk, the shape of the mission was controlled excessively by the requirement of missionary survival. In theory they had come to serve others. In practice it had to be that life revolved largely around their own needs. As one bright young missionary, fresh from Cambridge, described it:

The contrast will have struck you already. The people, to whom we have come to preach, lie on the ground or in a reed or grass hut, eat rice and a bit of dried fish (two cupfuls of rice and a handful of dried fish is a day's ration), carry a load under a burning sun for ten or twelve miles which I should be sorry to carry a mile in England, walk barefoot on the scorching ground, while we live in grand houses or tents (palaces to these people), sleep on beds as comfortable as any at home, eat chickens (carried in a box alive), preserved meat, green peas (preserved), tea, cocoa, biscuits, bread, butter, jam. Necessary for health perhaps . . . [16]

That was the comment of a newly-arrived in a particularly large and well-supplied expedition in 1890. Unfair for an earlier age, it represents all the same the way things were going.

At times it must have seemed to almost every missionary that the one thing there was no time or place for was formal missionary work. Travelling, obtaining supplies, arranging the dispatch of mail, building, gardening, digging irrigation canals, ensuring your water supply or your daily meal were all such engrossing and tiring occupations, let alone having babies, coping with illnesses, and

---

[16] 20 Apr. 1890, C. Harford-Battersby, *Pilkington of Uganda* (1898), 68–9.

learning a language. Yet all this was subsidiary to the great work they had come to do: preaching, the making of converts, the establishment of a Christian Church.

vii. *Missionary Teaching*

The early nineteenth-century Protestant missionary saw himself above all as a preacher and teacher of the biblical message of salvation. He thought rather little of what might follow conversion. He was seldom an ecclesiologist but often an eschatologist. He was anxious to preach to people as quickly and as frequently as possible, even when his grasp of any native language was—to say the least—tenuous. He would do it through an interpreter; whether the interpreter really understood the message and its more unexpected ideas, whether he had vernacular terms in which he could express them intelligibly, was not at once seen as rather unlikely. Or, if it was, this was not to be allowed to stand in the way of the great commandment, Go ye and teach all nations. Yet things were not that much easier when a language had, more or less, been learnt. Moffat wrote in April 1827, 'One afternoon I commenced conversing with about twelve women, who happened to collect before my wagon. I dwelt particularly on the coming of Christ, the raising of the dead and the end of the world. They really seemed in some degree alarmed.'[17] Three years later another LMS missionary, John Baillie, wrote in his journal at Lithako

We began to catechise them . . . I enquired (of an old man) what reason he had to think that he would go to heaven on dying, since he had lived always sinning against God. He replied that he had never committed any sin, and therefore he must go to Morimo, i.e. God . . . I then endeavoured to show him his lost and undone condition by nature and practice, and the impossibility of his ever going to heaven unless he should be converted from his present condition, but this seemed quite uninteresting to him.[18]

Franz Morland, a Catholic missionary at Gondokoro in the Sudan, commented on the same lack of interest in his diary in 1859: 'One teaches in school, one preaches in Church, the doors are always left open, the people who stand around with nothing to do are invited

[17] *Apprenticeship at Kuruman: Being the Journals and Letters of Robert and Mary Moffat 1820–1828*, ed. I. Schapera (1951), 265.
[18] G. Setiloane, *The Image of God among the Sotho-Tswana* (Rotterdam, 1976), 115.

in, but our doctrine, God's commandments, the creation, redemption, salvation, the immortality of the soul do not interest them.'[19]

Everywhere missionaries, Protestant and Catholic, attempted this direct approach, just as many a Franciscan had done in earlier centuries. Hinderer would walk round Ibadan or tour the neighbouring villages preaching in the open, week after week. It was standard form. 'With such interpreters and aids as we could obtain, we ceased not to lift up our voices to proclaim the Gospel . . . we itinerated by turn every Sabbath to the neighbouring villages; and very frequently after four and five miles walk could not get an individual to listen to the message of divine mercy.'[20] It cannot but be surprising to us that it was surprising to them. Why any African should be interested by such extraordinary assertions, uttered in broken and barely comprehensible language by a stranger, it would be difficult to say. It is clear that the doctrine immediately offered was at this period normally both a very Christ-centred and an individualistic one: the saviour, human sin, heaven and hell. Many a Protestant, Moffat included, made things even stranger by stress upon the resurrection of the dead, a stress which may well explain the millennial message of the Xhosa prophet Nxele in the 1820s. Consider this conversation:

'What!' he exclaimed with astonishment. 'What are these words about? the dead, the dead arise!' 'Yes', was my reply, 'all the dead shall arise'. 'Will my father arise?' 'Yes', I answered, 'your father will arise'. 'Will all the slain in battle arise?' 'Yes' . . . 'Hark . . . did ever your ears hear such strange and unheard of news?'[21]

This might well sound like the Xhosa king Ngqika, responding sceptically to the predictions of Nxele; it is in fact Makaba, Chief of the Bamangkhetsi, responding to Moffat on his first visit.

The Zulu were no less unpersuaded by millennialist teaching. Colenso on his first visit to them in 1854 was assured that the profession of Christianity had been much hindered by 'persons saying that the world will be burnt up—perhaps very soon'.[22] The millennialist assertions of many an early nineteenth-century Protestant missionary or even the ceaseless stress upon an afterlife seemed no less bizarre to his black hearers than they did to plenty of

---

[19] Francesco Morland, *Missione in Africa centrale: Diario 1855–1863* (Bologna, 1973), 193.
[20] R. Moffat, *Missionary Labours and Scenes in Southern Africa* (1842), 296.
[21] Ibid. 404.   [22] John Colenso, *Ten Weeks in Natal* (1855), 100–1.

people in Europe at the same time.[23] But if they got beyond their healthy scepticism and began to believe, the hermeneutical gap between white preacher and black hearer could still not be closed. The missionary, consciously or not, was distanced from the biblical events and images he dwelt upon in a way that his converts, hearing of these things for the first time, could hardly be. If angels frequently appeared in the gospel narrative which the missionary had thoughtfully translated into their language, then they could be expected to go on appearing in contemporary Africa, and so forth. People either did not believe the missionaries or they did. Either way the latter might well feel that their message had not got through. For most missionaries there was in reality a great gap between the biblical dispensation and the ecclesiastical dispensation of the Victorian Church. It was assumed but not explained. For their hearers it was only discovered when they later challenged the latter dispensation on grounds of their understanding of the former and found themselves in trouble.

The effective theology of missionaries varied a great deal, Evangelicals from Catholics, millennialists from non-millennialists, fundamentalists from a handful of relative liberals. The same society might include people with sharply divergent views as—by the late nineteenth century—was increasingly the case in the home Church, though Colenso proved too liberal in biblical interpretation to be acceptable to his colleagues. Missionaries almost always represented the more conservative end of current orthodoxy at home, but in the nineteenth century Protestant orthodoxy at least was changing perceptibly. Some were preoccupied with the devil; with others Satan hardly got a mention. Hell remained a much-stressed Catholic doctrine long after it was slipping out of Protestant sermons. Yet if missionaries grew less fundamentalist in their thoughts, they seldom admitted this too openly, and it almost certainly had little effect on what African Christians actually understood. The Bible message was accepted in its most literal form.

There appears, nevertheless, to have been a significant shift from initial concentration upon sin, salvation, and eschatology to one focused more upon God and creation, upon a linkage even with African traditional belief. For Catholics and High-Churchmen, this

---

[23] H. Fast, ' "In One Ear and Out at the Other": African Response to the Wesleyan Message in Xhosaland 1825–1835', *JRA* 23 (1993), 164–6.

came more naturally than for Evangelicals, but it was a matter of pedagogy as much as of theology. Bishop Mackenzie, in 1861, never preached at all to the unbeliever. He did not know enough of the language to dare to do so, and he did not trust the skills of his interpreters. The post–Tractarian university mind realized more easily the absurdity of the sort of brash preaching of the Christian mysteries in an alien language which an earlier generation had thought itself bound to engage in. John Colenso, admittedly a theological liberal, was already in 1865 criticizing missionaries for their stress upon salvation rather than the larger revelation of God. Callaway, writing in 1870, records the account a very old Xhosa man named Ulangeni gave of Van der Kemp's teaching: 'He made enquiries amongst us, asking "What do you say about the creation of all things?" We replied, "We call him who made all things Utikxo." And he enquired, "Where is he?" We replied, "In heaven." Uyegana said, "Very well, I bring you that very one (that is, all that relates to or concerns him) to you of this country."[24] Maybe that memory is coloured by subsequent Christian teaching, but it suggests that even in the first years of the century a highly intelligent, if idiosyncratic, Evangelical could start with creation and God, not salvation and Christ, and could use African beliefs as a bridge. 'Tell them', said Colenso in 1854, 'that their own names are excellent names for God; and we shall . . . come to tell them more about Him.'[25] Lavigerie would forbid his White Fathers even to mention anything derived from revelation and relating to Christ in the first two years of instruction, which were to be confined to 'fundamental truths of the natural order'.[26] It would be a command hard to keep, but it certainly pointed in a sane direction. When linked with the acceptance of a traditional African name to denote God (general, though not universal, among missionaries) such an approach could enable missionaries to begin to talk intelligibly, moving on from a common ground of belief, instead of flinging out at the start an extraordinary mix of salvific and eschatological doctrines.

Direct evangelism would not disappear, indeed many an African catechist or prophet would excel at it. They would, of course, ground it much better than could the newly arrived missionary within a context of local meaning. Sometimes, even with the

---

[24] Henry Callaway, *Religious System of the Amazulu* (1870), 67–8.
[25] Colenso, *Ten Weeks in Natal*, 134.
[26] Lavigerie, *Instructions aux missionnaires*, 109.

missionary, it seemed to work. Perhaps sometimes with Hinderer on a street corner in urban Ibadan. W. P. Johnson, far from a formal Evangelical, continued to favour it in the 1880s as part of his exceptionally eccentric model. He remained 'very free in speaking of our message wherever I went'. Colleagues had made clear to him 'what questions these miscellaneous preachings raised', but he still held that 'the original proclamation of the Gospel is a great work' and that 'it seems more honest and open on the part of the missionary to say at once what he has come for'.[27] He was not looking for conversions. He simply did not want to deceive people into thinking him anything other than what he was.

For the most part, however, early conversions came in other ways—through employment, protection, or just a desire to read. Most early converts were members of a missionary's household or otherwise within his circle and protection. His influence upon them was cumulative. The encouragement to be present at prayers, to attend his teaching on a daily or weekly basis, and to see things his way was the natural spiritual and intellectual concomitant of living within the community of a mission station. It was backed up by a host of subsidiary persuaders. Livingstone wrote home in 1856 about his porters on his transcontinental journey: 'The sight of ships and commerce has such a good effect on their minds, for when they see such examples of our superiority they readily admit that the Bible has something in it.'[28] 'Where have the white people got all this from, and why are they now superior to the black in so many things?', asked a Norwegian missionary of Zulus a few years later. 'Is it not the word of God which they have received which has worked these wonders among them?'[29] Again and again the power of Britain was appealed to as demonstration of the truth of the Bible. Victoria herself had done nothing less when she wrote to the chiefs of Abeokuta that the greatness of England depended upon the knowledge of Christ.[30] For the Victorian missionary this was no insincere appeal, simplistic as it must seem. The Victorian Protestant was intensely sure that Britain was the high heaven of human achievement and that the explanation lay in her Protestant faith.

[27] W. P. Johnson, *My African Reminiscences 1875–1895* (1924), 172.
[28] David Livingstone, *Missionary Correspondence 1841–1856*, ed. I. Schapera (1961), 310.
[29] J. Simensen, 'Religious Change as Transaction: The Norwegian Mission to Zululand, South Africa 1850–1906', *JRA* 16 (1986), 85.
[30] Stock, *A History of the Church Missionary Society*, ii. 105.

How little he knew about Victorian Britain! But his appeal was also to smaller, more immediately impressive things: the concertina, the gramophone, but especially the magic lantern, a favourite missionary possession. Livingstone carried one with him though when using it he was careful to make clear that there was nothing supernatural about its effects: it was the natural, scientific power of the white man which, he believed, pointed to the truth of Christianity, not anything supernatural, essentially supernatural as the core of his message undoubtedly was. His explanations meant little to his hearers: the magic lantern was clearly magical. But such things appealed too because they simply made life more enjoyable; they helped make it pleasant to share the missionary's company. They were a way to create initial interest, even a bit of excitement.

viii. *The Uses of Medicine*

Far more important in a missionary's repertoire, however, was his medical skill. Livingstone had early wished to be 'a medical missionary'.[31] At Koboleng he certainly spent much of his time working as a doctor, removing tumours and teeth, treating eyes, and advising on childlessness. 'Every morning numbers of patients crowded round our house.'[32] But in this he was in no way exceptional. He doubtless had a wider range of medical skills than his gardener father-in-law, Moffat, but he may not have spent so much more of his time on medical work. What is striking is how little he actually refers to it in his writings. Doctoring was nothing new for a missionary. The Jesuits in Ethiopia in the seventeenth century, for instance, had done quite the same. As Jeronimo Lobo wrote in his cool, detached way, 'The common country-folk of the land came to hold me in high repute as a doctor, thinking that was my profession and coming to ask for remedies, which I distributed liberally and authoritatively according to the instructions in a handbook I had.'[33] The only Jesuit who survived in Ethiopia after the débâcle of the 1630s was a German, Francis Storer, disguised as an Armenian doctor. Catholics continued this tradition in the nineteenth century. We hear of the first SMA fathers at Ouidah distributing medicines, treating sores, even performing minor operations. They were not doctors.

[31] Livingstone, *Missionary Travels and Researches in South Africa*, 5.
[32] Ibid. 114.
[33] J. Lobo, *Itinerario*, ed. M. G. da Costa and Donald Lockhart (1984), 262–3.

Protestants took over exactly the same approach. They may have been prepared with a little more medical training, but this was not seen as an activity distinct from that of the regular missionary. Schreuder, the Norwegian pioneer in Zululand, was allowed to settle there because of his successful treatment of King Mpande. The Norwegian mission had no trained doctor before 1874, but already in 1864 it was reported that 'They daily come to ask for medicines . . . often the entire morning is consumed by attendance to these people.' Here too a whole range of problems was being treated, from toothache to vaccination against smallpox, but sometimes all that missionaries could hand out were Eno's Fruit Salts or a spoonful of castor oil all round.[34]

The impression given by such remarks, often provided slightly on the side, is that the amount of medical work performed by the average nineteenth-century missionary was very much more considerable than we tend to imagine, but it was almost always unplanned and had no close connectin with conversion. It was a response to human need, often to emergencies, and was pressed on missionaries by Africa rather than deliberately pursued. To some it may have seemed almost a waste of time, delaying other more important occupations almost indefinitely. Medical knowledge was provided for the early missionaries more to safeguard their own health than to care at all systematically for others; even some of the first doctors were sent with this purpose still very much in mind. Cardinal Lavigerie may have been the first person to want to make of it a central element within an African missionary strategy although, paradoxically, in reality it came to be very much less central to White Father work than to that of many other groups. Africans expected religion and health to go together; indeed, 'religion' had little point to it apart from health. The missionary mix of the two fitted Africa precisely because it did not professionalize medicine too far away from the religious area. Missionaries may not have seen their approach as a holistic one, and for some it may have been little more than a matter of sharing the medicine they had brought for themselves with others when asked to do so. Even with the Scottish missions like Livingstonia and Blantyre, where a remarkable number of the leading missionaries were trained doctors, they were for long

[34] T. Jorgensen, 'Contact and Conflict', Ph.D. thesis (Oslo, 1989), 182–3; for Eno's Fruit Salts and the castor oil, see Duff Macdonald, *Africana* (1882), 2, 207–8.

anxious not to separate their medical work from the rest of their ministry. This approach must at least have looked holistic in the receiver's eyes. The missionary understood his medicines as working on purely 'scientific' grounds, the recipients understood them rather differently: for them the personal goodness of the missionary and his religious authority might have a lot more to do with it. There was a variety of missionary attitudes. On the Protestant side the CMS appeared to be least interested in medical work, the Scots the most. For Catholics it may have been more consciously conversion-orientated. 'Father Lutz is the doctor of the whole town,' lamented the CMS Dobinson from Onitsha in 1890. 'From 7–9 daily he receives sick folk and of course everyone goes whoever they may be.'[35]

The medical missionary was almost certainly more of a charismatic figure, even occasionally a miracle worker, than he imagined, especially when his medical expertise was less than his holiness. Livingstone's reputation among Africans was as a magician of exceptional power, and other missionaries who really made an impact could be seen as his younger brothers. An old Tanzanian priest, Canon Msigala, recalled in the 1950s an incident when he was very young involving one of the early UMCA priests, Canon Porter.

One day I was walking with him on parochial work when he saw a child, called Karowanga, a chronic invalid. He washed his sores, but had no bandage, so he said, 'Haven't we a purificator in church? Let us bind up this child'. By chance we had some suitable ones and he split these and bound the wounds of the child with them with medicine. For a time he prayed without uncovering them. When he uncovered them he was quite healed and his arm which had been bent was quite straight.[36]

That was an exceptional experience, but it may still express the way in which Africans frequently understood the effectiveness of missionary medicine.

Later on two things happened. The first was the development of a distinct 'medical mission' with its own rationale, staffed by doctors and nurses who would run hospitals and clinics, but not participate in missionary work of other kinds. It was only in the 1890s that this development got under way anywhere, and much later in many

[35] F. K. Ekechi, *Missionary Enterprise and Rivalry in Igboland 1857–1914* (1972), 77–8.
[36] K. Msigala, 'Reminiscences Started in July 1955', trans. from Swahili by C. Blood, quoted in T. Ranger, 'Godly Medicine: The Ambiguities of Medical Mission in South-East Tanzania 1900–1945', *Social Science and Medicine*, 15B (1981), 261–77.

places. Albert Cook, arriving in Uganda in 1896, is one of the first of the new breed. It involved a rationale which in some ways stressed the importance of medicine within missionary strategy far more than had been usual in the nineteenth century, but it also secularized it. The second development, perhaps in some reaction to the first, was the rise of independent Churches far more committed to Christian healing of a spiritual kind. While this can well be seen as the emergence within Christianity of more traditional African attitudes to healing and as a critique of the secularity of the twentieth-century medical missionary approach, it may also be seen as in deep continuity with the central perceived thrust of nineteenth-century medical mission.

ix. *Language and Translation*

While doctoring could be for many a time-consuming side occupation, the mastering of a new language and Scripture translation were—for the few capable of it—a missionary's central responsibility. Upon them preaching and teaching must be entirely dependent together with the whole subsequent life of the Church. They were certainly no less time-consuming. John Moffat remembered his father as spending 'most of his time' in his study, the rest of it doctoring the sick and being a general handyman.[37] Colenso, replying angrily to a suggestion by Bishop Gray that he had 'considerable gifts' for the study of language and in consequence it came easily to him, wrote testily,

I have no special gift for languages, but what is shared by most educated men of fair ability. What I have done, I have done by hard work—by sitting with my natives day after day, from early morn to sunset, till they, as well as myself, were fairly exhausted—conversing with them as well as I could and listening to them conversing—writing down what I could of their talk from their own lips, and, when they were gone, still turning round again to my desk to copy out the results of the day.[38]

Out of that work had come two grammars, a dictionary, four reading-books in Zulu, as well as Old and New Testament translations. Two years earlier Samuel Crowther wrote to Henry

---

[37] Cecil Northcott, *Robert Moffat* (1961), 131.
[38] J. Colenso, *Remarks upon the Recent Proceedings and Charge of Robert, Lord Bishop of Capetown* (1864), 44–5.

Venn, in December 1862, informing him of the tragic loss of his papers when his house was burnt down in Lagos:

I had always made it a rule that in case of a fire breaking out, not to hesitate but to snatch out the manuscripts of my translations the first thing, for security, and then I may try to save anything else if possible; but on this occasion I was not at home to put my resolution to practice. . . . Thus the manuscripts of nearly all the remaining books of the Pentateuch which I would have prepared for the press this quarter were destroyed. My collections of words and proverbs in Yoruba, of eleven years' constant observations since the publication of the last edition of my Yoruba vocabulary, were also completely destroyed. The loss of those is greater to me than anything else, in as much as it cannot be recovered with money nor can I easily recall to memory all the collections I had made during my travels at Rabba and through the Yoruba country, in which places I kept my ears open to every word to catch what I had not then secured, with which I had expected to enrich and enlarge my Yoruba vocabulary this year. Now all are gone like a dream.[39]

Crowther was himself a Yoruba. How much harder for any foreigner was the work of creating the first grammar, the first dictionary, the first collection of sayings. Pilkington, a Cambridge first in classics and the ablest of the CMS linguists in Uganda, wrote home that 'in most cases' it was 'worse than useless' to send a man without special training in language into a place where the language was not already mastered, yet that was what the societies had been doing from the start. 'I assure you,' he wrote, 'the majority of the men whom I've seen in the field closely, wouldn't learn a new language without help in twenty years.'[40] Moffat was very unusual among the major translators in knowing neither Greek nor Hebrew, but many— including Pilkington himself—translated large parts of the Old Testament without knowing Hebrew. Pilkington wrote much of the Luganda Bible in Ireland on leave. He was a confident man! Probably the Basle Germans were the ablest group of missionary linguists. The vast majority of missionaries of course knew no ancient language and most British missionaries knew none other than English. Pilkington rightly distinguished between the pioneer learning of a language and that by those able to use the grammars and dictionaries already produced by others. The Baptist Missionary Society in the Congo

[39] J. Ajayi, *Christian Mission in Nigeria 1841–1891: The Making of a New Élite* (1969), 128.
[40] Harford-Battersby, *Pilkington of Uganda*, 195–6.

put all missionaries on probation for the first three years while seeing whether they could pass the test of learning a language.

A very partial list of the corpus of nineteenth-century Protestant linguistic work can fittingly begin with Henry Brunton's *Grammar and Vocabulary of the Susoo Language*, printed in Edinburgh already in 1802 well before the missionary movement had really got under way in Africa. It shows well enough where the new priorities lay. Van der Kemp's pioneering language work with the Xhosa was being done at just the same time. If we move south from the banks of the Rio Pungas where Brunton had briefly worked, we may note Gustav Nyländer's work in Sierra Leone from 1806 on Bulom Sherbro, into which he had translated Matthew's Gospel by 1812, Johann Christaller of the Basel Mission on Akan and Twi, Schlegel on Ewe, Crowther, Bowen, and Hinderer on Yoruba, Schön on Hausa and Igbo, Goldie and Robb on Efik, Bentley and Nils Westlund on Kikongo, Boyce and Appleyard on Xhosa, Schreuder and Colenso on Zulu, Moffat on Tswana, John White on Shona, Johnson on Chinyanja, Krapf and Steere on Swahili, Pilkington on Luganda. Doubtless that list is not only brief, but fairly arbitrary, leaving out as many outstanding linguists as it includes, but it covers the most renowned names apart from S. W. Koelle, the Basel-trained CMS missionary whose amazing *Polyglotta Africana*, a comparative vocabulary of nearly 300 words and phrases in more than a hundred distinct African languages, was assembled entirely at first hand by the author from among the recaptives of Sierra Leone and published in London in 1854.

There is a Harrist hymn which runs, 'Each village has its own language; Take this then to pray to our Father!'[41] Language was Africa's greatest cultural glory. It was the missionaries who carried it across in scores of tongues from the oral to the written state and gave it a basic literature. They came to appreciate, as did very few other Europeans before the mid-twentieth century, its richness, copiousness, precision, yet also almost unbelievable diversity. Of course, as modern scholars like to stress, in writing it down missionaries also inevitably altered its pattern, standardizing certain forms as against others (insisting that neighbouring villages share a common form), stimulating even a sense of tribal division consequent upon the

[41] J. Krabill, 'The Hymnody of the Harrist Church among the Dida of South-Central Ivory Coast', Ph.D. thesis (Birmingham, 1989), 333.

enhanced sense of language difference. The fluidity of the oral across both time and space is diminished, though not entirely lost, by the reduction to writing and the consequent urge to standardize. Such is and has always been the consequence of literacy. The social effects of missionary linguistics could be considerable, but in this area at least missionaries did not take from Africans their heritage. Rather did they defend and enrich it, by opening it to a wider usefulness with both analytical self-understanding and the capacity to absorb the wisdom of other worlds.

Catholics had not shown such consistent linguistic determination, but with them too this increased in the course of the century. On nothing was Lavigerie more insistent than that his missionaries should be masters of the local language, and they were actually forbidden to speak to each other in anything else after being six months in a place.[42] It is doubtful whether that command was strictly adhered to, but it is certain that the White Fathers became, as a group, outstanding linguists. They were instructed to produce dictionaries, grammars, and catechisms. They were not urged to translate the Scriptures. They became excellent teachers in the vernacular, but they seldom produced a quantity of literature comparable with the Protestants, and never large translations of Scripture. Protestant vernacular Bibles had multiplied across the continent before the close of the century, Catholic ones were simply non-existent.

Undoubtedly for a correct evaluation of nineteenth-century missionaries, their linguistic work is crucial. It constituted the essential bridge. On the one hand it was the key work through which to commend the Word of God, so it was primarily evangelical. On the other hand, to understand a language intimately is also, almost inevitably, to enter into and appreciate its cultural context, the people who use it, have made it, and been made by it. It is hard to know an African language very well and not to be fond of the relevant culture and people. Through language we can experience an alien culture, both in its otherness and in its ultimate intelligibility and shared humanity. In the wrestling with construction, word, and meaning continuously involved in the learning of a language and the translation of texts, the claims of biblical primacy and cultural relativity could be wonderfully combined.

[42] Lavigerie, *Instructions aux missionnaires*, 70–1, 134–5, 145, etc.

x. *Christianity, Civilization, and Commerce*

Evangelism and Bible translation may seem a very long way from preoccupation with 'civilization'. How was it that a movement concerned with the one could so often harp upon the other? The nineteenth-century missionary fixation with civilization—and it sometimes seems little less—requires proper explanation. And that requires some return to eighteenth-century roots. A few quotations may help, chosen almost at random except that an African exile and a British Prime Minister have been chosen to lead the team.

In proportion to the Civilization, so will be the consumption of British Manufactures. (Olaudah Equiano, 13 March 1788, in a letter to the Committee of the Privy Council Examining the Question of the Slave Trade)[43]

I trust we shall not think ourselves too liberal, if, by abolishing the slave-trade, we give them the common chance of civilization with other parts of the world . . . If we listen to the voice of reason and duty we may live to behold the natives of Africa engaged in the calm occupations of industry, in the pursuit of a just and legitimate commerce. We may behold the beams of science and philosophy breaking in upon their land . . . and joining their influence to that of pure religion may illuminate and invigorate the most distant extremities of that immense continent . . . (William Pitt, Prime Minister, speech in the House of Commons, 2 April 1792)[44]

The authority of the British Crown is at this moment the most powerful instrument under Providence of maintaining peace and order in many extensive regions of the earth, and thereby assists in diffusing amongst millions of the human race the blessings of Christianity and civilization. (Earl Grey, 1853)[45]

There had been considerable advance in civilization since I left. Many cottages have sprung up to replace the windowless and chimneyless round conical-roofed huts. Trees have been planted, wagons purchased; the valley is nearly all reclaimed and cultivated. The effects of missionary influence are undeniable and striking. (John Moffat on Kuruman, 21 March 1859)[46]

We sympathize with your desire to introduce the law and order of civilized life, but we doubt whether the very extensive and rapidly developed changes in Lagos will produce anything but a forced compliance as far as British power extends and beyond it a fixed hatred and hostility to

[43] C. Fyfe, *Sierra Leone Inheritance* (1964), 111.
[44] *The Speeches of the Rt. Hon. William Pitt in the House of Commons* (1808), i. 395.
[45] *The Colonial Policy of Lord John Russell's Administration* (1853), i. 13–14.
[46] Wallis, *The Matabeleland Mission*, 55.

Christianity, Civilization and the white man. (Memorial from British subjects and foreign residents in Abeokuta (including CMS missionaries), 30 October 1863 to Lieutenant-General Glover)[47]

In the middle decades of the century almost everyone linked together Christianity and Civilization, adding—when occasion served—Commerce or Cultivation. It was by no means a specifically missionary characteristic. These Cs need some sorting out, if they are not to mislead. They represented the public values of the mid-Victorian age together with Science, for 'Civilization and Science' could be as easily linked as 'Civilization and Commerce'. In fact, in these four terms Christianity was really the odd man out, despite the rhetoric.

The bond between Christianity and civilizing goes back to the conversion of Europe's northern tribes in the Dark Ages, and it was very clearly present in the Portuguese conception of their overseas mission in the sixteenth century. Yet for Protestants what was decisive was the new eighteenth-century preoccupation with 'civilization'—a word which only then made its appearance in English. It was indicative of what the Enlightenment was all about. In 1728 Daniel Defoe in his *Plan of the English Commerce* declared that 'The Savage Part' (of West Africa) 'would be much civiliz'd . . . and the People learn to live to be cloth'd, and to be furnish'd with many things from Europe, which they now want; and by consequence would with their Manners change the very Nature of their commerce and fall in upon the consumption of the European Manufactures.'[48] Adam Ferguson, in his influential *Essay on the History of Civil Society* (1767), concerned with the advance of the human species 'from rudeness to civilization', saw civilization as a complex thing, at once political, intellectual, and commercial. Commerce, it was generally agreed, had a great deal to do with the spread of civilization, but Enlightenment thinkers were unlikely to suggest that Christianity had much to do with it.

The new missionary movement for its part had exceedingly little concern with civilization. Its working-class, Free Church originators were interested in evangelism, in the spread of faith and piety but not in the fruits of the Enlightenment or of British commerce. The gospel was something quite different. In 1815 the Methodist

---

[47] *Parliamentary Papers*, 1865, xxxvii (533) p.6 (540).
[48] D. Defoe, *A Plan of the English Commerce* (1728), 253.

Missionary Committee could still write emphatically to a missionary, 'As men of God and Ambassadors for Christ you must have nothing to do with trade in any way whatever.'[49] Here were two very different worlds. It is important for us not to confuse them in their starting-points, though in due course they did for a time confuse themselves and, in consequence, their interpreters. It was the Clapham group, high-minded, upper-middle-class Anglican Evangelicals with strong commercial connections who, consciously or unconsciously, did what many thoughtful Christians try to do in every age: adapt the current secular ideology to the service of Christian morality. They argued that legitimate commerce would be far more profitable for everyone (both Africans and Liverpool merchants) than one in slavery, that it would redound far better to the advance of civilization—which, on current thinking, commerce was supposed to do—and would (here they put their own oar in) spread Christianity too. This fusion took place in the 1780s when the new missionary enthusiasm had hardly even begun. It had little to do with mission, but it did provide the justifying ideology for the Freetown settlement and the Sierra Leone Company. Founded in 1791, its first instruction to its employees appealed to 'the true principles of Commerce' but added that they should also advance 'the introduction of Christianity and Civilization'. Here we have, in the late eighteenth century, and essentially unconnected with the missionary movement, the 'Three Cs' firmly in place, put there by a group of philanthropic businessmen and public figures. For them it was less a matter of making money than of exercising their public Christian responsibility. The Sierra Leone Company proved financially disastrous (partly as a consequence of the long war with France). Its success lay in harnessing contemporary ideology in an appropriate manner to the anti-slavery cause. It was also a way, especially in the mind of Granville Sharp, its originator, of being practically helpful to the poor blacks he saw in the streets of London.

In the course of the next twenty years this same group came to patronize the new missionary enthusiasm, and to extend to the latter the vocabulary of civilization. Missionaries, working class or not, were people of their age, imbibing almost unconsciously the assumptions of its ideology. The rationale for Britain's greatness

---

[49] Marsden and Watson to James Lynch in India, 29 Oct. 1815, Levee Kadenge, 'The Origins and Early Development of the Wesleyan Missionary Society', M.Th. thesis (Aberdeen, 1986), 149.

and, more generally, the world supremacy of western Europe was that of commerce and civilization. Commerce, it is true, could not mean much to the ordinary missionary, being for the most part too far removed from the opportunities of his station, but civilization was different. Missionaries were much concerned with vegetable gardens and fruit trees, clean houses and water, ploughs and forges, reading and writing, hats and shoes: the simple things which they had known at home but which were in no way new in Britain and hardly in the forefront of the minds of the civilization theorists. After all, many of them had been gardeners, hatters, or cobblers. Where the theorists thought of high international commerce, large companies, the development of factories in Manchester or Leeds, the missionaries translated civilization into the simpler terms of the more homely things they themselves had some knowledge of. They no less readily adopted the jargon of civilization for what they were doing. In practice they turned 'Christianity and commerce' into 'gospel and plough'. In this sense it was almost inevitable that they should be concerned with 'civilization', though Van der Kemp had had little interest even in that. James Read, more practical than Van der Kemp, was unpreoccupied with clothes but very preoccupied with ploughs (he may, indeed, even have originated the 'gospel and plough' formula) and with this or any other way of increasing the earning power of the Khoikhoi, with whom he had thrown in his lot.

By the 1830s 'Civilization and Christianity' had become the catch-phrase used by everyone from Ministers of the Crown, quite uninterested in pushing missions but concerned to present acceptably Britain's world-wide colonial enterprise, to the humblest missionary explaining the tiny developments of his own corner. John Philip, the theorist in the field, expressed a middle-of-the-road missionary viewpoint with his customary precision in a statement of 1833:

The civilization of the people among whom we labour in Africa is not our highest object; but that object never can be secured and rendered permanent among them without their civilization. Civilization is to the Christian religion what the body is to the soul . . . The blessings of civilization are a few of the blessings which the Christian religion scatters in her progress to immortality; but they are to be cherished for their own sake as well as for ours . . .[50]

[50] A. Ross, *John Philip* (Aberdeen, 1986), 217.

Of course, for many a non-missionary, colonial administrator or settler, it was very much the other way round: what mattered was 'civilization' (meaning, very often, commercial employability). The missionary was to be welcomed only so long as he did not push religion too much but made certain requirements of 'civilization' his first concern.

Disagreements over which those requirements were could be no less sharp. For Philip, as for Van der Kemp, the primary requirement was political justice, while for many who called for civilization that was almost the last thing they had in mind. Bishop Colenso of Natal began his South African career as a benign imperialist exuding a liberal confidence in the spread of civilization and even, like Livingstone, calling for a large increase in white settlement; he ended it battling against the British government for justice and independence for the Zulu kingdom. Bishop Mackenzie in 1861, fired with horror of the slave-trade, found himself engaged in fighting the Yao to liberate Manganja slaves. Twenty years later John Mackenzie of the LMS was so alarmed by Boer incursions on the Tswana that he helped persuade Britain to declare a protectorate over Bechuanaland. These various ways in which the missionary endeavour was politicized were all expressions of a concern for civilization, different as they may appear from ploughs or shoes or, for that matter, from buying shares in some Glasgow-based commercial company.

For whatever reason and in whatever form nearly everyone seemed for a time agreed that the concern to civilize was incumbent upon a missionary, and not only Britons. French colonial officials were complaining that French Catholic missionaries, unlike the Protestants, did too little to civilize. Poor Père Lossedat, a Holy Ghost Father in Gabon, wrote home in 1852 that 'Some Europeans (they say French Officers) have broken the rosaries of our catechumens. They object to our approach of teaching people to pray and to chant canticles. It is not thus, says M. Bouët, Commander of the *Adour*, that one civilizes people.'[51] In fact in his massive *Mémoire* of 1846 for Propaganda Fide on African missions Libermann had already firmly asserted the absolute need for civilization, and not just some low-level technical skills but the inculcation of science, 'les théories des choses'.[52] Turn to another sphere. In 1855 Alexander Crummell, a

---

[51] P. Coulon and D. Brasseur, *Libermann 1802–1852* (1988), 867.
[52] Ibid. 249.

black clergyman from New York with a Cambridge degree, delivered an address on 'The Duty of a Rising Christian State to Contribute to the World's Well-Being and Civilization' before the Common Council and citizens of Monrovia on the day of National Independence.[53] This duty, he declared, would be chiefly fulfilled through 'the elevating and civilizing influence of commerce'. The citizens of Monrovia were assured that 'The Carthaginians and the Roman merchants were noted for their sterling honesty and their love of justice. People who are uncommercial are given to dissimulation, fraud and trickery.'

Here we are back, if somewhat airily, at the virtues and rewards of commerce, but in reality commerce was one bit of the trio which consistently failed to pay off, even though it was the only one thought capable of stirring the effective interest of the normal British capitalist. The first attempt to activate it had been the Sierra Leone Company. Its failure had produced Britain's take-over of its debts and the rule of Sierra Leone itself in 1807. Thirty years later T. F. Buxton reactivated the idea with his book on *The Slave Trade and its Remedy*, published in 1839 first. Wilberforce's chosen successor, Buxton, had steered the abolition of slavery in the British Empire through Parliament in 1833, but the trade continued largely unaffected (carrying slaves to Brazil, Cuba, and the United States). Buxton now revived the idea of extinguishing it through the stimulation of alternative forms of commerce, and created enormous enthusiasm in Britain with a proposal to establish large commercial plantations— Read's 'plough' magnified a thousandfold. Out of the enthusiasm came the disastrous Niger expedition of 1841. It was simply not possible to set up a viable large-scale alternative commerce overnight.

After 1841 the commerce model was once more set aside until Livingstone revived it in the late 1850s, on returning from his great transcontinental journey. For the next quarter-century his message of 'the double influence of the spirit of commerce and Christianity' as being what was needed 'to stay the bitter fountain of African misery'[54] became again a widely accepted orthodoxy, especially in Scottish circles. Hence new trading companies like the West African Company formed in 1863, the African Lakes Company in 1878, and the British East Africa Company in 1888, all with close mission

---

[53] Alexander Crummell, *The Future of Africa* (New York, 1862), 57–104, passage quoted 71–2.   [54] Livingstone, *Missionary Correspondence*, 258.

connections. The Lakes Company's connections were particularly close—to the Livingstonia mission—and it was exceptionally unsuccessful. It is interesting that James Stewart, whose appeal it had been in 1874 to the Free Church of Scotland to establish 'a great centre of commerce, civilization and Christianity' in memory of Livingstone, was three years later writing, 'I hope none of my friends of the mission in Glasgow will have anything to do with *big trading schemes* for Lake Nyassa at present . . . Trade must grow little by little and a large expenditure at first means certainly a big loss.'[55] That was the voice of the missionary realist in contrast to that of the orator, but it was not harkened to. The Glasgow businessmen were resolved on a trading company and, perhaps, without the illusion of quick commerce they would not have backed missions as they did. In a sense the whole of this history is one in which missionary enthusiasts and their business friends deceived each other into believing in the possibility that profit and piety could be combined.

If missionaries of the late nineteenth century were, in the main, pretty cool about any link between their work and commerce, it was drink more than anything else which made them so. In August 1876 the steamer *Ethiopia* left Liverpool bound for the Nigerian coast, carrying one missionary, Mary Slessor, and a cargo of spirits. Six years later the *Ethiopia* was wrecked on rocks just off Loango and it is said that the rum seized as it was breaking up caused the deaths of 200 people. The first Baptist missionaries to the Congo arrived in 1879 on a boat loaded with gin. Earlier missionaries had arrived on slave-ships. Now 'legitimate' commerce had been substituted. In place of slaves, gin. It is hardly surprising that the late Victorian Evangelical shied away from Livingstone's enthusiasm for the commercial model.

In missionary jargon the word 'industrial' came much to be preferred to the word 'commerce'. 'Industrial' was a step up from the plough. It signified a more systematic stress on technical skills in a way that was only possible in larger centres like Livingstonia and Lovedale, though the name would come to be adopted by many smaller enterprises as well. The central missionary 'institute' became increasingly the ideal of the civilizing school—less ambitious and prone to corruption than the commercial company but rather more sophisticated than the 'gospel and plough' formula. The Industrial Mission is the late nineteenth- and early twentieth-century favourite

---

[55] McCracken, *Politics and Christianity in Malawi*, 43–4.

for people with this approach, aware of the dangers to which the commerce ideal almost inevitably led—drink, bankruptcy, or a take-over by European settlers. For white settlement is what Christianity and Commerce seemed inevitably to lead to if it was to succeed in terms of profit in the immediate term. And white settlement was, indeed, what Livingstone had had in mind. Maybe missionary recognition that this sort of culmination to the commercial pursuit would not be to the long-term advantage of Africans helped induce them to pull back from implementation of Livingstone's ideal. Yet in fact, on the west coast at least, the plough and the commercial marketing of its products by a new African farming class did actually succeed. We can see it particularly in the development of cocoa in Nigeria and then the Gold Coast at the turn of the century. In South Africa too and, later, in central Africa small-scale black commercial farming would have succeeded had it not been for white competitors determined that it should not do so. Settler farming needed black labour and did not want the rivalry of a profit-making black peasantry. Only where there were no settlers, as in the west or Uganda, did the commerce model finally work to black advantage: and to Christian advantage too, because in such cases the black community making profitable use of the plough was also the core of a local Church. So there proved to be, after all, a measure of sense in the commerce model. What was wrong with it was the narrow time-scale its backers in Britain inevitably looked for.

Nevertheless, there were always missionaries and, still more, missionary planners who had their doubts about this whole line of thought. 'Civilization' meant something different to everyone who used it. It secularized the mission and idealized Europe. A highly intelligent, rather sceptical, Italian Franciscan missionary, in declaring his preference in 1850 for Ethiopia over Italy, could refer mockingly to 'civilizzatissima Europa'.[56] The guide-lines of Propaganda Fide, ever since the seventeenth century, had been opposed to all unnecessary Europeanization, and what was the whole civilization school concerned with other than that? It is striking that Lavigerie, with all his devotion to the example of Livingstone, appears almost never to speak of civilization. On the contrary, he insisted, in his great *Instruction* to the missionaries of equatorial Africa of 1879:

---

[56] Letter of 26 Oct. 1850, cf. C. Conti Rossini, *Rendiconti della Reale Accademia dei Lincei*, 5/29 (1920), 216.

From the material aspect we must leave Africans as they are, that is to say truly Africans. We must shut our eyes and hearts to a false pity . . . and resign ourselves to see the young negroes close to us maintain the customs of their land, their wattle huts instead of houses, their bare earth in place of beds, sorghum and manioc instead of bread, grass waist bands in place of shirt and trousers.[57]

If Protestant missionaries seem to have been rather easily carried away by the 'civilization' model, it may be because they had so little of a real missionary doctrine to fall back upon, over and above a great enthusiasm for world evangelism. But so soon as they began to develop a doctrine, they started to recognize the danger. It is noticeable that Henry Venn had very little interest in civilizing, and indeed increasingly recognized how opposed it could be to the early realization of his ideal, the self-governing Church. The establishment of a native Church required the adoption of African ways, not the imposition of European ones. It is odd that it was Livingstone with all his African intuition who confused the whole movement by plunging back from a concern with native agency into one which ceaselessly harped on the vocabulary of civilization and pursued the goals of Western commerce and settlement. But at the very same time that he was reinvigorating the civilization school, Venn, Lavigerie, and others like Hudson Taylor, founder of the China Inland Mission, were guiding the central core of the missionary movement emphatically away from preoccupation with civilization towards the acceptance of cultural diversity and non-European ways as crucial to a missionary's central purpose.

By the 1880s an extreme point was reached by some radical Evangelicals following the Hudson Taylor line on adaptation. Two young upper-class English enthusiasts, Graham Wilmot Brooke and John Alfred Robinson, in proposing a new CMS mission up the Niger to the Hausa, were particularly outspoken. Brooke, a somewhat unbalanced extremist, had for years been trying to escape from any part of Africa affected by, as he saw it, the contaminating curse of Western commercialization and concern for the this-worldly values of civilization. 'We carefully avoid praising civilization or civilized powers to the heathen,' they wrote in 1891. 'If they themselves are extolling civilization we tell them that they should not set their affection on things below.'[58] Here was the

---

[57] Lavigerie, *Instructions aux missionnaires*, 98.
[58] CMS, Sudan Mission Leaflet, no. 18, Feb. 1891, A. Walls, 'Black Europeans, White Africans: Some Missionary Motives in West Africa', in D. Baker (ed.), *Religious Motivation, SCH* xv (1978), 347–8.

resurgence of pure evangelicalism with a vengeance, but it remained untypical of CMS men, even of that Keswick-influenced period, at least in so extreme a form.

UMCA attitudes were not all that different, and more consistent. 'Our desire is to distinguish very clearly between Christianising and Europeanising', wrote Bishop Smythies in 1892. 'What we want is to Christianise them in their own civil and political conditions; to help them to develop a Christian civilization suited to their own climate and their own circumstances. For instance, we do not allow any of the boys in our schools to wear any European clothing; it is not our business to encourage the trade in boots . . .'.[59] Next year the Synod of the Diocese of Zanzibar resolved to 'strenuously discourage all Europeanisms'.[60] Of course, this remained a minority position just as heavy civilizing remained a minority position. In between were the large majority, Europeanizing in some ways (and no book-learning could be done without a measure of Europeanizing), endeavouring to adapt to African ways in others. Dr Laws of Livingstonia was a distinguished but autocratic representative of the civilizing line while Archdeacon Johnson, who enjoyed at times the hospitality of Dr Laws when he was more than usually unwell and in need of a rest, was a fine and unusually unautocratic representative of the Africanizing. Both spent fifty years on Lake Nyasa and both have had their admirers, black and white. For Johnson, the Church must be above all 'a true native development and not a foreign intrusion. This must be insisted on by keeping its thought, its agents, its appointments as entirely native as possible.'[61] Laws, on the other hand, wanted to give the very best of Scotland to Africa—he even planned a tower at his Overtoun Institute just like that of King's College, Aberdeen! The Scots were the greatest of civilizers. Donald Fraser, a younger member of the Livingstonia Mission moving mildly in a different direction, could smile at Laws's dictum that to teach an African to lay bricks in a straight line was a great step towards civilization, but, of course, a lot of Africans were grateful for such lessons and without them the Christian Church and its institutions would have been far less attractive than they were. Johnson's far

---

[59] G.W. (Gertrude Ward), *The Life of Charles Alan Smythies* (1898), 190.

[60] Diocese of Zanzibar, *Acts of the Synods*, 1884–1903, 18; see also W. P. Johnson's defence in the *Nyasa News* of 1894 of this position, written as 'An Answer' to one who said 'You must accept your position as being not only messengers of the Gospel, but representatives of civilization', E. H. Barnes, *Johnson of Nyasaland* (1935), 106–7.

[61] Barnes, *Johnson of Nyasaland*, 140.

quieter, less disruptive, approach needed more time, and in late nineteenth-century Africa time was more limited than it may have seemed.

At the end of the day, Henri Junod, a remarkable Swiss missionary scholar, added up the pros and cons of 'civilization' in the conclusion of his *Life of a South African Tribe*, published in 1912. He listed the blessings of civilization, among them the disappearance of deadly famines, improved clothing (which he thought only a 'mixed blessing'), better seeds and agricultural implements, a broadening of ideas. But the 'curses of civilization' he judged far to exceed the blessings, at least in South Africa, and first among them he listed 'Loss of political interest and responsibility'.[62] For Adam Ferguson, in the eighteenth century, it was the political which, more than anything else, defined civilization. Now it is noticeable how consistently Johnson urged a scrupulous respect for African political authority, even of a rather minuscule form. Perhaps the 'anti-civilizers' had the deeper sense of civilization, even in terms of the Enlightenment, while the civilizers were continually in danger of disrupting civilization by concentrating upon the technical to the dissolution of the socio-political.

The ideology of the nineteenth-century missionary movement began with a simple evangelical individualism grounded upon the Bible first and last. As we have seen, it quickly joined to this a second more worldly thread which may loosely be characterized as 'civilization', an undefined additional component, formally rejected by rather few, but, equally, central to the thought of rather few. It seemed at least a happy way of persuading the secular scoffer that missionaries were a good thing earning their keep in terms of the public good. It also served to justify a great deal of highly 'secular' activity on the mission station which, in strictly evangelical terms, might be hard to defend. A secular component to mission seemed a natural enough adjunct to anyone other than the narrowest evangelist; for a minority it became a quite central concern. It could take an anti-slavery form with some, a struggle for political rights with others, a general interest in benevolent improvement with a third group, an alliance with Western commerce for the opening-up of the world with a fourth. Van der Kemp and Philip battled with the Cape government for Khoikhoi rights, Moffat irrigated the valley

[62] Henri Junod, *The Life of a South African Tribe*, ii (1912), 540.

of Kuruman, Livingstone encouraged grandiose schemes of European commerce, Bishop Mackenzie reluctantly led his missionary colleagues into various tiny wars for the freeing of slaves: these were extremely different approaches to the business of spreading civilization, but they concur in showing that part of the missionary task was a secular and worldly one.

xi. *The Three Selves and the Pursuit of Adaptation*

There was, however, a third important strand within missionary purpose, a strand which, present at first hardly more than implicitly, became at least for the theorists increasingly decisive. It developed in response to circumstance and experience, the exigencies of a second and third generation, pondered by the more far-sighted theorists sitting at home, responsible for planning the strategy of the main societies. Greatest of these upon the Protestant side was undoubtedly Henry Venn, Secretary of the Church Missionary Society from 1841 to 1872, though a very considerable influence upon Venn himself was Rufus Anderson, Secretary of the American Board of Commissioners for Foreign Mission. Venn's father, John, had been Rector of Clapham and first chairman of the CMS, so Henry was a natural heir to the central Anglican Evangelical tradition, yet in his own thought he would seem to distance himself from the more liberationist and civilizing preoccupations of the first Clapham generation.

The CMS was essentially a lay organization, and, while it stressed the use of 'Church' in its title, it had behind it and its early mission practice little more ecclesiology than that of the LMS. Its task, as it at first saw it, was to send out people, lay or clergy, men or women, to preach the gospel and spread a knowledge of the Bible. It is hardly surprising that the bishops were suspicious of it. Only the very year that Venn became Secretary did the archbishops accept a regular relationship with the Society after an agreement had been negotiated by Bishop Blomfield of London and Venn himself. This was important not only for a clarification of the Anglican character of the CMS at home, but, much more, as a step towards achieving a more genuinely ecclesiological understanding of the missionary enterprise itself.

For Anderson and Venn, it was becoming increasingly clear that the task of the missionary was not just to go abroad to preach and convert people or even to translate and spread afar the Scriptures.

There were far too many people to preach to; missionaries were seldom well equipped to evangelize in foreign languages; those that were sent too often died before they had done anything of much note. No, the task of preaching to the foreign multitude must belong to a local Church in each and every place. The task of the foreign missionary is to go where there is as yet no local Church in order to establish one. Once a native Church is functioning, he can and should move on. A self-governing Church is to be followed by the 'euthanasia' of the mission, a word of which Venn became fond and was already using by 1844. Once a self-supporting, self-governing, self-extending Church exists within a society, 'a Native Church under Native Pastors and a Native Episcopate' as Venn described it in 1858,[63] it is the duty of the foreign missionary either to advance to 'the regions beyond' or to integrate as some sort of auxiliary worker within the native Church. Until the middle of the century, Protestant missionaries had hardly at all thought in such terms; from then on they frequently did so, even if in many a case they remained deeply reluctant to implement the concept in practice. It was Venn most of all who brought about the change, particularly in a series of memoranda dated from around 1850.

The ordination of Samuel Crowther in 1843, first of CMS African ordinations, was already the indication of a new direction, and Crowther's outstanding intellectual and moral quality naturally reinforced it. People were soon suggesting his appointment to the episcopate. Over that Venn himself actually held back, only too aware of the reluctance of missionaries in the field to accept it but unsure too as to what his diocese should be. Crowther was made a bishop in 1864, the high point of achievement of Venn's strategy. The 'native agent' could now be seen, not as a useful supplement to the missionary, but quite the other way round, as the mission's goal and crown. A similar shift was going on in many non–episcopal missions, a shift in missionary thought from preacher to Church-planter. However, it was with Venn and the CMS that the shift was made most clearly, and just at the high time of the Victorian age when the Church of England was itself undergoing a shift in consciousness in the post-Tractarian era. Venn's position in this was somewhat paradoxical. While the CMS was self-consciously Evangelical, and Venn himself was always seen as a great Evangelical spokesman, he

[63] C. P. Williams, *The Ideal of the Self-Governing Church* (Leiden, 1990), 17.

was in this, the most crucial of his roles, in reality catholicizing, because ecclesiasticizing, what had been an overly Protestant activity.

In the first half of the nineteenth century, the most influential of missionary societies was the LMS. In the second half it was, undoubtedly, the CMS. The shift was only across a mile of London, from Blomfield Street in Finsbury to Salisbury Square, just west of St Paul's. In terms of personality it was from the slightly colourless Arthur Tidman to the more impressive and intellectually innovative Henry Venn. Yet Tidman's approach does not seem significantly different from that of Venn, and one can detect, for instance, in his correspondence with Livingstone in the 1840s, a certain impatience at how little the missionaries in the field were actually doing to further the 'important object' of native agency.[64] What made all the public difference was Crowther's episcopal consecration. In principle, and in practice too, Protestants were learning at this point much what Catholics had learnt a great deal earlier. One might see Henry Venn as the Ingoli of the Protestant world. But, just as Catholics failed to implement the vision effectively, so would Protestants find it exceedingly hard to do. The deep reluctance of missionaries actually to hand over, the evidence of native failings, the argument for caution and delay, all would be much the same on the one side as on the other. Yet Protestants were in some ways better placed to implement such a policy because they were at least not tied by Roman canon law, which again and again ruled out realistic adaptation to the needs of a viable local Church.

The 1840s, Venn's first decade as Secretary in Salisbury Square, was also a good decade for Catholic missionary rethinking. His nearest counterpart was Francis Libermann, whose missionary instructions written at various dates between 1840 and his death in 1852 were in their way as remarkable as those of Venn. It is true that his stress upon the importance of forming a native priesthood, strong as it was, did not differ from the Roman viewpoint as it had continually been stressed by Propaganda Fide. He took it over also through his friendship with Mother Javouhey, who had sent from Senegal a group of young men, three of whom were ordained in Paris in the seminary of the Holy Ghost in 1840. It would not be pointless to compare the achievements and frustrations in the life of Samuel

---

[64] See his letter to Livingstone of 6 Sept. 1847, or those of 30 Dec. 1845 and 23 Dec. 1848, Livingstone, *Missionary Correspondence*, 85–6, 109–10, 125–6.

Crowther with those in the career of the Abbé Boilat. One does, however, detect in Libermann a stronger sense than was customary in Catholic literature that the object was not just to ordain local priests but to establish 'la forme stable d'une Église':[65] 'a Church' is important, it is a phrase to be noted. Libermann stresses that the universal Church consists of 'particular Churches'. A Church outside Europe is not just a clerical extension of the one Church centred in Europe, it is a Church of its own and needs to become all that any one of the Churches in Europe may be. Above all, it must not remain 'a mission'. He recognized that the health of a Church is impossible without an adequate degree of civilization in its society, but, equally, he stressed that the duty of the missionary is not to impose his European mentality. It is, on the contrary, to reshape his own attitudes according to the culture he has come to. Hence that famous phrase of Libermann, to be found in the letter to the community of Dakar and Gabon of November 1847: 'Faites-vous nègres avec les nègres.'

Empty yourselves of Europe, of its manners and mentality; make yourselves blacks with the blacks, then you will understand them as they should be understood; make yourselves blacks with the blacks to form them as they should be, not in the way of Europe, but leaving them what is their own; behave towards them as servants would behave to their masters, adapting to the customs, attitudes and habits of their masters.[66]

Such spiritually and culturally radical teaching was doubtless most imperfectly implemented: the typical Holy Ghost Father of the late nineteenth century behaved quite otherwise. It is important to recall all the same that such teaching was given, and by one of the great missionary founders. It represents very much what, on the Protestant side, Van der Kemp had already been doing and what much later W. P. Johnson and Charles de Foucauld would endeavour to do, but only the most steely-willed masters of self-abnegation can realize such ideals.

Libermann was followed by Bresillac, Comboni, and Lavigerie, all of whom founded new missionary societies for Africa. They all stressed the need for a local priesthood, and their admirers have too easily in each case judged their hero as an innovator in this. They were not. Many had tried before, and the new societies, at least until

---

[65] *Mémoire* of Aug. 1846, Coulon and Brasseur, *Libermann*, 239.
[66] Ibid. 518.

well into the twentieth century, would have no more success, perhaps less, than missionaries of earlier ages. The bar remained canon law: the obligation to be fluent in Latin and bound to celibacy. As a matter of fact, Lavigerie's genius may be recognized, paradoxically, not in pushing a native priesthood, but in recognizing so clearly how unrealistic it was to hope for one in such circumstances. He therefore proposed to substitute for it an order of married medical catechists: 'There is no salvation outside marriage,' 'Il n'y a d'autre salut que le mariage.'[67] For him 'the most essential of all works' became the 'training of Christian doctors'.[68] When this, too, came to be seen as manifestly inadequate, Lavigerie suggested to the Pope in 1890 that Africa should be allowed a married priesthood.[69] Only after the rejection of that proposal, at the very end of his life, did he turn back with determination to the traditional attempt to develop a celibate priesthood.

Lavigerie is the best known and most praised of the nineteenth-century founders, largely because of the subsequent achievements of the White Fathers. He was an exceptionally powerful character with a continually probing intellect, but his principal ideas for a new missionary strategy proved largely misguided despite the imagination which went into them. A few doctors were trained in Malta, some of them remarkable men, but no one else was very happy with this project, and it was soon abandoned. Later on it proved hard enough for White Fathers to work with black priests; to have worked closely with an entirely new order of married black doctors would, indeed, have been miraculous. Again, Lavigerie's preoccupation with the conversion of kings and the establishment of a Christian kingdom was shared by others and there seemed some ground for it; yet, basically, it was a medieval throwback and, in the world of the British Empire, kings anyway usually preferred to be Anglican if anything. What his missionaries were left with was the common Catholic practice of buying young slaves to train in 'orphanages' and Christian villages. It was an enterprise which, while ostensibly part of an anti-slavery campaign, in fact merely encouraged the trade by producing regular buyers. It created an effectively captive Christian community, but seldom a very resilient one. Catholic preoccupation with this

[67] Lavigerie, *Instructions aux missionaires*, 99.
[68] Renault, *Lavigerie: L'esclavage africain et l'Europe* (Paris, 1971), i. 164.
[69] Ibid. 228.

approach through the latter years of the century only demonstrated how far they remained behind the better Protestant work.

Lavigerie's lasting legacy lay elsewhere: in his general insistence (in line with Libermann) upon establishing a viable Church, upon assimilating oneself to Africa, upon the learning of languages superlatively, and upon the re-establishment of a lengthy and structured catechumenate. These insistences served the White Fathers well; add to them the lesson of their unique Buganda experience and their taking to heart, more than anyone else, and that perhaps because of the impact upon them of the Baganda martyrs, the Roman insistence upon the development of a native priesthood, and one has the combination of qualities which made of the White Fathers a missionary force of unsurpassed vigour and consistency in the interior of Africa by the end of the nineteenth century. The Protestant example even drew them into rather more Scripture translation than was customary for Catholics.

Catholic and Protestant missionaries often behaved very differently in the nineteenth century, just as they generally looked different: a presence of cassocks and an absence of wives were both highly noticeable. Nevertheless, in fact, Protestants had moved in a distinctly 'Catholic' direction while Catholics had, for their part, learnt rather more than they might care to admit from Protestants. What remains most significant is that the main thrust of Protestant concern had shifted from the eschatological to the ecclesiological. While each could make some use of the language of 'civilization', for neither was it a central preoccupation. The eschatological tended to the destruction of African culture, the ecclesiological to be adaptationist. Venn and Lavigerie represent a common choice to put Church formation and cultural adaptation first. Neither, however, was a radical. They were both too near the centre of ecclesiastical power for that. Nor were their societies by any means fully faithful to their vision. Nevertheless, the CMS and the White Fathers became the two most influential missionary bodies at work in Africa, and the impact upon them of the ideas of Venn and Lavigerie was a major enduring factor in the shaping of African Christianity.

xii. *What Missionaries Thought of Africa*

What, finally, was the Victorian missionary's image of Africa, the image the missionaries themselves possessed, rather than that which popular missionary literature presented at home? 'O the blindness, the darkness, the foolishness of heathenism!', lamented Anna Hinderer in Ibadan in the 1860s.[70] 'Darkness' is unquestionably a recurring note in the missionary image of Africa. And it was easily taken over by the first generation of converts. 'Our mission stations', wrote Samuel Crowther a few years later, 'are as encampments from which we sally out to wage aggressive war with the powers of darkness.'[71] It would not be hard to multiply verbal examples a thousandfold. It was, in common parlance, the 'Dark Continent'. But here, as with 'civilization', we find a large variety of meanings. It was 'dark' because Europeans, or indeed anyone, knew little about it as a whole. Its vast interior was still largely unmapped when Hinderer and Crowther wrote. It was 'dark' because it lacked the indications of civilization which even the most emphatic upholder of the view that civilization depended upon Christianity could not deny finding in India or China. It was 'dark' because of European and Arab crimes perpetrated upon it over the centuries: the slave-trade and subsequent colonial oppression weighed heavily on the missionary conscience, producing a stress on the need for reparation. It was 'dark' most of all because it was 'heathen' and corrupted by all sorts of terrible practices. The heart of all this darkness in the European imagination combined atrocities both black and white, while for the missionary mind it was all bound up with the realm of the 'Prince of Darkness', the devil. Finally, it was 'dark'—though missionaries would mostly have found difficulty in focusing upon this underlying, more psychological, theme—because its inhabitants were 'dark'. Their colour mysteriously symbolized all other meanings.

Let us start with the last point by recalling Blake's poem 'The Little Black Boy'. Perhaps he had in mind one of those page-boys who appear quite often in portraits of the eighteenth-century aristocracy.

> My mother bore me in the southern wild
> And I am black, but O, my soul is white!
> White as an angel is the English child,
> But I am black, as if bereaved of light.

Undoubtedly Blake was struggling in the poem to find a positive point to negritude—'these black bodies' are 'like a shady grove', but we see here in the deliberately sympathetic poem of a radical mystic

---

[70] Anna Hinderer, *Seventeen Years in the Yoruba Country* (1872), 213.
[71] Ekechi, *Missionary Enterprise and Rivalry in Igboland*, 41.

an underlying European and Christian problem: in biblical and Christian symbolism 'white' is good, 'black' is bad; one signifies life, the other death. Africans (rather seldom so called) were Ethiopians, Negroes, characterized by their 'black' skins. They were thought, moreover, to belong to the race of Ham and to fall in consequence under the biblical 'curse' of Canaan (Genesis 9: 25–7). Some Catholic missionaries, at least, continued to believe that this curse applied to Africans well into the twentieth century. Blake's poem points to the Western linkage of skin colour and moral state. The black child is 'as if bereaved of light', suffering from some sort of spiritual blindness. Few missionaries if any will have thought this sort of thing out, but the almost platitudinous use of the word 'dark' for Africa probably owed as much to it as to anything else. As African cultures have, many of them, a similar pattern of colour symbolism, it was not hard for African Christians to take over the terminology rather easily.

The missionary use of 'darkness' is most often related to straight lack of Christian belief and, particularly, to such moral behaviour as seemed particularly awful, consequent upon 'superstition'. Anna Hinderer's outburst—and on the whole her judgements on African society were positive enough—was in connection with a human sacrifice offered on the outbreak of war. Human sacrifices, witch-hunts, the raids on their neighbours of warrior peoples like the Ndebele, were what most frequently prompted such remarks, and they very easily led in evangelical parlance to a reference to the diabolical character of the practices in question. Darkness and the devil went together. Undoubtedly the public moral evils of Africa were more glaring to missionary eyes than those of Europe, some of them hardly less awful. But the darkness which the missionary felt he had 'sallied out' to fight seems often a good deal vaguer than that. The New Testament and subsequent religious literature is so full of dark–light images, as of allusions to spiritual warfare, it was inevitable that highly committed Christians should identify their labours in such terms. Wesley was only too insistent upon the darkness of the villages and slums of England. There was often nothing so different about missionary references to darkness in Africa. It was no more than the common discourse of Evangelicalism. For Pilkington, speaking in 1896, there were 'three forms of darkness' to be fought in Africa, 'Heathenism, Mohammedanism and Popery'[72] and many an

---

[72] Harford-Battersby, *Pilkington of Uganda*, 224.

Evangelical would have agreed with that. Ireland and Italy were characterized as 'dark' in a not dissimilar way. In the end 'darkness' for the committed missionary came to have rather little to do with Africa as such. It had come to represent the unacceptable superstition of any religion other than one's own.

Much in the most negative and painful passages in popular Victorian missionary literature about Africa comes from the pens of mission organizers and backers who were never in the field. Nevertheless, there were undoubtedly many missionaries who produced an almost incredibly negative image of Africa. Bishop Knight-Bruce, Eton and Oxford, toured Mashonaland in 1888 to prepare the way for a mission. He does not seem to have been unkindly received, but could write, nevertheless,

No-one, who had not had dealings with the heathen savage, would credit what a repulsive degradation of humanity he is: seeming to combine the high development of rascality and cunning as found in the professional London thief with a shamelessness which few of them have, while their miserable stupidity, in nearly every case where their own interests are not concerned, is only to be appreciated by those who have been subjected to it.[73]

Yet he could also describe the Shona as 'a gentle, industrious and skilful people'. Knight-Bruce rapidly wore himself out as Bishop of Mashonaland. He had much of the self-confident arrogance of the late Victorian imperialist, but flashes also of a more humane discernment. At the end of his life he could write, 'I feel deeply how constantly I misjudged both my Christian and heathen natives.'[74]

Few missionaries were racialists. The very universalism implicit in their calling made it difficult for them to be so. They stressed again and again—often against fashionable Western opinion, with its increasingly racialist overtones—the intelligence, ability, rationality, and even high moral qualities of the unconverted people among whom they worked, and still more of course the achievements of their converts. They long expatiated on the virtues of a Khama or a Crowther. Occasionally they could delight in the closest of friendships, as Pilkington could write to his mother on the death of Sembera Mackay, 'Oh, Mother, you don't know how I loved him,

[73] C. Fripp (ed.), *Gold and the Gospel in Mashonaland 1888*, the first part being the Mashonaland Journal of Bishop Knight-Bruce, (1949), 54.
[74] G. W. H. Knight-Bruce, *Memories of Mashonaland* (1895), 161.

and love him still with all my soul; everyone loved him; the best, the bravest, the noblest, the wisest. Never to see his kind face in this world again or hear his cheery voice . . . I couldn't even bid him good-bye for the last time.'[75] 'Unreasonableness cannot be said to be a more obstinate hereditary complaint in Africa than in Ireland,' declared Livingstone provocatively. 'If one behaves as a gentleman, he will invariably be treated as such.'[76] In their approach to Africans, John Philip admitted in 1846, missionaries were of 'two different classes'.[77]

What is esteemed and practised as a virtue by one is viewed as a crime in the eyes of the other . . . Both parties would do the Coloured people good but in different ways. In order to raise the people James Read would treat them as brethren and to this Mr Calderwood says 'we object' . . . Both parties love the people but the one shows it in a way which the people like better than the other and they cannot be blamed for it. A missionary who was afraid of spoiling the people by shaking hands with them said to me the other day 'I never saw the like of these Hottentots, you can do nothing with them by scolding them, you may do anything with them by kindness'.

One kind of behaviour went with a deep sense of brotherhood and common humanity, the other with a sense of superiority over the 'savages' whom they had a mission to improve. The difference was probably less a religious or ideological one than the psychological ability or inability to identify, to recognize the existence of a common culture. In a similar way Gobat recognized it in Ethiopia twelve years earlier, but his colleagues did not. He compared his approach, a little sadly, with that of Isenberg. While he hoped to reach 'the heart of the Abyssinians' by adopting their way of eating, dressing, and so forth, 'Brother Isenberg hopes to have more influence upon them by keeping at a distance.'[78] Livingstone remarked that the stories he heard from his grandfather in the Highlands were 'wonderfully like those I have heard while sitting by the African evening fires'.[79] Perhaps a rural background helped more than an urban one in enabling the anthropologically untrained missionary make the great leap of cultural understanding across chasms of otherness to recognition of the 'wonderfully like' and

[75] Harford-Battersby, *Pilkington of Uganda*, 183.
[76] Livingstone, *Missionary Correspondence*, 298.
[77] Ross, *John Philip*, 93.
[78] D. Crummey, *Priests and Politicians* (1972), 40.
[79] Livingstone, *Missionary Travels and Researches in South Africa*, 1.

escape from the inclination of 'keeping at a distance'. The sheer will to identify was important, and married missionaries, when half settlers themselves and anxious to belong to a settler community, almost never had that will at all. But the most decisive factor may have been a real working knowledge of language. It is often hard to know when this existed, as the regular use of interpreters is easily omitted from the record. Inevitably when we discuss missionaries it is largely in terms of the more outstanding, most of whom were excellent linguists, but they were a small minority. There were many others who can never have had a really serious conversation in an African language. Without mastery of the language the stereotype of 'the savage' easily prevailed. With it and a growing awareness of the endless subtleties of the language the key to cultural admiration had been acquired.

Across a rich linguistic knowledge, and only across it, could some missionaries build up an organic grasp of culture, mentality, and religion, so that the impression of 'savagery' dissolved into one of a certain reasonableness. There were men, like Moffat, who could master the language but, despite his quite remarkable friendship with Moselekatse, could never quite master the culture. Without the language, the further step was hardly feasible.

François Coillard was someone who had lived for many years with the Basotho and then for many more with the Lozi. Like Livingstone he found it hard to co-operate with whites but was deeply sympathetic to blacks and close enough to each people to detect and to enjoy the differences. 'The Basotho, like the Athenians, are all, and always, on the scent of something new,' he wrote, yet they have too a 'grave and respectful politeness'. What struck him about the Lozi, on the other hand, was 'their incredible levity. They laugh and scoff at everything and everybody . . . Here, to live is literally to amuse yourself. All is frivolity.'[80] In comments like these one is being given an image of Africa by someone who has entered into its life in its rich diversity and sees it, as he might different nations of Europe, with the affectionate but critical eye of a real friend.

Livingstone's charming, and justly famous, little account of the conversation between a medical doctor and a rain doctor[81] is an early example of such fond interpretation by the outsider who has become

---

[80] Coillard, *On the Threshold of Central Africa*, 416–17.
[81] Livingstone, *Missionary Travels and Researches in South Africa*, ch. 1.

an insider. It must have helped many on the way to a more positive presentation of the African mind. Just a little later one cannot but be impressed by the very careful ethnographic account of the Dinka and the Bari by Fr. Anton Kaufmann, one of the remarkable group at Gondokoro in the late 1850s.[82] Then came works like Canon Callaway's *Religious System of the Amazulu* (1870) and Duff MacDonald's *Africana* (1882). Still more mature, as sympathetic anthropological interpretation, are John Roscoe's *The Baganda* (1911) and Henri Junod's *The Life of a South African Tribe* (1912). While these were published well into the twentieth century both men had been in Africa since the late 1880s.[83] For many of their missionary contemporaries such works were pointless. Archdeacon Walker condemned Roscoe's anthropological and historical researches as a matter of hunting 'in the dustbin and rubbish heaps of Uganda for the foolish and unclean customs of the people long thrown away'.[84] Yet Walker was an intelligent man with a great knowledge of the language and far deeper African sympathies than many, while Roscoe's anthropological concerns led him to give up missionary work and move to Cambridge. Sympathizing and belittling attitudes to Africans, their culture and history, could take a variety of forms but would continue to face one another, often ambiguously, within a single missionary society as they had done in Philip's time. That was true of both Catholic and Protestant, though upon each side there was a bad rump, with some missionary groups almost wholly uncomprehending.

Of the late Victorians the Swiss Protestant Henri Junod was *facile princeps*. No one else living in Africa before the arrival of the first academic anthropologists produced anything nearly as fine as his study of the Ronga people, *The Life of a South African Tribe*, comprehensive and comprehending. There was in truth no one missionary image of Africa any more than there was one missionary ideology, and one certainly finds some of the most racialist and uncomprehending of missionaries at just this time, the decades of the imperialist high tide. Yet if at times it is allowable to judge an

[82] A. Kaufmann, *Das Gebiet des weissen Flusses und dessen Bewohner* (Brixen, 1881) in part translated and republished in Elias Toniolo and Richard Hill, *The Opening of the Nile Basin* (1974) 140–95.
[83] Note too Junod's earlier 300-page work, *Les Chants et les contes des Ba-Ronga de la Baie de Delogoa: Recueillis et transcrits*, published already in Lausanne in 1897.
[84] J. Waliggo, 'The Catholic Church in the Buddu Province of Buganda', Ph.D. thesis (Cambridge, 1976), 272.

organization or a movement in terms of the finest it can produce, so long as that is not of a merely maverick nature but consistent with a wider achievement, then, exceptional as it remains, Junod's masterpiece may be allowed to represent the image of Africa as depicted by the Victorian missionary.

8

KINGS, MARRIAGE, ANCESTORS, AND GOD

i. *Monarchies and Christianization*

Kings dominated the nineteenth-century encounter between Christianity and Africa, and inevitably so. There were, indeed, exceptions to this and the exceptions may provide the quantitatively more considerable part of the conversion process. The exceptions were, however, in African terms at the margins of society, though in European terms at the centre of the new dispensation: in the urban society of the west coast and the ever-growing colonialized areas of South Africa. In these two regions, upon which we focused in Chapter 5, the dynamics of traditional Africa had already broken down under the Western impact by the middle of the century.

In this chapter we need to dismiss that impact from our minds so far as we reasonably can and to focus attention instead on African Africa, the great sweep of the continent still dominated until the 1880s by the internal norms of its tradition, diverse, conflictual, but black. They were, moreover, norms which, while politically undermined almost everywhere by the turn of the century, continued to control the cultural and social core of the real world of the vast majority of Africans through the greater part of the twentieth century. How far were the structures of culture inimical to the spread of Christianity, how far did they favour it or were, at least, capable of serving it? The history of the Christianization of Africa has usually been written within a context of the diffusion of European culture. That is not a false context; nevertheless, for most Africans it was a subsidiary one. The principal context was their own traditional, but not unchanging, thought-world. The fate of Christianity depended upon its ability to be reread in terms and with implications for the most part unimagined by its propagators.

The African Africa of the nineteenth century was not by any means everywhere a world of kings. Monarchies were, nevertheless, so powerful and so noticeable in western, eastern, and southern

Africa that they dominate the scene. While kingless societies remained numerous, many of them were much affected by their proximity to more aggressive and centralized states. Missionaries, like other outsiders, almost inevitably tended to concentrate their attention and their powers of persuasion upon royals. With some reason they saw the conversion of a king, or at least the achievement of his goodwill, as a prerequisite for the conversion of anyone else. They often imagined themselves in a situation comparable to that of the Europe of a thousand years before in which a royal baptism was followed by that of an entire people. In practice there was seldom much of an alternative. Their residence in inland Africa required authorization and protection. Kings were seldom agreeable to allowing a missionary to settle anywhere except at the court where he could both be put to practical use and kept under observation. Moreover, in a thinly populated continent where towns hardly existed—at least outside Yorubaland—as centres of industry, learning, or commerce, royal capitals were the only moderately dense centres of population, and missionaries naturally sought to locate themselves at a spot where a fairly numerous audience could be found within a radius of some fifteen miles.

For all these reasons the relationship of king to missionary was at the very heart of the early transmission of Christianity outside colonial enclaves. One could start with the meeting of Van der Kemp and Ngqika of the Xhosa in September 1799, the beginning of a relationship whose features would recur not infrequently in other such encounters. While Van der Kemp sought to convert Ngqika and his people to a gospel centred upon belief in another world, Ngqika, whose people were threatened upon every side, sought to find out what political use Van der Kemp might be. While colonial power had certainly begun to impinge upon the Xhosa state by 1799, it was still a society struggling to survive according to its own norms, if perilously close to the colonial frontier. While the missionary–king encounter we are considering implies the genuine survival of traditional power—sufficient at times to be used with impunity even against the missionary—the rumour at least of European power is almost always a part of the encounter's context. In the case of the western Xhosa it was already in 1799 far more than that.

Ngqika at times attended the services of Van der Kemp and hinted that, some day, he might be converted. In the meantime they discussed matters of many sorts. Van der Kemp appeared as somebody very different from other white people, a strange, powerful, prophetic figure, knowledgeable enough but less useful than many a later missionary. Though he departed quite soon, his memory remained strong for the King and his household, but, years later, Ngqika could declare emphatically to another missionary, 'You have your manner to wash and decorate yourselves on the Lord's day and I have mine the same in which I was born and that I shall follow . . . If I adopt your law I must entirely overturn all my own and that I shall not do.'[1] Seldom did a king spell out the truth of his predicament so starkly and uncompromisingly. Every side of an African monarchy and the ensuring of its power was tied to beliefs and practices unacceptable to missionaries. Yet the appeal of the missionary could still be remarkable. He not only had attractive presents and ongoing skills of a technical sort, he had a knowledge of the wider world and an ability to read and write letters which an African king could find invaluable. He was at times seen as someone of more than natural power, a mystery man, but he was also a rather secular figure, occasionally an almost official agent of the British government where it had no consul, even a 'Missionary of the Queen of England', as Glele of Dahomey described one Methodist,[2] but someone whom, with skill, you too could employ as your agent for foreign affairs. For many a king any religious role of the missionary was rather subsidiary. He might be a 'fetishman', but that was not really why one needed him.

There was, however, also the aspect of personal relationship. Missionaries at times became great admirers of the kings they lived with and observed, while kings undoubtedly enjoyed the regular presence of a missionary at court, an outsider of intelligence, experience, and moral stature who has learned one's language and agreed to live in one's capital, someone able to offer a friendship between equals of a sort that a king could hardly find among his own people. The missionary–king relationship was developed most memorably by Robert Moffat, not in other ways the most imaginative of missionaries, not only with Mothibi of the Tlhaping at Kuruman where he lived for most of his missionary career, but earlier with the Khoikhoi chief Jager Afrikaner and, later over many years, with Mzilikazi of the Ndebele. Livingstone's friendship with

---

[1] B. Holt, *Joseph Williams and the Pioneer Mission to the South-Eastern Bantu* (Lovedale, 1954), 80.
[2] P. Ellingworth, 'Christianity and Politics in Dahomey 1843–1867', *JAH* 5 (1964), 219.

Sechele of the Bakwena, Casalis's with Moshoeshoe of the Sotho, Coillard's with Lewanika of the Lozi, Thomas Birch Freeman's with Kwaku Dua of the Ashanti or with Ghezo of Dahomey, Colenso's with the Zulu king Cetshwayo, Lourdel's and Mackay's with Mutesa of Brfanda may all be recalled together with many other less well-known relationships.

Missionaries were seldom people who could have any political importance at home, even though the diplomatic skills they developed were in some cases considerable. They achieved in Africa on occasion a political status they had not sought but not unnaturally enjoyed. By influencing a king they could affect the lives of many, and they could themselves be affected with both fondness and admiration for an able and experienced ruler. They realized that kings appreciated them for their personal skills but seldom fathomed quite how politically inexpedient conversion was likely to be. Polygamy could be a political necessity, linking the king with powerful lineages; rain-making, either personally or through the patronage of specialists, could be his most significant social function; rituals of circumcision, of ancestor-intercession, or of witch-detection, provided the intelligible structures which shaped society and coped with its ills, and all might require his active participation. Even military leadership, especially when of an aggressive sort—hardly something alien to the Christian monarchical tradition of Europe—could be vitally necessary to the survival of a state and nevertheless seem pagan and highly unacceptable to the Evangelical missionary. As for human sacrifice or the public executions and royal disregard for human life which missionaries observed at the great courts of Buganda, the Zulus, Dahomey, or Ashanti, it could all seem simply diabolical. The social function of such bloody ruthlessness within a specific political or ritual system was seldom grasped in mitigation, nor was comparison made with the barbaric punishments still regularly used in European states in the first half of the nineteenth century. A problem with the missionary evaluation of African political realities was that the missionary mind had mostly been shaped in Europe in such a non-political way.

The difference between a self-interested patronage, including a genuine measure of personal affection, and conversion was a large one. Missionaries did recognize the gap, but hoped, usually unrealistically, that it might be bridged. Occasionally it was bridged, and the example of a Khama was there to prove that royal conversion was not an impossibility. The more likely scenario remained the one already described by Townsend writing realistically enough to Henry Venn from Abeokuta in 1850: 'I do not doubt but that the government of this country is set against the spreading of the Gospel . . . At the same time they want us without our religion . . . because they see that through us they are likely to . . . obtain trade and be well supplied with guns.'[3] In point of fact missionaries proved nearly always a commercial disappointment, particularly in the matter of guns. They had a few for their own use, but were almost never prepared to help with their supply or even their repair on a large scale. 'What do I want with a Gospel which gives neither guns, nor powder, not coffee, nor tea, nor sugar, nor workmen to work for me, nor any of the advantages I hoped for?', asked Lewanika bitterly of Coillard in 1893.[4]

Far from being suppliers of guns, tea, and coffee, most missionaries were in reality highly dependent economically upon their hosts. They depended upon them for labour, for materials for building, even for food. Again, they needed permission to talk to people, to travel around the country, to hunt, not only to arrive but also to leave. 'We are necessarily sadly too dependent upon him and he would wish us to be wholly so,' wrote Emily Moffat to her father of Mzilikazi.[5] That was how any sensible king wanted it: to remain in control of a game in which missionaries were additional pawns, rather than to become pieces within a game controlled exteriorly. As the nineteenth century moved to a close, we change in place after place from one game to the other, but what we are concerned with here are the dynamics of the first game.

If, initially, a king seemed the providential instrument for the conversion of society, he could in consequence of much of this, as realism prevailed in the missionary's mind, appear instead as the greatest of obstacles, the principal incarnation of everything that needed to be changed. 'The separation of the people from their tribal chief is, humanly, the only conceivable way in which they can be laid open to the reception of Christianity,' wrote Alexander Riddel of

[3] J. Ajayi, *Christian Missions in Nigeria 1841–1891: The Making of a New Élite* (1965), 100.

[4] F. Coillard, *On the Threshold of Central Africa* (1897), 508.

[5] 22 Jan. 1860, J. Wallis (ed.), *The Matabele Mission: A Selection from the Correspondence of John and Emily Moffat, David Livingstone and Others 1858–1878* (1945), 86.

[6] J. McCracken, *Politics and Christianity in Malawi: The Impact of the Livingstonia Mission in the Northern Province* (1977), 39.

Livingstonia in 1880.[6] The Jesuit Fr. Prestage regarded the Empandeni mission which he had founded among the Ndebele with Lobengula's permission in 1887 as a failure 'due to the overwhelming terror engaged by the system of government'.[7] The mission was closed, and Prestage soon after became a chaplain to Rhodes's pioneer column. It is striking how in some societies, especially in West Africa, even when the large majority of people have eventually become Christian in the course of the twentieth century, the monarchy itself has remained essentially pagan, continuing to require for its very existence the regular performance of rituals forbidden to a Church member.

It would, however, be mistaken to conclude from such examples that monarchies were always and necessarily an obstacle to Christianization. African monarchies varied enormously, and there is no single pattern in their response to Christianity. At one end of the spectrum we find the Zulu–Ndebele–Ngoni group. Most references to the independent African state as an insuperable barrier to conversion relate to this group of highly military peoples whose separate existence and whereabouts derive from the great wave of nineteenth-century migrations known as the *Mfecane* set off by the rise of the Zulu kingdoms under Shaka. The remarks of neither Riddel nor Prestage derived in point of fact from long experience, and Riddel in particular was to be proved wrong quite strikingly as the Ngoni turned Presbyterian pretty emphatically over the next couple of decades, but even in Matabeleland there were some committed Christians who suffered much in the Matabele war, and in a number of cases died for loyalty to their new faith. Nevertheless, it remains true that this type of highly organized, indeed totalitarian, monarchy, was highly suspicious of any suggestion of dual loyalty.

In striking contrast was the Sotho–Tswana group of kingdoms. Here the conversion of kings did actually happen. Mothibi of the Tlhaping was baptized as an old man in 1839; Sechele of the Bakwena in 1848 and Khama of the Ngwato in 1862 (when not yet king), and Moshoeshoe of the Sotho was about to be baptized when he died in 1870. It is certainly to be noted that the human culture of this group of monarchies was as different as could be from that of the Zulu with its democratic and rather civilian character. 'No one dreams of rising', Casalis observed, in the presence of the king. 'They

---

[7] N. Bhebe, *Christianity and Traditional Religion in Western Zimbabwe 1859–1923* (1979), 59.

are interrupted and contradicted without ceremony.' He contrasted this with the 'servile habits' of the Zulu and stressed how reluctant Moshoeshoe was to kill anyone.[8] An ethical congruity between Victorian missionary and Tswana king appears as part of the grounding of the conversion process.

François Coillard moved as a missionary from the Sotho to the Lozi. Lewanika was clearly a somewhat different sort of king from Moshoeshoe, more representative of what one may regard as the main group of central African Bantu monarchies, of which the Ganda provides another example. There appears here rather less convertibility than with the Tswana but little of the rigidity of the Zulu, despite a pervading cult of the royal ancestors linked with the need for rain-making. Lewanika's son Litia did in fact become a Christian in 1892 and Lewanika accepted the conversion. Though— like Sechele—Litia subsequently, if briefly, became a polygamist, he in due course succeeded to the throne as a Christian king. The Ganda monarchy only became Christian after the deposition of Mwanga and his succession by an infant son, Daudi Chwa, but here too the Christianization which had already been carried through by the principal chiefs of the kingdom could happen within a context still respectful of tradition. This does not seem to have been so possible in the more sacralized monarchies of the west coast. The Asantehene had major ritual obligations, such as those at the monthly Adae and annual Odwira ceremonies, all closely linked with the ancestor cult, which may explain why he and comparable rulers were unlikely to become Christians. Where, as in Dahomey, the cult of the royal dead required annual human sacrifice on a large scale, the royal culture might be quite unable to accommodate itself to missionary Christianity without self-destruction in a way that was not the case among the Lozi and had not been the case, in the past, for the Kongo. For all these monarchies, the abandonment of polygamy was a huge additional problem, involving the political loss of multiple marriage alliances which could do much to strengthen a king's position.

While some monarchs who were unable to convert could also not countenance their servants doing so, for others this was not the case. In the west, especially, where Islam had long been present, the

---

[8] E. Casalis, *My Life in Basutoland* (1889), 224–5, G. Setiloane, *The Image of God among the Sotho-Tswana* (Rotterdam, 1976), 25.

custom already existed of acquiescing in the presence of people of a religion of the book. Islam may well have made Christian conversion easier in many such societies. It would be naïve to expect any institution which had been based immemorially upon one belief system to be able to transfer easily or painlessly to another. What is remarkable is that some African monarchies, particularly some of the smaller ones, were capable all the same of doing so, and many more were capable of a considerable tolerance of Christianity among their subjects. In general the widespread missionary judgement at the close of the nineteenth century that traditional African power had to be broken before Christian faith could enter, a judgement accepted by some modern historians, does not appear valid. It was often based on quite brief experience, and experience reflecting only one of a number of very different forms that the African state had adopted. In the Kongo a traditional Bantu kingdom had retained for centuries a Christian commitment. The same could happen elsewhere. Kingship was both hindrance and helpmate to a process of Christianization, and that is hardly surprising when one recalls how central has kingship been to Christian experience in other ages and parts of the world. Missionaries were delighted to hand out crowns and develop rituals of Christian coronation. The perceptive king might foresee that it would not be all loss. Moreover, the perceptive commoner in stateless societies, the successful trader or teacher, might turn himself into something of a chief or king with missionary encouragement. Thus Bishop Shanahan's biographer writes firmly of the early Niger Missionaries, 'In one place—Aguleri—they actually succeeded in converting the king.'[9] The truth seems rather that Ogbuanyinya Idigo I of Aguleri was an influential trader who gave land for a mission, dismissed his wives, was baptized in 1891, became a catechist, but somehow turned into a sort of king too. In the flexibility characteristic of much of Africa outside the old established states Christianity could be more creative than destructive of kingly authority and only in a minority of African societies do kingship and chieftainship appear almost totally negative factors in the process of Christianization.

ii *Rain*

'Sorcerers or rain-makers', wrote Robert Moffat, were the strongest

[9] J. Jordan, *Bishop Shanahan of Southern Nigeria* (Dublin, 1949), 16.

opponents of the missionary task in southern Africa, 'the very pillars of Satan's kingdom'.[10] There is no doubt that for many a missionary they appeared as the most recognizable of enemies, one group of religious professionals in confrontation with another. Rain-makers were often outsiders, travellers, of varying reputation, powerful in what they achieved rather than in themselves, but rain-making in itself was much more than that: a decisive matter for the whole of society, something for which royalty had to be primarily responsible. You might challenge an individual rain-maker as an unsuccessful quack who overcharged and under-delivered, but if you challenged the principle of rain-making you challenged the king.

When Sechele became a Christian, he was caught in a quandary. Most kings called in the services of established rain-makers. They did not do the job themselves. But Sechele did and, most unfortunately, his conversion was followed by a drought. 'No rains', wrote Livingstone in his diary. 'Much discussion on rain-making . . . people intensely set on rain-making fooleries. The most insignificant persons in the tribe talk with great insolence to Sechele. No one doubts his ability to make it. Old men come to me to allow the chief to make rain. If I only do so all will come to meeting and all will pray to God together.'[11] Evangelical Christianity at its most uncompromising—only God can give rain—coupled with a lengthy drought coming at an inconvenient moment ended Livingstone's missionary career. Sechele reverted to polygamy. Livingstone 'cut him off' and packed up. The centrality of rain-making for society in much of southern Africa might then be seen as constituting a very large bar to Christianization. But that would be to misread reality. Sechele did not give up his new faith. Freed of a missionary presence and able henceforth to rule his own Church, he regularly preached on Sundays, expounding the Scriptures to the Bakwena, but he also resumed his old art of rain-making. Christianity and tradition were compatible after all.

That might appear as a merely schismatic or heretical example, at least as a withdrawal from missionary standards, but even thus to conclude would be to over-simplify. Livingstone provided in his *Missionary Travels* a splendid theoretical account of a rain-maker's viewpoint, characterizing it as 'remarkably acute'. Perhaps as a

---

[10] R. Moffat, *Missionary Labours and Scenes in Southern Africa* (1842), 305.
[11] *Livingstone's Private Journals 1851–1853*, ed. I. Schapera (1960), 300.

Christian missionary he was too much of a rationalist to be sufficiently adaptable. Anyway he would not, or did not, attempt to take over the rain-maker's role himself and step in with prayer where they had failed with bones. If kings were seldom their own rain-makers and missionaries were but willing to assume the ritual role of bringing rain through the nudging of supernatural power of one sort or another, everyone could still be happy. Back at the start of the century in 1800 Van der Kemp had already been under pressure from Ngqika to take on the job. He had refused at first: God would give rain when and only when he saw fit. However, the situation grew more desperate, the rain doctors failed, and repeated deputations had come to Van der Kemp. So holy a man could not fail to do the one thing which mystics were really needed for. He finally agreed to pray to God and declared in Xhosa, 'Jesus Christ, the Son of God, is Lord in Heaven. I will speak to him, and he will give rain. I cannot.' He prayed fervently, rain fell for two days and Ngqika's kraal was flooded out.[12] The Christian rain-maker had arrived.

Throughout the nineteenth century we find missionaries doing much the same. Moffat as a young man had argued in 1821 with a rain-maker that one simply could not do it—such effects could not follow such causes. The rain-maker insisted on the contrary that his operations had frequently been followed by 'abundance of rains'.[13] Most missionaries avoided the theoretical discussion. Pressed by popular demand they responded like Van der Kemp as best they could. Again and again it worked. Rain followed their prayers just as it followed the medicines of the rain-doctor. Thus Joseph Tindall, a Wesleyan, offered 'incessant prayer for rain' in April 1844 and it was followed by an 'abundance of rain'.[14] Henry Richards, one of the first Baptist missionaries in the Kongo, reported how on one occasion in 1881, 'They asked me to pray to God for rain, as I told them that it was no use to pray to their idols for it. I acceded to their request, and, although we had had no rain for a long time and the crops were suffering, a heavy shower came on in the afternoon.'[15]

A Dutch Calvinist, a Wesleyan, a Baptist, now for a Scottish Presbyterian. In January 1886 the prayers of Dr Elmslie of the Livingstonia Mission, offered at the request of the councillors of King

---

[12] I. Enklaar, *Life and Work of Dr J. Th. Van der Kemp* (Cape Town, 1988), 102.
[13] C. Northcott, *Robert Moffat: Pioneer in Africa* (1961), 76.
[14] *The Journal of Joseph Tindall*, ed. B. A. Tindall (1959), 57.
[15] H. G. Guinness, *The New World of Central Africa* (1890), 276.

Mbelwa of the Ngoni, produced a splendid shower to be long remembered. Back in Scotland the missionaries might play down any claim that the cloudburst was 'miraculous', but in Ngoniland they were happy enough to be accepted as effective rain-makers. One more example: among the Lozi Coillard's nickname was Mungole, literally 'the long rain'. 'You bring us rain and sleep, peace and abundance,' he could be greeted. Even though he had failed to bring the guns, coffee, and tea Lewanika claimed to want, he had brought what an African holy man was really meant to bring. Consider this splendid memory of an old man in 1974:

There was no rain; the land was dry. The Mbunda cast their bones in vain. Then *Mungole* called Lewanika and the people into the Church at Lwatile. Before them all, he preached and preached and preached. As he preached a cloud no bigger than a hand appeared on the horizon. Then *Mungole* began to sing a hymn. By the time he had reached the second verse, the sky was dark. By the time he ended, the rain fell so hard that people could not return at once to Lealui but had to remain waiting in the Church. Alas, there are not such men of power nowadays.[16]

We should not conclude from such stories (and there are plenty more of them) that praying for rain, let alone rain-making, was an important activity for nineteenth-century missionaries or for the Victorian religion, mostly of an evangelical hue, which they had learned at home. It might be truer to say that, faced with the activities of rain-makers, they had been driven to decide, quite pragmatically, 'If you can't beat them, join them', but of course they did believe that, with the help of God, they could beat them. And they were pretty sure that, time and time again, they had done so in a nearly miraculous way. They prayed and the rain came. Victorian Christianity had not rejected praying for rain, though it might be embarrassed at taking it too seriously. For us here, however, the important thing is not how the missionary interpreted these experiences but how Africans did so. The missionary was the new rain-maker and, if he did not always succeed, he was not dismissed on that account. His predecessors had done no better. The point is that rain-making needed to go on, and go on it did. Despite an initial

---

[16] G. Prins, *The Hidden Hippopotamus* (1980), 195 and 294. The incident in question probably happened in 1892. For an Anglican example see A. G. de la Pryne's rain-making achievements in 1907 in villages of the upper Shire valley, A. Anderson-Morshead, *The History of the Universities Mission to Central Africa* (1897) i. 237. For further discussion see I. Schapera, *Rainmaking Rites of Tswana Tribes* (1971).

conflict, worked out chiefly within the missionary's mind, rain-making provided no long-term obstacle to the spread of Christianity. On the contrary, with a little revamping it proved both a tool for its propagation and a context for its indigenization. Great Christian rain-makers of the twentieth century, like Shembe and Mutende, were here as elsewhere not rejecting their missionary inheritance. Rather were they the successors to the Elmslies and Coillards of the nineteenth.

iii. *Social Structure: Marriage, Circumcision, and Secret Societies*

For missionaries, African marriage custom undoubtedly appeared as about the greatest of obstacles in the way of realizing their ambitions, and when they said marriage they meant polygamy. It is worth recalling that the monks of medieval Ethiopia had already found it a problem as, of course, had the Capuchins in seventeenth-century Kongo. Throughout the nineteenth and first half of the twentieth century the theme recurs incessantly in missionary literature. While there are voices of moderation in the nineteenth and still more in the second half of the twentieth century, a crescendo of condemnation of the harshest sort built up in the years of the scramble and found expression in statements of the World Missionary Conference at Edinburgh in 1910:

Our correspondents in Africa view with unanimous intolerance conditions of life which are not only unchristian, but are at variance with the instinctive feelings of natural morality. With them there can be no 'question' of polygamy. It is simply one of the gross evils of heathen society which, like habitual murder or slavery, must at all costs be ended . . . In Africa polygamy is more prevalent than in other countries . . . indeed, the Christian law upon this subject may be said to be the greatest obstacle to the acceptance of our faith. In the face of this it is surprising to note, that it is in regard to the evidence from Africa alone that there is an almost complete unanimity of opinion. Every Mission within our review refuses admission to the Church in Africa to any man who is actually living with more than one wife.[17]

This was a remarkably unqualified position for a Protestant conference to take up, given that it is near impossible to ground insistence on monogamy upon any biblical text (as Lutheran

---

[17] *The Church in the Mission Field*, Report of Commission II of the World Missionary Conference (Edinburgh, 1910), 65–6, 69–70.

theologians in the sixteenth century, including Luther himself, already admitted) and that some Protestant missionaries, especially in Asia, but also in Africa, did receive polygamists to baptism through much of the nineteenth century. Set against the moral convictions of the missionary world at Edinburgh we have the reality of Africa, a continent in almost all of whose black societies polygamous marriage was actually the ideal, in which all rich and powerful people had numerous wives, many ordinary men had two, and in which no African saw it as a moral problem. No one thought he was doing wrong in entering into more than one public marriage, let alone did he see it as 'at variance with the instinctive feelings of natural morality'. One might conclude that the 'instinctive feelings' of Victorian Evangelicals had simply removed them from reality if they could denounce as equivalent to 'habitual' murder (and one wonders how murder can be 'habitual') the social practice of an entire continent, turning it into 'the greatest obstacle to the acceptance of our faith'. Or had they?

The apparent simplicity of a picture of stark confrontation does at least require a little modification. As a matter of fact, through much of the nineteenth century many missionaries had not thought it right that converts put away all wives but one. When Bishop Colenso first visited his diocese of Natal in 1954 he declared almost at once, 'I feel very strongly upon this point, that the usual practice of enforcing the separation of wives from their husbands upon their conversion to Christianity is quite unwarrantable and opposed to the plain teaching of Our Lord.'[18] It was indeed the usual practice in South Africa just as it had been the usual practice among Anglicans, as among Catholics, but it was by no means the invariable practice among Protestant missionary societies.

Consider this charming story from the American Baptist Missionary Union (formerly the Livingstone Inland Mission) in the Congo in 1888. After a service taken by Henry Richards at Mbanza Manteke a man named Nganvan Dimboini, accompanied by his five wives and a sixth lady to whom he was betrothed, asked to become a Christian. The missionary agreed that he might keep his five wives but not the sixth, and Nganvan refused, walking out of the missionary's room. An observer reported afterwards:

When he came into the garden, I watched him through a hole in the

---

[18] J. Colenso, *Ten Weeks in Natal* (1855), 140.

shutter. He took some steps towards the gate, stopped and pondered, took a few steps more and sat down on the ground. Inwardly, he evidently fought a terrible battle. His wives observed him with tense anxiety. But whether a decisive desire caught him, or that he was ashamed to not be 'following the fashion', he turned round, knocked on the missionary's door and asked in a humble voice if he might come in. The missionary wasted no time in opening. Nganvan pointed to the young girl and said that she was free and could go where she pleased, although it cost him many pieces of cloth. He was registered in the novices' book.[19]

In the Congo not only the Livingstone Inland Mission and the British Baptists but also the Swedish mission accepted polygamists, as had other missions elsewhere, such as the Bremen Mission in the Gold Coast.[20] And where a monogamous policy was enforced, it was often criticized. Thus in southern Africa as early as 1840 John Cameron, Chairman of the Bechuana District of the Wesleyan Methodists, wrote, 'I am very much in doubt whether it be the wisest plan and most likely to secure the happiest results, to force a polygamist embracing Christianity to put away all his supernumerary wives.'[21] Or, again, Traugott Bachmann, an influential German Moravian in Tanganyika, wished to accept polygamy during a transitional period, declaring, 'God does not make the ugly distinction between monogamy and polygamy', and this was to some extent adopted as Church policy in 1908.[22] But if the Moravians were moving towards tolerance in the early twentieth century, most other missions were by then moving in the opposite direction. John Colenso's *Letter to His Grace the Archbishop of Canterbury of the proper treatment of cases of polygamy as found already existing in converts from Heathenism* had been published in 1862. It was well argued, but had failed to convince Anglicans, who, at the Lambeth Conference of 1888, emphatically rejected tolerance. In the Congo there was a long argument on the subject among Protestant missionaries in the 1890s, and the Baptists continued to baptize polygamists while their most senior missionary, Holman Bentley, was

---

[19] S. Axelson, *Culture Confrontation in the Lower Congo* (Uppsala, 1970), 236.
[20] Guinness, *The New World of Central Africa*, 437, P. Coulon and P. Brasseur, *Libermann 1802–1852* (Paris, 1988), 362 n. 28; E. Grau, in C. Baëta (ed.), *Christianity in Tropical Africa* (1968). The 1876 *Church Rules* of the Bremen Mission are particularly explicit: 'a man who has several wives must be admitted to baptism and communion', Baëta, *Christianity in Tropical Africa*, 68.
[21] Setiloane, *The Image of God among the Sotho-Tswana*, 103.
[22] M. Wright, *German Missions in Tanganyika 1891–1941* (1971), 106, 132.

alive, but after his death in 1905 their rule was changed. So too with the Swedes in 1907. In this as in much else the years around the turn of the century saw a hardening of missionary attitudes of an unadaptive sort just as such attitudes were being challenged by increasingly outspoken voices within the African Christian community.

While Edinburgh's very hard line over polygamy does not then reflect the whole of nineteenth-century experience and reflection by any means, it cannot be denied that it does represent the normal missionary position, and Africans knew it. Without insistence on monogamy, Moshoeshoe had remarked, 'we should soon be Christians'. When Mzilikazi was asked why his people did not become Christian, he replied, 'We Matabele like many wives.'[23] More deeply instructive, however, is the case of Sechele. Here was a king with no more than five wives who had both learned to read and had brought his wives to study under Livingstone. He was a man of exceptional intellect and character who had taken to Bible-reading as a fish to water and appeared as quite the model of the convert king, while his wives Livingstone could describe as 'decidedly the most amiable females in the town, our best scholars too . . . Two of them were the daughters of under-chiefs through whose influence, after his father's murder, he had been enabled to succeed to the chieftainship. This circumstance made his parting with them assume the appearance of ingratitude.'[24]

Sechele's renunciation was received in his town with general consternation and when, two months later, he was baptized, many spectators were in tears. As Livingstone remarked, 'all the friends of the divorced wives became the opponents of our religion'.[25] Attendance at school and church diminished. Six months later Sechele made love to one of his superfluous wives, who, because she had a small daughter, had remained nearby. 'Never did man bid fairer for years to enter the Kingdom of God than he,' affirmed Livingstone, but now, instead, he was to be accounted 'an apostate'.[26] Despite expressing penitence, Sechele was cut off from

[23] Casalis, *My Life in Basutoland*, 225–7; Bhebe, *Christianity and Traditional Religion in Western Zimbabwe*, 43.
[24] 1 Nov. 1948, *Livingstone's Missionary Correspondence 1841–1856*, ed. I. Schapera (1961), 119.
[25] D. Livingstone, *Missionary Travels and Researches in South Africa* (1857), 6.
[26] *Livingstone's Missionary Correspondence*, 20.

communicant membership of the Church with no apparent likelihood of restoration, and Livingstone himself soon withdrew from Kolobeng. While the disastrous consequences of imposing monogamy upon already polygamous people as a condition of baptism could seem here excessively evident, Livingstone appears never to have questioned the rightness of his own behaviour, yet the contrast between the treatment of Sechele and of Dimboini, each with five wives, is striking. Just as Richards could act as a rain-maker but Livingstone could not, so Richards could receive a man and his five wives, Livingstone could not. But while some missionaries did prove capable of questioning the simplicities of Victorian Evangelicalism, Livingstone's spirit of enquiry was directed into other areas, geographical and social, rather than theological or pastoral, though whether ten years later he would really have agreed with his judgement of 1848 one may wonder. Yet it may well be that his authority and his well-advertised treatment of Sechele had a not inconsiderable influence upon the missionary mind of the next half-century, even if it was rejected by some, among them the Livingstone Inland Mission.

There can be no question but that missionary insistence upon monogamy created a sharp initial contrast between Christian and traditional models of domestic society and helped to deter many powerful people from becoming Christians, but how far did its consequences go beyond that? The general effect upon conversion can probably be overstressed. The fact is that many people in highly polygamous societies did become Christians. The effect was less to deter conversion than to ensure a long-term post-baptismal problem as polygamy re-emerged within the ranks of otherwise committed Christians. It was, then, less an obstacle to 'the acceptance of our faith', as Edinburgh put it, than to the subsequent development of the sort of Christian society the missionaries wanted. Sechele remained a Christian and a Bible-preacher, but also an embarrassment to the missionary. The African Church was thus provided with an ongoing area of dissension which in a hundred years was not to be resolved. Many African Christians, especially perhaps the married clergy of the mainline churches but also members of many independent Churches, agreed with missionaries and strongly insisted upon the importance of upholding monogamy. African Christianity has certainly adopted a monogamous culture both as a precious ideal and as something often lived by faithful Church members, but it has also continued to practise a polygamous culture. All in all the traditional polygamy of Africa operated less as an obstacle upon Christianization, at least in the longer run, and far more as an instrument of Africanization and as a focus of controversy about what Africanization should mean: and Christianity has often thrived upon internal argument.

It needs to be remembered that African marriage custom contrasted with Christian tradition in many other ways too, most obviously in the widespread giving of *lobola* or bride-wealth by a bridegroom and his family to the family of the bride as constituting the principal legal element of marriage. Again one must recall that marriage in Christian Europe had often been dominated by property considerations, if not so much in the class from which most missionaries came. For many of them bride-wealth was not a problem, especially in the earlier period. Thus Daniel Lindley, an American Congregationalist pioneer in South Africa, thought *lobola* 'the foundation of the structure of native society' and 'productive of a world of good',[27] but by 1878 younger missionaries within his society were promulgating a new set of rules to prohibit the custom. Much the same happened with the Norwegian Mission in Zululand. At first they accepted it and occasionally even helped young men to raise it while Zulu Christians simply took it for granted. Only in and after the 1880s did the missionaries turn against it, divisively but ineffectually.

Attitudes towards circumcision were not dissimilar in regard to some of the peoples who practised it, and it appears at times in southern Africa in the later nineteenth century to constitute as large a problem as polygamy. What African Christians might regard as an unabandonable piece of cultural identity became for some missionaries an offence against which they were resolved to set their face. The Xhosa poet Mqhayi tells how when he was studying at Lovedale about 1890, he went off as a teenager to be circumcised. As Canon Bevan at Phokwani among the Bechuana wrote at almost the same time, 'nearly all our young men whom we have brought up as Christians have gone to it'. For the mission authorities it was 'a great and unforgivable sin', 'apostasy', though none of the young men intended to give up Christianity for traditional custom, only 'to

---

[27] M. Dynnerstein, 'The American Zulu Mission in the Nineteenth Century: Clash over Custom', *Church History*, 45 (1976), 243.

combine the two'.[28] Yet here as everywhere we must beware of too wide a generalization. If for the Kikuyu or Gisu—as for Ethiopians—circumcision was a *sine qua non* of adult identity, whether or not one was a Christian, some peoples in the south abandoned circumcision in the late nineteenth century quite easily— in the Mpondo case without actually becoming Christian on any large scale. African culture certainly had its lines of almost unbreakable resistance; it also had a great but varying element of flexibility.

One could well imagine that if circumcision, bride-wealth, polygamous marriage, and many other customs, especially funereal ones but also dancing, bodily decorations, and much else, were all condemned by the run of missionaries, then they were bound to constitute a formidable barrier to evangelization. In some places and times this was undoubtedly the case. Nevertheless very often it did not work like that. Not only was custom often intrinsically far more flexible than accounts of 'African traditional culture' often suggest, but Christianity could flow over it rather than be dammed by it, and while missionaries went on endeavouring to eradicate what they regarded as unacceptable practices and disciplining native Christians in all sorts of ways in consequence, Africans themselves simply accepted a Christianity of Bible, baptism, and hymn but sat very much more loosely to such missionary regulations. It was not that they all or indiscriminately rejected the regulations. They did not. Many tried pathetically hard to satisfy their missionaries. Among the educated élite, James Johnson was hard on polygamists, John Knox Bokwe was scathing about circumcision, but these were people exceptionally close to the missionary mind. Collectively African Christianity simply did not make up its mind between missionary and traditional requirements. For the most part it did its best, somewhat unquestioningly, to embrace both. Z. K. Matthews, writing of his parents in his autobiography, remarked, 'There was never any apparent contradiction between my parents' yearning for traditional ceremonies and their Christian devoutness. There was no conflict because they saw none, in their minds the values common to both had blended and become a whole.'[29] As the twentieth century

---

[28] S. Dwane, 'Christianity Relative to Xhosa Religion', Ph.D. thesis (London, 1979), 105; *Historical Records of the Church of the Province of South Africa*, ed. C. Lewis and G. E. Richards (1934), 499–500.

[29] *Freedom for my People: The Autobiography of Z. K. Matthews* (1981), 15–16.

advanced the theological mind moved fairly steadily away from the simplicities of Edinburgh and back towards a recognition that bride-wealth, circumcision, even polygamous marriage, all had at least something to be said in their favour.

What matters to us here is not, however, how the missionary mind judged such customs, but how they appeared to the African mind. On this criterion they were far less of a major obstacle to Christianization than they may seem according to the missionary mind. They moulded the new community more significantly than they impeded it. Take one new example. The Nyakyusa of south-west Tanganyika lived in age-set villages. Once Christians began to multiply, their young people had to form generational villages of their own. These age-set villages adapted themselves to certain Christian requirements including the ideal of monogamy, and yet Christian living itself was profoundly adapted to a society in which teenagers went to live, no longer in the homes of their parents, but in a village of their own.

There were, however, some social structures which did for long constitute major bulwarks of anti-Christianity. Of these almost certainly the most powerful were secret societies and masquerades. In both West and central Africa these were popularist institutions without a hierarchical leadership, committed to the maintenance of traditional morality and certain rites of passage. They could control initiation and funerals. They were essentially educational societies with a strong public presence. They covered just the sort of ground the Church wanted to occupy. They were easily diabolized by missionaries, who found them particularly difficult to understand. Equally they were bound to see themselves as threatened by the advance of Church and school. Ogbonni among the Yoruba, Poro, Sande, and Humoi among the Mende, Nyau among the Chewa could be formidable powers. The stronger societies of this sort were among a people, the more difficult did any Christian advance remain. Christianity did not flow into and over them in the same way. They reflect too the wider nature of the diffused authority characteristic of the many stateless societies. Monarchies were in comparison easy to target and approach. In a relatively developed state there were, moreover, a range of classes and of interests—officials, traders, the poor. One group or another could well prove amenable to some message of the gospel. Converts might be found at least among the most underprivileged. Livingstone reported the perceptive comment of one chief that 'some profess Christianity because they like the new system which gives so much more importance to the poor'.[30] But in stateless societies the category of 'the poor' really did not exist. There appeared instead of royals and the poor a homogeneity far more difficult to fathom. Almost no one stood out and no one had any reason to be interested in missionary wares. School education appeared particularly pointless. Only when a society was threatened by a neighbouring state or by slave raiders might it turn rather readily to missionary patronage. In general and in the long term the supreme African social obstacle to missionary influence was not the kings, not the State, not marriage, but statelessness, amorphous and mysterious, lacking in centres political or commercial, lacking in any of the more familiar ambitions upon which a missionary could play.

Most negative of all were pastoral, semi-nomadic societies such as those of the Nuer, the Turkana, the Masai, or the Karamojong. The social shaping of this sort of Africa provided an almost total bar to the kind of religion the Western missionary had on offer. They could at best watch each other with an amused sympathy, but, for the most part, and for long, missionaries simply found they had plenty to do elsewhere.

iv. *Ancestors, Deities, and God*

None of this had much to do with religion as such. It was a matter of divergences within social structure, and of the way some structures were threatened by Christianity in a way others were not, at least to a comparable extent. But we cannot leave religion out of our discussion. How far were the religions of Africa in themselves a barrier to Christianization? How far, if at all, were they on the contrary some sort of secret ally, a spiritual fifth column preparing the way for a more definitive revelation? Had Africa in this sense any religion at all? Some missionaries doubted it.

Moffat called the Xhosa 'a nation of atheists'[31] and he quoted Van der Kemp in support. He thought the Sechuana no different. Bentley too believed that 'the people of the Congo, as we found them, were practically without religion'.[32] Of Shona religion Bishop Knight-Bruce declared, 'It is very hard to say that they have any.'[33] 'Among the Mashonas', agreed the Jesuit Fr. Hartmann, 'there

[30] Livingstone, *Missionary Travels and Researches in South Africa*, 93.
[31] Moffat, *Missionary Labours and Scenes in South Africa*, 40.
[32] W. H. Bentley, *Pioneering on the Congo* (1900), i. 247.
[33] G. W. H. Knight-Bruce, *Memories of Mashonaland* (1895; repr. Bulawayo, 1970), 43.

are only very faint traces of religion.'[34] Such judgements were common enough. They represent in part sheer superficiality of experience, in part a too limited concept of religion—biblical revelation was true religion, idols and temples were false religion. Anyone who appeared to have neither was easily judged to have nothing. Mackay remarked in 1878 on the difference between east and west: no people he had seen 'in east Africa make or worship idols. There is a strange contrast in this respect between the East and West coasts, for on the latter idolatry is everywhere.'[35] Moffat wrote that the missionary among the Sechuana 'has no idolatry to arrest his progress and his mind is not overwhelmed with the horrors which are to be found in countries where idols and idol temples are resorted to by millions of devotees . . . he seeks in vain for a temple, an altar, or a single emblem of heathen worship . . . A profound silence reigns on this awful subject.'[36] Inadequate as Moffat's understanding of Bantu religion surely was, it is obvious enough that a West African missionary could never have written like that faced with, say, the Mbari houses of the Igbo.

None the less, numerous missionaries always recognized both the religiosity and a fundamental monotheism in the peoples they encountered. In the mid-eighteenth century Thomas Thompson had already asserted, 'I never spoke with one of them (blacks) who did not confess belief in a Supreme Being.'[37] A century later the American T. J. Bowen could write of the Yoruba, stressing 'the pure theism of their natural religion. Everybody in that country believes in one true and living God, of whose character they often entertain surprisingly correct notions.'[38] Thirty years on again, D. K. Flickinger, another American, wrote of the Sierra Leonean peoples among whom he had worked, 'So far as I was able to learn, they all believe in the existence of a supreme Jehovah, who is the creator of the world and of all things therein; that he is almighty and just in all his ways.'[39] Livingstone was convinced that the Africans he knew had 'a tolerably clear idea' of basic religious truths and yet, perhaps partly in deference to his father-in-law, could still admit that they 'appear as

---

[34] T. O. Ranger, *Revolt in Southern Rhodesia 1897–1899* (1967), 3.
[35] *A. M. Mackay by his sister* (1890), 87–8.
[36] Moffat, *Missionary Labours and Scenes in South Africa*, 243.
[37] T. Thompson, *An Account of Two Missionary Voyages* (1758), 44.
[38] T. J. Bowen, *Adventures and Missionary Labours* (New York, 1857), 160.
[39] D. K. Flickinger, *Ethiopia; or Thirty Years of Missionary Life in Western Africa* (1885), 76–7.

among the most godless races of mankind known anywhere'.[40] The further north you go the more distinct, he thought, did African religious ideas become. By the first decades of the twentieth century missionaries, led by Henri Junod, Alexandre Leroy, Edwin Smith, and many other field scholars, were deciding that Africans were among the most religious of peoples. Earlier views may have been much affected by the deep reticence which, especially in the south, Africans exercised in regard especially to God, almost a discipline of the arcanum. Thus there can really be no doubt that the Xhosa name for God, Qamantha, was in use all along yet, despite a vast missionary contact with the Xhosa throughout the century, there is no written reference to the word before the 1870s.

The modern study of African religion has greatly depended, perhaps even excessively, upon Evans-Pritchard's *Nuer Religion*, in which he claims that Kwoth (regularly translated by him as 'God') was absolutely central to their experience and constantly on their tongues. Ray Huffman, a missionary for many years among the Nuer, published her *Nuer Customs and Folk-Lore* in 1931, some twenty years before *Nuer Religion*. It was introduced by the anthropologist Diedrich Westermann. In her account of Nuer religion Huffman makes no mention whatsoever of Kwoth but remarks, 'The Nuer has long feared and worshipped he knows not what.' In his introduction Westermann adds,

Very little is known about the religion of the Nuer. Miss Huffman mentions some names of their gods, but we learn little as to their significance in the lives and beliefs of the people. While I was studying the Shilluk people in the Sudan in 1910, yet another Nuer god, viz. Kot, was mentioned to me by a number of Nuer men . . . to Kot is attributed the creation of the world.[41]

Had Miss Huffman failed through all her years in Nuerland to hear the name which the two anthropologists heard so often? One cannot say, but this does suggest how hard it is to be confident not only about African religion but also about the interpretative skills of even deeply sympathetic missionaries, and anthropologists too. Lived and practised in a variety of ways but never written down, oral religion

[40] Livingstone, *Missionary Travels and Researches in South Africa*, 138–9; cf. *Livingstone's Missionary Correspondence*, 307.
[41] Ray Huffman, *Nuer Customs and Folk-Lore* (1931), viii.

may escape notice particularly from people gripped by a religion of the book.

Yet was there necessarily so total a contrast between biblical and African religion? When Equiano was first introduced to the Bible by a friend in 1759 he confessed himself 'wonderfully surprised to see the laws and rules of my country written almost exactly here, a circumstance which I believe tended to impress our manners and customs more deeply on my memory'.[42] In point of fact what proved for some missionaries a problem was less the religionlessness than the religiosity of Africans, because they themselves were now as much the apostles of science as of religion. The Bible and African religion might form more of an alliance than they really liked. The alliance they increasingly believed in was rather one between the Bible and science in which the more awkward parts of the former for the modern mind were quietly passed over: 'How much superstition a little science overthrows . . . To reveal a law where they expect a witch is our privilege.' So wrote an American missionary in Sierra Leone in the 1890s.[43] The secular benefits brought by the missionary could be clear enough. It was, paradoxically, his religious contribution which might be less obvious. Just as the missionary could fail to see African religiosity, so might Africans fail to see or to be impressed by a missionary's religiosity.

The missionary linked faith in God with a trust in 'secular' medicine. For Africans too religion had a great deal to do with health. They found it indeed impossible to separate the two, but also hard to see a difference between the theory of efficacy of their medicines and that of European ones. Why be compelled to reject the one and yet encouraged to make use of the other? African Christian religiosity tended, then, either to believe in the efficacy of both or to reject both. Either way one might judge their attitude more, not less, religious than that of the missionaries. Over medicine as over so much else, however, the conflict of contrasting understandings had to work itself out not so much in the initial leap of conversion as in the long run of the post-conversion years.

---

[42] *The Interesting Narrative of the Life of Olaudah Equiano or Gustavus Vassa, the African* (1789; repr. 1969, ed. P. Edwards), ch. 6.

[43] Alfred Taylor Howard, cf. A. Walls, 'Ruminations on Rainmaking', in J. C. Stone (ed.), *Experts in Africa* (Aberdeen, 1980), 146–51.

This particular issue would prove in point of fact one of the major factors in the spread of Christian independency.

Witchcraft is not unrelated to medicines. It provided a principal explanation for grave and unexpected misfortune. Belief in witches means belief in the existence of neighbours personally and secretly responsible for death, disease, and disaster. Prevalent throughout Africa, it was a belief activated a good deal more in some societies than others. People were executed for witchcraft, among them Lobengula's own sister Mngcengence, but in decentralized communities it probably made the least impact. It was where royal power and a machinery for finding and executing witches were linked together, as among the Ndebele and the Azande, that it had most fearful consequences. With the advent of Christianity there were several possible developments. Witch-finders tended to become a missionary's chief enemies, and early converts could casily be denounced as witches. People otherwise accused of witchcraft might at times seek missionary protection. Thus in general, from the viewpoint of traditional society, the witch-detecting industry was placed in opposition to Christianity, which was seen as a new source or cover for witchcraft. It may well be that what made it so hard for an Ndebele to become a Christian was the alliance between monarchy and witchcraft finders, rather than the nature of the former alone. However, as Christianity spread among a people, new alliances developed. In the period of social disorientation consequent upon the European take-over of Africa, the fear of bewitchment appears to have grown. If witchcraft was the most evil of things and Christianity was itself a struggle with evil and with the devil, then Christianity and witchcraft detection should be on the same side. Many of the waves of popular Christianity flowing across one part or another of rural Africa in the first half of this century shared in the characteristics of a witchcraft eradication movement. In one extreme case Tomo Nyirenda, a self-appointed evangelist with a slight Livingstonia background and Watch Tower inspiration, turned in Northern Rhodesia into an executer of witches on an horrific scale. Witch fears operated powerfully within Aladura, Lumpa, and many other independent churches and mass movements. Here again the content of traditional belief was carried over into the Christian community, powerful but neither unchanged nor unchallenged. Popular Christianity can in many places not be understood without a sense of this pervading fear, and yet, to cite one example to the contrary, the word 'witch' never once makes an appearance in the huge corpus of oral Dida Harrist hymns.[44]

The structure of traditional religious belief normally took either a twofold or a threefold form with some variety in the balance between the different elements. In east and south the principal form was the twofold one: God above, the ancestors and other fairly comparable spirits below. In many West African societies, however, as well as some others such as that of Buganda, a third group of divinities had come to dominate the scene, more powerful than the ancestors, closer and more activist than God.

The religion of the high god could merge with, perhaps indeed find full explicitness for the first time within, Christian or Muslim belief rather easily. Missionaries could be convinced of that, but the religion of the ancestors seemed to them, on the contrary, something profoundly opposed and there would in consequence be a constant strain over a multitude of domestic practices condemned yet frequently performed. Christian conversion was often painful above all because it appeared to demonstrate disloyalty to one's dead relatives. In doing so it separated one too both from the roots of social ethics and from much of the science for the interpretation of illness and the entire practice of divining. The whole complex of spirit cults, mostly focused upon ancestors—funerals, domestic oblations, spirit possession, oracles in their many forms—could not but seem the great ongoing enemy to Christianity at the village and domestic level, and in some societies it maintained a coherent barrier blocking any considerable Christian infiltration. If, for instance, after more than 100 years of quite considerable missionary presence in Pondoland Monica Hunter could find in the 1930s that not more than 4 per cent of the population were Christian, one can best explain it in terms of the intrinsic adequacy and power of resistance of a religion centred upon the cult of ancestral spirits. Political pressures were all the other way. The cogency of traditional Bantu religion woven through the whole of customary social life should not be underestimated, and it could of itself stand as a formidable barrier to Christian advance. Furthermore, many loyal converts shared the missionary conviction that to accept the new faith meant also

[44] J. Krabill, 'The Hymnody of the Harrist Church among the Dida of South-Central Ivory Coast 1913–1949: An Historico-Religious Study', Ph.D. thesis (Birmingham, 1989), 433.

rejecting the old. Some did so with fervour and in its entirety. Yet collectively, if and when a Christian momentum had developed, it hardly worked like that. The incompatibility was not in practice convincing. Most Africans remained committed to their ancestors. They could not see such a commitment as a reason for not becoming Christians once they felt an urge to do so. Neither did they subsequently see their Christian faith as a reason for not communing with their ancestors, though that faith did undoubtedly affect the relationship. A stronger eschatology proved one of Christianity's principal attractions, though a frequent missionary stress on hell was in itself far from attractive. It altered attitudes to death, making them a lot more positive, and it tied relationships with ancestors more explicitly into a relationship with God. Towards them it increased affection, lessened fear.

When Cetshwayo wrote to Colenso entreating 'all the ancestral spirits of his people . . . to help you',[45] he saw as a traditionalist no problem in offering such assistance to a Christian bishop. Most Christians continued in their hearts to think the same, though how far they went down the road of consulting ancestral spirits varied greatly. Mrs Igugu of Uzere in Isokoland, a convert to Catholicism, was condemned by the Church to go around the town every week for six weeks with a catechist and a gong confessing that she rang it 'because during the time of my baptism I pledged not to worship any other god or spirit and to abstain from all their works. But now, I have slaughtered a goat in sacrifice to the ancestral spirits of my husband's lineage when circumstances beyond my control forced me to do so . . .'.[46] A Lugbara Catholic elder, while not actively participating in the sacrifice of his lineage, sat nearby while it took place and commented, 'Some say these things are of Satan, but that is not true. They are good, the things of our ancestors.'[47] The theological and pastoral issues involved in how a Christian should relate to all this vast network of ritual and kinship relationships, upon which so much of social morality intimately depended, proved just one more section of the general business of inhabiting the two worlds of meaning which had come together in millions of humble lives. The point is that, despite a good deal of initial confrontation, carried

---

[45] Dec. 1877, G. Cox, *The Life of John William Colenso, Bishop of Natal* (1888), ii. 453, n. 1; J. Guy, *The Heretic: A Study of the Life of John William Colenso* (Johannesburg, 1983), 259.
[46] S. Akama, 'A Religious History of the Isoko People of the Bendel State of Nigeria', Ph.D. thesis (Aberdeen, 1981), 404.   [47] J. Middleton, *Lugbara Religion* (1960), 35.

over to many of the prophets of the twentieth century who were totally denunciatory of respect for ancestral spirits, this was not on the whole in most places a side of tradition which acted as a consistent break upon Christian conversion. Once again it was much more a question of Christianity flowing over it and then having to live with the consequences.

The cult of deities was very different. In the _orisa_ of the Yoruba, the _abosum_ of the Akan, the _lubaale_ of the Baganda, there was a developed system of worship with temples, rites, myths, systems of divination, an organized priesthood. In origin they had been royal ancestors, heroes of the past, or nature spirits. Their cult had almost inevitably to come into sustained organizational and ideological conflict with a Christian Church just because the two were so relatively similar. Such cults could not be assimilated into any recognizable Christianity. They were most extensive in the more established monarchies and in a number of cases, such as that of the Yoruba Cult of Esu, the Cult of Wamala and Kibuka in Buganda, and the royal worship in Dahomey and Ashanti, human sacrifice was an integral part of the system. Here religious confrontation, both between rituals and between people, was likely to be most complete, but quite apart from the aggravating element of human sacrifice—an element which had to disappear after the establishment of European power—we can identify a basic relationship of opposition between these particular cults and Christianity which would not go away. However, as such cults were far from universal—unlike ancestor veneration—and they could be, moreover, both fearful and feared, their significance for the confrontation of the two religions should not be overstated.

It has also to be borne in mind that while the cult of a deity could be exclusivist for its devotees, it did not effectively alter the general tolerance of the African religious culture of which they were part, a tolerance of inclusiveness comparable to that of Hinduism or the religious condition of the Roman Empire in the first centuries of the Christian age. If African religion tried—seldom very forcefully—to be intolerant of Christianity, it was less because of any confrontational character of its own than because of Christianity's inherent intolerance.

Only in regard to the reality of God was there a shared inclusivity. Here missionaries themselves increasingly recognized that in traditional belief they actually had an ally. It is hard for the historian to disagree. Maybe African traditional beliefs about the nature of God were not often as clear as some missionaries affirmed and many modern African Christian scholars tend to suggest. Duff Macdonald's remarks of 1882 may be as sound as any: after affirming that in scripture translation they always used the word 'mulungu' to translate 'God', though realizing that this is chiefly 'a general name for spirit' and often refers to the spirit of a dead man, he continued, 'Beyond their Polytheism the language contains a few expressions that remind us of Pantheism, and a great many that speak to us of Monotheism.'[48] Traditional usages could hardly not be theologically ambiguous, open to a development in clarity in quite different directions. Words for spirit had an inevitable fluidity of meaning. What matters for Christian history is that they were open to a Christian development and refinement which could generally take place without over-straining earlier meaning and with a sensed experience of spiritual continuity. This applied not only to god names but to other words as well, relating to human virtues or divine attributes. In almost every language group Christianity carried over from tradition its name for God—Olorin, Lesa, Nzambi, Mulungu, Katonda, Imana, or Modimo. It is true that missionaries were by no means always clear that it was right to do this. There was a great deal of argument, especially in southern Africa, and some quite sustained attempts to use an entirely European-rooted name—Jehovah, or even 'Godi'. Thus for years the Jesuits in Rhodesia stood out against the use of Mwari, insisting upon Jahve instead. Even as late as 1924 their Prefect-Apostolic could threaten to close a mission they had taken over from Mariannhill 'unless Mwari is eliminated and Jahve substituted',[49] but they were unusual in this and had finally to abandon it. 'Tell them', declared Colenso towards the Zulu, rejecting missionary caution in this matter as in others, 'that their own names are excellent names for God and we shall call Him by those names, and shall come to tell them more about Him. There was a general assent of "Yebo", "Yes".'[50] For the historian the crucial fact is simply that this happened and in happening helped shape the spirituality of the Christian Churches at the basic level of the orientation of divine worship and God-talk. It is difficult to disagree in point of fact with Henri Junod's judgement: 'It is wonderful to notice how easily the

---

[48] Duff Macdonald, *Africana; or, The Heart of Heathen Africa* (1882), i. 59 and 67.
[49] T. O. Ranger, 'Poverty and Prophetism', unpublished paper, 13.
[50] Colenso, *Ten Weeks in Natal*, 134.

idea of the God of Christianity is accepted by the Bantu.'[51] All the God proverbs and theophorous names common in many African languages could be adopted to strengthen a culture of religious continuity. Perhaps the Christian God was taught too often in terms less kind and more revengeful than the God of tradition, but if missionary doctrine might affect the traditional image of God in more than one direction, it is probably still more true that the latter continued to affect how Christians understood the former.

African religion, like African society generally, had then areas which were toughly resistant to the Christianization process, yet it had much else which could go along with that process more easily than many a rather condemnatory missionary had at first imagined or desired. In practice there was an oscillation between continuity and contestation both in the initial processes of conversion and within the subsequent development of church life and theology at almost every level. It may, finally, be best simply to illustrate the contrasts within that oscillation by a number of examples.

H. C. Monrad, a Danish chaplain at the fort at Christiansborg from 1805, visited an Ewe fetish mountain near the lower Volta. The priest who had accompanied him poured a libation to the local spirit before they descended and asked Monrad to do likewise. This he did 'with the hearty desire to God that a happier future would dawn for this corner of the earth which nature had so splendidly endued with beauty'. When later he went down with fever, a fetish priest in full dress murmured prayers over his bed and was rewarded with a glass of brandy.[52] Such an expression of ecumenism was, undoubtedly, wildly uncharacteristic of the nineteenth century, but it is interesting to know that at its start it was, all the same, possible.

'Sango cannot save. Oya cannot save, but Jesus Christ can,' declared early converts among the Yoruba.[53] Conversion tends to be confrontational. In nineteenth-century Africa it could be exceedingly so. Becoming a Christian almost inevitably involved public repudiation of the 'principalities and powers', the particular spiritual forces hitherto believed to dominate the world. When at Bonny in Nigeria late in 1874 Captain Hart decided to celebrate a festival in

---

[51] H. Junod, *The Life of a South African Tribe* (1912), ii. 410.

[52] H. Debrunner, 'Notable Danish Chaplains on the Gold Coast', *Transactions of the Gold Coast and Togoland Historical Society*, 2/1 (1956), 19.

[53] J. Peel, 'Conversion and Tradition in Two African Societies: Ijebu and Buganda', *Past and Present*, 77 (1977), 123.

honour of a deceased member of his family, three young Christians refused to take part and one, Joshua Hart, was put to death because he 'refused to partake of things sacrificed to the gods'. He was repeatedly tossed in the air and left to fall on the ground. He was then bound, hand and foot, taken in a canoe and thrown in the river. When he did not sink, his head was smashed with a paddle. The Bonny confirmation class used to pray, 'Give us the firmness of Joshua.'[54]

On the other side of the continent one day in 1882 the CMS missionary O'Flaherty was physically attacked by the medium of one of the gods, Namalere, and they fought with sticks until separated by a local official.[55] When a German missionary forced his way into the sacred grove of Lubaga of the Nyakyusa, it is said that there was a crash of thunder and he fled, afraid, leaving his jacket behind.[56] Michael Tansi, the Igbo Catholic priest, faced with a masquerade, took his stick declaring, 'The spirit has been confronted by a more powerful spirit' or even 'I will reduce you to ashes.'[57] Canon Buningwire, an early Anglican priest in Ankole, would go around the villages with two dogs dressed with fetishes and amulets, telling the people that those who trusted in such things were like dogs who cannot reason.[58] The mass destruction of fetishes by many a prophet like Harris or Babalola witnessed no less to an inherent confrontation which was surely in part unavoidable. These things were simply too powerful, just as the missionary claims for 'Christ alone' as mediator were too powerful, for there not to be plenty of immediate conflict in which some people died and many were threatened.

Yet for many Christians there were also elements of continuity, especially in personal terms. The Christian conversion of people with traditional spiritual authority was not unusual. They could carry their authority with them, and at least some early priests were able to say, 'If I had not been a priest, I would have been a diviner.'[59] The kings of Ankole depended profoundly upon their principal diviners, a dynasty of women chiefs at Ibanda, the religious centre of the

[54] E. Isichei, 'Christians and Martyrs in Bonny, Ora and Lokoja c. 1874–1702', in E. Isichei (ed.), *Varieties of Christian Experience in Nigeria* (1982), 62–8.

[55] D. Bukenya, 'The Development of Neo-traditional Religion: The Baganda Experience', M.Litt. thesis (Aberdeen, 1980), 71.

[56] M. Wilson, *Communal Rituals of the Nyakyusa* (1959), 29.

[57] E. Isichei, *Entirely for God: The Life of Michael Iwere Tansi* (1980), 55, 40.

[58] Bishop Jerome Bamunoba, oral information.

[59] J. Bamunoba, 'The Cult of Spirit in Ankole', MA dissertation (Makerere, 1973), 296.

kingdom. In 1902 Kiburuva succeeded her sister in the position, became a most enthusiastic Christian, and made Ibanda a major centre of Christianity. In 1904 she was baptized with her whole household, returned her instruments of divination to the palace where they were thrown on the grave of the last pagan king, and from then on until her death in 1951 patronized the church, made mats for the sanctuary with her own hands, provided money for the salary of catechists, and had a priest actually living in her household. Her influence was immense just because it was that of tradition.[60] The authority of Ibanda had been continued, not overturned.

Some missionaries saw the 'principalities and powers' of tradition as simply empty, imaginary things. For others, they were diabolical, just as they were for Tansi or Harris. But for many Christians they were real, far from diabolical, yet now replaced by a new, greater, but less approachable, power. A Christian Nyakyusa chief in the 1930s could affirm that 'in the old days Kyala heard men and agreed to their requests in this way. We went to ask for rain and food in the groves; the chief would kill a cow and Kyala agreed, food and rain came. Now that the Gospel has spread . . . Kyala refuses to agree . . .'.[61] For many Christians the old rituals were seen as having been necessary in the past, and, even now, probably remained necessary for non-Christians. Inevitably in times of drought or other crisis they could still fall back on them as 'necessary even for us'. They continued, then, to live in two worlds, between which the relationship was largely one of uneasy coexistence. One, nevertheless, was in process of displacing the other, sometimes by the sheer challenge of denial and destruction, sometimes as at Ibanda by a quieter transference, sometimes even through an amicable farewell.

Our final example illustrates the scenario of parting with an old friend and guardian, because a greater lord has arrived, rather touchingly. It comes from the Dida Harrists in the village of Yocoboué. The spirit Kpoto, who resided not far away in the river Boubo, had blessed the village with more children than any other spirit. It was necessary to sever his worship and the tie of dependence effectively but gratefully. A Dida witness years later described

the day when Pastor Jacob Towa announced in church that the worship service on the following Sunday would take place 'chez Kpoto' on the

[60] J. Bamunoba, 'The Diviners for the Kings (Abagabe) of Ankole', *UJ* 29 (1965) 95–7.
[61] Wilson, *Communal Rituals of the Nyakyusa*, 176.

Boubo River. Beginning already on Tuesday of that week, the villagers went to the spot and began cleaning up the area. From Tuesday to Saturday they worked, felling trees, burning the underbrush, sweeping impeccably the banks of the river, and then constructing an immense hangar of wood posts and palm branches, large enough to contain the entire village. The worship service on that Sunday was very long. There were songs and prayers and a lengthy sermon by Towa. And then, finally, came the moment which no one who actually witnessed it could ever forget, when Towa took water and baptized Kpoto in the name of the Father, the Son and the Holy Spirit, all the while beseeching God to hear him as he prayed: 'God, we want now to worship you, you alone, and none other. Send us the force we need in order to give you all of our praise. Protect us and give us the strength to remain faithful to you.' Then, addressing himself to Kpoto, Towa added: 'Go away now, far, far from this place. We will worship you no more. It is God alone who will receive our praise. We don't need you anymore.'[62]

Doubtless such events happened less frequently than those of confrontation and destruction. Yet interiorly and psychologically this scene may represent the larger reality better than that of Tansi waving his stick at a masquerader or Joshua Hart dying for his refusal to share in a sacrificial feast to his family gods. As a whole the Christian community moved beyond the rituals upon which its fathers had depended. Such a moving beyond was indeed a liberation from many burdens though, if only half believed in, it could also engender additional fears. Nevertheless, as it moved more confidently into a Christian world of meaning and practice, it did so for the most part without quite disbelieving in the reality and even the beneficence of the world it had hitherto inhabited. If destruction of the past was one inevitable dimension of the Christianization of society, it was a destruction coupled, not officially by the Church, but quite profoundly by many of its members, with gratitude for a religious inheritance which continued to shape in many ways their beliefs, their language, and their morality.

[62] Krabill, 'The Hymnody of the Harrist Church among the Dida of South-Central Ivory Coast', 392–3.

9

CHRISTIAN LIFE IN THE AGE OF BISHOP CROWTHER

i. 'Black Europeans'

On 26 July 1860, as part of the annual celebrations to mark Liberia's independence, Alexander Crummell, an Afro-American cleric working in Monrovia, delivered a speech before the citizens of Maryland County, Cape Palmas. His theme was the English language and its glories. It was a language, he claimed, which had for centuries been 'baptized in the spirit of the Christian faith', and he urged the citizens of Cape Palmas to spend a few hours daily reading Locke on the mind, Bacon's *Essays*, Butler's *Analogy*, or the *Life of Benjamin Franklin*. He pointed out that because they shared this inestimable benefit even black slaves in America had somehow been within 'a school of freedom' from which the German, the Italian, and the Frenchman had been excluded. Here in Liberia, he asserted, there was now 'a people possessed of Christian institutions and civilized habits, their only marked peculiarity being that in colour they were black' so that, if a stranger should land here, 'although sable are all the faces he meets with, the names are the old familiar ones he has been accustomed to in the streets of New York or London, viz. the Smiths (a large family in Liberia as everywhere else in Anglo-Saxondom) and their broods of cousins, the Johnsons, Thompsons, Robinsons and Jacksons . . .'.[1] Because of its English names and English language, Liberia was really just a part of Anglo-Saxondom, Crummell was defiantly asserting, and that represented the social and religious ideal of many a citizen in Freetown and further along the coast too. 'If our public worship in Cape Coast is not heaven come down to earth', declared Thomas Birch Freeman in 1854, 'it is pretty nearly that of England come to Africa.'[2] A little later an

[1] A. Crummell, *The Future of Africa* (1862), 12.
[2] *Report of the Wesleyan Methodist Missionary Society*, xii (1854).

Irishman, sometime Colonial Secretary, commented on Samuel Lewis, leading citizen of Sierra Leone in the second half of the century, that he was 'more English than the English themselves'.[3] While he may have said this a little sarcastically, Lewis almost certainly regarded it as a compliment.

Consider the great names of West African Christianity in this period: Samuel Lewis, Samuel Crowther, Samuel Johnson, Thomas Babington Macaulay, James Johnson, Nathaniel King, James Africanus Horton. Here indeed we find English nomenclature, English language, English manners, and clothes, come to Africa and vigorously adopted far more than imposed: clergy, doctors, lawyers, and soldiers all educated in and loyal to a London model. This mid-century Christian culture whose heart was in Freetown, with its parallel—more settler, less Africa-linked—in Monrovia, was by the 1850s spreading vigorously along the coast, above all around Lagos. The core experience of liberated slaves in the villages outside Freetown ensured an ethos that was intertribal yet not too abruptly cut off from local, pre-colonial, roots elsewhere. The founding fathers in Regent, Wilberforce, and Bathurst remembered their homes and their own languages. Some in due course returned to them. The vigour of the so-called 'Sierra Leoneans' of the second half of the century lay in this easy belonging to two worlds. They took on board as much of this Western, civilizing, Christianizing model as they wanted, the choice was essentially theirs, and some preferred Islam instead. Freetown was their own. There was no white settler society. Europeans died too fast and missionaries remained rather few. An African clergy, on the contrary, soon developed in remarkable numbers. Crowther was the first to be ordained, in 1843. At least 100 West African 'native clergy' connected with the CMS had followed him by 1899, apart from Methodists and Baptists. Most had been born in Sierra Leone. Fifty-five of them had been trained at Fourah Bay and eleven of these had received Durham University degrees (possible only after 1879). The rest were mostly untrained.

From the late 1830s some 'Sierra Leoneans' had begun to move back to their original lands along the coast, and by 1851 there were already some 3,000 returned 'emigrants' in Abeokuta alone. Samuel Crowther's reunion with his mother at Ochogu near Abeokuta in 1846 and her subsequent baptism were prophetically symbolic of the

[3] J. Hargreaves, *A Life of Sir Samuel Lewis* (1958), 61.

process whereby the homecoming 'Sierra Leonean' would seek to convert native inland Africa to the faith he had adopted in exile. It was, of course, by no means a typical experience, especially for the 1840s, any more than Crowther himself was typical of his contemporaries. Yet he was throughout his career supremely symbolic of the to-and-fro movement of nineteenth-century West Africa as of all that was best in the first blossoming of a basically self-propagating Christian community. Persistently loyal to England, to Canterbury, and the CMS, a devoted pastor and excellent linguist, Crowther was faithful throughout his life to the mid-Victorian missionary ideal, the link with civilization and commerce most especially. And—up to a point—he actually made it work. Consecrated in 1864 by the Archbishop of Canterbury as a missionary bishop for the Niger, he would remain one for over a quarter of a century, until well into his eighties. It might well be claimed that for all-round pastoral maturity he has no peer among nineteenth-century Anglican bishops in Africa. He certainly had no peer within his own community. A combination of learning, zeal, sound judgement, regular visits to Britain, and the towering status provided by his bishopric set Crowther in a place apart until the end of his life. For his contemporaries, both black and white, he appeared to represent all that they could hope for—the bestowal of trust by Europeans upon an African, the incarnation of Victorian Christian values in a black skin.

Yet he already represented a good deal more than that. A stress upon the special character of these 'Sierra Leoneans' has at times proved misleading. The slaves unloaded at Freetown were indeed from many parts. Nevertheless, a specially high proportion of them were Yoruba and it seems to have been the Yoruba alone who settled together in such large groups in the villages around Freetown that they continued to speak their own language. It is almost true to say that the Sierra Leonean Christian culture, at least in its expansive form, was a species of Yoruba culture. Almost all its principal figures—even those like Samuel Lewis, who always remained in Sierra Leone—were in fact Yoruba. Thus when in 1854 Thomas Babington Macaulay, back from studies in London, married Abigail Crowther, Samuel's daughter, it was a marriage at the heart of the new 'Sierra Leonean' reality, but it was no less a marriage between two Yoruba, and the newly-weds would soon be living near the ancestral Crowther family home in Abeokuta. Their son, Herbert

Macaulay, later to be hailed as the Father of Nigerian Nationalism, was generally dressed by his mother for the first years of his life in a suit of purple velvet knickerbockers with a purple velvet coat and shining silver buttons. Thus was the grandson of a Victorian bishop prepared for a career as father of black nationalism, the ambiguous 'black whiteman' who would in 1920 achieve a spectacular victory over colonial government in an appeal to the Privy Council. Anglicized as he might appear in his childhood clothes, he was in reality no less a Yoruba.

The crucial factor underlying the development of by far the most considerable and confident Christian community in West Africa in the later nineteenth century was the way in which Yoruba from Freetown, Christianized and in a way Anglicized yet not de-Yorubaized, returned through Badagry and Lagos into the interior to promote a style of Christianity which was increasingly their own and something well able to appeal to other Yoruba who had not had the Sierra Leone experience. Nowhere else did this happen to any considerable extent. Even in Sierra Leone—indeed in Sierra Leone most of all—it failed to happen. Christian Sierra Leone culture and life remained cut off from its hinterland, which for long it almost wholly failed to penetrate. Again on the Niger, Bishop Crowther's own diocese, it did not really happen. Here was missionary work run by a group of outsiders rather than confident re-entry of the returned native into his ancestral land bearing with him a faith he wished to share.

The Gold Coast experience was different again, although the area of penetration—among the coastal Fante in and around the British colony—was fairly small. The kingdom of Ashanti still provided a hard wall against any advance inland. The roots of nineteenth-century Christianity here are to be found less in the return of recaptives than among pupils of Philip Quaque and the Cape Coast Castle school, though little less important was the arrival of the Basel missionaries in 1828 at Christiansborg Castle. Methodism derived from the first, under the guidance of Thomas Birch Freeman, an enthusiastic pioneer, the son of an African father and English mother. Presbyterianism derived from the second. The Basel and Bremen missionaries were excellent linguists and more adaptive than the British. Johann Christaller in particular provided a series of outstanding translations in Twi in the 1850s and 1860s. There were nine African Methodist ministers by 1858, some of whom like John

Ahoomah Solomon and John Plange would go through to the 1890s. Joseph Dunwell, the first Methodist missionary, had arrived at Cape Coast on New Year's Day 1835. He died just under six months later. Freeman followed him in January 1838. Both his influence and his long survival on the West Coast derived from his Africanness. A consequence was that, for quite a while, he lost the confidence of Methodist authorities in Britain and ceased to be in the Church's employment. Nevertheless, when in 1885 the Jubilee celebrations were held in Wesley Church, Cape Coast, 'Father' Freeman was still there to preach the sermon.

Gold Coast Christianity avoided many of the strains of its Nigerian counterpart—strains connected with episcopacy, with the greater exuberance and sense of self-confident sufficiency of the 'Sierra Leonean' Yoruba, and with a more noticeable high-handedness on the part of Anglican Evangelical missionaries. Yet late nineteenth-century Fante society and its Wesleyan core shared closely the rather pan-African culture of the wider coastal world with its 'civilized' and Christian emphases, and it made considerable use of the educational facilities of Freetown. The political leaders of the Fante Confederation around 1870 were, all of them, Methodists. In men like R. J. Ghartey, elected President of the Confederation in 1869 and enstooled as King Ghartey IV in 1872, yet also a businessman and Methodist layman, one may find the first generation of 'Ethiopianism'—people successfully merging African political aspirations of a modern sort with a measure of traditional culture as well as of Christian commitment. In Casely Hayford, son of one of the most influential ministers of the 1870s, Joseph deGraft Hayford, Fante Methodism produced one of the leading figures of coastal politics and literary culture of the next generation. Nevertheless, the Nigerian scale was altogether larger and its areas of contention more dramatic. The Gold Coast model of Church development remained a more missionary one, while the decisive interest of the Nigerian model lay in the projection of Sierra Leone back into Yorubaland and the Niger. This inserted a highly original factor, one combining functional local autonomy with its own considerable missionary momentum, into the very heart of the picture. What happened in Nigeria comes in consequence to contrast with developments elsewhere quite strikingly and to achieve a far more than local significance for the history of the African Church.

The Nigerian experience in this period was, overwhelmingly, an

Anglican one, orchestrated by the CMS. The main educational institutions in Freetown were Anglican and, with the ordination of Crowther in 1843, an ideal was set to be followed by many. While Methodists were also numerous in Sierra Leone, they lacked anything educational comparable to Fourah Bay College, and their missionary society focused its wider attention upon Gold Coast and Dahomey. While it had established a post at Badagry already in 1842, further penetration of Nigeria was very limited. To the east the Church of Scotland founded a mission at Calabar in 1846 which grew to considerable importance, but, in this period, it remained quite apart from the main Nigerian story. Baptists and Catholics were also represented, but their impact was limited and late. The central theme of nineteenth-century Nigerian Christian history consists in the interplay of the CMS and the Anglican Yoruba. For the CMS the return of Christian Yoruba to their native land seemed a golden opportunity. It established a mission at Badagry in 1845 and followed it up with others at Abeokuta in 1846 and Lagos and Ibadan in 1852. Henry Townsend among the Egba at Abeokuta and David Hinderer at Ibadan were for more than twenty years missionaries of exceptional ability and influence. Indeed Townsend came near to controlling the policies of Abeokuta through the 1850s as secretary to its ruler, the Alake. But the wider spread of the Church depended upon the presence of the Saros, the returned, educated 'Sierra Leoneans', especially numerous at Abeokuta and, later, Lagos. Upon the one hand Townsend's authority was enhanced by the presence of the Saros, upon the other a rivalry between the two almost inevitably developed in which they resented his claim to monopolize the Christian voice while he felt confident that he understood the needs of the Egba far better than did the clergy or traders returned from Freetown.

ii. *Crowther and the Niger Diocese*

In 1864 Venn, Secretary of the CMS, persuaded the powers that be to make Crowther a bishop. His character and experience were clearly outstanding. He had published accounts of his travels, a Yoruba grammar, dictionary, and the translation of parts of the Bible. In Crowther, Venn saw the realization of his ideal, a chance to achieve the 'euthanasia' of the mission and the 'full development of the native African Church'.[4] Oxford gave Crowther a DD and the Archbishop

---

[4] J. Ajayi, *Christian Missions in Nigeria 1841–1891: The Making of a New Élite* (1965), 207.

consecrated him in Canterbury Cathedral. But of what was he to be bishop? The obvious answer was Yorubaland. He was a Yoruba. Yoruba Christians and clergy were reasonably numerous. Nowhere else was the 'euthanasia' of the mission remotely conceivable. But there were problems. The white missionaries among the Yoruba, Townsend especially, were emphatically opposed. Moreover, Crowther himself had been working on the Niger for several years and had been involved in all the Niger expeditions including the first and particularly disastrous one of 1841. He had survived. The CMS did not want to abandon the Niger Mission but feared to send white people to a region where they so rapidly died. By appointing Crowther Bishop of the Niger, Venn thought he could at one and the same time promote the man he believed in, solve the awkward problem of the Niger Mission, and avoid conflict with his missionaries in the field. Crowther was certainly a 'native' but he was not a native of the Niger. The degree of difference between the Yoruba and all the peoples east of Benin almost certainly escaped Venn's understanding. The unreasonableness of such an arrangement was overwhelming, its consequences in due course disastrous. That was not, however, how it looked at first. Crowther, declared the Act of Parliament requisite for the creation of a new bishopric, was to exercise jurisdiction over 'the countries of western Africa beyond the limits of our dominions',[5] while the English Bishop of Sierra Leone would retain within his diocese the various British colonies. As the British dominions were extremely limited in 1864, this should have given Crowther almost all Yoruba, including Abeokuta and Ibadan, and, indeed, Venn declared that their exclusion from his diocese 'can only be regarded as temporary'.[6] Crowther actually exercised some jurisdiction in his early years in Yoruba areas and even in Liberia. There was, then, a psychologically destabilizing ambiguity in the nature and boundaries of his diocese from the start. Crowther fixed his base at Lagos, absolutely reasonable if his jurisdiction was really as Parliament had declared it, but rather unfortunate if it was to be—as it came to be and by some had certainly been intended from the start to be—over the Niger and no more.

'I know that my new position sets me up as a kind of landmark, which both the Church and the Heathen World must needs behold. I am aware that any false step taken by me will be injurious to all the

[5] Ibid. 274.   [6] Ibid. 206.

Native Churches; yet, if God keeps me steadfast, the mouths of the adversaries will be silenced.'[7] Crowther's departing words in Salisbury Square to the Committee of the CMS before returning to Nigeria in July 1864 express both the lonely eminence to which he had been called and his profound sense of responsibility alike to the African Church and to the CMS: no missionary society ever had a son more loyal. But the facts were against him from the start. The Church in Yoruba, the one place where Venn's principles could reasonably be applied, remained under white control while Crowther and his very mixed bag of assistants were expected instead to be themselves missionaries in territories where they were, with few exceptions, far from native and with no firm base from which to operate, or adequate means to sustain their operations. It was a cheap arrangement. Yoruba was dissatisfied, while Crowther was left without the support needed to undertake a major missionary venture in a vast and difficult area. By 1875 Hinderer, who like Townsend had initially opposed Crowther's appointment to be bishop in Yorubaland, could ask, 'Has not the time come when the native bishop's jurisdiction should be further extended than the Niger, especially to his own native soil?'[8] But it was not to be. The history of the Church in both areas might have been very different if Venn had more firmly implemented his own principles instead of confounding them in an arrangement which led to ineffectiveness upon the one side and dissatisfaction on the other.

The very shape of the Niger Mission was a problem. It consisted, according to the plan as received from the CMS inheriting a Niger strategy stretching back to the planners of the 1841 expedition, of a series of stations along the River Niger. It related, not to society or language, but to the river as providing easy communications, a way into the continent's interior. In reality it provided a way to an Islamic interior unpropitious to missionary work. Apart from that it did little more than link together a number of rather insignificant places of different culture and language. The Yoruba Mission had a unity of language and culture. If Crowther had been instructed to evangelize the Igbo, his mission could also have had one. Instead he had the many peoples of the Delta in the south, the Igbo in the middle, the Nupe and other more Islamicized peoples including the Hausa in the

[7] E. Stock, *The History of the Church Missionary Society* (1899), ii. 457.
[8] Ajayi, *Christian Missions in Nigeria*, 230.

north. Nothing could have been worse from the viewpoint of making an impact anywhere. While the river linked the stations, it did so only if you possessed a reliable boat. For the first fourteen years Crowther had none. When a mission steamer did arrive, in 1878, it actually added to the problem: it had to engage in trading to pay its way and was handed over to a British assistant to manage, someone who failed to get on with Crowther and his agents. With or without a steamer, the mission was dangerously dependent upon trade and traders, especially the Niger Company. The riverside inhabitants could not conceivably be expected to make a sharp distinction between the evangelists and the traders (in the early years, largely traders in drink; in later years, largely imperialist bullies), who came and went in the same boats.

Whom could Crowther find to do the work of preaching and teaching? Here lay the largest problem of all. The Church in Yoruba was based on considerable numbers of Christian settlers home from Freetown, people who had not forgotten their own language in English-speaking Sierra Leone. There was no such group of any size for the Niger. Furthermore, Christian Yoruba were not particularly interested in, or suitable for, work quite outside their area. Crowther naturally recruited Igbo and others of eastern Nigerian background in Freetown. The general quality was far from outstanding. It is only too clear that there was considerable difficulty in finding enough suitable agents. Most of those selected were very poorly educated, some were old or physically unfit, some had no linguistic qualifications, a few were of quite dubious character.[9] The case of William John, recruited at Fourah Bay in 1874, was certainly untypical, but it provided ammunition for the mission's critics and was even debated in the House of Lords. First stationed at Brass, he was disconnected the next year on grounds of seducing the daughter of a leading Christian, but was re-employed by Crowther in a secretarial role. Two years later, now in Onitsha as assistant schoolmaster, he and his wife beat a slave-girl to death. On returning to Sierra Leone in 1882, he was tried for manslaughter. It was Samuel Lewis, a keen Sunday School teacher as well as an able lawyer, who acted as advocate for the prosecution and secured his conviction. John's behaviour was appalling in a missionary, but

---

[9] See the revealing list in app. III of G. Tasie, *Christian Missionary Enterprise in the Niger Delta 1864–1918* (Leiden, 1978), 250–6.

around Onitsha, where the Niger Company, whose employees were largely Sierra Leoneans, set standards which Crowther described in 1879 as 'Cruel and overbearing to the Natives; cruel to their native clerks',[10] it was less remarkable than in Freetown. If Crowther employed such people it was because he could not find better.

The bishop himself spent only a few months each year on the river. When problems grew in the 1870s he appointed his youngest son, Dandeson, Archdeacon of the Lower Niger and Delta, and Henry Johnson Archdeacon of the Upper Niger. That was in 1877. Both were Yoruba who had studied at the Church Missionary College in Islington and were far better educated than their Niger colleagues. It is striking that the bishop had to turn to Yoruba for reliable senior assistants. There was no one of similar calibre of eastern Nigerian origin. Nor was an Igbo, for instance, necessarily of much use in most of the diocese. With so many different languages—Hausa and Nupe in the north, Igbo and Ijo in the south, among others—there was no easy way to provide teaching of any quality. Even among Igbos the dialectal difference was considerable. It is noticeable that John Taylor, an Igbo and Crowther's earliest lieutenant, still used an interpreter at Onitsha. The knowledge of Igbo had not survived in Sierra Leone nearly as well as that of Yoruba. Moreover, the Sierra Leone Yoruba had arrived largely around 1820. When the movement to return to Yorubaland began in the 1840s many of those involved, like Crowther himself, were of the original generation. The Igbos had come earlier and people of Igbo extraction recruited in Freetown to return to their homeland in the 1870s were in a quite different position. Taylor was probably the best educated of the eastern Nigerians on the mission, but he resigned after some years and returned to Sierra Leone.

In the Delta the language problem was even worse. Only one or two of the agents—most notably J. D. Garrick—learned to speak the languages. Dandeson Crowther learned Igbo, but he was still using an interpreter in the Delta many years after becoming Archdeacon. All in all what remains remarkable was the number of little books the Sierra Leone agents published in a variety of languages. While Crowther himself concentrated on Nupe, he encouraged others to work at Igbo. Probably much of this work was not of high linguistic quality, but that was the case with most missionary first attempts in

---

[10] E. Isichei, *The Ibo People and the Europeans* (1973), 120.

hitherto unwritten languages. In Igbo, at least, the work of the Sierra Leoneans provided a useful base for the larger developments after 1890.

It was at Bonny and Brass, in the Delta, that the mission's evangelical purpose bore most apparent fruit. Brass was particularly receptive. It lay on the ocean side of the Delta and was prospering mightily for a generation before British commercial penetration of the river had advanced very far. Brass represented the successful coastal middleman who had succeeded in switching from slaves to palm-oil in the trade between the interior and Europe. Oil was exported, gin, brandy, cheap cloth, and trinkets imported. At this point in time Christianity and gin went together. Brassmen apparently felt that a modern economy required a modern religion and moved *en masse* into the Church in the 1870s. 'In no other place did I observe such a striking exhibition of the mighty power of the Gospel,' wrote Henry Johnson in 1877.[11] Old King Ockiya threw some of his fetishes into the river. The rest he handed over to Bishop Crowther, who saw how splendid they were and packed them off to London.[12] In 1876 he ventured so far as to give up eighteen of his twenty-five wives. The rest went three years later. By then, however, he was dying. Baptized Josiah Constantine Ockiya on 30 November 1879, he died two weeks later. But Christianity continued to flourish and a pagan reaction was vigorously defeated. 'Anything short of repelling force with force will give the heathens the advantage,' wrote Garrick to Crowther.[13] Brass became a Christian state and Salisbury Square was delighted with Crowther's principal evangelical achievement. The bond between Christianity and commerce seemed to be working.

It did not, however, go on like that. By the later 1880s the Royal Niger Company, controlled with a rod of iron by Sir George Goldie, a ruthless commercial racketeer and racialist, was taking over the government of the region. Of all the British chartered companies it was probably the most cruel and rapacious. Systematically ousting African middlemen, it imposed a monopoly of trade up the river.

[11] E. Ayandele, 'The Missionary Factor in Brass 1875–1900: A Study in Advance and Recession', *BSACH* 2/3 (1967), 251.
[12] One particularly magnificent one, 'Kakenga', is now to be seen in the Museum of African Art, Washington, DC: see the reproduction in P. McKenzie, *Inter-Religious Encounter in West Africa* (Leicester, 1976), facing p. 59.
[13] Tasie, *Christian Missionary Enterprise in the Niger Delta*, 67.

Meanwhile, it kept the CMS silent and supportive by its claim to oppose the drink trade, of which Brass was denounced as a principal culprit. The evil, degenerating consequences of the mass importations of gin into late nineteenth-century Africa were overwhelmingly evident. British missionaries have often needed some simplistic social cause upon which to focus their attention, and in the last years of the century they tended to regard the trade in spirits as the supreme evil against which a crusade needed to be mounted. Total abstinence became a necessary mark of Christianity. The prosperity of Brass collapsed. Its population in despair began to abandon the Church, and Crowther, tied as he was to the Niger Company, could do nothing to answer their complaints, except berate them for their infidelity. Commerce and Christianity had, in their experience, not worked after all, and Brass's new king, Frederick Koko, a former Sunday School teacher, abandoned the struggle to be a Christian king. Just a week after the bishop's visit in August 1890 he returned to ju-ju, chalked over his body, and took a second wife. At the height of its Anglicanism over half the Christians of the diocese were to be found in Brass. The apostasy of King Koko marks the collapse of Crowther's episcopate as well as anything. The prevailing cause lay in the demise of the age of independent African societies, in which Crowther and his mission had fitted well enough. In the particularly vicious and racialist form of colonialism which now, for a time, prevailed on the Niger, there was no room for him.

Samuel Crowther was a mild old man, devotedly evangelical, a scholar who studied languages indefatigably and learned a lot about the peoples he tried to serve. He was caught, none the less, between the triangular pressures of the CMS and its commercial allies in London, the limitations of the Sierra Leonean agents he could find to employ, and the inhabitants of his diocese. The consequence could only be disaster.

iii. *Yoruba Christianity*

Meanwhile, the job Crowther possibly could have done rather well, of leading the Church in Yorubaland, was being done by no one. It had no bishop other than the English Bishop of Sierra Leone. Nevertheless, even without a leader, it was wrestling with the problems of an African Christianity more freely and profoundly than the Church anywhere else on the west coast from the 1860s to the

1880s. Its experience of doing so in these last pre-scramble decades deserves our attention. The underlying factors in this wrestling were, upon the one hand, Yoruba traditional religion, upon the other, the special two-world identity of the Saros, the Christianized Yoruba from Sierra Leone who returned from the 1840s to their native land to become a confident bridge between their new faith and their old culture.

Take Yoruba religion first. It was, as even early missionaries recognized, an exceptionally tolerant form of the inclusivity of much African belief. Its tolerance reflected the uncentralized diversity of both Yoruba urban society and Yoruba polytheism. The towns were many, cults were many. At times, undoubtedly, the towns warred as the towns of medieval Italy warred, but they were still bound together by a common language and a sharing of divinities which could always make room for one more. While Christianity remained of its nature as absolute in its claims in nineteenth-century Yorubaland as in first-century Rome, it was met in each case by a society readier to be syncretistic than absolutist: and Yoruba lacked the imperial authority and its political cult which gave Rome its measure of intolerance. Christians, like Muslims already present among the Yoruba, adopted the name of Olorun, a Yoruba title for the creator God, to speak of the God of the Bible. While for them the worship of Olorun was to be sharply contrasted with that of lesser deities like Sango or Orunmila, for the traditionalist Yoruba it remained quite within their system if some should wish to transfer their worship from one of these deities, the *orisa*, to the high god, Olodumare—Olorun. The aggressiveness of the Christian preacher could appear ill-mannered and unnecessary. Within the context of a home Christian faith might well be persecuted and there was persecution of a sort in Abeokuta and elsewhere around 1850, but on the larger, public, scene this was greatly moderated by its deep incompatibility with both the religious pluralism of Yoruba tradition and its confident, almost democratic, urban authority.

In a remarkable judgement of July 1849 the Sagboa, or chief magistrate of Abeokuta, ruled on the persecution of a woman by her husband for attending Church:

Sagboa now speaks. With a prudent and calm speech he drew the minds of all to his subject. Then he began to ask: 'Did the Egbas ever know of so many country-fashions [indigenous customs] as they now do? No. Whether

Sango had ever injured any of such people, who do not worship him, and who of late have forsaken him? No. Are there not among us worshippers of Obbatala, Ifa, Orisako and of hundreds of Gods? And have we not many Mahomedans in the Land? Yes. Well then, did people ever express any illwill towards those differences? If we tollerate the one, we must of necessity tollerate the other also. Therefore my advice is this: that ye permit this woman to worship whom and what she pleases without the least interference.' And with this advice all agreed.[14]

In this the Yoruba attitude was not essentially different from that of African religious tradition in many other places. Yet it was more consciously pluralist than most, while being less closely tied to the authority of elders upon one side or kings upon another. It was in consequence rather easy for the Christian preacher to obtain a hearing. Ibadan's chief physician remarked only too positively to David Hinderer in 1859 that 'As soon as our church was built, he would be the first to attend it.' 'At last', added Hinderer, 'he carried me to an *Orisa* (Idol) grove of his own planting, there he said, when I have learnt your worship of God, there I will put it, by the side of all my other *Orisas*.'[15]

Yoruba tolerance made it rather easy for a Christian missionary to establish a small toe-hold within its world, and Hinderer was an unusually gentle person with the ability to do just this in a thriving town, where he remained someone respected but quite unimportant, a very different role from that of a missionary in some small southern tribal capital. Nevertheless, it did not make for any large-scale conversion, and it would be greatly to misunderstand the context to be surprised that no such thing developed. The advance of Christianity among the Yoruba necessarily followed ways reflective of Yoruba culture. That there was all the same an advance and the establishment of little communities of Christians in quite a number of places between the 1840s and the 1880s before the arrival of colonial rule was almost entirely due to the return of 'emigrants' from Sierra Leone, and their interaction with neighbours.

The Saros lived in two worlds. They had not been alienated from their native Yorubaland in the way that the black Americans settled in Liberia had been alienated from Africa. They were Yoruba-speakers, glad to be home, but they were also bearers of a new collective

---

[14] J. Iliffe, 'Persecution and Toleration in Pre-Colonial Africa: Nineteenth-Century Yorubaland', in W. Shields (ed.), *Persecution and Toleration, SCH* xxi (1984), 369.
[15] Ibid. 364.

culture and religion of whose merits and superiority they were very conscious. They had not, of course, all been equally Christianized in Sierra Leone. It is easy for us to concentrate on those who were, the ordained especially, and forget the thousands who merged far more completely with the Yoruba outlook. Nevertheless, ministers like James White and Samuel Pearse, while they were individual missionaries directly challenging Yoruba tradition in the name of Christianity, were also in a way chaplains to congregations of Saros. Their role as clergy was to ensure that the links with Freetown were retained, that there were schools and churches, that a Yoruba Christian world, strong in Lagos, Badagri, and a few other centres but mostly very weak anywhere away from the coast, was spreading and maturing. Such men had an authority as Yoruba which ordinary Yoruba could not easily disregard. It was possible in consequence for a dialogue to develop almost at once between Christian Yoruba and their traditional neighbours, in which the Christians could combine the assurance of still being Yoruba insiders with literacy, the theology of nineteenth-century Britain, and a range of other skills characteristic of the new coastal trading world.

The conversion of three *babalawo* in Badagri in the 1860s through the ministrations of Samuel Pearse, a Sierra Leonean Egba, illustrates both the ability of Christianity to convince and the way in which Sierra Leonean Christianity was able, given the right conditions, to pass quite quickly into something far more African and less British. A *babalawo* was a professional diviner of the cult of Ifa, a system of divination intimately associated with Ife, the traditional sacred centre of Yorubaland. Ifa priests had to master many hundreds of *ese*, texts used in divination and understood as messages from God, for Orunmila or Esu, the *orisa* or deity of divination, was regarded as being particularly close to the Supreme Being, Olodumare. Many *babalawo* were intelligent, well trained, religious professionals, capable of entering into serious philosophical discussion with a missionary, a discussion between two not entirely dissimilar views of divinity and human destiny.

The conversion of the three *babalawo* is described in the diaries of Samuel Pearse.[16] Pearse had arrived in Badagri in 1859 and met Akibode, 'chief *babalawo*', almost at once. He was in fact already

---

[16] J. Peel, 'The Pastor and the Babalawo: The Interaction of Religions in Nineteenth-Century Yorubaland', *Africa*, 60 (1990), 350–9.

attracted to Christianity, had sent his children to school, often attended services, and felt himself well on the way to becoming a Christian:

I am everywhere known as a *Babalawo*. I had made Ifa for money and am resolved the Lord help me when I make the final start, after having set my house in order, called my disciples, some of whom I am now drawing to Church, taken from them the Ifas I had made for them and pointed to Jesus the only Saviour. I will bundle them all up . . .

That was his position in 1859. In fact it would be another nine years before Akibode took 'the final start', but already in 1861 he was so sure he would be baptized that he had chosen the name he would take, Paul. Meanwhile, he introduced Pearse to other *babalawo* in his home. Among them was Masolowo, who had been one of Akibode's disciples and like him had accepted the basic message of Christianity yet for long could not be induced actually to abandon his Ifa. Like Akibode he visited Pearse, was fond of discussion and very friendly, but to give up both his work and his wives was another matter.

The third *babalawo* was Philip Jose Meffre, a different sort of person in that he was himself a returned ex-slave from Brazil. A highly skilled diviner with a great reputation, he came to be convinced by Pearse that he needed 'something superior to Ifa'. Meffre was keen to learn to read both in English and in Yoruba. As he read the Scriptures in Yoruba his commitment rapidly grew in the course of 1862. Encouraged by a dream in September he took his principal Esu, a great mud idol he had brought back from Brazil, and buried it in the ground. In November he handed over six other *orisa* to Pearse and two sets of Ifa at the January New Year's service. 'It yet remains two superior ones. The Lord will overcome them also.' He did so in February. It was a reproach to Akibode, who no longer used his Ifa but could not get himself actually to surrender them. Only in 1868 did he finally do so, to be followed almost at once by Masolowo.

These conversions are exceptionally interesting because they were highly personal, the intellectual and moral decisions of able, successful people who were losing a great deal in consequence: the principal source of their livelihood as well as their social prestige and their plural marriages. It says a great deal for Pearse that he was both so convincing and so patient. He could take his *babalawo* seriously within their own thought-world as so many a white missionary could not. He seemed able to argue convincingly the superiority of a

Christian theodicy, a Christian personal eschatology in regard to life after death, and a Christian pattern of morality, each in close comparison with Yoruba conceptions.

Meffre too was helped at a crucial moment by a dream in which a voice had ordered him to bury seven images, and he had actually done so. Dreams could be an important part of the conversion process. Many a prospective convert had one, and Sierra Leonean agents like Pearse at Badagri, James White at Otta, and William George at Abeokuta had no problem in taking them seriously. The mechanics of religious conversion within Yoruba society had moved rapidly away from the model British missionaries would themselves have inculcated. To some extent this was helped by the consequences of the Ijaye war between Ibadan and the Egba which raged through the early 1860s separating Ibadan Christians from Abeokuta Christians. European missionaries were expelled from Abeokuta and severely restricted elsewhere. As a result throughout much of Yorubaland the Christian ministry depended entirely upon Yoruba clergy and schoolteachers, almost all of whom were Sierra Leoneans, though in Ibadan they were joined by the first non-emigrant, Daniel Olubi, trained wholly in Nigeria and mostly in David Hinderer's household.

The maturity of this Yoruba Church by the mid-1870s was remarkable. It was not indeed in relation to the total population a numerous Church. Politically and socially it was insignificant, at least outside Lagos. Nothing like a mass conversion movement was to be expected. Many of the clergy had a fairly limited training while the lay Sierra Leoneans who had returned with them were, many of them, Christians in little more than name. All the problems characteristic of an African Church anywhere in relation to marriage, funerals, and traditional rituals structuring almost every side of social life were problems here too. What is remarkable, nevertheless, is how an evangelical momentum, begun in Freetown, was in many places maintained quite outside the sphere of British rule or a Westernized town, and how committed and imaginative the best clergy and laity were. It is interesting, for instance, to find at Otta by the late 1850s the development of hymns, both words and tune of local composition, encouraged by James White, who had been a catechist there since 1854 and was ordained in 1857. Henry Townsend described them that year as 'the first I have heard', and Crowther much later spoke of them as 'suitable Scriptural compositions of their own adapted to their native airs'.[17] This represented already a quite courageous break with the cultural norms of Freetown.

Nevertheless, while one kind of Africanization of Christianity was developing quite fast in up-country Yorubaland from the 1850s to the 1870s, another kind was being proposed more theoretically in Freetown and then in Lagos. Between 1871 and 1874 a controversy broke out in Sierra Leone. There had been a native church pastorate for a decade with nine pastors in charge of as many parishes, but supervision and authority remained finally in European hands. On the tenth anniversary of the pastorate, one of its clergy, J. H. Davies, appealed for a fully independent native Church: 'We request you to aim at establishing at Sierra Leone a pure Native Church . . . not only for our own and children's use, but for the use of Africa at large.'[18] But it was the arrival of Edward Blyden in Freetown in August 1871 which really triggered off the argument. Blyden had come from the Caribbean to Liberia as a very young man. There he had already held a large variety of posts including those of Professor of Classics at Liberia College and Secretary of State in the government. He was a man of extraordinary brilliance, a master of written English and much else despite a very limited formal education. He came now to Freetown, sent by Henry Venn and the CMS, to teach Arabic at Fourah Bay College and in general to prepare the way for a mission to the Muslim interior. It did not work like that. There were rumours that he had left Liberia on account of adultery with the President's wife. Bishop Cheetham and the white missionaries believed the rumours and suspended him at once. The African clergy disbelieved them and gave dinners in his honour. He soon began a newspaper, the *Negro*, through which he could disseminate his own great schemes: to bring more West Indians to Africa, to found a university in Freetown, to recognize the merits of Islam, and to free the Sierra Leonean Church from its dependence upon Britain and its missionaries.

The clergy of Sierra Leone at first responded with enthusiasm, James Johnson the principal intellectual among them particularly. Nevertheless, the enthusiasm was soon tempered with caution. Blyden's strident criticism of missionaries was simply too dangerous

---

[17] Ajayi, *Christian Missions in Nigeria*, 225.
[18] H. Lynch, 'The Native Pastorate Controversy and Cultural Ethno-Centrism in Sierra Leone 1871–1874', *JAH* 5 (1964), 396.

for people as basically dependent upon Britain as they were. Sierra Leone, so overwhelmingly a society of immigrants, could not function without Britain—something not at all true of Yorubaland. Moreover, Blyden's Islamic preferences were not easily shared. African Christians could admire the cultured sophistication of the author of *Christianity, Islam and the Negro Race* (1887), but for them Islam was a rival. For him it was something to be patronized. It is only too clear how when he visited Lagos in 1890 his Islamic opinions were really an embarrassment to his Yoruba Christian hosts, living in a city where they were outnumbered by Muslims. Blyden's personality was powerful but unstable. While he soon returned to Liberia the controversy he had helped stir up in Sierra Leone did contribute to securing the affiliation of Fourah Bay College to Durham University in 1876, but it resulted immediately in little else other than the transfer of James Johnson from Freetown to Lagos where in 1874 he became pastor of St Paul, Breadfruit.

Lagos could be the home of a movement to Africanize Christianity very much more effectively than Freetown, and we may well date the transfer of centrality from the one to the other within the history of the West African Church to the moment when James Johnson moves from Freetown to Breadfruit.

For the next thirty-five years, 'Holy Johnson', as he was called to distinguish him from various other Yoruba Johnsons, would be the principal leader of Nigerian Christian nationalism. At first he stood in the shadow of Crowther, later in the shadow of the independents whom he had not joined. A man of intelligence and commitment, and of sharp words rather than decisive deeds, Johnson was the clerical Hamlet torn between his Anglican priesthood and his African nationalism but at each point of separation finally loyal to the first. If that had been more obviously so, he might have succeeded Crowther as a diocesan bishop, though his years as superintendent of the Yoruba Churches of the interior in the late 1870s were hardly a success; if it had not been so, he might have headed a far larger secessionist Church than ever came into being. More painfully than anyone else Holy Johnson represents an Ethiopianism unable to repudiate its debt to European Christianity.

One of Johnson's church elders at Breadfruit was none other than Philip Jose Meffre, with whom he was soon working very closely. Here the two forms of Africanization—the one derived from the Yoruba grass-roots experience, an experience taking place entirely in the Yoruba tongue, the other more Sierra Leonean, an intellectual and English-speaking attempt to apply Henry Venn's model of the self-governing Church—were coming together to reinforce each other. Lagos Christian society was already ahead of Freetown's in the range of its innovations. The year before Johnson's arrival a group of people, including churchwardens at Breadfruit and Christchurch, had set up a Lagos Philharmonic Club, most of whose theatrical entertainments were in the Breadfruit schoolroom. Again, their productions fused the 'traditional' and the 'modern'. Soon there would be nationalistically inclined newspapers like the *Lagos Times* and the *Lagos Observer* which could count on far wider support than Blyden's *Negro*. A new culture was quickly emerging in which Christians could play a leading role, yet it was far from entirely Christian, and if it looked decidedly modernizing at the Lagos end, it was also quite consciously traditionalizing too. Yoruba society was essentially a mixed one, overwhelmingly traditionalist in religion, but with significant Muslim and Christian minorities, and a creative tension between the coast and the principal towns of the interior. This was simply not a society missionaries could control, but they resented their impotence. They could only have controlled the Christians if the latter were effectively excluded from society as a whole, but it was the great strength of Yoruba Christianity that this was not the case. Return from Sierra Leone had given them something of a privileged status, privileged at least in their greater grasp of the techniques of modernity, but it had left them still Yoruba, and, in the eyes of their fellow Yoruba, that was what mattered.

In Yoruba Christian history the conflicts and schisms of the late 1880s, 1890s, and beyond would grow almost inevitably out of the growing maturity of the 1860s and 1870s just as the developments in those decades which we have been illustrating grew out of the return of the Saros beginning in the 1840s and that again from the evolution of Freetown and its surrounding villages from 1810 to the 1830s. There is an internal dynamism here which missionaries hardly ever adequately recognized—though Hinderer did so when in 1875 he explicitly argued for an African bishop for the Yoruba on the grounds that things were now very different from what they had been a decade earlier.[19] Hinderer, however, had always been an exception-

---

[19] See his letter of May 1875, Ajayi, *Christian Missions in Nigeria*, 230.

ally sensitive missionary. It was the failure to find other Hinderers and to understand the intrinsic progression which the West African Church, and particularly the Yoruba Church, had achieved during fifty years that would bring about a series of quite unnecessary disasters, from the devastation of Bishop Crowther's diocese to the schisms which would divide Yoruba Christianity and take even the congregation of St Paul, Breadfruit, out of Anglicanism. Yet none of that would quite unravel the threads bound together in the consciousness of a James Johnson. Yoruba Christian history from 1860 to 1920 has a special fascination because it encapsulates so quickly, so vitally, and in a relatively non-colonial context almost all the deeper issues which the whole missionary movement and every African Church had sooner or later to face.

iv. *The South African Predicament*

Nothing might seem much more different from Yorubaland than the situation in South Africa. Yet go back to 1825 and west and south look not dissimilar. Probably, indeed, the local Christian leadership of men like Andries Waterboer, Andries Stoffels, and Jan Tshatshu was superior to anything indigenous to be found in West Africa. Move on sixty years and the position is quite other. While there was by the 1880s a remarkably confident Christian élite and numerous clergy in Freetown, Yorubaland, and on the Niger, nothing really comparable is to be found within the heartland of the new South Africa despite the far greater missionary resources. The principal reason for the difference lay, almost certainly, in the very multitude of missionaries. Already in 1843 David Livingstone remarked that in Cape Colony 'the number of missionaries of different societies is so large compared to the population it must strike everyone with astonishment'.[20] Yet they continued to multiply all through the century. By 1880, for instance, there were nine different societies at work in Natal and Zululand. No fewer than seventy-five mission stations were opened in Natal, Pondoland, and Zululand between 1844 and 1877.[21] Nowhere else in the world, it is claimed, with the exception of New Zealand, was so thickly populated with missionaries.

[20] Letter to Arthur Tidman, 24 June 1843, *Livingstone's Missionary Correspondence 1841–1856*, ed. I. Schapera (1961), 44.
[21] See the list and map, N. Etherington, *Preachers, Peasants and Politics in Southeast Africa 1835–1880* (1978), 26–7.

The consequence was obvious and inevitable: the more the white agency, the less the black. It was a shortage of white missionaries on the west coast and the health problems they encountered there which stimulated so fruitfully a multiplication of black ordinations. It was the multitude of white missionaries in southern Africa and the very healthy conditions they there enjoyed which inhibited the growth of an indigenous clergy.

It was not only a matter of numbers but also of a larger missionary method. Nowhere else was Christian life so long dominated by the 'station', the mission estate large or small, where Africans accepted a missionary landlord and a shaping of society according to missionary regulation. With the advancing wave of white settlement which was taking over the subcontinent, crushing the societies that had lived there and dispossessing them of a great part of their land, it was inevitable that the simultaneous wave of missionaries, with their own share of the land—even if not in all a very big share—should be seen and resented as part and parcel of the same thing. When land was granted by colonial authority to a mission, the people living on it sometimes simply migrated. Nevertheless, as settler land alienation continued, numerous Africans were bound to seek employment, security, and a home in the relatively benign atmosphere of a mission station. The contrast between mission Africans and those elsewhere soon became a sharp one. No people anywhere in Africa was more evidently divided by Christianity into two sections than the people who for long bore the main brunt of settler advance, the Xhosa. There were for generations the 'Red Xhosa' and the 'School Xhosa'. While the African Christian community did continue to grow, it thus did so in a fundamentally unhealthy and over-dependent way, as a social appendage to the white missionary community, itself an integral part of colonial society.

Missionaries conformed remarkably quickly to the dynamics and mentality of the colonial system whatever their origins. Initially Americans and Scandinavians, for instance, had been decidedly anti-imperialist. But such attitudes seldom lasted for long in South Africa. Again, Henry Callaway, an Anglican missionary of exceptional ability and understanding, was at first deeply concerned with the understanding of African culture and religion. As the years passed, however, he became less adaptationist, coming to believe instead in the necessity of the imposition of European ways for the accomplishment of evangelization. It is remarkable how monotonously alike in behaviour and outlook the great range of missionary societies in South Africa in fact became in this period. It was a monotony derived from an underlying conformity with the psychology and sociology of settler colonialism. The number of missions might multiply, but they only served to mask the void in development of a genuinely African Church. The functioning of such 'stations' consisted in the smooth running of a settlement of some hundreds of acres around a missionary's home and a school. There were plenty of people only too glad of the chance of a little land to cultivate and the simple facilities a mission provided. Mid-nineteenth-century South Africa was full of wanderers, dispossessed of their former homes by white settler encroachment or inter-black conflict. They were not locals and in consequence mission communities were often exceptionally intertribal in character. Christianity provided their common identity and, by doing so, greatly enhanced the developing consciousness of a common Africanness. The inhabitants of mission stations came to form something of a supertribe of their own, the Kholwa, the believers, as others called them. To begin with they prospered considerably, benefiting from schooling for their children and from missionary encouragement to take to ploughs, wagons, square houses, and cash crops. In 1864 the American missionary at Mvoti reported 48 upright houses, 22 ploughs, and 14 wagons owned by residents of the station. The following year a group of Mvoti people actually opened their own sugar mill—'a visible triumph of Christianity and civilization', as the satisfied missionary described it: 'Men with black skins who a few years ago were naked boys . . . are now competing with the white man in manufacturing sugar in a steam mill of their own from canes of their own cultivation and without any superintendence in the work.'[22] The gospel of sugar was a good one for the Kholwa just as the gospel of cocoa was a good one for Christian Yoruba. Each provided the economic undergirding and proof of this-worldly blessedness needed to stabilize a new religious and cultural community. Kholwa religion, like so much Protestant Christianity, combined a very explicitly other-worldly gospel with marks of very this-worldly achievement.

The Kholwa might be a small proportion of the total black population, but it could well be claimed that the proportion was not

[22] Ibid. 177 and 121.

a negligible one and that in social and religious terms the missions were having, collectively, a significant impact. At least the best of them were. They were empowering Africans in a new way within a colonial world. While we can most easily describe this in economic and educational terms, it could not have been done without acquiring a religious identity which provided an integrated sense of purpose, a typically African bonding of the spiritual and the material, and a sense of group unity between the inhabitants of many different stations. The evidence suggests that the denominational differences between the missions meant very little to their converts, who moved very easily from one to another. Some missions, however, managed to serve African needs much better than others. The Methodist clergy may have quarrelled enough among themselves, but their whole system of Church order with its stress on lay leadership and the 'class' system worked well for this sort of African society. The American Congregationalists were much the same, better than Lutherans or Anglicans. Lovedale, above all, did provide an exceptionally wide and effective education and a non-racial one. Tiyo Soga, John Knox Bokwe, John Tengo Jabavu, S. E. K. Mqhayi were among its many early graduates. Without Lovedale, its schools, and its printing-press, the development of a modern black culture in late Victorian South Africa would be almost unimaginable.

Kholwa did not necessarily stay in the stations where they discovered their new identity or in mission stations at all. Some at least carried their gospel and life-style to new, self-supporting, self governing villages in places where there were no missionaries. They made much use of the increasing number of secondary schools the missions were providing, at Lovedale, Adams College, and elsewhere, and they were rather over-appreciative of whatever they were offered which appeared European and academic. At Ladysmith Anglican school in 1879 42 students had attained an advanced level in English, German, and geography, 10 were studying elementary French, 62 were enrolled for Bible history. James Stewart's reaction at Lovedale against that sort of academic education may appear a little racialist, but it was rather a matter of practical common sense. A knowledge of Greek or French would not lead to a job, a knowledge of book-keeping or carpentry might do so. Xhosa and English were the languages upon which to concentrate. All in all in educational and other ways the black Christian community in South Africa in the 1870s was at least the equal of that on the west coast.

There were, however, severe limitations on what could be achieved. They derived from the completeness of white control over the institutional shaping of both Church and State. A first problem related to the missionary community's lack of sympathy with African culture. Nowhere was the identification of Christianity with the standards of the Victorian middle class more taken for granted. There had been exceptions. Colenso was one, Callaway, at first, another, as also some of the early American Congregationalists. But the whole nature of South African white society and the integration of most missionaries into that society produced a particular lack of sensitivity to African culture, manifest in such things as the hard line taken against circumcision and, increasingly, *lobola*. When people first settled on mission land, they often came more or less as outcasts willing to accept what was offered and the way it was offered. They were certainly not to be counted among the prosperous, Africa's natural polygamists. But as their ploughs multiplied and they grew richer and older, they thought and behaved increasingly like their non-Kholwa cousins. By 1871, six years after the opening of the sugar mill, Mvoti had so many polygamists that the missionary in charge was turning to government for assistance to drive them out. Two years earlier the station's founder, Alvin Grout, had written sadly, 'Up to that time when we opened our new chapel I always felt that I had a hold on the people and could lead them . . . Then they said "Heretofore we have been children and have followed our missionary, now we are men and may think and act for ourselves".'[23] The army of missionaries had brought about an impressively quick rise in a class of confident black believers. Ploughs and schools and vernacular Bible texts had been both effective and appreciated. The reply of the Mvoti people to Grout could be paralleled again and again. It was the missionary inability to think beyond a Western-controlled and highly paternalistic relationship, in which there was really no room for Africans to be at home constructing a culture of their own in some ways significantly different from that of Victorian whites, however immensely dependent it would remain upon it, which led on so very quickly to a mood of alienation.

The extreme limitation which missionaries imposed upon black initiative is shown most obviously in the reluctance to ordain Africans

[23] Ibid. 137–8.

in any circumstances, our second problem. The contrast between west and south over clergy ordinations is a striking one. William Ellis, an LMS missionary, wrote a report in 1855 on an institution established at Hankey a few years earlier for the training of teachers and clergy:

I deem it right to state that it does not appear to me that the important objects contemplated by the Directors, in commencing the Seminary, are likely to be realized without a cost of time and money greater than they will feel justified in appropriating to the same, especially if the uncertainty of the issue be taken into consideration.

The native Churches have not hitherto and do not now contain young men of piety and talent or attainments to render them suitable for becoming students for the Christian ministry . . . The want of materials out of which to train a native ministry is not confined to the Colony, but extends to the stations beyond it . . .[24]

The attempt to establish a theological college at Hankey had been one of the last expressions of the John Philip approach to mission in South Africa and it had been entrusted to his son, Durant Philip. However, with the passing of John Philip, the Ellis view was soon absolutely dominant in the southern missionary world though Durant Philip was still endeavouring to bring about the opening of a theological college in the 1880s. When Ellis wrote the above report in 1855 there was not a single ordained African in the south, yet in the west Crowther had been ordained in 1843. He had been followed by ten more Anglicans as well as several Methodists in both Sierra Leone and the Gold Coast by 1856 when the first black South African was ordained—Tiyo Soga in Glasgow. Soga, however, had not a single successor for eleven years, by which time more than twenty further ordinations had taken place in the west.

By the mid-1860s the Methodists in South Africa were beginning to feel that, perhaps, some Africans might be ordained and they set four men aside. They were 'received on trial' by the Annual Conference of 1866.[25] At that moment the American Revivalist William Taylor arrived in South Africa. It was the remarkable success of his interpreters, in particular Charles Pamla, one of the four, in becoming themselves preachers of the revival, and even more

---

[24] J. Sales, *Mission Stations and the Coloured Communities 1800–1852* (1975), 132.
[25] W. G. Mills, 'The Taylor Revival of 1866 and the Roots of African Nationalism in the Cape Colony', *JRA* 8 (1976), 108.

effectively than Taylor, which demonstrated how fruitful an African clergy might be. This led at last to a number of ordinations. Nevertheless, they remained both few and poorly trained, very different, indeed, from the best of those now finding ordination in the west, several of whom had studied also in England or elsewhere. By 1879 there were still only five functioning black ministers in South Africa. Soga was dead and there was just one Methodist, one Anglican, and three Congregationalists. Presbyterians and Lutherans had none between them. By that time not only had Samuel Crowther been a bishop for fifteen years, supported by a couple of Yoruba archdeacons, but the Methodists too, in Sierra Leone, had an African General Superintendent in Charles Knight (since 1874). Furthermore some clergy in the west were by the late 1870s beginning to obtain BA degrees of Durham University from Fourah Bay. The gap of forty years separating Fort Hare from Fourah Bay is decisively indicative of the difference in missionary attitude and black clerical achievement between the two areas. But the gap in Methodist practice is equally noteworthy.

Even when black clergy became rather more numerous in the south in the 1880s they were shaped as an inferior group, both educationally and in status. They entirely lacked the ecclesiastical and cultural significance of their colleagues in the west. One can find no equivalent at all to men like Charles Knight, Archdeacon Crowther, or Archdeacon Henry Johnson. Their standing within the Church and the treatment they were accorded by white clergy reflected only too exactly the character of colonial society and its increasingly sharp racial structuring. It is unsurprising that so many fell away. It is noticeable that in the west, despite the disillusionment produced by the treatment of the Niger diocese in the 1890s, none of the leading clergy went into schism. In South Africa, on the contrary, the black clergy quickly saw how inferior was the role they were accorded and schisms from their ranks were numerous.

The third problem was that white South Africans did not want economically successful blacks. In encouraging black entrepreneurs, missionaries were in fact getting out of the colonial line. The Mvoti missionary might be proud that his parishioners 'are now competing with the white man in manufacturing sugar', but that was not good news for immigrant whites, themselves struggling for prosperity. The only thing they wanted of blacks was cheap labour, certainly not a competition which the blacks were only too likely to win. And it was whites who decided government policy. Until 1880 the Kholwa could be legally exempted from Native Law and therefore able to compete on an equal basis. From then on the value of exemption almost disappeared, and the incipient prosperity of economically successful Africans was blocked by a white community rapidly increasing through immigration, always needing more land, and fully resolved to ensure that black people would not be in a position to compete with them. Even the education of the black community deteriorated in the final decades of the century. While missionary aspirations had clearly been somewhat different from those of their racial community, they were not sufficiently different to bring about a battle to protect the economic prosperity of the Kholwa. That was the sort of thing John Philip could see fifty years earlier, and it was seeing such things that got him branded a political priest. Only a very unified campaign of protest could have done anything at all, and the likelihood of that was simply non-existent. The politics and economics of an increasingly racialist state determined in this too the shaping of African Christian life without any significant missionary protest. It was their own earlier failure to deracialize the ministry which ensured that they would not now resist more subtle policies which were, nevertheless, undermining much of the achievement of which they had been most proud.

From such circumstances there was, for the African Church, no real avenue of escape. The black Christian was restricted to an increasingly boring existence inside a sort of cultural no man's land, neither African nor European: forced or persuaded to abandon the one society but refused admittance to the other. That the explosion of independency, the ideal of Ethiopianism, once it began, should develop so fast in South Africa, and to an extent far beyond anything experienced elsewhere, seems hardly surprising. It does not require much special explanation. The mission Churches had been married to colonialism so profoundly and painfully in South Africa that there was bound in time to be a divorce of massive and bitter proportions. One has only to think of James Stewart of Lovedale, the quintessence of over-confident paternalism, yet still representative of the better end of the South African missionary world, to realize how impossible it would have been not to have had a major explosion.

In two areas, however, something rather different had been happening. The first to consider is that of the northern Tswana peoples, inhabiting the northern frontier of the new South Africa and living in geographical conditions not over-attractive for either settler or missionary. Here the power of African kings, kgosi, remained considerable, and the few missionaries at work, mostly members of the LMS, were still able to identify with black society as a more or less functional reality in a way hardly possible in more colonized areas. Already in the first half of the century Mothibi of the Tlhaping and Sechele of the Bakwena had become Christians. Mothibi was old and near to death, however, while Sechele was quickly excommunicated by Livingstone and left henceforth without a resident missionary. In many ways that suited Sechele, who found himself free to combine in his own way Christian faith and Bible knowledge with a great deal of Tswana custom. Sechele thus became, in a way, a pioneer in African Christian kingship. He proved it possible to combine the role of kingship, tied though it necessarily was within the web of traditional custom and belief, with the new status which membership of the religion of the conquerors could give. Perhaps Sechele did not benefit as a king as much as he might have done by his conversion, but he had shown that Christian kingship was a possibility, that Christianity could be made somehow compatible with the continued tribal life of the Tswana.

The Bamangwato were neighbours of the Bakwena and Sekhoma, their kgosi, the contemporary of Sechele. Like many kings, he welcomed a group of missionaries to his capital but had no intention of adopting their religion. His eldest son and heir, Khama, however, did so, being baptized in 1862. Khama's close relationship with the LMS missionary John Mackenzie became from then on a crucial factor in central African history. Sekhoma and Khama came quickly into conflict over the latter's refusal to participate in the circumcision ceremony of *bogwera*. In due course Khama defeated his father and became kgosi of the Bamangwato in 1872. This he remained until his death in 1923. For the late Victorian and Edwardian world Khama was the model African Christian king, the jewel in the crown of the London Missionary Society, the man who led his country to Christianity and influenced all the kings around him. In 1895 he went to London with two other chiefs in a deputation backed by the LMS to establish a British protectorate over Bechuanaland and prevent Cecil Rhodes from obtaining control over their country as he had done over Matabeleland.

Khama, unlike Sechele, gave up rain-making but benefited from missionary prayers for rain. He totally abandoned the circumcision ceremonies, and *bogwera* died away among the Ngwato. He encouraged schools instead. He even forbade *bogadi* (bride-wealth). Missionaries praised him for making such 'a clean cut with the heathen past'[26] and for prohibiting alcohol as well. He did indeed do everything that the mainstream Victorian Protestant missionary wanted of an African king. Khama had proved himself a brilliant fighter in an old-fashioned battle with the Ndebele and, over many years, he would prove himself a brilliant diplomatist in new-fashioned battles with the powerful within a white-dominated world. He was in this rather like Menelik. His kingdom grew in size as did that of Ethiopia, and both rulers won the decisive battle over their European aggressor in 1895: Menelik at Adwa, Khama in London over Rhodes. If his kingship forfeited some of its traditional props through his emphatic Christianity, it clearly profited more than it lost. 'The Lord Jesus Christ . . . made me a chief,' he could declare to a missionary.[27] He had found it true and he had also found that it worked very well. He ruled in things religious almost as much as in things secular. While at first it must have appeared that he did what his LMS missionary told him to do, in due course the relationship was effectively reversed. What was established in his kingdom was a State Church, closely controlled by the king. Other Churches were not permitted to enter. Local clergy were very few. While it pleased the missionary world to have so Christian a monarch, as proof of the success of their work, it would appear that the Ngwato Church itself was anything but lively and extremely few Ngwato ever became Christians (only 7 per cent according to the 1946 census).[28] In Khama it could appear to be Tswana kingship which had triumphed—at a time when so many other African kings were losing their authority—rather than Christianity. Yet the legacy of his fifty years of reign left not only to his own people but to the whole of Botswana a public commitment both to Christianity and to modernization which has in fact served the country extremely well. Perhaps it would be appropriate to compare him not only with Menelik but with Afonso I of Kongo.

[26] F. Wilson and D. Perrot (eds.), *Outlook on a Century* (Lovedale, 1973), 186.

[27] Ø. Gulbrandsen, 'Missionaries and Northern Tswana Rulers: Who Used Whom?', *JRA* 23 (1993), 66.

[28] I. Schapera, *Christianity and the Tswana* (1958), 4. Among the neighbouring Kgatla, evangelized by a Dutch Reformed Mission, *bogadi* was compulsory for Christians. In 1946 they comprised 65% of the population.

The second area we need to consider is the heartland of Xhosa Christianity. When Ntsikana died in 1820 immediate leadership of his group of Xhosa Christians fell to Soga, a leading councillor of Ngqika, the paramount chief, but also a devoted disciple of Ntsikana. He led the group which came to be described as 'the congregation of the God of Ntsikana'[29] to the mission at Chumie, yet he himself did not settle down at the mission but some miles away, on his own homestead as headman of the area. His senior wife and his sons were baptized, but he retained his eight wives while continuing Ntsikana's practice of twice-daily prayer. He would only allow Ntsikana's own hymns to be sung in his services, he became a very successful farmer, the first person to use a plough, he still consulted diviners, he defended the wearing of red ochre, and he took a consistently Xhosa political line, fighting against the Colony in several wars, unlike most mission people. Missionaries could not ignore Soga. He and Jan Tshatshu were by far the most important Xhosa to have come under Christian influence, but he profoundly irritated them. He was so very independent a man.

Soga's sons were more evidently Christianized. One of them, Tiyo, became the very model of the missionary vision of African Christianity. From studying at Lovedale, he was sent to Scotland. After very successful studies there, he was ordained in Glasgow and returned to Africa with a Scottish wife to found a mission at Mgwali in 1857, in the aftermath of the great cattle-killing. In many ways the hysteria of that year, in which the slaughter of tens of thousands of cattle was expected by those Xhosa who believed in it to lead to the return of the ancestors and their cattle out of the depths of the earth, led to the destruction of the Xhosa kingdom more completely than anything else. It did so because the British Governor, Sir George Grey, exploited it quite ruthlessly to that end. Old Soga had not been one of the believers and he had strongly advised his paramount, Sandile, not to kill his cattle. But the unbelievers suffered in the end from British hands almost as badly as the believers. It was in that context that Tiyo began his ministry, gathering the core of 'the congregation of the God of Ntsikana' around him at Mgwali. Festiri Soga, Tiyo's elder brother, and Dukwana, Ntsikana's son, became two of his elders. When they had completed the building of a church of wattle and daub and the people gathered to open it with the

---

[29] John Knox Bokwe, *Ntsikana: The Story of an African Convert* (Lovedale, 1914), 55.

singing of Ntsikana's Great Hymn, Robert Johnson, a missionary who was hearing the hymn for the first time, reported that 'men as well as women were affected to tears. The sobbing competed with the singing and the service was in danger of being interrupted altogether.'[30]

Tiyo Soga combined the Ntsikana tradition of a very consciously Xhosa Christianity with all that was required of a Scottish Presbyterian minister. He saw at once that Christians should be living in the villages rather than at the 'station'. He could travel thirty miles with his notebook to record details of Xhosa history and custom, but he could still be much distressed when boys in his school (including, maybe, sons of Dukwana) organized a rite of circumcision. He had not been circumcised himself, unlike Jan Tshatshu's son. It is interesting that the unbaptized Soga had, in this, been more amenable to missionary teaching than the baptized Tshatshu. Tiyo wrote many hymns, translated Pilgrim's Progress into Xhosa as well as parts of the New Testament, and preached with considerable power, yet he recognized that Dukwana far excelled him both in eloquence and in a knowledge of Xhosa tradition. 'I would give anything to possess this power of Dukwana,' Tiyo whispered on one occasion to Johnson. 'He is the orator of our tribe and the orator of our mission.'[31] Johnson remembered too how, after a hard day's work, it was Dukwana who kept them up through the night listening spellbound to his stories and experiences.

Tiyo Soga died young, in 1871. Ill for some time but still struggling on with his New Testament translation, he laid it down at the end of chapter 23 of the Acts with a scribbled note of explanation, 'I have lost strength.'[32] 'He has gone to heaven to meet great men of his people who died in the faith from Ntsikana down,' it was declared in his Xhosa funeral oration.[33] In the end, even with the Glasgow-trained minister, that was the succession which counted. Tiyo's elder and colleague in the ministry of his parish, Dukwana, was to live another six years. Unlike Tiyo, Dukwana was not absorbed so coherently within the boundaries of missionary expectation. Yet he

---

[30] R. Johnson, 'Personal Reminiscences of Sandilli and Dukwana' *Kaffrarian Watchman* (16 Sept. 1878), quoted in J. Hodgson, 'Soga and Dukwana: The Christian Struggle for Liberation in Mid-Nineteenth Century South Africa', *JRA* 16 (1986), 201.
[31] Ibid.
[32] J.A.C. (J. A. Chalmers), 'Tiyo Soga: Minister', in Wilson and Perrot, *Outlook on a Century*, 52.   [33] Ibid. 53.

served the Church dutifully for fifty years. In frontier war after frontier war he had endeavoured to stand somehow between the two sides, remembering presumably the pacifism of his father. Finally in the Ninth Frontier War of 1877, he felt he could temporize no longer and he joined Sandile in fighting the British. 'I am not fighting Civilization or Christianity,' he declared, 'they have brought me great benefits; and most of all they have taught me how I may be saved. But I am fighting against the English who have robbed us of our country and are destroying our people.'[34] Unlike the rest of Sandile's forces, who wore the red ochre of tradition, Dukwana kept to his yellow cord trousers, his shirt, and his vest. Thus he died, defending his chief, and thus was his body found lying hidden in the bush. Old Soga, too, well into his eighties, was killed in this war, speared by a roving band of government auxiliaries.

Dukwana, Tiyo, and old Soga are important, not just because they were all three very remarkable people, but because they represent in three different ways a single tradition. Old Soga stands upon the one side, Tiyo upon the other, Dukwana somewhere in the middle. A half-century after Ntsikana they demonstrate that his legacy of a Xhosa Christianity spiritually free of missionary control remained a reality, hard as that was in the South Africa of the later nineteenth century. And behind Ntsikana one can still just detect the power of Van der Kemp, an influence so profoundly different from that of most of his successors. The tradition did not die with Dukwana.

It is striking to note how the appeal back to Ntsikana grows if anything stronger, and more varied, in the years after the death of the son who most resembled him. Little more than a year later John Knox Bokwe published an account of 'Ntsikana and his Hymn' in five instalments in the *Christian Express*. Bokwe, W. W. Ggoba, John Muir Vimbe, S. E. K. Mqhayi, Nkohla Falati, Alan Kirkland Soga (Tiyo's son), and William Kobe Ntsikana (the prophet's grandson) were all writers, poets, and teachers of the 1880s and 1890s consciously influenced by Ntsikana.[35] They represent what may well be called the Xhosa origins of 'Ethiopianism'. While the flowering of that movement would be after 1890, it was well rooted in the Xhosa Christianity of previous generations. If Ntsikana had provided the

---

[34] Hodgson, 'Soga and Dukwana', 204.
[35] J. Hodgson, 'Ntsikana: History and Symbol. Studies in a Process of Religious Change among Xhosa-Speaking People', Ph.D. thesis (Cape Town, 1985), 377–88.

root, Tiyo and Dukwana were the trunk carrying 'Ntsikana's Vision' (to make use of the title of a poem published in 1897 by one of Tiyo's sons and later set to music by John Knox Bokwe) across to the much enlarged Xhosa Christian community of the late nineteenth century. But they also themselves became part of the legacy. Ten of Tiyo's own hymns were included in a Xhosa hymn-book published shortly after his death. Mqhayi, when a schoolboy at Lovedale about 1888, recited the whole of the first chapter of Tiyo's *Pilgrim's Progress* in an elocution competition with such vivacity that onlookers wondered about his sanity. They were in fact listening to someone who was to become the greatest of Xhosa writers of both prose and poetry. For the development of Mqhayi, Bokwe, and their generation, Lovedale was absolutely needed to provide the books and the literary confidence, but Ntsikana and Tiyo were needed to provide the underlying, unitive inspiration.

From the origins of Xhosa Christianity in the early nineteenth century to the establishment of the Ntsikana Memorial Association in 1909 and beyond, a unifying mythology was provided by the figure of the prophet whom the Memorial Association would proclaim a saint. It was that symbol which empowered the culture of Christian Xhosaness actually to enhance its identity in the face of a ceaseless forward march of a racialist colonialism and of a missionary paternalism which could, especially at Lovedale, provide a useful education, but, once the education was given, could not adapt to the consequence of its own success. The 1870s and 1880s were not, in South Africa, an era of obvious black Christian achievement, despite the growth in number, wealth, and education of the Kholwa. The growth was too clearly threatened by the very forces which had encouraged it. Nevertheless, a growth in maturity can all the same be discerned, a growth which was at the same time, and quite especially, an exercise in perseverance.

v. *Buganda: Conversion, Martyrdom, and Civil War in the 1880s*

On 15 November 1875 a letter from Henry Stanley appeared in the *Daily Telegraph*. Written from the kingdom of Buganda, stretching along the the north-west shore of the vast inland sea we know as Lake Victoria, it described its monarch Mutesa, the conditions for an ideal mission, and the character of the missionary required: 'Mutesa would give him anything he desired, houses, land, cattle, ivory. He might call a province his own in a day . . . He must belong to no nation in particular, but to the entire white race.' Odd as this appeal may sound, it was very beguiling. Here apparently was something very different from the ill-populated, disordered, and poverty-stricken lands described in most of Livingstone's travels in eastern Africa. Buganda was highly populated, effectively governed, and very welcoming. Two great missionary societies, Protestant and Catholic, at once made up their minds to send men to Buganda—the CMS in London, the White Fathers in French North Africa. It deeply distressed the former that the latter were as bent as they on responding to Stanley's call, but neither would pull back, and in consequence the Christian history of Buganda would be character-ized from the start by a double identity: Anglican and British, Catholic and French. The CMS first arrived in June 1877, the White Fathers in February 1879, but, as the first CMS party did not stay long, its effective presence hardly began before Alexander Mackay's arrival in November 1878 only three months prior to that of his great rival, Simeon Lourdel.

Buganda provides us with the first really vigorous re-entry of Catholics into our story. It cannot be questioned that the middle part of the nineteenth century was above all a Protestant age, and it is Protestants that we have quite correctly been considering hitherto in this chapter, even exclusively. There was, however, a Catholic presence in various parts of the continent, so, before we continue with the history of Buganda, let us briefly survey Catholic Africa of the third quarter of the century—a survey not of missions but of local clergy as representative of Churches in some way equivalent to Crowther or Tiyo Soga. There are only three areas which really deserve attention: northern Ethiopia, Angola, and Senegal.

The most lively little Catholic Church in the middle of the century was that founded, as we saw in Chapter 6, by de Jacobis in Ethiopia. Its most distinguished priest, Gebra-Mika'el, died in prison in 1855, but around him was a whole group of others, some of whom were still active at the start of the twentieth century. De Jacobis ordained no fewer than forty-six priests between 1847 and his death in 1860, many of them married men. There was no other comparable body of local Catholic priests anywhere in Africa, but in Angola there was a succession of African clergy throughout the nineteenth century, among whom we may recall two, Pedro de S. Salvador, the son of

Garcia V of Kongo, who ministered in Loanda until his death in 1851, and Antonio Francisco das Necessidades.[36] The latter was the 'Canon of the Church' whom Livingstone encountered in Pungo Andongo in December 1854, 'a woolly-headed black, yet a dignitary of the Church, universally respected for his virtues'.[37] A native of Loanda, ordained in 1821, he had been Vicar-General in Kongo, 1845–7, had crowned Henrique II and baptized 107,890 persons, as well as instituting seventy Knights of Christ. He had then gone on a mission to Lisbon, accompanying a young Kongolese prince, before meeting Livingstone in Pungo Andongo. But, as Livingstone also reported, the mission stations inland from Loanda were now deserted, though the bedsteads still stood in the dormitories and fruit trees grew in their gardens. In 1835 there were still more than twenty African priests in Angola. Twenty years later there were five, and only some fifteen more were ordained between 1840 and 1870. The Church of Angola was slowly receding, much as the Church in the Kongo had earlier receded, effectively abandoned by the larger world while being quietly swallowed up by the beliefs of rural tradition. In Senegal too there were a few priests, though still less of anything that could be described as a local Church. Mother Javouhey had taken three young men to France and placed them in a seminary. David Boilat, Arsene Fridoil, and Pierre Moussa were ordained in Paris in 1840, but their ministry in Senegal ended when they were dismissed by the missionary authorities on account of some rather vague charges, though Boilat returned to France and worked there impressively for many decades.[38] Another Senegalese, Guillaume Jouga, was ordained in 1864 and ministered in Senegal until his death in 1875, to be followed by a few others.

Sudan, too, may merit a mention. The Sudanese mission produced two African priests in the later nineteenth century, though neither was able to work in his own country. Mgr. Comboni was accompanied in 1873 by a Benedictine, Dom Pio Giuseppe Hadrian of Subiaco. He was a Sudanese who had been carried as a child into

---

[36] See the list in A. Brasio, *Historia e Missiologia* (Luanda, 1973), 886–925, though curiously he excludes das Necessidades, for whom see L. Jadin, 'Les Survivances chrétiennes au Congo au xixe siècle', *RHA* 1 (1970), 137–85.

[37] *Livingstone's Missionary Correspondence*, 273.

[38] D. Jones, 'The Catholic Mission and Some Aspects of Assimilation in Senegal 1817–1850', *JAH* 21 (1980), 323–40, Y. Bouquillon and R. Cornevin, *David Boilat (1814–1901): Le précurseur* (Dakar, 1981). Boilat's work *Esquisses sénégalaises*, first published in Paris in 1853, was republished in 1984.

slavery, rescued in Cairo by an Italian priest, and taken to Rome. He was, however, already ill when he returned to Africa and died shortly after arriving at al-Ubayyid. About the same time Comboni freed a young Dinka slave, who was sent to Italy to study and later ordained in Cairo in 1885: Fr. Daniel Deng Farim Sorur, the first Dinka priest. He died in Egypt in 1899.[39] Elsewhere there were catechists who held little Church communities together in the absence of any priest, a pattern far more characteristic of Catholic ministry in Africa. Such a one was Pa Antonio, head of the Church in Lagos in the 1850s and 1860s. Born in São Tomé around 1800 and taken to Brazil as a slave, he was freed and taught by Carmelites in Bahia. He returned to Africa and shepherded the Catholic community in Lagos, which consisted mostly of returned Brazilians and Cubans. When an SMA missionary arrived in Lagos in 1866 he found Pa Antonio baptizing, blessing marriages and holy water, praying with the dying, and presiding over funerals.[40] Nowhere, however, in the 1860s or 1870s do we find what could fairly be described as a vigorous local Catholic Church in any way comparable with the Protestant Churches in the west and south. That is just one of the reasons why what happened in Buganda after 1879 represents for African Church history a very fresh beginning.

The Buganda in which the missionaries had arrived was a prosperous, well-organized, and militant kingdom, dominated by its kabaka or king, Mutesa. About that at least Stanley had been correct. Indeed the dominance was such that while Mutesa was glad enough to have no fewer than two groups of Europeans in his country to add to the Arabs already there, he made absolutely sure that they should never leave his court. Cardinal Lavigerie had promised that his White Fathers would stay well away from their Protestant rivals. It could not be. They were all to be firmly retained at Mengo, as Mutesa's mentors about the world, its politics and religion, pleasant conversationalists, or just playthings. Ganda government was highly centralized, but, unlike so many African societies, it was not at all gerontocratic. Each county or *ssaza* had its own chief, but these were appointed by the king and participated closely in the central

---

[39] E. Toniolo and R. Hill (eds.), *The Opening of the Nile Basin* (1974), 20, 196–203; see the photograph of Fr. Deng with Comboni reproduced in D. McEwan, *A Catholic Sudan: Dream, Mission, Reality* (Rome, 1987), 87.

[40] E. Isichei, 'An Obscure Man: Pa Antonio', in E. Isichei (ed.), *Varieties of Christian Experience in Nigeria* (1982), 28–33.

hierarchy of government headed by a chief minister, the katikiro. The religion of the country was a complex polytheism, somewhat similar to Yoruba religion, in which a number of powerful gods, the *balubaale*, had their own temples and priests, some of which practised human sacrifice. A high god, Katonda, had one or two small temples but appears to have been little attended to in the nineteenth century, whatever earlier may have been the case.

For fifty years before the arrival of the missionaries there had been Arabs at the court of Mengo and quite a number of Baganda had become Muslims. They had already adopted Katonda as the name for Allah, and in due course Christians would take this over without question. Mutesa had toyed with Islam as later he toyed with Christianity. His secretary was an Arab. A mosque had been built within the royal enclosure. Mutesa had once observed the fast of Ramadan and twice declared Buganda an Islamic state, but when Muslims at the court were too forthright, he had turned on them and executed a considerable number. Buganda in the 1870s was by no means a Muslim country, but it was one which looked likely to become one, little by little, much as many a West African monarchy was slowly Islamized. It was again in this not at all unlike Yorubaland at the same period.

It was the young men serving in and around the court of Mutesa, some of them drawn from the best families and training for chieftainship and war or already occupying minor offices, who had been attracted by Islam, but few of them were fully converted. Baganda appear as deeply averse to circumcision. It was among such people that the missionaries, Catholic and Protestant, quickly found hearers and readers. Standard missiology has portrayed the arrival of two competing societies, each prepared to denounce the other when necessary, as an evangelical disaster in a most promising field. The evidence suggests the contrary. It was the very tension between the two—as between both and Islam—which created a genuinely intellectual challenge and made Christianity so intriguingly appealing. It would not be very long before young Baganda could be heard discussing the merits and demerits of Henry VIII or of praying to Mary.

Cardinal Lavigerie sent instructions to his missionaries in 1879, forbidding them to baptize any convert, except in the case of the dying, before completion of a four-year catechumenate. So sure, however, were Lourdel and Livinhac of the quality of their best young men that before these precise commands arrived they had already baptized eight in March and May of 1880, hardly a year after their arrival. In 1882, after protests to Lavigerie and some mitigation in severity of the rule, they baptized eight more, including Joseph Mukasa Balikuddembe, Andrew Kaggwa, Luke Banabakintu, and Matthias Kalemba, four future martyrs. Later that year the White Fathers withdrew from the country to a station south of the lake. For some reason, not well identified, they had become discouraged and frightened, and for two and a half years, November 1882 to July 1885, they were completely absent from Buganda. In 1882 the first Protestant baptisms were performed and a good many more the next year. Mackay did not leave the country, and his influence remained considerable. Mutesa died in 1884, to be replaced by one of his young sons, the unstable Mwanga.

It is important for any understanding of the Christianization of Buganda to pause at that point, well before the beginning of any persecution, because what had happened was already quite remarkably out of line with missionary experience anywhere else. The behaviour of Mutesa can be closely paralleled by that of many another king. What cannot be paralleled is the speedy individual conversion, in a wholly non-colonial situation, of a large number— perhaps several hundred—of mostly young people who were not slaves or outcasts, who were not obtaining the protection of a mission station, but who represented many of the most intelligent among the up-and-coming governing élite.

It is impossible quite to explain the dynamics of conversion, whether personal or collective. In Buganda at this point when an immense process of change was just beginning, one has upon one side the personalities of the main missionaries, Lourdel and Mackay, both unusually interesting, and the dialectic of interaction of the two missions. Upon another side one can point out the quite exceptional interest the converts showed in learning to read and in the acquiring of new information. Different again was the appeal of a very other-worldly gospel, the message of heaven, and of a very high moral code embraced by many of the early converts with extraordinary enthusiasm. Put the stress where you will, already by 1882 a collective movement of conversion was under way which nothing would be able to hold back and over which the missionaries themselves had remarkably little control.

It is very striking how when the White Fathers left, after just over three years in the country, the little group of Catholics had already the confidence to stand on their own and grow still more numerous, rather than be reabsorbed in the company attached to Mackay. Several of them had in fact at the beginning regularly visited both missions. Thus all four of those mentioned above among the early Catholic baptisms had earlier been reading St Matthew's Gospel and the Acts of the Apostles with Mackay. In the absence of the White Fathers men like Mukasa and Kaggwa became both Church leaders and evangelists, baptizing the sick, catechizing new recruits. Mukasa in his early twenties was a trusted personal attendant to the King and took the lead among Christians in the inner court. Fifty miles away at Mityana, a place no missionary had ever visited, a considerable community was growing up around Matthias Kalemba, a most remarkable man in his forties. A Musoga who had been captured as a child by a Ganda raiding party, he had in time become the Mulumba or steward of the county chief of Ssingo. Of Kalemba, Lourdel reported in his diary for 7 June 1880: 'Yesterday, a young man among our catechumens, an overseer of the slaves of a great chief called Mukwenda, an ex-disciple of the Protestants and owner of a large number of women, sent them all away except one and then came to ask us to baptize him.'[41] Banabakintu was also in the service of the county chief at Mityana. The two were baptized together in 1882, and by 1886 there were, it was claimed, some 200 believing Christians gathered around them at Mityana.

It is clear that in each case strong early converts quickly built up a group in their vicinity. While Catholics and Protestants did not see themselves as sharply divided at this stage, they were in fact developing in separate areas. The presence of Mukasa Balikuddembe among the pages of the inner court ensured that this would be a predominantly Catholic area, and after his death leadership here was at once taken over by other Catholics like Charles Lwanga and Honorat Nyonyintono. In the stores, on the other hand, the leadership of the assistant treasurer, Apolo Kagwa, ensured a Protestant community. Outside the palace but in its close vicinity there was the important Catholic cluster at Natete around the houses of Kisule the gunsmith and Andrew Kaggwa, the royal bandmaster, while at Kasengezi there was a comparable Protestant meeting-place at the home of Nuwa Walukaga, the chief blacksmith.

[41] J. Faupel, *African Holocaust* (1962), 31.

The transformation in the Catholic community which Lourdel recognized on his return to Mengo in July 1885 was enormous. Everything that happens later derives from this very early experience of an almost self-directed and staggeringly confident Christianity. The court of Mwanga was, if anything, even more unpredictable than that of Mutesa. While the new Kabaka at first sympathized with his Christian age-mates in hostility to the older pagan chiefs and especially the Katikiro, Mukasa, whom he had inherited from his father, their clear dependence on an authority other than his own and their willingness even to speak in criticism of his behaviour quickly led him to turn back to seek the support of the Katikiro, a man increasingly worried by the Christian phenomenon and particularly by the influence of his namesake, Joseph Mukasa Balikuddembe.

At that point the Anglican Bishop Hannington was on his way to Buganda, approaching it not from across the lake as all the missionaries had done hitherto but overland from the east. It was regarded by the Baganda as dangerous to allow anyone to enter the kingdom that way while an English bishop sounded powerful and dangerous in himself. With every year that passed the stories of British power grew more impressive. Mwanga was frightened and gave orders that Hannington should be arrested and murdered, which he was at the end of October 1885. Once it was done, however, Mwanga was alarmed that his responsibility for the deed should be known by Europeans. Joseph Mukasa Balikuddembe he saw as to blame. Mukasa had rebuked him over the murder and must surely have passed on the truth to the missionaries. Mwanga worked himself into a fury and ordered Mukasa's execution. He was taken away, but the executioner hesitated to carry out the order, anticipating a possible reprieve for the King's close friend. The Katikiro, however, sent a further order to ensure that the execution took place without delay. It was carried out only a little before a reprieve did in fact arrive from Mwanga. Here, as in the large-scale persecution of six months later, the process was sudden, arbitrary, unsystematic. If Mwanga was responsible for part of it, the Katikiro Mukasa and other senior chiefs were also behind it. But neither had any desire systematically to eliminate the Christian community. The aim was rather to intimidate, to get rid of rivals, to make clear that the Kabaka should be obeyed, not foreign missionaries.

Mwanga was furious that his Christian servants refused to go to bed with him and were even attempting to subvert those of his pages still willing to commit sodomy. There was also anger that the newly baptized Princess Nalumansi, a daughter of Mutesa, on being appointed guardian of the tomb of Kabaka Jjunju, made a bonfire of all the pagan charms she found in the custodian's house. On 22 May 1886 her mother presented her with her umbilical cord, a symbol of the womb and of the totality of ancestral religion. The princess cut it up and threw it away. She, like the young men baptized with her, had all the religious ruthlessness of the newly converted, wholly uncompromising in both what she rejected and what she accepted. Such behaviour appeared outrageous to Ganda public opinion: this was what Christianity led one to. No more than twelve days later, 3 June, thirty-one Christians—both Catholic and Protestant—were burnt together in a great holocaust at Namugongo. Others were speared, hacked to pieces, or left to die by the roadside in agony.

Charles Lwanga had taken over the leadership in the court at Mukasa's death. That very day he had been baptized by Lourdel. He was burnt alone at Namugongo a few hours before the others. The constancy, indeed near ecstasy, with which many of these martyrs—there were probably towards 100 in all—went to their deaths was in part an expression of Ganda custom, but it was also a demonstration of the sheer strength of their Christian faith and ardent anticipation of heaven. 'Weraba, munnange. Goodbye, my friend, we shall meet again in heaven,' remarked Matthias Kalemba to Luke Banabakintu, shortly before he was killed with extravagant cruelty. 'Yes, with Katonda, with God,' replied Luke.[42] Yet, if some Christians almost sought the triumph of martyrdom, others prudently avoided it if they could. Moreover, if in the early stages of the persecution it was almost sufficient for one to be a Christian to be executed, neither Mwanga nor his councillors really intended to wipe out the Christian community. Once a number had died and anger had subsided, it could be safe for known Christians to return to court. Some were protected all along because they were too useful to lose or someone powerful was too fond of them. Kisule the gunsmith could not be spared, though, it seems, Walukaga the blacksmith could be. Apolo Kagwa, the storemaster, was flogged and wounded, but it seemed a pity to lose him. Honorat Nyonyintono, majordomo in the court, was castrated but survived. The Katikiro, regarded as a bitter anti-

[42] Ibid. 177.

Christian, in fact successfully protected two leading Christians, Nikodemo Sebwato and Alikisi Ssebowa, both in his service.

There was, then, no clear pattern of who died and who lived. The account of an incident in Apolo Kagwa's *Ebika Bya Buganda* shows it well:

Zakariya Kizito and Nuwa Walukaga remained where they were and prepared to be arrested. After a short time had passed, they saw in the distance the chief executioner as he was approaching to seize them . . . It was at this moment that Kizito was given to remember how it is written in Matthew 10: 22–3, 'That man will be saved who endures to the last. Only, if they persecute you in one city, take refuge in another.' And when he had remembered that, he stood up and said to his friend: 'Let us flee, because God has directed us to go.' But his companion refused. Then he turned to prayer a second time, and when he had finished praying, he stood up quickly and entered the place of Prince Kiwewa, where he hid himself. But when he had just left Nuwa Walukaga, the executioners came and seized Walukaga and took him away.[43]

Kagwa adds that Zakariya 'very wisely' decided to remain in hiding until the persecution was over. A couple of years before, he had for a while refused baptism because unable to give up all his wives. After the persecution he became one of the principal Protestant leaders, was ordained a deacon in 1893, and was appointed with Apolo Kagwa one of the kingdom's three regents in 1897. Zakariya proved, in time, like Kagwa himself, an able politician. Perhaps the note was already there in the young man of 1886. What is certain is that it was absent in the captains of the first line, in Lwanga, Kalemba, or Andrew Kaggwa. Their intense supernaturalism was very different from the politicism of the man who thought it 'very wise' to run away from martyrdom. Yet from the viewpoint of the community as well as that of the earthly career of Zakariya it was wise. At the time of persecution Walukaga was a very senior Christian as Zakariya was not. He was one of the first elders and a member since the previous year of the first Church Council. Before the incident described, Walukaga had already made up his mind. His wife and children had been sent to safety. He remained at home calmly awaiting his killers. He would be among the thirty-one to burn on the pyre at Namugongo. For Ganda Christianity it proved important that some like Walukaga stood their ground and died but that others like

[43] J. Rowe, 'The Purge of Christians at Mwanga's Court', *JAH* 5 (1964), 59.

Zakariya Kizito Kisingiri 'very wisely' escaped when they could. The one group canonized their cause, the other survived to fight another day.

The persecution quickly subsided though not completely for many months. It left a Church still with plenty of leaders as well as an increased sense of history and mission. Nyonyintono was soon back in favour at court, as influential as Mukasa Balikuddembe or Lwanga had ever been. He, Sebbowa, Kisule, and Stanislas Mugwanya were now the Catholic leaders, Apolo Kagwa, Sebwato, and Kisingiri the Protestant. The effect of the persecution was less to intimidate the Christians than to destabilize the State. Mwanga did not want to crush the young in favour of the old. He disliked the conservative chiefs who had been his allies in attacking the Christians, and soon veered back to favouring both Muslims and Christians. In the very confused conditions of the next two years, the number of the latter multiplied (though few were baptized), but quality declined as Catholics, Protestants, and Muslims began to arm and turn themselves—apparently at first with Mwanga's blessing—into 'regiments' or parties. Inevitably the King took alarm and planned to rid himself of these increasingly unrulable minorities. The plan failed and a *coup* followed.

In September 1888 Mwanga was deposed, and a joint Muslim–Christian regime appointed a new kabaka, Mutesa's eldest son, Kiwewa. Nyonyintono became Katikiro and the great offices of state were divided between Christians and Muslims. A month later the Muslims staged a second *coup*, this time against the Christians, who were outmanoeuvred and fled from the capital. The missionaries were at once imprisoned and deported. A few weeks later Kiwewa was also deposed and a genuinely Muslim kabaka installed, Kalema. Enforced Islamization of the country ensued.

Mwanga had fled on deposition south across the lake and soon found himself the penitent guest of the White Fathers in their station of Bukumbi. The Christians, meanwhile, had retreated westwards, throwing themselves upon the hospitality of the kingdom of Ankole. Each leader set off with his party of followers and as many guns as he could lay hands on. Soon they were numerous enough to advance back into the country, setting up a base on the border in Kabula. Over the next fifteen months civil war raged, with its fortunes going to and fro. The Christians needed a king and persuaded Mwanga to return as their sovereign. They also needed more guns. In both they were helped by Charles Stokes, who had come out to Buganda as a CMS missionary ten years before but had later taken an African wife and turned to trade in guns and ivory. It was Stokes who brought Mwanga across the lake together with guns and ammunition. The support of a gun-runner who had not lost his Christian sympathies may well have done more to save Christianity in Uganda than the work of any of his former colleagues.

Guns encouraged one, but they were seldom fired very accurately and battles were won far more by spears and the heroism of one or another leader. The Christians suffered a huge blow when Nyonyintono fell at the extremely hard-fought battle of Mawuki, and they never quite overcame their loss because Nyonyintono appears as the one man capable of holding Catholics and Protestants together. While Apolo Kagwa was fairly clearly the principal Protestant leader, the Catholics had no one else with the clear primacy of Nyonyintono or an ability to halt the increasing tension between the two groups. It was in Kabula that their political rivalry took shape. Only the Muslim peril held them together. If the Christians won, it was because the Islamizing policies and great cruelties of Kalema brought the mass of pagans increasingly to their side and to that of Mwanga, the legitimate king. Coupled with this was sea power. The pagans of the Ssese Islands backed Mwanga, and it was their control of the lake which gave the party of Mwanga, now established on Bulingugwe Island quite close to the capital, its chief superiority. Only across the lake could fresh guns and ammunition, needed by both sides, arrive. The Muslims endeavoured to break the blockade with two heavily loaded Arab dhows. When news of this reached Bulingugwe, Gabrieli Kintu, most audacious of the younger group of Christian leaders, led an attack on them just after their arrival at Entebbe and succeeded in setting both ablaze. By so doing he may well have won the war. In February as commander-in-chief of the combined forces of Catholics and Protestants, he finally recaptured the capital, driving out the Muslims and restoring Mwanga. Meanwhile, the missionaries had returned, first to Bulingugwe and then to Mengo, while the chieftainships were at once divided between Catholics and Protestants to the complete exclusion of Muslims and the almost complete exclusion of their pagan allies. Henceforth the king's power would essentially depend upon the consent of a new and Christian chieftainship. While the old rules of which clan could hold which office were fully respected, the most decisive rule henceforth for high office was not only being a Christian, but being a Christian who had gone through persecution and civil war. It mattered enormously that you had been in Kabula. It mattered enormously that you had fought bravely. But it mattered most of all that you were an accepted member of the Catholic or the Protestant Church.

Conversion in Buganda was from the start conversion at the heart of society. The inability of the King to convert had been side-stepped by a sufficiently numerous group of important people, mostly quite young, for whom Christianity had come to mean a very great deal. Some had given up numerous wives. Some had suffered severely in the persecution. They all reverenced the missionaries almost excessively. They had made the words of Scripture their law, often turning to it for guidance in moments of crisis. They felt themselves totally different from both pagan and Muslim, and they did their best to implement Christianity in any way they knew—by keeping Sunday, by declaring the abolition of slavery once they regained the capital, by instructing their followers and calling them to prayer. Few indeed in the Christian army were baptized, but all were expected to pray. It was in the course of the war that Christianity ceased to be the religion of an élite and became, instead, a mass movement. 'A sort of Twilight Christianity', the newly arrived CMS missionary Walker called it gloomily on Bulingugwe,[44] but it was a very determined Christianity for all that, and it had grown hugely in size just while the missionaries were absent. It had also grown, fairly devastatingly, in its rift between the two Churches and it would soon seem as hard for Protestants and Catholics to live together in one land—despite the fact that they shared the same clans, often the same family connections, and the same experience of persecution and war—as it had been for Christians and Muslims.

The intense spiritual experience of the 1880s would not be maintained by all the Christian pioneers. They would travel in various directions in the years of peace, but quite a few would continue doggedly faithful to the commitments of the era of heroism through a very long life. Ham Mukasa had lodged with Walukaga before the persecution began. In 1888 he had fled to Ankole. In 1889 he was a member of Kintu's attack on the Arab dhows at Entebbe. He

[44] M. Wright, *Buganda in the Heroic Age* (1971), 104. Wright's discussion of the subject is very helpful.

became county chief of Kyagwe in 1905, was a model if eccentric Christian patrician in all sorts of ways, and only died in 1956. For half a century and more Ganda Christianity would flourish, almost self-consciously, in the aura produced by the 1880s. It created the consciousness of a Christian nation with a high sense of mission but also an almost excessive pride in the superiority thus achieved. Christianity did not replace the traditional culture of Buganda. It merged with it, almost consecrating a commitment to tradition in regard to all sorts of things which elsewhere Christianity was more likely to challenge.

1890, where we leave this story for a while, remains a hinge year for Ganda Christianity as for so much in African history. It was the year the capital was recaptured. It was also the year that the two pioneer missionaries, Mackay and Lourdel, died while both still at work in East Africa. And it was the year that saw Captain Lugard of the British East Africa Company arrive in the capital in December. Nine days later Bishop Tucker arrived too, the first Anglican bishop to do so although the third to attempt it. For Lugard and Tucker what now appeared most important was a good, strong dose of *Pax Britannica* to bring all the feuding to an end. It did not work quite like that and Lugard's own share of responsibility for causing the next civil war, between Catholic and Protestant, in January 1892 should not be underestimated. Anyway, like it or not, independence was out, colonial rule was in, though to many people in London as in Buganda that was not immediately clear.

Probably no observer quite realized the wider significance of what had happened in Buganda in the 1880s. It was seen more as problem or as opportunity than as achievement—naturally enough, as so little had been done by the missionaries themselves. Yet a movement of religious conversion and political revolution had in no more than ten years provided for African Christianity as a whole a major new powerhouse, a new model of conversion, new saints to emulate. Nowhere else did such things ever happen so fast or so effectively. But for the effect of what took place in Buganda in the 1880s to be as widespread as it was over the next twenty years, it probably was necessary that *Pax Britannica* should intervene at that point. The Ganda Church and its amazing early self-confidence owed nothing to colonialism, and probably never could have existed like that if the colonial regime had arrived first. Having done it for themselves, however, the Baganda were able to take advantage of the arrival of the British Empire to spread their new beliefs far and wide upon less favoured peoples. More than any other nation, except the Ethiopians, they were ready to enter as partners into the wider scramble, ecclesiastical and political, now rapidly beginning. The 1880s had taken them a long way.

vi. *Revival in the Kongo*

In February 1878 two members of the Livingstone Inland Mission arrived at the mouth of the Congo. In July Thomas Comber and George Grenfell of the Baptist Missionary Society came on a reconnaissance expedition and were well received by Pedro V at São Salvador. A year later a Baptist mission led by Comber was established in the country with its main station at the capital. By 1882 the LIM (which would soon be taken over by the American Baptist Missionary Union) had sent out thirty-seven missionaries, the British Baptists nine.

Stanley had reached the mouth of the Congo River in August 1877 at the end of the transcontinental journey which had taken him through Buganda two years before. However, while the missions to Buganda were an almost direct consequence of his stay there and letter to the *Daily Telegraph*, the missions to the Congo were already being planned before he arrived at Boma. The publicity his journey produced turned public attention to the Congo, but the crucial missionary decisions had been taken a few months earlier. The Baptists on the Congo, just like Anglicans on the Niger, were fascinated by a strategy of rapid advance into the far interior, and they saw the coastal area chiefly in terms of a base. When São Salvador was recognized to be an unsuitable base, being far from the river, they actually almost abandoned it to the Catholic Portuguese priests who had also at long last returned there. Wisely, they did not do so. It is very clear that the Baptists were welcomed quite warmly within the area of the old Christian kingdom but found it very much more difficult to advance beyond. Yet they themselves wished to play down any continuity between their Church and the Catholicism of former days. In consequence, the development of the Baptist Church in the Lower Congo has never been adequately placed as it needs to be within the longer history of Kongo Christianity.

Its mission of São Salvador was located immediately beside the ruins of the old cathedral, and when a large Baptist church was built in the early 1890s, stones from the cathedral were taken for its construction. In Kongo eyes, the continuity implied by this was far closer than in European eyes. For the missionary these were simply ruins. For the African, they remained a holy place, the central religious shrine of the kingdom, the burial ground of generations of rulers.

In 1893 Holman Bentley completed the Kikongo New Testament upon which he had been working for some years. After 400 years of Christianity the Kongo was at last to receive the Scriptures in its own language. Bentley had made the translation in the closest collaboration with a young man named Nlemvo, whom the mission has traditionally regarded as its first convert, though not the first to be baptized. Nlemvo, Bentley wrote, 'has helped me in all my literary work'.[45] His uncle, who had brought him to work for Bentley as a boy, had a small brass crucifix, his Christo, before which he prayed. When he was dying he had the crucifix stuck up on the wall beside his bed where he could look at it. Nlemvo's uncle was known as a 'believer', a *munkwikizi*. This was still a recognized class, requiring crosses and holy water at funerals. How much it meant interiorly we cannot know. Bentley thought it meant quite a lot for Nlemvo's uncle. There were still public crosses in one or two places, while twice at São Salvador Bentley recalled someone rising after the sermon to urge the people to listen to the teaching because it was the same as old relatives had told them in the past. It is clear that there were quite a number of people like old Dom Afonso, the chief of Zamba, a skilled cotton-weaver, or Dom Garcia, the King's secretary, a fluent speaker and writer of Portuguese, who, while they might hardly be described as Christians, were still in a way representative of the old Kongo Christian culture. Many of the best early Baptists came directly out of this culture, men like the blacksmith Dom Miguel Ndelengeni, Dom Alvaro Mpanzu, or Dom Manuel Mangengo, the King's eldest son. Pedro V's favourite wife later became a deaconess. One of the mission's best young men working at Arthington Station on Stanley Pool was named Ntoni: it looked just like another African name but it was in reality the Kongolese form of Anthony, the most popular saint of the old Kongo Church, and Ntoni did indeed come from São Salvador.

For the English missionaries part of the problem of revivifying

---

[45] W. Holman Bentley, *Pioneering on the Congo* (1900), i. 35.

Kongo Christianity in a Baptist form was the presence of Portuguese missionaries, especially Fr. Barroso, at São Salvador in 1881–7, and of Portuguese colonial officials. The last glimmer of independence of the old kingdom was disappearing with the last glimmer of its former Christian tradition. But while the former did disappear, the latter did not, rescued just in time by the return of missionaries.

Dom Miguel, the blacksmith, was one of the first group to be baptized. A man with an extensive knowledge of Portuguese, he had been one of the first inhabitants of São Salvador to welcome the missionaries. He and Nlemvo may be regarded as the best bridge between the old and the new, but it was not just a matter of one or two individuals: the ease with which the school at São Salvador was got going, the zeal with which male members of the congregation were soon visiting neighbouring villages on evangelistic tours, even the courtesy and basically Christian attitudes of Pedro V—so different from his successor, Mfutila, an unquestionably 'heathen man'[46]—were all evidence of a genuine continuity. So too was the speed with which a mass revival could happen at the LIM station of Mbanza Manteke, to the north-west of São Salvador, with a mass burning of images. Henry Richards was writing from there in August 1885:

The bones that had been shaking for some time past began to stand up and show very evident signs of life. Truly the Pentecostal power came as I have never seen before . . . the people came up in large numbers to the station. The house became too strait, and we were obliged to hold the services in the open air, and have continued to do so up to the present time, and we have more than 700 converts. The glorious fact is this, that Banza Manteke is no longer a heathen country, but more Christian than any I am acquainted with.[47]

A year later something very similar was happening at São Salvador, and it was not unlike what had happened two centuries before in response to the preaching of some Capuchin. While in subsequent years disappointment would set in, it would be very hard not to explain this quite extensive popular enthusiasm for Christianity coming so soon after the missionary arrival other than in terms of the revival of an ancient religion still just alive, despite two centuries of decline and almost no ministry.

[46] Ibid. ii. 304.
[47] J. B. Myers, *The Congo for Christ* (1895), 152.

At a time when there were so many new beginnings, dependent for the most part upon the arrival of Europeans, there is considerable point in stressing elements of continuity, whether they go back only to the early nineteenth century or whether, as in this case, they go back much further still. And it is not merely a matter of a sort of religious archaeology, for it seems likely that it was the ease with which a Christian culture re-emerged in the Kongo in people like Nlemvo and Miguel that provided the root for a rather rapid wider expansion in the interior. Here as in west, south, or east, what made the expansion possible was that it was carried from and by a group already Christianized. The group that did this for the modern Congo was present and available because of what had happened in the ancient Kongo. Tenuous as the continuity might be, it remained creative.

vii. *The Niger Purge*

In the second half of August 1890 the Finance Committee of the Lower Niger Mission met at Onitsha.[48] Bishop Crowther was in the

---

[48] Over the last thirty years a very considerable literature has accumulated discussing the 'Niger purge' of 1890, its antecedents, and consequences. It has become the *cause célèbre* of 19th-cent. missionary and African history. One may start with the official CMS account in Stock, *The History of the Church Missionary Society*, iii. 383–401, and the factually inaccurate and one-sided summary of Stephen Neill in *A History of Christian Missions* (1964), 377–8. In reaction to that very paternalist note, the first wave of scholarly literature was almost entirely critical of the missionaries and defensive of the Niger diocese. The chief works here are J. Webster, *The African Churches among the Yoruba 1888–1922* (1964), 1–41, Ajayi, *Christian Missions in Nigeria*, 238–55, W. O. Ajayi, 'The Niger Delta Pastorate Church 1892–1902', *BSACH* 2/1 (1965), 37–54 (rather more lenient towards the CMS), E. Ayandele, *The Missionary Impact on Modern Nigeria 1842–1914* (1966), 205–38, and F. Ekechi, *Missionary Enterprise and Rivalry in Igboland 1857–1914* (1972), 57–69. From the later 1970s a slightly revisionist school re-examined the evidence, particularly in regard to the missionaries involved. On the one side were two studies written in Aberdeen: Tasie, *Christian Missionary Enterprise in the Niger Delta*, 83–135, and A. F. Walls, 'Black Europeans, White Africans: Some Missionary Motives in West Africa', in D. Baker (ed.), *Missionary Motivation, SCH* xv (1978), 339–48. On the other was a series of articles by Andrew Porter in the *Journal of Imperial and Commonwealth History*: 'Cambridge, Keswick and Late Nineteenth-Century Attitudes to Africa', 5/1 (Oct. 1976), 5–34, 'Evangelical Enthusiasm, Missionary Motivation and West Africa in the Late Nineteenth Century: The Career of G. W. Brooke', 6/1 (Oct. 1977), 23–46, and 'The Hausa Association: Sir George Goldie, the Bishop of Dover, and the Niger in the 1890s', 7/2 (Jan. 1979), 149–79. Still more recently C. P. Williams has carried out a most scrupulous re-examination of CMS attitudes and behaviour throughout the purge in *The Ideal of the Self-Governing Church* (1990), 146–97, and F. Ludwig has reassessed one of the principal actors in the drama in 'The Making of a Late Victorian Missionary: John Alfred Robinson, the "Purger of the Niger Mission" ', *Neue Zeitschrift für Missionswissenschaft*, 47 (1991), 269–90, while D. Johnson in 'Salim Wilson: The Black Evangelist of the North', *JRA* 21 (1991), 27–41, has thrown light on an earlier episode in G. W. Brooke's short life.

chair. His son, the Archdeacon, and one African agent were present at some of the sessions. The missionaries present included F. N. Eden, the Committee's Secretary appointed as such by the CMS as its representative, John Alfred Robinson, Graham Wilmot Brooke, and Henry Dobinson. Eden was 32 at the time, Robinson 31, and Brooke 24; the Bishop was about 84, the Archdeacon 52. Robinson had been rather over three years on the Niger, the other missionaries no more than a few months. The diocese had previously had no white clergy, but CMS worries about complaints in regard to its running had brought about a change of policy and a whole group of keen young Evangelicals arrived in February 1890. They were intended principally for the northern archdeanery. There they had quickly decided that the Church was no more than a home for drink and sexual immorality and had dismissed most of the clergy including the Archdeacon himself. Henry Johnson returned to Freetown.

Now it was the turn of the south. The old Bishop had just arrived from a dispiriting visit to Brass. He was faced by a group of young Britons determined to put the diocese to rights by sacking almost its entire staff. Brooke, the moving spirit in this ecclesiastical revolution, listed fifteen who had left in a letter home in October: three were dismissed for adultery, one for theft, five for incorrigible lying, two for incorrigible idleness. Two resigned, being 'shady' characters, and two left on account of ill health.[49] Two months before (just four months after his arrival in the mission) Brooke had written

There is no hope of success until we have first taken down the whole of the past work so that not one stone remains upon another. I mean that the pastors . . . must be changed, the communicants must be changed, the message preached must be changed, the time, mode and place of worship must be changed, the schoolchildren must be changed and the course in the schools must be changed.[50]

The climax of the Finance Committee came on 29 August when Eden declared it his 'solemn duty' to suspend the Archdeacon from his duties both as Archdeacon and as a missionary. The Bishop replied that the Secretary had no powers to disconnect his ordained agents and added 'the long and the short of it is that I disconnect myself'.[51]

What had happened to produce this extraordinary situation in a

[49] 21 Oct. 1890, Webster, *The African Churches among the Yoruba*, 17.
[50] 5 June 1890, Ekechi, *Missionary Enterprise and Rivalry in Igboland*, 65.
[51] Tasie, *Christian Missionary Enterprise in the Niger Delta*, 112.

diocese which had functioned for over twenty-five years and a bishop long revered both in Africa and in England? No other set of events has played so large a part in the African judgement of missionaries or the missionary judgement of Africans. Crowther's diocese effectively ceased to exist. The Delta defiantly established its autonomy under the leadership of the Archdeacon, while everything north of it was taken under total missionary control. But Robinson died at Lokoja in June 1891, the Bishop in December, Brooke the following March. Eden went to Britain on leave and, when it dawned on the CMS that a schism was imminent and he was hardly the best person to handle it, he never returned. By 1894 there was only one CMS missionary left on the Niger, Henry Dobinson. We have now to attempt to sort out the principal issues, causes, and consequences of these strange events.

We have seen how unsatisfactory the diocese of the Niger always was both in theory and in practice since its establishment twenty-five years before. What may remain surprising is how much was none the less achieved. If Bishop Crowther had retired at the age of 80 in 1886, his episcopate would still have been regarded as remarkably successful and he would probably have been replaced without argument by another African. What had happened to change things so drastically in his final years? The principal answer is undoubtedly a non-ecclesiastical one: the arrival of the high tide of the new imperialism represented on the Niger by the Company of Sir George Goldie, for whom a black bishop exercising considerable authority was a complete anachronism. There was simply no room for a Crowther in his Africa, and he set himself to undermine the Bishop's position both in London and on the river. The CMS was already far too closely tied to the Royal Niger Company and it was easy enough for him to play the anti-drink card. He was prepared to take a strong line against the drink trade, which by 1890 was the current missionary bugbear. Crowther's agents and native Christians in Brass and elsewhere could easily appear corrupted by drink. Crowther himself, tied to the Company through the CMS, was caught impossibly between the two sides.

With the new imperialist thrust came a new missionary temper. This is noticeable in many places, but perhaps nowhere else so emphatically as on the Niger. Eden, Robinson, and Brooke represent an uncompromising sort of upper-class evangelicalism. Many of this type (though not Brooke) were graduates. They were moral radicals, ruthless in condemnation of the slack compromises of earlier generations. They had a horror of drink and of anything they judged 'worldly'. For them the 'Christianity and Commerce' model was an absurdity. Robinson and Brooke were unusual in wanting to wear African dress and break away from the colonial trappings of missionary Christianity, though that was chiefly a personal preoccupation of Brooke. In general this school of missionaries, and Robinson was no exception, was very accepting of the new imperialism. What it was not tolerant of was anything but the highest standards of faith and behaviour among African Christians. The 'wholesale baptism of adults and of redeemed slaves'[52] was condemned. Indeed, as we have seen, for Brooke almost everything was to be condemned.

It was undoubtedly Brooke who set the tone of the attack and radicalized Robinson. By far the youngest, he was a man of limited education but limitless aggressive self-confidence. It was a self-confidence of a charismatic sort which carried others along with it unquestioningly. Brooke was not ordained and had pretty limited Anglican loyalties. It is odd that the CMS ever trusted him as much as it did. Without him the Niger purge would probably never have taken place, at least in so extreme a form, and, once he was dead, it was over. Only the pieces of a devastated diocese remained to be picked up so far as was possible. By 1896 Dobinson, now archdeacon, and the only survivor among the purgers, could publicly declare in Freetown: 'May God forgive us the bitter slanderous and slying (*sic*) thought we had against him (Henry Johnson) and others in those dark days of 1890 . . . we condemned others and we ourselves have done less than they did.'[53]

The purge was possible, and indeed easy, because of the Niger diocese's complete financial dependence upon the CMS. It had never in any way been self-supporting. Hence once a CMS Finance Committee, controlled by a group of young missionary hotheads, was established on the spot there was little most of the diocese could do to protect itself. Only in the Delta was there resistance. Here, where a steamer was not needed, the leadership of Archdeacon Crowther and the larger number of Christians made it possible to establish instead a native pastorate church funded largely from

[52] J. Robinson, June 1890. F. Ludwig, 'The Making of a Late Victorian Missionary', 285.
[53] Ekechi, *Missionary Enterprise and Rivalry in Igboland*, 68.

well-wishers in Lagos and Freetown. It was for a time an almost schismatic body, declared 'utterly irregular'[54] in a report produced for Canterbury, but the archdeacon had no desire to be other than an Anglican. In due course peace had to be made, and James Johnson, who had long argued that Crowther should be replaced by another diocesan bishop, eventually consented in 1900 to become an 'assistant bishop' for the Delta Pastorate, under Bishop Tugwell of Lagos.

The purge of 1890 remains a disaster, devastating the end of Bishop Crowther's career, damaging black–white Church relations for many years all along the west coast, and ensuring a misguided caution whereby there would be no other African diocesan bishop for forty years, until another such landmark was consecrated in 1939, this time not in Canterbury Cathedral but in St Peter's, Rome. Nevertheless, the limits of its significance need also to be stressed. African Christians did not respond to the attack on the Niger diocese in a unified way. Brooke and Robinson were not characteristic of all 1890s missionaries. The diocese did need reform. The purge did not, in the end, produce a schism.

Elsewhere, as in Uganda, CMS missionaries of the same period could behave rather differently. The 1890 Uganda CMS group led by Bishop Tucker certainly thought of themselves initially as something of a new broom, destined by Salisbury Square to develop the Church 'on somewhat different lines from those hitherto adopted'.[55] Their mood too was that of the new university evangelicalism, quick to stress the need for a higher spirituality and a disregard for earthly concerns, but quick too to line up with British imperialism when the need arose. Ganda Christianity with its civil wars and political intrigue could be written off easily enough as a worldly failure, and Mackay, who had just died, could be seen as its protector much as Crowther could be seen as the shield covering the worldly Christianity of the Niger. Yet in practice they never went far along this line. Tucker was from the start extremely supportive of his Baganda Anglicans while Douglas Hooper, the member of the party most closely linked to Brooke and Robinson, returned to England almost immediately. Faced with the immensely rapid growth of the Church coupled with Catholic rivalry, the missionaries really had

---

[54] W. O. Ajayi, 'The Niger Delta Pastorate Church', 44.
[55] Lang to Binns, 13 Dec. 1889, Tudor Griffiths, 'Tucker in Uganda 1890–1893', unpublished paper, 5.

little option. A policy more akin to that of the Niger would only too obviously have handed the whole country over to the White Fathers.

Still more significant for African Church history than the destruction of the Niger diocese was the fact that Archdeacon Crowther did succeed in keeping hold of the Delta Church. Further up the Niger there was anyway very little to save. The diocese was really not a viable entity to survive the Bishop's death. But the Delta Church did manage to soldier on, not particularly gloriously but as well as many a young Church elsewhere. The story as a whole is important for us not just in illustrating at its most arrogant the temper of a new missionary breed in the colonial high tide, but in suggesting how limited missionary power would nevertheless be, once an African Church developed a mind of its own. The Delta was saved for Anglicanism by the reluctance of the Archdeacon to abandon the denomination of his father, though it also required a considerable amount of give and take on the part of Bishop Tugwell in Lagos and the CMS authorities in London. It could then come to be seen, no longer as a consequence of CMS incompetence, but as an example of Anglican tolerance comparable with Dwane's 'Order of Ethiopia' in South Africa. Where denominational commitment or missionary tolerance proved less, schism would be only too easy. The Niger purge ends one era of our history while pointing forward somewhat prophetically to much that was to come.

PART III

1890–1960
THE CHRISTIANIZING
OF HALF A CONTINENT

10

A VARIETY OF SCRAMBLES: 1890–1920

THE CONTEXT OF CONVERSION

i. *The Why and How of the Scramble*

In the late 1870s Africa between the Sahara and the Limpopo was still, ostensibly, a continent divided, as it ever had been, into an almost infinite number of mini-states and stateless peoples, a network of villages battered at times by slavers, droughts, and tribal migrations but unrelated to anything Europe could recognize as sovereignty. Behind the appearance it was, nevertheless, a British continent in so far as Britain alone by trade, coastal possessions, and recognized interest dominated the whole. Portugal maintained a few antique claims around the Zambezi and Angola, while France held Senegal, but these were very limited areas. Beyond them a British hegemony, a paramountcy of implicit claim, was unquestionable and unchallenged. Occasionally, indeed, there was the suggestion of a sort of 'Monroe Doctrine' for Africa, whereby any other outside power was in principle excluded.

Perhaps if Britain had, in the decade following the Ethiopian expedition of 1867, set out to conquer Africa as a whole, for the sake of ensuring its informal empire of trade by the establishment of formal sovereignty, it could have done so. That is to say, it would have been little opposed by other European states. Its victories over the Ashanti in 1874 and the Zulus in 1879 were not won easily, but they were decisive, and few other peoples could have put up such a stout resistance as did those two. But it is, of course, unimaginable in terms of British politics that any government would have been willing to commit the resources required for such an enterprise or would have seen any point in doing so. Earlier than the 1870s the resources were not available. Later than the 1870s the European balance of power required that the continent be partitioned and not allowed to fall, as India had fallen, beneath the power of Britain alone.

Let us further consider the contrast between the earlier and later period. It is often suggested that up to the 1860s only 'informal empire' was pursued simply because it was economically profitable. There was no reason to push inland politically beyond the tiny points of the coastal colonies. That may be true, but it is also true that Britain had simply not the power to do so without quite disproportionate cost and, even then, probably unsuccessfully. A European army fighting in Africa against a Zulu, Ashanti, or Ethiopian army had fairly limited advantages and many grave disadvantages until well beyond 1850. The problems of a permanent internal occupation of Africa were overwhelming. From the middle of the nineteenth century, however, the balance of power came to change enormously in favour of Europe. Five things would bring about this change: the steam-engine, the breach-loading gun, the telegraph, quinine, and a coherent knowledge of the interior of Africa put together by explorers, missionaries, and geographical societies. Steamships would bring people and goods to and fro in a rapid and predictable way unimaginable in the age of sail; railways would make it possible to cross the vast interior of the continent in days instead of months; the breach-loading gun, especially the Maxim when it arrived, would render next to useless the thousands of old rifles which had been sold to Africa over the years and ensure that large armies could be mown down by a handful of properly equipped Western soldiers; the telegraph would make it possible for European governments to know within hours what was happening on every side of the continent; a coherent geographical picture of the interior would make it practicable to plan for the future as a whole; quinine would prevent repetition of the exceedingly heavy casualties from malaria still suffered in the 1840s. By the 1870s Africa was then, in principle, becoming conquerable by Europe in a way it had not been previously. Indeed the contrast between power and power-lessness was now so huge that conquest was not only possible but almost inevitable. In terms of the late nineteenth-century world there was an absolute vacuum of power in most of Africa and into a vacuum forces are inevitably drawn.

It was not, in fact, that the control of Africa was likely to be very profitable. To Britain, the country chiefly concerned, Africa never meant much. It wanted the Cape and Suez because of the East and its world naval role, and, once gold was discovered on the Rand in 1886, it wanted that too. The British government was always a reluctant taker of anything not obviously valuable. It had too many possessions elsewhere ever to feel that prestige required an extensive African empire. Even for other European governments sovereignty over large tracts of Africa was seldom a high attraction, although to any country becoming united and a 'major power' at that time, like Germany and Italy, the acquisition of colonial possessions could seem a piece of necessary prestige. For France too, humiliated by its defeat by Germany in 1870, the conquest of an African empire offered some compensation.

It was, however, far more self-propelled adventurers of every nation who forced the pace. De Brazza and Stanley, Goldie and Peters, Harry Johnston, Cecil Rhodes, and many more, were people who could not be held back, who could have made themselves independent rulers of colonial states—as Rhodes, indeed, almost did and King Leopold quite did—if European governments had not controlled the partition by authorizing it, at first through companies, then inevitably, when money ran out or their activities came under attack, by direct control. It had by that time become a matter of ensuring that rival powers were prevented from threatening one's own interests. The 1880s saw the sudden arrival of Germany, Italy, King Leopold, and a far more outgoing France upon the scene. They were united in determination to prevent Britain from increasing its world power at their expense by any total control of Africa, and their competition ensured that Britain lost important areas it had hitherto thought complacently to fall within its hegemony, such as most of the Sultan of Zanzibar's mainland possessions to Germany and Madagascar to France. Continental pressure produced in its turn a resurgence of British imperialism, even within government. It is striking that Portugal was allowed to hold such huge areas, despite its political and economic insignificance in terms of European power politics, and even more striking that King Leopold was allowed to get away with what might be regarded as the plum—a vast chunk of equatorial Africa. But this is in fact extremely revealing. When the partition arrived, the weakest did best. Britain, which could have had the Congo if it had really wanted it, was only too happy that Leopold should have it instead with all its problems, just because Leopold, king of what was not so much more than a British client state, could be no threat to Britain. Bismarck, for his part, had long been opposed to the acquisition of colonies and his late enthusiasm for it did not last. It had become important, not so much for its own sake, but because, once some sort of partition of Africa had become manifestly inevitable, German prestige and possible future interest might suffer if Britain and France alone shared the continent.

The plans were made in the 1880s. The actual partition took place mostly in the 1890s. By 1900, of the African political world as it had been for centuries only Ethiopia retained its independence. A new political geography, imposed quite arbitrarily by European power in a matter of fifteen years, had created in principle an extraordinarily different context for every side of human activity, religion as much as anything. The history of African Christianity could not possibly escape the consequences of the colonial revolution.

It remained, for the most part, a cheap and feeble colonialism, in which European governments invested the minimum they could get away with. At times, it was all the more brutal for that. Fervent colonialists had always claimed that Africa could be profitable. It seldom proved so and most of the chartered companies had soon fallen into financial difficulties—the investment required for inland profitability was too considerable, the return too slow in coming. Even Leopold, the greatest of believers in an African El Dorado, was driven to countenancing an increasingly cruel regime in order to make his Independent State pay its way. If, in the short run, the very underlying feebleness and lack of sustained imperial will produced shoddy, tyrannical governments, it also led speedily enough to the use of subcontractors other than commercial companies: both 'chiefs' and missions. 'Indirect Rule' through native authorities, traditional or invented, to handle local government, on the one hand, and a privileged role for the missions in education and medical services, on the other, were both inevitable consequences of the reluctance of European governments to give African colonies a high priority. For France they mattered most, for Britain least. Hence France could afford to lean less than Britain on subcontractors.

Until well into the 1890s most Africans will have been hardly aware that anything had altered. Only in the middle of the decade did European rule really begin to press on people outside the perceived centres of local power as rural administration was set up, hut or poll tax demanded, new chiefs appointed, forced labour on roads required, land alienated for settlers and their plantations. The two decades after 1895 were ones of extensive misery and dislocation as the hard reality of alien rule manifested itself in ever wider circles. In many places the colonial presence only arrived about 1895 or even later and, as it weighed on more and more people, resistance which had at first been remarkably slight increased, including a series of major rebellions. In Namibia the Herero people rose against German rule in 1904, killing over 100 German settlers and traders. The German commander, General von Trotha, retaliated with an out-and-out war aimed simply at extermination, and 70 per cent of the Herero were killed and almost as many of the Nama. Nowhere else was colonialism quite so brutal, but almost everywhere it tended towards an unrestrained brutality as soon as it was challenged. And challenged it inevitably was as people saw their traditions, land rights, historical polity, and moral norms continually flouted by arrogant foreigners who had so suddenly and strangely seized control of their society.

The consequences of resistance could be devastating. Southern Tanzania took decades to recover from the suppression by the Germans of Maji Maji, but if straight resistance could not succeed, colonial brutality seldom worked either. Even German colonials in South West Africa needed a labour force and had soon to be importing workers from South Africa to replace the Herero they had slaughtered. The tyranny of early colonialism certainly demonstrated in many cases a total denial of common humanity, at times even defended in terms of the racialism of a social Darwinianism. This was particularly the case where European settlers were arriving in numbers, needed a cheap labour force, and government looked principally to their supposed interests. But in most of Africa the settlers were few, the climate too unfavourable in comparison with America or Australia to attract them. There was little colonial alternative, at least north of the Zambezi, to seeking the health, education, goodwill, prosperity, and profitability of the African population, and, while steps to achieve such ends could be slow in coming and often at first ineffectual, the direction of policy of most colonial authorities to pursue them was clear enough by 1920, and in many places still earlier. If the devastation caused by colonialism among the Herero can hardly be overstated, among many of the great peoples of West Africa the colonial impact was of a far slighter order and one quite soon channelled into essentially progressive directions and ones inherently laid down by African society itself.

While almost numberless effects of European occupation of the African interior might well be listed, a few may here be singled out as of particular importance. First must come the collapse of the existing system of authority and power. It was not, on the surface, a complete collapse, especially in areas where 'Indirect Rule' was favoured. There would still be a Kabaka of Buganda, a Sultan of Zanzibar or Sokoto, though for years there would be no Asantehene or Oba of Benin. Some glitter, some social privilege, a good deal of manipulative power might remain, but sovereignty, any ability actually to decide issues of moment, had entirely departed. Moreover, as political authority had for the most part been inextricably bound up with religious and moral authority, these too were in principle mortally wounded where the bonding had been close. It may well be that it was the stateless, kingless, chiefless peoples who were the least deeply affected in their social psychology by the colonial take-over. Their symbols of power were not so easily trivialized. Missionaries could still not afford to disregard chiefs in the new order. Their willingness to give land, send their children to school, or even attend church themselves remained of considerable importance, but they no longer exercised anything of the near total control over the fortunes of a mission, which in the past had often been the case. And if they behaved unreasonably their decisions might well be overruled brusquely enough by the District Officer.

The old authorities—many, many hundreds of independent entities—were reduced or disappeared. In their place were the colonial states of modern Africa, a division into a relatively small number of countries, a demarcation of frontiers which would be largely decisive until today. In terms of late Victorian modernity, the pre-colonial units of Africa were impossibly small. Their sudden aggregation into potentially modern states was ordered in terms of European convenience, straight lines on maps in Berlin or Brussels, the odd manœuvrings of tricksters who had persuaded chiefs to sign treaties with this country or that. The important point is that once the new political geography was set up, it remained to dominate everyone's consciousness, black and white.

From this viewpoint, as from many others, the First World War was the final act of the scramble. It deprived Germany of its four African colonies, and ensured that German would not be one of the languages—apart from some continued use in Namibia—of modern Africa. English, French, Portuguese would. In no way was the scramble more permanently decisive than in the imposition of a European language map which ensured that Akan, Mende, Yoruba, and Igbo would be anglophone, Bambara, Mossi, Fon, and Fang francophone. This was not just a matter of language-use but of systems of education and administration, the shaping of a literary culture and a political tradition. The missions too were enormously affected by where they happened to have fallen. In some cases they were harassed or even not allowed to continue because their country of origin or form of Christianity or both did not please the new rulers. If one form of political control over religion collapsed with the fall of the old kingdoms, another at once replaced it. But the sheer fact of the formation and established identity of the colonial states was the most decisive of legacies, one simply taken over— despite a few border hesitations—by post-colonial nationalism. If Nigerians, Ugandans, Zaïreans, and Zambians exist as such at the end of the twentieth century, so that Yoruba and Igbo are united in being Nigerians while Fon or Akan never can be, if Chagga and Sukuma are united in being Tanzanians over against the Kenyan identity of Kikuyu or Kamba, it is due to the arbitrary decisions of colonialists at the end of the nineteenth century.

The widest immediate impact of the new regime upon the ordinary people came from the imposition of tax. Africans were suddenly precipitated into a new kind of economy, in which they were forced to earn in order to pay tax and, thereby, forced too to seek employment in plantation, mine, or government service. Furthermore, the complexities of the new order were clearly related to pieces of paper on which rules were laid down whose infringement could be disastrous. Everything profitable or powerful seemed now to require literacy. In the past learning of a Western sort had been largely a waste of time. Now it appeared as the key to Western magic, to avoiding punishment, even to wealth, perhaps to the retention of sanity within an upside-down world. For the most part, at least in British, Belgian, and Portuguese Africa, the only people to offer a way to literacy were missionaries, and for them perhaps the greatest consequence of the partition of Africa was that in place after place there was suddenly a huge demand for schools, mission schools. What had been almost unwanted was now fought for between villages. The need to read and write in the colonial order quickly transformed the whole relationship between mission and society.

To function with even moderate efficiency across the African interior, the colonial system required a basic new structure of communication. The Uganda railway, which reached Lake Victoria from Mombasa already in 1901, transformed the ability of Europeans to control and develop not only Uganda but Kenya too. Indeed its economic impact on German East Africa was soon very considerable—and drove the Germans to counter it by building their own parallel line from Dar es Salaam to Tabora and Ujiji. Railways made the entry of Europeans and their goods infinitely easier; they also made it possible for African peasants to export their produce and achieve a certain prosperity or to travel to distant towns in search of work. They could, of course, and often did, do that simply by walking, but the railways were used by Africans far more than by Europeans. They created a new mobility and helped develop a new sense of a wider society. By 1910 almost every part of Africa's interior was somehow served by a line of rail while the rail lines themselves were served by the new road system, largely created by forced labour and often at the price of great suffering.

If the new communications system served government, the economy, and very ordinary Africans, it served the missions too. The slow, exhausting marches up from the coast which had been the start of every missionary's experience until the late 1890s were replaced by a railway journey of a couple of days. European leave became infinitely easier. The missionary life ceased to be so much a romantic and dangerous adventure into the unknown and rather more a prosaic, well-organized affair. The pioneering spirit was not gone, but scope in which to exercise it was decidedly more limited.

The organization of large states, symbolized by government houses whose grandeur must have been quite astonishing to many who saw them, the railways, the newspapers, the cathedrals, the sense of now falling beneath the authority of some remote potentate of seemingly infinite resource, the King of England or the Emperor of Germany, the sheer enlargement of scale, power, and knowledge within a space of twenty years, and the very numerous possibilities of participation within this new system of things, inevitably precipitated a pursuit of new systems of meaning, truth, philosophy, and religion. The religions of tradition were not unchanging. They were not incapable of incorporating new elements and experience. But they were closely tied to relatively small-scale communities and, very often, to authorities which had now been deeply discredited. They had been appealed to and had failed to halt the white invasion. The new school learning ignored or mocked them.

Despite all this, most people would for a time turn all the more fervently to the invisible powers they were familiar with, but a more reflective, modern-minded minority was no less bound to seek for spiritual and moral alternatives. All the conquerors claimed to be Christian, and at the end of the nineteenth century it seemed overwhelmingly obvious that power, riches, and knowledge belonged to Christian nations. It would have been very strange if Africans did not, in the situation of conquest, seek to share in the beliefs of their conquerors. If the process of Christianization was now to be greatly accelerated, it was not just that there were vastly more missionaries about, with plenty of privileged opportunities for proselytism, it was because Africans themselves had been placed in a situation of objective intellectual unsettlement and were thoughtful enough to seek appropriate positive answers of a religious as well as a technical kind to their current dilemmas.

The answers which presented themselves most obviously in the twenty years following partition were mostly two: Christian and Muslim. And these two had much in common. Both religions had a great deal of continuity with the religions of Africa, above all the continuity of belief in a finally single personal God of creation and providence; but both too had the continuity that they were already held by Africans. This was most obviously true of Islam, whose African presence was already enormous, but it was also significantly true of Christianity. It was the grip which black Africans from Sierra Leone, or Cape Colony, or, indeed, Ethiopia, already had on Christianity which made it a great deal easier for black Africans elsewhere to appropriate it quite quickly and confidently in the age of partition. Christianity, even in the worse moments of the scramble, was seldom simply a religion of the whites.

ii. *Islam within the Scramble*

The relationship between Islam and the new colonial order was a different one, and it is important that it not be misunderstood. The Islamization of much of West and East Africa had been steadily advancing in the later nineteenth century in a quiet but noticeable manner. Some peoples were highly resistant, like the Ashanti, who had a large and influential body of Muslim merchants in their midst but who were themselves almost never converted. The Yoruba were different, and the growth of a large Muslim community in many parts of Yorubaland was one of the more important developments in

African religious history of this period. In East Africa, in the wake of Arab slave-traders, Islam had for the first time established indigenous communities far inland—as around Tabora and Ujiji or among the Yao and the Baganda.

For the most part the European colonialist came to Africa with no hostility whatsoever towards Islam. Quite the contrary. There were exceptions. As a group the Portuguese and the Belgians may have tended to see Islam as an enemy. The closer the formal links between a body of missionaries and the colonial state, the more likely this was to be the case. But even the links between Portugal and the Catholic Church were historic rather than contemporary. Again, Leopold's Congo Independent State had used the Arabs in its eastern parts as sub-imperialists in its early days and had no reason to turn anti-Muslim until its alliance with the Catholic Church developed in the last years before the official Belgian annexation.

For the British, the French, and the Germans an anti-Muslim note was even rarer. Some French administrators did see the spread of Islam as potentially a threat to French control of West Africa; they were, however, rather few and uninfluential. In general all three nations recognized how powerful Islam already was in areas they wished to control, and the last thing they wanted to do was to provoke a Muslim-inspired anti-colonial movement. At this point missionaries and administrators found themselves quickly at cross purposes, and their lack of a common ideology was usefully revealed.

German rule in East Africa was first firmly established on the Muslim, Swahili-speaking coast, and its administration, as it moved inland, carried its coastal ethos with it. Germany was quite used to religiously neutral state schools at home and its government schools opened along the coast, and, catering mostly for Muslims, provided the original core of its native administrators and teachers. Swahili was adopted as an official language and its use quickly spread across the territory into parts where hitherto it was almost unknown. Islam had certainly never previously spread so fast as it did in the early colonial period, but its East African growth was not only within German territory. The Yao, mostly in Malawi and Mozambique, had been closely associated with the slave-trade and began to turn Muslim at that time, but it was in the last decade of the nineteenth and the first decade of the twentieth century that they became a predominantly Muslim people, as did the Zaramo and other groups a little inland from Dar es Salaam.

Experience in India and elsewhere had long trained British administrators to treat Islamic susceptibilities, particularly where rulers were Muslims, with quite special sensitivity. The role of the Sultan of Zanzibar in the east and of the sultans of northern Nigeria in the west was here of primary importance in shaping the British attitude to African Islam on both sides of the continent. So anxious was Britain not to upset Muslim rulers that Christian missionaries were hardly permitted to enter northern Nigeria at all, although in fact many of the subjects of Muslim sultans were by no means Muslims. The French attitude was little different, and official French use of Arabic in West Africa until 1911 had much the same effect as German use of Swahili in East Africa. The colonial regime objectively favoured the mobility of people and of ideas, and Muslims were among the most mobile of Africans. The colonial authorities found among them useful co-operators, people already literate; like Blyden they widely regarded Islam as Africa's most sensible religious choice: superior to traditional religions because emphatically monotheist, literate, and universalist, while more indigenous and less difficult to understand than Christianity, as well as being unwedded to a seemingly futile attack upon polygamy. It may have been a facile judgement but it was an understandable and influential one, helped by the fact that the Muslim community was on the whole turning for a time away from the jihadic and Mahdian intransigencies which had widely characterized its history through much of the nineteenth century and resuming an alternative Islamic face, accommodating, pietistic, and other-worldly.

There were colonialists who disagreed with a benign interpretation, but, for the most part, French Catholic missionaries felt dismayed by how favourable to Islam were French administrators, such as William Merlaud-Ponty, Governor-General of French West Africa from 1908 to 1915, while British Protestant missionaries were no less dismayed by how favourable to Islam were British administrators such as Sir Charles Temple, Lieutenant-Governor of northern Nigeria in 1914–17. The laws of an effective imperialism seldom mesh too well with the requirements of a proselytizing religion. Before long colonial cities like Dakar, Freetown, and Lagos, which had started life with a strongly Christian character, would find themselves with a Muslim majority, though Christians for their part would become a noticeable minority in old Muslim strongholds like Dar es Salaam and Mombasa. The colonial order, in fact, was intrinsically pluralist at least in its British, French, and German forms. Pluralism can benefit many people, but among its principal religious beneficiaries in the early colonial period Islam was certainly to be counted.

iii. *Missionaries and the Politics of Partition*

The nineteenth-century missionary was invariably instructed to avoid politics and, with few exceptions, he intended most sincerely to do so. Nothing interested him less—at least so he thought. But politics and religion are almost never separable and there was no way in which the average missionary could avoid politically significant behaviour. Romans 13 remained his guide, and few missionaries will have doubted in principle that this covered both independent African and colonial authorities. He intended to be loyal to government, but government, whether colonial or African, often found it rather convenient to make more use of him than that. Many missionaries were glad enough to be so used. Established Churches were still the norm in Europe, and while as many missionaries derived from a free as from a State Church, this often made them just a little more pleased to be patronized and made use of by a colonial government. Again, every African ruler's approach to a missionary was a matter of political stratagem, and even the most insignificant missionary could become a person of political consequence at the court of an African king. Robert Moffat was someone particularly concerned in his own mind not to play politics. His visits to Msilikazi were for him a case of personal friendship in the cause of evangelization, yet they inevitably gave him a suprapolitical role of considerable importance, one recognized and respected by other whites.

Until the 1880s it did not occur to most missionaries that the whole of Africa might shortly be ruled by one or another European state. They did not expect it, nor work for it, although at times they undoubtedly hoped for some sort of backing from Britain to assist and even protect them in difficulty. The typical nineteenth-century Protestant missionary did not separate the role of Britain from the providential opening of the world to the gospel in which he was taking part. The British Empire appeared as clearly part of the divine plan for the evangelization of the world, and while it was not his task to extend the Empire, yet a missionary nudge at the right moment to those responsible seemed appropriate enough. Nevertheless, here and now, 'Caesar' might be black and his authority was certainly to be respected within limits.

There was a variety of reasons why a nudge might be appropriate. It would be hard to argue that John Philip was an apolitical person. Orthodox Evangelical of some social standing as he was, he had acquired the easy linking of high political and moral causes with religion characteristic of the Clapham Sect. The abolition of the slave-trade was not a party issue. It had been backed by both Pitt and Fox. Nor for Philip, throughout his thirty years as Superintendent of the LMS in South Africa, could justice for its native inhabitants and the struggle against racialism be a party issue. The justice he sought was an imperial justice, his intention to uphold the highest standards of British liberalism as he saw it. But Philip was a strategist preoccupied not only with the colony's inhabitants but also with the lands beyond, societies increasingly threatened by white pressure, both Boer and British. His intention was to protect them as independent states, building up their resources through a missionary presence. But he could see too in some cases that this was unrealistic, and the only way to protect their inhabitants against white settler invasion and loss of land seemed incorporation in some form within the Empire. Livingstone's denunciations in the 1850s of Boer outrages against the Tswana tribes in his area carried the same message.

There was thus a fairly coherent line leading from missionary defence of Khoi liberties within Cape Colony through missionary advocacy of independent black states on to the establishment of British protectorates over large new areas. John Mackenzie, the most influential LMS man in southern Africa by the mid-1870s, employed this logic pretty forcefully in his appeal to Britain to establish a Bechuanaland Protectorate, which it did in 1884, and Mackenzie became for a while the Deputy Commissioner. In truth he distrusted chiefly power as well as Boer expansionism, but the logic of his imperialism was that nothing else could save Africans from white settler rapacity. It was exactly the same logic as that of Philip and Livingstone, though its tone was more stridently imperialist, a reflection of the wider secular mood of the 1880s. His two-volume 1887 publication, *Austral Africa: Losing it or Ruling it*, suggests an informed, confident, expansionist note. Like Philip, and like many later missionaries, he had a rather large confidence in the moral purposes of London.

Further to the north missionaries were politicized not by a white settler threat but by the Arab slave-trade. In general, missionaries were more anti-slavery-minded in the second half of the century than the first. The spiritual legacy of the British anti-slavery campaigns of the Wilberforce years had percolated through the movement and been revitalized by Livingstone's accounts of the ravaging of East Africa by the slavers. So when in 1861 the first UMCA men led by Bishop Mackenzie went up the Shire River, their encounter with caravans of slaves incited them to carry out the work of liberation by force. A series of tiny wars followed, leaving the missionaries to cope with the pathetic groups of people they had freed, and a horrified public in Britain to protest against missionaries engaged in organized warfare, whatever the cause.

The basic problem remained throughout much of East Africa for the next thirty years. Nominally these were the lands of the Sultan of Zanzibar, whose law sanctioned slavery. The CMS missionaries in Freretown on the mainland opposite Mombasa were in constant trouble for harbouring runaway slaves throughout the 1880s, just as Blantyre and other missions were. They were blamed by the British Consul at Zanzibar for doing so, and the Arabs of Mombasa threatened, and at times took, retaliatory action. But in Europe a horror of slavery was being whipped up in ever wider circles by Cardinal Lavigerie in a new anti-slavery crusade, and King Leopold was adopting this as one of the planks in his own plans for a Congo Independent State. The White Father expedition of 1878 included six armed lay auxiliaries (four Belgians, former papal zouaves, and two Scots, recruited via the *Tablet*!). In future, Lavigerie would bless the sword he presented to each such missionary in the service of departure in Algiers. Six zouaves, however, were not going to achieve much and their very presence could prove a problem for the missionaries. By what authority did they fire their guns? Bishop Mackenzie's problem would also be Lavigerie's, and the Cardinal quietly wound up the exercise in 1885 soon after the Congress of Berlin. If the slave-trade was to be eliminated it could only be by a much larger show of force, and this must mean European annexation. Even after that did happen, it would take the British several years to overcome the Arab slavers powerfully ensconced at the northern end of Lake Malawi.

The Portuguese continued slaving long after other European nations had turned against it, but their slavers on the upper Zambezi were also highly indigenous, their long Portuguese names implying only a small amount of Portuguese blood. They were no less the first line in the renewal of Portuguese claims to the interior of central Africa. The Scottish missions established at Blantyre and Livingstonia since the mid-1870s found themselves in consequence threatened by a Portuguese colonial take-over which might in practice mean more slave-trading rather than less. The Church of Scotland's Foreign Missions Committee appealed to the Foreign Secretary, Lord Granville, in 1884 to block Portuguese advances in the Shire River area. In 1889 the campaign culminated after mass meetings in Glasgow, Edinburgh, and Aberdeen in the presentation to Lord Salisbury of a petition signed by 11,000 ministers and elders of the Scottish Churches. No Church carried more political weight in Britain than the Church of Scotland when it had made up its mind on a matter, and the government could not afford to disregard it. An ultimatum was sent to the Portuguese to withdraw their soldiers from the Shire, and in September 1889 John Buchanan, who had been the Blantyre gardener and was now Britain's Acting Consul, declared a protectorate over the Shire highlands. It was certainly missionary interference which brought this about, yet its point had not been as such to turn African rule into British rule, but to prevent Portuguese annexation. Boers, Arabs, or Portuguese: in each case fear of their rule turned missionaries, not unreasonably, into becoming more active imperialists than they had first intended.

Most missionary influence in the scramble—and it was seldom as effective as in Nyasaland—was within that sort of context. When partition became a certainty, missionary lobbies related less to the question whether, than to that of by whom and how. They could still appear questionable. Take the case of Uganda. The Imperial British East Africa Company was established in 1888. It sent Captain Lugard to Uganda in 1890 in time to participate in the latest round of civil war and ensure that when the King and the Catholics fought the Protestants, the latter won despite being the weaker group. Before the Battle of Mengo took place in January 1892, however, the Company had run out of money and decided to evacuate Uganda. The effect of this upon the work of the CMS might well have been disastrous, and in a special meeting at Exeter Hall in October 1891, Bishop Tucker of Uganda appealed for money to give to the Company to enable it to stay on in the country. Within a few days the necessary £15,000 had been raised, and the Company agreed to delay its departure for a year. But that was a mere breathing-space.

Either the British government accepted direct responsibility or the Company would still withdraw, leaving a highly unstable situation in which the Protestant hegemony established after the Battle of Mengo was unlikely to survive. Britain had at the time a Liberal government, most of whose members favoured withdrawal but in which the Foreign Secretary, Lord Rosebery, a new-style Liberal imperialist, disagreed. In the latter part of 1892 an intense campaign was waged in Britain, largely stimulated by the CMS and its allies within the Church of England, to press the government to retain Uganda. In due course it decided to do so. Almost certainly, after three years of Company rule—of a sort—and the settlement it had produced, the upset resulting from withdrawal would not have been to the good of anyone. Nevertheless, nearly all the reasons put forward in the numerous petitions for retention were unfounded. In this campaign we find the whole package of 'Christian civilization', the honour of Britain, the commercial prospects, the suppression of the slave-trade, set forth somewhat dubiously but very effectively by a missionary lobby to secure the protection of a seemingly successful mission which had in reality gained a political position far in excess of its local strength and was now in danger of losing it.

There was one other, very different, motive behind some missionary pressure for colonial annexation. We find it among some of the Norwegian Lutherans in Zululand in the 1870s, among the LMS in Matabeleland ten years later, and then more widely in Rhodesia in regard to the Matebele war of 1893. It was resentment that years of missionary presence had been unavailing, belief that this was due to the refusal of the king to allow conversions, and the conclusion that the Zulu or Ndebele state needed to be 'broken' so that grace and a more amenable regime could enter in. The British Army or the soldiers of Rhodes's British South African Company then became the providential nutcracker for the preaching of the gospel. This was never a universal position. Bishop Colenso denounced the war on Zululand as quite unjustified, and struggled manfully to defend King Cetshwayo, as Cetshwayo fully appreciated. It was also not a very effective one in terms of its impact upon the colonization process. The LMS men in Bulawayo, Helm especially, allowed themselves to be used as tools by Rhodes in securing the Rudd concession in 1888, but they were little more than tools and there is little reason to doubt that Helm thought he was advising Lobengula in the Ndebele best interest. He could anyway not have affected the outcome of Rhodes's drive north of the Limpopo. Here as in many other places a pre-existing missionary presence somewhat eased the colonial advance—it eased it for the colonialists, in some cases it also eased it for Africans.

The partition being basically decided upon, missionaries participated in it as intermediaries. Some were enthusiastic about what was going on, some more hesitant, but few had the power much to influence it. Essentially they shared in the expansionist imperialism of the age, an easy belief that within the providence of history Africa had now to be conquered for its own good. Their immediate concern was that it should be conquered in a humane way and by the right power. By the latter most Protestant missionaries meant Britain, though once Germany had entered the imperialist game German missionaries naturally transferred their loyalties to it, while most Catholic missionaries more hesitantly meant France, though once Italy had entered the game Italian missionaries naturally again transferred their loyalties.

In very few cases could the missionary factor actually make a difference to how partition proceeded, though as we have seen it did in a few. The conditions for effectiveness were, first, that a mission was already well established in a particular area, secondly, that it was of the same nation as a possible colonial power and in a position to influence it at home. These conditions were fulfilled in the case of the Scottish mission in Nyasaland and the CMS in Uganda, but in very few other cases. There was an easier natural channel between missions of the British Established Churches and their government than between almost any other missions and governments. Curiously, by the late nineteenth century, Britain was the most quietly clericalist of major European states, and British missionaries could profit from a traditional relationship which, elsewhere and especially in France and Italy, had been eroded by anticlericalism.

But a negative case may be instructive too. The area of the Cameroon River had long been a British Baptist mission, and its inhabitants had petitioned for a British protectorate. There was no German mission in the area. While the German take-over in 1884 was thoroughly unwelcome to the missionaries, Baptists had not the political clout in Britain of the Church of Scotland, nor was the Cameroon of any great interest to the British government. Furthermore, Germany could not be threatened, as could Portugal. The Baptists were therefore quite unable to affect the process of partition and withdrew the following year to be replaced by Germans of the Basel Mission: an early example of the reformation of the missionary presence in consequence of European political control.

In German East Africa too there had, previous to partition, been no German mission. There were English UMCA missionaries in one part of the area, CMS in another, LMS in a third. On the Catholic side there were French Holy Ghost Fathers and White Fathers. Both the nationalist impact of partition on the character of the missions and an increase in scale is here apparent. The LMS withdrew across the border to Northern Rhodesia and the CMS to Kenya and Uganda. Only the UMCA, for whom it was their principal missionary area, stuck it out on the Protestant side. At least five German missionary societies were, on the other hand, soon seriously at work within the territory: the Bethel Mission (earlier named Berlin III), the Moravians, the Berlin Missionary Society (Berlin I), the Leipzig Society (which took over the CMS stations in the north-east), and the Catholic Benedictines of St Ottilien. By 1893 all five were established in one or another part of Tanganyika, producing a predominantly German quality within the missionary force at least upon the Protestant side.

The Rhodesian case is equally illustrative of the speed and shape of the ecclesiastical scramble. At the beginning of 1890 there was still no white missionary settled in Mashonaland and only the LMS stations at Inyati and Hope Fountain in Matabeleland. The Jesuits after ten fruitless years north of the Limpopo had just withdrawn from Bulawayo and Empandeni. They returned with Rhodes's Pioneer Column in its march northwards to occupy Mashonaland in search of gold and to found Fort Salisbury in 1890. There came soon afterwards a group of Dominican nursing sisters under Mother Patrick Cosgrave from County Meath. Knight-Bruce, Anglican Bishop of Bloemfontein, had already visited Mashonaland in 1888 and in 1891 became its first bishop, establishing an important station in the east of the country at Penhalonga. Three other missions entered Mashonaland in 1891—the Salvation Army, the Wesleyan Methodists, and the Dutch Reformed Church of South Africa, each occupying part of the central territory. In 1893 the American Board established a mission in the south-east, near Mount Silinda, in 1894 the Seventh-day Adventists arrived in Matabeleland, and in 1897 the American Methodist Episcopal Church began work in the east around Umtali. Thus within seven years the single mission of the

LMS was joined in what had now become Rhodesia by eight other, ecclesiastically quite distinct, mission bodies.

Take one other example. In 1900 Kavirondo (at the time the eastern province of Uganda, later transferred to Kenya) had not a single mission. In December 1901 the railway from Mombasa reached Kisumu. By 1908 there were six different missionary societies at work in the region: the Quakers at Kaimosi from 1902, the Mill Hill Fathers a few months later, the CMS early in 1905, the South African Compounds and Interior Mission late 1905, the Nilotic Independent Mission and the Seventh-day Adventists, both in 1906. On the Protestant side, by 1908 there were five different societies occupying eight stations, twenty-one missionaries in all.

Equally rapid growth and the effective subdivision of countries and regions into a number of segments of missionary influence was going on in most parts of the continent apart from the strongest Muslim areas. The British remained the most tolerant colonial power in regard to national and denominational diversity, and as their territory was by far the most extensive, especially in regard to population, the element of colonial control over missionary expansion was hardly— apart from the special case of the protection of Islamic areas—a decisive factor on a large view, though locally it could be so. British tolerance was a natural consequence of the size and character of the British Empire, the diversity of Church life within Britain, and government recognition that, while England still saw itself at the end of the nineteenth century as a Protestant State with an established Protestant Church, any discrimination against Catholics could only be disastrous. Not only had Ireland—then within the United Kingdom—a large Catholic majority, but other important parts of the Empire like Malta and Quebec were overwhelmingly Catholic.

Britain had learnt from long experience that imperialism required religious tolerance, but even here there could be hiccups. The brief civil war between Catholic and Protestant Baganda in 1892 could be seen as a war between French and English influences. Reflecting the nationalities of the White Fathers and CMS missionaries present in Buganda, the one party named itself the Bafransa, the other the Baingleza. Basically, any identification between British rule and Protestant evangelization was antipathetic to long-standing British policy, yet an 1890s imperialist like Rosebery could get out of line sufficiently to suggest that French missionaries had plenty of French colonies to work in without poaching on British territory. If that remained an un-British approach, the Catholic reaction to it in Uganda was still significant: bring in British missionaries (of the Mill Hill Society) to supplement, though not replace, the French White Fathers and so demonstrate to Africans that Britishness and Catholicism could go together.

When Gabon became French territory, the well-established American Presbyterian mission quickly withdrew and handed over to French Protestants. French Holy Ghost Fathers in the Congo Independent State were forced by an agreement between Leopold and the Vatican to give way to Belgians of the newly founded Society of Scheut and to Belgian Jesuits. Even Lavigerie had to promise Leopold that White Father missions in the Congo would be staffed from their Belgian province. But Leopold had not a strong enough position to drive out British and American Baptists and Presbyterians or Swedish Lutherans, given the almost entire absence of Protestantism in Belgium to provide a national replacement, and his commitment, required by the Congress of Berlin, to freedom of religion. The odd consequence of his insistence upon Catholic missionaries being Belgians, coupled with the undeveloped state of missionary concern in Belgium, was that Catholic missions in the Congo remained far less widely spread than Protestant until almost the end of the century. Leopold had no particular religious preference and was at first quite happy to co-operate with Protestants as they were with him—until the 1890s and the growth of missionary criticism of his regime. Even in Portuguese Angola considerable British and American Protestant activity dating from the 1880s, Baptist, Congregationalist, and Methodist, continued freely enough—perhaps unsurprisingly, given the increasing anticlericalism of the Portuguese State and its deep economic dependence upon Britain.

Hitherto missionaries, at least Protestant missionaries, throughout Africa had tended to use English as the European vernacular, though in places on the west coast it had never quite replaced the traditional Portuguese. Now the new authorities insisted upon the use of German or French instead, but, so long as rather minimal requirements were complied with, early relations between colonial officials and missionaries of any nationality tended to be good: British officials with French or Dutch missionaries, Belgian officials with American or Swedish missionaries, German officials with British or French missionaries. This is hardly surprising as the officials were extremely few and hard-pressed and naturally turned for assistance to any white person around, so long as he was not openly hostile, while the missionaries for the most part welcomed the colonial era as bringing them vast new opportunities for proselytization. In French West Africa, nevertheless, an almost monolithic national pattern did emerge, as Protestant missions hardly appeared and all the Catholics were French, while in Belgian Africa a monolithic pattern was—as we have seen—imposed in regard to the principal, and increasingly privileged, missionary Church: privileged, it was claimed, not because Catholic but because Belgian. In this case most of all an impression of intrinsic diversity between missionary Church and colonial State was seriously eroded. Elsewhere differences of national origin helped render recognizable deeper differences of nature and purpose to the observant local eye. Thus, for instance, the early Catholic missionaries on the Niger were favoured in Igbo eyes precisely because, unlike the CMS, they did not appear to be linked to the oppressions of the Royal Niger Society.

iv. *The Changing Shape of Missionary Endeavour*

The huge numerical increase in the missionary force in the quarter-century following 1885 deserves some explanation. Undoubtedly the general European interest in Africa generated by the Congress of Berlin, the discovery of gold on the Rand, and a heightening of imperialist cravings stimulated the sense of missionary calling in a similar direction among religious people. Occasionally, perhaps most of all in Germany and a little later in Belgium where the colonial urge was new and especially intoxicating, missionary responsibility was drummed up quite consciously as part of the national colonial destiny, though Gustav Warneck, greatest of German missiologists, at once denounced any attempted nationalizing of the Christian mission. But, in general, heightened missionary interest was simply a natural expression of religion in a post-Livingstone and expansionist age. The growth in numbers even of old established societies like the CMS is notable, though a great deal of it was due to a new willingness to accept women, and the latter would soon become the majority. On the Catholic side, at least, it is clear enough that the numerical growth cannot be tied too closely to political developments. For celibate orders requiring a lifetime's commitment, recruitment and training involved quite a few years. Societies like the White Fathers, Mill Hill, and Verona, all founded in the late 1860s, were bound to take a while before they could send many members abroad. The numerical growth of missionaries both in training and in the field pre-dates the scramble and would have continued to happen whatever the political history. But not to the same extent. Political pressures brought societies to Africa which would otherwise most probably not have come—Belgian Jesuits, Premonstratensians, Redemptorists, or Benedictines to the Congo, German Pallottines to Cameroon, German Fathers of the Divine Word to Togo. On the Catholic side in particular there was a large drafting-in of new nationalities. The French and Italian pioneers were being supplemented by Belgian, Dutch, and Irish contingents.

The Irish were slow in coming. Secular priests from Dublin had been serving white immigrants in South Africa, especially in the Port Elizabeth area, through much of the nineteenth century, but entry into the missionary apostolate belonged instead to the early twentieth. Joseph Shanahan, Irish pioneer among the Holy Ghost Fathers in Nigeria, arrived in 1902; Thomas Broderick of the SMA left for the Gold Coast in 1906. Their contribution would be as born English speakers to a mission hitherto over-tied to the French language; they did not, however, noticeably contribute any special sympathy with the colonized such as might have derived from Ireland's own experience.

On the Protestant side, Afro-Americans deserve special mention, though they were never very numerous. Black Jamaicans took a significant part in the early Baptist mission to Cameroon and Congo while Afro-Americans were, of course, early involved in Liberia—as settlers rather more than as missionaries. From the 1880s they went to Sierra Leone and then to South Africa in the African Methodist Episcopal Church (a black Church founded in 1787 in Philadelphia), but some also worked, chiefly in the Congo, in Baptist and Presbyterian missions. While they undoubtedly felt a natural sense of racial unity with Africans and contributed, especially through the AME, but also through Chilembwe's Providence Industrial Mission in Nyasaland and otherwise, to a challenging of the heavy white dominance of this period, they were themselves mostly too immersed in the Westernizing orientation of the main American missions to offer any very distinctive message. There was no successor to Blyden. Nevertheless, if there was one missionary group of which colonial authorities tended to be suspicious, it was that of American blacks. In an age of white supremacy they at least appeared to be inherently unreliable.

By 1910 the Christian missionary army deployed throughout Africa numbered some 10,000 men and women, over 4,000 Protestants, nearly 6,000 Catholics. Over 1,500 of the Protestants were in South Africa where denominations multiplied and overlapped and the climate was very pleasant; on the other hand there was but a handful in French West Africa. Over half the Catholics were nuns and over half of those (1,667) were again in South Africa—mostly serving the white population. Thus the Catholic missionary total might better be given as some 4,000. Nevertheless, it is clear that, outside South Africa, Catholic missionary numbers now well exceeded Protestant, though they had been far smaller than the latter thirty years earlier. Their recruitment was also rapidly increasing while Protestant recruitment, at least in Britain, was already severely in decline. They were also co-ordinated in a way Protestants never could be. The ecclesiastical scramble for Africa coincided with the massive institutional revival of the Catholic Church world-wide in the post-Vatican I era on strictly ultramontane and Rome-guided lines. The contribution of Catholic missionaries was seldom a very creative one, but it was highly disciplined and committed, it learned from Protestants more than it would admit, and its ever-growing strength would prove fairly decisive for the shape of African Christianity in the twentieth century.

It was good to be a missionary in 1910. The movement had grown not only in numbers, but in education and organization, in quality, stature, and confidence. Its impact upon the Churches at home was now very considerable. Western domination had unlocked the doors of the non-Western world as never before. The Student Volunteer Movement, launched in the United States in 1886, was drawing thousands of graduates into the ranks. German professors of missiology were providing academic depth. In 1906 a Strasbourg philosopher, theologian, and organist of high renown, Albert Schweitzer, had decided to spend the rest of his life as a missionary doctor in Africa. In 1910 the first World Missionary Conference gathered more than 1,200 delegates in Edinburgh. No meeting of Protestants on such a scale had ever taken place before. It received messages from the King, the Imperial German Colonial office, and Theodore Roosevelt. It included the Archbishops of Canterbury and

York. It was chaired by John R. Mott, an American Methodist layman, a person of apparently impeccable judgement and the soundest evangelical credentials to whose 'absolute and indeed infallible *ex cathedra* rulings', in Temple Gairdner's slightly mocking words, everyone seemed able to defer. There were even Chinese, Japanese, Korean, and Indian delegates, who took an active part in the discussions and who could be described by Gairdner as 'certainly by far the most significant figures of all'. He named some of them, but, though his general comment applied to 'the Oriental and African delegates', when he at last arrived at the latter all he could find to refer to was one, unnamed, 'negro of immense size glorying in his African race, from Liberia'.[1] Edinburgh 1910 had much to say about Africa, but its mood was, only too clearly, patronizing rather than attentive.

There were no Roman Catholic delegates at Edinburgh, though there was one delightful letter of support from the Bishop of Cremona. The tension between Catholic and Protestant missions in Africa was in many places considerable. In principle Catholics refused to agree to 'comity' arrangements of territorial division with Protestants, though in practice such separations were often imposed at least initially by colonial authorities. In practice, too, relations were at times often less than cordial between Protestant missions themselves and inter-mission agreements delimiting 'spheres' often broke down, especially in urban areas. Africans seldom liked them anyway. But the degree of rivalry with Catholics was vastly greater. It was not always and everywhere so. Coillard could write affectionately about Jesuits on the Zambezi in the 1880s: 'You would have been very much astonished to see me, a descendant of the Huguenots, holding serious converse with this disciple of Loyola, on the experiences of the Christian life, the evangelization of the world, of Africa in particular, on the approaching coming of our Saviour, on true conversion . . .'.[2] Bishop Crowther even passed land at Onitsha, ceded to him, to Fr. Lejeune: 'I acquired this land for God's sake, take it.'[3]

Samuel Crowther was a generous man. He was certainly in this deed an unusual missionary bishop. Again and again the haste in the

[1] W. H. Gairdner, *'Edinburgh 1910': An Account and Interpretation of the World Missionary Conference* (1910), 200, 56 and 58.
[2] June 1885, F. Coillard, *On the Threshold of Central Africa* (1897), 187; see also 132–3, 198–9.   [3] E. Isichei, *The Ibo People and the Europeans* (1973), 147.

missionary scramble was fuelled by an intense desire to keep the other side out. 'Our principal duty at present is to occupy the country by rural schools', wrote Bishop Vogt, a Holy Ghost Father, in 1912, 'in order to close it to Islam and the Protestants.'[4] 'Saturate the people with the Word of God', wrote Dr Laws to Bishop Maples of the UMCA, 'and you will stop both Mohammedanism and Roman Catholicism.'[5] A. G. Macalpine, another Livingstonia man, reported in 1914 that teachers were being posted across a wide swathe of land from Mwenzo to Kasungu 'to claim the country for Christ and save it from heathenism and the Pope'.[6] Such remarks appear almost endlessly in unpublished letters from every side. Occasionally missionaries came into face-to-face confrontations, like Mackay and Lourdel at Mengo or Bentley and Barroso at São Salvador in the 1880s, but mostly they kept severely apart. It is true that there were major differences between them. There were also centuries of post-Reformation misinformation and, in most cases, much more in common than either side recognized. Without the rivalry neither side would have worked so hard. For ecumenists it seems a shocking way of spreading the gospel, but it had at least the merit that it provided Africans with a certain freedom of religious choice and even standards of evaluation to judge each particular missionary package which they could not otherwise have had. Missionaries had to explain themselves more than otherwise and too great high-handedness might lead to mass desertion to another Church. Missionary rivalry put limits on missionary power and, in the early twentieth century, that was no bad thing.

What probably best characterized the day-to-day work of most missionaries in these years in contrast to that of the previous generation was enhanced mobility. The functioning of a large central 'station' had undoubtedly tended to produce a missionary 'as stationary as his station', to quote the comment of a critical observer of 1906.[7] But the cutting edge of mission growth was now in the villages, their schools, and catechists. To help that happen yet still keep it somehow under control one needed to travel a great deal

[4] J. Iliffe, *A Modern History of Tanganyika* (1979), 218.
[5] W. P. Livingstone, *Laws of Livingstonia* (1921), 291.
[6] J. McCracken, *Politics and Christianity in Malawi: The Impact of the Livingstonia Mission in the Northern Province* (1977), 126.
[7] W. G. B. de Montmorency, quoted in R. Slade, *English-Speaking Missions in the Congo Independent State 1898–1908* (Brussels, 1959), 180.

more. In pre-colonial times the long initial journey left little energy for a continually peregrinatory ministry. Steamship, rail, and a new road system made the big journeys very much briefer and less demanding, but what transformed the ongoing local work and indeed made a regular peregrinatory ministry possible for the normal missionary was the bicycle. Robert Ashe may have been the first to introduce one to the far interior on his return to Uganda in 1892. He is pictured on it as a great novelty in his *Chronicles of Uganda* of 1894. Then came George Pilkington in 1896. He rode much of the way from the coast to Uganda, gaining five weeks in consequence on the rest of his party. He thought thirty-five miles 'a nice day's ride'.[8] In 1898 the arrival of the bicycle in Togo heralded a new missionary age.[9] The same year Douglas Pelly and his wife were riding around Penhalonga, to the amazement of locals so that 'at intervals we had to get on our machines and ride in and out of the huts for the benefit of fresh comers'.[10] Donald Fraser brought one back to Nyasaland in 1901 and Joseph Shanahan to Nigeria a year later.

By 1912 the veteran missionary Dan Crawford, writing his *Thinking Black: Twenty-two Years without a Break in the Long Grass of Central Africa*, could praise the endless bush paths, 'only eighteen inches wide', as splendid tracks for the cyclist.[11] Of course, many continued to walk, ride a donkey, or even be carried in a *machila*. 'The donkey is really a splendid acquisition,' wrote Arthur Douglas at Kota Kota in 1903.[12] Canon Lloyd of St Faith's, Rusape, was still riding a donkey over great distances in the 1920s. Bishop Hine spent four months in 1910 walking a good 1,300 miles around his diocese of Northern Rhodesia, and even in July 1922 Frank Weston could write, 'I've walked a 1000 miles since December 15.'[13] Anglo-Catholics were somewhat self-consciously anti-modernity, but by the 1920s long walks were becoming old-fashioned even for backward Tanganyika. 'The tenth bicycle in Angoniland' was hailed by a White Father diarist in Nyasa in September 1909,[14] only two years after

---

[8] C. Harford-Battersby, *Pilkington of Uganda* (1898), 312.
[9] K. Müller, *Histoire de l'église catholique au Togo 1892–1967* (Lomé, 1968), 55.
[10] J. Farrant, *Mashonaland Martyr: Bernard Mizeki and the Pioneer Church* (1966), 226–7.
[11] Dan Crawford, *Thinking Black: Twenty-two Years without a Break in the Long Grass of Central Africa* (1912), 381–2.
[12] B. W. Randolph, *Arthur Douglas: Missionary on Lake Nyasa* (1912), 112. There is a photograph of 'Mr Douglas on his donkey' on the facing page.
[13] H. Maynard Smith, *Frank Bishop of Zanzibar* (1926), 276.
[14] K. Hannecort, *Intrepid Sowers: From Nyasa to Fort Jameson 1889–1946* (1991), 53.

their Superior-General, Mgr. Livinhac, had grudgingly allowed them to be used. In Tanganyika the White Fathers seem to have turned *en masse* to the bicycle around 1912, and it transformed their ability to get to grips with their particularly extensive, thinly populated vicariates. Bishop Léonard, appointed to Tabora in 1912, would ride around his vicariate with a frying-pan on top of his luggage and a mitre tied to the handlebars. 'I should like to put everyone on a bicycle—it is more necessary than bread,' he wrote in 1916.[15] In more advanced circles, the motorcycle was even beginning to make an appearance. Mgr. Lamaître, another White Father, introduced one to the French Sudan in 1911. As his companion on the road had only a bicycle, he attached a rope from one to the other. Bishop Shanahan brought a motorcycle to Nigeria the next year and pulled his companion on a push-bike in quite the same way. Bishop Guillemé introduced it to the Nyasa vicariate in 1913. The importance of all this is that the bicycle and its successors transformed the whole balance of the mission Church away from the centre, and its large buildings to the periphery and its countless village communities. That transformation was required by an almost spontaneous process of growth, but missionaries could hardly have risen to its challenge without at least a bicycle.

The transformation of concern from centre to periphery took time, and, for missionaries other than the most clear-sighted, it was a far from obvious development, involving, as it had to, a very different relationship between missionary and convert, between Church and village society. The element of control largely disappeared. For many missionary groups the immediate concern in the aftermath of the scramble was, however, still the establishment of large stations, the larger it seemed the better. If the UMCA had already learnt that the vision of the 'Christian village' was a delusion by 1890 (see Chapter 5, Section vi), few newly arrived groups had heard that message. Catholic missionaries remained particularly prone to the vision of a little world ruled over by them, an agricultural and technical oasis in which the gospel of work was learnt and from which both pagan custom and European bad influence could be excluded. Nowhere was that more true than in the great Catholic Belgian missions, the *chrétientés*, multiplying in the Congo, though even here by 1911 the

---

[15] F. Nolan, 'Christianity in Unyamwezi 1878–1928', Ph.D. thesis (Cambridge, 1976), 291–2.

Jesuits in Kwango had recognized that their system of 'fermes-chapelles' could not work and needed to be transformed into a simple Christian presence within the traditional village. By then they had already been subject to considerable criticism at home for attempting to create in Kwango 'un Petit Paraguay', yet in Rhodesia under the influence of a Frenchman, Fr. Loubière, Jesuits were still endeavouring to create 'Christian villages' as late as the 1920s.[16]

v. *The Ownership of Land*

All missionaries needed land. But how much? The normal way to obtain it was through negotiation of gift or sale with a local chief. There was plenty of empty land in Africa, but missionaries needed to be close to the more highly inhabited areas where available land was bound to be limited. Where the people wanted them, a grant of ten to fifty acres was seldom a problem, though the terms on which it was originally negotiated might prove later to have been differently understood by the two sides. Basically, however, an African grant of land could strengthen the missionary position and people might be proud that they or their parents had given a piece of land for church or school. That was the normal pattern in West Africa and in many other places too. But the 'Christian village' missionary syndrome, which had developed especially in the south, required a much larger amount of land. The Kuruman model was the ideal for every newly arrived missionary. So Colenso in Natal in 1854 at once applied for an estate of 8,500 acres, granted him—he stressed—by 'His Grace the Duke of Newcastle'.[17]

The mature Colenso may perhaps in his later years have had second thoughts about such an approach, but it became the norm in the atmosphere of the scramble. Commercial companies tied the Churches to their chariot wheels—or hoped to do so—precisely by large grants of land. No one more so than Cecil Rhodes. It seems odd that groups like the Salvation Army and the Quakers, or a 'faith mission' like the AIM in Kenya, should want to own estates of thousands of acres, but few societies were not affected by land lust. There was a range of missionary motivation behind this. A first

---

[16] For Kwango and the Paraguay comparison see G. Ciparisse, 'Les Origines de la méthode des fermes-chapelles au Bas Congo 1895–1898', *BIHB* 43 (1973), 802; for Fr. Loubière see A. Dachs and W. F. Rea, *The Catholic Church and Zimbabwe* (Gwelo, 1979), 79-84.   [17] J. Colenso, *Ten Weeks in Natal* (1855), 70.

motive was simply the desire to implement the current dominant southern model, which required space for a large village with plenty of land to cultivate over which missionaries could exercise control. The aim, however, was becoming rather the provision of boarding-schools and 'central' institutions for people permanently residing elsewhere than the establishment of homogeneous settlements—the Livingstonia model, in fact, rather than the Blantyre. The boarding-school, wrote Archdeacon Willis of Nyanza in 1909, 'secures what the old monasteries secured in the Middle Ages and in its measure it effects what they effected'—a place of protected Christian teaching and living 'amid a sea of temptation',[18] but residence within it was essentially temporary.

A second motive was a desire to cultivate a large estate profitably in order to make the mission self-supporting. Profitable cultivation, such as the development of a commercial plantation, however, almost always proved incompatible with the first aim. A third aim might in some cases actually be to allow Africans to remain unthreatened on their land through missionary ownership of what might otherwise fall to settler control and expropriation. It seems likely that this was more of a subsequent missionary justification for large landholdings than an original motive for acquiring them. However, it does look a little as if the Jesuits, having singularly failed to evangelize people effectively north of the Limpopo in the pre-colonial era, then backed white conquest but subsequently salved their consciences by seeing huge estates like Chishawasha and Empandeni as 'reductions' of a Paraguayan type in which they could not only convert and educate the natives but also protect them from injustice. They certainly did not see it in terms of large commercial gain. Still more clearly, when Arthur Shearly Cripps acquired over 7,000 acres outside Enkeldoorn, it must simply have been to provide a large area of protection for tenants who paid no rent and did as they chose. Chapepa, to give him his African name ('He who cares for people'), lived himself in a thatched hut beside his church.

On the Protestant side, however, concentration upon profitability, the ownership and development of an estate in just the same way as might a settler or commercial company, could go far in crossing the bridge into settlerdom. Not only did missions seek estates of quite

[18] Archdeacon Willis, *Annual Letter*, Nov. 1909, Willis Papers, CMS Archives, Birmingham.

huge size, individual missionaries sometimes acquired estates in their own name. Again, some missions after acquiring estates for a Church purpose then sold them unabashed for profit to settlers, some settlers claimed to be missionaries when acquiring estates even though unsponsored by any recognized society, and some missionaries of recognized societies still managed to acquire estates in their own name and then gave up missionary status to become settlers. In African eyes, in Rhodesia or Kenya, the differences between the two groups of intruders could hardly be perceptible.

In Rhodesia over 400,000 acres were owned by the missions by the 1920s. Of these 325,730 acres had been granted them by the British South Africa Company, the rest acquired subsequently. The LMS held 24,000 acres at Dombodema, the Jesuits 12,000 at Chishawasha, the American Methodists 13,000 at Old Umtali, and the British Methodists 10,000 at Tegwani. Groves commented on Rhodes's generous grants that this created 'a situation to which no other territory in Africa could offer a parallel'.[19]

Kenya, however, did offer something of a parallel. The missions there held over 90,000 acres by 1910. By far the biggest single estate was the Church of Scotland Mission's huge holding of 64,000 acres at Kibwezi. The CSM also held more than 3,000 acres at Kikuyu, the CMS 1,200 at Freretown (explicable in terms of the ex-slave settlement) and 1,123 at Taveta; the Quakers had 1,000 at Kaimosi, the Consolata Fathers 3,000 at Nyeri, the Methodists 6,000 at Tana River, and the White Sisters 5,000 at Mangu. After 1908 and the arrival of the Canadian Governor Girouard, the colonial authorities attempted to put a stop to this, limiting new grants to no more in normal circumstances than ten acres.

The history of the use of missionary land in Kenya is a pretty sorry one, in which again and again missionaries found themselves in conflict with Africans. The Scottish mission obtained its huge Kibwezi estate in 1891 for nothing from the IBEA, with which it was effectively linked, and for some cloth and brass wire from the Kamba it found there. It never attempted to use the land and leased it to a sisal company. The story at Kikuyu is worse, as this was a highly

---

[19] C. P. Groves, *The Planting of Christianity in Africa* (1952), iii. 104; *Report of the Land Commission 1925*, para. 206; C. M. Brand in M. Bourdillon (ed.), *Christianity South of the Zambezi*, ii (1977), 70–1; C. Zvobgo, 'The Wesleyan Methodist Mission in Zimbabwe 1891–1945', Ph.D. thesis (Edinburgh, 1977), 219. For an account of life at Chishawasha under the Jesuits see Laurence Vambe, *From Rhodesia to Zimbabwe* (1972).

populated area in which initially, in 1898, the local chief refused to sell more than 44 acres though pressed for 100. A few years later D. C. Scott, head of the Scottish mission, persuaded the government to turn it into 3,000, while leaving the Africans on the land as a captive population now to be defined as 'squatters'. In 1909 H. E. Scott, D. C. Scott's successor, was imposing labour agreements on his 'squatters' whereby they were obliged to work for the mission for three months a year, received one acre as a personal plot, but had to sell surplus products to the mission at current market prices, if the mission so wanted.

D. C. Scott had come to Kikuyu from the Church of Scotland Mission in Nyasaland, where he had built a huge Church in Blantyre at the centre of another immense missionary landholding—two and a half square miles. The Blantyre estate was obtained initially from an African chief before the colonial state arrived, and, probably for this reason, it never produced the same resentment. It constituted a large African investment rather than a large European robbery. Clement Scott did not detect the difference—strangely for someone who, in Nyasaland, had criticized European land-grabbing and had written in 1894, 'if the Europeans take the land they practically enslave the native population'.[20] In Kenya, in 1904, he even obtained a further 1,000-acre estate for himself, which was sold privately by his nephew after his death.[21]

'Settlers' were, beyond all else in African eyes, seizers of the land. It was inevitable that in those places where missionaries behaved in the same manner they would be identified with settlers: 'Gutiri mubia na muthungu', 'There is no difference between missionary and settler'. The Kikuyu saying reflected basic realities. It is clear that in the early colonial period, where missionaries were established in this way, they reacted also in a typically settler manner over such issues as labour. The land grants in Rhodesia and Kenya of Rhodes and Mackinnon, one an atheist, the other a devout Scottish Presbyterian, did much to paralyse the freedom of the missionary Church in any role of social criticism.

[20] A. C. Ross, ' "The African—a Child or a Man": The Quarrel between the Blantyre Mission of the Church of Scotland and the British Central Africa Administration 1890–1905', in E. Stokes and R. Brown (eds.), *The Zambezian Past* (1966), 348.
[21] T. Price, 'The Church as a Land-Holder in Eastern Africa', *BSACH* 1 (1963), 8–13, and R. Githige, 'The Mission–State Relationship in Kenya 1888–1938', Ph.D. thesis (Aberdeen, 1982), ch. 4.

vi. *Missionaries as Critics of Colonialism*

The range of models in the relationship between missionaries and the early colonial state remained, nevertheless, considerable: from fawning subservience to deep distrust and open disagreement. One important factor in the relationship was whether the mission had arrived significantly prior to colonial authority. Where it had done so and had achieved something of a genuine relationship with African authority, it tended both to take a more independent line and to be more critical of colonial actions. It had a status within society other than that of colonial dependant, and it tended to continue the role it had already in places fulfilled of counsellor and spokesman for native authority. This was not always the case—the Rhenish Mission in South West Africa provides one sad exception in the Herero war—but it often was, and nowhere more so than in Nyasaland where the Blantyre Mission of the Church of Scotland could be described by Acting Commissioner Sharpe in 1894 as 'in the eyes of the natives of this Protectorate an Opposition Party to H. M. Administration'.[22]

The Blantyre missionaries had done a great deal to bring about the establishment of British rule over the Shire highlands, but when that rule came there were several things about it they did not like. For a while it looked rather too much like rule by Cecil Rhodes; it led to a wave of British settlers; it brought a heavy hut tax and pretty arbitrary punishments for any group of Africans who failed to co-operate; and it inevitably brought to a close the civil jurisdiction which the Blantyre missionaries had previously, if illicitly, exercised within their area. Above all, it consistently ignored African customs, authority, and dignity. 'We ask for a constitutional mode of dealing with the native life around us,' Alexander Hetherwick of Blantyre wrote in 1891. 'We ask that the authority and influence of the native chiefs in the country be recognized and their counsel sought in dealing with the people.'[23] Hetherwick was not an easy person, and, in many places, British colonial authority would come to recognize the authority of native chiefs more than some missionaries would like. Nevertheless, Blantyre in its controversy with the administration in the 1890s not only demonstrates well enough a basic non-coincidence of view of the two groups, but it also illustrates some specific issues. Here as elsewhere missionaries, with few exceptions,

[22] Ross, 'The African—a Child or a Man', 332.
[23] Ibid. 341.

accepted a colonial take-over as both inevitable and desirable, but they wanted it in large part precisely to protect Africans from other aliens—Arab slave-traders, Boers, the Portuguese, Cecil Rhodes. They saw their role as one of guiding African society for its own good rather than for the good of Europe.

The CMS in Buganda had a not very dissimilar approach. They too had been in the country for a dozen years before British rule arrived, but they had never possessed a settlement mission of the Blantyre sort and had never exercised any sort of civil jurisdiction. Bishop Tucker and Archdeacon Walker were also, perhaps, more diplomatic in their approach than Hetherwick or Scott. In consequence while Sir Harry Johnston as Commissioner in Nyasaland had come to regard the missionaries as the cause of half his problems, in Uganda he welcomed their influence as the counsellor of the Ganda chiefs in the negotiations leading up to the Uganda Agreement of 1900. Church–State relations in early colonial Buganda are interesting as representing one pole, a rather neo-traditionalist pole, of a wide spectrum. British Anglican missionaries in a British protectorate, the CMS had all the advantages of belonging to the Established Church of the colonizing state. But they also had the incomparable advantage that the leading chiefs were all already Christians. Here it seemed possible to realize that dream of a Christian kingdom of an early medieval type which so many missionaries carried in their hearts. When the young King Daudi Chwa was crowned in 1914 by the Anglican bishop, it could seem that, with colonial approval, the missionary dream was being achieved. Up to a point. African authority was being hallowed rather than ignored—the secular policy of 'indirect rule' here fitted in well enough with missionary principles—and there were no white settlers nor even other more or less discordant Protestant missionary societies to disrupt the model. Unfortunately there were Catholics, a lot of them, and British policy could not be seen to favour Anglicans against them, especially as some of the Catholic missionaries, including their bishop, were also English. But British colonial policy, anyway, was deeply against carrying the 'Establishment' which survived in England (though terminated in Ireland and about to be so in Wales) to the colonies. The apparent closeness of Church–State relations as created in Buganda in the early colonial period suited Anglican fantasy and African expectation well enough, but not the underlying secularism and pluralism of a modern empire.

In very few other places was there, nevertheless, any such relationship. The French West African experience may be considered in comparison. In the interior of West Africa French administration arrived before the missionaries, but all the latter were French and there were no Protestants. In the years following France's 1870 defeat by Prussia, the French sought compensation in colonial expansion. A quite traditional attitude to Christian missions still existed, not so unlike that of pre-nineteenth-century Portugal, and there was a natural alliance between soldiers and missionaries. Though the latter, mostly White Fathers, were ultramontane rather than Gallican, they were happy enough to see their work as one which facilitated the French conquest. The French government wished to ensure that the missionaries would be French, and, on that condition, it provided a good deal of direct material support for the White Fathers, as it had for long done to the Holy Ghost Fathers. Undoubtedly there were differences of viewpoint: the missionaries were deeply disappointed that the administration did not at once abolish slavery, and they endeavoured to distance their stations geographically from government posts; the administrators had doubts about allowing the missionaries to settle in some Muslim areas and wanted them to use French in teaching while the missionaries concentrated instead upon Bambara, Kissi, or Malinke. Nevertheless, the missionaries saw their work as being French as well as Catholic, while the administrators respected the local knowledge and pacifying skills of the White Fathers.

Then came a decisive change. The political situation in France brought an abrupt end to this age of ambiguity. The Waldeck-Rousseau government let loose a new anticlerical campaign in 1899. The bonds of Church and State were severed, religious orders were expelled from France, diplomatic relations with the Vatican terminated. While missionaries were not expelled from French Africa, their subsidies were terminated, their schools closed, and, deprived of State assistance, they were expected to pack up and go. They did not, discovering instead a new freedom. This proved a decisively important experience for the central core of the Catholic missionary movement, freeing it in a few short years from the attitudes of the seventeenth century and propelling it into a more genuinely twentieth-century mood. It was hardly a revolution sought by the Vatican, which indeed continued to favour the old model of the domestication and subsidization of Catholic missions by national states, as the twentieth-century concordats with King Leopold and Salazar, the latter as late as 1940, showed only too well. It is true that with the coming of the First World War efforts were made upon both sides to restore a union of the two, but they were partial and fleeting. Mgr. Bazin had remarked in 1906 that 'the blacks are far from ignoring that the colonial authorities are hostile to us and that our religion is not that of the whites who live in the [French] Sudan'.[24] Basically the requisite distance between the two realities was achieved, and seen to be so in black eyes, though this achievement was the product less of missiological or colonial doctrine than of French domestic politics.

In British East Africa, as in French West Africa, one of the earliest issues over which missionaries and colonialists fell out was that of slavery. The former had been fighting it, as much as they could, long before the latter arrived, and the principal justification in their eyes for the colonial take-over as agreed in Berlin or Brussels was to end this fearful abuse once and for all. Yet here were French, British, and German authorities refusing to free slaves, even insisting upon the return of escaped slaves to their masters just as the pre-colonial powers, themselves involved in the slave-trade, had done.

The quarrel remained particularly intense around the CMS mission of Freretown, and it continued for years after the establishment of the British Protectorate. The missionaries were allied with the London Anti-Slavery Society while colonial officials like Sir Arthur Hardinge, the first Commissioner for British East Africa, upheld the existing laws of Zanzibar. Hardinge opposed in particular any immediate tampering with slavery on the grounds that it was a 'fundamental principle of the social system of Islam'.[25] The point at issue was not so much immediate general abolition as the enforced restitution of runaway slaves. Many missions had for long been sanctuaries for them, but once colonial administrators arrived this disturbed their law-abiding minds. By harbouring slaves, missionaries were undoubtedly condoning a breach of local law. The facts that the claim to sovereignty of the Sultan of Zanzibar over any area of the mainland outside Arab-settled towns was a somewhat mythical one (there had been no administration of any sort), that the slaves ran away of their own accord and if they chose to run further

[24] J.-R. de Benoist, *Église et pouvoir coloniale au Soudan français* (Paris, 1987), 217.
[25] Hardinge, 26 Feb. 1895 in Githige, 'The Mission—State Relationship in Kenya', 81.

than Freretown there was no way at all of recovering them, that the missionaries anyway exercised little effective control over comings and goings in a large settlement like Freretown, and, finally, that the slaves in question were African, their masters Arab, were all disregarded by officials endeavouring to establish British rule by bolstering up the 'local' authority of Zanzibar. What they could less easily disregard was that, if slavery remained part of the law of Zanzibar, it was outlawed within the British Empire. Officials maintained their duty to apply the one law, missionaries appealed to the other, and the British government at home, faced with a strong anti-slavery lobby in Parliament fuelled by missionary reports, had to restrain its East African officials, whose sympathies were with the Arab coastal authorities, not with missionary meddling. With the passing of time this particular issue faded away. It remains significant as illustrating a basic difference of perspective.

Missionary concern with the political in the early colonial period was fitful and unplanned, but in a number of places it was far from insignificant, despite seldom questioning the basic colonial premiss. For the large majority, who were not on the way to becoming settlers themselves, African interests were paramount, and they found it painful to remain mere onlookers if those interests were too flagrantly disregarded. Nevertheless, only a handful had the ability to think through or express their view in a way that differentiated them coherently from their colonialist contemporaries.

Near the end of his life in 1889, Mackay of Uganda remarked perceptively, 'In former years the universal aim was to steal the African from Africa. Today the determination of Europe is to steal Africa from the African.'[26] 'Africa for the Africans', wrote D. C. Scott of Blantyre five years later, opposing a proposal to settle Indians in Africa to improve the labour supply, 'has been our policy from the first, and we believe that God has given this country into our hands that we may train its peoples how to develop its marvellous resources for themselves':[27] paternalistic maybe, but hardly settler-inclined. W. P. Johnson in 1896, commenting on the rather mild words of his newly appointed bishop—when he himself had been passed over—wrote 'I could have wished for a triumph of Liberty, Equality, Fraternity or Death. Rights of the People . . . but the current is too

---

[26] *A. M. Mackay by his sister* (1890), 450–1.
[27] Ross, 'The African—a Child or a Man', 340.

strong . . . It may be that Bishop Hine will enter into the real meaning of Africa for the African Church better than I could have done.'[28] By then 'Africa for the African' had become almost a war-cry for Joseph Booth, an exceptionally radical independent missionary in Nyasaland, and he used it as the title of a book he published in America in 1897. Four years later Arthur Shearly Cripps arrived in Rhodesia, a young Anglican priest soon to become the most uncompromisingly radical Christian voice in that country for half a century. When he too, in 1927, published a book entitled *An Africa for Africans*, he dedicated it to the native Africa he had come to know and love in the last twenty-six years.

Booth and Cripps were not then entirely isolated, though their histories and idiosyncrasies sometimes give the impression that they were. There were many who shared their essential viewpoint, if less vociferously. John White and Edgar Lloyd in Rhodesia, for instance, Basel missionaries in Cameroon, Baptists and Methodists in Angola among others adopted an essentially similar line. There was, indeed, another wing. The Methodist George Eva declared in 1896 that the Ndebele needed a sound 'thrashing'; even more incredibly the Jesuit Fr. Biehler at Chishawasha declared in 1897 in regard to the Mashona, 'it seems to me that the only way of doing anything at all with these natives is to starve them out, destroy their lands and kill all that can be killed'.[29]

That was a very atypical missionary viewpoint, even for a moment of crisis, but it has to find its place in the unsettled spectrum of the 1890s. The typical Catholic approach almost everywhere did, however, remain more apolitical than that of many Protestants and less willing to speak up publicly for African rights, let alone encourage Africans to speak up for themselves. 'Of all the missionaries the Roman Catholics did the least harm,' wrote a white settler in 1911, representing the deep settler hostility to most missionaries, 'for they never preach equality, nor allow the natives to approach the level of equality in any way. Therefore, politically as well as socially the Roman Catholic missionaries are to be congratulated.'[30] Yet even Roman Catholics could at times protest vigorously enough over colonial injustices. The attitude of Fr. Richartz, the Jesuit superior at Chishawasha just a few years later, was

---

[28] B. H. Barnes, *Johnson of Nyasaland* (1933), 151.
[29] T. Ranger, *Revolt in Southern Rhodesia 1896–1897* (1967), 295, see also 3.
[30] C. Mansfield, *Via Rhodesia* (1911), 256–7.

as different from that of Fr. Biehler as could be. He protested strongly in 1901 over forced labour and again, in 1902 and 1903, over the raising of the hut tax. To move to West Africa and a German colony Mgr. Bücking in Togo made vigorous protests over retaliatory punishments and other abuses. While the position of Fr. Richartz was not endangered by his protests, Mgr. Bücking was forced by the German government to resign. Perhaps the very recognition of Catholic apoliticism strengthened the hand when protests were made—at least within the British Empire.[31]

In 1911 Arthur Douglas, a UMCA priest in Mozambique, a Marlborough boy who had studied at Oxford and Ely Theological College, was murdered by a Portuguese official. He had tried to prevent village girls from being carried off for 'a life of sin'. It was a simple concern for which he died and hardly of a very political kind, yet it was basically no different from that which made quite a number of missionaries across Africa in the early colonial period appear a bit like 'an opposition party to the administration'. It was really no different too from that which took them into their one extended, if still deeply reluctant, public crusade: the protest campaign over the administration of the Congo Independent State.

The Congo Independent State was a very odd invention, a piece of pure capitalist colonialism masked in various devious ways. Leopold wanted to be an altogether greater king than the constitutional monarchy of Belgium could allow, and he had long been convinced that you could make a vast fortune somewhere, in Asia or Africa, if you put in a bit of money first. His royal status plus a great deal of philanthropic verbiage about abolishing the slave-trade enabled him to convince the powers to let him take control, sovereignty, of a huge area of Africa to be developed essentially as a piece of private property—or so he conceived it. It was ruled as an absolute monarchy and administered, especially at first, by a very internationally mixed group of adventurers starting with Stanley. The Belgian dimension only grew gradually.

Relations between Leopold's state and the various Protestant missions at work in the area began well enough. Leopold had great ability to charm and to convince. In the field there was a good deal of co-operation. Missionary leaders like the Baptists George Grenfell

---

[31] For Fr. Richartz, see Dachs and Rea, *The Catholic Church and Zimbabwe*, 57–9; for Mgr. Bücking, Müller, *Histoire de l'église catholique au Togo*, 65–7.

and Holman Bentley long believed in his high philanthropic purposes and put down maladministration (at times perfectly correctly) simply to the inadequacies of the handful of local officials. The missions were provided with the sites they required, some received considerable material assistance from the administration, and they were perhaps relieved to find that Leopold's determination to keep French Catholic missionaries out of the Congo effectively gave Protestants a missionary monopoly in many areas.

It is true that even in the early 1880s there were Swedish missionaries in the Lower Congo who reported on the violence and cruelty with which Stanley and Leopold's other pioneers were setting up the new state, but methods were not equally bad everywhere and, until after 1890, there was very little voiced Protestant criticism. Even as late as 1900 Holman Bentley's *Pioneering on the Congo* appears excessively laudatory of the king and his government. The missionaries were conscious of how dependent they were upon Leopold's goodwill while working in an 'absolute monarchy'. Open criticism might have little effect while being highly disadvantageous to their work.

By the 1890s the Congo State had come to cost too much and Leopold developed a new policy to ensure that, at last, his kingdom would produce profits not losses: a State monopoly over ivory and wild rubber was established in large parts of the country, and Africans were compelled both to provide a food tax and to collect adequate amounts of rubber under pain of fearful punishment—hands were cut off, villages burnt down, if quotas were not met. The Congo soon became profitable, but some missionaries in the worst-hit areas (and, of course, with the size of the Congo, there were huge areas of the interior with no missionary presence at all) began to protest both to the local officials and by writing home. 'These poor people died', wrote a Swedish missionary, Gustav Palmer in 1896, 'as if they had been sentenced to extermination and no more to exist as a nation.'[32] It was another Swede, E. V. Sjöblom, employed by the American Baptist Missionary Union, who first sent home for publication a detailed report of atrocities, also in 1896. He sent it to Britain, the United States, and Sweden. Cautious mission authorities in the first

[32] S. Axelson, *Culture Confrontation in the Lower Congo* (Uppsala, 1970), 265.

two countries decided not to publish it. In Sweden, however, they did so and Sjöblom's report was soon reverberating round Europe.

There can be no doubt that the systematic abuses in the Congo administration were appalling, despite a number of genuine but quite inadequate attempts at reform. They failed, however, to produce for quite some time any great wave of Protestant protest. Missionary leaders for long remained convinced of Leopold's good intentions, and they doubted whether any campaign would have other result than to terminate or restrict their own presence in the country. In fact, in retaliation for the protests they did make, they ceased to be given new mission sites: the government did not wish their presence to be spread any wider than it was already. It may be noted that while Belgian supporters of Leopold tended to blame British missionaries for the growing international attack on the Congo State, suggesting that it was in order to get British rule established in the Congo (moreover, these were the years of the Boer War and most Belgians sympathized with the Boers), in fact the British missionaries were slower than either Swedes or Americans in voicing any sort of public protest.

At the beginning of 1900 one of the most senior and responsible of the American Presbyterian missionaries in Kasai, William Morrison, published a devastating account of recent atrocities, but what really changed the situation was the appearance of E. D. Morel, a young Englishman with no Church connections but a burning concern for justice in Africa and outstanding skills in organizing a publicity campaign. By 1900 there was much international dissatisfaction, and some Belgian dissatisfaction too, with the way the Congo was run, but it was only Morel, beginning with a series of unsigned articles on the 'Congo Scandal', who turned this disquiet into a crusade. In 1904 he founded the Congo Reform Association and published his massive *King Leopold's Rule in Africa*, centred upon an analysis of 'the new African slave-trade'. He could not have mounted his campaign without missionary evidence, but it was he, not they, who had done the homework, putting the evidence together from many sources to create a coherent picture, and then drawn the leadership of the missionary societies into public support for reform. It was because of this that the British government, also reluctantly enough, sent its consul, Roger Casement, to tour the interior and write a report, fully vindicating missionary accounts. Its publication was dynamite.

It was the mounting indignation in Britain, America, and

Germany which forced the Belgian government to end the 'Congo Independent State' by annexing it in 1908 and reform its administration fairly decisively. Nevertheless, the Congo Reform Association continued to function until 1913, endeavouring to ensure that Belgium really did implement the necessary reforms and to prevent Britain from recognizing Belgium's sovereignty over the Congo until that had been done. The Baptist Missionary Society remained a firm supporter of the Association all that time. There can be no question but that Leopold was forced to abandon his powers and Belgium to undertake a major programme of reform by British and American pressure which would have been unimaginable without missionary provision of evidence and sustained support for the campaign. Yet the missionaries could not have done it on their own. The campaign itself was the child of Morel and depended greatly on a radical lobby in the House of Commons. There were many abuses elsewhere in colonial Africa, and nothing in the Congo was worse than the near genocide of the Herero in South West Africa, but nowhere else was there so systematic and long-standing a regime of oppression as in Leopold's Congo. Again, at no other point did a large group of missionaries, including several nationalities and societies, enter so publicly and for so long into the arena of politics. The missionaries in question were not naturally politically minded— far less so than many Church of Scotland or CMS men—and they entered the campaign slowly and reluctantly, but the contribution they made thereby to a very general improvement of life and liberty for the mass of Congolese people was none the less considerable, and its evaluation must remain central to any understanding of missionary participation in the African scramble.

THE SHAPING OF CONVERSION

vii. *Black Evangelism: Some Southern Examples*

We can chart the movement of Christianity into the interior of Africa rather easily with reference to European missionaries. We know their names, their backgrounds, the Churches and societies to which they belonged, the places they lived in. We have their journals, their letters home. But the reality of the young Churches was a largely different one and far less easy to chart or to describe. The Christian advance was a black advance or it was nothing. It was one in which ever so many more people were involved but very few of whom we can even name. It used and depended upon the missionaries to some extent, and it was used by them to a very considerable extent, but in general the black advance was far more low-key and often entirely unplanned and haphazard. When occasionally very high-key, it was because its prophetic dimension suddenly set the forest aflame.

The African spread of Christianity consisted for the most part in outreach from places where it had already long taken root, such as West African coastal towns or certain districts in South Africa. It should be understood in terms of two or three trees with ever longer branches rather than hundreds of separate trees each planted anew by a white missionary. Thus in the south and centre of the continent black missionaries, initially Xhosa, Tswana, or Sotho, moved very easily to work among new peoples. Every established mission had its local evangelists or catechists and it was very natural that these should be sent to open up areas where there was no available missionary or simply decide to do so on their own, while at the same time trading or working for government. Whether in time a missionary did actually arrive might make rather little difference to the work of preaching, teaching, conversion, the brunt of which was almost always borne at primary level by black teachers. The missionary negotiated with chiefs and colonial authorities, arranged the building of houses, the translation and printing of texts, taught the teachers, punished irregularities, supervised the overall advance of the mission—all important functions but ones which by themselves do not at all explain the actual process of conversion.

For the latter we have to turn primarily to the way in which black Christians passed on their new faith, whether formally or informally, while remembering that they too by no means always made any lasting impact. Thus there was a quite considerable number of evangelists, Sotho and others, who worked among the Shona before 1890, sent by the Church in Lesotho, the Dutch Reformed Church, the Swiss Mission Vaudoise, and the Berlin Missionary Society. They were often well received by chiefs, but there was seldom much progress made. The insecurity of society affected by Shona–Ndebele conflict had something to do with it, but the evangelists seem simply to have had too little to offer to persuade Shona people to alter in any serious way their traditional beliefs. One of the early Sotho evangelists in Shonaland, Aaron, who had originally been placed there by François Coillard in 1877, moved on with him to the Lozi in 1886. An elderly man who had never attended school, he was one of a number of Sotho who worked with Coillard at Sefula. Two years later he returned to Lesotho. Though Coillard praised him exceedingly, one has the impression that hard as it had been for Aaron at Seleka, left for years, as Coillard puts it, 'deprived of all help',[33] yet he found the deprived state more satisfying than the undeprived one as assistant to an autocratic, if benevolent, missionary like Coillard. Whether he was more effective as an evangelist in one situation or the other, we may not be absolutely sure. What we can say is that for ordinary Africans, encountering Christianity whether at Seleka or at Sefula, it was the Aarons not the Coillards of the Church that they encountered.

William Koyi was a Xhosa educated at Lovedale and had, most probably, belonged to the circle within which the Ntsikana tradition was strong. He was one of four South Africans who volunteered to join the Livingstonia Mission in 1876. They travelled there with Dr Stewart. Koyi could converse with the Ngoni and soon became Dr Laws's 'right hand in many a serious and delicate piece of work'.[34] His, undoubtedly, was the prime achievement of persuading the Ngoni to accept teachers, upon which the whole subsequent expansion of the Livingstonia Mission depended. So great was the impact he made that, after his death, one young man believed for a while that Koyi must have died for the Ngoni as Jesus died for the whites, and should now be worshipped by them.

When, after 1890, white missionaries multiplied in Shonaland, they too were accompanied by interpreters and catechists from the south. Thus Bishop Knight-Bruce, landing at Beira in 1891, came with one elderly white carpenter but six Africans, among them Bernard Mizeki and Frank Zigubu, upon whom the development of the Anglican Church would largely depend in the following years. Mizeki was murdered five years later in the Shona uprising, just a week before his Methodist Sotho evangelist friend Molimile Molele was also murdered. These particular men had been selected, commissioned, and controlled by missionaries, but there were many others who were quite uncontrolled. Zigubu, Mizeki's Zulu

---

[33] Coillard, *On the Threshold of Central Africa*, 338.
[34] Livingstone, *Laws of Livingstonia*, 222; D. Fraser, *The Autobiography of an African* (1925), 82; T. J. Thompson, 'Fraser and the Ngoni: A Study of the Growth of Christianity among the Ngoni of Northern Malawi 1879–1933', Ph.D. thesis (Edinburgh, 1980), 57–62.

companion in Rhodesia, eventually turned farmer. In practice evangelists had largely to maintain themselves, and the difference between evangelists who farmed or traded and traders or farmers who evangelized may have been a clear one on missionary ledgers but was hardly so in real life. R. A. Coker, the Anglican Yoruba clergyman who presided over the Ijebu conversion movement in the 1890s, wrote in December 1897, 'We often have pleasant surprises of adherents in many places we little dreamed of. Again, as the converts are all traders, they go as preachers of the Word taking with them their Bibles and Prayerbooks.'[35]

Samuel Kona, a Fingo from the Transkei and a preacher at home, migrated to Rhodesia and settled at Tebekwe mine in Selukwe, where he set about preaching, joined the Methodist Church, and in 1899 built a little church by the compound. Here a young man named Mantiziba, a 'kitchen boy' in the compound, listened to Samuel preaching on John 3: 3, the need of a 'New Birth'. He attended Samuel's evening classes, learnt to read and write, but in 1903 moved as storekeeper to another mine. With his savings Mantiziba bought a Zulu New Testament, built a church, formed a congregation, and spent his earnings on hymn-books and spelling-books. He called Samuel to visit him, who found to his surprise 'a singing and praying congregation'. In 1905 the local Methodist missionary opened the new church and, three months later, Mantiziba was baptized and given the name Peter.[36] Years later he was, exceptionally for such evangelical pioneers, actually ordained a minister. Such unplanned Christianizing was happening everywhere. 'Down comes a man with a long string knotted into more than thirty knots,' wrote Dan Crawford, describing an odd experience at about this time, of someone from the mountains of Kundlelungu in Zaïre. 'Each of the knots represents a man or woman who has professed conversion to Christ', and when the missionary got there 'to verify the strange news', there they were, mostly women, 'praising God among the rocks'.[37]

By 1901 Dr Laws, home on leave, could tell the Assembly of the United Free Church of Scotland that there were now 'three hundred or four hundred native Christians' preaching the gospel every

[35] J. D. Y. Peel, 'Conversion and Tradition in Two African Societies: Ijebu and Buganda', *Past and Present*, 77 (1977), 125.
[36] Zvobgo, 'The Wesleyan Methodist Mission in Zimbabwe', 87–90.
[37] Crawford, *Thinking Black*, 354–5.

Sabbath in as many villages around Livingstonia.[38] Yet, by and large, this sudden vast multiplication of African preachers and teachers had not been planned or prepared for by missionaries. It had simply happened, theoretically commissioned in some places, uncommissioned in many others, at a time when the training of native agents was still far from high on the normal missionary agenda.

Within this almost universal phenomenon, let us consider in more detail, first, the origins of the Protestant Church in Mozambique and, second, some of the mass conversion movements of West Africa, before turning to what we may term the classical case, the conversion of Buganda, and attempting to obtain some overall understanding of how conversion functioned on a large scale in the early colonial period.

A new missionary society was set up by the Free Evangelical Church of the Canton of Vaud in Switzerland in 1869. In 1872 its two first missionaries, Ernest Creux and Paul Berthoud, arrived in South Africa and established themselves among the Tsonga people in the northern Transvaal at a place called Spelonken, with the help of three Sotho and two Pedi evangelists. The first baptism was in 1876. In September 1878 two brothers, Yosefa and Yacob Mhalamhala, were baptized. Both had worked in the mines and now set themselves to learn to read and write. The greater part of the Tsonga still lived in their original home on the coast of Mozambique, from where the Transvaal Tsonga had emigrated, and Creux, for the time being alone as Paul Berthoud had returned temporarily to Switzerland on the death of his wife and children, decided to send Yosefa and some companions to the coast to see whether a mission to it would be feasible. The report they brought back was favourable, and so in April 1882 Creux ordained Yosefa in exactly the way he had himself been ordained in Switzerland and dispatched him, his wife and daughter, together with his sister Lois Xintomane, her husband Eliachib Mandlakusasa, and their daughter Ruti Holene, as evangelists to the coastal Tsonga.

The dispatch of this all-African mission within ten years of the beginning of the Swiss mission and less than four years since the baptism of its ordained leader was—in missionary history—a highly unusual event. It went remarkably well. Two years later the Church at Spelonken sent Yosefa's brother Yacob to report on developments,

---

[38] The *Missionary Record of the United Free Church of Scotland*, i (1901), 321.

and the account he brought back was highly favourable. The next year, a Swiss missionary, Paul's brother Henri, was sent to do the same and again returned with a thoroughly positive account of the growth of the Church in several different places and of the ministry of Yosefa.

Meanwhile Lois and Eliachib had settled separately at Rikatla, and the Church there began to grow much more than at Yosefa's mission of Antioka. Indeed a 'revival' broke out around Lois, Ruti, and another young woman named Mareta, all of whom had become very literate and made use especially of the one work now printed in Tsonga, the *Buku*, containing extracts from Scripture and a collection of hymns. Soon Rikatla had become a centre for conversions and for ecstatic services in which the participants were seized by the Spirit. Many people stayed for long periods and it was seen as a miracle that there was always sufficient food—provided through the diligence of Lois's agricultural arrangements. Meanwhile, she divided them into groups of between twenty and forty persons, to which she read a part of the *Buku* and then preached. The teaching of literacy was part of her programme, but, while the keeping of Sunday was important, traditional practices like polygamy and the dowry—unacceptable at Spelonken—were admitted. The authority of Yosefa was not challenged and he alone baptized, but it was, perhaps, the leadership of the women, Lois, Ruti, and Mareta, that in contemporary Christian missionary terms was most striking. Ruti and Mareta in particular were regarded as having power to drive out evil spirits. But there were limits to what was acceptable in the experience of possession and when in a service a girl in ecstasy spoke with the voice of the Mother of Jesus, she was seriously reprimanded by her elders.

At this point the missionary conference decided, despite the continued misgivings of some of the missionaries, Henri Berthoud especially, about white interference, that a Swiss missionary needed to be based on the coast and Paul Berthoud, who had returned with a second wife, was the one chosen. He was not the most sympathetic of people and, after his arrival at Rikatla in July 1887 with a new group of Spelonken evangelists, there was inevitably a good deal of tension. Numbers fell. In due course Yosefa was sent back to Spelonken, the spirit of the coast was brought into conformity with that of the Transvaal, and Paul Berthoud was confirmed in his conviction that the controlling presence of a white missionary would be required for a very long time. Nevertheless, schism was avoided and Lois Xintomane in particular, 'the prophetess of Rikatla', retained her confidence in the missionaries and died immensely respected by them, in March 1894. 'Dear mother,' wrote one of them, 'what blessings I have received through her.'[39]

It could be argued that more than almost anywhere Rikatla achieved an instant 'African Christianity' in the period prior to Paul Berthoud's arrival, and yet it never quite developed into an independent Church, despite having almost all the features which could so easily have led to it, including missionary misgivings. A sense of continuity between catechist and prophet, white missionary and black female diviner, here survived, despite the missionary re-establishment of control over the fruits of African evangelization. It is a sense which needs to be retained if elsewhere apparently discrepant phenomena are not to be too divisively interpreted.

viii. *West African Conversion Movements in the Age of Harris*

Late in 1913 a strange barefooted figure, carrying cross, calabash, and Bible, crossed the frontier from Liberia to Ivory Coast to begin the most effective evangelical crusade in modern African history. His name was William Wade Harris. He was a Grebo, a native Liberian, of about 50 years of age. He had been brought up a Methodist but later worked for many years as a teacher for the Protestant Episcopal Church, a man who could speak and read some English and had rather prided himself on his European clothes. Involved in Liberian politics in opposition to the Afro-American rule which did so little for his native fellow countrymen, he had been put in prison after attempting a revolution which would have brought the black 'independence' of Liberia to an end and handed the country over instead to the more enlightened rule of Great Britain. In prison he saw a vision of the Archangel Gabriel, who proclaimed him a prophet to prepare the way of Jesus Christ, but commanded him to abandon his European dress, and, in particular, the shoes he had recently ordered from America. Their rejection was proof of his conversion and the symbol of a quite other way of demonstrating Christianity.[40]

---

[39] J. Van Butselaar, *Africains, missionnaires et colonialistes: Les origines de l'église presbytérienne du Mozambique (Mission Suisse) 1880–1896* (Leiden, 1984), 112.

[40] For Harris's letter, dated Oct. 1907, ordering the shoes, together with the illustrated advertisement for them to which he was responding, see D. Shank, 'A Prophet of Modern Times: The Thought of William Wade Harris', Ph.D. thesis (Aberdeen, 1980), app. xiv.

Harris as prophet taught a fairly straight message about God and Christ as vanquishing and replacing the spirits of tradition. Harris was proclaiming the imminent return of Christ, which was to be prepared for by a radical conversion of life. The Decalogue and Sunday must be observed, the authority of the Bible accepted, the 'fetishes' of traditional religion burnt. Those who believed were to be baptized. Once baptized they should enter whatever Church missionaries provided for them. Christ was coming and those, black or white, who rejected his prophet, ignored the Sabbath, or otherwise despised his commandments would be punished. Polygamy was not to be condemned, and Harris himself would appear to have had several wives. The response to his message in villages all along the Ivory Coast and into western Gold Coast, where he spent several months in 1914, was amazing. Tens of thousands of people abandoned their fetishes, were baptized, and from then on endeavoured to live like Christians. Early in 1915 he was arrested by French officials, treated very roughly, and expelled to Liberia. He lived for another twelve years, preaching on occasion in Liberia and Sierra Leone, but never with quite the same extraordinary effect he had had in those few months between the Cavalla River and Axim. There can be no doubt of his effectiveness. It was reported at once by observers, white and black, Protestant and Catholic, missionaries and administrators. Not only did the fetishes go up in great bonfires, not only did Christian communities spring up and survive quite stably in countless villages where there had never been a missionary, the very social habits of the people had changed. 'The sanitation of the villages between Half Assinie and Ancobra Mouth improved to a truly amazing degree during 1914,' wrote the District Commissioner in the Axim Record Book. 'This is largely the work of the "prophet" as he was called . . . He impressed upon them that next to Godliness is cleanliness.'[41]

There is extremely little in the teaching of Harris which was not straight missionary doctrine, the stock-in-trade of any evangelist. That he was no longer under the precise orders of a clerical missionary mattered little. He had now the higher orders of an archangel instead. But many another catechist too had had visions and dreams to strengthen his resolve. Harris was outstanding in the quality of his self-confidence and in the degree to which his

[41] G. Haliburton, *The Prophet Harris* (1971), 90.

appearance and the externals of his mission had escaped a European model. Yet he cannot have known the languages of the peoples he addressed. For the most part he must have taught in pidgin English, and—though the Ivory Coast was now being shaped as a French colony—the Bible he carried with him was the English Authorized Version. The Lord's Prayer as passed on to his disciples began 'Ow farder wish art in ebi Alloi be die nam Die kingdom cong'. It became known simply as 'What you say to Nyam'.[42] Harris was offering a simplified but not an alternative African Church. He was not teaching a gospel other than that he had learnt from missionaries. It was rather that his visions had provided the biblical message with a greater immediacy. He believed himself, indeed, to be an Elijah, a John the Baptist, but he expected his converts to become Methodists or Roman Catholics, and many of them did. Where there was no European mission, they developed inevitably into Churches of their own, which as the decades passed became known by the name of their founder.

Many hundreds of miles along the coast to the east, in the Niger delta, probably in the course of 1915, a lesser 'prophet' by the name of Garrick Braide prompted a very similar evangelistic crusade in an area where the Anglican Niger delta Pastorate had long functioned, not too dynamically or effectively, using the foreign Igbo language and staffed almost entirely by 'Sierra Leoneans' headed by the Yoruba, Archdeacon Crowther, and Bishop James Johnson. Braide was a Niger delta native, baptized in 1910, and his preaching in his native language, done at first with Anglican approval, brought a wave of mass baptisms, the destruction of fetishes, and the opening of bush schools. P. A. Talbot, the local District Commissioner, complained of 'a holocaust of untold numbers of irreplaceable cult objects',[43] while the Revd A. W. Banfield, Secretary of the British and Foreign Bible Society, who was visiting the area, reported that Braide's services were like 'an old-fashioned revival meeting, where people were to be seen prostrated on the floor calling out for forgiveness, while others were praying and confessing their sins'.[44] Not surprisingly most of the clergy, and particularly Bishop Johnson, reacted negatively. Braide, it

[42] Shank, 'A Prophet of Modern Times', ii. 608 n. 46.
[43] P. A. Talbot, 'Some Beliefs of Today and Yesterday', *Journal of the African Society*, 15 (July 1916), 305–6.
[44] F. Ludwig, 'Elijah II: Radicalisation and Consolidation of the Garrick Braide Movement 1915–1918', *JRA* 23 (1993), 302.

seems, like Lois Xintomane and Harris, tolerated polygamy. He claimed to be Elijah II. He himself appointed evangelists. However, he was functioning too close to an established, clerically controlled Church for such things to be allowed to go unchallenged. Braide was condemned by his Church and arrested by the colonial authorities for causing disorder. He died a little later. The movement then seems to have lost momentum, though many of his followers set up a Church of their own, the Christ Army Church. What is striking here is less the evangelical prowess of Braide—other preachers were soon said to be drawing greater crowds than he—than the collective readiness of the population for conversion. 'There are over 8,000 souls now wandering in their spiritual matters and panting for some reliable Christian body' at Abonnema, a pathetic appeal from some of the converts to the Wesleyan Methodist Mission reported.[45]

Both Harris and Braide had their assistants. Among those of Harris was an elderly man named John Swatson, who continued the ministry of his master in the border areas of the Gold Coast and with not uncomparable results. He had been an agent of the Wesleyan Methodist Church. By 1915 he was styling himself 'Bishop Swatson' in a letter to the District Commissioner of Sefwi in which he informed him of his intention to go to Wiawso 'to break all fetishes and idols and turn the population to the Christian faith'. The DC replied that while he was quite free to visit Wiawso, 'angelic visitations could not be made an excuse for breaking up people's household gods',[46] but he admitted that Swatson did make 'an astonishing number of converts'. A little later Swatson appealed to the Anglican Church to adopt him and his followers. It agreed to do so, and Archdeacon Morrison of Kumasi set off to visit the Denkyera and Sefwi areas Swatson claimed to have converted. After a three-week trek Morrison reported back to London in June 1916:

Throughout the whole trip my loads were carried and I and my servants were fed with no cost to myself. I was received with joy by these simple folk, who escorted me with hymn-singing to their well built churches, where day by day at dusk and dawn they meet for worship and prayer conducted by their own illiterate leaders. They have picked up Fanti hymns of all sorts from any clerks passing through from the Coast, and they have a delightful tuneful form of extempore hymns as well as extempore prayer.

[45] G. Tasie, *Christian Missionary Enterprise in the Niger Delta 1864–1918* (Leiden, 1978), 180.
[46] Haliburton, *The Prophet Harris*, 218.

Their leaders made most earnest prayers and the congregations said Amen like claps of thunder.[47]

A little later, around 1920, another still less instructed prophet named Samson Oppong restarted Swatson's crusade in another part of Ashanti, this time to the benefit of the Methodists. His converts were even more numerous, his anti-fetish fervour even more unbounded.

If we move once more eastwards to Nigeria, to the country of the Isoko just west of the Niger, we are with a people who in 1910 had still been totally untouched by any missionary agency. There was, so far as is known, no Christian of any sort present in the area before Mr Edda Otuedo was sent in 1909 to Uzere as court clerk. An Itsekiri-man, Otuedo had attended a CMS Church for four years in Benin, but was not baptized. In 1910 with the aid of a portable 'organ' which he is said to have bought at Asaba Ase he started to preach to the Uzere people outside office hours, to organize Sunday worship, and to run a small school for boys. A couple of years later, however, he was transferred to a post outside Isokoland. By then an Ijo woman, Bevebolo Bribrina, who had been converted to Christianity some years before, and had later demonstrated her commitment by refusing to allow one of her twin children to be put to death—for which she was banished from her community—settled at Igbide with a trader, whom she married, and began to preach the gospel to her neighbours. Persecution forced them to leave Igbide and with convert friends they founded a new Christian settlement, Obhodo (the 'new town'). Obhodo soon became the centre for Christianity in Isokoland. At much the same time, Christianity was entering the country from other directions. In Ozoro town a local trader named Akwa, who had become a Christian while residing in Warri, returned to his home to carry the message. His first convert, a woman named Ezihobo, was soon joining in his public preaching. These, and others, are oral traditions about very humble people, none of whom had anything of the charismatic power, the genuine knowledge, or the wide-ranging ministry of a Harris or even a Swatson. Yet by the close of 1914 the one missionary who had visited the area, J. D. Aitken, could report 'Lack of men and means alone prevent this country from being a Uganda on a small scale. Agents without supervision! Converts without anyone to prepare them for baptism! Churches without pastors! Schools without teachers! A

[47] Ibid. 223.

harvest unreaped! A judgement to come!'[48] A couple of years later an elementary crash training for evangelists was being begun at the nearest mission, Patani, but it is quite clear that the mass movement among the Isoko had nothing to do with local missionary stimulation or almost any other factor normally offered to explain such events.

The Christian life of the first converts was enthusiastically confrontational. At first even the traditional Isoko name of God, Oghere, was rejected, as were all deities and ancestor spirits. The new Christians worshipped Egode or Ijohiva through Jesu Kriti and each group was led in its worship by the first male Christian in the place, who became its 'olori', a name used equally for leaders in non-Christian cults. At the initiation of a new Christian, the congregation would gather at his home, outside which all his 'fetishes', previous religious symbols and statues of any sort, were set on fire, while the Christians danced around the flames, proclaiming the power of God and the impotence of the spirits of the past. Here is one of their songs.[49]

Othihikpe! Othihikpe!	Destruction! Destruction!
Othihikpe! Othihikpe!	Destruction! Destruction!
Emo ichoche	The children of the Church
Ithihi edho kpere;	Have destroyed the gods,
Othihikpe!	Destruction!
Emo Ijohura	The children of Jehovah
Ithihi edho kpere;	Have destroyed the gods,
Othihikpe!	Destruction!
Emo Jesu Kriti	The children of Jesus Christ
Ethihi edho kpere;	Have destroyed the gods,
Othihikpe	Destruction!

The convert thus became a 'child of God' (*omo Egode*), memorized the Lord's Prayer and the Ten Commandments, and paid an entrance fee of 3*d*.

It is hardly surprising that the elders of the Isoko endeavoured to crush this extraordinary movement, all the more so as the efforts of the Christians were seriously undermining the trade of the local guilds of image-carvers. But such exciting new convictions, linked with all that was changing in the world around, could not possibly be suppressed.

[48] E. S. Akama, 'A Religious History of the Isoko People of the Bendel State of Nigeria', Ph.D. thesis (Aberdeen, 1981), 268.   [49] Ibid. 236.

When we compare these four examples of conversion movements, all taking place along the West African coast between 1912 and 1916, we are faced with profound similarities and relatively superficial differences. It would be impossible to see the movements effected by Harris having any influence upon those around the Niger and very unlikely that the Braide movement had much effect upon that of Isoko. Furthermore, it seems clear that for most of his life after 1915 Harris achieved rather little, that in the wrong environment he could simply produce scoffing, and that Swatson, Oppong, and Braide too had very short careers as powerful evangelists. These four movements, furthermore, while all 'independent' of missionary control, could not have been, in African eyes, significantly different from, for instance, the mass movement which had already been taking place for some years in Ijebu, the Yoruba area immediately inland from Lagos, harvested by African evangelists of the Lagos Native Pastorate, an Anglican body. By 1899, it was reported, Christianity was spreading here 'like a prairie fire'. No white missionary was involved and almost no African clergy: even in Ijeshaland, where the conversion was most intense, there was a single Anglican priest between 1896 and the 1920s, R. S. Oyebode, assisted by a few catechists.[50] Again a Nigerian, T. J. Marshall, established Methodism around Porto Novo, preaching the gospel along the Dahomeian coast for over thirty years up to his death in 1899. Only after that did a white missionary come to live in the country. Remarkable as Harris undoubtedly was, his difference from many another evangelist was probably far less than historians of a later age may imagine, and the success of his work depended at least as much upon a mysterious ripeness for conversion in society as upon the intrinsic qualities of the prophet.

Let us now cross east of the Niger to look at a fifth and last example—the interior of Igboland. It is remarkable how seldom what happened among the Igbos is compared with what happened in southern Ivory Coast. One is seen as part of missionary history, the other as a case of African prophetic history. Moreover, the Igbo conversion is treated as special, for West Africa, in the degree to which conversion was to the Catholic Church; special too in the sharpness of the Catholic–Protestant competition that there

[50] *Proceedings of the CMS 1899*, 59–60, Groves, *The Planting of Christianity in Africa*, iii. 216; J. Peel, *Ijeshas and Nigerians* (1983), 166–8.

prevailed. These were, of course, also the characteristics of conversion in Buganda. Once more, however, in African eyes, the difference between the Igbo case and the other West African ones may have seemed little more than that the number of missionaries accorded the Igbo ensured a far larger increase in the schools they saw opened within a quite short space of time.

TABLE 1. *Catholics in Igboland 1906–18*

	1906	1912	1918
Catholics	1,488	5,563	13,042
Catechumens	1,322	5,368	37,929
Scholars	2,057	6,578	22,838
Teachers	33	124	552
Schools and churches	24	86	355

Here too 1913 is the crucial year. It was the year Father Shanahan wrote, 'At last the era of Patrick is being realised in Igboland. As we move from town to town, idols are toppling of their own accord and the Cross of Christ is being erected in their place. How much more astonishing would the miracle be, if we only had more priests to increase our contact with the people.' The years 1912 and 1913 are looked back upon as 'the two most fruitful in the history of the Catholic Church in Southern Nigeria'. The statistics shown in Table 1 are indicative of what was happening.[51] In twelve years a Catholic community of under 5,000 had grown into one of 74,000 and it was the period after 1912 which really saw the mass movement, Shanahan's 'miracle'. This is only part of the story as Anglican and Methodist numbers were growing almost as fast. Shanahan himself, we are told, after a fruitless visit to Europe to find more priests in 1913 entered upon 'his greatest span of stern and relentless trekking from town to town'.[52] It would be interesting to compare a contemporary African evaluation of Shanahan with one of Harris. They had much more in common than might be supposed. Shanahan's very lack of sophistication in terms of a modern missionary apostolate added to this. He had the advantage in time

[51] J. Jordan, *Bishop Shanahan of Southern Nigeria* (Dublin, 1949), 109 and 140.
[52] Ibid. 122.

span, in a minimum of government assistance, and in the army of untrained teachers who followed behind him, though he certainly could not rival Harris in ability to produce an instantaneous impact. But the basic phenomena of charismatic, peregrinatory evangelist and mass conversion, a 'toppling of idols of their own accord', among a decentralized coastal people being opened up simultaneously to the local pressures of colonial administration seem essentially the same.

Once more, however, it would be mistaken to overstate the degree to which European missionaries, Holy Ghost Fathers, or whoever 'converted' the Igbos. All the evidence suggests that, for perhaps mysterious reasons, the Igbos converted themselves. Shanahan's part was not so much more than to hurry along the process, enticing villages to opt for the Catholic rather than the Protestant fold by offering to open up a multitude of bush schools. What brought about the conversion was, instead, a combination of the influence of catechists, 'warrant chiefs', and an atmosphere of expectation among the young engendered by the appearance of 'new men'—policemen, traders, clerks. Here again it was the already existent commitment of a very small minority which sparked off the mass movement. Igbo chiefs were not traditionally decisive figures, but it was often their preferences which decided which way—Catholic, Anglican, Methodist—a particular village went. But it was above all the catechists who made conversion seem both desirable and possible. Statistics make this clear enough. In 1906 there were 31 Catholic missionaries east of the Niger (12 priests, 9 brothers, 10 sisters). In 1918 there were 30 (19 priests, 7 brothers, 4 sisters). Moreover, it is doubtful whether many of the latter could speak Igbo with even partial fluency (the early French missionaries in Igboland mastered the language, their Irish successors mostly failed to do so). What had changed in those twelve years was the number of catechists, 33 in 1906, 552 in 1918. Their organization was described a few years later: 'Each village is a substation with its own chapel and catechist. Several substations depend on a principal station having at its head a chief catechist. Above the chief catechist is a visiting catechist in charge of a district.'[53] Initial evangelization and subsequent pastoral care depended almost as wholly upon the African agents here as in the Ivory Coast of Harris. They all carried with them Fr. Vogler's

[53] C. A. Obi, *A Hundred Years of the Catholic Church in Eastern Nigeria* (Onitsha, 1985), 140 and 144; I. Ozigboh, *Roman Catholicism in South-Eastern Nigeria 1885–1931* (Onitsha, 1988), 226.

Katekism ak'okwukwe Nzuko Katolik N'asasu Igbo, printed in Strasbourg in 1903 and capable of recitation in a rhythmic singsong manner. Before 1913 there was no catechist training centre but here, as elsewhere, that mattered little. It may even have been an advantage. The power of the barely literate evangelist clutching his one book proved sufficient to convert a nation.

'See how all the villages hastened to abandon their fetishes; see all the roads littered with fetishes of all kinds. People confessed their sins. Drums were broken, dancing forsaken. People struggled to seek out teachers. Churches were built overnight in all the villages.'[54] That is a passage in a Kimbanguist doctrinal text of the late 1950s describing what happened in the Lower Congo in 1921. It might easily be judged a somewhat mythical account of events as imagined long after. In fact we should judge it substantially accurate, not only for the countryside around Nkamba in 1921, but also for the whole series of phenomena we have been considering. When Sir Hugh Clifford, Governor-General of Nigeria, bewailed in 1920 'the extraordinary irruption of "hedge-schools" which has of late years occurred throughout the southern provinces',[55] he was referring to essentially the same thing. What the Kimbanguist text does, however, suggest is how decisive such events were, not only at the time, but also in the memory of those who recalled them a couple of generations later.

It is necessary, then, to beware of any conclusion which would too sharply isolate what was happening on the West Coast in 1913 to 1916 from conversion movements elsewhere in Africa, then or in other years. What happened in those years had happened very similarly, over the two previous decades, in Ijebu and in and around Buganda. It was happening, if just a little less dramatically, in Kasai (central Congo) and in Manicaland, the eastern part of Rhodesia where Anglicans, Methodists, and Catholics were all multiplying fast by 1910 and where the pace was very clearly being set by African demand rather than by missionary hard work. By 1923 a Methodist agriculturalist could comment, 'The success of our native people in agriculture is really wonderful. Some of our best stations like Gandanzara where the new methods of agriculture have taken a firm grip are a wonderful demonstration. At this particular station every

---

[54] Wyatt MacGaffey, 'The Beloved City: Commentary on a Kimbanguist Text', *JRA* 2 (1969), 138.

[55] *Education in Africa*, the first Phelps-Stokes Report, ed. T. Jesse Jones (New York, 1922), 175.

person who has any cattle has a plow and there are forty-three plows owned by the people there.'[56] Ploughs are important, but we should not allow them to stop us seeing how underlyingly similar was the conversion movement in a society where it took this particular form and in another where, perforce, the plough or any comparable technique was not available. The movement in Manicaland was as basically spontaneous as that in Isoko and neither was primarily economic. What was happening in place after place was a spiritual revolution sparked off by native evangelists in conditions created by the unsettlement of early colonial rule.

ix. *The Catechist and his Tools*

'Evangelist' suggests a more peregrinatory ministry, catechist a more settled one. The former is also more of a Protestant title, the latter more commonly Catholic. The practical difference between the Churches was not considerable, but the difference between a missionary, evangelizing role in the early days and the stabilized village ministry of a later period was. Evangelists were characteristic of the age of the scramble, catechists of the post-First World War decades. Before 1890 neither was of great importance, at least not of great independent importance, being more of an interpreter and companion of the missionary. The expansion of the 1890s necessitated the multiplication of the catechist well beyond that of the missionary, and largely separated the two. It was in the areas of mass response that the change came first. We see it in Uganda in the early 1890s, in the Jesuit mission of Kwango and around Livingstonia by the later 1890s, but not very generally until after 1900.

In movements of conversion such as those we have been considering, what may first be underlined is the role of the evangelist as precipitant rather than any formal status: at times a prophet, at times a catechist formally trained and sent on mission, very often a trader or government clerk who had experienced Christianity in one place with some relish and found it absent in another. The status does not matter. His conviction, enthusiasm, reshaping of the message, and what he carried with him do. He was never alone. His power was linked to a book. The early converts of

[56] G. A. Roberts, *Journal*, 1923, 67, T. Ranger, 'Religions and Rural Protests in Makoni District, Zimbabwe, 1900–1980', in J. M. Bak and G. Beneche (eds.), *Religion and Rural Revolt* (1984), 320.

Isokoland travelled to Patani to obtain a Bible to place under their pillow as protection against evil spirits. In the temporary constructions where they worshipped, a copy of the Bible was placed upon an altar on a cloth. It was for them as for Harris the great symbol, but it did not remain for anyone just a symbol: it was indeed a source of authority. Harris knew his Bible or at least parts of it pretty well, so did the Tsonga evangelists know their *Buku*, the Igbo catechists their *katekisma*, Peter Mantiziba his Zulu New Testament, and every other evangelist some portion of the Scriptures or other booklets obtained from a missionary.

There was here a dual authority. The primacy lay with the book and what the book signified, but what was immediately operative was not the book but the man, and what the man (or woman) lacked in training he made up in conviction, courage, sheer inspiration. He certainly needed courage to challenge both the spirits and the elders, to seize and burn fetishes, overturn beer pots, endeavour to break up dances, to stand up like Daniel against all the powers that had been. 'Dare to be a Daniel, Dare to stand alone,' went the old evangelical hymn. 'You are like Daniel,' the angel told Harris.[57] 'I shall go and take their hoes, that they may not dishonour God's day,' declared a Livingstonia catechist.[58] A Sotho evangelist among the Lozi, Paulus Kanedi, at Christmas 1894 preached 'like one inspired, addressing all classes of his audience by turns'. Unfortunately his prophetic spirit carried him too far and he pointed with his fingers at his hearers, even the king, an unacceptable action even from one inspired. There was an explosion of anger and Kanedi had to apologize.[59] In 1894 kings could still be kings and evangelists had to acknowledge their power, but, as the years passed, the confidence and authority, indeed at times arrogance, of the catechist increased as those of the chiefs whose wings were being clipped more and more by colonial control no less declined. 'What a teacher says is law,' it could be claimed as late as 1927, 'what chiefs and messengers say is for heathen only.'[60]

Evangelists, catechists, and teachers mattered so much because there were so few ordained African clergy. In 1910 there were—as there had long been—a fair number of black clergy in the Anglican and Methodist West Coast Churches mostly of Sierra Leonean

[57] Shank, 'A Prophet of Modern Times' 1. 324.
[58] McCracken, *Politics and Christianity in Malawi*, 130.
[59] Coillard, *On the Threshold of Central Africa*, 577–8.
[60] T. Ranger, 'Poverty and Prophetism', unpublished paper (1981), 4.

background, 100 black clergy in Liberia of Afro-American background, while the Basel Mission in Gold Coast and the Bremen Mission in Togo had also made steady progress. In South Africa there were by then a considerable number of Methodists. In three other areas Anglicans had been successful in developing an African clergy. In Uganda since the 1890s the CMS had ordained 33 priests, in Tanganyika and Nyasaland the UMCA had 23. The latter figure was particularly remarkable in areas where there had been no mass movement of conversion. It began with the priestly ordination of Cecil Majaliwa as early as 1890, and it was certainly demonstrative of the determination of UMCA men to establish a genuinely African Church. Thirdly, in the Transvaal the Community of the Resurrection arrived in 1903 and almost immediately opened St Peter's College, Rosettenville, to remedy the great Anglican lack of African clergy within South Africa. By 1920 it had trained 31 black clergy, 15 of whom were already priests.

Elsewhere, there were strangely few. Protestant Churches in Cameroon, Congo, Angola, and German South West Africa had in 1910 16 ordained local clergy between them.[61] Blantyre ordained its first in 1911, Livingstonia in 1914, the latter thirty-nine years after its foundation. The Belgian Congo with sixteen Protestant missionary societies had still only 5 ordained pastors in 1925. Even more unbelievably, the Dutch Reformed Church, established at Morgenster near Great Zimbabwe in 1894, ordained its first African minister only in 1938, the African Inland Mission at work in Kenya from the 1890s ordained its first African in 1945, and Coillard's Paris Evangelical Mission in Bulozi, founded in the 1880s, made its first ordination in 1950. The neurotic missionary anxiety about ordaining men who had not been proved by many years of theological study and controlled pastoral experience—an anxiety which, while not universal, probably grew rather than declined in these decades—coupled with the speed of Church growth—ensured that the characteristic minister throughout the interior of Africa would be the unordained, poorly trained, and almost unpaid evangelist or catechist.

The missionary, based in the larger central stations, toured the villages when time could be found to do so. But the minister of the new myriad village congregations was the catechist, at first more peregrinatory, then more settled, in due course increasingly a

[61] Figures in B. Sundkler, *The Christian Ministry in Africa* (1960), 62–7.

schoolteacher. Bishop Dupont described his Bemba catechists early in the new century as follows: 'A score of intelligent men . . . with impeccable manners and total devotion . . . they hardly know how to read or write but they all have good memories.'[62] Such was the new local symbol of spiritual and intellectual authority, the possessor and interpreter of a book, the teacher of literacy, the person who could and did converse with white men, who represented modernization, who showed by his whole life-style not only a belief in angels and hymn-singing, but also in cleanliness, improved cultivation, and the basic skills which could lead on to employment as clerk or policeman. All these things formed a package, pushed by Harris just as much as by the most carefully controlled paid evangelist. It was in origin almost entirely a missionary package, but in presentation and reception, in the vigour with which different elements within it were stressed, it was almost equally entirely the package of the evangelist-catechist-prophet who strode the stage of village life in the early decades of the twentieth century. The missionary's preoccupation was its control through training and supervision. That worked in a way at Livingstonia or in a well-run White Father vicariate where the European personnel was considerable, but in many a place the number of the converts and the geographical area in which they proliferated so exceeded the resources of available missionaries that it could not. Ivory Coast and Isokoland appear special less in regard to the primary phenomenon they experienced and more in regard to the extreme paucity of missionaries anywhere around to cope with its consequences.

The community created was from its beginnings and more than all else a hymn-singing one. The hymns might be vernacular translations of 'Abide with me' or 'Holy, Holy, Holy'. 'Lo, He comes with clouds descending' was the favourite hymn of both Harris and the Ndebele Zionist Elias Mhlangu. 'Onward Christian soldiers, marching as to war' was what Kimbangu's followers sang, at the top of their voices, in May 1921 at a moment of confrontation with the colonial administrator, just as it was what a congregation of Lagos Anglicans had sung twenty years earlier at a moment of confrontation with their English bishop.

Less commonly the hymns were new creations. Ntsikana's hymns had spread across southern Africa and been supplemented with

---

[62] Garvey, *Bembaland Mission*, 96.

others. William Koyi seems to have carried the tradition to Nyasaland, and Donald Fraser was commenting upon some 'particularly beautiful' new Ngoni compositions by 1902.[63] Anywhere that a missionary hymn-book was not quickly provided, a new hymnody could spring into being, as among Harris's converts or those of Isokoland. It was the hymn that made the Christian—and converts had at times little else, being nearly always illiterate.

For the most part the community's members long remained unbaptized—Harris was exceptional in the confidence that he had the authority to baptize at once upon conversion. Nothing in his ministry so offended missionaries. But the desire for baptism was universal and with it went another desire, often unfulfilled, the desire to read. Christianity was potentially everywhere a reading community. The *Buku* was its focal point, the proof of its power. You may see this as but the replacement of one fetish by another, yet that is not quite correct. It might be treated with all the respect of a traditional fetish, but it was known to contain not only the supernatural but also the key to earthly wealth and power. Its devotees aspired to read its pages as most catechists could already do—more or less. Nothing is clearer than the passion for reading which gripped each convert: 'The wild desire to read and possess a book has seized the whole country. . . What we want are books, not thousands, but millions of books', wrote Pilkington in Uganda in 1892.[64] 'Teachers, teachers, teachers, are what the natives are demanding', wrote Bishop Gaul in Rhodesia just a few years later.[65] In many languages, east and west, the word for reading became one and the same as the word for being a Christian. Thus in Luganda, 'asoma' means 'he or she is reading', but it means no less 'he is praying', 'he is a Christian', 'he goes to church'. Reading and Church affiliation were essentially synonymous, just as the catechist, the *musomesa*, was at once the person who taught reading and who led praying. A church might be used as school, a school might be used as church, the shade of a tree might initially be both. In the early days it was all one and all provisional.

The enigma within this process was its combination (though hardly recognized for its oddity by anyone) of extremes, of secular

[63] Thompson, 'Fraser and the Ngoni', 211.
[64] Harford-Battersby, *Pilkington of Uganda*, 220.
[65] N. D. Atkinson, 'The Missionary Contribution to Early Education in Rhodesia', in A. J. Dachs (ed.), *Christianity South of the Zambezi* (Gwelo, 1973), i. 89.

modernity and traditional supernaturalism. A little booklet containing the first chapters of Matthew's Gospel was a vade-mecum to the
modern world. With it you could learn to read and write. There
manifestly were the skills which gave power to all the great men who
now ruled the world. Everything appeared to depend on paper.
Master this and you could become teacher, clerk, or new-style
farmer. The sky was the limit. And it went with lots of other quite
secular things: elementary mathematics, hygiene, bicycles, things
clearly linked with the still-greater mysteries of train, car, electric
power. In most up-country parts even these greater things largely
appeared, in so far as they did at all, under missionary patronage.
Thus in 1905 Livingstonia began to operate a water-driven turbine to
provide electric light. All very modern and scientific, but actually
read what was offered as a key to it all—the Gospel of Matthew or of
Mark, painstakingly translated into the local vernacular—and what
you get is an account of angelic visitations, of miracles and prophets,
offered by missionary to convert as the revelation of God, more true
than anything. The average missionary could have had almost no
conscious theology to fill the gap between his unhesitating assertion
of the truth and relevance of the Scriptures and his equally
unhesitating disbelief in anything quite comparable actually
happening in modern times. For the convert that gap simply could
not exist. What was so exhilarating about the Scriptures was that they
were so comprehensively supernaturalist, so supportive of belief in
spirits of various sorts, and yet also so manifestly useful in secular
terms. The ministry of Harris, but of many another less known
evangelist too, was in consequence far more consonant with the
Scriptures the Protestant missionary was resolved to distribute in as
many languages as possible than was the rest of the ministry of the
Protestant missionary. Alphabetization and hygiene might reconcile
more agnostic colonial officials to the worth of the controlled
catechist, visions and orgies of image-breaking might alarm the same
officials in the work of the more uncontrolled, but in African eyes
any gap between them did not really seem significant. Most prophets
preached modernization, most catechists had dreams.

   The primal character of a Christian community in contrast with a
traditional one was not confined to hymn-singing, monogamy, or
even school-learning. It went equally with a newly shaped week.
Sabbath-keeping's most revolutionary effect derived from its
substitution of a seven-day week for a four-, five-, six-, or ten-day

week—four, arranged around market days, being very common. This meant in principle the substitution of a liturgical week—one centred upon a day of worship—for an economic one. To such basic things were quickly added a style of clothes, of houses, of recreation. It was, in most places, a community of youth, a great deal less gerontocratic than traditional society, a world in which novelty rather than custom was favoured. It too would have its regulations, some of them troublesome enough, about the Sabbath, marriage, dancing. The negativity of Protestantism might appear very strikingly in the list of all that Christians could be required to withdraw from—dancing, beer-drinking, the chewing of cashew nuts, the paying of bride-wealth, every kind of customary ritual. Yet the early experience of Christian conversion outside the restrictions of the 'mission village' was likely to feel liberating rather than restrictive, in abandonment of fetish, taboo, and cult. Quantitatively the true village Christian had at first little to put in place of a myriad of customary practices. Sometimes very little indeed.

Once baptized, my father asked Harris what he should do. The Prophet cited for him the ten commandments, not to kill, not to steal, not to worship idols and to reserve one day each week for praying to God. When my father asked Harris what day that was, the Prophet said the seventh, and counted on his fingers, one, two, three . . . up to seven so that he would never forget. When father got back here he did his best to follow the Prophet's orders. Taking an empty bottle, he filled it each week with seven stones. On the first day he would remove one stone . . . when all the stones were gone he would call the family together in his courtyard and tell us 'This is the day the Prophet said to worship God. Go, wash yourselves, and get ready for prayer.'[66]

The sheer simplicity of the moral and ritual requirements with which a conversion experience began is well communicated in that Dida reminiscence. Sunday-keeping was so important because it seemed to be the one ritual act absolutely required within the new dispensation.

If traditional dancing was banned, an alternative was quickly provided. In the UMCA mission diary of Magila for 17 September 1884 is the first recorded football match in Tanganyika. By the close of the century British missionaries were enthusiastically encouraging football everywhere. Donald Fraser, a missionary in the east of the

---

[66] J. Krabill, 'The Hymnody of the Harrist Church among the Dida of South-Central Ivory Coast', Ph.D. thesis (Birmingham, 1989), 222–3.

continent, publishing *The Future of Africa* in 1911, could illustrate it with the photograph of a West African football team, winners of the 'Calabar Cup', with their European minister in a dog-collar sitting well satisfied in their midst. On the football field, it was being suggested, lay the road to a healthy Christian Africa, whether in east or west. Furthermore, football crossed the denominational divide; the football match was becoming as much part of the Igbo Catholic catechists' annual retreat as the 'group rosary' or the talk on 'customs that should be retained or abolished'.[67] A village church might even be less of a necessity than a playground for football, close to school and catechist's home.

Christian clothes were trousers and skirts. Beyond that, it depended on prosperity. Catholics, Protestant Igbo believed, were 'people who wore trousers without shoes'.[68] They had the essential Christian character but lacked the prosperity. They were also, most likely, the less Europeanized ones. In general Catholics were, anyway, less keen to Europeanize. Perhaps that is why in Buganda, where their influence was strongest, the best Christians did not wear trousers but a *kanzu*. In this, as much else, Buganda would offer a new model, one least consonant with the ethos of the mission village.

Names mattered. Unlike an earlier generation the Christians of this period did not abandon their African names, but they added to them new ones—a quite African thing to do. Non-Christians in Ankole could even be nicknamed Abelziina rimve (one-named or single-named) and compared to dogs which have but one name. Christian identity now required that one had both: a double name for a double belonging.

Ploughs. In the south they had long been a characteristic of Christian communities, ever since the time of James Read. They were, as we have seen, becoming a noted feature of Methodist life in eastern Rhodesia by the 1910s. And if not ploughs at least agricultural improvement of some kind. Oyebode's demonstration plot of cocoa, oranges, and plantain, behind his Iloro parsonage, was an integral part of his apostleship of Ijeshaland. Christianity brought prosperity if it was allowed to do so, and congregations needed to support Church, school, and even catechist. Agricultural development—the growing of cocoa, coffee, cotton, or whatever—

[67] V. A. Nwosu, *The Laity and the Growth of the Catholic Church in Nigeria: The Onitsha Story 1905–1983* (Onitsha, 1990), 31.		[68] Ibid. 91.

remained the one economic part of the civilizing mission almost all missionaries still believed in. Very often, too, Christians in the villages simply imitated what went on in the central mission stations and the old 'Christian villages' which had depended for survival upon agricultural production of a Western sort. In many places the first Christians in the villages had previously lived in missionary-controlled settlements, but had moved away when colonial order made it seem safe to do so. They naturally carried with them upon a small scale the new pattern of cultivation but not the regimentation.

x. *Logics of Conversion*

In the nineteenth century Christian converts tended by and large to be ex-slaves, outcasts from their society, refugees looking for a safe haven, though this book has concentrated attention so far as possible on people who did not fall into such categories. By the early twentieth century the picture was different. While the Christian community tended to be young, in most places it was drawn from central elements within a settled society, though its initiators were often outsiders, traders, clerks, or migrant workers. In a world where the skills which Christians learned were quickly becoming politically and economically valuable, there was anyway an automatic adjustment of status. In background and early personal history, a catechist might not have been someone of social importance, but he became one because of his new religious status. Very few chiefs of any importance became Christians in this period—though some village headmen did so—but increasingly they sent their sons to be educated by missionaries. They could see where the new power lay, and their very action in ensuring that their own offspring could participate in it validated it socially for others.

It remains extremely hard to see quite why some areas and peoples suddenly turned in strength to Christianity on a scale and with a note of spontaneity which can merit the term 'mass movement' while others failed to do so and advanced no further than a predictable response to specific missionary initiatives; why Manicaland, for example, was by 1910 seeing something of a mass movement building up, as it was not elsewhere among the Shona. Why did one people take so heartily and suddenly to Christianity, others more slowly and unenthusiastically, others again hardly at all? If Ijebu and Buganda from the 1890s, Igboland, Isokoland, and Manicaland from the 1910s, be chosen as areas of notable mass conversion, it is not easy to find convincing common factors differentiating them from other far less responsive societies.

Some missionaries claimed before the conquest that kingdoms which would not harken to the message in independence needed to be broken to do so, but there is little evidence to suggest that a bruising conquest encouraged Africans to turn enthusiastically to the religion of the victors and little reason psychologically to expect them to do so. It may well be that areas which were brought rather gently under colonial rule were in the following decades more amenable to the gospel than those who had fought hard and lost. It is true that manifest defeat could call in question the power of the old gods more forcibly than the establishment of a fairly mild form of protectorate, and there is reason to think that colonial conquest could undermine old beliefs pretty badly and prepare people for a quite drastic change of spiritual allegiance. Yet there is also evidence to suggest reluctance to adopt the religion of such conquerors, and it must not be forgotten that, for instance, parts of Igbo society were bitterly and violently resisting the imposition of British rule at the same time as other parts were turning *en masse* to Christianity and, especially, Catholicism. In Chinua Achebe's *Things Fall Apart*, its hero, Okonkwo, remains to death a resister, but his son Nwoye runs away to become a Christian and a catechist.

Ijebu may have turned so soon after British conquest to Islam still more than to Christianity, just because while different from the beliefs which had propped up the old order Islam was precisely not the religion of the British. A majority of Baganda may have preferred Catholicism to Anglicanism not because there were more Catholic than Anglican missionaries in the field—conversion being anyway more dependent on catechists than on missionaries—but because the Catholics were just sufficiently differentiated from the new British rulers. It was, in its way, an act of defiance while becoming an Anglican was rather more obviously the path of the collaborator. The same may be true for the Igbo. Catholicism and Islam, it is being suggested, shared in British Africa the advantage of being a world religion without being that of the colonialists. In the Belgian Congo it was of course the other way round: being a Baptist and, even more, being a Kimbanguist might be attractive precisely because it combined conversion to a world religion with cocking a snook at the colonial–Catholic alliance. The success of Harris or Oppong may be related to quite the same sort of logic. While the old gods which had failed were rejected, it was at the command not of a colonialist but of an African who was manifestly uncolonial. A 'world religion' was accepted, but by no means in the form the conquerors provided. Even where colonialism did stimulate large-scale conversion it should be seen less in terms of military conquest than in the new opportunities resulting from the imposition, some years later, of a stable local administration.

What seems also to be the case is that mass conversion almost always depended upon the presence and activity of a core of previously existing Christians. There seems almost no direct relationship between mass conversion and missionaries. It was Harris and his Fanti clerks who could set fire to the Ivory Coast, Xhosa, Sotho, and Pedi Christians from the south who could break through in various areas north of the Limpopo, traders or black clergy from Lagos who could arouse Ijebu. Or again it was the handful of one generation within a society who could lead the next in a movement of mass change, both in Buganda and around Livingstonia in the 1890s. Nevertheless, in places it also seems clear that a popular desire for change was so great that it could burst forth—as in Isoko— with the slightest of encouragements from anyone, white or black, yet it could also be fuelled pretty directly by intelligent missionary co-operation as in the case of Bishop Shanahan's schools policy in Igboland, or simply by a charismatic missionary figure who trekked through the villages. Africans were not racialists in regard to whom they were willing to hear. On the contrary, where a fluent and charismatic missionary linguist really got near them, he or she could be extremely influential.

In economic and educational terms, there were very real differences distinguishing these movements and the immediately resultant Christian communities. The preoccupation with schools among the Igbo, with ploughs among the Manyika, or with political power among the Baganda cannot be matched at all among the Isoko or the Dida and Ebrie converts of Harris. Yet, despite such undoubted divergences, which make any neat theory of mass conversion so awkward to get right, the common character of all these movements is unquestionable, and it does not seem so different from religious movements in quite other parts of the world, such as that of evangelicalism in the rural Wales of the eighteenth century. In the coming years, something similar would happen in many other parts of Africa. We have here been reviewing a selection of the earlier and more striking cases. We have, however, hitherto almost entirely omitted consideration of the most impressive of all, that of Buganda. This may have looked rather too like a study of *Hamlet* without the Prince of Denmark, but it seemed right to examine the other evidence on its own precisely to avoid allowing the Ganda story to dominate the rest. To it we have now to turn, shifting back from a focus on the 1910s to one on the 1890s.

xi. *Buganda: Mass Conversion in the 1890s*

Buganda is the only place in Africa where there was both large-scale conversion to Christianity in the pre-colonial era and a mass conversion movement within the early colonial age. The latter was most certainly dependent upon the former, and, while the arrival of British rule in the early 1890s facilitated it, the explanation for what happened is to be found less in any colonial logic than in the initial conversions and stormy events of the 1880s, leading up to the political and military triumph of the Christian minority in a situation when British rule was certainly not anticipated, at least upon the African side. When Bishop Tucker reached Kampala on 27 December 1890, just nine days after Captain Lugard and nineteen days after his Roman Catholic opposite, Mgr. Hirth, their joint arrival can well be seen as marking the start of the colonial age, but it was in no way the start of Christianity. Bishop Tucker on his first Sunday was delighted by the numbers who came to Church, but surprised that they all brought their guns with them. Understandably he knew little of the true state of the country, still in the midst of several years of civil war, a war in which the Christians had finally defeated the Muslims, but were themselves about to break apart. At the Battle of Mengo in January 1892 the Catholic forces allied with the Kabaka Mwanga and led by Stanislas Mugwanya fled before the fire of Lugard's Maxim gun, brought into action to prevent a Protestant defeat. Effective control of the country was then seen to have passed into the hands of the representatives of Britain and its most reliable local allies, headed by Apolo Kagwa, the new katikiro.

All the new leaders of the nation had come through the struggles of the 1880s, but they had been marked out as members of the ruling class before their Christian conversion and before the wars began. They were in many ways determined to maintain Ganda custom but no less to convert the nation to Christianity, excluding both traditionalists and their Muslim opponents so far as they could, but ensuring too their own oligarchic ascendancy in the face of both a debilitated monarchy and colonial power.

The armies who had fought for them were 'Christian' by allegiance to one or another warlord. They were not only unbaptized but almost uninstructed, yet already largely committed to an either Protestant or Catholic identity. That large-scale, if almost mythical, commitment had come about at a time when there were no missionaries in Buganda, and it was manifested already in 1892 when Lugard divided the country, giving the great western county of Buddu to a Catholic chief, Alikisi Ssebowa, but most of the rest to Protestants. In consequence, there was a massive redistribution of population in the course of 1892; 15,000 to 20,000 'Catholics' migrated westwards, some in large armed parties, some singly, while smaller numbers of Protestants marched east. Already by April Protestants were singing jubilantly

> I don't want to sit where a papist sits
> I don't want to eat where a papist eats
> I don't want to dip my fingers in the same plate with a papist
> For we the English defeated the papists.

The Catholic drums could only respond more wistfully:

> Leave them alone, we shall share later, we shall share later.[69]

For both sides martial energies were now to be transformed into evangelical ones. The newly arrived missionaries were overwhelmed by the sheer scale of the demand for baptism and instruction. 'No sooner', wrote Bishop Tucker,

> was a reading sheet mastered than at once the learner became a teacher. It was the same with the Gospels: every fact noted, every truth mastered, was at once repeated by groups of eager enquirers. It was a most touching sight to see little groups scattered about here and there in the church, each of which had in its centre a native teacher who was himself, at other times in the day, an eager learner.[70]

Exactly the same enthusiasm was found upon the Catholic side,

---

[69] J. Waliggo, 'The Catholic Church in the Buddu Province of Buganda 1879–1925', Ph.D. thesis (Cambridge, 1976), 84–5.
[70] J. Taylor, *The Growth of the Church in Buganda* (1958), 63.

especially in Buddu. It had almost nothing to do with the arrival of the missionaries. The conversion movement was well under way before they returned. An old blind man, formerly a flute-player in the royal palace, doubtless a member of Andrew Kaggwa's band, came to Henri Streicher, the first Catholic missionary in Buddu, at Villa Maria, already in May 1891. He had come to beg for baptism: 'I have prayed for five years. It is a long time since I mastered the catechism.' He added that as he had heard that the missionaries favoured for baptism 'those who teach others to pray' he had brought with him thirty-two people whom he had taught.[71] Thus the self-appointed catechist came first, but both Catholic and Protestant missionaries saw that the only conceivable way they could respond to the situation was to send forth an army of catechists. Bishop Tucker had already commissioned a first group in January 1891, and the Catholics followed a little later, but both were blessing an existent reality rather than erecting something new.

As this movement spread out across the countryside, it depended very largely upon the favour of the chiefs. While they might not be able to stop a determined evangelist, they could greatly facilitate the work of conversion. The most enthusiastic were indeed themselves evangelists, but it was the forceful patronage of Nikodemo Sebwato, county chief of the eastern county of Kyagwe, and later of his successor Ham Mukasa, which turned it into a Protestant heartland, and that of Ssebowa in Buddu and most of the *gombolola* chiefs beneath him which made Buddu ever after the stronghold of Catholicism in which the conversion movement, already under way in 1891, was reinforced by the arrival of Ssebowa himself and of the Catholic exiles from the east who were settled in some 950 villages throughout the county. When in 1893 Sir Gerald Portal rectified the religious division of the country by giving Catholics the additional counties of the Ssese Islands, Mawokota, and Buwekula, Daniel Ssematimba, the new chief of Mawokota, left Buddu with a retinue of over 800 Catholics, and Cypriano Mutagwanya went with several hundred to take over Buwekula.

In the new Buganda to be a senior chief you not only needed to be a Christian, but you really needed too to have been among the exiles in Ankole in 1888. Only four among the three ministers and twenty county chiefs at the time of the Uganda agreement of 1900 had not

---

[71] Waliggo, 'The Catholic Church in the Buddu Province of Buganda', 96–7.

had this experience. They were the victors in a revolutionary war, but it is also true that they were by upbringing appropriate office-bearers. They had been *bagalagala*, royal pages, when young, and had proved their quality in war. They also made sure that clan traditions were scrupulously followed in the division of offices. Yet evangelization was now almost a function of chieftainship. So too, less easily, were piety and marital propriety. Christian chiefs were expected to go to Church regularly, avoid drunkenness, be faithful to one wife, and in general lead their peasantry into the way of Christian living. It is remarkable how many did so. Ssebowa and Mugwanya, Sebwato and Ham Mukasa, remained models of Christian rectitude—preachers, leaders in public prayer, even in Ham's case writers of biblical commentaries. But many others were not so perfect. The moral backsliding of chiefs upon whom the forward movement of Christianity so largely depended became increasingly a missionary headache. Kagwa might be Prime Minister and a highly skilful political leader of Protestantism, but his personal life was anything but impeccable in Christian eyes. He was, however, far too powerful and his support far too important for evangelical missionaries to complain publicly. Kakunguru, the most brilliant of Protestant war leaders, turned into an egocentric and increasingly idiosyncratic private empire-builder. Gabrieli Kintu, the most fiery of Catholic war-leaders, found missionary discipline fairly intolerable and was prone to heavy drinking. The French White Fathers with a fairly Jansenist moral theology were considerably less willing than Anglican Evangelicals to overlook the sins of those in power. In the Lent retreat of March 1894 shouts of the 'most scandalous type' were heard from the houses of some of the chiefs, a catechist was beaten up when he tried to interfere, and next morning Kintu and others were ordered by Streicher not to make their Easter communion, and indeed to pack up and go home. 'Tears prevent me to speak more about it,' Streicher confided to the mission diary, but next day Gabrieli and his men returned to beg for pardon 'because they have been unable to eat or sleep'.[72]

There were tensions here between aristocratic lay black leadership—the leadership which had in fact brought the Churches through the years of war and engendered the movement of mass conversion—and a white clerical leadership which was now striving

[72] Ibid. 129–31.

to achieve control of the Church and quietly end much of the spirit
of independence which had characterized the preceding years but
seemed quite alien to a proper Church, missionary and colonial.
Tucker, who was and remained faithful to the Venn CMS tradition of
the self-governing Church, far more so than most of his colleagues,
resolved very quickly to establish a local clergy and ordained the first
six deacons in 1893. Four of them also functioned as chiefs including
two county chiefs, Sebwato of Kyagwe and Zakariya Kizito Kisingiri
of Bulemezi. That, undoubtedly, was a brave attempt to consecrate
rather than replace the leadership which had naturally developed in
the Church, but Sebwato died two years later, and few chiefs were
in Church terms as reliable as he. Increasingly those who were
ordained gave up, or never exercised, a significant chiefly role, but
it was immensely important that a quite considerable group of
ordained priests was being built up by 1900 as a core within the far
larger body of catechists and as providing some sort of parallel
leadership, closely related to, but independent from, that of white
authority.

xii. *Buganda as a Model for its Neighbours*

The Ganda evangelical movement swept almost at once beyond the
borders of Buganda. Already in 1891 Nathaniel Mudeka, a nephew
of the old Prime Minister Mukasa, who had been much behind the
persecution of 1885 but had finally been murdered in the Islamizing
terror under Kalema, had volunteered and left to evangelize the
Sukuma south of Lake Victoria. In the following years the flow went
out in all directions. To understand this aright Buganda's claim to
some sort of paramountcy over its neighbours must not be
overlooked. The new Ganda leadership was anxious to use both
British rule and Christianity to extend the effective size of their
country, incorporating neighbouring lands into the kingdom. As the
tiny British administration battled to establish its control over the
peoples around, the appointment of Christian Baganda as chiefs over
non-Baganda seemed a good initial step. To the east where there was
no comparable chiefly system it worked for a while to colonial eyes
with apparent efficiency. In fact Kakunguru, who in the early 1890s
had been used again and again to command the Ganda levies needed
to support British expeditions, was temporarily given an almost free

hand to colonize Teso and Bukedi with the help of British-supplied ammunition. With him went a horde of Ganda adventurers looking for land, cattle, and subchieftainships as well as many a catechist who seldom made any effort to learn the local language, regarding Luganda as the chosen tongue of Christianity and civilization. The closer the missionary movement was tied to Ganda sub-imperialism, the less successful it was.

To the west things were more complicated in the Bantu kingdoms of Bunyoro, Toro, and Ankole, whose language and structure were far more similar to those of Buganda. Protestant success here too, if in a different way, was often closely political. The Ganda Protestant leaders Kagwa and Kisingiri exercised a great influence upon the new kings who for various reasons came to office in these years. No long-established ruler here, any more than in Buganda, adopted Christianity, but as British power became incontestable the model of Christian, and especially Anglican, chieftainship now dominant in Buganda, the principal state in the area, was accepted by each new king as part of the package of survival. Kasagama of Toro was baptized in 1896, Kitehimbwa, the young Mukama of Bunyoro, his sister, and the regent Byabacwezi in 1899, Kahaya, the Mugabe of Ankole, and his chief minister, Mbaguta, in 1902. At once they and their subchiefs became patrons too of Ganda catechist and local conversion, if seldom with the degree of personal commitment manifested by some at least of the Ganda leaders they were emulating. Tensions could subsequently arise, Baganda catechists be driven out, demands be made for a local translation of Scripture and prayer-book, but the fact is that here and still further afield the spread of Christianity would have been unthinkable without the Baganda evangelists, who were to be found by 1910 not only throughout most of what is today Uganda but also in Rwanda, eastern Zaïre, southern Sudan, western Kenya, and northern Tanzania. If in some cases they were cultural sub-imperialists, arrogant and unwilling to use another language than their own, in others they proved the most committed and disinterested of missionaries. In the case of the Catholics, moreover, they were less often (at least outside Rwanda and Tanganyika) assisted by any sort of political alliance. While the Catholic missionaries who had, as much as the Anglicans, sought the conversion of chiefs and were often bitterly disappointed to be deprived of the fruits of erastianism, they in due course found themselves instead beneficiaries of the fruits of freedom and, perhaps, of a certain preference on the part of ordinary Africans for a Church not so closely associated with the colonial state. Nevertheless, Catholicism too, even within British territory, and not only in Buddu, could advance under chiefly protection. Thus the muganda who first reduced Kigezi to colonial order was a Catholic, Yowana Ssebalijja, and when the first Catholic catechist arrived, he took up residence to begin with at Ssebalijja's. Years later in retirement Ssebalijja could proudly claim, 'Yohana Kitagana is the father of the first Bakiga to profess Christianity. I am their grandfather.'[73] In the lands around Lake Victoria chief and catechist constituted the two linked hands of Christian expansion.

The most outstanding figures in the early Ganda evangelization of neighbouring lands were Kitagana and Apolo Kivebulaya. As a character, Kivebulaya was the odd man out in this story: baptized in 1894, he was, unlike most of the famed Ganda Christian leaders of his generation, quite clearly not a chiefly type. He had rather an insignificant air. He cut little ice at home, but when he volunteered to serve in Toro, the offer was gladly accepted. Ordained a deacon in 1900 and a priest in 1903, he spent many of his years of apostolate in the Congo serving the people around Mboga. But it was as apostle to the pygmies of the forest that he is above all remembered and that particularly peregrinatory mission he took on in consequence of a vision of Christ in 1921. He 'appeared to me in the form of a man and stood beside me . . . He said to me "Go and preach in the forest because I am with you".'[74] This Apolo never married. He remained a model of poverty and of apolitical devotion to the very insignificant people among whom he evangelized. He died at Mboga, after thirty years of ministry, in 1933. It could be said that the entire Anglican province of today in eastern Zaïre has grown out of Kivebulaya's work, a work wholly untouched by the pursuit of power, wealth, or any physical satisfaction whatsoever. Any evaluation of Ganda Protestantism of the first colonial generation has to extend all the way from Apolo Kagwa to Apolo Kivebulaya. The distance is considerable.

Yohana Kitagana is a less well known but not less interesting figure. A tall, dignified, highly intelligent man in his mid-thirties, the husband of five wives, Kitagana was baptized a Catholic at the Kisubi

[73] Yowana Ssebalijja, 'Memoirs of Rukiga and other places', in D. Denoun (ed.), *A History of Kigezi* (Kampala, 1972), 179–99.
[74] A. Luck, *African Saint: The Life of Apolo Kivebulaya* (1963), 123.

mission in 1896. He had already abandoned all his wives and declared that he would have no more: 'God must suffice for me.' He then settled in Mawakota, receiving a chiefdom, but in 1901 announced his desire to become a missionary to peoples other than his own, and later that year, having resigned his chiefship and distributed all his property to the poor, set off for Bunyoro. Soon afterwards he was brought back to Lubaga to take the year course at the newly opened school for catechetical training, after which he went back to the west, being placed in the kingdom of Bunyaruguru beyond Ankole, which the British were at the time endeavouring to pacify through the imposition of some Ganda chiefs. The project was not a success. The Banyaruguru rose in revolt, the Baganda fled, only Kitagana remained, even continuing his work among the insurgents, despite the manifest danger he was in.

In 1911 Kitagana was moved to evangelize the mountainous district of Kigezi, and for more than ten years, before the arrival of three White Fathers in 1923, he preached and directed the work of other resident catechists, continually trekking through its valleys and hills, dressed only in an animal skin—apart from the white gown he kept for Sundays—and becoming truly the apostle of Kigezi as he was already that of Bunyaruguru, a man about whom many wonderful stories came to be told. Kitagana and Kivebulaya were at the height of their apostolic prowess at just the same time as Harris and Swatson, and in very comparable circumstances—the early years of colonial rule in societies hitherto almost untouched by any European presence. Kitagana's emphatic teaching of God, his destruction of fetishes, a simple concern with hygiene, the very poverty of his appearance, armed only with staff and rosary, may all remind one of Harris, though his spirit seems more gentle, without that touch of charismatic madness which differentiates a 'prophet'. He certainly did not have the power to effect change overnight. Harris functioned through the immediacy of unmitigated absolutes: destroy your fetishes now, be baptized now. It was a therapy of instantaneous conversion. For Kitagana this was not possible. For him, as a catechist of the White Fathers, baptism could only come—except in danger of death—after a lengthy catechumenate. Even fetishes might be kept for a little. In one charming story, when a sorcerer begged him to come at once and burn all his charms in front of his brothers, Yohana replied, 'Gently, my friend. Do not harm your protecting gods, for fear could take hold of you.' They waited a week and then Yohana burnt the objects to the chanting of 'Veni Creator'.[75] Over the years his journeyings may have been little less decisive for Kigezi or Bunyaruguru than were those of R.S. Oyebode for Ijeshaland or of Harris for the Ebrie or the Dida, but the main point which needs stressing is that, rather than isolated heroes, they are all three representative of a class of 'apostle' to be found in these years throughout the length and breadth of sub-Saharan Africa.

In Buganda itself the movement of conversion had inevitably passed by this time into a more prosaic, less exciting, even disillusioned, process of ecclesiastical construction under missionary control. In the Church of Uganda a rather dreary argument was going on between Bishop Tucker and his missionary colleagues over the establishment of a constitution for the Church with a regular synod. Tucker wanted the white missionaries to be fully in, and therefore under, the local Church. They were mostly reluctant to agree, arguing that it would be like 'giving school children control of their master'.[76] By 1908 a compromise was achieved which, if it did not go as far as Tucker had hoped, still did give the Church of Uganda a very much stronger position and more self-government than almost any African Church had at the time. In practice, nevertheless, it left the missionaries largely outside, and therefore above, its control. This was symbolic of a missionary failure, perhaps basically a racialist failure, to trust sufficiently a Church which had come into existence in so remarkable a way and with so little effort on their part.

Upon the Catholic side it would have been impossible to be anywhere near so far advanced in selfhood as, despite its faults, the Anglican Church's constitution proclaimed it to be. Yet, in Catholic terms, the Ugandan achievement was still more remarkable. In 1908 a Protestant missionary published a book about Uganda in which he remarked of the Catholics, 'They have no native clergy connected with their mission and are not likely to have any unless they can remove the obstacle of celibacy.'[77] That sounds a fair judgement and it tallies with Catholic experience elsewhere. Apart from the clergy of Angola of earlier days, mostly of mixed race, and a few individuals

[75] J. Nicolet, 'An Apostle in the Ruwenzori: Yohana Kitagana', unpublished paper, 9.
[76] H. B. Hansen, 'European Ideas, Colonial Attitudes and African Realities: The Introduction of a Church Constitution in Uganda 1898–1909', *IJA* 13 (1980), 255.
[77] C. W. Hattersley, *The Baganda at Home* (1908; repr. 1968), 220.

trained and ordained in Europe, the Catholic Church in Africa had proved wholly incapable of developing a local clergy despite the constant Roman insistence upon the importance of doing so. Everywhere the difficulties produced, upon the one hand, by the use of Latin for the celebration of mass, the recitation of the breviary, even the teaching of theology, and, upon the other, by the law of priestly celibacy seemed simply too great to overcome in societies where literacy was so limited and a life of celibacy derided. Yet almost at once Mgr. Hirth began a seminary, and when Mgr. Streicher was consecrated at Bukumbi in 1897 he declared to the thirty-three seminarians who crossed the lake to assist at the ceremony that it was his top priority. Rome had insisted that 'a mission that can produce martyrs can produce priests'.[78] Despite a great reluctance on the part of many of the missionaries, Streicher pressed on. The boys who entered the seminary were, for the most part, selected by Catholic chiefs to do so, including in some cases their own sons. To make the exercise possible, a great many books were required, both in Luganda and in Latin, including a large Latin–Luganda dictionary, used in manuscript form already for many years before its printing at Bukalasa—632 pages of a *Lexicon Latinum Ugandicum*—in 1912. In due course what seemed an unrealistic dream became a reality when the first two Baganda priests, Victor Mukasa and Bazilio Lumu, were ordained in 1913 in a ceremony witnessed by 15,000 people. By 1920 there were ten (including three from Toro and Bunyoro) and many more on the way, and the example was being followed elsewhere.

In 1910 a congregation of Ganda nuns, the Bannabikira, began its existence—in response not to missionary pressure but to the insistence of a large number of African women, including one of Stanislas Mugwanya's daughters, Angela Nabbogo, among others. Already in 1886 a first woman, Munaku, the sister of one of the martyrs, Noe Mawaggali, committed herself to perpetual virginity on the day of her baptism. She and others who joined her became auxiliaries in the missions and female catechists. Out of this group, the formal congregation began and grew by about a dozen a year. At the time of Munaku's decision there had not been a single white nun in the country to inspire her vocation. In this, as in so much else, early Ganda Christianity was both radical and spontaneous.

---

[78] White Father *Notice nécrologique* of Mgr. Streicher, 22.

Thus the conversion movement of the early 1890s in Buganda had come a long way by 1920, producing upon both Catholic and Anglican sides far more of a genuine Church, with a leadership and an intellectual life of its own, than one can find in so short a space of time anywhere else. And this had happened wholly within the vernacular culture. It was in no way an English-language Church. Many of its leaders indeed spoke little or no English. But it was a Church which had already made a quite considerable contribution outside its own language area to the Christianization of its neighbours, and from this came a recognizable unity within a conversion movement covering almost the whole area around Lake Victoria. As we have seen, the monarchies immediately to the west of Buganda all adopted Christianity around 1900. By 1910 the local White Father Superior on Ukerewe was able to bless the new king of that little island south of the lake. In 1919–20 all the eight kings of Buhaya suddenly became Christians, and their people followed them: 'Ekishomo kyomukama', 'to believe as the king believes' or 'to read the king's book' was how they put it.[79] In the 1930s it was the turn of Rwanda and Burundi to experience mass conversion. By 1940, then, a very large section of East Africa centred upon Buganda was predominantly Christian and, quite largely, Roman Catholic. A common character to this whole movement had been provided by a number of things: Ganda catechists were to be found throughout it, though their influence was far from being everywhere decisive, and in some areas, such as Burundi and parts of eastern Uganda, it may well have been counter-productive. It was certainly withdrawn well before the mass movement began in many places. Yet, in a larger way, the model set by Buganda—a particular mix of modernization, Christianization, and royalist traditionalism—was the one generally adopted.

Underlying the unity within the conversion movement lay a common type of Bantu culture. It was a civilization of monarchies, and while the conversion movement undoubtedly spilt out beyond the borders of that region, it did so somewhat uncertainly and unsuccessfully. It would be hard to regard the non-Bantu peoples of northern Uganda as genuinely included within the movement, and impossible to see the Wasukuma, the principal people directly south of the lake, as being so. Yet the unity of the movement was also

[79] B. Sundkler, *Bara Bukoba* (1980), 63–5.

established by the main missionary societies involved, the CMS and—still more—the White Fathers. For both bodies the experience of Buganda was profoundly formative. It is clear, in particular, how far White Father strategy was transformed by their Ugandan achievement. Orphanages were abandoned, catechists and bush schools multiplied, seminaries opened, the village rather than the central station cultivated—all because this was seen to succeed in Buganda. The process was helped by the fact that important bishops elsewhere, men like Hirth and Gorju, had been in Buganda first and sought to replicate the Ganda experience in their new fields. Moreover, Mgr. Livinhac, the society's first Superior-General, who presided over its very considerable shift in apostolic methodology in the quarter-century following the death of Cardinal Lavigerie in 1892, had himself been superior of the Ugandan mission and naturally thought that what was achieving so much in Buganda should be adopted elsewhere. As the White Fathers had been entrusted by the Catholic Church with such a huge area of east central Africa, extending southwards to the northern parts of Northern Rhodesia and Nyasaland and west into the Belgian Congo, the Buganda impact was felt very far—even if in some places, as among the Wasukuma, it simply brought no response. Outside White Father territory, however, its influence was slight.

xiii. *A Comparison between Conversions*

Buganda was then the new model, and a highly influential one. Nevertheless, it would be a great mistake to conclude that what happened in Buganda in the 1890s was simply replicated in, for instance, Rwanda in the 1930s, during the conversion movement the White Fathers there described as a 'tornade'. As Buganda and Rwanda had so much in common in size, the power of the monarchy, and the rapidity of a mass conversion movement when it came, it is worth pausing for a movement to reflect upon the deep divergence between the two. The Ganda movement was overwhelmingly self-started, at a time when there were few missionaries in the country and colonial rule had hardly begun. Missionaries and the colonial state responded to something they had certainly not created and could barely control. In Rwanda, the 'tornade', on the contrary, was produced by years of heavy missionary pressure and, finally, the forcible removal of the old pagan king Musinga in 1931.

Conversion in Kigezi, again, had a quite other face, derived in part from its very different social character, consisting of a number of non-monarchical units. While its early evangelization by an outstanding Ganda catechist links it with the conversion of Buganda, the character of the process involved was by no means the same. Moreover, while some of the secondary examples—particularly the kingdoms to the west first affected by Buganda—did themselves send out evangelist-catechists, this happened far less spontaneously and strikingly. It is remarkable that the remembered 'apostles' of peoples west of those kingdoms are names not from them but from Buganda. The Ganda experience, then, while greatly influential over a far larger area, was not as such replicated elsewhere.

What made it unique? The first answer to that question lies in the depth of its pre-colonial Christian experience. The mass movement of the 1890s is unimaginable without the individual conversions, martyrdoms, and civil wars of the 1880s. One may say that the early colonial situation provided a highly favourable environment for the working-out of a movement already under way. It certainly did not create it. Nowhere else did a conversion movement cross the hinge of colonialism in this way, feeding upon the opportunities and new horizons of the new regime without being intimidated by it. If the stimulus was not primarily colonial, nor was it primarily missionary—less so, undoubtedly, than in Igboland twenty years later, though more so than in the Ivory Coast of Harris or the villages of the Isoko. Here the missionaries, still after all quite few in relation to the scale of the movement, could to some extent channel and teach it, but they did not produce it and could not—at least for quite a while—control it. The balance was probably a good one. What did control it, at least initially, were the chiefs. Nowhere else in Africa did major chiefs, and not one or two oddities but a whole group, enter into, indeed initiate, a mass conversion and do so, not out of a sense of diplomatic advantage in relation to foreign powers, but from one of personal involvement. They had not indeed been chiefs before conversion, but they were in the class of those at court who were marked out for chieftainship in the near future. Undoubtedly conversion brought with it, after a lot of struggle and including not a few deaths in battle as well as on the execution pyre, both power and land. It was a political revolution as well as a religious one, but it was the religious change which came first, and, in purely political terms, these men still looked like a bunch of conservatives. If some of them hardly lived up afterwards to the personal ideals of their new public allegiance, others did so to a quite remarkable degree.

The Ganda experience was unique too in the speed, scale, and sheer enthusiasm of its early missionary movement to the peoples beyond. Nothing quite similar can be found elsewhere and if, without question, it at times degenerated into a sordid piece of subcolonialism, it also rose to produce some figures of exceptional holiness. Again it was unique in its production of an ordained clergy—more than twenty Anglicans by 1900, ten Catholics by 1920. Both were quite remarkable. On the Catholic side especially, Buganda showed that it was possible to produce priests against all expectation and provided a yardstick by which every other mission would subsequently be judged. The development of a community of sisters was no less impressive. And both went with the quick emergence of an ongoing leadership, lay as well as clerical, within both Churches which can again hardly be paralleled. The production of an early Luganda Christian literature by Ham Musaka, Apolo Kagwa, Alifonsi Aliwaali, Fr. Yozefu Ddiba, and others was quite exceptional. It was all part of the creation of a new rounded, thoroughly living national culture at once traditional and Christian, a culture which included within it all the clan differentiations of the past, the Catholic–Protestant divide the first missionaries had brought them, a unique and quickly mythologized religio-political history of its own, and even characteristic clothes. In Buganda the good Christian did not wear trousers, but a *kanzu*, just like Muslim or traditionalist. In nothing perhaps is the self-confidence of Ganda Christianity better expressed, but it was doubtless helped in this by the not very different dress of the White Fathers. In most places from the early nineteenth century on an African Christian, a missionary, and a settler all dressed alike, in European style, wholly distinguishable from non-converts. In Buganda this was not so. Colonialist and Protestant missionary wore trousers, but African Christians of both Churches adhered to the clothes of tradition, and if the Catholic missionary was judged—as he often was—an honorary 'non-European', it was in part at least because he almost dressed as one. Clothes remain a crucial part of consciousness, culture, and group identity.

When one considers the conversion of Buganda, it is essential not to see it simply as a mass conversion movement but as one which pushed straight on into the shaping of a diversified African Christian life. It may well be true that nowhere else were there so many exceptionally able missionaries, exceptional particularly as linguists, both Catholic and Protestant, and their contribution to the total process should in no way be undervalued. Nevertheless, they were, far more than they realized or quite liked, secondary to a phenomenon which as a whole from the 1880s to the 1920s remains one of the most decisive, unexpected, and still inadequately understood chapters within the Christian history of Africa.

xiv. *Varieties of Ethiopianism*

In March 1896 an Italian army invading Ethiopia under General Baratieri was decisively defeated by the Emperor Menelik at Adwa. A wave of sympathetic pleasure could, to the horror of colonialists, be felt throughout Africa. The white man was not invincible. It is odd how difficult then and even recently Europeans have found it to comprehend what came to be called 'Ethiopianism'. Why should Africans in the south or west wish to identify themselves with the name of a primitive kingdom thousands of miles away from them? Ethiopianism of course by no means began with Adwa. News of the victory merely reinforced its sense of confident identity. And the identity was, after all, in its way a Western imposition. For centuries Europeans had regularly described every part of black Africa as Ethiopia. It comes again and again in the titles and contents of books written in Portuguese or English from the sixteenth century onwards. In 1512 King Afonso I of Kongo had already been taught to refer to 'the peoples of these kingdoms and all the chiefs of Ethiopia'.[80] From then on instances of its use are innumerable. Kongo and Angola were parts of 'western Ethiopia', Mozambique and Mutapa parts of 'eastern Ethiopia'. When T. J. Hutchinson published in 1861 his *Ten Years Wandering among the Ethiopians from Senegal to Gabon* or D. K. Flickinger entitled his 1885 volume *Ethiopia; or, Thirty Years of Missionary Life in Western Africa* (in fact in Sierra Leone) they were only doing what all missionaries were accustomed to do. Their use of the line of Psalm 68 'Ethiopia shall stretch out her hands to God' to refer to Christian conversion anywhere in Africa was again common form. It was apparently the

[80] *Correspondance de Dom Afonso, roi du Congo 1506–1543*, ed. L. Jadin and M. Dicorato (Brussels, 1974), 54.

favourite text of James Stewart of Lovedale, hardly someone sympathetic to Ethiopianism. An equally popular missionary text was Acts 8 on the baptism of the Ethiopian eunuch. So it is hardly surprising if African Christians accepted an Ethiopian identity. 'Africa is to rise once more, Ethiopia is to stretch out her hands to God; her tears are to be wiped off her eyes; her candlestick is to be replaced,' said James Johnson in a memorable 1867 sermon in Freetown.[81] 'I stand up for the Ethiopian,' Harris told Benoit near the end of his life in 1926.[82] 'Ethiopianism', then, as such, had nothing special to do with ecclesiastical independency in the narrow sense. It referred to a natural sense of cultural and political identity of black Christians anywhere on the continent, drawing upon the Bible on the one side and the surviving strength of a black Christian state in the horn of Africa on the other, to inspire confidence at once religious and political over against the pressure to conform in all things to the white man, missionary or colonialist. But it was natural too to carry this across to provide a name and justification for independent African Churches: Ethiopian was, after all, a better name than those the missionaries had brought with them: Anglican, Methodist, or Presbyterian. Which of these was to be found in the Bible? Of which could it be said, as it could of Ethiopia in reference to Zion, 'This one and that one were born in her' (Psalm 87: 4–5)? Ethiopia and Zion, be it noted, were not contrasting but overlapping points of reference: Ethiopia had always for Ethiopians been a relocation of Zion. Now for black people everywhere it would symbolize a biblical and historical pathway to Zion.

When in 1892 Mangena Mokone, a Wesleyan minister in Johannesburg, resigned in opposition to racial segregation within the Wesleyan Church and established a new 'Ethiopian Church', something quite decisive was happening for African Church history. It was not the first secession in South Africa, but it was the first to endure in a way which mattered and to point the road for many others to follow in quite rapid succession. In fact similar secessions were taking place at just the same time in Nigeria. In each case some people within the now quickly expanding African Christian community were finding missionary control and a certain inbuilt racial discrimination intolerable. But many other Christians, while

[81] E. Ayandele, *Holy Johnson* (1970), 45.
[82] Shank, 'A Prophet of Modern Times', iii. 1114.

not dissenting from the sentiments of the secessionists, did not agree with their conclusions. Bishop James Johnson was an obvious Nigerian example. 'Why should not there be an African Christianity as there has been a European and an Asiatic Christianity?', he asked in 1905 in his annual report to the CMS as auxiliary bishop in the diocese of Lagos.[83] Johnson, undoubtedly, was an 'Ethiopian', but he was not a secessionist, while in point of fact none of the early Nigerian 'Independent' Churches adopted the name 'Ethiopian'. Again, when in 1900 Mokone's forceful colleague James Dwane led a group of his Church members via the black American African Methodist Episcopal Church back into communion with a mission Church—the Anglican Church in South Africa—they retained the Ethiopian nomenclature, becoming the Order of Ethiopia. Being an Ethiopian did not exclude being also an Anglican or whatever, but it did imply an unwillingness to be Europeanized in religious culture or bossed by white missionaries, and it went with a strong committedness to the cause of African political freedom as well as ecclesiastical.

For many indeed it was more a political than a religious movement. Ethiopia and Ethiopianism signified the African perception, arrived at very quickly, that Christian commitment did not need to include being a colonial stooge or a 'black European'. Most missionaries were uncomprehendingly horrified, none more so than the paternalist patriarch James Stewart of Lovedale, horrified to see his hitherto dutiful son P. J. Mzimba, the Free Church of Scotland's first ordained black successor to Tiyo Soga, found the African Presbyterian Church in 1898. For him the Order of Ethiopia, to which the Anglican bishops had agreed, was 'a cave of Adullam for the restless and dissatisfied'.[84] For the Victorian Anglo-Saxon Protestant, strong on efficiency, civilization, and white control, Ethiopia signified the antithesis of all he had sought to achieve. For the African Christian, to the contrary, it symbolized the identity and the dignity one could never quite find in a missionary's world. It is noteworthy that the figure of Ntsikana was seminal to South African Ethiopianism, the symbolic name to which almost everyone appealed. If two of his great-grandsons, Burnet and Ntsikana Gaba, founded a small independent Church, the Ntsikana Memorial Church at Pirie in 1911, a far larger number of people, most of them

[83] Ayandele, *Holy Johnson*, 304.
[84] J. Wells, *Stewart of Lovedale* (1908), 292.

firmly within mission Churches, were involved in the establishment of the Ntsikana Memorial Association in 1909, a body more cultural than religious and a seed-bed for the African National Congress. By the 1920s it had canonized Ntsikana. The decade after Adwa proved the great age of Ethiopianism just as much as it was the great age of colonial and missionary expansion. The one was indeed, in terms of African Christian experience, the immediate, natural, and inevitable corollary of the other, but it was not simply a reaction. It was rather the flowering at a time of increased stress of a spiritual tradition which already went back in some places nearly 100 years.

Ethiopianism produced, moreover, one outstanding cultural artefact—'God bless Africa'. Mankayi Enoch Sontonga composed both music and words of 'Nkosi Sikelel' i-Africa' in 1897. A Lovedale Presbyterian, he threw in his lot with Mzimba and the hymn was first sung in 1899 by a choir of the African Presbyterian Church. The first meeting of the South African Native National Congress sang it in January 1912 and the ANC adopted it as national anthem in 1925. It has since become the official anthem of the Transkei and, in translation, the national anthem of both Zambia and Zimbabwe. In influence it is the only hymn which can rival Ntsikana's 'Great Hymn'. Through it the spirit of Ethiopianism, at once religious and nationalist, has been carried for a century across the Churches and political parties of the whole of southern Africa.

In July 1897 Mwanga, the Kabaka of Buganda, left his palace, secretly boarded a canoe, and crossed Lake Victoria to Buddu to unleash war upon the British. Buddu was now the heart of Ganda Catholicism, and though its pokino (county chief) Alikisi Ssebowa remained faithful to the British, his deputy, the equally devout Catholic Lui Kibanyi, became Mwanga's katikiro for the period of struggle. Mwanga was supported in his 'revolt' against the British by a great number of Catholics and Protestants as well as traditionalists and Muslims, for colonial rule had proved deeply unpopular. It was in a way a rising in favour of the old against the new, for Ganda tradition against European innovation, and many churches were burnt as representing alien invasion, particularly as the missionaries—French Catholics as much as British Protestants—condemned the rising unhesitatingly. It was 'against Europeans, Christianity, civilization and progress', wrote George Pilkington uncompromisingly in August.[85]

---

[85] Harford-Battersby, *Pilkington of Uganda*, 317.

Yet the numerous Christians who supported Mwanga for a variety of reasons did not see it like that. Many of them in no way regarded themselves as betraying their religion, though there were others who sympathized but did not join them because religion held them back. For some who had gone with Mwanga loss of the sacraments was too much. 'Go back and get your chiefdom,' said the King bitterly to Matayo Bakaluba. 'For me, my lord,' Matayo replied, 'I am not going to take a chiefdom, I am going to practise my religion, though perhaps I may find a chief to give me meat if I am faithful.'[86] Gabrieli Kintu, who had always been the fiercest and most successful of the Catholic war-leaders, became Mwanga's most effective general. His excommunication by name was read out in churches throughout the county on 10 October 1897, but, as he wrote later to Bishop Livinhac, 'I never stole anything belonging to the Church, never burned any church, I never stole a Christian woman.'[87] While the more prudent of Christian leaders—Apolo Kagwa and Zakariya Kizito Kisingiri, Alikisi Ssebowa and Stanislas Mugwanya—remained emphatically committed to British rule and missionary guidance, those who threw in their lot with Mwanga did so above all out of simple loyalty to their king. Certainly they included the drunkards and the adulterers, the bhang-smokers and the polygamists, but they also included a few at least of the most sincerely Christian of the chiefs. Lui Kibanyi was hanged for his leadership in the 'revolt' after receiving communion, crucifix and rosary in hand. 'You will soon know', he declared unabashed to Kagwa and Mugwanya, 'who the true rebel was, myself or you . . . Judge for yourselves if those who obeyed their king were the rebels and not you who obeyed the Europeans.'[88]

The Ganda Christian chiefs in 1897 were having to work out in a hurry and the heat of war issues of religious and political loyalty of great complexity and with exceedingly little help from outside. In most comparable resistance movements, such as the simultaneous Shona rebellion or Maji Maji in Tanganyika, the inspiration of traditional religion, of prophets like Nehanda and Kinjikitile, was wholly preponderant. Buganda was exceptional in being already so Christianized that the Christians could and did take part in

---

[86] M. Wright, *Buganda in the Heroic Age* (1971), 179.
[87] Waliggo, 'The Catholic Church in the Buddu Province of Buganda', 152–3.
[88] Ibid. 154.

anticolonial revolt, following the South African example of Dukwana a generation earlier. But the underlying issue was not dissimilar from that which 'Ethiopians' in south and west were facing increasingly openly in the same years, to the alarm of many a missionary. Did Christian faith necessarily imply loyalty to the colonial order in all its forms? What is remarkable is how quickly black Christians were able to answer 'no' to that question in defiance of missionary advice. In the following years, in the Bambata Rising in Natal in 1906 and the rebellion against the Germans in South West Africa, for example, Christians would again be found among the resisters as well as among the collaborators. They would, however, be among the first of the resisters to recognize that simple reaction could never succeed and that the triumph of Ethiopian ideals would come through schools, journalism, and political associations rather than through the outdated guns of Mwanga or Bambata. The wider secular value of the Ethiopianism which attracted such attention in the first decade of the century was that it helped provide the seed ground for a constructive realignment of African resistance in directions which reconciled the pursuit of freedom with the requirements of modernization.

Charles Domingo had been brought as a boy from the coast of Mozambique by William Koyi to serve with the Livingstonia Mission. He was educated by Laws and became an elder in the congregation and an unordained minister. For a while he was the hope of the Mission, but just as Mzimba disappointed Stewart at Lovedale so Domingo disappointed Laws at Livingstonia, though— perhaps curiously—his breach with the mission came about through confrontation not with the authoritarian Laws but with the more liberal Donald Fraser. In 1908 Domingo withdrew from the Scottish mission and, a little later, came under the influence of the quintessential missionary 'independent' Joseph Booth, who encouraged him to set up in Nyasaland an African Sabbatarian Church, the Seventh-day Baptists. Despite receiving a little support, channelled through Booth, from America, it was not a great success. Domingo's Ethiopianism combined an assertion of African competence, Sabbatarianism, and the attempt to run an educational mission on Livingstonia lines. It could not work in so poor an environment, despite his own considerable ability and hard endeavour. The very same letter which could express the hope that they 'make whole

Nyasaland be The Seventh Day Nyasaland' complained that his wife, no longer at home, had nothing to clothe herself and her children.[89] Here as often within the Ethiopian enterprise the gap between aspiration and attainment was singularly wide. All the more striking was the clarity of judgement upon the situation around him in passages some of which have become deservedly famous, and none more so than one of September 1911:

There is too much failure among all Europeans in Nyasaland. The Three Combined Bodies: Missionaries, Government—and Companies or Gainers of money do form the same rule to look on a Native with mockery eyes. It sometimes startle us to see that the Three Combined Bodies are from Europe and along with them is a title 'CHRISTENDOM'. And to compare or make a comparison between the MASTER of the title and His Servants it pushes any African away from believing the Master of the title. If we had power enough to communicate ourselves to Europe, we would have advised them not to call themselves 'CHRISTNDOM' but 'Europeandom'. We see that the title 'CHRISTNDOM' does not belong to Europe but to future BRIDE. Therefore the life of the Three Combined Bodies is altogether too cheaty, to thefty, too mockery. Instead of 'Give' they say 'Take away from'—from 6 am to 5 or 6 pm there is too much breakage of GODS pure law as seen in James' Epistle V:4. Therefore GOD's vengeance is upon The Three Combined Bodies of Nyasaland.[90]

Despite the struggle with language, that passage presents a quite remarkably powerful analysis of the colonial situation in the early twentieth century by an extremely isolated person, yet one fully in line with a vastly much wider Ethiopianism.

Livingstonia continued to regard itself, and to be generally regarded, as an exceptionally progressive mission. But Scottish progressivism here as at Lovedale or Blantyre was not incompatible with a deeply, almost racistly, authoritarian treatment of those it was determined to uplift. Three years later it conducted its first ordinations. The case of Y. Z. Mwasi is instructive. First appointed a Livingstonia evangelist in 1902, a fellow student of Domingo, he was one of the three selected for ordination in 1914, yet just a few months later he was suspended for insubordination and only permitted to resume work 'on the distinct understanding he will obey the minister in charge as to how he is to carry out his work, and

[89] *Letters of Charles Domingo*, ed. H. Langworthy (Zomba, 1983), 58 and 60.
[90] Ibid. 16.

where he is to work, and whatsoever other directions he will receive'.[91] That minute of the Livingstonia Presbytery is dated 13 February 1915, just twelve days after the death of John Chilembwe. While the Livingstonia missionary Donald Fraser would have repudiated indignantly the accusation that he looked on African ministers with 'mockery eyes' and, indeed, defended Domingo personally a few months later before the government Commission of Inquiry into the Chilembwe Rising, could one be surprised if Mwasi saw his ordination when hedged around with such severe instructions as 'altogether too cheaty'? At the time he did, however, accept the conditions imposed, and even became some years later Livingstonia's first African Moderator, before, in the 1930s, breaking away to found the Blackman's Church.

Domingo was then by no means unusual in his evaluation of how missionaries regarded Africans: 'Gutiri mubia na muthungu'—'There is no difference between missionary and settler'—the Kikuyu saying simply summarized Domingo's analysis. The very same year, 1911, on the other side of the continent Joseph Casely Hayford, the Gold Coast lawyer, published his *Ethiopia Unbound*, probably the most distinguished literary expression of early twentieth-century Ethiopianism. Casely Hayford had spent years in London where his book was produced. He was a man of vastly higher formal education than Domingo. He did not join an independent Church (though his brother endeavoured to found one), and his approach to both Christianity and African traditional religion was characterized by a slightly whimsical and playful detachment. But his fictional picture of the missionary Silas Whiteley was at least as bitter as Domingo's. So 1911 (the year following the *annus mirabilis* of missionary consciousness, self-confidently epitomized in the Edinburgh Conference) gives us two damning anti-missionary texts stemming from Ethiopianism. But it also gives us a third with a rather different note.

At almost exactly the same moment as Domingo was writing his scathing indictment of 'the Three Combined Bodies' an Anglican catechist in Southern Rhodesia of very comparable qualifications was making his indictment of measures of forced labour whereby government officials were forcing Africans to work for white farmers. In November 1911 Matthew, the senior teacher at St. Faith's, Makoni, was teaching at the kraal of Gushiri, sent there by Canon

[91] J. Parratt, 'Y. Z. Mwasi and the Origins of the Blackman's Church', *JRA* 9 (1978), 196.

Edgar Lloyd. It was to Lloyd that Matthew reported the complaints of Gushiri's people, and when Lloyd vigorously took them up with the government and a Commission of Inquiry was appointed, Matthew declared firmly to the Commission: 'I consider it my duty should I hear of any irregularity by officials of the Native Department to report to the head of the mission. In my opinion the Native Commissioner exceeded his authority . . . If the Native Commissioner acted wrongly I should like to see him punished.'[92] Matthew's voice is not unrecognizably Ethiopian. The difference between him and Domingo was that he was working with a quite exceptionally enlightened missionary in Edgar Lloyd. In consequence the forces and sense of anticolonial grievance at work in Ethiopianism could here actually enhance the life and witness of a mission Church.

More famous than Domingo, Mwasi, or Matthew was Chilembwe. In 1892 a young man named John Chilembwe sought work as a cook boy from the missionary radical Joseph Booth of the Zambezi Industrial Mission established at the time in the Shire highlands. From a cook boy he became a son, and in 1897 Booth took him to America where he entered a Negro college in West Virginia and returned to Nyasaland in 1900 with Negro Baptist backing to begin what they named the Providence Industrial Mission. It was not an independent Church. It was indeed directed for a time by black American Baptist missionaries. It was a very typical example of the restrained Ethiopianism which hoped to develop an African Protestantism, in this case very little adapted culturally, free of white control: committed to Western forms of schooling, monogamous marriage, Moody and Sankey hymns, long dresses, black suits, and a pretty mild form of political protest, the kind of Ethiopianism in fact that Afro-Americans had come to prefer, progressive but seldom 'cheeky'.

For fourteen years Chilembwe laboured in the Providence Industrial Mission at Chiradzulu by Magomero. From 1906 he did so without Afro-American supervision and he did so successfully. There were many hundreds of children in his schools, the brick church he completed in 1913 was exceptionally impressive, and an African Industrial Society had been launched. There were, however, growing problems, especially shortage of money and tension with the Bruce Estates, the huge Scottish agricultural development which

---

[92] T. Ranger, 'Religions and Rural Protests in Makoni District, Zimbabwe', 325.

'owned' most of the land around Magomero. Ironically the Bruces who owned the estate were David Livingstone's son-in-law and, later, grandson. Livingstone had appealed for British settlement to develop central Africa and the Bruce Estates represented the response of pious, commercial Scotland. The Bruce Estates wanted cheap labour. Chilembwe's congregation were, for the most part, 'squatters' on Bruce lands, and the estate management appears to have burnt the grass-hut churches which his flock erected here and there near their dwellings. Even an instinctively moderate African Church was being driven to radicalism by its settler-colonial context. In 1913 the centenary of David Livingstone's birth was celebrated in Blantyre, and A. Livingstone Bruce of the Magomero Estates presented to its church a bronze memorial plaque on behalf of all Livingstone's grandchildren. Beside him for this occasion stood William Jervis Livingstone, the estate manager and—in the eyes of the humble Christians of the Providence Industrial Mission—the tyrant who abused their lives. While commerce at Magomero could thus still appeal devoutly to the heritage of Livingstone, nowhere was it more painfully at odds with the reality of an African Christianity. The very place where Livingstone's most ambitious piece of missionary strategy, the UMCA expedition led by Bishop Mackenzie, had failed disastrously fifty years earlier, would shortly become the scene of an even more painful débâcle for a vision of conversion linking Christianity with the commerce of colonialists.

xv. *The Impact of World War*

From 4 August 1914 Britain, France, and Russia were at war with Germany and Austria. This meant that in Africa too there would be war, in fact four different wars, in east, west, and south, relating to Germany's four African territories. Of these the longest and most severe was the war for Tanganyika and Rwanda–Burundi, a war affecting all the territories around—Kenya and Uganda, Northern Rhodesia, and Chilembwe's Nyasaland. Already in September a considerable number of Africans had been killed when the King's African Rifles encountered the German forces for the first time at Karonga near the northern end of Lake Nyasa. European armies in Africa required a mass of African auxiliaries, both soldiers and tens of thousands of porters. African society was now to be press-ganged to provide the muscle without which white officers could not march around, to kill and be killed. Far more porters died than soldiers. The British alone 'employed' more than half a million porters and admitted to the death of 44,911 from disease, probably a great underestimate. In November as recruitment was getting under way, Chilembwe, perhaps the black man in Nyasaland with the most standing, took it upon himself to write a letter of protest to the *Nyasaland Times*, which the newspaper actually printed:

A number of Police are marching in various villages persuading well-built natives to join the war. The masses of our people are ready to put on uniforms ignorant of what they have to face or why they have to face it . . . Will there be any good prospects for the natives after the end of the war? Shall we be recognised as anybody in the best interests of civilisation and Christianity after the great struggle is ended? . . . In time of peace the Government failed to help the underdog. In time of peace, everything for Europeans only. And instead of honour we suffer humiliation with names contemptible. But in time of war it has been found that we are needed to share hardships and shed our blood in equality.[93]

Unsurprisingly the government immediately confiscated the issue of the newspaper which included this scathing protest. Two months later, on 23 January 1915, a group of Africans led by Chilembwe rose in revolt. A few of them marched over to the European houses in Magomero, decapitated William Jervis Livingstone, and bore his head back upon a pole to place it in the church at Chiradzulu. A couple of other Europeans were murdered, but their wives and children were not harmed and no real strategy of attack was apparent. As government forces advanced, the rebels disintegrated, Chilembwe himself being killed as he fled towards Mozambique. For several years Eliot Kamwana had been spreading the millennialism of Watch Tower throughout Nyasaland, and Watch Tower had prophesied the end of the world for 1914. Had Chilembwe's followers reinterpreted this prophecy to anticipate divine intervention if they rose in revolution? More mundanely, the Germans were at the frontier. Had they expected German assistance? Had they hoped for a general rising and been disappointed by how little support they in fact received? Were they making no more than a symbolic gesture of protest after which they would die as martyrs? Was Chilembwe in fact out of his mind, distraught by debt and the impact of war? The

[93] G. Shepperson and T. Price, *Independent African: John Chilembe and the Origins, Setting and Significance of the Nyasaland Native Rising of 1915* (Edinburgh, 1958), 234–5.

macabre service he is reported to have held before the head of Livingstone could suggest it. It seems impossible to answer such questions with any certainty. Chilembwe has proved vastly more powerful in death than in life: the strangest of mini-risings largely unsupported in a land not excessively ill governed has become in the retrospect of mythological history a famous expression of proto-nationalism and Christian resistance. What is very difficult is to understand how the rather mild-mannered Ethiopian churchman was transformed in his last weeks into the instigator of murder and anarchy. Perhaps the sheer awfulness of the prospect of war and his own deep isolation combined to craze the mind of a sensitive man long embittered by a colonial system which bore particularly painfully on the few who were as educated as he. The first reaction to the rising of the white settlers, Livingstone Bruce above all, was to denounce the missions in general, and especially the more liberal of the Protestant missions, as the cause of much evil. The missionary reply, formulated by Laws of Livingstonia and Hetherwick of Blantyre, was adequately convincing. It may at least have helped demonstrate a certain degree of distinction between missionaries and the other sides of the white establishment.

Harris, a prophet of a very different sort, was disturbing the Ivory Coast at exactly the time Chilembwe was disturbing Nyasaland. The French could not tolerate prophets in wartime and he was hastily deported. In Uganda too a group of Anglicans, Malaki Musajjakawa, Yoswa Kate Damulira, and the formidable Semei Kakunguru, began in 1914 a movement of spiritual revolution which rejected European medicine—the Church of the One Almighty God or the Bamalaki as they were commonly called—and tens of thousands of Christians were joining them. Chilembwe, Harris, and Malaki did not have so much in common, but all three represented a new and populist level of African Christian initiative, quite removed from missionary control, an Ethiopianism taken to the market-place of a sort which could only worry missionaries exceedingly.

There were in 1914 only some twenty Catholic missionaries in the Ivory Coast. They had hitherto achieved little, yet just as the preaching of Harris was providing both a challenge and an opportunity to enrol his converts in their congregations—as he himself recommended—nine out of the twenty left at once on 7 August to enlist in the French army. Three more followed soon, leaving for a while just six priests to man their eight stations. Despite this the number of Ivory Coast Catholics multiplied in the following years, and, much as the missionaries disliked Harris, they had to admit that it was he who had brought it about. Up to 1914 missionaries had been rapidly increasing in number almost everywhere. Now they still more rapidly diminished. The German authorities arrested British missionaries. The British authorities arrested German missionaries, while French missionaries, even when arrested by no one, showed their loyalty to a country which had been abusing its clergy by returning to France to join the army.

The effect of all this upon the African Churches was varied. Where missionaries, like Fraser in Nyasaland and Arthur in Kenya, backed recruitment they could incur considerable unpopularity, but in general the war may well have temporarily diminished (except in South Africa) the white–black strain which had been mounting in the previous years. In practice it left Africans much freer to get on with things in their own way. Many Churches found themselves with no missionaries at all. African teachers carried on in their place, in a few instances hastily ordained before the white clergy departed. In some cases, such as the old Basel Mission in the Gold Coast, white control was never really recovered. Where there had been very few converts some Churches disappeared altogether, but where there was already a moderately strong Church the freedom of the war usually made it a great deal stronger. The self-leadership, self-propagation, and self-support which missionaries had so often talked about, but so seldom been willing to try out, actually worked when they had to. Moreover, the leaders who emerged in these circumstances often showed a quite particular loyalty to the denominational tradition in which they had begun. Absence made the heart grow fonder, and when South African Wesleyans, for example, tried to poach the Bukoba Lutherans left pastorless by their German missionaries, the local Christians remained firmly Lutheran, boycotting the Wesleyan mission. The social disturbance of the war and the further strains produced by the great influenza epidemic of 1918 actually encouraged religious conversion while diminishing internal Church tension. The growth of Islam was encouraged too at least in areas, such as the coastal hinterland of Tanganyika, where it already had a foothold. In Africa, as elsewhere, war then proved good for religion.

Despite the huge loss of life, it was in a way also good for society. It was the last phase of the scramble—the phase in which Germany lost all its possessions to be redistributed between France and Britain,

Belgium and South Africa. But it also, more decisively, brought the whole era and atmosphere of the scramble to a close. The League of Nations was inaugurated in January 1920, and the former German colonies were not simply to be taken over by the victors. They became instead 'mandated territories' for which their rulers had to answer to the League. The powers of the League were not really very strong, but legally the position was a new one, and the sense of moral responsibility intrinsic to the mandate came to be extended to the older colonies as well. The philanthropists of the Phelps-Stokes Commission on Education in Africa, funded from New York, had set sail for the west coast already in August 1920. In South Africa the College of Fort Hare had just been founded. One age had ended and another begun, though many a missionary and colonial official might hardly realize it.

'Will there be any good prospects for the natives after the end of the war?', Chilembwe had asked pessimistically. In fact the answer was 'yes'. Colonial power was weakened, the world forces of anticolonialism greatly reinforced. Africans themselves were stronger, more knowledgeable, more experienced, and among them no group was growing faster in knowledge and experience than Christians who had had in many places to cope largely on their own, while drawing their own conclusions from the conflict of white Christian nation with white Christian nation. In 1921 Tengo Jabavu lay dying at Fort Hare. A member of its governing council, he had done as much as anyone to bring it into existence as a college, and future university, for all Africans regardless of tribe. For many it was simply his college, I-Koleji ka Jabavu. As breathing grew difficult he endeavoured to sing Tiyo Soga's hymn 'Lizalis' idinga Lako', placing himself at death within a formed tradition of African spirituality.[94]

> Fulfil Thy promises,
> O God, Lord of truth
> Let every tribe of this land
> Obtain Salvation.

In 1921 it could fairly be claimed—as it could not when Soga wrote it more than fifty years earlier—that such a prayer was about to be fulfilled. In 1871, when Soga died, almost the only Africans to have seriously appropriated Christianity and so identified themselves as

---

[94] Francis Wilson and Dominique Perrot (eds.), *Outlook on a Century* (Lovedale, 1973), 182.

radically 'Ethiopian' were Sierra Leoneans and some Yoruba and Fante in the west, some Khoi, Xhosa, and Tswana in the south, a handful of Bakongo clinging to ancestral memories in the middle. They had been joined in 1921 by a quickly growing multitude of Zulu and Baganda, Igbo and Shona, Fipa and Ebrie, Basotho and Bahaya, Ngoni and Bemba. A history of the African Church has largely to be a history of particular peoples, but from the turn of the century there are really too many major movements for it to be any longer possible to chart them individually in a work of this sort. We can attempt to comprehend the pattern, we can no longer list the instances.

11

FROM AGBEBI TO DIANGIENDA: INDEPENDENCY AND PROPHETISM

i. 'African Churches' in Nigeria and South Africa 1888–1917

David Brown Vincent was a Yoruba born in 1860, the son of a CMS agent returned from Sierra Leone to Nigeria. His entirely English name expresses well enough the tastes of the first generation of Sierra Leonean Christians. In the early 1880s in a wave of revivalism he joined the Baptist Church in Lagos and was soon employed as a teacher in its Academy, an educational institution of some prestige. It was an American mission. In 1888 Vincent became one of a group of leading Lagos Baptist laity to disagree with their white American missionary and establish an independent Native Baptist Church. In itself, and in terms of Baptist polity, this looks like a quarrel within a Church rather than a schism from a Church, but in terms of a growing dissatisfaction on the part of Nigerian Christians with missionary control, it is to be seen as the first of a series of secessions from the mission Churches of Lagos which continued for twenty-five years and produced a considerable group of African Churches deriving from Baptist, Anglican, and Methodist parents.

The underlying cause of all these separations, here and in South Africa, was tension between an African Christian community with more than fifty years of tradition to it and an increasingly self-conscious sense of identity, an ethos of its own, and the quickly expanding number of white missionaries sharing in the expansionist self-confidence of Europe in the age of the scramble and mostly quite unimpressed by what had hitherto been accomplished. They were disposed to believe that the time was very far from ripe for the sort of independence which African Christians deriving from an earlier evangelism had come to think their due. In West Africa the collapse of Bishop Crowther's Niger Episcopate under the hammer-blows of young CMS enthusiasts set the stage for what was to follow: a reassertion of white control within the mission Churches, the determination to establish independent Churches on their own terms among many of their more disaffected members. 'Ethiopians' turned into 'Independents'.

'There are times when it is more helpful that a people should be called upon to take up their responsibilities, struggle with and conquer their difficulty than that they should be in the position of vessels taken in tow. . . for West African Christianity, this is the time.' So wrote James Johnson, the most learned and respected of the African Anglican clergy, in July 1892.[1] Nevertheless, neither Johnson nor many of the clergy took part when it came to it. Despite bitterness with the way things were going in the post-Crowther era, denominational loyalties, theological doubts, perhaps simply pragmatic recognition of the difficulties involved, held back most of the potential clerical leaders of an independent African Church and left its direction largely in lay hands.

D. B. Vincent and James Johnson may well be contrasted: the one took the decisions which the other only advocated. Vincent became easily the most distinguished of the secessionists, and the most thoroughgoing. In 1894 he abandoned all his Western names, becoming instead Mojola Agbebi. He also rejected European dress, even when visiting Europe. In both he was endeavouring to symbolize the underlying motivation of the African Church movement, escape from the culturally Westernized model of Christianity which had been so enthusiastically embraced by the first Sierra Leonean generation. The African Churches were not challenging the doctrine, theology, or liturgy of the mission Churches—for the most part they held indeed to these only too tenaciously—but they were seeking a measure of synthesis with African culture and mildly anticolonialist politics.

Agbebi was the founding pastor of the Native Baptist Church in Lagos, but in character and activity he was far more of a layman than Johnson, a prolific writer and propagandist, the editor at one time or another of every newspaper appearing in Lagos between 1880 and 1914. First president in 1913 of the African Communion of independent Churches, he was something of an international figure known in both Britain and America, while at the same time continuing until his death in 1917 an unsuppressible propagandist for a non-missionary version of African Christianity. Already in a

[1] J. Webster, *The African Churches among the Yoruba 1888–1922* (1964), 1.

pamphlet of 1889, *Africa and the Gospel*, he had appealed to his fellow countrymen not 'forever to hold at the apron strings of foreign teachers, doing the baby for aye'.[2] 'The foreigner is not fitted to construct an African Church,' he insisted in 1892.[3] In a sermon of some distinction preached in December 1902 at the celebration of the first anniversary of the Lagos African Church, an Anglican secession, he appealed in memorable words for the rejection of 'hymn-books, harmoniums, dedications, pew constructions, sur-pliced choir, the white man's names, the white man's dress, so many non-essentials, so many props and crutches affecting the religious manhood of the Christian Africans', and added, 'In one of the Churches planted up-country, I have found it necessary to advise that for seven years at least, no hymn-books but original hymns should be used at worship.'[4]

Agbebi's policy of Africanization was not wholly unacceptable to missionaries. We have seen, that very same year, 1902, Donald Fraser on the other side of the continent encouraging the production of 'original hymns' most effectively. The CMS had already some twenty years earlier minuted the resolution that Africans should be encouraged to retain African names, and James Johnson, at that time pastor of St Paul's, Breadfruit, had thereupon refused to baptize children with names other than African, though equally he refused to change his own. His refusal to import European names was not, in fact, popular with Lagos Christians. The culture of a new society— and Sierra Leonean Christianity was a new society—could not be reversed by sudden perception of a different vision. Agbebi was in reality isolated enough in his whole-hogging embrace of Africaniza-tion, and the African Churches, especially in Lagos, would be criticized precisely for their unyielding fidelity to Western norms on many a non-essential.

Where the African Churches did in theory diverge fairly significantly from the mission Churches was over polygamy. Yoruba society was particularly polygamous. Insistence on monogamy is not 'good news' for polygamists, whose marriages are in consequence

[2] E. Ayandele, *The Missionary Impact on Modern Nigeria 1842–1914* (1966), 200.

[3] H. King, 'Co-operation and Contextualisation: Two Visionaries of the African Church—Mojola Agbebi and William Hughes of the African Institute, Colwyn Bay', *JRA* 16 (1986), 17.

[4] M. Agbebi, 'Inaugural Sermon', in J. Ayo Langley (ed.), *Ideologies of Liberation in Black Africa 1856–1970* (1979), 74.

broken up. The year of the first significant Nigerian secession, 1888, was also the year of the Lambeth Conference which laid down emphatically that persons living in polygamy be not admitted to baptism. Crowther was there and had approved. While only confirming what was normal mission policy against liberals like John Colenso who had wished to modify it, the Lambeth resolution indicated a hardening of the missionary view about the unaccept-ability of polygamous marriage just at the moment that it was being increasingly challenged by African Christian opinion. In reality the mission Churches had proved a good deal more accommodating than the Lambeth pronouncement might suggest. In Nigeria, in particular, while polygamy was condemned in theory, a blind eye was often turned in practice so long as not more than one wife and family was baptized in the same Church, but to some clergy this was unacceptable. Thus at a Methodist circuit leaders' meeting in 1917 the ten top men of Ereko Church were named as polygamists. Admitting their 'guilt', they were removed from membership. Another member then stood up and asked why these ten were singled out when so many were guilty. On being told that evidence was available only for these, forty-five others stood up to provide evidence against themselves. They too were removed from the roll. The result was the emergence of the United African Methodist Church, a small but wealthy group of Lagos polygamists. While no other African Church in Nigeria seceded precisely upon the issue of polygamy, the case for its more public tolerance very much formed part of the independent agenda. Nevertheless, here too there were disagreements—between a policy of toleration of polygamists and a policy of full acceptance, as between allowing or not allowing polygamous marriage to the clergy. On the whole African churchmen in Lagos held closer to the missionary view, while in the country, especially around Agege, the alternative 'evangelical' school advocated the acceptance of polygamy as a key to Christianization and resistance to Muslim advance.

For a large part caution, and mission ideals, prevailed, but it remained one of the issues on account of which the African Church movement was deeply fragmented. It was probably also one of the few issues dividing Bishop James Johnson, the continuing Anglican, from Dr Mojola Agbebi, the theorist of independency. But the intellectual and practical line separating the two camps, Christians who put up with missionary control and those who repudiated it, was seldom a hard one. Few Christians who belonged in any way to the Sierra Leonean tradition were in practice interested in going to Agbebi's lengths. Johnson remained their natural leader. A man of stature and some learning, but both angular and indecisive, he had stood for a while on the verge of secession but never quite got there. The advantages of not seceding, spiritual and institutional, for an educated man and still more a cleric or a bishop, were too considerable. In 1901 at the moment that Johnson was assuming his new role as assistant bishop on the Niger, the core of his old parish of St Paul's, Breadfruit, was moving into schism over the issue of the appointment of his successor. Here as elsewhere the hard division was between lay independents and white missionaries and it was a division over control, not over doctrine or liturgy. Indeed the continuing loyalty to denominational tradition in regard to the latter subsequently inhibited attempts to bring the various groups of independents into unity. A sense of Anglican, Baptist, or Methodist identity remained too strong.

While the African Churches grew to some significance, including by 1920 about a third of all Yoruba Christians, it cannot be said that the promise in Agbebi's appeal was fulfilled. In hymnody and politics their contributions were not negligible. Their Lagos church buildings were impressive enough, their success in rural evangelization in places quite considerable, but in general their continued division and further subdivision in small units, coupled with a natural inability to evaluate with theological maturity the legacy they had carried over from the missionaries, inhibited effectiveness. They reflected the circumstances, particularly the urban circumstances, of a generation of Christians still within the Sierra Leonean tradition if disillusioned with its ethos. From the early 1920s the role of Africanizing challenger to missionary Christianity would increasingly be taken over by a new, and very different, wave of prophet Churches.

In South Africa the story appears not dissimilar. Here too the end of the 1880s was a time of increasing ecclesiastical unrest, culminating in the establishment in Pretoria in 1892 of the Ethiopian Church of Mangena Mokone, a Wesleyan minister. A few years later, encouraged by Mokone's friend James Dwane, they joined the black American African Methodist Episcopal Church (AME) and in 1898 an AME bishop, H. M. Turner, visited South Africa. His five-week preaching tour excited Africans and infuriated Europeans. Turner was, declared the *Christian Express*, the newspaper of Stewart of Lovedale, an 'Arch-mischief-maker'.[5] The same year a large secession of Presbyterians took place from Lovedale led by P. J. Mzimba, while, both in 1890 and 1896, there were also Congregationalist secessions: to form the Zulu Mbiyana Church in the former year, the Zulu Congregational Church in the latter. Disagreements over polygamy mattered less in South Africa; here as in Nigeria the underlying issue was one of control. It was expressed in conflicts relating to the career prospects and life-style of black ministers and to race relations within the Church as a reflection of race relations within society. In both countries a basic alienation in sympathy derived from the concern of thinking black Christians with issues of African political and social rights at a time when the imperialist bandwagon was moving forward most unrestrainedly and missionaries for the most part tended to share uncritically in its enthusiasms. There was, nevertheless, a large difference between the ecclesiastical context of the two movements. In West Africa there were by the 1890s numerous black clergy, not a few of some distinction. There were also considerable areas of at least partial autonomy—the native pastorates of Freetown and Lagos as well as that of the Niger delta. While much of this appeared threatened by the attack on Crowther's diocese, it was still from a position of relative strength that the African Church movement in Nigeria developed. Indeed, it was just because of that position that many natural Ethiopians, like James Johnson, in fact never felt called to secede. In South Africa almost none of this existed. Ecclesiastical Ethiopianism here sprang from depression with a far more intensive pattern of white control. Existing clerical resources were far more limited, and the movement might hardly have had the strength to emerge as it did had it not been for the Afro-American assistance it received at the start.

It is important here to remind ourselves that secession was not an inherently African phenomenon. The kind of issue upon which most of these schisms actually took place was hardly at all different from ones which had caused the British Methodist movement in the nineteenth century to split again and again, or which had worked in the United States to multiply denominations. They were in a sense endemic to Anglo-Saxon Protestantism once it ceased to be a State Church. Its missionaries had carried their seed to Africa only too

---

[5] S. Jacobi (ed.), *Black Americans and the Missionary Movement in Africa* (1982), 179.

faithfully, and it would be misguided to see in this wave of so-called Ethiopian separatism a merely African phenomenon uncharacteristic of contemporary Protestantism.

In South Africa and in West Africa what was decisive in bringing about this particular wave of secessions was nevertheless a loss of interracial confidence heightened by the atmosphere of the scramble. Yet in the south as in the west many people who shared that loss of confidence remained within a mission Church. If James Dwane eventually established his Order of Ethiopia within Anglicanism, if J. Tengo Jabavu, outspoken editor of the Xhosa newspaper *Imvo*, but critic of the Turner visit, remained a Lovedale Presbyterian, it was not because they entirely liked the way things were in a white-ruled Church, but because they recognized that the mission option was still the wiser one for people who valued the kind of religious and social life, the educational· opportunities, even the international links, which the main Churches continued to stand for. The independent Churches in the period up to 1910 were sufficiently numerous to alarm missionaries and to establish an alternative ecclesiastical option, but it remained very much a minority option even for people who shared interiorly almost all of their presuppositions. It remained so precisely because, while rebelling against control by missionary personnel, it was still so closely controlled by a missionary model of religious life.

ii. *The Rise of Zionism*

It was the role of the prophets to forge a new model, even though they too began often enough under missionary inspiration. Consider, for instance, the little network of Protestants in South Africa who had linked together the name of Zion, a commitment to faith-healing, the solemnity of baptism in a 'Jordan' river or sea, and, in due course, the Pentecostalist gift of tongues. All this is to be found especially in the enthusiastic but unstable ministry of P. L. Le Roux, an Afrikaner who had come under the influence of the Scottish revivalist Andrew Murray, who had done so much for the Dutch Reformed Church. Le Roux began work as a missionary to the Zulus. It was from Murray above all that he had learnt of faith-healing. Le Roux's little chapel at Wakkerstroom was already a 'Zions Kerk' because in it they sang the hymns of Zion, the *Zions Liedere*, a Dutch hymn-book of Moravian inspiration. In 1903, however, he went further, resigning from the Dutch Reformed Church to join, instead, a group dependent upon the Christian Catholic Apostolic Church founded a few years before by John Alexander Dowie at Zion City near Chicago. 'I am going over to Zion. Those who wish to follow me may do so,' Le Roux wrote in a letter in Zulu to one of his parishioners, Jonas Hlatshwayo, dated October 1902.[6] A strength of Le Roux lay in his close and happy relationship with Africans. It proved to be a bridge carrying the religious ideals and nomenclature of a tiny, not very significant group of white Christians across to a far larger group of black Christians. He now called his congregation the Zionist Apostolic Church.

This Zionist form of missionary Christianity, for so we may term it, proved unusually attractive. It seemed indeed to share so many themes with African traditional religion that once it had adopted an African persona and broken any organizational links with its white genitors, it was easily forgotten that it had anything but an African origin. Yet Le Roux and his colleagues Edgar Mahon and Daniel Bryant provide the necessary link between the 2,000 or more black Churches in South Africa eventually calling themselves by the name of Zion and historic Christianity. Not that use of the name of Zion could only have come by such a route. Rather its scriptural resonance and the spiritual need of biblical religion to reinvent Jerusalem in one's own land have time and again inspired Christians to claim a Zionist identity. This would be the case in Africa not only in the south where a precise missing link is identifiable but also in other parts of the continent. And just as the missionary root of African Zion could easily fade from view, so could that of many other aspects—millennial, ritual, and so forth—but may again and again be discovered in a Watch Tower pamphlet or some passing contact between white and black enthusiasts.

One of Le Roux's most faithful disciples was Daniel Nkonyane. Around 1908 Le Roux had another crisis of religious identity. This time he decided that he must join a Pentecostal Church, the Apostolic Faith Mission (the new wave of Pentecostalism had only just begun in Los Angeles in 1906), and leave Zion. Nkonyane replaced him at this point as the latter's principal leader in South Africa, but the fast-growing Zionist tree quickly divided into numerous branches, all of which were initially led by men who had

---

[6] B. Sundkler, *Zulu Zion and some Swazi Zionists* (1976), 24–5.

been directly influenced by Le Roux or Mahon such as Paul Mabilitsa, Elias Mhlangu, and Eduard Lion.

By 1920 Zionism had spread in many directions. If its greatest strength was among the Zulu, it had also entered Swaziland—where in time it would become almost the national religion—while Lion, a Sotho, established a 'Zion City' in Basutoland in 1917. By the 1920s Ignatius Lekhanyane, a Pedi who for a time worked with Lion, had started his own Zion Christian Church in the northern Transvaal, and Andreas Shoko, Samuel Mutendi, and other Rhodesian workers in South Africa carried it further north into Rhodesia. Both Shoko and Mutendi had been baptized in 1923 in a 'Jordan' near Pretoria by Lekhanyane. Zionism would be misinterpreted as a Zulu creation. It was the development among several peoples of a particular form of missionary Christianity which may have seemed attractive because of apparent parallels with traditional religious culture. Nevertheless, almost all its most characteristic elements—even such points as a very open tolerance of polygamy—in fact derive from Le Roux or Mahon. It was the sheer lack of white control due to the small number of missionaries involved and the personality of Le Roux which made it so easy for a white-led movement to become a wholly black one to such an extent that its missionary roots, while recalled by Zionists themselves, could be almost ignored by observers.

Zionism was then far less a movement of 'schism' or 'independency' than is normally imagined. Indeed it could well be argued that if there was a seceder at its origins it was Le Roux, who moved out of it into the Apostolic Faith Mission, and not Nkonyane or Mabilitsa. Again, any contrast with 'Ethiopian' Churches of a sort that is regularly offered can easily be overstated. Zionism did not begin with prophets, it began with its own species of missionary just as any other Ethiopian Church did. Again, it retained the doctrine and liturgy of its missionaries, continuing to use the missionary hymn-books which provided the chief content of the latter. Nevertheless, the very limited structure of the original mission provided space for African Zionism as it developed to do so in its own manner with a large and easy indigenization of organization, appearance, and ethos, so that the white-robed Zion of the 1920s with its prophetic staffs and food taboos was already looking very different from the Protestant sectarianism of Le Roux and Mahon. By 1930 Zionism was firmly established in Zululand, Swaziland,

Basutoland, the Transvaal, and Rhodesia as an essentially single and wholly black movement of Churches, multiplying and dividing according to prophet leaders, tribe, and language, and spreading naturally outwards. As a form of Christianity it represented a degree of independence and of Africanization very threatening to most missionaries, particularly perhaps in its liberation from the missionary preoccupation with literacy, for which it had substituted a more traditionally grounded concern for healing.

It was around 1910 that almost all the main strands of Zionism appeared in South Africa, not only the central tradition identified with the Nkonyanes, but the Church of the Light of Timothy Cekwane, centred upon its Zion at Ekukhanyeni high in the Drakensburgs, and the Amanazaretha of the most famous of Zionist prophets, Isaiah Shembe. The latter was indeed rather different, and some would deny his Zionist status. Here there is no comparable missionary genealogy, though it is clear that Shembe came under some of the same influences as the more orthodox Zionists before establishing the Church of the Nazarites, centred upon Ekuphaka-meni, just north of Durban, in 1911. While it could be argued that the principal Zionist leaders were Pentecostalist ministers rather than prophets, Shembe has undoubtedly to be categorized first and foremost as prophet. Yet as what makes both prophet and Pentecostalist is direct experience of spirit in visions, dreams, or other phenomena, the difference is not necessarily a great one. But while the Pentecostalist's ministerial calling and experience may not begin with the paranormal impact of spirit, that of the prophet must do so. Shembe had in fact frequently experienced revelations in the years before 1911 while he was for a time working with the African Native Baptist Church, and he was already famous as a healer. It is this combination of revelation and healing power which constitutes the African prophet.

What came to distinguish the Amanazaretha most particularly from other Zionists were two things: the figure of Shembe and the richness of the liturgical cycle he devised. That Shembe was seen as a prophet and, more than a prophet, a Zulu messiah, is hardly questionable. His relationship to his Church is very different from that of Nkonyane, Mabilitsa, or even the more charismatic Mutendi. 'Shembe, the Servant of the Lord, will wipe the tears of his people.'

Our Liberator,
We Dingaan's people
We have heard him,
He has come,
The Liberator has arrived
You, Zulus, we have heard him.[7]

Again, what makes Amanazaretha worship significantly different from most other Zionist worship has been the possession of its own hymnal, much of it written by Shembe, and the character of its hymns in which Zulu and biblical motifs are woven integrally together. It is noticeable too how seldom Jesus is mentioned in the *Izihlabelelo zama Nazaretha*. It is the figure of Shembe himself who is central in a way that would not be liturgically possible in Zionist worship with its continued use of a highly Christ-centred hymnody. This does not mean, however, that Shembe has replaced Christ theologically; rather that he is for Zulu Christians of the twentieth century a vivid representation of what God and Christ are thought to signify. In the same way Ekuphakameni becomes the living, here-and-now relocation of Jerusalem, both the earthly and the heavenly, to which some fifty of the 250 hymns in the Nazarite hymnal are devoted.

I remember Ekuphakameni
Where is assembled
the saintly congregation
of the Nazarites.

I remember Ekuphakameni
where the springs are
Springs of living water
lasting for ever.[8]

Here and elsewhere one finds a creative reweaving of biblical texts and themes in the context of a highly realized eschatology. In the July festival at Ekuphakameni and the January festival on the mountain of Inhlangakazi, in the services of baptism, washing of the feet, and healing, the Amanazaretha developed a symbolically and emotionally highly charged liturgy which is undoubtedly extraordinarily different from the rather impoverished worship of late nineteenth-century Protestantism. To a considerable extent all Zionists have done the

[7] From no. 134 and 214 of the Nazarite hymn-book, B. Sundkler, *Bantu Prophets in South Africa* (1948), 282.   [8] No. 102, ibid. 292.

same. They may occasionally have consciously borrowed elements they have seen within the Catholic Church, but for the most part it is simply the product of a merging of biblical—especially Old Testament—inspiration and African consciousness. While the details of different Churches vary hugely, there remains a striking similarity between 'New Jerusalems' all across Africa, most of which did certainly not influence each other.

iii. *Elliot Kamwana*

It was in 1908 that the most influential of central African religious enthusiasts began his ministry, Elliot Kenan Kamwana. A Tonga who had studied for a few years at Livingstonia's Overtoun Institute, had worked in the mines of Johannesburg, and come under the restless influence of Joseph Booth, Kamwana had spent some years as an Adventist before following Booth into the world of the Watch Tower Bible and Tract Society. It was as a Watch Tower preacher that he returned to Nyasaland in 1908. In the next six months, in a phenomenally successful campaign, Kamwana baptized some 9,000 people around Nkhata Bay, people mostly on the fringes of the Livingstonia Mission. His teaching was an Africanized form of Watch Tower millennialism: Christ was to come in October 1914, only those who were baptized would be saved, the whites would leave, and taxes would end. 'Kwacha Africa Yuka'—'It is dawn, Africa, arise'—he would stand up and shout emotionally.[9] That may sound millennial, but it could also be little more than an expression of Ethiopianism very appropriate in 1909. Ethiopianism was hardly millennialist and not over-prophetic. Kamwana depicted as prophet and millennialist could seem very far away from Ethiopianism, but his years in South Africa may have injected into him attitudes deeper than Booth's Watch Tower doctrines, which he was ostensibly preaching. It was, anyway, a fusion of the two which produced his own specific message.

For his converts in Nkhata Bay the main attraction may have been less the one or the other than the sheer availability of immediate and unconditional baptism. While missionaries imposed lengthy catechumenates and tiresome tests of knowledge and morality, Kamwana

---

[9] J. Chakanza, 'Continuity and Change: A Study of New Religious Movements in Malawi 1900–1981', D.Phil. thesis (Oxford, 1985), 120.

gave baptism to all who desired it. Livingstonia had produced a thirst for this new rite of initiation without being able or willing to satisfy it so summarily. However, while easy baptism did not distress the colonial authorities unduly, an approaching millennium in which Christ would remove white rule most certainly did. Kamwana was arrested, and many of his converts returned to Presbyterianism.

From Kamwana's mission derived a tradition of millennialism and numerous little Churches including the one he established himself when he returned in the 1930s from twenty years of exile in the Seychelles, no longer a Watch Tower preacher. The millennialism within Chilembwe's rising in 1915 may also derive from the inspiration of Kamwana. Yet, as with Zionism or with Chilembwe and Domingo, we have to note how what may well appear to the observer—and indeed was—an explosion of prophetic independency looked to its initiators—and was no less—an attempt at continuity with a particular strand of Western religion.

iv. *Harrists and Kimbanguists*

Just at the time that Zionism was spreading in and around South Africa under the influence of Nkonyane, Shembe, and Cekwane, some not dissimilar Churches were appearing in West Africa under the impact of Harris and Garrick Braide. Even less than the South Africans was Harris a schismatic or a deliberate founder of Churches. He never interpreted his prophetic calling as one to create a separate denomination of his own. He was, as much as Kamwana, both a millennialist and an instant baptizer, though his conditions for baptism appear more genuinely demanding. While the missionary Churches did not like to receive those so hurriedly baptized, again and again he had instructed his converts to go to the Methodist or the Catholic Church or simply to wait for missionaries to come. Nevertheless, in fact a series of Harrist Churches did develop across the Ivory Coast and it is instructive to examine how it happened. His converts had to do something, and while many undoubtedly joined existing Churches almost at once—Catholic in Ivory Coast, Methodist in the Gold Coast—this was simply not an option open to villagers across much of the territory through which he passed. What he seems regularly to have done, after destroying fetishes, administering baptism, and providing elementary instruction, was to appoint twelve apostles in each place to lead the new Christian community. What followed depended largely upon the quality of these leaders. While some of the outsiders, the 'clerks' who had attached themselves to the prophet as his lieutenants, proved far from satisfactory, the impression is that most of the village leaders carried on the religious revolution which Harris had inaugurated with extraordinary perseverance. Their knowledge was inevitably limited. Among the Dida where there was no mission presence for many years and the Church flourished remarkably, much was due to one man, Latta Gnandjoué, whom Harris had appointed in January 1915 and who remained leader until his death in 1931. He alone in the *cercle de Lahou* had a Bible which the prophet himself had given him, an English Bible. He could read little of it, but his young nephew Ledjou N'Drin could read a good deal more and accompanied his uncle on his preaching and baptizing tours. They built chapels, they—women chiefly—composed hymns, they preached a simple gospel about God, Jesus, and love. They continued to spread. Like Harris, they stressed the Ten Commandments but fully accepted polygamists. Thus a new Church developed with its own beliefs and customs, its ministry, its history and traditions, or rather a series of new Churches because there was no contact between, for instance, the Harrist Christians among the Dida and those among the Ebrie.

When a Methodist missionary, W. J. Platt, 'discovered' the Harrists in 1923 and set about their integration into Methodism, the prophet's original instructions to obey white missionaries when they should come had by no means been forgotten, yet conflict was almost inevitable. There was at first great enthusiasm: 'Village bands, whole villages bedecked with flags, street arches of palm leaves, all formed part of the outward signs of the people's enthusiasm and longing.'[10] In the village of Ebonou, for instance, Platt was conducted to a long church filled with 600 people, whose leader at once asked him to accept this church and that of eight neighbouring villages into his Society. Nevertheless, the issue of the polygamous presented a formidable problem about which the Methodists were unwilling to be accommodating. In other things, however, they were adaptable enough. The offices of twelve apostles, of 'Peter of the Church', and suchlike were retained, and in fact many thousands of Harrists became and remained Methodists. This illustrates once more the way in which a prophet movement and its fruits were, as such, neither

[10] Platt's second report, G. Haliburton, *The Prophet Harris* (1971), 176–7.

schismatic nor anti-missionary. Nevertheless, after ten years of developing in their own way, there were many Harrists who were no more attracted by Methodism than they had been in earlier years by Catholicism. Harris had not preached Harrism, but a Harrist Church had been the result.

Even more quickly had Braide's preaching in the Niger delta led to a new Church, though here it was not missionaries but quite independent-minded African churchmen who could not stomach his mix of self-assertion, fanaticism, and the tolerance of polygamy. It was on Christmas Eve 1915 that some Bonny chiefs presented Garrick Braide to Bishop James Johnson with the words, 'Your Lordship, this is the young man, in other words the prophet we have come to present to you for recognition and induction.' To this Johnson replied, 'Don't call him a prophet. Change that name. I shall listen to you when you have changed the name.' Each side refused to budge. Braide picked up his walking-stick and walked out of the Bishop's court.[11] Thus within a wholly African encounter did Ethiopianism, of an Anglican kind, and prophetism diverge. A normal Church's degree of adaptability, even when led by a venerable African bishop, was simply insufficient to stop prophecy from leading to independency.

Towards the end of his life Harris received two visits at his home at Cape Palmas in Liberia. The Methodists surmised that their task would be much helped if it had the explicit backing of the prophet. Hence in 1926 they sent Pierre Benoit to see the old man, and he returned with a photograph of the two of them standing side by side together with a series of instructions for particular places. Those amongst the Harrists who did not wish to be Methodized responded to this by sending representatives of their own to see Harris, Solomon Dagri and Jean Ahui. They arrived in March 1929 in Cape Palmas. The message they brought back was inevitably a different one, and they too returned with a photograph of themselves and the prophet. A few months later Harris was dead. Out of his preaching both Methodist and Catholic Churches had grown considerably, but it had also left in the Ivory Coast a Harrist Church, in the Gold Coast the Church of the Twelve Apostles, as well as a wave of secondary prophets, many of them propounding pretty bizarre messages such as

---

[11] F. Ludwig, 'Elijah II: Radicalisation and Consolidation of the Garrick Braide Movement 1915–1918', *JRA* 23 (1993), 296.

that of Yessu, another Liberian who appeared in the Ivory Coast in 1918, declaring that he had come from Jerusalem in the belly of a fish called 'Captain': 'Don't smoke pipes, only cigarettes. Don't weep for the dead or your villages will be burnt by fire from Heaven. Don't dress the dead for burial'.[12] In evaluating the prophet phenomenon it is essential to recall that while in retrospect only the more weighty figures are remembered, in fact at the time a situation of popular religious flux, of mental and social uncertainty, was often fed upon and stimulated by large numbers of other self-appointed prophets and teachers, some of whom were in it for money (which Harris never asked for) and were certainly remote enough from any recognizable standard of Christian orthodoxy.

This was very much the case in the Lower Congo in 1921. We are here once more upon the frontier of a fairly well-established Protestant Church, that of the Baptists, whose roots in the ancient Kongo tradition of Catholicism we have already explored (Chapter 9, Section vi). Here too was a disorientated society, whose beliefs and structures had crumbled under the blows of a particularly cruel colonialism, but which still needed moving by something less cerebral and methodical than even the best of Protestant missions. But here too, within Kongo religion, was a tradition of the *ngunza* or prophet. Simon Kimbangu, a villager from Nkamba, some ten miles from the mission of Ngombe Lutete, had been baptized with his wife at the mission in July 1915. He was about 26 years old. We know little of his early life except for one memorable incident. A missionary, G. R. Cameron, journeying in the 1890s on the Ntontani–Nkamba road, had been attacked by villagers and took refuge in the house of a woman, Kinsembo, who gave him some water. Before leaving he blessed the woman and her child, who was Kimbangu. For Kimbangu and his followers subsequently that event was something to appeal to, and a group of Baptist deacons in prison in 1923 could write to him, 'You, Mr Cameron, can rejoice in these things, and know that the things which you asked of God for this Congoland, He has done them, and especially in the matter of the blessing of the woman who helped you when you were in danger.'[13] The accounts of many prophets claim supernatural events setting them aside in childhood, or even before birth. It is remarkable that

---

[12] Haliburton, *The Prophet Harris*, 163.
[13] C. Irvine, 'The Birth of the Kimbanguist Movement in the Bas-Zaïre 1921', *JRA* 6 (1974), 74.

Kimbangu is the recipient of special blessing already in childhood, but remarkable too that it is not as such a supernatural event and that it is in fact well authenticated. This does, moreover, help to locate the Kimbanguist movement firmly inside the Baptist Church and its oral history.

Cameron's blessing of Kinsembo did not, however, determine Kimbangu's sense of vocation according to the tradition. It was only after his baptism that he had a dream vision calling him to teach, and he was in fact accepted as an evangelist or lay preacher in 1918. His weakness in reading was an obstacle to promotion, but a recurrence of his dreams affected him still more, and apparently in an effort to escape them he set off to work in Kinshasa. His time there was clearly disturbed, and after a few months fellow Bakongo persuaded him to return home. His visions had continued, and he interpreted his troubles in Kinshasa as consequent upon his failure to respond to them. He then hoped to be appointed the Church's evangelist at Nkamba, but he was rejected for this and his stepbrother appointed instead. It was at that moment that he had a vision of a new order no longer calling him, as he saw it, to a given and lowly office within the Church's hierarchy, but constituting him 'an apostle', someone replacing the 'apostle' Cameron by right of the blessing he had received from Cameron. He was also, by right of his visionary calling, prophet and healer, fulfilling, as he and his disciples constantly insisted, the miraculous expectations of Mark 16: 16.

It was in the middle of March 1921 that Kimbangu's healing ministry began. The immediate response to it was twofold. On the one side, large numbers of people began coming to Nkamba to be healed, apparently as far as from Kinshasa, abandoning hospitals, Catholic missions, whatever. It is clear, even from Kimbanguist sources, that far from everyone was cured, but it is clear too that many people thought they were or that other people had been. The second immediate response was that of senior African members, deacons and others, of the Baptist Church. They visited Nkamba, decided that what was going on was indeed 'the work of God', and from then on included it within the structures of the Church. It would seem that, strictly, the Kimbanguist movement did not begin with Kimbangu's first 'miracle' but with the moment, some weeks later in April, when the Church approved of it. Kimbangu himself was its prophet but hardly its leader. He and the deacons around him did, furthermore, emphatically separate themselves from many of the other 'prophets' who were springing up around him. Nothing is clearer in the fascinating work going under the name of Nfinangani and written within the first three months of the movement than its insistence upon the difference between the true prophet, Kimbangu, and others filled with false spirits. It is in terms of biblical exegesis that the claims for Kimbangu are already here made. He and the community around him are wrestling both through dreams and through discussion with specific biblical passages, but the text as a whole is redolent with a sense that what was happening in lower Zaïre was a renewal and fulfilment of what they had read about in the Bible and what the missionaries, they believed, had taught them to expect.

Such a highly charged and quickly growing movement could not, however, in white eyes be left entirely in black hands. Nevertheless, the local missionary, R. L. Jennings, was slow to make up his mind. Kimbangu visited him at Ngombe on 19 April and he visited Nkamba in May and saw no miracles. The local administrator, Morel, also visited Nkamba in May and, again, saw little to agitate him greatly: no cadavers being brought for resuscitation, no huge crowds. Neither witnessed any healings. Kimbangu undoubtedly preached about the imminent return of Christ, but so did many a missionary. Meanwhile, prophets of all sorts were multiplying throughout the region and some were recommending the non-payment of tax, a Catholic chapel was vandalized at Kiwembo, European estates were denuded of workers. Catholic missionaries and Belgian settlers were alike urging the government to suppress the movement at once, and early in June Morel returned to Nkamba to arrest Kimbangu, which he did, but then, in the general confusion, the prophet escaped. The next day the village was sacked by the soldiers. When the people returned to see it, they sang together the Baptist hymn 'See the man of sorrows now'.[14]

Many Baptist deacons and others were at once arrested and quickly sentenced to years of hard labour. A missionary who saw a group of them chained at a railway station and shook their hands in a friendly way was violently denounced in the colonial press. Kimbangu returned to Nkamba early in September and was arrested there. Put on trial at the beginning of October, he was sentenced to death, but King Albert at the request of the Baptists commuted the sentence to

---

[14] Ibid. 43.

one of life imprisonment. The hard core of Kimbanguists which had also been the hard core of the Baptist Church was sent into exile in the upper Congo, and little by little order returned.

It is clear that some of the other prophets had been Baptist catechists, but many were marginally, if at all, Christians. They were *ngunza*, spirit-possessed people typical of Kongo and other traditional religion. Kimbangu's behaviour too fitted, at least in part, the *ngunza* type, but his own interpretation of it—and still more the interpretation of the non-charismatic deacons who believed in him—was Christian, not traditional. So far as we can judge, it had nothing politically subversive about it; nevertheless, it is unquestionable that the teaching of many of the other prophets was politically subversive and that the millennialism which Kimbangu did preach as did other prophets was at least potentially explosive here as anywhere. It was recognized by everyone that it was Kimbangu who had set off the movement as a whole and that the others were largely imitating what they imagined him to be doing. It was not, then, entirely unreasonable, to call for his arrest. The sentence of death or even of life imprisonment was, however, a monstrous perversion of justice upon a man against whom no serious charge could in reality be sustained. Hardly less unjust were the sentences of five, ten, or twenty years' penal servitude on people who had supported him in a purely pacific way. Unlike prophet movements in some other countries, this had, in fact, led to no uprising of any sort. What violence there was, apart from attacks on one or two Catholic chapels, appears to have been wholly that of the State.

Outside observers at the time and many a sociologist since have been unable to distinguish between what we can reasonably call Baptist Kimbanguism and a far wider prophet movement which came for decades to be labelled Kimbanguist but was essentially Ngunzist. In fact the true Kimbanguists saw themselves as Baptists, distinguished Kimbangu from other 'false' prophets, proposed no teaching which they did not believe they had received from their missionaries, and were only sad that, as they saw it, the missionaries had abandoned them at the time of trial. In the letter which Ntima, Kuyowa, and Mbandila wrote from prison to 'our old Teacher, Mr G. R. R. Cameron' in June 1923 the purpose was emphatically to deny the charge that they had accepted 'new teaching' of any sort. It was simply that the miracles the gospels promised had actually happened. People had believed and thrown away their fetishes. Even

Mr Jennings, they claimed, 'saw one miracle', on his own admission. All the books of the New Testament and hymn-books were sold in a single month. 'Since the first coming to Congo there was never seen such a buying of the book of God.' This immensely moving epistle was written in Kikongo to their old missionary in response to the one and only letter which had got through to 'your old boys, we, deacons and elders and members of the Protestant Church of the BMS bound for the word of God on the Upper Congo'. It told of some who had died from their beatings but could still declare 'we are well, we get beaten with canes and have other troubles but Jehovah is our shepherd, and he tends us well in all our afflictions'.[15] Kuyowa and Mbandila had in fact been two of the most senior and experienced deacons in the Baptist Church. They were far from charismatic prophets themselves, but in their following of Kimbangu they illustrated the continuity between the first generation of Kongo Christians and the Kimbanguist community.

Basically the Kimbanguist movement appears, like others we have considered, far more as one of mass conversion to Christianity than as one of schism within a Church, of resistance to colonialism, or even of a new African form of Christianity. If it had not been for the heavy hand of Belgian colonialism, things could have been very different. Yet it could be that the government intervention in fact excused the missionaries from responding to a movement about which they were themselves increasingly worried, and that, if it had been left relatively free by the State to proceed, schism within the Baptist Church would quickly have become inevitable for reasons other than it did. It is possible but not certain, and it should be noted that the sort of issues which elsewhere separated 'independents' from mission Church such as the acceptance of polygamy or female circumcision never arose in this case.

The Baptist deacons who led early Kimbanguism had been quite well instructed and they carried into it the faith of the missionaries who had instructed them. What separated them from the Baptists was the conviction that Jennings had betrayed them. Kimbangu's original attitude to his Church seems to have been clear enough: 'Stay with your white men, for they are your husbands and you are their wives; you cannot desert them.'[16] By the time of his arrest his attitude had

---

[15] Ibid. 75–6.
[16] D. Mackay, 'Simon Kimbangu and the BMS Tradition', *JRA* 17 (1987), 151.

changed. 'He who is not for you is against you,' he now insisted, declining to join the congregation at Ngombe. That night he spent at the home of the deacon Kuyowa. The next day he went on to Nkamba and arrest. Whether all his followers understood that they were now to separate from the mission is unclear, but some certainly did and acted accordingly. For the next thirty years Kimbanguism was in part an inchoate Church of its own, unaccepted in law and without an even internally recognized leadership, in part a movement of dissent within the mission Church. In this it was not unlike Methodism *vis-à-vis* the Church of England in the latter years of the eighteenth century. Inevitably, as the years went by, the recusant Kimbanguist tradition would be affected internally by, and from the outside identified with, all sorts of other prophet movements, such as that of Simon Mpadi, different in spirit as most of them were. Nevertheless, the idea that a relatively 'pure' Kimbanguism survived the long years of oppression and exile was not simply a validating myth of the resurrected Church led by the prophet's sons from the end of the 1950s, it is also an historically tenable hypothesis. But it is also true that by the 1940s it was the recent 'Khaki' movement of Mpadi and others which was most forceful and evidently at work. While partially modelled on the organization of the Salvation Army and highly eclectic in what it had embraced from traditional and Catholic sources as well as Protestant ones, its adepts continued to pray in the name of Simon Kimbangu. What survived of the original Kimbanguist tradition was meanwhile for the time being less widely influential or, at least, a great deal quieter and less observed by civil authority.

v. *Aladura*

In western Nigeria in May 1920, just a year before the beginning of Kimbangu's ministry, something not dissimilar was happening. At the first synod meeting of the new Anglican diocese of Lagos a complaint was made that 'persons styling themselves "prophets" . . . have been allowed to speak or preach in one of our churches, and then have quoted this as a reason for having the same opportunity elsewhere'.[17] With Harris to the west of them and Braide to the east of them, it was hardly surprising if prophets were multiplying among the Yoruba

[17] H. Turner, *African Independent Church* (1967), i. 10.

as well. They had in fact been doing so for some time and in much the same sort of way that we have seen elsewhere: catechists who have dreams, illiterate converts who assume the role of evangelist, the gravely ill who pray and get better.

One of the most memorable was Moses Orimolade, an early convert who had been ill for seven years and, after seeing a vision, had partially recovered. By 1916 he had become a wandering preacher, welcomed at times in Anglican churches, at others by the African Church and even by Muslims. Whether he was one of those complained of by the Lagos Synod we do not know, but it is likely. One member of the synod was also a subject of complaint, Joseph Sadare, a leading Anglican at Ijebu-Ode, forty miles south of Ibadan. He had formed a prayer group during the influenza epidemic in response to a dream which he later called, again in obedience to a dream, the Precious Stone Society. Like many such societies, it was at first welcomed by the Church but then became a problem: its members were rejecting medicines whose use they saw as a lack of faith. They were also rejecting infant baptism. By 1922 they had slipped out of the Anglican Church and briefly joined themselves instead to a small faith-healing Church in Philadelphia called Faith Tabernacle, whose tracts they were reading. Similar groups arose elsewhere so that by the mid-1920s there was a small network of Faith Tabernacle communities in Yorubaland led by Sadare, Isaac Akinyele, and J. A. Bamatope among others. Akinyele too had been a lay member of the diocesan synod and his brother was a priest and Principal of Ibadan Grammar School. Bamatope had been a catechist. From Faith Tabernacle they were confirmed in faith-healing, but otherwise they carried into their new Church probably as much core Anglicanism as, a generation earlier, the secessionists from St Paul's, Breadfruit, had carried into the African Church. When the American Faith Tabernacle fell apart a few years later, the Nigerians severed their connection but twice more tried to connect themselves to a Western Church. They succeeded for a while in submission to the British Apostolic Church, a Pentecostalist group, but found that they could not quite agree about medicine. Hence, from 1940, they ceased the search for overseas authorization and took their final name, the Christ Apostolic Church.

The people who were gathering themselves around Sadare and Akinyele came to be called in a general way 'Aladura'—praying people. They prayed more than others and more visibly. Moreover, by rejecting the use of medicine, they confined themselves to the power of prayer. But Aladura were not all in Faith Tabernacle. Another network was developing around Moses Orimolade and a remarkable young woman, Abiodun Akinsowon, who at the Corpus Christi procession in Lagos in 1925 saw under the canopy by the host an angel who followed her home where she entered a trance. The pastor of St Paul's, Breadfruit, Archdeacon Ogunbiyi, was sent for but proved unable to help. Orimolade was sent for and Abiodun recovered. Soon there developed around the two the Seraphim Society, later to be called the Cherubim and Seraphim. It too for a while remained, if uneasily, within Anglicanism. Archdeacon Ogunbiyi praised their commitment to praying but feared that they were turning Orimolade, Baba Aladura as he was now known, the 'Praying Father', into an authority rivalling that of the Church.

None of this represented any large-scale Yoruba movement before 1930. Up to that point, Aladura meant no more than a number of small praying groups of committed Christians functioning on the edge of, or just outside, the main Churches, especially the Anglican, strong on faith-healing, on the value of dreams and visions, and very much opposed to traditional religion. Unlike the African Churches of a generation before, there was with Aladura no conscious suggestion of sympathy or compromise with tradition. 'We stamp Satan under our feet,' sang the Seraphim in the streets of Lagos, and by Satan they meant the gods of the Yoruba.[18] The leaders of the Faith Tabernacle were more educated than those of the Seraphim but still less disposed to compromise. The Seraphim accepted polygamists. Faith Tabernacle refused them. Meanwhile, the mission Churches were expanding fast in the Nigeria of the 1920s and Aladura added little to that expansion until 1930, the year of Babalola's 'Revival'.

Joseph Babalola was born in 1904. In 1928 he was a steamroller driver, an employee of the Public Works Department on the road between Akure and Ilesha. His roller stopped working and he heard a voice call out his name three times and tell him to leave his job and preach the gospel. He did so, returning to his home town, naked and covered with ashes. He was in consequence lodged for a while in the local gaol. A year later, 19 December 1929, Babalola was baptized in the sea at Ebute Metta to become almost at once Faith Tabernacle's

[18] J. Peel, *Aladura* (1968), 74.

leading evangelist. The revival began at Ilesha in July 1930 at a Faith Tabernacle meeting to which Sadare, Akinyele, and Babalola had come. It was then that Babalola's powers of preaching were revealed. Several times a day, armed with Bible and handbell, he called on the people to bring out all their idols and juju to be burnt. God alone was sufficient. Never in Yorubaland was there such a mass movement and never such bonfires of the implements of traditional religion. Suddenly Aladura expanded into one of the major religious groupings of the Yoruba, although many of the converts of the Babalola revival undoubtedly found their way into Anglicanism and Methodism. Here again religious division between 'independency' and the mission Churches was by no means a hard one. There had been no rending schism. There was no political banning of the new movements, the British attitude to them being essentially different from the Belgian. There was also no single major issue upon which separation hinged. There was simply the emergence of a new religious ethos among a group of people confident enough to stand their ground against missionary criticism but in a quite unantagonistic way.

One of those who joined in the preaching of the 1930 revival was Josiah Oshitelu, again an Anglican by baptism, who during the 1920s had developed at his home in Ogere in an Aladura direction through prayer, fasting, and visions. But his visions included a special dimension which would soon present a problem. He began to use all sorts of strange 'holy names' beginning with his own personal holy name, Arrabablalhhubab. While, for other Aladura, dreams and visions could help one understand the Scriptures or how to apply them in one's life, for Oshitelu they brought a new and esoteric knowledge of holy things. When he first joined the other Aladura in the great revival, Oshitelu was both welcomed and admired. Akinyele and Babalola both visited him in Ogere, and it appeared as if his group of Aladura and the older established tradition of Faith Tabernacle were joining to become one. In fact, however, the other Aladura leaders soon became uneasy with what they saw of Oshitelu, a man who more than any other Aladura appeared to seek and expect a position of personal primacy.

At seven in the evening of 23 January 1931 the leaders of Faith Tabernacle were gathered with Oshitelu in the house of Akinyele in Ibadan for a discussion which ended after 3.30 the next morning. The basic issues were threefold. The first was that Oshitelu in his healing services identified witches. The second was that he permitted polygamy. The third that he used 'holy names' derived from his own revelations. None of these three was acceptable to the leaders of Faith Tabernacle. Sadare's pragmatic discussion of witchcraft confessions with its sceptic conclusion 'knowledge that somebody is a witch can bring no benefit to anybody' was remarkably different in approach to Oshitelu's fervent appeals to people to admit their witchcraft. No less remarkable was Akinyele's treatment of the 'holy names' issue. 'In a dream I heard these words: "Incline thine heart to keep this law. These names can bring no forgiveness, salvation, or benefit of any kind to anybody." I therefore conclude that there is no use in calling these names.'[19] The result was separation. Oshitelu went his own way back to Ogere to found the Church of the Lord (Aladura) and to claim the right to seven wives, while Akinyele and Babalola went on to lead the main body of Aladura, which insisted on monogamy and became in due course (July 1941) the Christ Apostolic Church with Akinyele its first President and Babalola its General Evangelist.

The importance for us of this well-reported meeting within the ranks of Aladura is that it focused so precisely on some of the central issues with which the prophet movement was wrestling almost everywhere: how far could dreams and visions have a revelatory role comparable even with the Bible? How far could faith-healing accept the medieval categories of traditional religion, including the existence of witchcraft? How far could an independent Church adopt the marriage pattern, including polygamy, of traditional society? While there were independent churchmen such as Oshitelu and many others who could give a positive answer to all three questions, it is important to recognize that there were also those who could say an emphatic 'no'. In this the Christ Apostolic Church would be not at all unlike the Church of Simon Kimbangu.

Isaac Akinyele had been born in 1881 into one of the oldest Anglican families of Ibadan. His elder brother was an Anglican priest and, from the 1930s, an assistant bishop. Isaac had been for a while a civil servant, rising to be Secretary to the Council of the Ibadan Native Authority and Chief Clerk for the 1921 census. By the time of his conversion in 1924 to the Faith Tabernacle he was a cocoa farmer, a man of very considerable means, and a lay member of diocesan synod, from which he now resigned. He never again took

---

[19] Turner, *African Independent Church*, i. 22–3.

medicine of any sort. While meetings were often held in his house, doubtless because it was roomier than most, he was not in the early days one of the principal leaders of the movement, but his balance, his clarity of mind, integrity of character, and social status brought him to the front and to preside over the Christ Apostolic Church when it came into existence. He poured his own money into the Christ Apostolic Grammar School in Ibadan, sometimes paying the salary of teachers from his own pocket, and it was believed that he would go out at night incognito to distribute clothes and money to the destitute. By the 1950s he would be the Olubadan (king) of Ibadan, the largest city of black Africa, and would be knighted by Queen Elizabeth. By that time his brother would be almost equally revered as the Anglican Bishop of Ibadan, and the two were very close. Aladura and Anglicanism did not, in the Akinyeles, seem so far apart. They represent a third generation in the remarkable history of Yoruba Christianity. The first generation was that of Samuel Crowther and his associates, the second of Mojola Agbebi and James Johnson, the third of Aladura. It is a history which, as a unitary development, has not as yet been adequately described.

Isaac Akinyele was, of course, exceptional in his social standing, but, while the prophet movement in Ivory Coast or the lower Zaïre might appeal above all to the illiterate or almost illiterate, in Yorubaland Aladura appealed at least equally to youth within the progressive, urban, literate class. Orimolade was indeed an old and illiterate prophet, but for that very reason his leadership was quickly threatened among the Seraphim. Aladura represented from the start a kind of Africanization of Christianity which was not opposed to modernization, being faithful in this to the well-established traditions of the Yoruba Churches. While the 1930 revival had seen already the usual multiplication of prophets of every sort and led, especially through the very fissiparous model of Cherubim and Seraphim, to a multitude of small Churches, in some of which bodily healing became the very centre of their life, it also led in the Christ Apostolic Church, easily the largest of Aladura bodies, to a fairly traditional kind of Protestant denomination. The CAC was as emphatically opposed not only to polygamy but to dancing, drumming, and drinking as any mission Church. It was also committed to schooling, and it built up a considerable educational network of its own from primary to grammar schools and teacher training-college.

vi. *East and Central Africa: From Kunyiha to Lenshina*

Turn from Nigeria to Kenya and one finds that here too the very end of the 1920s was a crucial time. The previous years had seen a considerable growth in Christianization and a concomitant desire for schooling, but had also witnessed increasing tension between the races basically caused by the expansion of white farming and settlement in the highlands. There is, in consequence, a bitterness in Kenyan history not to be found in Nigerian. Yoruba society was not threatened in the way Kikuyu society was. Here the main movement of independency focused upon two issues: African control of schools and the circumcision of girls. Missionary opposition to the latter, especially the campaign against it organized by Arthur of the Church of Scotland Mission, a man highly influential with government, to secure the suppression of what nationalist Kikuyu could see as an integral mark of their identity as a people, was the spark which provoked secession and the establishment of the African Independent Pentecostal Church (the AIPC, not in fact Pentecostalist). While its origins may go back a few years before that, it was the 1929–30 crisis over circumcision which made thousands of Church members, Presbyterian, Methodist, and Anglican, move into the AIPC. The educational issue, however, was no less fundamental so that the other side of the AIPC was KISA, the Kikuyu Independent Schools Association, which was certainly established in 1929. Johana Kunyiha would for long be its president. He had been a district councillor since 1928, a member of the District Education Board since 1930. For him the independent movement was intended to differ from the mission Churches on the right of Christian girls to be circumcized but on nothing else, and it is noticeable that in 1933 a petition was actually sent to the Anglican Bishop of Mombasa to allow some ministers to be trained in the diocesan theological college. The request was refused.

At the same time, however, other movements of independency were developing in the very same places, notably that of the Arathi, 'prophets', or the Watu wa Mungu, 'the people of God'. The culture of the Arathi was far closer to tradition. These were people with no interest in schools or any other aspect, other than the Bible, of the European intrusion which was dispossessing the Kikuyu of so much of their land. European dress was rejected, white robes (or even just skins) and turbans adopted; the taboos of Kikuyu tradition were reshaped by Levitical law; Western medicine, Western schooling, Western housing, all was to be avoided. Later on this spirit movement split on whether polygamy should be accepted or not, on whether Sunday should be replaced by Saturday, on the degree of radicalism in rejection of the European-mission style of life, which was seen as so alien to Kikuyu consciousness in a way that the Bible, the Old Testament particularly, was not. While the Arathi worried the colonial authorities, who judged them at least as 'potentially subversive' of civil order—particularly after a clash in 1934 in which Joseph Ng'ang'a, the original leader and two others were shot and killed by the police—they were not proscribed and in due course came to be recognized as a group of unusually hard-working and puritanically moral country folk. The gap between Johana Kunyiha and Joseph Ng'ang'a was undoubtedly a very considerable one in religious, cultural, and educational terms, but once more it is important not to divide different tendencies within Christian independency too rigidly, just as it is important not to overstress the difference between the Christianity of much of it and that of the mission Churches. The Roman Catholic missions, and, at least in some parts, the Anglicans continued to allow female circumcision. The bitterness in the division in Kenya was considerable, but it was a bitterness which reflected the African reaction against white control in an increasingly settler world rather than theological principle.

In Rhodesia too the early 1930s were years which saw the rise and spread of new movements of importance over and above the Zionism which had entered the country a decade earlier and had been spreading especially in the area south and east of Fort Victoria (Masvingo). It was characteristic of Zionism that each group became quickly focused on its own district and precise ethnic identity, with a holy healing 'city' of its own and rather little appeal to people beyond its specific area. The new movements of the 1930s arose particularly in eastern Rhodesia in places which had been much affected by the near mass conversions into the mission Churches of twenty years earlier, but had hardly been touched by Zionism. It is one of the oddities of our history that the two eastern movements in question not only looked so much alike, in at least their earlier stages, but began so close together that it is hard to say which came first. Johane Masowe and Johane Maranke—John of the desert and John of his own district, Maranke—both had visions some time in the middle of 1932 in which it was revealed to each that 'You are John the Baptist' sent by God to preach. For Maranke the experience has been dated to 17 July. For Masowe (formerly named Peter Shoniwa) the date does not appear to be known, but a police report dated 1 November makes it clear that it was some months before that. The former had something of a Methodist background (with, perhaps, some Zionist influence), the second an Anglican. Each claimed a complete personal revelation. In Maranke's case it is to be found written down in a book, the *New Revelation*, which supplements or even replaces the Bible. The element of dream or vision, used elsewhere including mission Churches simply to provide personal guidance for the interpretation of Scripture or to add to Scripture in a fairly minor way, has here gone far further. Indeed Masowe, at least at first, ordered his followers to destroy their Bibles.

The Churches of these two Johanes were Churches of 'Apostles'—the Vapostori of Maranke, the Apostolic Sabbath Church of God of Masowe, better known as the VaHossana from their extensive use of 'Hosannah' in worship. What characterizes them in contrast with the Zionists is a number of things. First, the greater, almost messianic, authority of the founder. A Zionist prophet stressed his authorization through a chain of ordinations back to Zion City, Illinois, and beyond. For Maranke and Masowe authority came directly, and only, through personal revelation and the power of the Spirit. Secondly, as a Church each became far more outgoing and spread far further afield than did a typical Zionist community. The Vapostori were soon to be found in several different countries, as far away as Zaïre. The VaHossana travelled even further. Thirdly, while both Churches of apostles developed a very rich, symbolically complex liturgy, neither developed a holy city, or central location of any sort, and healing was a much less important element in their life. While baptism was important for both Zionists and apostolics (though Masowe allowed no one but himself to baptize), the latter developed liturgy as a whole in a more original and creative way with the 'Paska' of the Vapostori and the Sabbath celebration of the VaHossana, especially as carried out by the 'Ark' of the sisters, a sort of convent of praying nuns at the heart of the Church.

The figure of Masowe is one of the strangest in this history. For much of his life he simply disappeared. In his earlier period he led the core of his apostles first to Bulawayo and then into South Africa where they settled temporarily in the Transvaal and then in 1947 in Korsten, a suburb of Port Elizabeth. By the early 1950s they had become well known as the Korsten Basketmakers. In fact they did far more than make baskets, they installed their own electric generator and had developed an entire mechanical complex in which they made furniture and metalware of every sort. Then they were banished from South Africa as aliens and had to set off again, this time northwards to establish their headquarters, first in Lusaka, then in Nairobi, but always with the intention of arriving finally in Jerusalem. Ruled by the 'Twelve', the central body of VaHossana had become a highly disciplined and industrious group of polygamists, with their symbol, a seven-branched candlestick set above the world. The industrial development of the VaHossana can be compared with the even more remarkable case of the community of the Holy Apostles at Aiyetoro in Nigeria, but their 'ark' of praying nuns and their extraordinary peregrinatory existence across at least four countries has no parallel.

The majority of Masowe's apostles always remained in Rhodesia but were outnumbered by the more numerous Vapostori of Maranke, which soon became the largest independent Church in central Africa. But other Churches of various types continued to multiply. It would not be helpful to refer to them all individually. We can, however, usefully glance at two further groups. The first is what we may call secessions of the 'Ethiopian' type in the 1930s and 1940s. In the early 1930s there was a series in Nyasaland from the Livingstonia Mission, each headed by an ordained minister. Yaphet Mkandawire founded the African Presbyterian Church in 1932, Yesaya Mwasi the Blackman's Church of God in 1933, and Charles Chinula the Eklezia Lanangwa (the Church of Freedom) in 1934. All three had personal difficulties, but they were among the most senior, able, and committed of the not very large group of clergy which Livingstonia had produced. To them we may join Wilfrid Gudu, a teacher of the Seventh-day Adventists, who established the Ana a Mulungu (Children of God) Church in 1935. A little later came a number of Rhodesian examples: Mheke Sengwayo, an evangelist of the American Board, began the African Congregational Church (Chibarirwe) in 1940; Francis Nyabadza, an Anglican catechist of St Faith's Mission, was excommunicated by it and formed his own Church of St Francis, Rusape, in 1942; Madida Moyo, a preacher of the Apostolic Faith Mission Church, left it to found his own in 1945; and Esau Nemapare, a Wesleyan Methodist minister, tendered his resignation in 1947 to launch the African Methodist Church. We can join Johana Kunyiha in Kenya to this little list and we could without much difficulty find others such as Matthew Ajuoga and the group of clergy who left the Anglican Church in 1957 in western Kenya to found the Church of Christ in Africa.

All of these men had been working for years under white missionaries as clergy, catechists, or teachers. They were not charismatic and they did their best to continue in their new Churches almost all the practices of the mission but without the mission's resources. In most cases they were probably not worse off personally for their secession because most clergy and catechists were paid no more than a pittance, if that, in the 1930s and 1940s. There were particular issues at stake: Madida was shocked that a mission which forbade the eating of pork should be making a profit from farming and selling pigs. Nyabadza found his mission slack on drunkenness. Kunyiha could not accept the banning of the circumcision of girls. But underlying such relatively trivial issues was the wider one of control and confidence. This was still not an age in which the missionaries were, at all often, giving signs of bowing out or of heeding the mature judgement of African Christians. What had happened in Lagos and Lovedale in the 1890s was happening now in a great many other places as black frustration mounted with the restrictions of life within what was structurally still a mission Church though in reality it was now an established, indigenous Church. It is true that in several cases the immediate problem was an inter-black one, but it remained a fact that behind certain blacks stood a system of white power. The moving indictment of Y. Z. Mwasi in *My Essential and Paramount Reasons for Working Independently* was widely felt to be true: 'The time has now come for the Native Church to take up its responsibilities alone as the individual Churches, planted by the Apostle Paul did, without fear that absence of mission is death of the Christianity of the soil.'[20] Yet most of these Churches remained small. The missions suffered from the secessions but could not really be rivalled as providers of educational and medical services or even of a structured parish life. Many who remained within them are unlikely to have dissented strongly from the viewpoint of those who left. Pragmatism rather than principle in fact most often prevailed upon either side, and the pragmatism of the

[20] Y. Z. Mwasi, *My Essential and Paramount Reasons for Working Independently*, ed. J. K. Parratt (Zomba, 1979), 3.

late colonial age was still for the most part a pragmatism of submission. As Mwasi bitterly complained, too many of his fellow ministers deferred to their missionaries on the grounds that they were the 'ruling race you know'.[21] But that was soon to change.

The last example we will consider is once more a prophetic one, that of the Lumpa Church of Alice Lenshina Mulenga among the Bemba of Zambia (Northern Rhodesia) in the 1950s. Mulenga was a young woman who had studied in the primary school at the Presbyterian Mission of Lubwa beside Kenneth Kaunda, whose father had been its catechist and then, briefly, its first African minister. In 1953, like many another prophet in the making, she had an experience of death and resurrection out of which sprang a mission which for a little while she exercised within the Presbyterian Church. She began to compose hymns of a traditional Bemba type and great popular appeal. Within two years, however, the nature of her movement with its strongly anti-witchcraft character and millennialist note brought about a break with Presbyterianism and the development of her village of Kasomo as 'Zioni' with a vast church, larger than any mission church in the district. Whole villages of Lumpa devotees grew up, cut off so far as they could be from the rest of society, though the many Lumpa members on the Copperbelt continued to mix freely with other mortals. Lumpa was fiercely opposed to 'pagan' practices of every sort, witchcraft and sorcery most certainly, but also to polygamy and beer-drinking. It represented the 'prophetic' type of Church, with its revelations, its hymns, its holy city, its segregation, but in the most explicitly Christian of forms. While in some others of this type the cultural mode was more traditionalist or Old Testament, Lumpa was intensely Jesus-centred—both the Jesus of history and the Jesus who would soon return. It was Jesus whom Lenshina had met in her experience of death, and references to Jesus abound in her hymns.

Around 1958 there was a veritable exodus both of Presbyterians and of Catholics into Lumpa, at a time when white domination still seemed secure and the general population felt alienated by the imposed regime of the Central African Federation. While the Guta ra Jehova of Mai Chaza in Southern Rhodesia dates from about the same time and the Maria Legio in Kenya from some years later, Lumpa may reasonably be regarded as the last major prophetic

21 Ibid. 1.

movement to arise in colonial Africa, and it is not surprising that this should happen in Zambia, one of the last countries to be effectively missionized. Nevertheless, it may be that the particularly Christian character of Lumpa reflects the wider spread of Christianity in society by the 1950s. Lumpa appears also as a feminist Church, not only led by a woman but expressing feminine aspirations, a woman's view of the ideal society, more than others. This was expressed in its opposition to polygamy, but also in the symbols it made use of in its hymns deriving from the mind of Lenshina. In the 1960s with the advent of political independence Lumpa would take up a strongly negative stance, linked with its opposition to the spread of schools, and would end in a bloody confrontation with government, but in the 1950s when our story ends this could hardly have been anticipated. Indeed in its anti-mission stance it appeared at times as a populist ally of the nationalists.

vii. *Independency in the 1950s*

The 1950s were important in most parts of Africa more for a consolidation and institutionalization of existing movements than for wholly new outbreaks. This was the result in part of political preparations for national independence. Thus the whole Belgian attitude to African religious movements changed in the mid-1950s from repression towards a gradual acceptance, part of a new more liberal colonial attitude developing after the Second World War. It is still far from clear exactly how the Church of Jesus Christ through his prophet, Simon Kimbangu, actually emerged in this period, but from about 1954 Joseph Diangienda, Kimbangu's youngest son, a well-educated and capable civil servant, assumed the role of direction in concert with his two elder brothers. Diangienda was only a baby when his father's imprisonment began. It ended thirty years later when Kimbangu died in Elisabethville in October 1951. Diangienda must have been brought up by his mother and other devoted disciples with a sense of mission to lead the Church which his father, perhaps without realizing it, had brought into existence, and it was shortly after Kimbangu's death that Diangienda began to link up with the now elderly survivors of the movement of 1921. By 1956 a Council of the Kimbanguist Church had been formed and, after a final bout of persecution, toleration was officially accorded in December 1957. In April 1960, just before the political independence of the country was declared in June, the body of Simon Kimbangu was brought back from Elisabethville and solemnly interred in the mausoleum at Nkamba, the Kimbanguist New Jerusalem.

The public appearance of a Kimbanguist Church led by his sons inevitably involved the making and breaking of frontiers upon two sides. On the one hand there was an exodus of covert Kimbanguists from Protestant Churches, involving an often bitter conflict of expulsion as well as of withdrawal. On the other hand there was the refusal of many Kimbanguists and other 'Ngunzist' dissidents to join the Church of Diangienda. Thus while the latter was developing on fairly recognizable 'Protestant' lines, monogamous and in very real continuity with the Baptist practices of Kimbangu's own background, Simon Mpadi returned from twenty years of imprisonment to preside over a Church in which polygamy was in principle compulsory and in which he was able to relate the wonderful story of his own fourteen resurrections. In 1959 as in 1921 Congolese prophetism was something far wider than the prophetic experience of Kimbangu and the teaching of his sons. A battle over 'authentic' Kimbanguism had inevitably to be launched.

In Ivory Coast too the later 1950s were a time in which the hitherto largely hidden life of the Harrist Church surfaced, acquired a constitutional character, and was for a time hailed as almost the national Church by the nationalist movement. We have seen how well established in the figure of Sir Isaac Akinyele was Aladura by the 1950s. In South Africa too Zionism had settled down in fairly stable forms, on the one hand more urbanized on the Rand, on the other so closely linked with the King of Swaziland as to be part of its established religion. In the 1950s the presence of Bishop Nkonyane at the annual Swazi Incwala was taken for granted. Yet at the same time as some of the principal 'prophet' movements of a generation before were hardening into an almost 'Ethiopian' model, there was as ever a multitude of other tiny spiritual groups springing up around them, each serviced by a prophet whose functions were mostly those of ritual healing. While the great prophets of the first generation were above all evangelists, the multitude of their successors were healers rather than preachers. Healing, in the meantime, had become a slightly secondary dimension of the main Kimbanguist or Harrist traditions. Independency could not mean the same thing in 1958 as it had meant forty years earlier, but equally it could not mean the same thing for a movement that was new, like Lumpa, as for a movement which had gone through a considerable history of persecution and spiritual maturing like the Kimbanguist. The character of a movement at its origins did not determine its character a generation later, but, equally, there could be an intrinsic biblical or Christian commitment which survived but might nevertheless look rather different when translated from an almost illiterate to an urban and partly educated society. Nevertheless, it is clear that basically similar religious movements could spread in very different social and political contexts. Zionism might be the characteristic religion of the South African underclass in a racist society, but Aladura, not all that different in religious terms, was always a religion of aspiring and literate urban artisans and clerks under no sense of political alienation.

viii. *Causes and Motivations*

Some further discussion of the causative factions at work within the movement is necessary. First of all, it was clearly a very Protestant movement, emerging for the most part within denominations—Methodist, Baptist, Presbyterian, among others—in which secessions had been fairly numerous in Britain and the USA, secessions—such as the Great 'Disruption' of 1843 within the Church of Scotland—which were an important and much emphasized part of their history. Separation on grounds of truth was, after all, an almost intrinsic principle of Protestantism as a historical phenomenon, and the fact that this was recognized and applied by African Protestants suggests a priori not that they had not heard the missionary message but that they had heard it. The theoretical Protestant appeal to the Bible was also an inherently fruitful ground for division. Africans received the Bible and its authority as good Protestants, but they inevitably read it through cultural and social spectacles different from those of the missionary. The missionary believed in angelic visitations, miracles, and what have you in their biblical context, but had in most cases ceased to believe in any continuity between the biblical and the contemporary, strongly as he will have affirmed his to be a purely biblical religion. It could entirely nonplus the missionary that his African Christians claimed to experience dreams and visions of a revelatory sort. Again, many missionaries had made insistence upon monogamy into a very corner-stone of the Church, precisely in reaction against the polygamy they saw around them and which, more and more, they regarded as both vicious and pagan. But they could not give any convincing biblical argument for this insistence. On the contrary, African Christians could point to the polygamists of the Old Testament, whom the Bible never blamed. Most Protestant missionaries had absolutely no theological equipment to respond convincingly to this argument. They only had the weight of Western convention and the experiential certitude that a monogamous union was the mark of both civilization and Christianity. Finally, secessions multiplied in places where Protestant missions overlapped and very seldom happened where there was a single mission in operation. South Africa, Lagos, southern Nyasaland, central Kenya were all places where half a dozen or more missions, not very different from each other in appearance, were all functioning as separate and mostly uncommunicating Churches. If white Christians could be so divided, why should not black Christians?

None of these things was applicable to Catholics. Within their own history they had no tradition of separation. Separation was what other people did and it was invariably wrong. The Bible, with all its strange revelations, mattered far less to them either in theory or in practice. Indeed even by the 1950s there was no complete Catholic translation of the Old Testament into any African language. Catholics had, moreover, in the Church and the papacy an authority effectively above the Bible from the viewpoint of its interpretation. They were also so different from Protestants that the presence of Protestant missionaries in the same place as Catholics did not encourage the idea of the acceptability of secession from Catholicism in the way that the proximity of, say, Presbyterians and Methodists within the one area made it seem ecclesiastically feasible to set up another Church of the same sort but with an African name. Catholics were also, by and large, more tolerant of African custom than Protestants. There were secessions from the Catholic Church such as the Bamutima in Northern Rhodesia and (in the 1960s) the Maria Legio in Kenya, among others, but their number and significance were tiny in comparison with those from Protestantism. In this we may well conclude that African Catholics were being good Catholics (putting the unity and authority of the Church first), African Protestants were being good Protestants, members of a tradition in which Church unity had always taken second place.

African independency cannot, however, be understood without the consideration of three other major factors. The first was that of colonialism and racialism. In most of the more deliberate secessions this was a factor of importance. It was not just the racialism in colonial society, most evident in South Africa. It was, still more, the racialism within the Church, the impression—in most cases very well grounded—that even able and experienced African ministers remained second-class members of the Church, always inferior to even the most junior missionary recently arrived from Britain. This was a matter of authority exercised, of salary, of details of human behaviour such as the sharing of meals. The missionary Churches were so integrated into racialist society, especially in South Africa, that their membership was profoundly alienating for black people. By itself, this seldom produced a secession, but it prepared the way for secession on other, often trivial, grounds.

The second factor was the pressure of traditional African religion and culture upon young Churches. Few missionaries understood the way even their most committed converts understood and appropriated what they were taught. Appropriation had to be within the thought forms which already structured their minds and the kind of religious experience, ritual and spiritual, with which they were already familiar. In the well-disciplined Christian village ruled over by a missionary, such thought forms might seem almost to disappear. However, once the necessity of a mass Christianity developing within ordinary villages well away from a mission was accepted, it was inevitable that the overall interpretation of Christianity would shift imperceptibly but quite quickly from a missionary model to an at least partially indigenous one. The shift, moreover, was greatly assisted—as we have already seen—by a certain correspondence between biblical and traditional African experience. The correspondence was not, of course, complete. Nevertheless, it was sufficiently striking to create a sort of biblical-African alliance against the rather more rationalist, but also simply more rigidly Victorian denominationalist, missionary which provided the springboard for much of the prophetic side of independency. On many issues the Old Testament in particular appeared to justify both African tradition and African Christian aspirations against missionary regulations. The pursuit of a Hebraic model within an African context was as clear in Shembe's Amanazaretha or Kivuli's African Israel as it had been in the Ethiopia of centuries earlier. The prophet criticized the missionary for not being biblical enough, and, while such criticism might seem simplistic, the missionaries seldom had the theology to contend with such an approach or to recognize its genuine strengths.

Where the pressure of Africa mattered most was in the area of health and healing. African religion was, to a very large extent, health-orientated. Missionary Christianity was not. In fact as we have seen the early missionaries, often with little if any medical training, spent a great part of their time tending the sick. Africans may have read into this more than Europeans intended, but around the turn of the century several things happened. Missionary societies became a great deal more preoccupied with professional medicine. Their medical standards went up, but in consequence the hospital was in its way secularized and divorced from the Church as such. The great majority of missionaries could be excused further participation in healing. At the same time in many areas African religion was tumbling and Christianity spreading like a bush fire. Who now was to care for the sick? Village life was too far away, anyway, from the rare mission hospital for the latter to fill the gap left by the collapse of traditional healing amongst the newly converted. The rise of movements of Christian healing was inevitable. Moreover, new plagues had swept the continent including in particular the 1918 influenza pandemic. Western medicine had proved unable to cope. Missionaries had long commanded their Christians to shun African medicines. Why not shun European ones as well and turn to God alone through prayer and holy water? The new prophetic movements all had within them a strong element of miraculous healing and faith-healing. It was a little less central for Harris or Babalola than it was for Kimbangu, but it was strongly present through most of independency. If the mission Churches came to look more and more like a network of schools, the independent prophetic Churches came to look like a network of hospitals and health clinics. And many an African found both attractive.

The third factor was that all this was happening upon an expanding frontier in which the mission Churches were already growing faster than they could cope. Independency, as we have seen it, was often hardly, if at all, distinguishable from a primary movement of mass conversion. It is the continuity between the one and the other which is important. Mass conversion movements were not set off by missionaries but by a concatenation of circumstances within African societies, at once buffeted by the new pressures of colonialism and enlightened by African 'evangelists' of one sort or another who were able to mediate just sufficient of Christian wisdom to be understood and effective for the masses. Such a movement could end up with almost any denominational form, but the form taken should almost always be seen as an attempt to reproduce missionary Christianity rather than to reject it. The prophet was essentially taking on the missionary's task because it seemed so important. He based it on the missionary's book, the Bible, and focused it most often upon the missionary's most symbolic action—baptism by immersion. Again and again early missionaries had insisted upon river baptism and this was true of Churches like the Anglican which did not practise baptism by immersion at home. Thus the first Anglican to be baptized among the Mashona, a young man named Shoniwa, was immersed in a river near Umtali and given the name of John in July 1896.[22] Thirty years later another Shoniwa in quite the same place would take the name of John and become one of the great prophet-baptizers of central Africa. In baptism, as in much else, it is the continuity in experience rather than any discontinuity between mission and independency which requires recognition; however, while almost all missionaries reasonably insisted upon a quite lengthy baptismal preparation, the desire for instant baptism had become so great in some quarters that it almost generated prophetic baptizers to respond to it.

It was inevitable that either the complete absence of any missionary Church in some places or a rigidity in the missionaries available in others forced many movements to generate permanent congregations, hierarchies, and rituals of their own. The years between 1910 and 1940 witness a flow of mass conversion movements across many parts of Africa. Their details vary, and it is on account of the details that some such movements produced areas solidly Catholic, others equally solidly Lutheran or Anglican, others again of a much more mixed complexion, including independent Churches like Aladura and Kimbanguism. Although secession from an established Church is undoubtedly what happened in some places, nevertheless, primarily this process was one of conversion, not one of secession. Conversion had to lead to a structured pattern of Church life of one sort or another, and the combination of factors listed above ensured that the pattern would not always be, even on the surface, one known already within Western Christendom.

[22] J. Farrant, *Mashonaland Martyr: Bernard Mizeki and the Pioneer Church* (1966), 228.

A word should be added here about 'negative cases'. The 1914 upsurge of the Bamalaki in Uganda was a major movement involving for a few years tens of thousands of Anglicans, but it did not last except in a minuscule form. One other, later, Ugandan secession from the CMS Mission joined the Greek Orthodox Church. It was not large, but its very shunning of independency is significant. In Uganda by the 1950s independent Churches were so small as to be effectively non-existent. Even more striking is the Christian history of Tanzania. Almost every independent Church in Tanganyika in the 1950s was a cross-border extension, of no great size, of a body based elsewhere, in Kenya or Nyasaland. Both Uganda and Tanganyika had exceptionally large Christian communities by 1960. In each case considerable parts of the country were predominantly Christian. They also had the Bible translated into their principal languages, something claimed by some interpreters as almost inevitably leading to independency. But in neither country was there any significant locally based independent movement. If we ask why, we can find three fairly evident possible factors. The first was that in each the majority of Christians was Roman Catholic; the second that in most of Uganda there was only one Protestant missionary society and while there were several in Tanganyika they did not overlap; the third that in neither was there any considerable white settler presence. We can observe the same absence and the same possible causes in Rwanda and Burundi.

By the 1950s something like a third of all black Christians in South Africa belonged to independent Churches. Elsewhere it was seldom nearly so large a proportion, nevertheless, there were now two kinds of country, in one of which independency was significant, in the other it was not. South Africa and Swaziland fell into the first category, Basutoland and Bechuanaland (Lesotho and Botswana) into the second; the Rhodesias (Zimbabwe and Zambia) were in the first, Tanganyika in the second; Kenya in the first, Uganda in the second; Nigeria (at least western Nigeria) in the first, Cameroon in the second; the Belgian Congo (Zaïre) in the first, Rwanda and Burundi in the second. No single factor correlates well with that division, but in general the rule holds that where Christianity began with a multiplicity of Protestant Churches and where there was a considerable white settler (and ostensibly Protestant) presence, there independency grew; where Christianity was predominantly Catholic, where Protestant missions did not overlap, and where white settlers were few or none, there it hardly emerged. It is at least in such terms and not in those of the character of traditional religion that its growth has chiefly to be explained.

Independency appealed to different classes in different circumstances. Its 'Ethiopian' end appealed to the new élite of clergy and laity, literate and school-minded, but irritated by European control. Its other, 'prophetic', end is harder to define socially. Mostly it was the very poor who wanted the power of Christian faith but had little interest in schools and none in élitist self-improvement. They were opters-out into a religious world of meaning when the secular world was so dominated by white foreigners and a colour bar. Even in Northern Rhodesia at the end of the 1950s it looks as if the progressively minded were turning to nationalist politics and even a mission Church, while the unschooled, often from the same families, went for Lumpa. But it would be dangerous to press this too far. Zionism may have been in South Africa the refuge of the very poor. That is not so obvious in Swaziland, while in Yorubaland it has been demonstrated that Aladura appealed on the contrary to up-and-coming urban youth, both literate and skilled. Those responding in their thousands to the preaching of a Harris or a Swatson will have sought whatever the prophet had to offer, and it was not a package so different from that of the missionary.

ix. *The Character of Prophetic Christianity*

The Bible remained somehow central in almost every case, even if you could not read it. Harris laid his tattered Bible on a convert's head at baptism. So powerful was the mystique of the heavenly book that additional books of revelation abound in many prophetic traditions. Lenshina was given a Bible by God when ordered to return to earth. Maranke produced his *New Revelations of the Apostles*. Only Masowe confined biblical reading to himself. Prophetic religion was then at least implicitly literate. Moreover, even if they began socially at the bottom, the members of an independent Church could rise very noticeably within a generation. The economic miracle of Aiyetoro was exceptional, but the Basketmakers of Masowe were not so far behind. The tiny Church of St Francis, founded by Francis Nyabadza near Rusape, was as poor as could be when it began, but hard co-operative work gradually changed that. The farm was enlarged, a tractor and truck bought, a trading store opened, then a butchery, then a twice-weekly sale of produce under a tree in Rusape town. Later it would have a grinding-mill and two diesel electricity generators. The polygamous Vapostori of Maranke became well known as prosperous farmers. The Arathi in Kenya, viewed as wholly rejecting everything of Western ways in the 1930s, were judged particularly reliable labourers on Western standards by the 1950s. The work ethic and a commitment to the material improvement of the group had in each case prevailed. As they did so prophetism, except in terms of fairly well-controlled healing services, declined and was replaced by a well-structured hierarchy in which each member knew his or her place.

A crucial moment could be the death of the founder. Leadership tended to the hereditary, and in a number of Churches one of the prophet's sons took over his authority effectively, with reduced but still recognizable charisma coupled with a greater bureaucratic efficiency. Thus Johannes Galilee Shembe succeeded his father Isaiah in 1936, and Diangienda inherited the authority of Kimbangu, but in other cases the prophet's death could result in schism and disintegration. Bureaucratization, routinization, the ownership of buildings, the more professional study of the Bible, could all become characteristics of a Church which in its origins thirty years earlier would have scorned such things. Again, it would be a mistake to generalize. Developments which were possible within a large community such as the Kimbanguist Church, over which Diangienda presided by 1960, were not possible, nor necessarily desired, within far smaller groups. And if a few larger Churches are those most noted by the historian, it is the multitude of tiny groups, breaking off from one another, often with a minimum of knowledge, that continue to dominate the scene in many places. It is not unreasonable to question whether some of them could fairly be described as Christian and a few explicitly repudiated the claim. The intricate mix of village religion focused so often upon one type or another of healing ritual, including spirit possession, cannot usefully be categorized or defined in a single way. That was already the case when the movements started—the Lower Kongo is a good example—and it remains true through the period. Some Churches might indeed prove, as Sundkler claimed in the first edition of his *Bantu Prophets*,[23] to be a 'bridge leading back' to traditional religion;

---

[23] B. Sundkler, *Bantu Prophets*, 2nd edn. (1961), 302.

but others became increasingly Christian over the years, until they came to look much like any other small Protestant congregationalist denomination.

The main prophetic movements and Churches do, however, tend to share a number of characteristics which, placed together, create a new, rather African, form of Christianity. Healing, visions and dreams, a holy city, the sacralized figure of the founder, certain kinds of ritual, food taboos: such a list includes the principal elements. The prophet's staff was the symbol of the authority with which it all began, a very important part of the repertoire of almost every prophet, whether in West, central, or southern Africa. In every photograph, even those at the end of his life with Benoit and Ahui, Harris is portrayed gripping his staff. At a crucial moment when confronting the District Administrator, Kimbangu found he was without his staff, and hurried back to collect it. 'Who is it if not Nzambi (God) who has given me this *mvwala* (staff) and set me to lead his sheep?', asked a little-known Congolese prophet, Mavonda Ntangu, in 1943.[24] The title given to Kimbangu's sons is actually that of *Mvwala*: they continue his authority because they have his staff, just as a century before the dying Ntsikana had described his son Dukwana as his staff. Where does this very widespread way of denoting the prophet come from? From the staff of Moses (Exodus 14: 16, 17: 5, 17: 9) or apostolic precept as in Mark 6: 8? Yet as a whole the Hebrew Scriptures do not stress the need for a prophet to have a staff. It would seem to be rather a motif of African tradition whose retention is justified by the Mosaic example and, perhaps, by the episcopal use of a crozier.

If the staff denotes the prophet, the prophet's total characterization, particularly subsequent to his death, requires a great deal more to it and undoubtedly takes different levels of sacralization. Some are a John the Baptist for Africa, pointing to a Christ who remains explicitly central. Others are rather a successor to Christ but not a replacement, more like the comforter Christ promised his disciples. A third possibility is to take the place of Christ either functionally or absolutely in regard to Africa, a particular people, or the modern age. Harris may be seen as prototype for the first, Kimbangu for the second, and Shembe for the third. Yet they merge into each other, being essentially functional, not ontological, categories. A successor

[24] E. Andersson, *Messianic Popular Movements in the Lower Congo* (Uppsala, 1958), 146.

as well as a replacement functions through similarity. What Christ did for the world, Kimbangu has shown forth here, for blacks. So all the attributes of Christ can be reproduced as well—the widow of Kimbangu stands in for Mary, Nkamba becomes the New Jerusalem, there are Resurrection visions. If Shembe and even Kimbangu may be at times described in hymns in apparently divine terms, a missionary bishop may fare little differently. A Bemba hymn for the White Father Bishop Dupont, 'our Redeemer' (Mulubushi wesu), describes how he 'gives life to our children and nurtures them with food. He hurls down the lions and heals our ailments,' while a Dinka hymn saw Bishop Eduardo Mason of Wau as the supreme Master of the Fishing Spear: 'The Great Mason is the Master of the Christians of the Bahr al-Ghazal, And he is the Master of the World'.[25] The point is that the song of praise tends to hyperbole. It is not a safe source for the finer points of belief.

There may appear greater conformity to a single type in regard to the holy city than in regard to the figure of the founder. Modern Africa has thrown up numerous New Jerusalems, replicating the Aksum and Lalibela of Ethiopia, from Mozano and New Tadzewu in Ghana to Ekuphakameni and Ekukhanyeni in Zululand. But again analysis reveals significant differences. The holy city is a place of pilgrimage, liturgy, and healing; it is the centre of the Church, the place where the founder is buried, and it is symbolically identified with the historic Jerusalem. Nevertheless, the balance varies. In some small, rather segregated, Churches, it is in principle where the members actually live. It is the Church. Against this, in a large Church like the Kimbanguist, Nkamba becomes only a place of pilgrimage and not even the administrative headquarters. Diangienda lived in Kinshasa. Healing may be the city's dominant activity, as in the Mount Zion or Mount Moriah of Bishop Mutendi, but again that dominance can diminish after the death of the founder. His successor may be far less renowned as a healer. With Shembe that is clear. Healing did not disappear with his son, but its character altered and its centrality in the activities of the city was diminished. The significance of the city remains tied to the significance of the founder: the more messianic or Mosaic the latter, the greater the

[25] H. Hinfelaar, 'Religious Change among the Bemba-Speaking Women in Zambia', Ph.D. thesis (London, 1989), 50–1; L. and N. Sanderson, *Education, Religion and Politics in the Southern Sudan 1899–1964* (1981), 405, quoting F. M. Deng, *The Dinka and their Songs* (Oxford, 1973).

symbolism of the former. John the Baptists do not have holy cities. Nor indeed do prophets—or apostles—claiming a lower profile still, yet they and their Churches constitute a very large part of the whole movement. Only more marginal groups of Aladura have holy cities. They would be alien to the religion of a Babalola or an Akinyele, equally to the Zionism of an Nkonyane. While the holy city and functional messiah present a fascinating type of African Christianity more colourful than most others, and one found in all the main regions of Africa, it is nevertheless a minority type, even within the more prophetic end of independency. And it is to be noted that Kimbanguism, while remaining somewhat ambiguous about the status of its originator, in point of fact moved under the leadership of Diangienda fairly steadily away from this type of religiosity and towards that adhered to quite consistently by the Aladura Christ Apostolic Church.

Churches with a holy city—but some others too—tend to dress in special uniforms; they may reject shoes; they stress a symbolic apartness. They tend to maximize taboos and to retake the Levitical laws of the clean and the unclean. Here too there is a frequent fusion between the taboos of African traditional custom and the taboos of the Old Testament, though again it has been noted for the Kikuyu Arathi, for instance, how in point of fact where the two differ, it is the Levitical rule, not Kikuyu tradition, which prevails. Western missionaries, anyway, brought various taboos of their own—against alcohol and tobacco, for example, or even against pork. The rejection of pork is exceedingly widespread. Agbebi already excluded it, so did the Kimbanguists, Kivuli of the Kenyan African Israel Church Nineveh, the Vapostori of both Maranke and Masowe, Nyabadza's Church of St Francis, George Khambule in South Africa, and many others. Where a biblical prohibition emphatically reinforced a traditional one, it might be embraced with especial enthusiasm, particularly if it reinforced one's own biblical purity against the defects of missionaries. Madida in Matabeleland could denounce the Apostolic Faith Mission of South Africa, from which he had broken, precisely as a 'Church of Pigs'. In contrast to all this we may note that the Balokole Revival of Uganda, Rwanda, and Kenya particularly denounced food taboos. They were part of the list of sins to be challenged together with smoking, drinking, charms, incest. The theology of the Revival here stressed a discontinuity with both the biblical and the African 'Old Testament' but a more emphatic continuity with the spirit of the New.

The theology of a prophetic Church is functional, not ontological, and, like much traditional religion, it can vary according to context and to whom one is speaking. Vernacular hymns and an apologia in a European language are not likely to say quite the same thing, but they diverge without dishonesty. The hymns of ultramontane Catholic pilgrimages hardly accord very precisely with textbook Roman theology. The hymns of the Amanazaretha may appear to leave Jesus out and to give all to Shembe, but a carefully prepared sermon by his son Johannes Galilee can right the balance. It is an ongoing process of affirming the importance of the particular in the context of the universal, and the brief observing visitor or pernickety theological analyst may easily come away with the wrong impression or, if not wrong, at least one too partial.

By 1960, while new movements were still arising, the older ones, whether Zionist, Aladura, Kimbanguist, or Harrist, were stabilizing their faith and self-understanding. In Nigeria, benefiting from British colonial tolerance, Aladura had long been able to do this, but in the Congo circumstances were only now permitting it, and a text of the late 1950s illustrates rather well the need to defend one's own tradition both by linking it with the great things of the Christian past and by differentiating it from other movements of the localized present. It was written by Dialungana K. Salomon, the second son of Kimbangu and guardian of the holy city of Nkamba, and was entitled *Zolanga Yelusalemi dia Mpia*, 'Being Loyal to the New Jerusalem'.[26] It was composed about the time the body of Kimbangu was returned to Nkamba and in relation to the struggle of the sons of Kimbangu to establish firm leadership over a movement which had begun with their father but which had now developed in many conflicting directions. Our text was therefore a plea for recognition of the unique status of Nkamba and for the centralized Church which was being organized by the prophet's family. It was a plea grounded upon the biblical history and status of Jerusalem, city of David, the centre of pilgrimage, the object of so many psalms. The black people are 'the most dishonoured of all races whom God created in this earth', transported to America in ships 'like sardines in cans' or killed by the

---

[26] W. MacGaffey, '*The Beloved City*: Commentary on a Kimbanguist Text', *JRA* 2 (1969), 129–47.

thousand in the colonial Congo 'while they carried loads from Matadi to Leopoldville'.

Then in 1921 God raised up a prophet, Simon Kimbangu, through whom 'God our Father and his Son Jesus Christ are returned to us'. Miracles were performed, but only in order that wickedness should cease, hearts be converted, prayers and hymns be said, the Bible be read. All this happened in Nkamba, clearly identified by such events as the New Jerusalem spoken of in prophecy. Inevitably there was resistance from 'the hill of Satan'—false prophets, missionaries, and the Belgian government. Just as Jesus and his disciples were persecuted, so were Kimbangu and his followers. For all these reasons Nkamba is to be loved and the children of Kimbangu obeyed as against the many others who 'have bestowed prophethood upon themselves . . .and set themselves up as the equals of Simon Kimbangu'.[27] They dissuade people from going to the true Jerusalem, claiming instead their own holy cities, but God has rejected them.

In this moving text, Kongolese and biblical history are woven together. One renews the other, being essentially the same thing. Within a single sacred history we move through soteriology to ecclesiology. While the colonial government has crumbled, the false prophets are still a 'hill of Satan' very much in existence. Kimbangu himself did in fact declare other prophets to be false. His sons renew the claim of a divine intervention, a divine love which has been manifested within black history but is both particularized and institutionalized. Come to Nkamba and experience it. Not many Churches might have expressed their theology quite so well, but we have in this text an integration of African experience and biblical spirituality which is essentially common to many Churches other than the Kimbanguist, and it may well provide the best theological expression of the type of Christianity characteristic of the African prophetic movement in every part of the continent. It was a view of things by no means unfaithful to what had happened forty years earlier, yet controlled by the needs of a very different age in which colonialism was passing and the prophetic and millennialist mission required reinterpretation by a Church in which the miraculous healer was being replaced by the cooler hand of preacher and administrator.

[27] 141.

12

CHURCH, SCHOOL, AND STATE IN THE AGE OF BISHOP KIWANUKA

THE STATE AND THE MISSIONARY

i. *The 1920s and Education*

By 1920 armed African resistance to colonial rule was almost a thing of the past and colonialism itself was beginning to mellow. The National Congress of British West Africa, meeting in Accra in March 1920 under the leadership of Casely Hayford, was symbolic of the advance of political debate and a realignment in the African response to foreign rule. The last great uprising had been that of the Makombe in 1917 in the particularly ill ruled and poorly developed territory of Mozambique. Elsewhere the sheer brutality of treatment meted out to the Herero, Bambata, and Maji Maji risings in the early years of the century could hardly be imagined in the 1920s. If one reason for this was that African resistance was effectively over and replaced by an apparently at times even enthusiastic collaboration, another was that the climate of world opinion had greatly changed. The sheer blood-letting of the First World War between European and European had produced not only a revulsion against violence and a great diminution of imperialist fervour but also positive new approaches to the whole business of running the world. Weak as the League of Nations would prove to be when faced with hard issues, its very existence, together with that of the International Court of Justice and the International Labour Organization, set up new standards for the unacceptable in political behaviour. Thus, while Britain, France, Belgium, and South Africa divided control of the German colonies in Africa, they had to hold them as 'mandates' on behalf of the League with the obligation of maintaining certain standards and of submitting an annual report to the Council of the League. Furthermore, the setting-out of what was appropriate government for 'mandates' could not but affect neighbouring colonies to some extent. Governors were moved from one to the other. When in 1923 the Duke of Devonshire as Colonial Secretary recommended that in Kenya 'the interests of the African natives must be paramount',[1] something like this was already happening, even though in reality their interests were still often far from paramount. A philosophy of 'trusteeship' was coming to occupy the moral high ground.

Within British Africa the new approach was expressed in terms of 'Indirect Rule', a concept first developed by Lord Lugard with northern Nigeria in mind. Where chiefs exist, rule through them; where they do not, invent them. Yet the hasty creation of all sorts of new authorities could, in traditionally democratic societies especially, prove extremely unwelcome. As ultimate power remained very firmly in white hands, there was, anyway, an element of charade in the system, but there was also an element of realism, of an underlying recognition that Africa could, after all, only be ruled by Africans and in an African way. What, however, was the African way? Colonial administrators needed to find out, hence a greatly increased interest in custom and the writing of important books by some of them, such as P. A. Talbot's four volumes published in 1926 on *The Peoples of Southern Nigeria* or R. S. Rattray's 1929 *Ashanti Law and Constitution*. The commencement of the quarterly *Africa* in 1928 was another sign of the change in climate. It was intended as a forum in which missionaries, academics, and administrators could learn to understand Africa in a way they were now conscious of not having done hitherto. At the same time the old military governors were passing away, to be replaced by at times quite progressively minded civilians like Hugh Clifford in Nigeria and Donald Cameron in Tanganyika.

The rehabilitation of tribal custom could, however, be no long-term substitute for modernization. Here education was increasingly recognized to be the key. Previous to 1920, French Africa apart, schooling had been almost entirely left to missionary initiative. It could be so no longer. The Phelps–Stokes Reports (1920 and 1924), financed by an American fund, both surveyed existing educational provision country by country across the continent and pointed the way to a future in which governments accepted a large responsibility

[1] *Indians in Kenya*, Memorandum presented to Parliament by Command of His Majesty, July 1923, 9.

in this area. The thrust of the reports was to encourage an industrial rather than a literary education, and the intention of their principal originator, the American Jesse Jones, may even have included a racialist concern to ensure that Africans were not educated above their station. The effect, however, was very different. In practice both industrial and literary education were needed and both were developing. While governments now sought to control standards and encourage new initiatives by the provision of funds and some inspection, they remained largely dependent upon the missions for most of the work and the finding of personnel. In British tropical Africa in 1945, 96.4 per cent of pupils attending schools were in those of a mission. In consequence, in both British and Belgian Africa a close working alliance developed between Church and State, functioning mostly to the satisfaction of both (though in Belgian Africa this only applied to Catholic missions until after the Second World War). The colonial mind was now concerned less with guns than with blackboards.

The shift within the colonial order towards the benevolent and the developmental was, nevertheless, both patchy and bounded. The inclusion of James Aggrey, a Ghanaian, on the Phelps-Stokes Commission was remarkable because it was so unusual. For many an African in central and southern Africa to see this black man eating with whites and treated the same was quite extraordinary. It had never happened before in their experience and would not happen again for quite some time. Moreover, while a wide commitment to educate was new and very important, it did not reach far at secondary level until well into the 1930s in most countries. In Belgian Africa it did not do so even then. Indeed the African with more than primary education could still be seen as inherently undermining Indirect Rule and the maintenance of 'traditional' authorities. Of course such people were already quite numerous in the principal towns of the west coast as in South Africa, but colonial orthodoxy tended to condemn missionaries who pushed secondary education for 'spoiling' Africans and turning black men into white.

Even more was the educated African seen as a threat by the white settler. Across much of southern, central, and eastern Africa a very different development was in progress. In more and more places settler communities were establishing themselves, acquiring large stretches of land which required for their cultivation a cheap black labour force and erecting around themselves the sharpest of colour bars. The one relatively liberal tradition within white Africa, that of Cape Colony as it had developed by the later nineteenth century, was quickly cut back after the Union of South Africa came into existence in 1910 and the more racialist attitudes of the Transvaal and the Orange Free State came to prevail. In 1923 Southern Rhodesia became internally self-governing, a settler community whose attitudes were fundamentally those dominant in South Africa. The settlers in the Kenya highlands were hoping for no less, and the even smaller groups in Nyasaland, Northern Rhodesia, and Tanganyika had comparable aspirations for the more distant future. While total numbers remained very limited until after the Second World War, the pressure of settler politics seemed considerable everywhere in the continent south of Uganda, being quite as noticeable in the Belgian and Portuguese possessions as the British. Undoubtedly that pressure held back African advancement and especially African education above primary level.

The most important change in African consciousness wrought in these years by Western education was, however, precisely at primary level. It is to be situated in the almost indefinable area of a popular culture deeply affected by literacy. The expansion of bush schools run by teachers often barely literate themselves was not much approved of by government or by educational theorists and it may have brought no great range of examinable skills to the general population, but it did bring within reach of millions an awareness of what reading and writing were about, tools both for new forms of culture and economic advancement. As there was still so little vernacular literature other than that which missionaries had produced, this created a vast, diffuse conditioning of the common mind favourable to the spread of Christianity. It also enhanced the status and spread of a number of major African languages while contributing to their greater internal uniformity. In some cases new languages were almost constructed in the process, a process running parallel to the attempts of colonial governments to establish suitable media of communication. Africans were quite used to speaking more than one language, so the wide use of standardized forms of a relatively small number of languages for administrative and educational purposes did not much affect the usage of a vastly larger number of more local languages. What was happening was not the destruction of traditional cultures but the organic implantation within them of a new and potentially decisive element centred upon 'Book', Shona, Swahili, Igbo, or

English. It was much fostered in some places by the spread of vernacular newspapers, the Xhosa *Imvo*, the Luganda *Munno*, the Kikuyu *Muigwithania*, and on the West African coast the English-language papers like the *Gold Coast Independent* and Azikiwe's *West African Pilot*. By 1940 reading was an important element within the popular culture of very many, though not all, African peoples.

It went with an enhanced social mobility. There had always been more travelling than many an outsider imagined. Nevertheless, the change in these years was very great. Railways helped make it possible, so did the bicycle, which by the 1930s was becoming the cherished possession of the slightly better-off, but improvement in the roads helped the basic business of walking and many people walked extraordinary distances. As labourers travelled they carried religion with them. A European whose train had halted at a wayside Kenyan station one evening in 1920 heard the words of a Kavirondo hymn being sung by a group of workers from a Nakuru farm returning to their homes. The hymn completed, they recited the Lord's Prayer and one pronounced the 'grace'.[2] The pull of education took many on to the road. The pull of employment and the earning of money in mine or plantation drew still more. Catechists might abandon their almost unpaid work to find money on the Copperbelt for a bicycle, yet the pull of religion could also lead to remarkable journeys. In 1933 John Membe as a young AME minister walked from Broken Hill to Abercorn—some 570 miles, he thought—and back, and later wrote, somewhat bitterly, to his superintendent: it is a 'very hard and important thing for a person to walk from there to Broken Hill or to Ndola by walking only'.[3] Three years later a group of discontented Christians in eastern Rhodesia heard from a passing Malawian about the Church of God in South Africa and sent one of their number, Achem Charangwa, to find out more. He cycled all the way, contacted the Church, was ordained a deacon, and cycled back again.[4] By the 1930s countless ordinary Africans took books, trains, and bicycles very much for granted as part of their own lives. They could have homes in northern Nyasaland and work on the Rand, or in Tanganyika and work in Uganda or Kenya. They spoke more languages than most missionaries. The very uniformity of the

---

[2] *CMS Report 1919–1920*, 36–7.
[3] A. Hastings, 'John Lester Membe', in T. Ranger and J. Weller (eds.), *Themes in the Christian History of Central Africa* (1975), 187.
[4] T. Ranger, 'Poverty and Prophetism', unpublished paper (1981), 40.

colonial order, the lack of manned frontiers, passports, or a clear sense of citizenship, all helped the emergence of an almost continent-wide new society. When a successful small entrepreneur who had one wife in Tanganyika and another in Uganda, and himself sailed back and forth across Lake Victoria visiting them, was challenged as to whether he did not think this an odd way to live, he replied, 'No, not at all: the Union Jack flies in both countries.'[5] Here was a new consciousness burgeoning well below the level of secondary education and generally without even minimal fluency in a European language, but deeply dependent, nevertheless, upon the structures and opportunities provided by the colonial order.

Secondary education, all the same, was becoming increasingly important, however rare it remained quantitatively. The famed mission boarding institutions were in the age of their greatest influence. They were places to which students came from hundreds of miles: Mfantsipim in the Gold Coast, Alliance High School in Kenya, King's College, Budo, in Uganda, Adams College in Natal, and St Peter's, Rosettenville, had the power of creating an almost cosmopolitan atmosphere, a sense of intertribal fellowship and of continuity with all the intellectual endeavour of the civilized world from Plato to Einstein. 'What Lovedale really does, whether it teaches carpentry or Latin, is to put its students into a historical succession and to give them a sense of belonging to a distinguished company,' wrote an observer in 1929.[6] The Scottish missionaries at Lovedale had in fact already generated their own mini-university next door, Fort Hare, from which between 1923 and the mid-1930s some fifty BAs graduated. Its Principal from 1918 to 1948, Alexander Kerr, probably represents all in all missionary influence in this period at its most intelligently benign. One year after the first degrees at Fort Hare, the Prince of Wales College was opened in 1924 in Achimota by the Governor of the Gold Coast. Here too a Scottish missionary was the Principal, A. G. Fraser, but James Aggrey was Vice-Principal and in the official photograph the Governor's hand rests on Aggrey's shoulder. At Achimota as already at Fourah Bay a handful of West Africans were gaining their BAs, while a growing stream of others were finding their way to the universities of Europe and America. Nevertheless, for the time being it was the missionary boarding-

---

[5] A. Richards (ed.), *Economic Development and Tribal Change: A Study of Immigrant Labour in Buganda* (1954), 135.
[6] A. V. Murray, *The School in the Bush* (1929), 98.

school itself, rather than the university, which stood at the perceived apex of the educational pyramid with all the prestige and attraction that this involved.

ii. The Second World War and the Triumph of Nationalisms

The world depression, the emergence of new conflicts in Europe, and the increasingly manifest inability of Britain to control its primary empire in India were all undermining the dynamism of imperialism by the later 1930s. On the surface things were quiet enough, but beneath the surface signs were building up to point in two quite contrary directions: in countries like the Gold Coast, Nigeria, and Uganda some form of black rule must return in the indeterminate future, but elsewhere from Nairobi to the Cape there could seem a rather greater likelihood of a series of white-controlled self-governing states emerging as successors to an empire ruled from Europe.

At this point European ambitions again took over and with great violence. Italy had long wanted more of an African empire. It had sought one in Ethiopia in the 1890s and been routed by the armies of Menelik. Now under Mussolini and an expansionist Fascism it was determined to get its revenge and establish itself as a major imperial power. Ethiopia was invaded in October 1935. Despite the feeble protests and ineffective sanctions of the League of Nations the country was conquered within a few months with great brutality. Nothing like this had happened in Africa for a quarter-century and its impact upon other parts of the continent, especially the west, was considerable. Among the many appalling atrocities committed by the Italians, none can have been worse than the massacre of the entire monastic community of Dabra Libanos and the destruction of its monastery on 19–20 May 1937. Done on the personal command of Marshal Graziani, who ordered its 'liquidazione completa',[7] it exactly repeated the events of 14 July 1532 in the jihad of Ahmed Gran.

While constituting the last major expression of colonial aggression, the Italian conquest of Ethiopia was nevertheless more significant in being the prelude to the Second World War, once more an essentially inter-white conflict. In consequence the Italian occupation of Ethiopia was to last only five years. Once Mussolini had joined Hitler

---

[7] A. del Boca, *Gli Italiani in Africa orientale*, iii (Rome, 1982), 106.

in fighting Britain and France in 1940, British forces—including Nigerian, Gold Coast, and East African regiments—marched into Ethiopia. Its emperor, Haile Selassie, who had meanwhile taken refuge in England, was returned to his throne in Addis Ababa in May 1941 to address the people from the balcony of Menelik's palace, surrounded by guards of honour made up of West, East, and South African troops. It was the first great act of decolonization and symbolic of all that was to come.

Elsewhere the Second World War was less traumatic for Africa than the First but it was at least as consequential. The European colonial powers were revealed as the emperors without any clothes. France and Belgium had been overrun, Britain was struggling for its life. All three had actually to appeal for African support. The prestige of France, in particular, suffered in a way that could never really be mended. Furthermore, thousands of Africans fought in the armed forces in Ethiopia, Asia, and elsewhere and returned with a wider experience of the world and a much diminished respect for the European. No less important, the war ended with the establishment of the United Nations, located in the United States, which had not lost its traditional anti-imperialist sentiments. The colonial powers were henceforth under continual and mounting pressure to justify themselves. While in the immediate aftermath of war colonial rule had to continue for there was no alternative, henceforth a large question mark hung over its future such as no one would have expected twenty years earlier.

Advances in higher education again suggested a different kind of public future. Ibadan was founded as a university college in 1948, to be followed almost at once by Legon in the Gold Coast, Makerere in Uganda, and Khartoum. In the Belgian Congo Lovanium was founded in 1949 as an offshoot of the Catholic University of Louvain, but the lack of secondary education in the Congo upon which to build meant that its strictly university courses could only begin in 1954. In Dakar the *Institut des Hautes Études* was established in 1950. These were to become within a very few years the decisive institutions in the formation of a new professional élite.

In West Africa nationalist parties were developing at the same time with a power which they had not known in the pre-war years. Here the Gold Coast took the lead under the inspiration of Kwame Nkrumah and his Convention People's Party, which won a landslide victory in the elections of 1951 over its more cautious and earlier established rivals with the programme of 'self-government now'. There could be no turning back. Post-war Britain simply did not have the political will to stand up to continuous nationalist agitation, and the Gold Coast became independent as Ghana in March 1957.

Meanwhile, in South Africa a not incomparable movement of white Afrikaner nationalism had led, for black people, to very different consequences. In 1948 the Nationalist Party led by Dr Malan came to power with a policy intended to reshape South Africa on lines which would ensure that black people should never pose any conceivable threat to white supremacy. South Africa had, ever since 1910, been a clearly racialist state, but the implementation of its racialism had been pragmatic rather than principled and there always remained the possibility that a government led by Jan Smuts might start to move in a different, more liberal, direction. That possibility was now to be excluded and on the firm ground of religious belief: do not make equal what God has not created equal.

In 1950 Dr Hendrik Verwoerd, the supreme theorist of apartheid, became Minister of Native Affairs. The son of a missionary but a man who had come under considerable Nazi influence, he was entrusted by Malan and then Malan's successor, Strydom, with the systematic implementation of 'the struggle for racial purity' in every side of the country's life. Most significant was the Bantu Education Act of 1953 and subsequent policy to secure total government control of all African schools in receipt of State aid. The intention was to remove the mildly liberal influence of missionaries and ensure that Africans received in future only 'a training' to 'suit the requirements of their own people'[8] as Verwoerd explained the following year in the House of Assembly. Lovedale and Fort Hare were taken over by the State, Adams College and St Peter's, Rosettenville, closed permanently. Thus the sort of black society open to the world's highest achievements which had been fostered by the more progressive wing of the missionary movement was being flattened in South Africa just as it was beginning to scent the achievement of power in the rest of the continent.

In East and central Africa there remained a few years of uncertainty as to which way the future lay. White settler communities had grown considerably in numbers in the post-war years, but black nationalist

---

[8] 3 June 1954. *Debates of the House of Assembly,* Union of South Africa (Cape Town, 1954), 86, 6220.

organizations grounded upon far more than 90 per cent of the population were spreading everywhere with the example of the Gold Coast before them. The first half of the 1950s witnessed two victories for the former and defeats for the latter. In January 1953 a conference in London, from which every African representative had withdrawn, recommended the establishment of a Central African Federation, uniting the two Rhodesias and Nyasaland. Essentially this extended local white control from Southern Rhodesia to its two northern neighbours and constituted a major settler victory. The same year the Mau Mau rebellion broke out among the Kikuyu of Kenya, reacting tenaciously and bitterly to the settler expropriation of so much of their land. It took three years to suppress. It is noticeable how Mau Mau, like other 1950s nationalist movements in Buganda and elsewhere, very easily assumed an anti-Christian and still more an anti-missionary face. In the heat of the moment Christianity could be damned as the fourth wheel of the white man's chariot.

It would be a number of years before it became clear that the Central African Federation could not survive against the opposition of the African population of Northern Rhodesia and Nyasaland, and that Kenya was after all going to emerge as a black- and not white-ruled land, but by the end of the decade both were obvious. Give or take a few months here and there, 1960 provides the symbolic line between past and future, north and south. In January of that year, Harold Macmillan, Britain's Prime Minister, declared to an unenthusiastic audience in Parliament in Cape Town that 'the wind of change is blowing throughout the continent'.[9] The government of South Africa remained adamant that it should not blow there. It was a determination shared in Rhodesia and by the government of Portugal in regard to Angola and Mozambique. A new triple alliance of the south was about to be forged. In March 1960 sixty-nine people were shot and killed by the police in less than one minute during a demonstration at Sharpeville. The following month African political parties were permanently banned in South Africa. There would be no wind of change in a land now governed by Verwoerd. 'Never in history', he declared in an emotional address in September 1958, 'at least not in the history of the past two thousand years, was the position of white society (*blankdom*) in danger to such an extent as now.' His government, he continued, remained

[9] Harold Macmillan, *Pointing the Way 1959–1961* (1972), 475.

determined to defend 'everything which has been built up since the days of Christ . . . for the salvation of mankind'.[10]

To the north of the Zambezi the opposite was happening. Black nationalism had pushed over the walls of colonialism with extraordinary ease, particularly in the Belgian Congo where almost nothing had been done to prepare for the change and where, inevitably, near anarchy was soon to prevail in consequence. The Congo, Nigeria, and most of French Africa became independent in the course of 1960. The countries of eastern Africa followed a year or two later. The era of colonial rule had an ending as hurried and ill planned as its beginning. In less than a single lifetime it had, in most places, come and gone. The degree of its impact had varied, least in a great western society like that of the Yoruba where there was no white settlement or plantation farming, most where the whole economic map had been transformed as by the creation of the Copperbelt in a hitherto almost uninhabited area. Everywhere, however, it had changed the context of living by laying down political borders, capital cities, railway networks, administrative structures, Western educational norms, and the dominance of specific European languages.

All this had proved fundamental to the process of Christianization. Few colonizers had wanted to Christianize. Many among them, even believing Christians, had thought it profoundly inappropriate. That was not true of the Belgians, nor, theoretically, of the Portuguese though in reality the Portuguese did less to Christianize than anyone, basically because they did less than anyone to modernize. It was the context of modernization in latter-day colonialism which proved, in African circumstances, so enormously favourable to the spread of Christianity, though hardly less in places to the spread of Islam, and it is to the relationship between the missionary Church and the late colonial state that we must now turn.

ii. *Protestant Missionary Priorities in the Oldham Era*

The Edinburgh Missionary Conference of 1910 was in its way the apogee of the modern Protestant missionary movement. While Edinburgh was intended to point towards great further growth, in

---

[10] W. Kister, 'The 16th of December in the Context of Nationalist Thinking', in T. Sundermeier (ed.), *Church and Nationalism in South Africa* (Johannesburg, 1975), 85–6.

fact henceforth it would be downhill all the way, though out of it
grew a new and different movement—organized interdenomina-
tional ecumenism. The missionary decline was produced from two
different factors, intellectual and economic. On the intellectual side
lay a great theological shift within the central body of Western
Protestantism from fundamentalism to liberalism, a shift taking place
quite quickly in the thirty years before the First World War. The
typical nineteenth-century missionary was other-worldly, scripturally
fundamentalist, and frequently millennarian, yet he came from the
central sectors of the main Protestant Churches. He still believed in
hell and preached about it. The famous watchword of the late
nineteenth-century Student Christian Movement was 'The evangelization of the world in this generation'.[11] It knew what it meant by
evangelization and it knew that it was urgent. That was still
Edinburgh's message but was quickly dropped thereafter to be
revived only by conservative evangelicals half a century later.

The shift towards more this-worldly preoccupations, schools,
hospitals, race relations, was epitomized by J. H. Oldham, most
influential of Protestant missionary strategists of the first half of the
twentieth century. A Scotsman who had worked for a few years in
India, Oldham was Secretary of the Edinburgh Conference, of its
Continuation Committee, and then of the International Missionary
Council, which came into existence after the war. He was also editor
of the *International Review of Missions* and the principal organizer of
the first great missionary gathering after Edinburgh, the International
Conference of Jerusalem in 1928. Everything that mattered in the
field of mission for twenty-five years found its way on to Oldham's
desk, and he himself moved quietly but steadily from evangelizing to
wider social concerns. By the 1930s he was planning the great 1937
Oxford Conference of the 'Life and Work Movement' on 'Church,
Community and State', whose purpose was both to challenge
Fascism and to agree to establish a World Council of Churches.
Oldham was the statesman who always had the ear of the Archbishop
of Canterbury and usually that of the Colonial Office too. He did
much of his work in the Athenaeum, adroitly selecting and
marshalling the forces of Christian and liberal opinion for the
achievement of a better world. Oldham was convinced that the

---

[11] H. Hans Hoekendijk, 'Evangelisation of the World in this Generation', *International
Review of Mission*, 59 (1970), 23–31.

interests of Empire and Church, blacks and whites, settlers and natives, could all be harmonized. While at times willing to orchestrate a campaign of public protest, as over forced labour in Kenya, he far preferred the non-confrontational victories of back-stairs diplomacy.

Oldham was undoubtedly the most influential missionary planner in regard to the African Church for several decades and was even the first Administrative Director of the International African Institute, set up in 1926, a highly prestigious organization in the world of governments and academia, but one largely derived from missionary initiative. Oldham had never lived or worked in Africa. While greatly successful in all sorts of negotiations such as those relating to the post-war return of German missionaries, he seldom perceived how starkly different realities could be on the ground from the high-flown philanthropic statements of government and settler leaders. His benevolence was limitless, but its tone was profoundly paternalistic, very appropriate for the 1920s but anything other than radical. Radicals of one sort or another like Roland Allen, Norman Leys, and Arthur Shearly Cripps inevitably found Oldham's leadership uncongenial: it subordinated evangelicalism, the self-governance of the African Church, and even protest against settler injustice too much to a long-term 'civilizing' strategy within an imperial context. But it was he, not they, who represented the central missionary mood of the inter-war years.

At the same time the missionary movement was in economic trouble. While there were always more 'openings' there was also nearly always less money to meet them. This was already becoming the case before the First World War, but that made it a great deal worse. The 1920s did not improve matters, while the Depression made them worse again. The Church Missionary Society had 1,385 missionaries on its active list just before the First World War, 1,085 just before the Second World War. Even conservative evangelicals, who had rebelled against the liberalizing of the message and walked out of the Christian Student Movement, were in a trough in the 1920s, though it was in this sector that the only Protestant missionary growth is to be detected—much of it American—especially in the latter part of our period. CMS numbers were going down, but those of the Sudan Interior Mission and the Sudan United Mission, for instance, were going up. Yet again and again in the inter-war years one finds Protestant missionaries of the older societies crying out that they were being forced to retrench just when they needed to extend their work and when they saw Roman Catholics advancing upon every side.

The missionaries who were coming out were for the most part professionally trained teachers, doctors, nurses, very many of them women. The most productive side of the new mission was, undoubtedly, the educational. Oldham was behind the Phelps-Stokes Reports, the British government paper on educational policy of 1925, and the Le Zoute Conference of 1926. All of these were intended to push both colonial commitment to African educational progress and co-operation therein between administration and mission. They largely succeeded, at least in regard to British Africa. In South Africa missionaries were already spearheading African education at Lovedale, Fort Hare, and elsewhere. The characteristic contribution of the educational missionary in this period was the boarding-school, teaching a Cambridge syllabus and modelling itself on an English public school. It may not have been a very imaginative contribution, but it remained, quite probably, what Africa needed most and wanted most: some at least of its sons and daughters to be provided with the educational and social confidence inherent in the ways of their masters. For the most part these were rather happy communities, to which in after days African politicians would look back as providers of the cradles of the new nationalism. Headmasters like Carey Francis of Alliance High School in Kenya could be seen and loved as liberal mentors of a free Africa. When Francis died in Nairobi in 1966 his old pupils Oginga Odinga, Tom Mboya, Charles Njonjo, and Ronald Ngala, now political rivals, nevertheless united to act as pallbearers.

The other main concern of Le Zoute was African culture. The conference's chairman was Donald Fraser, back in Britain after thirty years in the Livingstonia Mission. He was hardly a profound thinker but someone much more sympathetic to African ways than Dr Laws, Livingstonia's head, an unapologetic Westernizer. Edwin Smith, who produced the Le Zoute book, was a still better example of a missionary whose heart had moved into the field of language, translation, and culture. The International African Institute was in large part his brain-child. He had written major works on the Ila language and peoples, and the same year as Le Zoute he published what could well be regarded as the most authoritative textbook for African missiology in the inter-war years, *The Golden Stool*. Here far more explicitly than in earlier works it was suggested that

Christianity should be presented as not antagonistic to, but the fulfilment of, African culture, religion, and tradition. It was now no longer hard to go out to Africa with a reasonable and positive knowledge of African culture. There were plenty of books available, some of them written by missionaries like Roscoe and Cullen Young, others by anthropologists like the Seligmans or administrators like Rattray. The Jesuit Fr. Dubois in his 1932 Roman handbook *Le Répertoire africaine* urged every mission to have one or two trained anthropologists. Doubtless there were many missionaries who never opened a page of such books and many missionary societies which never encouraged it. There was least response among conservative evangelicals and in places where there were white settlers. Nevertheless, much of the movement in its leadership, literature, and influence was becoming genuinely affected by a certain sympathy for African beliefs, which we can see in works like Shropshire's *The Church and Primitive Peoples* (1938) or Edwin Smith's symposium on *African Ideas of God* (1950).

Where the inter-war missionary may appear least attractive is in his insistent retention of control. The growth of Christian numbers was, in many places, formidable. Mass movements of all kinds were bringing them in, and the ever-growing network of bush schools was producing a new generation of young people for which Church affiliation of some sort could be taken for granted as part of village life. The normal missionary response to this state of things was one of almost reluctant welcome. Numerous conversions could not but please, yet to the missionary of the time they needed a great deal of careful handling, and his missionary society had almost never the resources to respond adequately to new opportunities. One thing the missionary of this period never doubted was that, however conversion had come about, newly converted Christians could not safely be left without control. 'The African', wrote Donald Fraser in 1911, 'is most efficient as an evangelist when guided and controlled.'[12] Handley Hooper, Africa Secretary of the CMS after ten years in Kenya, wrote in 1929 for many, 'This is the paradox . . . we want to see the beginning of a genuinely indigenous Church, but we do not believe that Africans are yet ready.' If they were to be released from tutelage there would be a 'general lowering of standards'.[13] 'Nothing but a rod of iron is any use for these people,'

[12] D. Fraser, *The Future of Africa* (1911), 206.
[13] R. Strayer, *The Making of Mission Communities in East Africa: Anglicans and Africans in Colonial Kenya 1875–1935* (1978), 69–70.

wrote the Jesuit Fr. Jerome O'Hea, still more uncompromisingly, in
1930. He was responding to criticism by Catholic Manyika of the
imposition of language changes over which they had not been
consulted.[14] Roland Allen, author of *The Spontaneous Expansion of the
Church*, was the great missionary critic of such authoritarian
determination to retain control, in the inter-war years, but Allen
did not work in Africa any more than did Oldham. Those who did
were seldom exactly imaginative. It is hard to name Protestant
missionaries of stature for these years. As the generation of the
pioneers died away in the 1920s it was replaced by a generation who
were seldom very close to Africans, who believed that the colonial
order was going to last a long time and that the achievement of 'a
genuinely indigenous Church' could safely be left for a while.
Administrative efficiency, good bookkeeping, heading off schism,
getting a tiny élite through the Cambridge School Certificate was
what mattered now.

It is strange how little attention was still being paid to the
formation of an African clergy. In comparison with other schools
remarkably little effort was put into theological colleges and any
raising of their standards. It was almost as if a rise in the number of
the ordained, especially if reasonably educated, was regarded as a
threat to be held off as long as possible. The very schisms of an
'Ethiopian' sort which had taken place and were still taking place
could be seen as grounds for avoiding any more by the multiplication
of clergy. It is certainly striking that in 1950 not a single Anglican
African diocesan bishop had been appointed since the death of
Crowther. The new leadership the Churches were fostering through
the best of their schools would, in consequence, become in the 1950s
a contester for political control but only very occasionally for
ecclesiastical control. In most places it simply was not strong enough
for the latter. Nevertheless, it is also true that, while African clergy
did not grow in numbers to the extent one would have expected in
this period, they did in a way come to exercise authority simply
because a vacuum had been created. White missionaries had moved
steadily upwards into central institutions or higher administration.
Black Church numbers had multiplied. The people actually doing
pastoral work on any scale were a large number of catechists and a
small number of ordained Africans. Inadequately trained and in

[14] Ranger, 'Poverty and Prophetism', 16.

theory subject to white control, they were in practice by the 1940s the only functioning pastors in a great many Churches. Leslie Brown became the Anglican Bishop of Uganda in the 1950s. 'When I arrived in my own diocese', he later wrote, 'I found one priest, with no ordained assistant, responsible for ninety congregations, but I suppose the average with us may be about fifteen.'[15] The consequence of a long policy of holding back on ordination was less to maintain white control than to create an impossible strain upon the few Africans who were ordained and to establish a state one may describe as 'sacramental famine' across the young Churches of the continent.

Kenya presents an interesting case for this period in that its political fate seemed the most uncertain. It had the largest settler community of any colony not ruled by settlers. Here, more than elsewhere, missionaries were in a way in a balancing position. In Rhodesia they could criticize but hardly challenge the policy of a settler government, and after 1930 hardly any one except Cripps even criticized it. In Uganda and Tanganyika colonial rule was fairly clearly geared to the long-term interests of black society. In Kenya the country stood upon a knife-edge in which, while the settlers were extremely powerful, they were not in control and direct appeal to London on behalf of African interests could be effective in a way it could no longer be in South Africa or Rhodesia. Church history in Kenya was dominated in this period by two figures, Arthur of the Church of Scotland Mission and Archdeacon Owen of Kavirondo. They were both powerful extroverts, self-confident people who have received a great deal of attention, and between them they may illustrate well enough the strengths and weaknesses of the missionary Church in this period.

In August 1921 the Council of the Church of Scotland Mission drafted a resolution with reference to Indians in Kenya: 'Missionaries, in partnership with a British Colonial government and with Christian white settlers, held a sacred trust for the material, spiritual and intellectual uplift of Africans. No member of another race or culture, be he Christian or otherwise, could be permitted to share in the exercise of this trust.'[16] Racialist in regard to Indians, anti-ecumenical in regard to the Church in India, blind in regard to the

[15] L. Brown, *Relevant Liturgy* (1965), 53.
[16] B. G. McIntosh, 'The Scottish Mission in Kenya 1891–1923', Ph.D. thesis (Edinburgh, 1969), 365–6.

reality of settler behaviour, intensely paternalistic in regard to Africans, and pompous in regard to missionaries, this resolution reveals the mind of Arthur through and through. The Church of Scotland missionary, whether of the Established or the Free Church, had a strong tendency to be insensitively autocratic. One can see it in Stewart at Lovedale, Laws at Livingstonia, D. C. Scott at Blantyre and then in Kenya, but most of all Arthur in Kenya. He had established a strong power base through the organization of Protestant missions in an Alliance, the organization of the Progressive Kikuyu Association, of which he was President, and as a member of the Legislative Council nominated to represent African interests. He was even for a time on the Governor's Executive Council. At home he had the powerful backing of the Church of Scotland and of such lay admirers as the Duchess of Atholl, an MP and a strong Church of Scotland member, who appears at times little more than Arthur's mouthpiece.

It was not surprising that the CSM saw white settlers as its allies. No mission was more settler-minded and no mission had obtained ownership of more African land. D. C. Scott had actually been a Vice-President of the Planters' and Farmers' Association. The settlers were intensely anti-Indian and Oldham's quiet appeals to the missionaries in 1926 not to get involved in an anti-Indian campaign were hardly heeded, though he had succeeded the year before in pulling them back from supporting a memorandum from the Governor to the administration which implied that labour on settler farms should quietly be made compulsory. It was, however, a few years later over the issue of female circumcision that Arthur made the greatest attempt to use his public position to achieve a Protestant missionary goal—its abolition. He forced it through the Mission Alliance and caused a major schism among Christian Kikuyu, but he failed to get the government to go along with him. He had even to resign from the Executive Council, which he did in 1929 rather bitterly. Arthur dominated the missionary scene in central Kenya for a good fifteen years. The result was sharply to divide the Kikuyu, producing a bitter anti-missionary reaction which helped lead on to Mau Mau. No one had done more to identify, in African eyes, the missionary with the settler and, for a while, with the government, though the latter proved in due course more prepared to defend African rights than Arthur.

Compare Owen. Not a university man, he had left school early and advanced up the missionary ladder of the CMS mostly in Uganda until he became Archdeacon of Kavirondo, now the western province of Kenya, in 1918. He retained that position until 1944 and became in Kavirondo as influential as Arthur was for a time in Kikuyuland. He too established a native association, the Kavirondo Taxpayers' Welfare Association, of which he was President, so when he wrote to the government protesting about this or that, which was often, it was as much in the role of President of the KTWA as in that of Archdeacon. Professor Ogot has written that Owen 'entered fully into the social life of the people and became every man's lawyer, solicitor, doctor and midwife. He stood for the Christian principle of the sacredness of human personality . . .'.[17] Perhaps unsurprisingly, one Provincial Commissioner described him as an 'out and out Bolshevist'.[18] 'Anyone', Owen wrote in 1931, 'who attempts to voice the cry of a people who are almost inarticulate, is apt to be regarded, not as a peacemaker, but as a public nuisance.'[19] Owen was not concerned as was Arthur to achieve some large piece of moralistic social engineering. Both came into conflict with the administration: Arthur because the government declined to impose highly unpopular rules upon the people, Owen because he defended the people against highly unpopular impositions. Both could act as they did because of the considerable status a missionary leader, especially if British, could attain in this period within British Africa alike with the government and with the people. Both functioned well within the system while trying to bend it to their purposes. In comparison with Oldham in London, the one went further in a settler direction than he would have advised, the other in confrontation with the powers that be than he thought wise. But the difference between the three should not be overstated. They could and did co-operate.

One man in Southern Rhodesia was more fundamentally awkward. Arthur Shearly Cripps worked there for half a century until his death in 1952. As a young missionary he had already written in 1901 a play entitled the *The Black Christ*. He spent his life in extreme poverty fighting battles quixotically enough over African land rights or the hut tax when not writing one of his numerous novels or poems. Cripps was the visionary who rejected the system,

[17] B. A. Ogot, 'British Administration in the Central Nyanza District of Kenya 1900–60', *JAH* 4 (1963), 264.
[18] Strayer, *The Making of Mission Communities in East Africa*, 107.
[19] L. Spencer, 'Christianity and Colonial Protest: Perceptions of W. E. Owen, Archdeacon of Kavirondo', *JRA* 13 (1982), 55.

refusing government subsidies for his schools and even the bishop's licence. A high Anglican, he was also in his way a white independent. Even the round hut at Maronda Mashanu in which he lived expressed his rejection of the whole philosophy of imposing a Europeanized model of Christianity upon Africa. He had allies and admirers in the Methodist John White and the Anglican Canon Lloyd, but in his protest against colonial practice he went far beyond either—impractical and unreasonable in the judgement of most whites, a saint who really did become one of us in the eyes of most blacks. His grave is now a place of pilgrimage. He is remembered where most others are forgotten. J. W. Arthur and Arthur Cripps were close contemporaries. Both gave their lives to missionary work in Africa with exceptionally single-minded zeal, but in the way they did it they were as different as might be.

iv. *The Catholic Breakthrough*

Catholic missionary history in these years was considerably different and is seldom well understood. It proved a decisive period in which the Protestant missionary predominance in many parts of Africa was effectively reversed, and just at a time when African society was opening up far more widely and easily to missionary influence than was the case before the First World War. Pius XI, Pope from 1922 to 1939, became known as the Pope of the Missions because of the great increase in Roman concern for the Church in the non-European world manifest in this period. It was a concern Pius inherited from his predecessor, Benedict XV, whose influential missionary encyclical *Maximum illud* had stressed both the formation of a native clergy and the need to avoid identification with the imperialist intentions of one's own country. The missionary exhibition in Rome in 1925, the appointment of the first Chinese, Japanese, and Indian bishops of modern times, and a general pressure upon the Church in Europe and America to participate more actively in missionary work were all evidence of the new priority. The theology and spirituality of the missionary movement, however, were in no way changed and would not be until well into the post-Second World War period. They were narrowly neo-scholastic, papalist, and Marian. Hell was not questioned, Protestants hardly noticed except as rivals, social and political issues avoided unless they were greatly affecting Catholics or the conversion process. The element of control and unquestioned obedience internal to the system was decisive. It was highly self-sacrificing, unself-questioning, supremely confident in the mission committed to it and the divine approbation of every element of the Catholic Church exactly as it stood. It had little time for Scripture. While the number of complete Bibles and, still more, New Testaments, in African languages was increasing rapidly due to the work of the Protestant Bible societies, Catholic Scripture translation remained minimal. Thus in East Africa at the end of the 1950s there were thirteen complete Protestant translations of the Bible and nearly fifty New Testaments to be compared with just three complete Catholic translations of the latter.[20]

This does not mean that Catholic missionaries were never good scholars or linguists. On the contrary, some were outstanding, especially among the French and the Germans. In general they were more tolerant than Protestants not only of native beer, but of native culture. They printed dictionaries and grammars, catechisms and Church histories, potted accounts of the Scriptures, even a complete gospel. They were also good on local history, books of fables, proverbs, and suchlike. They did, then, much to create a vernacular literary culture, while the greatest names, men like Bishop Cuvelier and Fr. Van Wing in the Congo, Fr. Crazzolara in Uganda, Fr. Aupiais in Dahomey—to mention but a few—were scholars of African culture and history of outstanding quality.

New groups of missionaries arriving in these years were not always so good at language. They can be considered under two heads, institutional and national. Both new missionary societies and old orders without an existing missionary commitment were being pressed by Rome to take over some area of Africa. Thus the Swiss Bethlehem Fathers came to central Rhodesia, the Irish Capuchins to Barotseland, the Italian Franciscan Conventuals to the Copperbelt in the 1930s, the Irish Pallottines to Mbulu in central Tanganyika in the 1940s, and the American Maryknoll Fathers and Sisters to Musoma in northern Tanganyika in the 1950s, among many other new arrivals. Some of these were new missionary institutions, such as the Bethlehem Fathers in Switzerland and Maryknoll in the United States. In Ireland the Society of St Patrick (the Kiltegan Fathers) developed from an appeal of Bishop Shanahan in the 1920s to

[20] J. Bessem, 'Scripture Translations in East Africa', *AFER* 4 (1962), 201–11, see also J. Vermeulen, 'Scripture Translation in Northern Rhodesia', *AFER* 6 (1964), 66–73.

Maynooth priests to work in eastern Nigeria. It is only after the First World War that the Irish missionary flood, in particular, really flows into Africa, especially Holy Ghost Fathers and SMA Fathers into West Africa and the former also into Kenya. The Irish, Americans, French Canadians, and Swiss were reinforcing a missionary body which had at first been overwhelmingly French, Italian, and German, and then Dutch, Belgian, and British. All this apparently almost ceaseless growth in missionary numbers was dependent upon the continuing world-wide growth of religious orders within the great ultramontane century, stretching from Pius IX to Pius XII.

As so often, especially in regard to Catholic history, it is of males that one has been speaking, yet the increase in the number of sisters was at least as striking, but the still greater multiplicity of congregations and the anonymity they have cultivated makes it exceptionally difficult to summarize their advance. Medical work was gravely hampered by the prohibition of canon law for nuns to be midwives, a prohibition only lifted in 1936. The Medical Missionaries of Mary were founded in Drogheda the same year by Mother Mary Martin. It was only then, and still more in the 1950s, that the medical sister could become a central figure in the missionary world.

Most important of all, however, was probably the increase in numbers within the main well-established missionary societies. To give just one example from Northern Rhodesia. Quite apart from the arrival of Capuchins for the Lozi and Conventuals for the Copperbelt, the number of White Father missions was mounting extremely fast and each mission contained at least three fathers. Thus the new vicariate of Lwangwa expanded from a single station (Chilonga) at its foundation in 1933 to eight by 1938. Again in the Luapula area, which had formerly been practically a Protestant preserve, White Father missions were founded at Lufube (1930), Kabunda (1932), Mapula (1933), Twingi (1938), and Kasaba (1942). Real evangelical work and the quick growth of Catholicism continued to depend upon the catechists, rather than the foreign fathers; nevertheless, the latter were there in more and more places to train, supervise, and urge on the former.

In consequence of this great growth in numbers, Catholic missionaries did not move out of pastoral work to the extent that Protestants did. Nevertheless, like the latter, they did move increasingly into educational work and the provision of post-primary institutions. The Catholic Church had not, hitherto, been much concerned with schooling of other than the simplest sort but, in the age of the Phelps-Stokes Reports, it could no longer afford to leave such work to others. Arthur Hinsley, Rector of the English College in Rome, was appointed in 1927 as special Visitor-Apostolic to the Catholic missions throughout British Africa with the simple message of the necessity of co-operating with the government's educational policies. 'Collaborate with all your power', he told a conference of bishops and other leading missionaries at Dar-es-Salaam in August 1928, 'and where it is impossible for you to carry on both the immediate task of evangelisation and your educational work, neglect your churches in order to perfect your schools.'[21] The impact of Hinsley's mission was enormous. Protestant educational work of the highest quality precedes the Phelps-Stokes Reports, but there was absolutely no Catholic equivalent to Lovedale in South Africa, Waddilove in Rhodesia, or the Hope-Waddell Institute at Calabar. The 1920s see government taking up the Protestant example and then Hinsley making Catholics do the same. It is rare to find any Catholic institution one could describe as of secondary standard prior to his mission. Certainly the Irish Holy Ghost Fathers among the Igbo who had based their mission above all on schools had none, until Christ the King College at Onitsha was opened in 1933.

In regard to this new challenge of secondary education the Irish and, to a lesser extent, the Canadians, proved invaluable. The Irish were poor linguists, but as apostles of the British educational system and its use as an instrument of Church growth they were incomparable. Nigeria, above all, became an area of dominantly Irish activity in which priests were regularly described as 'managers'. By 1960 it could proudly be claimed that the bishops have 'more than thirty thousand Catholic teachers on their payroll'.[22] Igbo Catholicism, so considerably an achievement of the Irish Holy Ghost Fathers, flourished on the school.

In British Africa the Catholic Church was treated generously enough, obtaining a very fair share of scholastic subsidies within a vast unofficial concordat relating the missions to the colonial State. In French Africa the hostilities of the pre-First World War period were not resumed, but a certain distance remained. The Church was far

[21] R. Oliver, *The Missionary Factor in East Africa* (1952), 275.
[22] J. P. Jordan, 'Catholic Educators and Catholicism in Nigeria', *AFER* 2 (1960), 61.

from established in France, but colonial officials knew that Catholic missionaries in French Africa were French, while Protestant missionaries were inevitably mostly of some other nationality. They much preferred the first. Belgian Africa was another matter. The Concordat of 1908 had established the Catholic missions in a highly privileged position. As Belgian missions they received subsidies denied to the very extensive Protestant bodies throughout the country. The discrimination here was systematic. It did, of course, in some ways help the Protestants, who were seen to be different and not identified with colonial power in a way that Catholics were. The triangle of the administration, the big mining and agricultural firms, and the Catholic mission was a very close one. Catholic missionaries used their privileged status to convert by little less than force, compelling children to attend school, converts to attend the catechumenate, everyone to conform to the moral law as interpreted by themselves. Nowhere else in Africa was so much force used, even in the 1930s and 1940s, to achieve a religious end as in many Belgian Catholic missions in the Congo.[23] They would pay for it in due course with the number of missionaries murdered subsequent to Independence.

With the conquest of Ethiopia, including a quite extraordinary degree of barbarism in the treatment meted out to the Orthodox Church, the government of Italy offered another privileged area for Catholic evangelists, but only to Italian missionaries. Non-Italians were all expelled, including the aged French Bishop Jarosseau, who had spent more than forty years in the country and was immensely respected by the Emperor. It is sad to have to state that the Vatican agreed in 1937 to reserve the Ethiopian mission to Italians alone. In practice it had little choice in the matter, yet for Rome a privileged status could still mean rather more than justice or freedom. This was seen again only too clearly in the Concordat and Missionary Agreement negotiated with Portugal in 1940, which tied the Catholic Church exceptionally tightly to the Portuguese State in Angola, Mozambique, and Guinea-Bissau: privileges and salaries in return for control. Rome's ulterior purpose was here clear enough. Mozambique in particular, while one of the oldest Catholic mission areas in Africa, remained one of the least developed. The Jesuit missionaries there, who had returned in the late nineteenth century

[23] See e.g. M. Douglas, *The Lele of the Kasai* (1963), 264–6.

after their first expulsion in the eighteenth century, had been expelled once more by Portugal's anticlerical government in 1911. Mozambique was still without a single diocese or vicariate in 1940, something hardly surprising in view of the very slight interest of the Portuguese Church in missionary work and the continued exclusion of non-Portuguese. The aim of the Missionary Agreement on the Roman side was, then, to obtain permission to send workers of other nationalities into the Portuguese territories. It had to pay for this by guaranteeing that all bishops would be Portuguese and that Church activity would conform particularly closely to government policy. The 1940 Concordat is in its way the last endorsement of the mind-set of an era stretching back many centuries, in which democracy and the rights of others had mattered not at all to the Vatican. The war would effect a great alteration in Catholic political consciousness. Jacques Maritain became the recognized teacher of the post-war Church, and much that had seemed normal in the age of Pius XI, but was in fact only a belated legacy of Counter-Reformation behaviour, soon came to be recognized as anachronistic. Already in the 1950s, well before the Second Vatican Council, the common mind of the Catholic missionary world had begun to move well away from such models of the past.

In terms of African history the questionable uses of colonial power to further missionary conquest remain important for an understanding of the twentieth-century Catholic apostolate, but not too important. Indeed, outside the Belgian Congo, they were fairly peripheral. What was decisive for the central and lasting achievements in areas like those around the great lakes was the quality of the missionaries, and it is necessary now to turn to some of them, people who built up the great Catholic Churches in countries like Uganda, Tanganyika, Rwanda, and Burundi. In the longer run it was the model of the core areas which was naturally communicated to less developed places. Thus Masaka in Uganda might be one small area, but its success as a vicariate wholly staffed by an African bishop and clergy was an inevitable challenge, and one steadily used by Rome, to push on less effective missionaries elsewhere. Masaka and similar places were only possible because of the missionaries who had made them so, and it is helpful to look at a few of them rather more carefully.

They were above all White Fathers. Catholic missionaries remain far too anonymous in African history, but, without a sense of the generation of men and women who struggled for decades, often without any significant break, in single-minded purpose to build up the Catholic Church throughout sub-Saharan Africa in the first half of the twentieth century, it would be impossible to understand the Christian history of this period. Many of them were outstanding linguists and highly knowledgeable about local customs and history. They lived a good deal closer to village life than did most other missionaries, and, without this commitment to a deep Africanization of their work, learnt from their founder Lavigerie and insisted upon with an almost military discipline, they could not have achieved what they did.

Let us consider two examples. Henri Streicher was born in Alsace in 1863. He arrived in Uganda early in 1891, just before the Catholic-Protestant civil war, and was sent to found the first mission in Buddu, Villa Maria, the mother station of what later became Masaka diocese. In 1897 he was chosen to be bishop. Refusing to return to Europe for consecration, he was ordained bishop by a single colleague, assisted by two simple priests in the humble church of Kamoga. He ruled his vicariate of Buganda and western Uganda for the next thirty-six years, during which the number of his Christians increased from 30,000 to 303,000, forty-six priests were ordained, and a sisterhood with 280 members established, together with an order of local teaching brothers. He had also established a secondary school and invited Canadian brothers to staff it, well before the arrival of Hinsley. When he retired in 1933 at the age of 70, he was leaving a mission almost incomparably beyond anything else in Catholic Africa at that time. Even then he did not leave Uganda, remaining there until his death nearly twenty years later. By that time he had seen his intentions fulfilled and part of his vicariate, Masaka, handed over in 1939 to the first Catholic African bishop of modern times, Joseph Kiwanuka. The significance of Kiwanuka's consecration was demonstrated by its being carried out in St Peter's by Pius XII himself, but Streicher was invited to assist the Pope. He then returned once more to his original mission of Villa Maria near Masaka to be available as Kiwanuka's councillor, and when he finally died in 1952 he was buried within the great church at Villa which he had himself built in the 1890s. Cardinal Costantini, no mean authority in missionary matters, described Streicher as 'the greatest missionary of the twentieth century'.[24] He did in fact establish the

---

[24] *Monseigneur Henri Streicher (1863–1952), Notice nécrologique* (Rome, 1952), 47.

model to which everyone else in Africa had perforce to conform. For sheer effectiveness as well as for length and single-mindedness of commitment it would be hard to find a rival.

Jan van Sambeek (1886–1966) was a Dutchman, one of a family of ten. Three of his brothers became priests, one of his sisters a nun. Ordained a White Father in 1911, he arrived in Northern Rhodesia in 1919 at the mission of Chilubula in the vicariate of Bangweolo. Over the next twelve years he was especially responsible for building up the Catholic school system in close co-operation with the government. To attend educational meetings in Livingstone, the opposite end of a huge country to his own, he would bicycle for some ten days, at times sleeping under the stars. In the same period he wrote, edited, and published a whole series of books in Bemba including three school-readers, *Ifya Bukaya*, written by African teachers at his college, containing a mixture of Bemba history, games, songs, and fables as well as gospel stories, geography, and whatever. They came enormously to influence the way Bemba saw themselves.

In the early 1930s van Sambeck was moved to the Tukuyu area of Tanganyika where he at once set about producing a dictionary in Kinyakusa and a grammar in Kisafwa. In 1933 he was sent back to Northern Rhodesia as superior of the new mission territory of Lwangwa (later Abercorn, then Mbala) where he founded the great mission of Ilondola. He also found time to compose a Bemba grammar. Then in 1936 he returned to Tanganyika to become Vicar-Apostolic of the whole western part of the country in succession to Mgr. Birraux, who had just been elected Superior-General of the White Fathers. After ten years there presiding over what was fast becoming in Ufipa an almost wholly Catholic peasant community, he divided his vicariate into two, himself retaining Buha, its more undeveloped northern half. In his final phase as Bishop of Kigoma for twelve years until 1958, he once more set himself to language work, writing a book on local customs and translating the Psalms, Epistles, Gospels, and much else into Kiha. After retirement he still remained in the diocese, dying at Kabanga in 1966. Here sheer length of service and a formidable knowledge of languages is linked with a certain Dutch pragmatism, the ability to co-operate effectively with the British government and even with Protestant missions in the educational enterprises of the inter-war years.

Not every White Father, or even every White Father bishop, had the longevity or the far-sightedness of a Streicher or a van Sambeek.

Nevertheless, the careers of Johanny Thévenoud in Upper Volta and Leon Classe in Rwanda, for example, were very comparable among the bishops. What is more important is that they were exceptional as a group for the extent to which they shared a common approach to their work as well as for linguistic ability. Collectively the White Father impact on Africa in the first half of the twentieth century proved a major factor in its religious history, but it is one which historians tend not to notice, geared as they continue to be into the dynamics of the Protestant rather than the Catholic story.

v. *The Missionary of the 1950s*

The 1950s were a good age for the missionary movement. Protestant decline was not yet too evident while the Catholics were still going from strength to strength. Missionary enthusiasm was in fact central world-wide to the Catholicism of the period. For Protestantism its vigour was surviving only in the rather marginal counter-culture of conservative evangelicalism, though here it was expanding. But among both Catholics and Protestants probably no other decade in missionary history could lay claim to such intelligent vitality. This was as true of Africa as anywhere. The rather ponderous, slow-thinking, paternalistically benevolent but heavy-handed note of the inter-war years was giving way to something altogether sharper, more self-critical, more willing to recognize that God had always worked as much outside the Christian Church as in it. Max Warren, General Secretary of the CMS since 1942, was now the principal Protestant strategist, a scholar of considerable historical and cultural sensitivity. To sense the quality of the missionary spirit in post-war Africa one could well put together some such collection as Geoffrey Parrinder's *West African Religion* (1949), Bengt Sundkler's *Bantu Prophets in South Africa* (1949), Trevor Huddleston's *Naught for your Comfort* (1956), and John Taylor's *Christianity and Politics in Africa* (1957). Doubtless all these books could be criticized, but they and others of the same period collectively show a much more open and immediate recognition of the weight and validity of African human and religious experience as of the political rights of Africans and the missionary responsibility to be critical of colonialism and still more of racialism.

The new missionary mood could be sharpest and most to the point where the African identity was being most painfully repressed—in South Africa. There was, of course, still plenty of racialism in the missionary Church of the 1950s, both in South Africa and elsewhere. Indeed Trevor Huddleston, Michael Scott, Ambrose Reeves, and other vocal Church critics of racialism and especially of the policies of the new Nationalist government were largely regarded by fellow Church workers, from Archbishop Clayton of Cape Town downwards, as trouble-makers. They certainly did not represent most, or even many, white Christians within South Africa. Nevertheless, in terms of moral passion, gospel conviction, and even sheer political long-sightedness, they won the debate hands down against the moderates within the Church who stood for a more measured approach or even just an inability to recognize that the issues in question, basically ones of human dignity and racial equality, were more central than anything specifically ecclesiastical to the health and credibility of the Church.

The Catholic scene was not too dissimilar, though it was still characterized more by continued post-war growth in missionary numbers than by any profound rethinking. The latter would have to wait another ten years. Nevertheless, there was an increasing liberalism in approach, brought about in part by the large number of lay missionaries now serving in Africa, particularly in organizations like Ad Lucem, a graduate fellowship originating in France. Fr. Placide Tempels's profound and stimulating *Bantu Philosophy* (1945) had had a considerable influence if, perhaps, not always a beneficial one—his stress on the centrality of 'force vitale' in the African philosophy of life could be misinterpreted by missionary colleagues to confirm their conviction that Africans only understood force of a very crude sort. Fr. Mosmans, the Belgian Provincial of the White Fathers in the later 1950s, was one among a number of writers pre-dating in the mission field the *aggiornamento* which would blossom forth so rapidly after John XXIII became Pope in 1958. Again, the replacement in 1956 as General of the White Fathers of the rigidly conservative Bishop Durrieu by the more open-minded Dutchman Leo Volker helped a larger shift in attitudes, while Joseph Blomjous, another Dutchman and Bishop of Mwanza in Tanganyika from 1948, was highly unusual among missionary bishops in being a theological scholar who built a large library for himself on the shores of Lake Victoria, an ecumenical liberal who held the confidence of his fellow bishops. He was largely responsible for the commencement in 1959 of the *African Ecclesiastical Review,* a quarterly published in Uganda but intended for the whole of English-speaking Africa as a means of decreasing the extreme intellectual isolation from which the Catholic missionary world suffered. Its editor was a third Dutchman and White Father, Joop Geerdes. Volker, Blomjous, and Geerdes represent what we may call the Dutch age of Catholic mission, a fairly brief age, vigorous, open-minded, ecumenical, which was just beginning as our story ends.

Such developments, however, were in 1960 only starting to affect the basic attitudes of the majority of missionary bishops, priests, and sisters. Many continued to hold without question that every unbaptized person must go to hell, that Protestants were unquestionably wrong, that—beyond perhaps some minor reforms such as a greater use of the vernacular—the Roman Catholic Church neither could nor should change. The mental gap between ordinary Catholic and Protestant missionaries was still quite enormous at the end of the 1950s, though rumbles of impatience could be heard and were tolerated rather more than in earlier decades. It was Pope John, the Council, and the need to respond to African independence which would change it, and nowhere did the Council have a more startling effect than in the African missionary field, but that again is a story which goes beyond the frontiers of this history.

Africa and its Churches north of the Zambezi were clearly turning to the 'left' by the end of the 1950s, but south of the Zambezi the political direction would remain equally emphatically to the 'right'. Scott, Huddleston, Reeves, and their like were all removed from South Africa or silenced within it, and for a while in the 1960s they had few obvious successors in that dark age of black hopes. They were, of course, all English priests. Afrikaners had for a century been decrying the interference of English people in South African affairs. Clerics of this sort were seen as simply an anachronistic example of the British imperialist spirit which had crushed the Boer republics. In the nineteenth century the Dutch Reformed Churches had at times put brakes upon the racialism of their members. By the 1930s it was rather the other way round. In 1938, for example, the mission secretary of the Nederduitse Gereformeerde Kerk, J. G. Strydom, could already describe apartheid as an 'issue of faith' at a mission congress at Bloemfontein. This was at a time when the use of the term 'apartheid' was only just beginning. The mildly liberal theology of the English-speaking Churches had done next to nothing to hold back the advance of racialist legislation in the age of Smuts, but it had been a piecemeal, untheorized advance. Now Christianity itself, in one of its forms, was justifying the implementation of a coherent racial apartheid through a simplistic but heavy-handed and fundamentalist neo-Calvinist theology, which had only quite recently emerged within the spiritual context of Afrikaner nationalism.

It was obvious that after the Nationalist victory of 1948 it would appear more than ever intolerable that a handful of rather high church English clerics should assert the unchristian character of racialism with an inspired clarity never before achieved. At the time they certainly appeared to fail in their struggle. Yet, on the one side, the struggle would quickly be taken up again, even by Afrikaner Christians. In the late 1950s Dr Beyers Naudé, Vice-Chairman of the Transvaal Synod of the NGK and a member of the Broederbond, thus someone from the very heart of Afrikanerdom, was just beginning his own lifetime of public protest against the theory and practice of apartheid. On the other side, Huddleston had been decisively heard and would be remembered by the blacks he had served in Sophiatown and elsewhere, just as Scott would be remembered by the Hercro on whose behalf he went year after year to speak in New York at the UN. Desmond Tutu would never lose the impression made upon him as a boy by the sight of Fr. Huddleston raising his hat to his mother in the street and visiting him as a sick child in hospital. The black archbishop of the 1990s might never have found his Christian calling without the radical white priest of the 1950s and his sustained expression of human caring. Such apparently inconsequential actions would be proved worth while, not only because their stand would in due time be vindicated by the march of secular history but also because they established within the Church they had come to serve a cherished memory, a protest against racial tyranny so intense that it actually did something to redeem the shoddy racialist record of almost all the Churches over many decades. It may seem unrealistic for the historian to pick out such things from a very complex series of events, yet religious history is constructed more than most by myths, symbols, and a tradition of empowering memories. When myths ring true they can be very powerful indeed. Twenty-five years later South Africa would be teeming with radical clergymen, but not in the 1950s. Yet it was then when the star of racialism was rising, not when it was setting, that such witness was historically significant.

North of the Zambezi, colonialism was now rapidly and benevolently crumbling. Equally, the missionary movement was sitting ever more loose to colonialism. At times they had seemed horse and rider, now the missionary preferred not to stress the acquaintance. The warning of China, with its communist take-over and expulsion of missionaries, had to some degree at least been imbibed. The 1950s were in the Western Church as a whole a fairly conservative epoch. Its missionary groupings together with other people particularly concerned with Africa could seem for the moment its more radical wing. It was in Africa that the perceptive could discern a new world about to arrive, a world of great poverty, underdevelopment, and exploitation, yet possibly a rather Christian world—but only if the Churches could show that their colonialist links might fairly be forgotten or forgiven. Could they now serve creatively instead in the development of a new and independent Africa? Many missionaries throughout the 1950s saw such prospects only with foreboding, expressions of the advance of 'communism'. And many African nationalists were still unsure whether the missionary Churches should be seen as friend or foe. The 1950s were, obviously enough, a time of transition in which Churches of a highly colonial type subsisted side by side with signs of rapid change. By and large missionary leadership recognized the challenge just in time, and a new independent Africa which needed missionary personnel and expertise only too obviously was disposed in most places to believe in its good intentions and accept its collaboration in the long march that had now to begin.

THE CHARACTER OF THE CHRISTIAN COMMUNITY

vi. *Catholic Masaka*

'Tulidde Buddu'—'We have eaten (taken possession of) Buddu'— was the triumphant cry of the Catholic priests of Buganda in March 1934 when it was announced that Buddu and its neighbouring counties of Kkooki, Mawogola, and Kabula were being handed by Rome to the native clergy to be entirely staffed by them with no missionary control other than that of the bishop. They chose Joseph

Mpagi as episcopal vicar of the district of Masaka. Five years later, it became a full vicariate with Joseph Kiwanuka as the first African diocesan bishop of the twentieth century.

It is worth looking rather more at how this came about and why it mattered so much. There had been a fairly steady stream of Ganda ordinations since 1913, and already in 1921 Bishop Streicher had handed over the first mission to African clergy to run on their own, Narozari. In the following years several more were entrusted to them while at the same time he was giving other Ganda priests additional administrative training. Thus he made Timoteo Ssemogerere his secretary. In 1925 in his five-year report to Rome he declared it was time to start arranging for his vicariate to be divided and one part given to the African clergy. The establishment of Masaka with its own bishop in 1939 was then the culmination of lengthy preparation upon the part of both Streicher and Rome. While it was possible only because Streicher's insistence upon the development of a local clergy had been acted upon by numerous White Fathers on the staff of the seminaries of Bukalasa and Katigondo, it has also to be said that many were deeply opposed to the whole plan. They were also shocked when, in 1934, Buddu, the most favoured part of their whole mission, and not some more marginal area—as had earlier been planned—was chosen, very fittingly, for the local clergy. In the context of the 1930s it was an almost staggering series of decisions. Kiwanuka himself had been ordained in 1929 and sent by Streicher to study in Rome with Ssemogerere. That too was a genuinely radical decision. They became the first African doctors of canon law. At every point in this process Streicher, the Ganda Church, and Masaka itself were far ahead of anything else in African Christianity, and success was possible only because on the one side Streicher was so very unusual in both his vision and his perseverance and on the other the local clergy as a group thoroughly justified his confidence. They formed indeed an exceptionally able, well-educated, and responsible body.

For twelve years after 1939 Bishop Kiwanuka was the sole African Catholic diocesan bishop. There was equally no Anglican. It is in itself highly surprising that in a matter of this sort the Catholic Church was now actually ahead of any other, and this points both to the loss of Africanizing momentum after the death of Bishop Crowther and to the way in which the Protestant–Catholic balance had been altering during the first third of this century. Kiwanuka represents an age in which Catholicism had moved to the centre of African Christianity in a way that was not at all the case in the nineteenth century. But it was the success of Masaka that ensured the extension of what could be seen as an experiment. Kiwanuka was as conscious as Crowther had been seventy years before that he had been appointed as 'a kind of landmark' for the wider Church. He proved a model bishop who worked with the laity, pressed forward with the education of his clergy, gave sage political advice, and tempered episcopal autocracy with basic democracy through the development of elected parish councils and school parent associations. Few missionary bishops achieved so much.

Masaka was in consequence a model waiting to be exported elsewhere, and its many dozens of very adequately educated, hard-working, celibate priests a standing reproach to missionaries in so many parts of Africa who had done little if anything to develop a local clergy. Thus there were whole countries like Rhodesia where, until Bishop Chichester arrived in 1931, absolutely no attempt had been made to train a single priest. Moreover, Katigondo, the regional seminary for half of Uganda and north-west Tanganyika as well, lay inside Masaka. All the clergy educated there were bound to be anticipating the moment when their dioceses too would go the way of Masaka. Again other large regional seminaries run by the White Fathers—Kipalapala in Tanganyika, Nyakibanda in Rwanda, Kachebere in Nyasaland—could not be unaffected. All were responsible to Propaganda Fide, and in Masaka Rome had shown its model for all their futures. Ever since the sixteenth century, the more far-sighted Catholic missionaries in Africa had sought to achieve just this. Now for the first time it had actually been done, following quickly upon the example of China, India, and Japan, and despite the conviction of most missionaries that the time was not yet ripe.

The shadow of Masaka lay across the continent and from the early 1950s other similar dioceses would be established, beginning with Lower Kagera, a district of Tanganyika directly next to Masaka, over which Laurean Rugambwa was appointed bishop in 1951, and Nyundo, a section of Rwanda not far to the west, with Aloysius Bigirumwami as bishop in 1952. At much the same time the first Anglican diocesans since Crowther were appointed in West Africa, A. B. Akinyele in Ibadan and Bishop Dimieari in the Niger delta. It may be noted that being Bishop of Ibadan, like being Bishop of

Masaka—and even more so—was a position of importance. It was still more symbolic that the Niger delta where Archdeacon Crowther had made his stand for African autonomy after the death of his father should be among the first to be allowed once more a black diocesan. Lower Kagera and Nyundo were not comparable. In their cases, Roman missionary strategy had fallen back, not quite on tokenism, but on the cautious handing-over of a very marginal area indeed. When Kiwanuka had the courage to protest that Rugambwa's see was not Bukoba, he was put in his place. He was nevertheless right, but at that point the daring logic which had brought him to Masaka twelve years earlier had still not been recovered.

In theory, Catholic Masaka was clearly quite abnormal for the years before 1951. Here alone was a Church of any size free of direct missionary control but served and led by its own people. Nevertheless, in reality the difference was not so clear-cut. If almost everywhere else on the Catholic side missionary control remained fairly tight, on the Protestant side missionary withdrawal upwards was leaving increasingly large areas of African Christianity to cope with its problems largely on its own.

Let us look at one example where hundreds might be offered: the Abaluyia section of the Nyanza rural deanery of the Anglican diocese of Mombasa.[25] By 1946 it had five pastorates served by five priests, all African, plus fourteen lay readers and 138 teachers and evangelists. There were no regular training courses for either the lay readers or the teachers and evangelists. Between them these five pastorates consisted of 204 separate congregations, each with its own church. All this had developed almost entirely by a process of 'spontaneous combustion' since the foundation of a mission at Butere in 1913, as a missionary described it in the 1930s.[26] Not surprisingly in March 1949 the Nyanza Ruridecanal Council produced a document entitled 'The Needs of the Growing Church', expressing its deep discontent with a system that left them with priests serving in some cases more than fifty churches, a Church which had in point of fact been Africanized but remained constrained by the control of a single bishop who visited it once every twelve to eighteen months.

'Africanization' could take many forms, and our purpose here has to a considerable extent to be an analysis of its diversity. Take Masaka

[25] W. Omulokoli, 'The Historical Development of the Anglican Church among Abaluyia 1905–1955', Ph.D. thesis (Aberdeen, 1981).
[26] E. Richards, *Fifty Years in Nyanza 1906–1956* (Maseno, 1956), 60.

once more. This was not simply a case of black faces replacing white ones in a certain number of missions. The style was different too. Undoubtedly White Fathers were good at living off the land; nevertheless, the African clergy had to be still more self-reliant. The gardens of their missions were a most necessary object of their care. Their relationship with the people was different, linked as they were in innumerable kinship relationships. They knew more and could indeed be more severe in application of the norms they had learnt in the seminary just because it was more difficult to pull the wool over their eyes. The clergy of Masaka with their mastery of Latin and the theology of their textbooks were an object of incomparable admiration in the 1930s and 1940s. Their English was less good than their Latin. Their domestic culture was essentially vernacular, their one normal source of external knowledge being the Church newspaper *Munno*. In this they were very like many a diocesan clergy in Italy or Spain. The diocese of Masaka was, then, in its way very deeply Africanized, but this did not signify the slightest deviation from missionary norms. On the contrary, its clergy were meticulously faithful to the 'Statutes' regulating the details of their daily life, drawn up on missionary authority. If it had not done so, it would have spelled undoubted disaster and been used as an argument against the success of the 'experiment'. Even so, missionaries could write to Rome that 'in all the Buddu missions entrusted to African clergy, we have observed an evil spirit. Priests manifest nationalism. They want to be on their own, manage their own affairs.'[27] Masaka succeeded just because, ecclesiastically and theologically, it was so unnationalist, so persistently faithful to missionary norms and ultramontane theology. In this model of Africanization there could be no room for anything else.

vii. *Conversion, Community, and Catechist*

Masaka represents, clearly enough, a clerical and Roman model. The 'Africanization' which was going on far more widely among the laity of many quickly expanding Churches took a rather different form. The Nyanza rural deanery may here be a good deal more typical, though in Masaka too the reality of the villages, well away from clergy houses, was probably much the same. What differentiated

[27] Annual Report 1937, J. Waliggo, *A History of African Priests* (Masaka, 1988), 134.

Buganda was two things: one, the exceptionally early date for its mass
conversion; the other, the speed with which a quite numerous
clergy—Anglican and Catholic—was subsequently developed. But
the underlying character of the Christian community was not all that
different, and we have to move now from clergy to community, a
community in most places largely clergyless until well after 1960.
Understandably we tend to concentrate upon areas of early mass
conversion, like the Ganda and the Igbo. Their history has a special
memorableness because of its priority. The Luyia were undergoing
their 'spontaneous combustion' thirty or so years later. It is much less
remembered in consequence. What we need is a map, decade by
decade, of the ongoing advance of large-scale conversion movements, but it would be a very complicated map because the process
enjoyed a different tempo and character in different places. Nor did a
particular people necessarily move as one. Nevertheless, it is clear that
the 1930s were a time when numbers were going up fast over rather
wide areas. One may think of the 'tornade' in Rwanda and Burundi,
but that was only an extreme case of a far wider shift in public
religious commitment. What was happening was that the fairly tight
Christianity established in pockets around older missions was
suddenly coming to be adopted, if rather more superficially,
through the expansion of a network of schools or the conversion
of a king, by far larger hinterlands. Take some fairly unsensational
examples from Tanganyika: the Moravians claimed 1,087 baptized
Christians in 1910, 5,653 in 1927, but 19,153 by 1939; the Berlin
Mission in the southern highlands was no different: 2,227, 5,183, but,
by 1938, 17,695. The Lutherans in the north-west around Bukoba
had 3,000 catechumens in 1930, 25,000 in 1945.[28] Such figures
indicate just the start of a large quantitative growth which would
continue through the 1940s and 1950s, and which provides, in its
way, the backdrop for the emergence in each place of a new, more
populist, shape to the 'mission Church', a shape less and less
effectively controllable by the missionary.

Two more sensational mass movements of the 1940s will remind us
that the pattern was not only one of faster development on old
foundations but also still of new beginnings as fresh and fervent as any
of those near the start of the century. Both, be it noted, were towards

---

[28] M. Wright, *German Missions in Tanganyika 1891–1941* (1971), 221; B. Sundkler, *Bara
Bukoba: Church and Community in Tanzania* (1980), 31.

the north, the Sudanic belt, which the missionary movement was late in taking seriously. In the north-west of the Gold Coast the Dagarti around Jirapa and Nandom were beginning a sudden, almost total, conversion as a people to Catholicism, falling into the delighted arms of the White Fathers, who were able to respond with rather more flexibility than would have been the case a generation earlier. The first 1930s convert, a young water-diviner named Peter Dery, became in 1951 the first Dagarti priest and in 1960 the first Dagarti Bishop of Wa, an almost Roland Allen-style achievement.

Our second example is that of Churches in southern Ethiopia dependent upon an initial input from the Sudan Interior Mission. The SIM entered Ethiopia at the end of 1927, led by Dr Thomas Lambie, intent on opening a network of mission stations in the south-west of the country towards Lake Rudolf. Obtaining permission from the Ethiopian government for a Protestant mission was a slow business, especially in the period before Ras Tafari became Emperor Haile Selassie in 1930, but work eventually began in Sidamo and Wallamo provinces and around Hosanna. These were fringe areas of the Ethiopian Orthodox Church. The first four converts were baptized at Homatcho in Sidamo on Christmas Day, 1932. Over the next six years forty-eight people were baptized in Wallamo and perhaps 100 in all. After the Italian conquest all Protestant mission property was expropriated, all Protestant missionaries withdrew, and the small groups of Ethiopian Protestants were subjected to particularly ruthless persecution. Thus most of the students in the Bible Church Missionary Society's school at Addis were killed in cold blood. However, the small groups of SIM converts led by a young man named Biru, who had in fact been the guide of the first SIM party, persevered and multiplied. They grew to be divided into fifteen sections, each with a Ruling Elder, while each section was divided into its own areas, and churches with four or more elders to each church. A monthly meeting was held in which the Ruling Elders and three or four representatives from each church gathered to decide, among other matters, the time for the monthly communion celebrated simultaneously in every church. At the same time baptisms took place and, though all the traditional practices of dancing and merry-making were otherwise banned, all were allowed, including horse sports, in the baptismal procession to and from the river—a remarkable example of the immediate modification of missionary puritanism by traditional popular culture.

When the Italian occupation was ended and the Emperor restored in 1941 a former SIM missionary, Laurie Davison, who was in the British army in Addis, made contact with the Church in Wallamo to discover that there were now hundreds of congregations and many thousands of Christians. 'We have found here', he reported, 'as indigenous a Church as Roland Allen ever dreamt about.'[29] It continued to grow. If there were 80 churches in Wallamo by 1942, there were 334 by 1960, 150 in all in 1942, 800 by 1960, despite intermittent persecution by local Orthodox authorities.

In Sidamo and Wallamo the new Church with all its young evangelical fervour had still to fit into a world in which there were and had long been Christians of other traditions, in this case of a tradition which was at once ancient, nationalist, monopolistic, and ignorant. But a 'mixed' Christianity of one sort or another, and often very mixed indeed, was emerging all across the continent. The long struggle of the early missionary to establish firm lines between converted and unconverted, between Catholic and Protestant, had grown less and less successful. There were, of course, areas overwhelmingly one-denominational: Catholic areas like Masaka, Ufipa (the core of van Sambeek's vicariate of Karema), Burundi, and suchlike. There were more occasional Protestant areas, like the Baptist stronghold of Ogbomoso in Yorubaland, Congregationalist Bechuanaland, and much of Lutheran Namibia. Even these, however, were frequently eroded, and Africans themselves showed a marked dislike for 'comity' arrangements agreed between Protestant societies whereby any particular area would be designated for a single denomination. African society had become too peregrinatory for that to be acceptable.

A report from the Bangweulu vicariate, Northern Rhodesia, for 1937 tells of a particular family. Its head was a polygamist of the old school, a bon viveur not much interested in religious innovation. He had two wives, Salome, a Catholic, and Judith, a Protestant. His eldest son, Potiphar, was a fervent member of the Watch Tower Society while his eldest daughter, who would have liked to maintain the Catholicism of her mother, was married to an evangelist of the African Church. Another son of 17, baptized a Catholic, was now studying to be a teacher in a Protestant school while his sister, Tabita, who had been baptized a Protestant, was engaged to a Catholic and

---

[29] F. P. Cotterell, 'An Indigenous Church in Southern Ethiopia', *BSACH* 3 (1969–70), 86.

under instruction. Of the younger children Salome's were to date Catholic and Judith's Protestant.[30]

The Tswana had in the past been something of a preserve of the Congregationalism of the London Missionary Society, yet a missionary report of 1929 presents an equally confused picture: 'Church work seems to progress slowly. The opposition of the Roman Catholics, the Seventh Day Adventists, the Church of England, the Wesleyans, and the Independents, not to speak of the Ethiopians, seems to have taken much of the vigour out of the remaining workers in the LMS Church.'[31] Much of the confusion derived from the almost automatic acceptance of a school's religious identity by the children who went to it, but there was also plenty of 'conversion' from one denomination to another produced by marriage, accessibility of a place of worship, missionary behaviour, or the level of church tax. In 1924 the wedding of Esau Oriedo took place in the village church of Ebwah in the Nyanza province of Kenya. It was a Church of God mission, and Christians in the village were mostly its members. After the wedding there was a good deal of dancing and music, which proved unacceptable to the Church of God missionary, Mr Kramer. He closed the church while awaiting an act of contrition. The people turned instead to the Anglican Church and presented Archdeacon Owen with a list of 115 names who wished to become Anglicans. What had hitherto been an area outside their influence became from then on a pillar of Anglican strength.

Church membership was something capable of many degrees. Next to the missionaries came the local clergy, catechists, and communicant members. Here was the solid core of the Church, though even that core may need to be qualified. Some catechists and, still more, some devoted patrons of a local church were not communicants, being excluded on marital grounds. Beyond them were a large number of the baptized who either never had been communicants or were not now. Under public discipline in a Protestant Church, excluded from communion in the Catholic Church, a growing proportion of the baptized community were permanently marginalized. The marital grounds for this could be polygamy, but equally it could be breakdown of church marriage followed by a customary marriage, or simply marriage to someone of

[30] B. Garvey, *Bembaland Church* (Leiden, 1993), 125–6.
[31] B. A. Pauw, *Religion in a Tswana Chiefdom* (1960), 229.

another denomination which had made impossible a wedding in church. It might even be none of these, but simply a lack of money or will-power to transform a customary marriage (validated by bride-wealth) into a church marriage blessed by a recognized minister.

The White Father diarist at Mua mission in central Nyasaland remarked on 1 January 1952:

> It is the fiftieth anniversary of the founding of the mission. We now have 6,140 baptized Christians, 1,579 families, 639 of these are broken marriages. Only 2,100 of our 3,334 adults are allowed to receive the sacraments, 2/5ths of our parishioners never receive communion. Out of a total of 2,516 children and youngsters, 750 are illegitimate, from adulterous liaisons. And this is only the children we know about. For the Christians who remain faithful, what indifference to the things of God. Let us hope that 1952 will see an increase in their fervour.[32]

The Chewa people of Mua were not very polygamous but their marriages were traditionally unstable. Nevertheless, the proportion of Church members still able to receive the sacraments in Mua was in fact relatively high. John Taylor, a few years later, found that over 80 per cent of Anglicans in Buganda were excommunicated.[33] For Ganda Catholics it may have been about 60 per cent. This is what 'control' had come to mean: the statistical precision and sacramental discipline of the Mua diarist represents it most accurately. Mua in 1952 remained a well-run mission—not too large in size or numerous in its parishioners to be out of control for three energetic White Fathers. The statistics and the communions could still be controlled, only the 'indifference' could not. Elsewhere things could already be a good deal worse.

When, however, we have gone so far, we are still far from through all the degrees of Church membership because we have not considered the many who had for years been enrolled in a catechumenate but were never, for one reason or another, actually baptized. Again there were many people who had not seriously entered a catechumenate at all, but who regarded themselves as Catholic, Anglican, or Methodist because a parent, child, aunt, or whatever, actually was a member of such a Church, and they wanted to be something. If an ordained Luyia priest of fairly limited

---

[32] I. Linden, *Catholics, Peasants and Chewa Resistance in Nyasaland 1889–1939* (1974), 189.
[33] J. Taylor, *The Growth of the Church in Buganda* (1958), 245.

education had fifty congregations to serve, with only the assistance of various untrained and mostly unpaid lay readers and evangelists, is it surprising that the complexities of individual life histories when placed against the requirements of Church regulations were often beyond his time and ability to work out?

If such problems were to be worked out, it would be done by the catechist. He was the Church's one local man, and in this regard the age of the catechist lasts well into the 1950s. It was the catechist and no one else who ensured that the vast numbers of Christians multiplying across the first half of this century became, most of them, Catholics, Anglicans, or Presbyterians and not members of an independent Church or millenarian cult. The catechists continued to represent in the context of innumerable villages Ecclesia Catholica, the universal fellowship of Christians, as well as literary modernity, the three Rs in fact: Reading, Writing, and Religion. He was not entirely local. Catechists might be moved. They might even have a bicycle. Almost unpaid by the Church, they often supported themselves by trade unless they were doubling as teachers paid by the State. A few would be promoted. To us they stand for the local. To their people, and even to themselves, they stood for and were linked with a world of religious and secular power, the world of the bishop, of a cathedral, even of the Pope. They were far-flung outposts in a new ecclesiastical geography growing up around them. They visited their diocesan headquarters from time to time, and the way things were there was the way things should be in the village too. Protestant or Catholic, biblicism or papalism, he had somehow to represent these great things to his fellow villagers, standing for values, ideas, and powers whose authority he could sense but whose meaning he could hardly begin to apprehend.

Jedida Asheri describes her catechist father at Kikai in western Cameroon in the 1930s as owning a sewing-machine and sewing his family's clothes as well as trading. He would set off on foot hundreds of miles to sell his kola-nuts. Greatly respected by his fellow villagers, he was 'Massa' (Master), whose calabash had to be filled at the spring before theirs, and he lived a little apart even from his family in 'Papa's house', whose principal room was the parlour, the office of his ministry, containing table, two chairs, and magazine pictures on the three walls. Here cleanliness and tidiness had a high priority. 'Massa' was a Catholic. His contemporary Benjamin Paul Apena was an Anglican. Both had been born in the 1890s. Apena, an Isoko from

Ikpidiama, was in the Nigerian army in the latter years of the war. In 1921 he felt the call to become an evangelist and interpreter for the missionaries. Over the next twenty years he was promoted and sent on courses for further training until in December 1939 he was ordained a deacon and became the first native Isoko pastor. Twenty-five years later he would be its first archdeacon.[34] The Catholic catechist could never advance beyond his parlour, the Protestant might conceivably—but not until after 1960—end his days as an archdeacon. But in this Apena was quite abnormal. Massa, with his tidy parlour, the respect of the village, and the struggle to make ends meet, remained the model of the many thousands of catechists who held the Church together but never advanced a step higher up the ecclesiastical ladder.

Sometime in the 1930s an English woman recorded this scene from eastern Nigeria, a Methodist Sunday service led by its catechist:

The Church was crowded, behaviour irreproachable. The leader of the service stood, or sat upon a collapsible wooden chair behind a small square table over which was thrown crookedly a torn piece of cloth. He read from the Bible in Union Igbo and commented thereon; he gave an extempore prayer; he led the singing, also in Union Igbo . . . I had expected the very simplicity of the setting would have lent dignity, the very naiveness of the worshippers would have brought some charm, the very fact that this handful of Christians was ringed about by the cohorts of paganism would have awed and inspired . . . Instead, I found it ugly, alien, *dull*. I think that was what struck me most. How could those people sit through that halting reading of which, even with the leader's comments, they could hardly have understood a word (I remember the last readings I heard were from Malachi and Hebrews), that ear-splitting singing of words which, set to a western tune, must have lost (Igbo being a tone language) all their meaning? . . . There was no whispering nor fidgeting nor squabbling for a seat on the narrow mud benches, the faces were immobile, the eyes fixed brightly and intently on the leader.[35]

How to evaluate such experiences or the comment of an alien observer? The limitations of the catechist are as clear as his authority and both are related to the impossible task of the barely literate teaching the Bible to the illiterate. This particular observer found a

---

[34] In retirement at the end of the 1970s Apena wrote 'The Life History of Venerable Benjamin Paul Apena JP as Compiled by Himself'. Cf. S. Akama, 'A Religious History of the Isoko People', Ph.D. thesis (Aberdeen, 1981), app. D, 495–6.
[35] S. Leith-Ross, *African Women* (1939), 121–2.

Catholic mass with its Latin less alien than a twisted Igbo and 'to the outsider there seemed more of God',[36] but a Catholic mass was not a normal village service, and the Catholic service led by a catechist, though it probably did not try to take Malachi on board, may have been little different from the Methodist. There was certainly an absence of the charismatic, the exciting, or the spontaneous in most village worship of this sort. The criticism 'dull' remains a telling one.

Missionaries had been making considerable efforts to train catechists in the inter-war years. It was on this, rather than clergy training, that they concentrated, though for Protestants in theory at least the one could lead to the other. Catechist and teacher in this period were essentially one and the same, though with White Fathers, for instance, the stress was more on the catechist, with Holy Ghost Fathers more on the teacher. The catechist's primary task was to care for the local church, its services, and its catechumens. The teacher's primary task was to run the local school. Little by little the two fell apart. In 1956 Roland Oliver remarked, 'the village catechist and teacher is still today the corner-stone of the African Church'.[37] That was still true but it was also a slightly anachronistic judgement because by the 1950s catechist and teacher were coming to separate. Governments were raising the educational level of the teacher by leaps and bounds but also their control over his or her work. The catechist remained the Church's almost unpaid and increasingly unvalued servant. Almost every catechist training centre had been closed, and missionaries could write them off ungratefully as uneducated and inadequate, 'a bunch of riff-raff', people who 'only destroy our work'.[38] Yet there was still no one else actually to keep the village church functioning. Before the First World War catechists were already 'the corner-stone' of the African Church. In between the wars the truth of this was recognized and much effort was put into training them. After 1945 it was again forgotten. Training and appreciation diminished, but the fact remained. There was no one else and it was, in a way, to the good that the regular minister of the local congregation was not ordained and that in consequence its regular service was not a communion one. As most of its members were likely to be excluded from communion, the absence of the ordained kept the congregation together as one for

[36] Ibid. 169–70.
[37] R. Oliver, *How Christian is Africa?* (1956), 10.
[38] B. Sundkler, *The Christian Ministry in Africa* (1960), 155–6.

almost all their services. Priest and communion could only be divisive. While more priests might mean the regularization of more marital problems, the large majority of the latter were—given Church law and the realities of African society—bound to remain impervious to the ministry of the former.

viii. *Dreams*

Samuel Ntara was a young teacher in a Dutch Reformed mission school in Nyasaland who won a prize in the early 1930s from the International Institute of African Languages and Cultures for his novel *Man of Africa*. With his prize money he purchased a cow for his mother and a bicycle for himself while giving one-tenth to the Church. Ntara was a model teacher-catechist at the high point of its role. His novel is about the conversion of a young man, Nthondo, to Christianity, a conversion achieved almost wholly through a series of dreams. It is the authority of the dream quite as much as the authority of the Bible which is here at the root of conversion, and it is the status of the dream within emerging African Christian life that we need again to consider.

'All the natives of this land, Moors, heathens or Christians, attach great credit to dreams.' That perceptive remark about East Africa was made by Friar João dos Santos in his *Etiopia oriental*.[39] It was based on his observations in the 1590s. Ntara was simply demonstrating that 350 years later it was still true. Almost more surprising is the evidence of Donald Fraser's biography of Daniel Mtusu, *The Autobiography of an African*, published in 1925. Mtusu was an early Ngoni teacher-evangelist, and Fraser recounts no fewer than three remarkable occurrences in Mtusu's life: a dream, in which he was emphatically forbidden six times to become a polygamist, leading to his conversion, a vision of Jesus in his hut after baptism, and a further vision of angels shared with a friend. Alexander Hetherwick, another fairly staid Presbyterian Scot, accepted that it was often a dream which brought his candidates into the catechumenate.[40] 'Those dreams were sent by Mulungu,' a Christian teacher explains to Nthondo (in *Man of Africa*).[41] Such was the conviction of many ministers in this period who believed it was through a dream that

[39] G. M. Theal, *Records of South-Eastern Africa* (Cape Town, 1898–1903), vii. 224.
[40] A. Hetherwick, *The Gospel and the African* (1932), 117.
[41] Samuel Ntara, *Man of Africa* (1934), 172–3.

they discovered their vocation. 'I am glad if and when any of our candidates mention anything else but dreams when applying for ordination,' an East African bishop remarked to Bengt Sundkler, while Bishop Akinyele of Ibadan said the same: the majority of candidates offering for the ministry 'had seen themselves in a white surplice and therefore wished to be ordained'.[42] Dreams tend to dominate the early experience of the prophets and to remain crucial to the life of their Churches, so it is important to note that it was not something original to them. It was already part of life in the mission Church they had known. Thus the fascinating early Kimbanguist text put together by Nfinangani records how a Baptist catechist, Samuel Mowala, had a dream in which he saw that he should read Matthew 25: 1 on the ten bridesmaids and preach about it holding a clean bowl in his right hand and a dirty jerrycan in his left. This he did the next day, but Kimbangu, who was listening, believed that he had misunderstood the true meaning of the dream.[43] The point for us here is that it is already the Baptist catechist who is applying his dream for the understanding of the gospel. We find the usage of dreams everywhere, among Anglican catechists in Nigeria, Lutheran deacons in Bukoba, Catholics both within the movement of Jamaa in the Congo and in Igboland as affected by the figure of Michael Tansi.[44]

The striking thing about this acceptance of dreams as in some way revelatory or vocational is, then, that it is so wide-ranging. Faced with the very considerable reference to dreams in both the Old and New Testaments, missionaries seem to have felt unable to condemn their use. It is certainly striking to find it in West, East, central, and southern Africa, among Catholics, Protestants, and Independents.[45] There is plenty of patristic evidence to show that dreams were a factor in conversion in the early Church. Yet it was hardly something stressed in nineteenth-century Western Christianity, though

---

[42] Sundkler, *The Christian Ministry in Africa*, 25.
[43] J. Pemberton, 'The History of Simon Kimbangu by the Writers Nfinangani and

[44] P. McKenzie, 'Dreams and Visions in Nineteenth-Century Yoruba Religion', in M. C. Jedrej and R. Shaw (eds.), *Dreaming, Religion and Society in Africa* (1992), 126–34, Sundkler, *Bara Bukoba*, 98–112, W. De Craemer, *The Jamaa and the Church: A Bantu Catholic Movement in Zaire* (1977), 85, 93–7, 110, E. Isichei, *Entirely for God: The Life of Michael Iwere Tansi* (1980), 57.
[45] B. Sundkler, *Bantu Prophets in South Africa*, 2nd edn. (1961), 265–75. For further discussion see S. Charsley, 'Dreams in a Ugandan Church', *Africa*, 57 (1987), 281–9, and Jedrej and Shaw, *Dreaming, Religion and Society in Africa*, esp. 135–76.

missionaries too could at times connect their calling to dreams.[46] If the dream so quickly takes on prominence within African Christianity, it must be because Africans themselves were already prone to make use of dreams as well as finding in the Bible encouragement to go on doing so. It is thus a quite significant example of the early Africanization of Christianity, an example unresisted by missionaries.

ix. *Church and Society*

As the mission Churches multiplied in membership and in the number of congregations, two things almost inevitably happened. On the one hand was a steady reduction in the contact between missionary (or even ordained local minister) and the average Christian. The conditions of the catechumenate were reduced, but a quickly growing proportion of Church members had not been through any real catechumenate at all, only a couple of classes in a bush school. Their ongoing link with the historic mind of their Church might consist in no more than the hymns they sang, the memorized answers of a catechism, the weekly preachings of a catechist, increasingly rare encounters with an ordained minister. On the other hand lay a steady reduction in the sense of separation between Church and society. This was not true for the more sectarian groups particularly in their earlier years. But membership of a large, well-established Church could by the middle of the century be little differentiated from the membership of ordinary society. Yet the customs of ordinary society had not greatly changed. Any not over-enthusiastic and well-trained Christian had simply to live in the two societies, largely accepting the rules and assumptions of both, even though such rules and assumptions were often contradictory. Some people bothered more about the one, some more about the other, but most people would to some extent respect both. They were not in consequence real traditionalists, but equally they were not—in missionary eyes at least—very good Christians.

The degree of tension depended both upon the society in question and the exigencies of a particular Church. The head-on conflict which arose among Kikuyu Christians was over a custom—female

---

[46] See J. T. Hardyman, 'Dr Phillips' Dream of Madagascar', *BSACH* 2 (1967), 207–23.

circumcision—not practised among most peoples. In attacking it Protestant missionaries could feel all the righteousness of a modern liberal denouncing something manifestly retrograde and even dangerous. They could see themselves as defenders of womankind. Catholic missionaries were less modern-minded and more tolerant than they would have been in the past. They were not in consequence prepared to make of its rejection, as the Presbyterians were, a condition for continued Church membership. Anglicans caught, as often, in the middle mostly went along in theory with the Presbyterians, but a few thought that even female circumcision could better be Christianized than attacked head on. Here was a case when something seen as quite central to Kikuyu cultural identity upon the one side was judged wholly incompatible with Presbyterian Christianity upon the other. In earlier days male circumcision, far more widely practised in Africa than female, was condemned almost as strongly by missionaries, and it could still be so in a few places. In 1924 two teachers of the CMS Buwalasi mission in the strongly circumcizing people of the Bagisu reneged from their position in order to undergo circumcision. They had found that, uncircumcized, they were accorded little respect by their pupils. In the 1920s Christian Bagisu had still to persuade the mission that circumcision was in itself an acceptable 'custom'. In Tanganyika, where there had long been a more adaptationist approach common among missionaries than was to be found in Uganda or Kenya, Bishop Lucas of Masasi was already convinced, and endeavoured in the 1920s not too successfully to develop a Christian ritual of initiation which incorporated circumcision.

Again, burials almost always included rites which the Church condemned but which many Christians were unwilling to forgo: they feared the effect of omission upon the fate of the deceased or the way the deceased's spirit might treat them. They had also to cope with the pressure of relatives. The conflict between two ways of life could never be a private matter. Life in a village is public and at every point a particular issue must be seen as something fought out between two groups of communal pressure. But funerals once over might be put behind one. While undoubtedly problems at this point could express a profound clash between two sets of belief concerning death and the afterlife, a return to traditional funerary practice seldom permanently affected a Christian's Church status in the way that marriage matters tended to do. The preoccupation of the

Church, both Catholic and Protestant, with the regulation of marriage is nothing special to Africa, but it was inevitable, given such a preoccupation, that the African Church would become more or less permanently afflicted by a conflict between marital law and practice. 'One wife for a teacher. But a chief should have more.'[47] So should any rich man who wished to conform to a chiefly model. Missionaries greatly admired chiefs who remained genuinely monogamous, but they were few and far between. There were too many good social reasons for having more than one wife, and a senior wife herself might expect the additional help and prestige provided by junior colleagues. Christian matrimony, ring marriage, was regarded by missionaries as a great liberation for women, but there is plenty of evidence from the inter-war years that women themselves did not always see it that way. Teachers would lose their job if they failed to conform socially to mission requirements, but for almost everyone else the requirements of custom were very much superior. Over polygamy few Africans were ever convinced by the missionary case and hardly surprisingly. It was not an obviously strong one. But many ordinary men never wanted to be polygamous anyway, and in some societies, such as the matrilineal peoples of central Africa, polygamous marriage seems never to have been much practised outside chiefly circles.

It is rather in the enactment of marriage itself that the tension between custom and Church may best be seen. Almost every mission insisted that its members marry in church in front of a minister. Nothing else would be accepted as a valid Christian marriage. The rites of customary marriage were being rejected as inadequate because they never explicitly included a commitment to monogamy. Yet customary marriage continued to constitute marriage in the eyes of society. It is only too clear that for almost all Christians, at least those not in Church employ, customary marriage was essential, marriage in church an attractive extra which it would be nice to have sooner or later. But it could also be difficult and expensive, something which in many countries involved going a considerable distance to the principal mission church because it could not be performed in the village. A ring, a white dress, bridesmaids, a hired lorry to take them all to church: people were not opposed to all this, but they often did not get round to it. Moreover, if you were a

---

[47] R. Sweeting, 'The Growth of the Church in Buwalasi', pt. 2, *BSACH* 3 (1969–70), 24.

Catholic and marrying a Protestant, then it would not be possible anyway. Such a monogamous marriage between two Christians, unrecognized by the Church and incurring their lifelong excommunication, was now a quite common phenomenon, but customary requirements had been fulfilled and no African doubted that it was marriage.

Such matters of personal status did not, however, generally or necessarily challenge publicly the growing hegemony of Christianity. With a little duplicity they could be contained within it and it simply meant that some Christians remained unprotestingly non-communicant. Even matters of ancestral veneration, of shrines for the spirits, and occasional offerings were a personal or household matter. They might quietly be retained by otherwise diligent churchgoers. Such things seldom led to confrontation. What did lead to confrontation were traditional associations of one sort or another, a phenomenon of enormous public importance in many parts of Africa though absent elsewhere. They could take many forms. Not everyone was a member. Entry into a society could be a costly and time-consuming business. Their task was to uphold customary morality in one area or another of life. They were often responsible for wider rites of initiation into adulthood. They demonstrated their presence and power by dances and masquerades. They inevitably appealed to customary religious belief. Membership could be a *sine qua non* for recognition as someone of importance. Take the example of Ozo in Igboland. Only men who had taken the Ozo title could be accepted to hold political office, participate in village councils, or preside over the settlement of a dispute. But the Churches, particularly the Catholic Church, saw membership of Ozo as something essentially pagan. Title-holders on conversion had to renounce their titles and burn the insignia and cult objects connected with them. As Christians became more numerous, the consequent social problems grew more awkward. Some Christians took Ozo and were excommunicated in consequence. In 1942 the traditional ruler of Onitsha, Obi Okosi II, appealed to Bishop Heerey to agree to a 'settlement' whereby Christians could take the Ozo title. It would be stripped of all 'pagan, sacrificial and superstitious practices', it would give Christian candidates 'no powers to perform pagan priestly functions'. There would simply be payment of the cost of title, presentation of staff (the insignia of titleship), and an invitation by the candidate to members to a feast and dance. No, replied Bishop

Heerey, the staff is 'the very symbol of Ancestor-worship, which the very first of the Divine Precepts forbids'.[48] In reality Catholics continued to take the title, thus in 1948 the Catholics of Umuoji appealed again to Heerey. 'The "Ozo" title is a "sine qua non" in the rank and dignity of the Ibo man so much so that no Christian is allowed to claim his rights and privileges if he is not a member of this aristocratic order. In view of this some lukewarm Christians bowed themselves to it . . .'.[49] But they would have to wait until the different atmosphere of the mid-1960s for their petition to be heard.

It may be true that Catholic missionaries were on the whole less negative to African custom than Evangelicals, but that was more likely to be true of Frenchmen and Germans than of the Irish. Thus, Fr. Moreau, a French Jesuit who had founded the mission of Chikuni in Northern Rhodesia in 1905, could write in 1932:

Last Thursday there was a great gathering at Monze's grave at least 1,500 people. I went there myself and I preached to the crowd from a heap of stones . . . I told them about Monze whom I had known thirty years ago, who was then living on the very spot where they were gathered. I told them that if they his children gather now and then at his grave there was nothing wrong in that. If they gather together to pay honour and show loyalty to the departed chiefs there was nothing wrong. In that the Batongo meet us, we all believe that our departed friends are still in communication with us.[50]

Moreau was an unusually open-minded priest, and it seems that he actually wished to permit polygamous people to become practising Catholics. When he died in 1949 he was given a splendid traditional funeral with drumming, dancing, and feasting. It was a great honour, but the Irish missionaries who had now taken over Chikuni were deeply horrified at such 'pagan' rituals and a ceremony of reparation was held with sermons to condemn what had taken place. Clearly Moreau and Heerey saw the relationship of Christianity and tradition very differently, perhaps because one knew an African language extremely well, the other very poorly, but probably too because one had an underlying inclusivist, the other an exclusivist theology. But until the 1960s it was the viewpoint of Heerey that mostly prevailed.

Nowhere was confrontation stronger than in central Nyasaland

---

[48] V. Nwosu, *The Catholic Church in Onitsha 1885–1985* (Onitsha, 1985), 58–9.
[49] Ibid. 60.
[50] B. Carmody, 'Secular and Sacred at Chikuni 1905–1940', *JRA* 21 (1991), 134.

where the missionaries, both Catholic and Dutch Reformed, found themselves faced with the Chewa Nyau societies. They were male societies whose masked dances were performed at female initiation rites and at funerals. Their songs were sexually very explicit, their masks represented the spirits of bush and lineage. They reinforced traditional order and morality by staging its reversal. They could also be violent. Independent of chieftainships, of the State, and of the Church, they represented like many other societies especially in West Africa a populist power which was also secretive and in part oppressive. Catholic missionaries disliked Nyau exceedingly, particularly because it began enrolling schoolchildren, and they endeavoured to persuade the administration to ban it just as Presbyterians endeavoured to do the same in Kenya for female circumcision. District Commissioners, however, could not see the harm. Church advance was in consequence punctuated by battles with Nyau initiates over funerals as well as for the control of the young. It was not that traditional religion in central Malawi was in belief more profoundly opposed to Christianity than elsewhere; it was rather that the opposition was in many places diffused, while in others, as here it came to be, concentrated in a particular institution which enjoyed a greater power of public survival and to which missionaries had taken up a sharply hostile attitude. To no institution were they more opposed than a mask society. The opposition passed across to committed Christians. Fr. Tansi in the Igboland of the 1940s was confronting masquerades as fiercely as Legion of Mary activists like Peter Kalilombe (father of a future bishop) in Nyasaland at the same time. Yet modernization went on, schools increased, and the real influence of Nyau declined. As we approach the middle of the century, the importance for Church history of traditional beliefs comes to lie less in their ability to motivate external confrontationary forces (except in temporary alliance with political nationalism) and more in the internal reshaping of the Christian mind.

Salathiel Madziyire's account of Jeche Munyani Garajena may help us here. Madziyire was an Anglican priest in the Marandellas (Marondera) area of Rhodesia and Jeche was a prophet and rain-maker possessed by a Mhondoro spirit whom Madziyire had known well for many years and whose marvellous deeds, including the ability to spend hours at the bottom of a deep pool, snuff in hand, he records unquestioningly. Jeche, he tells us, could foretell the future, either by dreams or when he was possessed. He could foretell drought, rains, fortunes, misfortunes, illness. This wonderful man foretold the truth about the 1947 famine in Southern Rhodesia . . . In the 1950s, before his death, he told me of something that was to happen to me during my lifetime. I waited for it to happen and everything came true. I kept all this in my mind to test the type of tribal spirit that possessed him.[51]

In his youth, Madziyire continues, Jeche had been the first man to welcome missionaries. The first mass in the country had been celebrated in his mother's hut, but it was only in his final illness that he felt called to baptism and was given the new name of Abraham. Suitably for such a great rain-maker, there were three days of torrential rain at the time of his death and a great thunderstorm during his burial service. The point for us here is the integration of the two religions, old and new, both in Jeche and in Madziyire. It is the carrying-across of the religious consciousness of Jeche into that of Madziyire which matters. In the literature it may appear exceptional. Here the confrontatory rejection of the old by Fr. Tansi or Peter Kalilombe is the norm. But in life it is almost certainly the other way round and the more normal is rather that the deeply Christian consciousness of a Madziyire yet draws more than it is generally willing to admit upon a real validity in pre-Christian experience. Madziyire may be exceptional in admitting to it so openly but not in accepting it. It is at least another form of Africanization.

x. *Associational Religion: From Welfare Group and Manyano to Balokole and Jamaa*

The people who began to stand up to Nyau within Chewa village life were the Catholic activists of the Legion of Mary, a movement which was beginning to spread in Catholic Africa by the 1940s but would grow a good deal more in the 1950s: 45 presidia in Calabar diocese in 1939, 68 in 1952, 148 in 1957. Its significance lies in being a lay association, something of itself comparable to Nyau and therefore able to replace it. Where Christianity grows strong, where it escapes the dullness we have detected in none too intelligible services, a puritanical morality, and a preoccupation with schooling

---

[51] S. Madziyire, 'Heathen Practices in the Urban and Rural Parts of Marandellas Area and their Effects upon Christianity', in Ranger and Weller, *Themes in the Christian History of Central Africa*, 77.

which is useful but hardly for most people the business of a lifetime, it does so by sprouting a variety of associations. To some of these we will now turn.

Between 1910 and 1940 one finds in many parts of eastern and central Africa the emergence of local welfare associations, some temporary enough. At times missionaries actually founded them or became a president or vice-president, such as Owen and Arthur in Kenya. Elsewhere they simply encouraged their founding. Thus Dr Laws advised the first members of the North Nyasa Association to hold their meetings in public, send the minutes of their proceedings to the Resident Magistrate, and limit membership to men of good character and education. And on the whole this is what they did. The North Nyasa Association became the model for many others in Nyasaland and Northern Rhodesia, so Levi Mumba, its principal founder, was widely influential. He had been appointed the first African teacher of commercial subjects and bookkeeper at Livingstonia's Overtoun Institute in 1905 and was for many years Laws's right-hand man in business matters. Of the fifty-one members of the Mombera Association at Ekwendeni in 1924, twenty-two were mission teachers, eight government clerks (of whom seven had previously been mission teachers), two were ordained (but former teachers), two were chiefs (again, both ex-mission teachers).[52]

When associations grew up in towns rather than in the countryside, their membership was more diverse, but their character and aims changed relatively little. Intended to promote the corporate interests of the new group of English-speaking mission-educated people, they grew out of the more liberal Protestant missions— particularly missions like Livingstonia which had pushed secondary education hard—and reflected their political culture. The educators of Livingstonia and its like were educators for freedom, democracy, and secular progress, however cautiously its missionaries proposed such values and however slow they were to apply them to their own institutions. They gave what they had and they had nothing else. For Laws the Overtoun Institute was intended to replicate Aberdeen University. Inevitably it passed on the political culture of a free Scotland. At the same time the welfare associations sought a larger measure of elbow-room than mission life itself afforded. Their aims

[52] D. Cook, 'The Influence of Livingstonia Mission upon the Formation of Welfare Associations in Zambia 1912–1931', in Ranger and Weller, *Themes in the Christian History of Central Africa*, 103.

were secular, though their tone was often mildly ecclesiastical, but then the aims of Livingstonia were largely secular too. The welfare associations were essentially 'a place to feel at home' for the new Protestant-trained élite. Catholic missions contributed nothing to such a culture.

Welfare association members, nevertheless, could grow increasingly disillusioned with the missions which had nurtured them. Levi Mumba actually helped found the African National Church in 1929, and later still, in 1944, was the first President-General of the Nyasaland African Congress. Some association members joined independent Churches, some the African Methodist Episcopal Church, but the greater part probably had their eye too firmly on the secular city to wish to change ecclesiastical allegiance. Basically they represented a moderately independent way for the new Christian élite to shape itself, a way which in every country led on by the 1940s and 1950s to the formation of political parties. The leadership of each new congress, whether it was that of Levi Mumba or Dr Banda or Kenneth Kaunda, came in central Africa preponderantly out of the Livingstonia stable, just as in South Africa it had already come preponderantly from Lovedale and Adams College and in West Africa from Fourah Bay, Mfantsipim, and other Protestant institutions, Presbyterian, Congregationalist, Methodist, or Anglican. The relationship between the Churches and political parties is too complex for adequate treatment here and it would take us too deeply into wider political and social history. But it is absolutely true and extremely important to stress that African political life as it developed in English-speaking Africa was not only unimaginable without the input of the main Protestant missions but also long continued to function as, in a very real way, part of their life. Men like Luthuli, Z. K. Matthews, and indeed, among a younger generation, Oliver Tambo, belonged at one and the same time to a Church world and a political world. They did not see the two as contradictory. On the contrary one had both prepared them for the other and continued to provide some support for the other. It would be quite wrong to over-secularize the South African ANC before the end of the 1950s, though the bonds were undoubtedly weakening. When, however, any congress acquired a mass membership, and entered the business of pursuing immediate power, the mission Churches could come to look very different: their liberal areas small and tepid, their wider influence thrown firmly behind the colonial status quo. Hence the sort of nationalist–church tension, even the burning of missions, which erupted at times in the late 1950s. It was essentially a superficial and short-lived dimension of the independence struggle. Once the latter was over the earlier relationship was quite easily revived. The developing associational history of African nationalism, at least within English-speaking Africa, in the decades up to 1950 has to a considerable extent to be seen as the way in which Christians combined the African need for societies and the ideals of liberal Protestant secondary schools to create for themselves a context at once for personal advancement and political action.

They were entirely a matter for men. Neither custom nor the Church did much to encourage women in these years. Missionaries lamented the backwardness of female schooling, just as the Phelps-Stokes Reports had done, but they certainly did not succeed in greatly altering the sexual balance in education. Yet perhaps for that reason the female associations which were beginning to proliferate were all the more religious, as well as being in African terms innovative. The development by the 1940s of a network of societies of quite considerable size wholly controlled by women was a revolution for most of Africa even if the Manyanos of South Africa, the Rukwadzanos of Rhodesia, and comparable bodies elsewhere hardly look revolutionary to us. Deriving chiefly from Methodist inspiration, they were uniformed societies of respectably married women committed to the virtues and duties of Christian domesticity and to supporting one another in the troubles of life. The Rukwadzano member was committed to teaching her children Christian customs, to not cooking beer, smoking tobacco, or working in a tobacco field. She was committed to cleanliness, to sewing on the buttons of her husband's clothes, to hospitality, and to Church work. The founders and leaders were the wives of ministers, but ministers in no way controlled the Manyano and indeed were often irritated by it. Its regular meetings and collection of money were nevertheless coming to be recognized as a principal source of strength for Churches which had it. The very success of such an organization, as in Rhodesian Methodism, could, however, make the Church as a whole appear a 'women's Church' and be criticized accordingly. Certainly female Church attendance could proportionately be far higher for Methodism than elsewhere. Women were in fact less likely to be excommunicated for marital offences than men, they were less likely to be away as migrant labourers, they were less likely to be preoccupied with politics or drink. They were more likely to retain a commitment to the Church, and Manyano concretized that commitment. They were effectively excluded from Church office, but office was coming to mean less in ordinary African Christian life than association.

The same message is true if we turn to the East African Balokole 'Revival', by far the most famed of Christian associational movements to have emerged in these years. It grew out of the Rwanda Mission, an intensely conservative evangelical wing of CMS, largely staffed by Cambridge men, recruited from CICCU, Cambridge's Christian Union, of whom the most influential was Dr Joe E. Church, who arrived in Rwanda in 1927, imbued not only with Keswick Evangelicalism but also with the Oxford Group practice of public confession. Church became very friendly with Simeoni Nsibambi, a wealthy Muganda landowner, and his brother Blasio Kigozi. As a result Church at his hospital in Gahini, Rwanda, was helped by a flow of young Ganda Christians coming to work in Rwanda. The interaction between Church and his Ganda assistants produced Revival, whose first convention was held in September 1931 at Gahini. Annual conventions followed in different places, always with the same pattern: impassioned appeals to 'Awake', sin, repentance, 'Coming out of Egypt', separation, the Holy Spirit were its favourite topics, leading up to public confessions of guilt. At Kabale in September 1935 we read 'many had dreams, sometimes receiving strong impressions to read certain verses of the Bible which led them to put away some sin, beer-drinking for example'.[53] The sudden death of the deacon Kigozi in 1936 made him into a sort of patron saint of the Revival.

Church, Nsibambi, and their allies had two targets. One was the so-called 'dead' state of the Ganda Church fifty years after its mass conversion—a mix of establishment Anglican attitudes and Ganda traditionalist ones. It was criticizable for its tolerance of chiefly polygamy, traditional religious practices, and a preoccupation with power where the King and Prime Minister were publicly Protestant but hardly evangelical. The other target was 'modernism', which Church and other Rwanda missionaries with their CICCU background discovered in everyone a little less fundamentalist than themselves and especially in J. C. Jones, warden of the theological

[53] L. Barham, in J. Church, *Quest for the Highest* (1981), 117.

college of Mukono. There was at times an almost hysterical confession of 'sin', a fixation on the saving 'blood' of Christ, and unqualified condemnation of everything the Balokole or 'saved ones' did not regard as acceptable. To their neighbours the impression the Balokole gave could be much the same as that which members of a spirit Church produced elsewhere: an at times almost uncontrollable and infectious frenzy of enthusiasm.

Let us picture a group of revivalist preachers arriving at the village of Karuhembe in Ankole on an April morning in 1939, the first experience there of these *abomwoyo*, 'people of the spirit', as they were called, or *abarabukiirwe*, 'people who have received a revelation'. A crowd of young men and women, gathered by the local catechist, waited for them from nine o'clock. At two they arrived, singing exultantly:

> Hariyo ensi eshemeire
> There is a clean world
> Belonging to the saved only
> We perceive it clearly
> Jesus prepared it for us
> Oh, how beautiful it is.

A Mr Betsembire then preached on Genesis 3: 9 (God's question 'Where are you?' to Adam when he had sinned), and in the excitement of his presentation people began to confess their sins. We know of the occasion from its description by one of those converted, vividly remembered fifty-one years later.[54] Young revivalists in consequence threw away their bracelets and necklaces, they denounced the spirit cults practised in their homes, they ate taboo foods, red ants, and grasshoppers. They refused to go to dances. They cut down their beer banana plants and even their coffee trees, claiming that they sought no riches on earth.

In October 1941 thirty Balokole, including William Nagenda, the brother-in-law of Nsibambi, were expelled from Mukono theological college for refusing to obey its warden. They would not desist from imposing their ceaseless preachings on other students. While Bishop Stuart supported Jones he tried hard to reconcile the Balokole and avoid total schism. For many Christians the arrogant denunciations of worldliness by the young revivalists were deeply

---

[54] Y. Bamunoba, 'The Development of the Anglican Church in West Ankole 1900 to 1990', M.Phil. thesis (Leeds, 1990), 150–5.

shocking. One old clergyman who had been through Mwanga's persecution testified in Synod to how hard it was to have a lifetime's faith so cursorily dismissed. Here as so often there were two underlying models of Christian life, one stressing separation, the other inclusivity, and both can be seen as expressions of that elusive concept 'Africanization'. The revivalists were protesting at one, inclusivist, model of it and imposing another, because radical cleansing is as much a recognizable phenomenon within African religion as retentiveness. The most remarkable thing is, perhaps, that separation did not quite win the day with the Balokole themselves. They continued within the Church and in fact came to provide most of its leadership for the next generation.

Its influence continued to spread. Already in 1937 the Revival held a convention in Kenya. In 1939 there were conventions in the Sudan and Tanganyika. By 1953 Nagenda and Church were travelling to America, drawn there by the tentacles of the Billy Graham organization into which they could perfectly fit. There was in fact from one point of view absolutely nothing characteristically African in Revival. Joe Church can be said to be the father of every aspect of its doctrine and methods. Yet it can equally well be seen as a remarkable expression of African Christianity and a highly influential one, decisive for the spirit Protestantism would assume in several different countries and among Kenyan Presbyterians and Methodists and Tanzanian Lutherans as well as among Anglicans.

It was essentially a lay association, an ongoing fellowship linked by ethos and the singing of its famous Luganda hymn 'Tukutendereza Yezu', 'We praise you, Jesus, Jesus the Lamb. Your blood has cleansed me. I am grateful, Saviour.' Except for some relatively small cases in western Kenya and north-western Tanganyika it avoided becoming a Church of its own and avoided hierarchicalism. If most of the clergy at the time opposed it, most of the first group of African bishops later came from its ranks—Sabiiti, Shalita, Kariuki, Luwum, Kivengere—but it was not clerical and it crossed divides: black–white, tribal, and sexual, as well as denominational. Women were important in the movement and in general male–female relations among the Balokole were relatively egalitarian.

The Balokole were, above all, anti-traditionalist. While African theologians of the 1960s castigated missionaries for being so intolerant of African custom in what they required of the first generation of Christians, the Balokole castigated that same generation for their tolerance in accommodating the unchristian. They rejected bride-wealth and all the customary food taboos which other Christians still practised. When the Kabaka Daudi Cwa died in 1939 and his widow, the Namasole, became pregnant and wished to remarry, Bishop Stuart agreed to perform the ceremony. By tradition the Namasole must not remarry and most Ganda Christians were horrified at his action, but the Balokole supported him. It is clear that the Revival was on the one hand a huge protest against one form of Africanization of Christianity and yet on the other hand can rightly be seen as itself a major wave of Africanization—an appropriation of Christianity not through hierarchy or school but through a very typically African thing, a decentralized association unified by its singing and certain basic forms of behaviour. The breaking of food taboos and the very refusal to give or receive bride-wealth were themselves highly unifying things. It established a separation but also a new community. The closest comparison remains with Aladura in its principal Christ Apostolic form, but whereas in Nigeria the movement broke apart from Anglicanism, in Uganda it was contained.

The Revival found its most bitter moment of confrontation with tradition—or rather with neo-traditionalism—in the Kenya of the Mau Mau. Few of its members can have failed to sympathize with the defence of Kikuyu land against settler occupation, which provided the underlying will-power of Mau Mau, but the rising was not just a black–white war, it was also a Kikuyu civil war in which respected Kikuyu leaders like the murdered Chief Waruhiu and Harry Thuku took an outrightly anti-Mau Mau stance. This was very much a Christian position maintained by clergy like the Presbyterian Wanyoike Kamawe and the Anglican rural dean Obadiah Kariuki, himself a brother-in-law of Kenyatta. But it was in the villages that resistance was hardest, and it is clear that here it was very much a matter of the commitment of Balokole to their own vision of life. What was required by Mau Mau was the taking of its oaths sealed with blood, whether the blood of a goat or of the oath-taker himself. The blood of Christ was the central symbol of Revival. Through it, every Mulokole sang in the 'Tukutendereza' hymn, he or she was saved. 'I have drunk the blood of Christ, how then can I take your blood of goats?'[55] was a frequent reply of Christian Kikuyu

---

[55] E. Wiseman, *Kikuyu Martyrs* (1958), 45, cf. 38 and 40.

villagers who refused to enter Mau Mau. Some died in consequence. The Revival was one association. Mau Mau was another. Their meaning was symbolically incompatible.

Isoko in the Niger Delta had been swept by a movement of mass conversion between 1910 and 1920, as we saw in Chapter 10. A remote, low-lying land, it had never been other than intensely unhealthy for white people, and twenty years later its Christian communities almost entirely lacked any ordained ministry. By 1940 there was for a time not a single CMS missionary in the area. This was the context in which Anglican Adam's Preaching Society (AAPS) took its origins.[56] Adam Cornelius Igbudu, the son of a Christian polygamist with five wives, had little formal education but learned to read and write. He joined the CMS Church choir and soon became choirmaster. About 1928 he founded a 'prayer band' of young people who would descend dressed in flowing white robes on a particular community, singing and whistling. Adam's preaching was punctuated by dancing, while the hymns sung were mostly composed by the group members themselves. After their open-air campaigns, the group members would go round Christian homes to inspect their sanitary arrangements and the cleanliness of cooking utensils. Their message, like that of Harris twenty years earlier, was always one of this-worldly as well as other-worldly cleanliness. As the group grew and became more influential it encountered opposition from such older Church leadership as existed, but on the whole such missionaries as came to Isoko and, later, the Nigerian Bishop of Benin, Agori Iwe, supported Adam, who by the 1940s was also becoming a healer and miracle-worker. Adam's ministry may be compared with that of Mother Paul in the Transkei at much the same time. Both crossed Church frontiers while remaining basically Anglican, but what is interesting for us here about the AAPS is as a development among mostly illiterate people of an association, held together by singing, dancing, or dress, something in various ways comparable with the secret societies of traditional society. Its descent upon an Isoko or Urhobo village may not have seemed so different from that of Nyau among the Chewa. In comparison with the Balokole, it was a great deal less purely evangelical. It had almost no input from outside and no educated membership, yet it fulfilled the

[56] Akama, 'A Religious History of the Isoko People', 294–315.

same function of creating within the missionary Church a fellowship in which its members could feel at home.

One further lay association developing in these years may also be considered: Jamaa. Here, as with the Balokole, we start with a European founder, Placide Tempels, the author of *Bantu Philosophy*. His own encounter with African experience moved on from that rather cerebral work, through a sort of second conversion, to a realization that the Christianity he sought to communicate was much more a matter of love than of understanding. We find this emphasis on love already in his 'Catéchèse Bantoue' of 1948. By 1953 Jamaa was being born in his mission at Ruwe, near Kolwezi, in the interaction between Tempels and a group of married couples which later, in the myth of its origins, became the 'Seven', the first perfect Jamaa community. Tempels left Africa in April 1962. A few other Belgian Franciscan priests were intimately involved in the movement, but essentially it went on to become an almost secret association of many thousands of committed married Christians, practising a pattern of prayer, instruction, and moral and ritual behaviour which Tempels had modelled fairly deliberately upon the secret societies of the Luba, as seen through the spectacles of a Flemish mystic. More than any other of our examples, Jamaa developed a language and esoteric doctrine of its own, centred upon a series of initiations separating members from non-members and involving an 'encounter', interpersonal, spiritual, but also profoundly sexual. The attractiveness for Africans of Jamaa's Franciscan overtones and the primacy of love may be demonstrated too by the remarkable movement developing at just the same time over the border in Northern Rhodesia led by a catechist and ex-seminarian, Emilio Mulolani. The similarities in spirituality are striking. Emilio's followers were forced out of the Catholic Church and became in 1958 the independent Bana ba Mutima, but his sister and close confidant for many years, Mother Bernadetta Stuart Chanda, became the first Mother-General of the Sisters of the Infant Jesus, and his brother, Leo Makumbi, President of the Third Order of St Francis. The appeal of Franciscan spirituality and an African-led community is clear for all three. The completeness of separation between Emilio and Catholicism should not, then, be overstressed. Jamaa, too, was more than once on the verge of complete episcopal condemnation.

The relationship of husband and wife in Jamaa was renewed by a sort of mystical marriage between the husband and Bikira Maria, the wife and Bwana Yezu Kristu, which had to be achieved through a dream experience. Authoritative interpretation of the complexities and obscurities of Jamaa teaching and practice, distinguishing the original intentions of Tempels from their development in the so-called 'Katete', deviationist groups, is well beyond us here. Some priests were enthusiastic members, others deeply suspicious. What matters for our argument is the way a Christian life originally offered by missionaries in a very hierarchical manner, leaving room for little but extreme passivity on the part of most people, became transformed in the context of a sort of semi-secret voluntary association, which functioned not as a separate Church but as an additional society controlled by its members.

Jamaa and the Balokole derive from white prophets, Tempels and Church, belonging to opposite ends of the spectrum of European Christianity. Yet they had a surprising amount in common. Each was a missionary charismatic founder with quite exceptional ability to cross the colour bar and create an intense feeling of fellowship wholly transcending it. Both movements were emphatically lay with a high view of marriage—Western and nuclear rather than African—and a low view of hierarchy. Both were very apolitical with a spirituality of separation, not transformation. Both were intensely Christ-centred. Both seemed often on the edge of schism, but remained profoundly uninterested in making, or being driven to, a formal break.

Almost certainly the most significant development within African Christianity in the period from 1920 to 1960 consists in the emergence of a range of such movements. Some do turn into independent Churches, some into almost secular bodies, but many remain emphatically within the context of a mission Church. Some stress a certain secrecy. Some flaunt their uniforms. Most are in a way evangelistic, but, still more, provide an integrated context for weekday living.

Zionism and Manyano in southern Africa, Aladura, a submerged Kimbanguism, the Balokole, Anglican Adam's Preaching Society, and Jamaa were all associated movements, holding considerable numbers of people in active Christian commitment. Between them they contained a very large part of whatever vitality African Christianity had in the 1950s. There was generally some measure of external input, but each developed in a specifically African way to become something very different from what might be found elsewhere. Basically they were all at the time lay movements, that is to say hardly if at all dependent upon professional clerical leadership. In all of them women were important—far more important than within the Church's missionary-shaped structures. Such movements, when within a mission Church, all constituted a degree of threat to its unity, and, still more, to clerical and missionary control. As movements they were of their nature one-sided, preoccupied with certain things, unconcerned with others, and open to criticism as such. Yet each, if allowed to remain, provided in the longer run strength rather than divisiveness, the strength both of a committed base and even of a new leadership. The fact is that only through such movements, perilous as each seemed to missionary eyes, could a Church switch from depending upon abroad for its vitality to finding it within its own lay roots. The history of African Christianity in this period really needs to be a history of how far this was happening and of where it was not happening.

Of our several examples, only Jamaa had a Catholic background and it is significant that it is the last to appear and the most clerical in originating influence. While Catholicism had grown so immensely in Africa since the First World War, both numerically and institutionally, its particularly hierarchical ethos and its ever greater number of professional missionaries were still inhibiting the associational development where in the long run strength could only be found. In a way the later phasing of its missionary expansion permitted a later phasing too in associational response. Nevertheless, two associational aspects of Catholicism which were making much progress by the 1950s deserve a mention. On the one side was the Legion of Mary and various other organizations of lay Catholic Action favoured in the latter years of Pius XII. While the Legion's Dublin model was in no way modified for Africa, it was taking extensive root in many places. It was certainly Legion of Mary activists among the Bemba who prevented the Catholic Church from being almost swept away by Lenshina's Lumpa, just as it was Chewa legionaries who were willing to stand up in central Nyasaland to Nyau harassment.

The other aspect was the growth of sisterhoods. Progress here was very varied, again like the clergy more in parts of East Africa than elsewhere. By the mid-1950s there were still hardly 100 African sisters in eastern Nigeria, but far more than 500 in Buganda alone. While modern Catholic sisterhoods in one way certainly represent a clericalized and hierarchical control of women in imitation of male clericalism, they also represent where they have become numerous an associational model of Christian life open to women. While their existence might be seen to inhibit more free-flowing associational developments it fulfilled some at least of the needs met elsewhere by such societies. Mother Chanda's Sisters of the Infant Jesus should not be seen as wholly different in aspiration and achievement from the third order of St Francis of one of her brothers or the Bana ba Mutima of the other.

x. *A Modern Leadership*

If Catholics in the 1950s had still contributed relatively little to any Africanization of Church life, they had also made little of an intellectual contribution. Here again it is to Protestantism that we have first to turn and, not unnaturally, to one of the countries of West Africa where Protestant Christianity earliest took root and which also developed most strongly a Western-style cultural life. The Methodist and Presbyterian Churches of the Gold Coast were well established by the end of the nineteenth century. Indeed, in Casely Hayford's *Ethiopia Unbound* one can detect already in the first decades of the twentieth century a slightly precious, almost post-Protestant Western culture. In Aggrey we have, on the contrary, in the 1920s the white missionary's ideal black man, the educational co-operator trusted on all sides, the man whose quintessential message was that to play a good tune on the piano you needed to use both sets of keys, the black and the white. When the lawyer and journalist J. B. Danquah published his *Akan Doctrine of God* in 1944, in explanation and defence both of African monotheism and of the ethical system of ancestor veneration, he was doing so as a good lay Presbyterian and someone who at almost the same time was helping to found the United Gold Coast Convention. When in 1949 the University of Legon was founded, the Presbyterian minister C. G. Baëta, who had studied his theology in Basel and at King's College, London, and attended the great missionary conference at Tambaram, India, in 1938, became at once a lecturer in its Department of Divinity. The same year F. L. Bartels, a Methodist layman, became headmaster of Mfantsipim, most prestigious of mission schools in West Africa. Later he would write a distinguished history of Ghanaian Methodism. When in 1955 the Christian Council of the Gold Coast sponsored a conference on 'Christianity and African culture' it was another

Methodist layman, Dr Kofi Busia, a Professor of Sociology and a little later Leader of the Opposition in Parliament to Dr Nkrumah, who appealed to the Church to come to grips with traditional practices and with the world-view that these beliefs and practices imply. Busia, Baëta, Bartels, and Danquah represented a mature Christian élite, deeply committed to their Protestantism, nationalist through and through yet very moderately so in expression, mildly anxious to reassert the values of traditional religion and culture.

Looking at such people it seemed obvious to the more perceptive that a full transfer of leadership, organizational and intellectual, from missionary to African, could not be much longer delayed. The atmosphere of the 1950s was to this extent one of harvest, of a sense of recognized achievement. When the International Missionary Council met in Ghana in 1958 its greatest theoretician, Professor Freytag, practically appealed for 'fewer and fewer missionaries'. 'Who would want', he asked, 'to impede the development of Churches which in some degree depends on the absence of missionaries?'[57] The first meeting of the All African Conference of Churches, taking place in Ibadan in January 1958 under the chairmanship of Sir Francis Ibiam, a Presbyterian Igbo, demonstrated both the desire to share the Gold Coast model continentally and the way in which west coast Protestantism was naturally taking the lead. Suppression of the African voice in South Africa left no alternative. Sam Amissah, another Ghanaian Methodist layman and educationalist, would become its first General Secretary.

While the Methodist and Presbyterian Churches of Ghana and Nigeria, as they stood in the late 1950s, provided in a very real way a model for the future to which many Churches throughout the continent would come in some way to conform across the next three decades, they also stood in considerable contrast to the immediate reality of most places. The most strident contrast was to be found in South Africa, where a quite opposite model was being enforced, despite a fully comparable group of black leaders, many of them men of deep Christian commitment and considerable academic and political maturity. Such a one was Albert Luthuli, President of the African National Congress from 1952. In accepting that position he made clear that for thirty years he had been 'knocking in vain

<hr />

[57] Walter Freytag, 'Changes in the Patterns of Western Missions', in R. Orchard (ed.), *The Ghana Assembly of the International Missionary Council* (1958), 140.

patiently, moderately and modestly at a closed and barred door'.
Now, instead, he would take the path of Congress while recognizing
that 'The Road to Freedom is via the Cross.'[58] Luthuli had been a
Vice-President of the Christian Council. His combination of
commitments to Church and Congress was not exceptional. James
Calata, for instance, had combined being Anglican parish priest at
Cradock with being General Secretary of the ANC all through the
1940s. He was also, for good measure, President of the Saint Ntsikana
Memorial Association. Consider Z. K. Matthews and D. D. T.
Jabavu, two others among a distinguished group of black South
Africans at their peak of achievement in the 1950s, a group very
similar to that in the Gold Coast which we have been discussing, but
destined here not to an extension but an extinction of their role.
Jabavu was the first member of staff of Fort Hare University College,
appointed in 1915, its Professor of African Languages. The existence
of the college had owed much to the exertions of his father. He was a
Methodist lay preacher, a patron of the Saint Ntsikana Memorial
Association, a prolific writer in both Xhosa and English, an attender
at numerous international conferences. His colleague, Z. K.
Matthews, Acting Principal of Fort Hare, had formerly been a
colleague of Luthuli on the staff of the Congregationalist Adams
College in Natal. All three had been tolerant gradualists, men of the
Church and of education before entering, if at all, into politics. But
Matthews, like Luthuli, had joined the leadership of the ANC. Both
were among the 156 people arrested in December 1956 and charged
with treason. In due course, several years later, every charge was
quashed, but Matthews was then again arrested after the Sharpeville
massacre in 1960 and held uncharged for five months. Meanwhile,
Jabavu had died and Fort Hare had been seized by the government.
Z. K. resigned from an institution whose character as a genuine
African university had ceased to exist. In 1961 he joined the staff of
the World Council of Churches in Geneva, his exile from South
Africa symbolizing the end of an era in its black leadership.

Among the 156 arrested in 1956 was a much younger man, Oliver
Tambo, a teacher at St Peter's, Rosettenville. He had considered for a
time applying for ordination. He was, instead, to become one of the
principal leaders of a radicalized ANC. The pressures of the political
struggle would distance it from a Church unwilling to challenge

---

[58] A. Luthuli, *Let My People Go: An Autobiography* (1962), 238.

racial injustice to a comparable extent, yet Tambo's own close friendship with Trevor Huddleston, established in youth when they worked together at Rosettenville, would survive a long lifetime and significantly affect the relationship between black nationalism and Christianity. For a long time, however, both Huddleston and Tambo would be exiles from South Africa.

Upon the Catholic side there had been no comparable development of either lay leadership or a political, literary, or theological culture anywhere in Africa. In 1956, with quite startling suddenness, a book of essays entitled *Des prêtres noirs s'interrogent* was published in Paris. A dozen young black priests studying in Europe and coming from Dahomey and Togo, Cameroon, the Belgian Congo, and Rwanda were its authors. The principles of missionary adaptation as it should be but failed to be in practice, the relationship between the African and the biblical mentality, the rites of traditional religion upon the one hand, of the Roman liturgy upon the other— here for the first time we find a theological voice within African Catholicism interested in, and willing to question, every aspect of the Church's life and teaching as missionaries had been establishing it. Not that these essays were anything but orthodox, distressed as many missionaries undoubtedly were by their publication. All the more remarkable then that the book included a preface written by Marcel Lefebvre, Archbishop of Dakar and Apostolic Delegate to French West Africa. A seal of Roman approval was being placed upon public expressions of opinion by African priests of a sort which would have been unthinkable a decade or two earlier. It must be noted that, unlike the Protestant adaptationist theology in the Gold Coast, this volume grew out of no institution existing in Africa and its thinking was not shared by a Catholic laity in the way that was the case with that of Baëta or Amissah. The culture of its construction was entirely clerical. Its authors had studied their theology in Rome, Louvain, or Paris and had been influenced not by missionaries but by the new wave of West European progressive theology, the writings of Congar, Danielou, and De Lubac. When they returned to Africa they would have the greatest difficulty in establishing an institutional milieu for their ideas in Churches which had developed with a very different orientation and in seminaries still for the most part directed by missionaries of a very different school of thought. It would take the Second Vatican Council and a good deal more to earth the themes of *Des prêtres noirs s'interrogent* within the African Church. Nevertheless, its authors, far from being suppressed, were soon being made bishops or, like Vincent Mulago at Lovanium, professors in the newly developing universities. Here, even more than elsewhere, the 1950s was a decade less of achievement than of promise.

It was, after all, a decade in which control of the Church remained hierarchically, almost everywhere, in foreign hands. There was not a single black archbishop, Catholic or Anglican, throughout the continent, before 1960. Only in Ethiopia had the change occurred when, after more than a thousand years of Egyptian abunas, an Ethiopian, Basilios, was consecrated in Cairo. Nevertheless, the Rome of Pope John XXIII had come to recognize that, with political independence on the way, the future of a young but quickly growing Church must now lie with African leadership. As the Second Vatican Council was about to begin a considerable number of black archbishops suddenly appeared: Yago in the Ivory Coast, Zoungrana in Upper Volta, Gantin in Dahomey, and Amissah in Ghana. Zoa would soon follow in Cameroon and Mabathoana in Basutoland. Joseph Kiwanuka, Bishop of Masaka for more than twenty years, was moved to become Archbishop of Kampala. It symbolized the end of an era. He and his clergy had in a way been on trial for those twenty years, for most of them almost alone. Now African bishops were multiplying upon every side and Kiwanuka himself would move to preside over the great cathedral at Lubaga in Uganda's capital, awaiting the arrival in 1962 of political independence. A little later he would be joined by the first Anglican Ugandan archbishop, Erica Sabiiti, a member of the Balokole.

A new age of the African Church was about to begin. An initial reaction would be that with political independence the Churches mattered less. As one young railwayman put it a couple of years later, 'One of the good things about Independence is that it means you don't have to go to Church on Sundays.'[59] But amusement with that expression of relief might induce us to miss the point. Political independence helped liberate the Churches from their colonial links without in any way diminishing their usefulness or attractiveness. Indeed the new states would come to find they needed the Churches and even the missions too, even more than had the old ones; moreover, the people would find that, when their governments grew

[59] R. D. Grillo, *African Railwaymen* (1973), 152. The field-work was done 1964–5.

tyrannical, the Churches might be the only institutions able to mitigate or challenge the new bondage.

Independence also provided a further spur for Africanization. In many ways and in most places the 1960s constituted almost a golden age for African Christianity, an age of optimism and progressive thinking in which black and white co-operated more affectionately than they had ever done before. It was a decade in which missionaries would still retain an undeniable importance but were all the same inexorably passing into the wings of the stage. At the centre stood men like Kiwanuka, Sabiiti, and younger colleagues like Zoa and Gantin. Nearly all these men had experienced the rein of missionary control and had at times fretted under it. What, nevertheless, is striking about them is the continuity they represent with their white predecessors. The new ecclesiastical leadership had grown out of the soil of the old. Kiwanuka and Sabiiti are two examples of men with decades of spiritual and pastoral experience obtained within a Church firmly contained within the colonial order. While they wanted more black priests and black bishops, they were too loyal to their formation to seek any sudden or startling change. If change was to come it would be due much more to the pressures of the new political order and of the theological revolution about to sweep across the world Church in the wake of the Second Vatican Council. Where in the Catholic Church there was but one black bishop in Africa of the Latin Rite in 1950 and only about twenty when Pius XII died in 1958, there would soon be many hundreds. At every level and in almost every denomination the quantitative growth of African Christianity would be formidable. A new era had begun, ecclesiastical as much as political, an era whose closure is not in the early 1990s yet evident.

African Church history 1960–90 undoubtedly grows out of the experiences we have examined in the late colonial period, but the scale, the challenges, and the context are so different that 1960 remains the most appropriate point to call a halt to this particular chronicle, a point many of us can still well remember and yet one already quite remote from the African Church of the 1990s. Yet that very remoteness can enable us to achieve an historical focus too elusive in regard to happenings more recent. Here then in the late 1950s we will call a halt, contemplating Churches which had already attained a size, a strength, and a leadership missionaries of a half-century earlier could hardly have imagined possible. Yet the scale by then achieved may in its turn seem slight in comparison with that of the 1990s when African Christianity had doubled and redoubled to become one of the largest and most lively segments of the world Church. Desmond Tutu, ordained a priest within a white-ruled Church and a racialist state of the late 1950s, would be Archbishop of Cape Town and a figure of world-wide renown by the 1990s. The problems of the African Church might multiply, but its prayerful character and its cheerful hopefulness would not diminish and would continue to constitute of themselves a very African contribution to the life of Christianity in an age of depression. Whatever else had happened and for whatever reason, it would certainly seem true that from the age of the scramble to that of independence Ethiopia had held out its hands to God.

APPENDIX 1

KINGS OF ETHIOPIA AND KONGO
REFERRED TO IN THE TEXT

ETHIOPIA

Ezana	Mid–4th century
Caleb	Mid–6th century
Zagwe Dynasty	12th–13th century
Yimrha-Kristos	
Lalibala	
The New 'Solomonic' Line	
Yikunno-Amlak	1270–85
Yagbe'a Seyon	1285–94
Amda Seyon	1314–44
Sayfa–Ar'ad	1344–71
Dawit	1380–1412
Tewodros I	1412–13
Yishaq	1413–30
Zara Ya'iqob	1434–68
Baida Maryam	1468–78
Eskender	1478–94
Na'od	1494–1508
Lebna Dengel	1508–40
Galawdewos	1540–59
Minas	1559–63
Sarsa Dengel	1563–97
Jakob	1597–1603, 1605–7
Za Dengel	1603–5
Susenyos	1607–32
Fasiladas	1632–67
Yohannes I	1667–83
Iyasu I	1683–1706
Takla Haymanot	1706–8
Takla Giyorgis	1779–1800, intermittently
Tewodros II	1855–68
Yohannes IV	1872–89

Menelik   1889–1913
Haile Selassie I   1930–74

KONGO

João I	Nzinga Nkuwu	?–1506
Afonso I	Mvemba Nzinga	1506–43
Diogo I	Nkumbi Mpudi	1545–61
Bernardo I		1561–67
Alvaro I	Nimi Lukeni	1568–87
Alvaro II	Mpanzu Nimi	1587–1614
Alvaro III	Nimi Mpanzu	1615–22
Pedro II	Nkanga Mbemba	1622–4
Garcia I	Mbemba Nkanga	1624–6
Garcia II	Nkanga Lukeni	1641–61
Antonio I	Vita Nkanga	1661–5
Pedro IV	Nsamu Mbemba	1695–1718
Garcia V	Nkanga Mbemba	1803–30
Pedro V	Elelo	1859–91

APPENDIX 2
MAPS

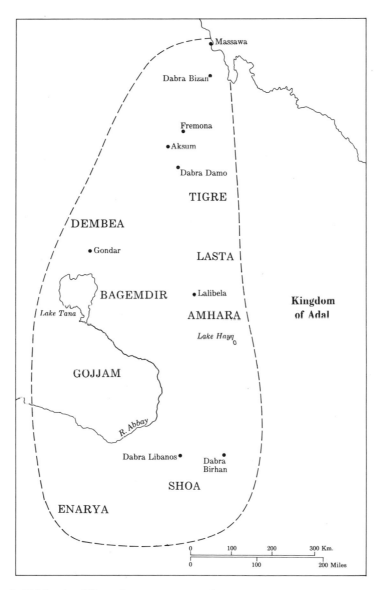

Map 1. Ethiopia, fifteenth to seventeenth centuries

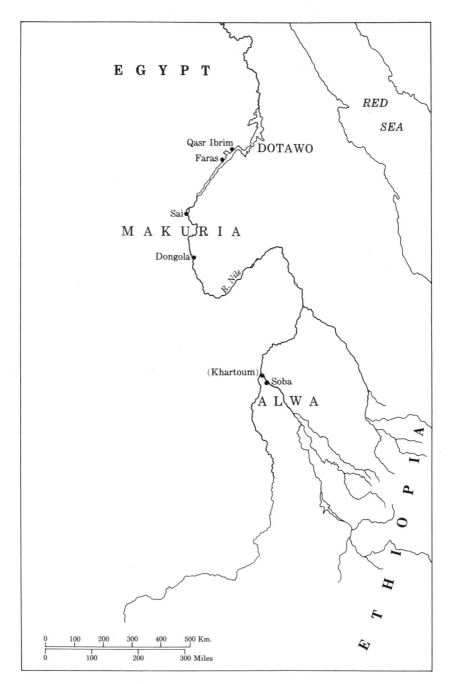

Map 2. Christian Nubia

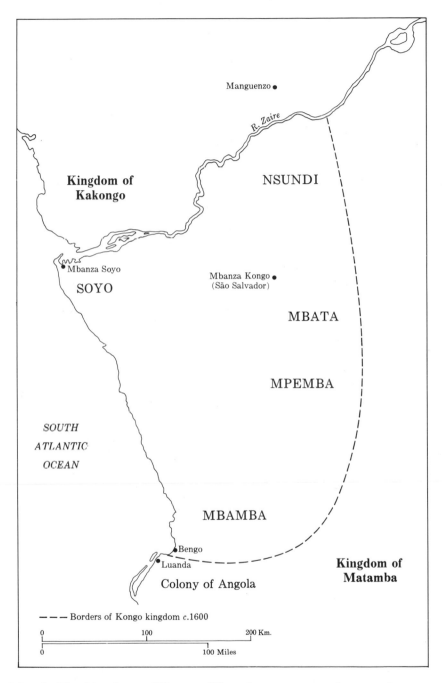

Map 3. The kingdom of Kongo, fifteenth to seventeenth centuries

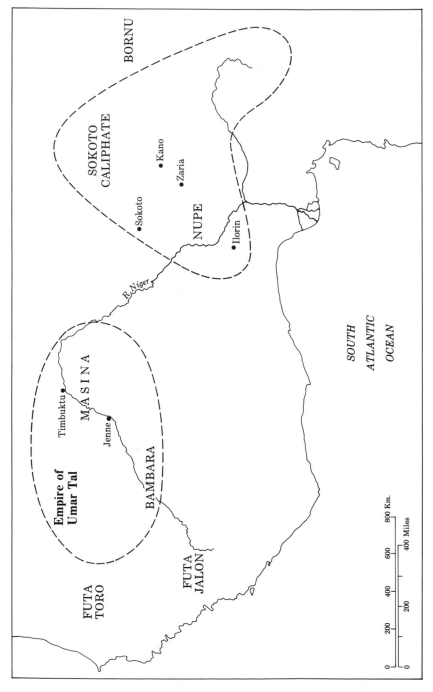

Map 4. Islam in West Africa and the nineteenth-century Fulani empires

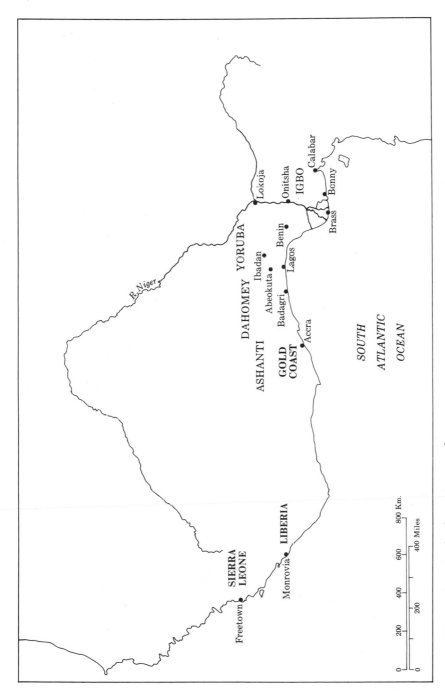

Map 5. West Africa in the late nineteenth century

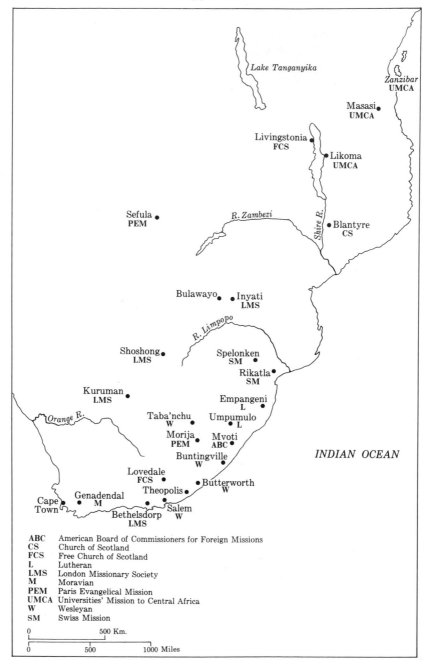

Map 6. Protestant missions in South and East Africa established by 1885. This includes only a small proportion of those in Cape Colony and Natal

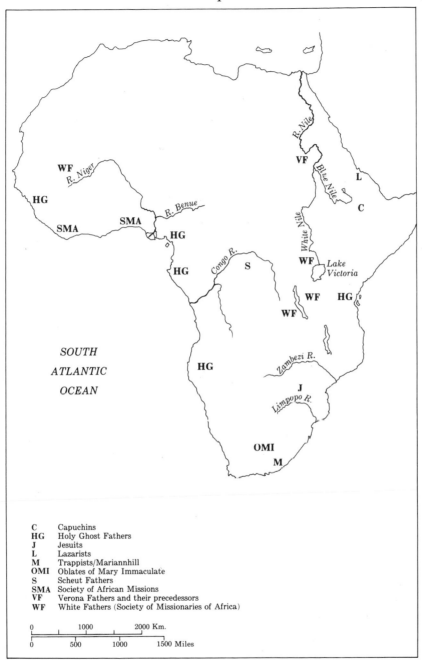

C Capuchins
HG Holy Ghost Fathers
J Jesuits
L Lazarists
M Trappists/Mariannhill
OMI Oblates of Mary Immaculate
S Scheut Fathers
SMA Society of African Missions
VF Verona Fathers and their precedessors
WF White Fathers (Society of Missionaries of Africa)

Map 7. The principal Catholic missionary societies at work in Africa between 1850 and 1890

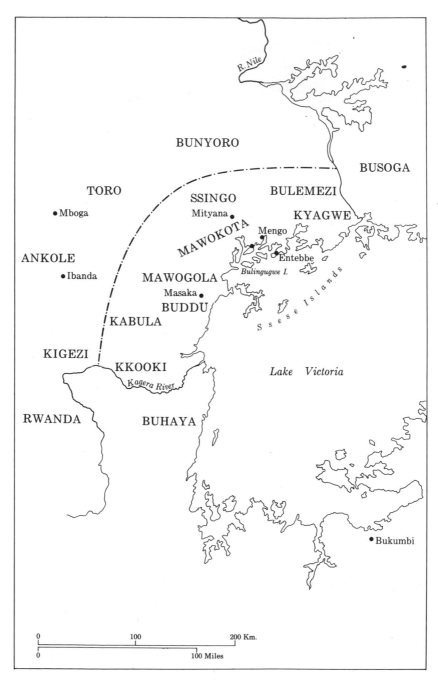

Map 8. Buganda and its neighbours, late nineteenth century

BIBLIOGRAPHY

Place of publication is London unless otherwise stated.

GENERAL

African history, apart from that of the Mediterranean and Ethiopian areas, had hardly started to be taken seriously until the 1950s. Before that there was little more than the history of white people—Arabs and Europeans—in Africa. A fair date for the effective beginning of the new African historiography is 1960, 'the year of Africa' in which so many countries became independent, including black Africa's two giants, Nigeria and Zaïre, but also the year in which the *Journal of African History* began. In consequence, in this field, more than in most areas of history, one has largely to limit a useful bibliography to works published within the last thirty years.

1. *General Histories*

There are two standard general histories of the continent, each in eight volumes: J. D. Fage and Roland Oliver (eds.), *Cambridge History of Africa* (Cambridge, 1977–86) and the *UNESCO General History of Africa* (1981–). These are invaluable for reference at every point of our story but can best be supplemented by the main regional histories. The earliest of these is the three-volume *History of East Africa* (Oxford), i, ed. R. Oliver and G. Mathew (1963), ii, ed. V. Harlow, E. M. Chilver, and Alison Smith (1965), iii, ed. D. A. Low and Alison Smith (1976). The other major regional histories are: J. F. Ajayi and Michael Crowder (eds.), *The History of West Africa*, 2 vols.; this was very considerably rewritten for the third edition (1985), which must be used; Monica Wilson and Leonard Thompson (eds.), *The Oxford History of South Africa*, 2 vols. (1969); and the youngest of the series, David Birmingham and Phyllis M. Martin (eds.), *The History of Central Africa*, 2 vols. (1983). J. D. Fage, *A History of Africa* (1978) and Basil Davidson, *Africa: History of a Continent*, rev. edn. (1972), magnificently illustrated, may be the best of the single-volume histories, though the latter at least is somewhat dated in its perspective. J. D. Fage, *A Guide to Original*

Sources for Precolonial Western Africa published in European Languages (1987) and G. S. P. Freeman-Grenville, *Chronology of African History* (1973) are useful tools. The annual *Africa Bibliography* (Manchester, 1984–90; Edinburgh, 1991–) is indispensable.

Among an almost infinite number of other general works the following regional collections of selected documents may be recommended: G. S. P. Freeman-Grenville, *The East African Coast: Select Documents from the First to the Earlier Nineteenth Century* (Oxford, 1962), Thomas Hodgkin, *Nigerian Perspectives: An Historical Anthology*, 2nd edn. (1975), and John Hargreaves, *France and West Africa: An Anthology of Historical Documents* (1969). Finally, John Iliffe, *The African Poor* (Cambridge, 1987) provides a fascinating overview of a particular theme.

2. *Missionary and Christian History*

The only other major recent history of Christianity in Africa as a whole is Bengt Sundkler and Christopher Steed's forthcoming *Africa: A Church History* (Cambridge). C. P. Groves, *The Planting of Christianity in Africa*, 4 vols. (1948–58) remains extremely useful, at least from the late eighteenth century on, for the amount of information it contains as a thoroughly reliable survey of missionary developments; a massive and very careful work, it came a little too early to benefit from the new historiography. To these may be added three symposia: C. G. Baëta (ed.), *Christianity in Tropical Africa* (1968), Giuseppe Ruggieri (ed.), *Église et histoire de l'église en Afrique* (Paris, 1988), and O. Kalu (ed.), *African Church Historiography: An Ecumenical Perspective* (Berne, 1988), together with Adrian Hastings, *African Catholicism* (1989), Richard Gray, *Black Christians and White Missionaries* (1990), and two shorter essays of interpretation: Noel King, *Christian and Muslim in Africa* (1971) and Adrian Hastings, *African Christianity* (1976). See also, for a critique of what had gone before, the influential appeal of J. Ade Ajayi and E. Ayandele, 'Writing African Church History', in *The Church Crossing Frontiers: Essays on the Nature of Mission in Honour of Bengt Sundkler* (Uppsala, 1969), 90–108. Two recent West African surveys are L. Sanneh, *West African Christianity* (1983), and J. K. Agbeti, *West African Church History*, 2 vols. (Leiden, 1986 and 1991).

Two much-used works of missionary history by masters in their field, chiefly upon the Protestant side, may also be noted: K. S. Latourette, *A History of the Expansion of Christianity*, 7 vols. (1937–45), and Stephen Neill, *A History of the Christian Missions* (1964; rev. 2nd edn. 1986). Both authors were more at home in other parts of the world and the African sections of these books are not among their stronger parts but the long chapter in Latourette, vol. v, on missionaries in nineteenth-century Africa, remains useful. On the Catholic side are the rather uneven four volumes of Mgr. S.

Delacroix (ed.), *Histoire universelle des missions catholiques* (Paris, 1956–9). The five large volumes of Josef Metzler (ed.), *Sacrae Congregationis de Propaganda Fide Memoria Rerum 1622–1972* (Rome, 1971–6), are essential for Catholic missionary history from the seventeenth century on.

3. Bibliographies

No less necessary for Catholic missionary history are the African volumes of Robert Streit, OMI and Johannes Dindinger, OMI (eds.), *Bibliotheca Missionum* (Freiburg, 1951–4), listing all known documents and publications by year. These volumes, entitled *Afrikanische Missionsliteratur*, are divided as follows: 15, AD 1053–1599; 16, 1600–99; 17, 1700–1879; 18, 1880–1909; 19 and 20, 1910–40. In addition to this, publications since the early 1930s are listed in the indispensable annual *Bibliographia Missionaria* (Vatican City), first published in 1934 and now edited by W. Henkel and J. Metzler, OMI. For an account of the development of both *Bibliotheca* and *Bibliographia* see Willi Henkel, 'The Legacy of Robert Streit, Johannes Dindinger, and Johannes Rommerskirchen', *IBMR* 6 (1982), 16–21. For the Jesuits use may also be made of Laszlo Polgar, SJ, *Bibliographie sur l'histoire de la Compagnie de Jésus 1901–1980* (Rome, 1986), ii, Africa, 507–30. In the last twenty years the *Bibliographia Missionaria* has become increasingly ecumenical but remains predominantly Roman Catholic.

The nearest Protestant equivalents are to be found in the quarterly review of missionary literature in the *International Review of Mission* (Geneva) and in the regular missiological abstracts of *Missionalia* (Pretoria). For South Africa, Lesotho, Swaziland, Botswana, Namibia, and Zimbabwe there is a 6,000-entry bibliography entitled *History of the Church in Southern Africa: A Select Bibliography of Published Material to 1980*, ed. J. W. Hofmeyer and K. E. Cross (Pretoria, 1986).

4. Guides to Archives

For archival research the following guides to manuscript material are available. An eight-volume *Guide to the Sources of the History of Africa* has been published with UNESCO support by the International Council on Archives (1970–83), country by country. The first volume, *Quellen zur Geschichte in den Archiven der Bundesrepublik Deutschland*, has a useful section on the archives of the *Rheinische Missionsgesellschaft* at Wuppertal-Barmen, 115–22. But the most valuable volume for our purposes is vol. vii, *Guida delle fonti per la storia dell'Africa a Sud del Sahara negli Archivi della Santa Sede e negli Archivi Ecclesiastici d'Italia* by Lajus Pasztor (1983). In this, besides an invaluable 150-page survey of African material within the Vatican's principal *archivio segreto* (including an important section on the nunciature of Lisbon, 211–32), there are particularly useful sections on the archives of Propaganda Fide (253–60), the Jesuits (302–13), the White Fathers (388–413), and the Capuchins. For the last named, this includes not only their *archivio generale* (337–42) but also the Italian provincial archives (463–82). To this, for Catholics, may be added J. C. Baumont, 'Une source de l'histoire du xixe et du debut du xxe siècle: Archives et publications de l'Oeuvre de la Propagation de la Foi', *HIA* 3 (1976) (an archive in Lyons), and the two volumes of S. Luciani and I. Taddia (eds.), *Fonti Comboniane per la storia dell'Africa nord-orientale*, i (Bologna, 1986), ii (Cagliari, 1988).

The five-volume series of *Guides to Materials for West African History* is also invaluable: Patricia Carson on Belgium and Holland (1962), A. F. C. Ryder on Portuguese archives (1965), J. R. Gray and D. S. Chambers, Italian archives (1965), Patricia Carson, French archives (1968), and Noel Matthews, United Kingdom archives (1973). T. W. Baxter and E. E. Burke, *Guide to the Historical Manuscripts in the National Archives of Rhodesia* (Salisbury, 1970) is of help for Zimbabwe, while Noel Matthews and M. Doreen Wainwright, *A Guide to Manuscripts and Documents in the British Isles relating to Africa* (1971) is useful, particularly for the archives of the Church Missionary Society (30–48), the London Missionary Society (75–80), the Methodist Missionary Society (81–5), and the United Society for the Propagation of the Gospel (145–50). It should, however, be noted that the location of these missionary society archives has altered: the CMS archives are now in Birmingham, the LMS and MMS at the School of Oriental and African Studies in London, and the USPG at Rhodes House, Oxford. To these should be added *A Survey of the Archives of Selected Missionary Societies*, covering nineteen societies, published by the Historical Manuscripts Commission (1968), M. Cason, 'A Survey of African Material in the Libraries and Archives of Protestant Missionary Societies in England', *HIA* 8 (1981), 277–307, and *The Joint IMC/CBMS Missionary Archives, Africa and India, 1910–1945 Inventory* (includes material as far as 1950) (Zug, 1979). The latter too are now housed at the School of Oriental and African Studies.

For German-speaking missions, besides the UNESCO volume above, there is W. Haas and P. Jenkins, *A Guide to the Basel Mission's Ghana Archives* (Basel, 1979) and D. Maier, 'The Norddeutsche Missionsgesellschaft Archives', *HIA* 8 (1981), 335–7.

For the United States see Aloha South, *Guide to Non-Federal Archives and Manuscripts in the United States Relating to Africa*, 2 vols. (1989) and Robert Shuster, 'Documentary Sources in the United States for Foreign Missions Research: A Select Bibliography and Checklist', *IBMR* 9 (1985), 19–29. For Canada there is K. V. Ram, 'Survey of Canadian Protestant Missionary Archives Relating to Africa', *HIA* 7 (1980), 359–65.

5. Reference Books

Among reference books the following, among others, may be helpful: J. D. Fage, *An Atlas of African History*, 2nd edn. (1978), Roland Oliver and Michael Crowder (eds.), *Cambridge Encyclopedia of Africa*, (Cambridge, 1981), Jocelyn Murray (ed.), *The Cultural History of Africa* (Oxford, 1981), E. Livingstone (ed.), *Oxford Dictionary of the Christian Church*, 3rd edn. (Oxford, forthcoming), S. C. Neill, Gerald Anderson, and John Goodwin (eds.), *The Concise Dictionary of the Christian World Mission* (1970), M. Eliade (ed.), *Encyclopedia of Religion*, 16 vols., (1987), and John Hinnells (ed.), *Penguin Dictionary of Religions* (1984). For Catholic subjects one may consult the *New Catholic Encyclopedia*, 15 vols. (Washington, DC, 1967), together with its three supplementary volumes (1974–89).

For Islamic matters consult both the old *Encyclopedia of Islam*, 5 vols. (1913–32), and the still-unfinished *New Encyclopedia of Islam*, 5 vols. (1960–86), as also I. M. Lewis (ed.), *Islam in Tropical Africa* (1966), J. Cuoq, *Les Musulmans en Afrique* (Paris, 1975), and various volumes by J. Spencer Trimingham: *Islam in Ethiopia* (1952), *Islam in West Africa* (1959), *History of Islam in West Africa* (1962), and *Islam in East Africa* (1964). For full bibliographies see S. M. Zoghby, *Islam in Sub-Saharan Africa: A Partially Annotated Guide* (Washington, DC, 1978), and the *Index Islamicus* (1958 with later supplements).

6. Journals

Useful periodicals include the *Journal of Religion in Africa* (Leiden, 1967–), the *Journal of African History* (Cambridge, 1960–), *African Affairs* (London, 1902–), the *International Journal of African Historical Studies* (Boston, Mass., 1968– ; until 1972 called *African Historical Studies*), *Études d'histoire africaine* (Kinshasa and Louvain, 1970–), the *Journal of the Historical Society of Nigeria* (Ibadan, 1956–), and the *Bulletin de la Société d'archéologie copte* (Cairo, 1935–). Two rather short-lived periodicals should also not be forgotten: the *Revue d'histoire des missions* (Paris, 1924–40) is of considerable value for Catholic history, just as the *Bulletin of the Society of African Church History* (Aberdeen, 1963–70) is chiefly useful for Protestant.

CHAPTER I

THE ETHIOPIAN CHURCH IN THE AGE OF ZARA YA'IQOB

1. Introductory

The most useful modern books are Taddesse Tamrat, *Church and State in Ethiopia 1270–1527* (Oxford, 1972), Edward Ullendorff, *Ethiopia and the Bible*

(London, 1968), Jean Doresse, *L'Empire du Prêtre-Jean*, 2 vols. (Paris, 1957), and Steven Kaplan, *The Monastic Holy Man and the Christianization of Early Solomonic Ethiopia* (Wiesbaden, 1984). The first three have extensive bibliographies, as has the article 'Éthiopie' by Bernard Velat, in *Dictionnaire de spiritualité*, ix (Paris, 1961), cols. 1452–77. See also for items in English Jon Bonk, *An Annotated and Classified Bibliography of English Literature Pertaining to the Ethiopian Orthodox Church* (Metuchen, NJ, 1984). The *Rassegna di studi etiopici* (Rome, 1945–) and the *Journal of Ethiopian Studies* (Addis Ababa, 1963–) are invaluable. See, in particular, K.-R. Zelleke, 'Bibliography of the Ethiopic Hagiographical Traditions', *JES* 13 (1975), 57–102.

2. *Primary Texts*

The principal surviving royal chronicles are G. W. S. Huntingford (ed.), *The Glorious Victories of Amda Seyon* (Oxford, 1965), Jules Perruchon (ed.), *Les Chroniques de Zar'a Ya'eqob et de Ba'eda Maryam* (Paris, 1893), and J. Perruchon (ed.), 'Histoire d'Eskender, d'Amda-Seyon II et de Na'od, rois d'Éthiopie', *Journal asiatique*, 9/3 (1894), 319–66. To these should be added the following basic texts: Abu Salih, *The Churches and Monasteries of Egypt and Some Neighbouring Countries*, ed. B. T. A. Evetts (Oxford, 1895), *The Queen of Sheba and her Only Son, Menyelek, being the 'Book of the Glory of Kings' (Kebra Nagast)*, ed. E. A. Wallis Budge (London, 1932), Gigar Tesfaye, 'Inscriptions sur bois de trois églises de Lalibela', *JES* 17 (1984), 107–26.

By far the largest collection of printed primary texts is that of the more than 70 volumes of the Scriptores Aethiopici, in the *Corpus Scriptorum Christianorum Orientalium*, printed with Ethiopic text and translation into one or another European language. They are referred to here according to their numbering in the *CSCO*, not their additional numbering for the Sc. Ae. For the fifteenth-century Church particularly enlightening are the *Actes de Marha Krestos*, ed. Stanislas Kur, *CSCO* 330–1 (1972), the *Actes de Samuel de Dabra Wagag*, ed. Stanislas Kur, *CSCO* 287–8 (1968), and the *Acta Sancti Abakerazun et Sancti Takla Hawaryat*, ed. C. Conti Rossini, *CSCO* 56–7 (1954). All these (except *Abakerazun*) are of the House of Takla Haymanot. To them should be added the lives of the principal Ewostathian leaders, 'Il "Gadla Filpos" e il "Gadla Yohannes" di Dabra Bizan', ed. C. Conti Rossini, *Atti della Reale Accademia dei Lincei*, 1900 5/8 (1903), 61–170, and C. Conti Rossini, 'Note di agiografia etiopica Abiya-Egzi', 'Arkaledes e Gabra-Iyasus', *Rivista degli studi orientali*, 17 (1938), 409–52 (only the third, Gabra-Iyasus, was an Ewostathian). For the Stephanites besides Abakerazun (above), there is André Caquot (ed.), 'Les Actes d'Ezra de Gunda Gunde', *Annales d'Éthiopie*, 4 (1961), 69–121, and Aleksander Ferenc (ed.), 'Les Actes d'Isaie de Gunda Gunde', *Annales d'Éthiopie*, 10 (1976), 243–94. For

Giyorgis of Sagla see C. Conti Rossini, 'Due capitoli del libro del Mistero di Giyorgis da Sagla', *RSE* 7 (1948), 13–53, G. Haile, '*Fakkare Haymanot* or the Faith of Abba Giyorgis Säglawi', *Le Muséon*, 94 (1981), 235–58, and Yaqob Beyene, 'La dottrina della chiesa etiopica e il "Libro del Mistero" di Giyorgis di Sagla', *RSE* 33 (1989), 35–88.

Some of the writings of Zara Ya'iqob are also to be found in the *CSCO: Das Mashafa Milad und Mashafa Sellase des Kaisers Zara Ya'qob*, ed. K. Wendt, is in *CSCO* 221–2, 235–6, the *Mashafa Birhan*, ed. C. Conti Rossini and L. Ricci, *CSCO* 250–1, 261–2 (1964–5). For Zara Ya'iqob's writings see also C. Conti Rossini, 'Il libro di re Zar'a Ya'qob sulla custodia del Mistero', *RSE* 3 (1943), 148–66, E. Cerulli, 'La festa del battesimo e l'eucaristia in Etiopica nel secolo XV', *Analecta Bollandiana*, 68 (1950), 436–52, G. Haile, 'A Preliminary Investigation of the *Tomara Tasbat* of Emperor Zar'a Ya'eqob of Ethiopia', *Bulletin of the School of Oriental and African Studies*, 43 (1980), 207–34, G. Haile, 'Power Struggle in the Medieval Court of Ethiopia: The Case of Bätargela-Maryam', *JES* 15 (1982), 37–55, and G. Haile, *The Mariology of Emperor Zär'a Ya'eqob of Ethiopia: Texts and Translations* (Rome, 1992).

3. *Judaic Tradition*

The nature of the original Christian conversion of Ethiopia is examined by Steven Kaplan, 'Ezana's Conversion Reconsidered', *JRA* 13 (1982), 101–9. For the subsequent relationship with Judaic tradition see, besides Ullendorff above and a review of it by L. Ricci in *RSE* 24 (1969–70), 273–83, E. Ullendorff, 'Hebraic-Jewish Elements in Abyssinian (Monophysite) Christianity', *JSS* 1 (1956), 216–56, Maxime Rodinson, 'Sur la question des "Influences Juives" en Éthiopie', *JSS* 9 (1964), 11–19, Ernst Hammerschmidt, 'Jewish Elements in the Culture of the Ethiopian Church' *JES* 3 (1965), 1–12, I. Shahid, 'The *Kebra Nagast* in the Light of Recent Research', *Le Muséon*, 89 (1976), 133–78 (a very important reassessment), G. Haile, 'The Forty-Nine Hour Sabbath of the Ethiopian Church', *JSS* 33 (1988), 233–54. On the Falasha there has been an avalanche of recent work. See Steven Kaplan and Shoshana Ben-Dor (eds.), *Ethiopian Jewry: An Annotated Bibliography* (Jerusalem, 1988), W. Leslau, *Falasha Anthology* (New Haven, Conn., 1951), K. Shelemay, *Music, Ritual and Falasha History* (East Lansing, Mich., 1986), Steven Kaplan, '"Falasha" Religion: Ancient Judaism or Evolving Ethiopian Tradition?', *Jewish Quarterly Review*, 79 (July 1988), 49–65, and James Quirin, *The Evolution of the Ethiopian Jews: A History of the Beta Israel (Falasha) to 1920* (Philadelphia, 1992). Shelemay's work is an original research contribution of major significance for matters far wider than its title. Steven Kaplan, 'Indigenous Categories and the Study of World Religions in Ethiopia: The Case of the

Beta Israel (Falasha)', *JRA* 22 (1992), 208–21, and R. Pankhurst, 'The Falashas, or Judaic Ethiopians, in their Christian Ethiopian Setting', *African Affairs*, 91 (1992), 567–82, provide the most recent overviews.

4. *Religious Life, Liturgy, and Doctrine*

For varied aspects of religious life, liturgy, and doctrine, see Stefan Strelcyn, 'Prières magiques éthiopiennes pour délier les charmes', in *Rocznik Orientalistyczny*, xviii (1955), S. A. B. Mercer, *Ethiopic Liturgy* (1915), E. Hammerschmidt, *Studies in the Ethiopic Anaphoras* (Berlin, 1961), Bernard Velat, 'Études sur le Me'eráf, commun de l'office divin éthiopien', *Patrologia Orientalis* (Paris, 1966), E. Cerulli, *Il libro etiopico dei miracoli di Maria* (Rome, 1943), J. Leroy, *Ethiopian Paintings in the Late Middle Ages and under the Gondar Dynasty* (1967), and Bernd M. Weischer, 'Historical and Philological Problems of the Axumitic Literature (especially in the Qerellos)', *JES* 9 (1971), 83–93.

Among important shorter studies of our period the following may be noted: Enrico Cerulli, 'Gli abbati di Dabra Libanos', *Orientalia*, 12 (1943), 226–53, 13 (1944), 137–82, and 14 (1945), 143–71; A. Van Lantschoot, 'Abba Salama metropolite d'Éthiopie (1348–88) et son rôle de traducteur', in *Atti del convegno di studi etiopici* (Rome, 1960), 397–401; T. Tamrat, 'Some Notes on the Fifteenth Century Stephanite "Heresy"', *RSE* 22 (1966), 103–15; Robert Beylot, 'Un épisode de l'histoire ecclésiastique de l'Éthiopie: le Mouvement Stephanite', *Annales d'Éthiopie*, 8 (1970), 103–16; T. Tamrat, 'The Abbots of Dabra-Hayq 1248–1535', *JES* 8 (1970), 87–117; T. Tamrat, 'A Short Note on the Traditions of Pagan Resistance to the Ethiopian Church (Fourteenth and Fifteenth Centuries)', *JES* 10 (1972), 137–50; Roger Schneider, 'Notes sur Filpos de Dabra Bizan et ses successeurs', *Annales d'Éthiopie*, 11 (1978), 135–9; G. Haile, 'From Strict Observance to Royal Endowment: The Case of the Monastery of Dabra Halle Luya', *Le Muséon*, 93 (1980), 163–72; G. Haile, 'The Letter of Archbishops Mika'el and Gabre'el Concerning the Observance of Saturday', *JSS* 26 (1981), 73–8; Robert Beylot, 'Estifanos hétérodoxe éthiopien du 627xv^e siècle', *Revue de l'histoire des religions*, 198 (1981), 279–84; G. Haile, 'Documents on the History of Ase Dawit 1380–1413', *JES* 16 (1983), 25–35.

For external relations, especially with the rest of Christendom, see E. Cerulli, *Etiopi in Palestina* (Rome, 1943); O. G. S. Crawford, *Ethiopian Itineraries ca. 1400–1524* (Cambridge, 1955); G. Wiet, 'Les Relations égypto-abyssines sous les Sultans Mamlouks', *Bulletin de la Société d'archéologie copte*, 4 (1938), 115–40; Joseph Gill, SJ, *The Council of Florence* (Cambridge, 1959); E. Cerulli, *Tiberius and Pontius Pilate in Ethiopian Tradition and Poetry* (1973); S. Chojnacki, 'Notes on Art in Ethiopia in the Fifteenth and Early Sixteenth Century', *JES* 8 (1970), 21–65; S. Tedeschi, 'Profilo storico di

Dayr as-Sultan', *JES* 2 (1964), 92–158; R. Lefevre, 'Presenze etiopiche in Italia prima del Concilio di Firenze del 1439', *RSE* 23 (1967–8), 5–26; Otto Meinardus, 'Ecclesiastica Aethiopica in Aegypto', *JES* 3 (1965), 23–35; Diana Spencer, 'Travels in Gojjam: St Luke Ikons and Brancaleon Rediscovered', *JES* 12 (1974), 201–20.

CHAPTER 2

AFRICA IN 1500 AND ITS CHRISTIAN PAST

1. *Introductory*

To the works referred to in the general section above, the following may be added for the political state of Africa before and around 1500: R. S. Smith, *Kingdoms of the Yoruba* (1969), R. E. Bradbury, *Benin Studies* (1973), P. S. Garlake, *Great Zimbabwe* (1973), D. N. Beach, *The Shona and Zimbabwe 900–1850* (1980), G. S. P. Freeman-Grenville, *The Medieval History of the Coast of Tanganyika* (1962), and M. S. M. Kiwanuka, *A History of Buganda from the Foundation of the Kingdom to 1900* (New York, 1972).

For stateless societies Robin Horton's chapter in Ajayi and Crowder (eds.), *History of West Africa*, i, 87–128, is particularly valuable. For some modern examples of stateless societies see E. E. Evans-Pritchard, *The Nuer* (1940), M. Fortes, *The Web of Kinship among the Tallensi* (1949), and Mary Douglas, *The Lele of the Kasai* (1963).

In regard to African religion again only a very small selection of what is both available and helpful can be offered: Dominique Zahan, *The Religion, Spirituality and Thought of Traditional Africa* (Chicago, 1979), Meyer Fortes and Robin Horton, *Oedipus and Job in West African Religion* (Cambridge, 1984), Evan M. Zuesse, *Ritual Cosmos: The Sanctification of Life in African Religions* (Athens, Ohio, 1979), E. W. Smith (ed.), *African Ideas of God* (1950), D. Forde (ed.), *African Worlds* (1954), J. Omosade Awolalu, *Yoruba Beliefs and Sacrificial Rituals* (1979), Wande Abimbola, *An Exposition of the Ifa Literary Corpus* (Ibadan, 1976), E. E. Evans-Pritchard, *Witchcraft, Oracles and Magic among the Azande* (1937), Jack Goody, *The Myth of the Bagre* (Cambridge, 1972), Godfrey Lienhardt, *Divinity and Experience* (1961), and D. I. Nwoga, *The Supreme God as Stranger* (Ahiazu Mbaise, 1984).

2. *Islam*

For Islam in West Africa up to 1500 the most comprehensive and reliable study is Joseph Cuoq, *Histoire de l'Islamisation de l'Afrique de l'Ouest, des origines à la fin du xvie siècle* (Paris, 1984), to which may be added J. Spencer

Trimingham, *A History of Islam in West Africa* (1962) and Peter Clarke, *West Africa and Islam* (1982). The available Arabic sources are to be found translated in N. Levtzion and J. F. P. Hopkins (eds.), *Corpus of Early Arabic Sources for West African History* (Cambridge, 1981) and J. Cuoq, *Recueil des sources arabes concernant l'Afrique occidentale du VIIIᵉ au XVIᵉ siècle: Traduction et notes* (Paris, 1975). To these the following may be added: N. Levtzion, 'Patterns of Islamization in West Africa', in N. Levtzion (ed.), *Conversion to Islam* (1979), 207–16, J. O. Hunwick, 'Religion and State in the Songhay Empire 1464–1591', in I. M. Lewis (ed.), *Islam in Tropical Africa* (1964), 124–43; J. O. Hunwick, *Shari'a in Songhay: The Replies of al-Maghili to the Questions of Askia al-Hajj Muhammad* (1984), J. O. Hunwick, 'Notes on a Late Fifteenth-Century Document Concerning "al-Takrur"', in Christopher Allen and R. W. Johnson (eds.), *African Perspectives* (Cambridge, 1970), 7–33, Elias Saad, *Social History of Timbuktu* (1983), Ralph A. Austen, 'The Trans-Saharan Slave Trade: A Tentative Census', in Henry A. Gemery and Jan A. Hogendorn (eds.), *The Uncommon Market* (1979), 23–76, Allan G. B. Fisher and Humphrey Fisher, *Slavery and Muslim Society in Africa* (New York, 1971), and Robin Law, *The Horse in West African Society* (1980).

For Islam in eastern Africa there is J. Spencer Trimingham, *Islam in East Africa* (1964) and Freeman-Grenville, *The Medieval History of the Coast of Tanganyika*, as above. For Ethiopia we have J. Cuoq, *L'Islam en Éthiopie des origines au XVIᵉ siècle* (Paris, 1981) and J. Spencer Trimingham, *Islam in Ethiopia* (1952).

3. *North African Christianity*

W. H. C. Frend provides an overview of ancient North African Christianity including Egypt in 'The Christian Period in Mediterranean Africa AD 200–700', *CHA* ii. 410–89. For its western, Latin-speaking half, the foundational work remains P. Monceaux, *Histoire littéraire de l'Afrique chrétienne*, 7 vols. (Paris, 1901–7). W. H. C. Frend, *The Donatist Church* (1952) is the most authoritative study on its subject but for a review of more recent literature see R. A. Markus, 'Christianity and Dissent in Roman North Africa: Changing Perspectives in Recent Work', in D. Baker (ed.), *Studies in Church History*, ix (1972), 21–36, and W. H. C. Frend, 'The Donatist Church: Forty Years On', in C. Landman and D. P. Whitelaw (eds.), *Windows on Origins* (Pretoria, 1985). For Augustine and his Church see Peter Brown, *Augustine of Hippo* (1967), Peter Brown, *Religion and Society in the Age of Saint Augustine* (1972), Henry Chadwick, *Augustine* (1986), and R. A. Markus, 'Afer Scribens Afris: The Church in Augustine and the African Tradition', in R. A. Markus, *Saeculum: History and Society in the Theology of Augustine* (Cambridge, 1970), 105–32. The best complete survey of the evidence for the decline of Christianity in North Africa is Joseph Cuoq, *L'Église d'Afrique du Nord, du deuxième au douzième siècle* (Paris, 1984).

4. Christianity in Egypt

There are regular bibliographies entitled 'Christian Egypt' in the *Journal of Egyptian Archaeology* between vol. 1 (1914) and vol. 26 (1940) which are invaluable. See also the *Bulletin de la Société d'archéologie copte* (Cairo) beginning in 1935, together with many other publications of the society, especially its series Textes et documents, as well as the subseries Scriptores Coptici within *CSCO*.

Colin H. Roberts, *Manuscript, Society and Belief in Early Christian Egypt* (1979) is a stimulating discussion of origins, while H. I. Bell and H. Thompson, 'A Greek–Coptic Glossary to Hosea and Amos', *Journal of Egyptian Archaeology*, 11 (1925), 241–6, provides a fascinating glimpse of the Christian crossing of the Greek–Coptic divide. See also C. W. Griggs, *Early Egyptian Christianity, from its Origins to 451 CE* (Leiden, 1991), Mario Naldini, *Il Cristianesimo in Egitto: Lettere private nei papiri dei secoli II–IV* (Florence, 1968), and W. H. C. Frend, 'Athanasius as an Egyptian Christian Leader in the Fourth Century', in his *Religion Popular and Unpopular in the Early Christian Centuries* (1976).

For Coptic Christianity monasticism became absolutely central. It also provides the indispensable background to Ethiopian monasticism, while comparison with movements in modern African Christianity may also be enlightening. Derwas Chitty, *The Desert a City* (Oxford, 1966) provides a vivid and wide ranging interpretation, and C. C. Walters, *Monastic Archaeology in Egypt* (Warminster, 1974), a survey of the physical remains. For an accessible edition of the earliest texts see Benedicta Ward, *The Sayings of the Desert Fathers* (1975) or O. Chadwick (ed.), 'Sayings of the Fathers', in *Western Asceticism* (1958), 33–181. There is an English translation of Athanasius' *Life of Anthony*, ed. R. T. Meyer (1950) and Derwas Chitty has translated *The Letters of Saint Anthony the Great* (Oxford, 1989). For Pachomius, the basic texts are L. T. Lefort, *Œuvres de S. Pachôme et de ses disciples*, CSCO 159–60 (1956) and L. T. Lefort, *Les Vies coptes de saint Pachôme et de ses premiers successeurs* (Louvain, 1943). In English we have Philip Rousseau's fine study, *Pachomius: The Making of a Community in Fourth-Century Egypt* (1985), as also the two volumes of Armand Veilleux, *Pachomian Koinonia* (1982) and J. E. Goehring, *The Letter of Ammon and Pachomian Monasticism* (1986). An account of Egyptian monasticism in the late fourth century, the *Historia Monachorum*, is translated and discussed in B. Ward, *The Lives of the Desert Fathers* (1980). For the later tradition of the White Monastery see *Sinuthii Vita et Opera Omnia*, ed. I. Leipoldt and W. Crum, CSCO 41–2 (1906–8), and David N. Bell, *The Life of Shenoute by*

Besa (Kalamazoo, Mich., 1983). For the Ethiopian text see G. Colin (ed.), *La Version éthiopienne de la vie de Schenoudi, CSCO* 444–5 (1982). For Besa himself see Besa, *Letters and Sermons*, K. H. Kuhn (ed.) CSCO 157–8 (1956) and K. H. Kuhn, 'A Fifth-Century Egyptian Abbot', *Journal of Theological Studies*, NS 5 (1954), 36–48, 174–87, and (1955), 35–48. For the Coptic view of Saturday, of interest for later Ethiopian controversy, see J. Muyser, 'Le Samedi et le dimanche dans l'église et la littérature coptes', in Togo Mina, *Le Martyre d'Apa Epima* (Cairo, 1937).

For the last period of Egyptian Church history prior to the Arab conquest the best account is W. H. C. Frend, *The Rise of the Monophysite Movement* (Cambridge, 1972), together with his chapter in *CHA* ii. 410–89. Bibliographies and a general review of the theology and literature of the later Coptic Church can be found in *Dictionnaire de théologie catholique*, x (1929), article entitled 'Monophysite (Église copte)', 2251–306, in *DTC* viii (1925), 'Kabar, Ibn', 2293–6, and in the *Dictionnaire de spiritualité*, ii (1953), 'Copte (littérature spirituelle)', 2266–78, and iv (1960), 'Égypte chrétienne', 532–58. Other studies of Coptic history and life include Murad Kamil, *Aspects de l'Égypte copte* (Berlin, 1965), with 120 fine photographs, Sylvestre Chauleur, *Histoire des Coptes d'Égypte* (Paris, 1960), Edward Hardy, *Christian Egypt: Church and People* (New York, 1952), Maria Cramer, *Das christlich-koptische Aegypten einst und heute* (Wiesbaden, 1959), valuable for bibliography and for another large collection of photographs and plans, and Otto Meinardus, *Christian Egypt Ancient and Modern*, 2nd edn. (Cairo, 1977).

5. *Christian Nubia*

Knowledge of Christian Nubia has been transformed in the last twenty-five years through excavations undertaken in haste before the flooding of the whole area by the Aswan High Dam, but for a sensitive treatment of what earlier archaeological finds already suggested see J. W. Crowfoot, 'Christian Nubia', *Journal of Egyptian Archaeology* 13 (1927), 141–50. P. L. Shinnie, 'Christian Nubia', *CHA* ii. 556–88 (plus bibliographical essay, 712–15 and bibliography, 764–6) and S. Jakobielski, 'Christian Nubia at the Height of its Civilization', *GHA* iii. 194–223, provide a reliable account of present knowledge, but U. Monneret de Villard, *Storia della Nubia cristiana* (Rome, 1938) remains a foundational work. G. Troupeau, 'La "Déscription de la Nubie" d'al Uswāni', *Arabica* 1 (1954), 276–88, relates to a valuable tenth-century Arabic account of Nubia, mostly lost, while Togo Mina, *Inscriptions coptes et grecques de Nubie* (Cairo, 1942) is a basic collection of texts. Two important recent collections are K. Michalowski (ed.), *Nubia, récentes recherches* (Warsaw, 1975) and J. M. Plumley (ed.), *Nubian Studies* (Warminster, 1982). K. Michalowski, *Faras: Centre artistique de la Nubie chrétienne* (Leiden, 1966) describes the most spectacular of the archaeological discoveries and J. M. Plumley, *The Scrolls of Bishop Timotheos* (1975) another hardly less exciting. Both relate to northern Nubia. D. A. Welsby, 'Recent Work at Soba East in Central Sudan', *Azania*, 17 (1983), 165–80, describes excavations at the southern capital of Alwa. Stefan Jakobielski, *A History of the Bishopric of Pachoras on the Basis of Coptic Inscriptions* (Warsaw, 1972), John Vantini, *The Excavations at Faras* (Bologna, 1970), S. C. Munro-Hay, 'Kings and Kingdoms of Ancient Nubia', *RSE* 29 (1982–3), 87–137, and J. Cuoq, *Islamisation de la Nubie Chrétienne, viie–xvie siècle* (Paris, 1986), should also be consulted. The possibility of some survival of Christianity west of Nubia even in the eighteenth century is discussed by R. Gray, 'Christian Traces and a Franciscan Mission in the Central Sudan 1700–1711', *JAH* 8 (1967), 383–93.

CHAPTER 3

THE KONGO, WARRI, MUTAPA, AND THE PORTUGUESE

1. *General*

The principal source of published primary material for West Africa, Kongo, and Angola is the massive twenty-volume *Monumenta Missionaria Africana* (Lisbon), ed. Antonio Brasio, with fifteen volumes in series 1 (1952–88) and five in series 2 (1958–79). Volumes i–iv of series 1 and i–iii of series 2 contain material prior to the end of the sixteenth century, vols. v–xiv of series 1 and iv–v of series 2 cover the seventeenth century. Volume xv of series 1 is a final supplement covering both centuries. There is nothing comparable for the eighteenth century. For eastern Africa the main collection of primary material remains the rather dated nine volumes of G. M. Theal (ed.), *Records of South-Eastern Africa* (Cape Town, 1898–1903), to which must be added the far better-edited *Documents on the Portuguese in Mozambique and Central Africa 1497–1840* (Lisbon, 1962–89), of which nine volumes, containing original texts and English translation and arriving at 1615, have so far been published.

H. Livermore, *A New History of Portugal*, 2nd edn. (Cambridge, 1976) provides an introduction to the major colonial and missionary power of this period. For Portugal's overseas empire and missionary policy C. R. Boxer, *The Portuguese Seaborne Empire 1415–1825* (1969) and C. R. Boxer, *The Church Militant and Iberian Expansion 1440–1770* (Baltimore, 1978) are indispensable. See also A. de Silva Rego, *Portuguese Colonisation in the Sixteenth Century* (Johannesburg, 1959). C.-M. de Witte, *Les Bulles pontificales et l'expansion portugaise au xve siècle* (Louvain, 1958) provides a full account of the ecclesiastical significance of the pre-Vasco da Gama era bulls. It is also to be found, in article form, in the *Revue d'histoire ecclésiastique* 48 (1953), 49 (1954), 51 (1956), and 53 (1958).

There is a vast modern literature on the development of the Atlantic slave-trade in this period. See especially P. D. Curtin, *The Atlantic Slave Trade: A Census* (1969), James Rawley, *The Transatlantic Slave Trade* (1981), 21–50, and Paul E. Lovejoy, *Transformations in Slavery: A History of Slavery in Africa* (Cambridge, 1983). For slavery in Africa itself see also C. Meillassoux, *The Anthropology of Slavery* (1991); for slavery in Portugal see A. C. de C. M. Saunders, *A Social History of Black Slaves and Freedmen in Portugal 1441–1555* (Cambridge, 1982), and for Portuguese Africa, Joseph Miller, 'The Slave Trade in Congo and Angola', in Martin Kilson and Robert Rotberg (eds.), *The African Diaspora* (1976), 75–113, and J. Miller, *Way of Death* (Madison, Wis., 1988). For the papal position see J. R. Gray, 'The Papacy and the Atlantic Slave Trade', *Past and Present*, 115 (May 1987), 52–68.

For Catholic missionary organization in the seventeenth century the first of the five volumes of *Sacrae Congregationis de Propaganda Fide Memoria Rerum* is essential. See in particular J. Metzler, 'Foundation of the Congregation "de Propaganda Fide" by Gregory XV', 79–111, and Willi Henkel, 'The Polyglot Printing-Office of the Congregation', 335–50. The documents in the appendices of the last volume, iii/2 (1976), are also important. S. Delacroix (ed.), *Histoire universelle des missions catholiques*, ii (Paris, 1957) is helpful, especially chapters 6 and 7 by A. Perbal on Propaganda Fide and the beginning of Vicars Apostolic.

For an overall view of Catholic missionary history in Africa in this period, from a Roman viewpoint, see L. Jadin, 'L'Œuvre missionnaire en Afrique noire', *PFMR* i/2. 413–546, and, for the eighteenth century, Josef Metzler, 'Missionsbemühungen der Kongregation in Schwarzafrika', *PFMR* ii. 882–932.

2. *West Africa*

The lasting impact of missionary activity in West Africa, apart from Warri, was minimal. The principal studies on Warri and Benin have been made by A. F. C. Ryder: 'Missionary Activity in the Kingdom of Warri to the Early Nineteenth Century', *JHN* 1 (1960), 1–26, 'The Benin Missions', *JHN* 2 (1961), 231–59, and *Benin and the Europeans 1485–1897* (1969). T. Hodgkin, *Nigerian Perspectives*, 2nd edn. (1975), 171–89, includes valuable Warri documents. To these should be added Vittorio Salvadorini, *Le missioni a Benin e Warri nel XVII secolo* (Pisa, 1972).

For early seventeenth-century Sierra Leone there is a great deal of material available in English, mostly due to Professor P. E. H. Hair. See his survey article, 'Jesuit Documents on the Guinea of Cape Verde and the Cape Verde Islands 1585–1617 in English Translation', *HIA* 16 (1989),

375–81, together with the following articles, all by him: 'Alvares at Mitombo 1611', *Africana Research Bulletin* (Institute of African Studies, University of Sierra Leone), 11 (1981), 92–140; 'Hamlet in an Afro-Portuguese Setting: New Perspectives on Sierra Leone in 1607', *HIA* 5 (1978), 21–42; 'The Abortive Portuguese Settlement of Sierra Leone 1570–1625', in *Vice-Almirante A. Teixeira da Mota in memoriam* (Lisbon, 1987), 171–208. A very considerable collection of shorter documents is to be found in *Jesuit Documents on the Guinea of Cape Verde and the Cape Verde Islands 1585–1617*, translated by P. E. H. Hair (Liverpool, 1989). For two longer documents see André Donelha, *Descrição da Serra Leõa e dos Rios de Guine do Cabo Verde 1625* (An Account of Sierra Leone and the Rivers of Guinea of Cape Verde 1625), ed. A. Teixeira da Mota and P. E. H. Hair (Lisbon, 1977) and Manuel Alvares, SJ, *Etiópia Menor e descrição géografica da Província da Serra Leõa c. 1615* (Ethiopia Minor and a Geographical Account of the Province of Sierra Leone *c.* 1615) an interim translation by P. E. H. Hair (Liverpool, 1990).

For the Ghana area see Ralph Wiltgen, *Gold Coast Mission History 1471–1880* (Techny, Ill., 1956) and for part of what is now Benin, Henri Labouret and Paul Rivet, 'Le Royaume d'Arda et son évangelisation au xviɪ^e siècle', *Travaux et mémoires de l'Institut d'ethnologie* (Paris, 1929), and Robin Law, 'Religion, Trade and Politics on the "Slave Coast"', *JRA* 21/1 (1991), 42–77.

For a late eighteenth-century French mission to the coast, just north of the river Zaïre, see the Abbé Proyart, *Histoire de Loango, Kakongo et autres royaumes d'Afrique* (Paris, 1776). Its first half is translated into English in J. Pinkerton, *A General Collection of . . . Voyages and Travels*, xvi (1814), 548–97. Unfortunately this does not include the history of the mission and account of the discovery of the community of Manguenzo Christians. See, too, the important collection of related documents in J. Cuvelier, *Documents sur une mission française au Kakongo 1766–1775* (Brussels, 1953).

3. Kongo and Angola

The earliest major published collection of documents is Paiva Manso's *Historia do Congo (Documentos)* (Lisbon, 1877). While Brasio's *Monumenta Missionaria Africana* is by far the most comprehensive of collections of the shorter documents, some of the same material is to be found, more approachably for many, in French translation. For the late fifteenth and sixteenth century, Willy Bal (ed.), *Le Royaume du Congo aux xve et xvie siècles: Documents d'histoire* (Brussels, 1963) and L. Jadin and Mireille Dicorato, *Correspondence de Dom Afonso, roi du Congo 1506–1543* (Brussels, 1974). For *c.* 1580–1630 there is J. Cuvelier and L. Jadin, *L'Ancien Congo d'après les archives romaines* (Brussels, 1954); thereafter there are the three volumes of L. Jadin, *L'Ancien Congo et l'Angola 1639–1655, d'après les archives romaines, portugaises, néerlandaises et espagnoles* (Brussels, 1975).

To these must be added the principal available contemporary accounts. The earliest is that of Rui de Pina, edited by Leite de Faria, *Una relacão de Rui de Pina sobre o Congo escrita em 1492* (Lisbon, 1966). For the sixteenth century the most important is Filippo Pigafetta, *Relazione del reame di Congo*, first published in Rome in 1591 and re-edited recently by Giorgio Cardona (Milan, 1978). For an excellent French edition see Willy Bal (ed.), *Description du royaume de Congo et des contrées environantes par Filippo Pigafetta et Duarte Lopes* (Louvain, 1963). The first English translation was published in 1597 with a dedication to Archbishop Whitgift! A modern translation by M. Hutchinson (1881) was reprinted in 1970.

Next in line comes the early seventeenth-century *Historia do Reino do Kongo*, now identified as the work of Mattheus Cardoso, SJ. First published in full by A. Brasio in *Studia*, 27–8 (1969), 425–509, it is most accessible in French translation in vol. iv of *EHA* (1972), F. Bontinck and J. Castro Segovia (eds.), *Histoire du royaume du Congo*. For the later seventeenth century we have a considerable number of important accounts by Capuchins, beginning with that of Giovanni Francesco da Roma, *Brève relation de la fondation de la mission des Frères Mineurs au Royaume de Congo par Jean-François de Rome*, ed. François Bontinck (Louvain, 1964). This first appeared in Rome, from Propaganda's own press, in 1648 and went through seven editions in three years, including immediate translation into French and Spanish. It should be seen as a very effective piece of official publicity for the new mission. To it should be added Giovanni Antonio Cavazzi, *Istorica descrizione de tre regni Congo, Matamba et Angola* (Bologna, 1687), translated into French by J. B. Labat (Paris, 1723) and into Portuguese and edited by P. Graciano Maria de Leguzzano, *Descricão de Congo, Matamba et Angola*, 2 vols. (Lisbon, 1965), as also Calogero Piazza, *La prefettura apostolica del Congo alla meta del XVII secolo: La relazione inedita di Girolamo da Montesarchio* (Milan, 1976), French translation, O. de Bouveignes and J. Cuvelier (eds.), *Jerome de Montesarchio, apôtre du vieux Congo* (Namur, 1951). These constitute the principal witnesses (together with Hildebrand on Georges de Geel and the unfortunately still unpublished manuscript of Antonio de Teruel, written in 1663–4) for the first twenty years of the Capuchin mission to the Kongo prior to the disastrous battle of Ambuila. The 'Voyage to Congo' of Michel Angelo of Gattina and Dionigi de Carli of Piacenza provides a glimpse of Bamba in the year immediately following the battle: A. and J. Churchill, *A Collection of Voyages and Travels*, i (1704), 611–50, reprinted in J. Pinkerton, *A General Collection of . . . Voyages and Travels*, xvi (1814), 148–94.

Available Capuchin accounts are more numerous for the last forty years of their systematic work (roughly 1685–1725) in the very different and disintegrating political conditions of that period. They concentrate particularly upon Soyo. These include the narrative beginning in 1682 of Girolamo Merolla, *Breve et succinta relatione de viaggio nel regno di Congo nell'Africa meridionale* (Naples, 1692), translated in A. and J. Churchill, *A collection of Voyages and Travels*, i. 655–754, and Pinkerton, *A General Collection of . . . Voyages and Travels*, xvi. 195–316; Romain Rainero, *Il Congo agli inizi del settecento nella relazione di P. Luca da Caltanissetta* (Florence, 1974); a French translation of the same text, ed. F. Bontinck, *Diaire congolais (1690–1701) de Fr. Luca da Caltanisetta OFM Cap* (Louvain, 1970); J. Cuvelier (ed.), *Relations sur le Congo du Père Laurent de Lucques 1700–1717* (Brussels, 1953); Antonio Zuchelli, *Relazione del viaggio e missione di Congo nell'Etiopia Inferiore Occidentale* (Venice, 1712); C. Piazza, *La Missione del Soyo (1713–1716) nella relazione inedita di Giuseppe da Modena* (Rome, 1973); Andrea da Pavia, beginning in 1685, and Bernardo da Galla, beginning in 1694 (for the last two see Jadin, below, 1961 and 1970).

As important, and unique of its kind, is the Kikongo catechism of Mattheus Cardoso, SJ, first printed in Lisbon in 1624. There is an excellent modern edition, including both French translation and the original Kikongo and Portuguese texts: F. Bontinck and D. Ndembe Nsasi, *Le Catéchisme Kikongo de 1624: Réédition critique* (Brussels, 1978). This *Doctrina Christiana* can be compared with another translated, far less competently, into a West African language, Popo, and printed side by side with the Spanish in 1658. See H. Labouret and P. Rivet, 'Le Royaume d'Arda' (previous section). For the eighteenth century a guide to missionary practice written in Italian *c.*1747, probably by Fr. Hyacinto da Bologna, is enlightening. It has been published in French translation: *La Pratique Missionnaire des PP. Capuchins italiens dans les royaumes de Congo, Angola et contrées adjacentes* (Louvain, 1931).

No less valuable as a source of available primary material for the seventeenth and eighteenth centuries, as well as for a careful commentary upon it, is a lengthy series of studies by Louis Jadin in the *BIHB* between 1961 and 1970: 'Le Congo et la secte des Antoniens: Restauration du royaume sous Pedro IV et la "Sainte-Antoine Congolais" 1694–1718', 33 (1961), 411–615; 'Aperçu de la situation du Congo et rite d'election des rois en 1775, d'après le P. Cherubino da Savona, missionnaire au Congo de 1759 à 1774', 35 (1963), 343–419; 'Le Clergé séculier et les Capuchins du Congo et d'Angola aux xviie et xviiie siècles, conflits de jurisdiction, 1600–1726', 36 (1964), 185–483; 'Rivalités luso-néerlandaises au Soyo 1600–1675', 37 (1966), 137–359; 'Pero Tavares, missionnaire Jésuite, ses travaux apostoliques au Congo et en Angola 1629–1635', 38 (1967), 271–401; 'Relations sur le Congo et l'Angola tirées des archives de la Compagnie de Jésus 1621–1631', 39 (1968), 334–454; 'Voyages apostoliques aux missions d'Afrique du P. Andrea da Pavia, Prédicateur capucin, 1685–1702', 41 (1970), 375–454.

Anne Hilton, *The Kingdom of Kongo* (1985), provides what is probably the most informative recent account of Kongolese history from the fifteenth to the eighteenth century, but the diversity of viewpoints in modern Kongo-related scholarship is considerable and the following general studies are all noteworthy: J. Cuvelier, *L'Ancien Royaume du Congo* (Brussels, 1946), over-pious but remarkable for its date; Georges Balandier, *Daily Life in the Kingdom of Kongo* (New York, 1968), over-reductionist; Sigbert Axelson, *Culture Confrontation in the Lower Congo* (Uppsala, 1970), too critical of the Capuchins; David Birmingham, *Trade and Conflict in Angola: The Mbundu and their Neighbours under the Influence of the Portuguese 1483–1700* (Oxford, 1966); and two excellent wider studies: W. G. L. Randles, *L'Ancien Royaume du Congo, des origines à la fin du XIXe siècle* (Paris, 1968) and John K. Thornton, *The Kingdom of Kongo: Civil War and Transition 1641–1718* (Madison, Wis., 1983). An important reassessment of the early period is to be found in John Thornton, 'Early Kongo–Portuguese Relations: A New Interpretation', *HIA* 8 (1981), 183–204, while two other interesting studies relating to Afonso's work are C.-M. de Witte, 'Henri de Congo, évêque titulaire d'Utique (\dag *c.*1531) d'après les documents romains', *Euntes Docete*, 21 (1968), 587–99, and F. Bontinck, 'La Première "Ambassade" congolaise à Rome 1514', *EHA* 1 (1970), 37–73.

Besides the articles of Jadin, listed above, which all include much primary material, a number of more specifically ecclesiastical studies are to be noted. Pierre Sérouet, *Jean de Brétigny (1556–1634), aux origines du Carmel de France, de Belgique et du Congo* (Louvain, 1974) includes a fascinating account of proposals for a Carmelite mission in the early seventeenth century. The indispensable tool for a study of the Capuchin missions is Teobaldo Filesi and Isidoro de Villapadierna, *La "Missio Antiqua" dei Cappuccini nel Congo 1645–1835: Studio preliminare e guida delle fonti* (Rome, 1978), to which should be added the three volumes of P. Graziano Saccardo, *Congo e Angola con la storia dell'antica missione dei Cappucini* (Venice, 1982–3). Antonio Brasio, *Historia e missiologia* (Loanda, 1973) provides a learned discussion of many aspects of Angolan mission history. Père Hildebrand, *Le Martyr Georges de Geel et les débuts de la mission du Congo 1645–1652* (Antwerp, 1940) is useful for the primary material it includes. Two works by Teobaldo Filesi focus on the relationship with Rome: *Le relazioni tra il regno del Congo e la Sede Apostolica nel XVIe secolo* (Como, 1968), *Roma e Congo all'inizio del 1600: Nuove testimonianze* (Como, 1970). There is a brief study of the most interesting native-born Kongo priest of the seventeenth century, Manuel Roboredo, by Laurenz Kilger, 'Der erste einheimische Ordenspriester in der alten Kongo-Mission', *Neue Zeitschrift für Missionswissenschaft*, 14 (1958), 50–2. Richard Gray reassesses the Catholicism of Soyo in '*Come Vero Principe Catolico*: The Capuchins and the Rulers of Soyo in the Late Seventeenth Century', *Africa*, 53 (1983), 39–54 (reprinted in R. Gray, *Black*

Christians and White Missionaries (1990), 35–56) and John Thornton, the whole sweep of Kongo Catholicism in 'The Development of an African Catholic Church in the Kingdom of Kongo 1491–1750', *JAH* 25 (1984), 147–67.

For the Antonian movement there is now a considerable literature. The fullest discussion, together with all the primary texts in their original Italian, is to be found in Teobaldo Filesi, *Nazionalismo e religione nel Congo all'inizio del 1700: La setta degli Antoniani* (Rome, 1972). Cuvelier's French edition of Lorenzo da Lucca provided the first published account of the movement and Jadin's 'Le Congo et la secte des Antoniens' the first publication of the most important piece of evidence, the report of Bernardo da Gallo. Both Thornton, *The Kingdom of Kongo*, 106–13, and Randles, *L'Ancien Royaume*, 157–9, provide valuable comment, as does Wyatt MacGaffey, 'The Cultural Roots of Kongo Prophetism', *History of Religion*, 17 (1977), 177–93. The wider literature includes R. Batsikama, *Ndona Béatrice: Serait-elle témoin du Christ et de la foi du vieux Congo?* (Kinshasa, 1970), a plea for Beatrice's canonization, Bernard Dadié, *Beatrice du Congo* (Paris, 1970), an opera, and Ibrahim Baba Kake, *Dona Beatrice: La Jeanne d'Arc congolaise* (Paris, 1976), an imaginative retelling of the story.

4. Eastern Africa

Volumes vii and viii of *Documents on the Portuguese in Mozambique and Central Africa* includes the source material for Goncalo da Silveira and his mission, while viii. 324–429 contains the *Relação* of the Jesuit Fr. Monclaro on the expedition of 1569. Later material can be found in G. M. Theal (ed.), *Records of South-Eastern Africa* (Cape Town, 1898–1903), including in vol. iii a report by Manuel Barreto, SJ, dated 1667, 436–508, while almost the whole of vol. vii is devoted to the first three books of *Ethiopia Oriental*, a long and interesting account of Mozambique and Mutapa written by the Dominican João dos Santos, who worked there in the 1590s. It was printed at Evora in 1609. A report by another Jesuit in 1648, Antonio Gomes, entitled *Viagem que fez Padre Ant Gomes, da Comp de Jesus, ao Imperio de Manomotapa* (1648) is to be found, ed. A. E. Axelson, in *Studia*, 3 (1959), 155–242. The 1696 'Tratados dos Rios de Cuama' of the Augustinian Antonio da Conceicao, together with his 'Petição que fez o Administrador da Christiandade de Moçambique e Rios ao Conselho da Junta das Missões', are printed in *O Chronista de Tissuary Periodico* (Nova Goa, 1867). They are valuable as being written just after the Changamire had driven the Portuguese out of the Zimbabwe area. Eric Axelson, *The Portuguese in South-East Africa 1488–1600* (Johannesburg, 1973) and *The Portuguese in South-East Africa 1600–1700* (Johannesburg, 1960) provide an indigestible but well-referenced blow-by-blow account of developments from a European viewpoint. The best recent studies are W. G. L. Randles, *The Empire of Monomotapa from the Fifteenth to the Nineteenth Century* (Gwelo, Zimbabwe, 1981), M. D. Newitt, *Portuguese Settlement on the Zambezi* (1973), and S. I. G. Mudenge, *A Political History of Mumhumutapa c.1400–1902* (1988). See also Bertha Leite, *Goncalo da Silveira* (Lisbon, 1946), Antonio da Silva, SJ, *Mentalidade missiologica dos Jesuitas en Moçambique antes de 1759* (Lisbon, 1967), P. S. Garlake, 'Excavations at the Seventeenth-Century Portuguese Site of Dambarare, Rhodesia', *Proceedings and Transactions of the Rhodesia Scientific Association*, 54/1 (1969), 23–61, W. Rea, SJ, *The Economics of the Zambezi Missions 1580–1759* (Rome, 1976), and S. I. G. Mudenge, *Christian Education at the Mutapa Court* (Harare, 1986).

For the coast north of Mozambique there is G. S. P. Freeman-Grenville, 'The Coast 1498–1840', in Oliver and Mathew (eds.), *History of East Africa* i. 129–68, J. Strandes, *The Portuguese Period in East Africa*, ed. J. S. Kirkman (1961), John Gray, *Early Portuguese Missionaries in East Africa* (Nairobi, 1958), C. R. Boxer and C. de Azevedo, *Fort Jesus and the Portuguese in Mombasa 1593–1729* (1960), J. Kirkman, *Fort Jesus* (Oxford, 1974), and G. S. P. Freeman-Grenville's edition of the canonization proceedings begun for those murdered at Mombasa in 1631, *The Mombasa Rising against the Portuguese 1631* (1980).

CHAPTER 4

RICHES TO RAGS: ETHIOPIA 1500–1800

1. *Primary Sources: The Sixteenth Century*

For the sixteenth century the principal Ethiopian chronicles are W. E. Conzelman (ed.), *Chronique de Galawdewos (Claudius) roi d'Éthiopie* (Paris, 1895) and the exceptionally interesting and well-written work by C. Conti Rossini (ed.), *Historia Regni Sarsa Dengel (Malak Sagad)*, CSCO 20 and 21 (1907, repr. 1955). Other important Ethiopian texts available are E. Cerulli (ed.), *Scritti teologici etiopici dei secoli XVI–XVII*, 2 vols. (Rome, 1958 and 1960), E. J. van Donzel (ed.), *Enbaqom, Angasa Amin (La Porte de la Foi): Apologie éthiopienne du Christianisme contre l'Islam à partir du Coran* (Leiden, 1969), L. Ricci (ed.), 'Le vite de Enbaqom e di Yohannes abbati di Dabra Libanos di Scioa', *RSE* 13 (1954), 91–120, 14 (1955–8), 69–108, 22 (1966), 75–102, 23 (1967–8), 79–219, 24 (1969–70), 134–232; see also L. Ricci, 'La "vita" di Enbaqom e l' "Anqasa amin"', *RSE* 24 (1969–70), 233–41, C. Conti Rossini, 'L'autobiographia de Pawlos monaco abissino del secolo XVI', *Rendiconti delle Reale Accademia dei Lincei*, 5/27 (1918).

For the *Jihad* of Gran there is one Arab text of the greatest value: René

Basset (ed.), *Histoire de la conquête de l'Abyssinie par Chihab Eddin Ahmed Ben Abd El Qader*, 2 vols. (Paris, 1897). This does, however, come to an end a full five years before the death of Gran. The Portuguese sources for this period begin with the exceptionally important account of Francesco Alvares, published in English as *The Prester John of the Indies*, ed. E. F. Beckingham and G. W. B. Huntingford, 2 vols. (Cambridge, 1961), describing Ethiopia in the 1520s. For the 1540s we have Miguel de Castanhoso, *The Portuguese Expedition to Abyssinia in 1541–1543*, ed. R. S. Whiteway (1902). Whiteway has included in this volume a translation of the mendacious 'Short Account' of João Bermudez, together with a number of selected letters. Volumes i and x of C. Beccari, *Rerum Aethiopicarum Scriptores Occidentales* (Rome, 1903–1917) contain sixteenth-century material relating to the Jesuits.

2. Primary Sources: The Seventeenth Century

For the seventeenth century the principal surviving Ethiopian chronicles are *Chronica de Susenyos, rei de Ethiopia*, ed. F. M. E. Pereira (Lisbon, 1892–1900) and *Annales Iohannis I, Iyasu I et Bakaffa*, ed. I. Guidi, *CSCO* 1 and 2 (1903). The most important other historical text is that of the *Acta Sanctae Walatta Petros (1594–1644)*, ed. C. Conti Rossini and C. Jaeger, *CSCO* 68 (1912), Ethiopic text, and *Vita di Walatta Pietros*, tr. L. Ricci, *CSCO* 316 (1970), Italian translation.

For the first half of the seventeenth century the fifteen volumes of Beccari provide a massive collection of Jesuit materials, divided as follows: i, various; ii–iii, P. Paez, 'Historia de Ethiopia'; iv, three works by Emmanuel Barradas; v–vii, E. D'Almeida, 'Historia Aethiopiae', largely based on Paez but carrying on the story beyond Paez's death; viii–ix, A. Mendez, 'Expeditio Aethiopica'; x, sixteenth-century letters; xi, seventeenth-century letters up to 1623; xii, letters 1622–35; xiii, letters 1633–72; xiv letters 1697–1708, 1782–1815; xv, index. Sections of Almeida have been published in English by C. F. Beckingham and G. W. B. Huntingford, *Some Records of Ethiopia 1593–1646* (1954). Beccari did not include one major Jesuit source, that of Jeronimo Lobo. His *Itinerario* was first translated into English by Dr Johnson. There is a definitive modern edition based on the original text, only recently rediscovered, ed. M. G. da Costa and Donald Lockhart (1984).

3. Primary Sources: The Eighteenth Century

The surviving chronicles, besides *Annales Iohannis I, Iyasu I et Bakaffa*, ed. Guidi, are as follows: *Annales Regum Iyasu II et Iyo'as*, ed. I. Guidi, *CSCO*

61 and 66 (1910 and 1912) and *The Royal Chronicle of Abyssinia 1769–1840*, ed. H. Weld Blundell (Cambridge, 1922). The last-named is a wonderful work, comparable in vitality with the chronicles of Amda Seyon and Sarsa Dengel, but it chiefly relates to Takla Giyorgis. The principal external sources for the eighteenth century are the accounts of two visits: that of the Frenchman Charles-Jacques Poncet to Gondar in 1699–1700, whose *Journey to Ethiopia* was first published in English in 1709 and republished in W. Foster (ed.), *The Red Sea and Adjacent Countries at the Close of the Seventeenth Century* (1949), 89–165, and that of the Scotsman James Bruce in 1770–1, *Travels to Discover the Source of the Nile* (1st edn. 5 vols., 1790; 2nd, posthumous edn. 8 vols., 1804–5). Extracts from Bruce have been published under the same title, ed. C. F. Beckingham (Edinburgh, 1964). Bruce remains the most entertaining but not the most reliable of travellers in Ethiopia. For Poncet see S. Tedeschi, 'Poncet et son voyage en Éthiopie', *JES* 4 (1966), 99–125.

4. Modern Historical Works

There is a great lack of modern critical historical writing on this entire period. Most of the wider writing of a generation ago can be seriously misleading from one aspect or another, for example the learned volumes of J.-B. Coulbeaux, *Histoire politique et religieuse d'Abyssinie* (Paris, 1928) are deeply affected by the author's RC missionary commitment. C. Conti Rossini was probably the greatest of twentieth-century Ethiopicists but, unfortunately, he never carried his history of Ethiopia beyond the Middle Ages. For recent work see the two summary chapters in *CHA* with their bibliographical essays and bibliographies: T. Tamrat, 'Ethiopia, the Red Sea and the Horn', iii. 98–182, and M. Abir, 'Ethiopia and the Horn of Africa', iv. 537–77.

Joseph Cuoq, *L'Islam en Éthiopie des origines au xvie siècle* (Paris, 1981) is authoritative on its subject; see also J. S. Trimingham, *Islam in Ethiopia* (1952), and, for the *Jihad*, Asa J. Davies, 'The Sixteenth Century Jihad in Ethiopia', *JHN* 2 (1963), 566–92, and 3 (1964), 113–28.

For relations with the Catholic Church in the sixteenth century see P. M. Chaine, SJ, 'Un monastère éthiopien à Rome au xve et xvie siècle', *Mélanges de la Faculté orientale* (Beyrouth, 1911), v, 1–36, Renato Lefevre, 'Documenti e notizie su Tasfa Seyon e la sua attivita Romana nel secolo XVI', *RSE* 24 (1969–70), 74–133, S. E. Euringer, 'Der Pseudopatriarch Johannes Bermudes (1639–56)', *Theologie und Glaube*, 17 (1925), 226–56, A. Brou, SJ, 'Saint Ignace et la mission d'Éthiopie 1545–1556', *RHM* (1936), 341–55, J. Brodrick, SJ, *The Progress of the Jesuits* (1947), 236–67, L. Lozza, *La confessione di Claudio, re d'Etiopia* (Palermo, 1947), and Girma Beshah and

Merid Aregay, *The Question of the Union of the Churches in Luso–Ethiopian Relations* (Lisbon, 1964).

For relations with the Catholic Church in the seventeenth century, besides the basic texts in Beccari and in Beshah and Aregay, *The Question of the Union of the Churches in Luso–Ethiopian Relations*, see P. Caraman, *The Lost Empire* (1985), and a chapter by Metodio Caribbio da Nembro, 'Martirio ed espulsione in Etiopia', in *PMFR* i/1. 624–49; for the eighteenth century, see a further chapter by da Nembro, 'La missione etiopica nel secolo XVIII', in *PMFR* ii. 463–95, vol. xiv of Beccari, two articles by T. Somigli, 'La francescana spedizione in Etiopia del 1751–54 e la sua relazione del P. Remedio Protky di Boemia O.F.M.', *Archivum Franciscanum Historicum*, 6 (1913), 129–43, and 'L'itinerarium del P. Remedio Protky, viaggatore e missionario francescano (Alto Egitto) e il suo viaggio in Abissinia, 21 Febbraio 1752–22 Aprile 1753', *Studi Francescani*, NS 22 (1925), 425–60, and Z. Maly, 'The Visit of Mlartin Lang, Czech Franciscan, in Gondar in 1752', *JES* 10/2 (1972), 17–25. M. Pacelli, *Viaggi in Etiopia del P. Michelangelo da Tricarico, Minore osservante* (Naples, 1797) is important for the mission of Mgr. Tobias in the 1790s. A chronicle of Catholic activity between the departure of Mendes in 1632 and that of the Abune Tobia in 1797 is provided by K. O'Mahoney, 'Abune Tobia and his Apostolic Predecessors, in Commemoration of the Bicentenary of an Ethiopian Bishop's Consecration', *Quaderni di studi etiopici*, 8–9 (1987–8), 102–71.

G. Haile, 'A Christ for the Gentiles: The Case of Za-Krestos of Ethiopia', *JRA* 15 (1985), 86–95, publishes the texts for a unique piece of Ethiopian religious history. For the christological controversies of the seventeenth and eighteenth centuries see Mario da Abiy-Addi, *La dottrina della chiesa etiopica dissidente sull'unione ipostatica*, Orientalia Christiana Analecta, 147 (Rome, 1956), Yacob Benene, *L'unzione de Cristo nella teologia etiopica*, Orientalia Christiana Analecta, 215 (Rome, 1981), I. Guidi, 'Uno squarcio della storia ecclesiastica di Abissinia', *Bessarione*, 49–50 (1900), 10–25, and G. Haile, 'Materials on the Theology of Qebat or Unction', in G. Goldenberg (ed.), *Ethiopian Studies: Proceedings of the 6th International Conference* (held in Tel Aviv, 1980) (Rotterdam, 1988).

For wider cultural and social dimensions see *inter alia*: E. Cerulli, *La letteratura etiopica*, 3rd edn. (1968); J. Leroy, 'L'Évangeliaire éthiopien illustré du British Museum (OR510) et ses sources iconographiques', *Annales d'Éthiopie*, 4 (1961), 155–80, and S. Chojnacki, ' "Flemish" Painting and its Ethiopian Copy: The Iconography of the Pietà in Ethiopia in the Seventeenth and Eighteenth Centuries', in S. Uhlig and B. Tafla (eds.), *Collectanea Aethiopica* (Stuttgart, 1988), 51–73, illustrate developments in Gondarine art; E. van Donzel, *Foreign Relations of Ethiopia 1642–1700* (Leiden, 1979) is of wider significance than the title might suggest, as is M.

Aregay, 'Society and Technology in Ethiopia 1500–1800', *JES* 17 (1984), 127–47. David Mathew, *Ethiopia: The Study of a Polity 1540–1935* (1947), Sylvia Pankhurst, *Ethiopia: A Cultural History* (1955), J. Doresse, *Ethiopia* (1959), and A. Bartnicki and J. Mantel-Niecko, 'The Role and Significance of the Religious Conflicts and People's Movements in the Political Life of Ethiopia in the Seventeenth and Eighteenth Centuries', *RSE* 24 (1969–70), 5–39, are all somewhat dated but remain well worth consulting.

CHAPTER 5

EQUIANO TO NTSIKANA: FROM THE 1780S TO THE 1820S

1. *Anti-Slavery*

Equiano's autobiography was first published in London (1789), by himself as *The Interesting Narrative of the Life of Olaudah Equiano, or, Gustavus Vassa, the African*. It was reprinted in 1969, ed. Paul Edwards and an abridged edition, also by Edwards, appeared in 1967. Ottobah Cugoano's *Thoughts and Sentiments on the Evils of Slavery* (1787), was also reprinted in 1969. P. Hoare (ed.), *Memoirs of Granville Sharp* (1820), includes reference to both men.

For the anti-slavery campaign and Evangelicalism in general see E. Howse, *Saints in Politics: The Clapham Sect and the Growth of Freedom* (1971), S. Jakobsson, *Am I not a Man and a Brother?: British Mission and the Abolition of the Slave Trade and Slavery in West Africa and the West Indies 1786–1838* (Uppsala, 1972), R. Anstey, *The Atlantic Slave Trade and British Abolition 1760–1810* (1975), C. Bolt and S. Drescher (ed.), *Anti-Slavery, Religion and Reform* (Folkestone, 1980), D. W. Bebbington, *Evangelicalism in Modern Britain: A History from the 1730s to the 1980s* (1989), and E. Wilson, *Thomas Clarkson* (1989).

2. *West Coast Protestantism and Sierra Leone*

For the eighteenth-century Protestant presence on the west coast prior to the Sierra Leone colony, see T. Thompson, *An Account of Two Missionary Voyages by the Appointment of the Society for the Propagation of the Faith in Foreign Parts* (1758; repr. 1937), F. L. Bartels, 'Philip Quaque, 1741–1816', *Transactions of the Gold Coast and Togoland Historical Society* (Achimota), 1, part v (1955), 153–77, H. W. Debrunner, 'Notable Danish Chaplains', *Transactions of the Gold Coast and Togoland Historical Society*, 2 (1956), 13–39, F. L. Bartels, 'J. E. J. Capitein 1717–1747', *Transactions of the Historical Society of Ghana*, 4 (1959), 3–13, H. Debrunner, 'Sieckentroosters, Predikants and Chaplains: A Documentation of the History of Dutch and English Chaplains to Guinea before 1750', *BSACH* 1 (1965), 73–89, M. Priestley,

'Philip Quaque of Cape Coast', in P. D. Curtin (ed.), *Africa Remembered* (1968), 99–139.

The essential studies of Sierra Leone are Christopher Fyfe, *A History of Sierra Leone* (1962) and J. Peterson, *Province of Freedom* (1969). C. Fyfe, *Sierra Leone Inheritance* (1964) is a useful volume of primary documents. *An Account of the Colony of Sierra Leone, from its First Establishment in 1793: Being the Substance of a Report Delivered to the Proprietors* (1795) gives a valuable early official account of developments, while A. M. Falconbridge, *Two Voyages to Sierra Leone during the Years 1791–2–3* (1794) gives a lively unofficial one. M. Knutsford, *Life and Letters of Zachary Macaulay* (1901) includes much material on the early years. There are a number of important articles in the *Sierra Leone Bulletin of Religion*: A. F. Walls, 'The Nova Scotian Settlers and their Religion', 1 (1959), 19–31; C. Fyfe, 'The West African Methodists in the Nineteenth Century', 3 (1961), 22–8; C. Fyfe, 'The Countess of Huntingdon's Connection in Nineteenth-Century Sierra Leone', 4 (1962), 53–61; C. Fyfe, 'The Baptist Churches in Sierra Leone', 5 (1963), 55–60; P. Hair, 'Freetown Christianity and Africa', 6 (1964), 13–21. To these should be added A. H. M. Kirk-Green, 'David George: The Nova Scotian Experience', *Sierra Leone Studies*, NS 14 (1960), 93–120, A. F. Walls, 'A Christian Experiment: The Early Sierra Leone Colony', in G. J. Cumming (ed.), *The Mission of the Church and the Propagation of the Faith*, SCH vi (1970), 107–29, and E. G. Wilson, *John Clarkson and the African Adventure* (1980).

3. *Islam*

For the jihad of Shehu Usuman dan Fodio and Islam in early nineteenth-century West Africa, the most authoritative recent studies are Mervyn Hiskett, *The Sword of Truth: The Life and Times of the Shehu Usuman Dan Fodio* (1973), Murray Last, *The Sokoto Caliphate* (1967), H. A. S. Johnston, *The Fulani Empire of Sokoto* (1967), B. G. Martin, *Muslim Brotherhoods in Nineteenth-Century Africa* (1967), M. Kane, *The Islamic Regime of Fuuta Tooro* (East Lansing, Mich., 1984), and David Robinson, *The Holy War of Umar Tal: The Western Sudan in the Mid-Nineteenth Century* (1985). There are selections of texts in Hodgkin, *Nigerian Perspectives*, 244–56, and J. Hargreaves, *France and West Africa* (1969), 119–34.

4. *The Kongo*

For the Kongo in the late eighteenth and early nineteenth centuries see L. Jadin, 'Relation sur le royaume du Congo du P. Raimondo da Dicomano, missionnaire du 1791 à 1795', *Bulletin des séances de L'Academie royale des sciences coloniales* (Brussels), NS, (1957), 307–37, T. Filesi, 'L'epilogo della "Missio antiqua" dei cappucini nel regno del Congo 1800–1835', *Euntes*

Docete, 23 (1970), 377–439, L. Jadin, 'Les survivances chrétiennes au Congo au XIXe siècle', *EHA* 1 (1970), 137–85, and Susan Broadhead, 'Beyond Decline: The Kingdom of Kongo in the Eighteenth and Nineteenth Centuries', *IJA* 12/4 (1979), 615–50. Garcia V's correspondence is to be found in L. Jadin, 'Recherches dans les archives et bibliothèques d'Italie et du Portugal', *Bulletin de l'Academie royale des sciences coloniales*, 2 (1956), 958–69.

5. *South Africa*

B. Kruger, *The Pear Tree Blossoms* (Genadendal, 1966) is authoritative for the Moravians in South Africa. See also H. Bredekamp and H. Plüddemann (ed.), *The Genadendal Diaries: Diaries of the Herrnhut Missionaries H. Mansveld, D. Schwinn and J. C. Kühnel*, i, 1792–1794 (Bellville, SA, 1992). For early London Missionary Society work the volumes of the *Transactions of the Missionary Society* (1795–) are valuable, as is I. H. Enklaar's *Life and Work of Dr J. Th. van der Kemp 1747–1811* (Rotterdam, 1988).

For South African mission history in general in this period see P. Hinchliff, *The Church in South Africa* (1968), R. Lovett, *The History of the London Missionary Society 1795–1895* (1899), Harry Gailey, *The LMS and the Cape Government 1799–1828* (Los Angeles, 1957), P. Hinchliff, *A Calendar of Missionary Correspondence from the Colony of the Cape of Good Hope 1800–1850* (Pretoria, 1967), Jane Sales, *The Planting of the Churches in South Africa* (1971), B. Holt, *Joseph Williams and the Pioneer Mission to the South-Eastern Bantu* (Lovedale, 1954), J. Sales, *Mission Stations and the Coloured Communities of the Eastern Cape 1800–1852* (Cape Town, 1975), and V. C. Malherbe, 'The Life and Times of Cupido Kakkerlak', *JAH* 20 (1979), 365–78. The thirty-six volumes of the *Records of the Cape Colony 1793–1831*, ed. G. Theal (1897–1905) contain many mission-related documents.

Among contemporary accounts of the state of the mission in the two decades following Van der Kemp's death are John Campbell, *Travels in South Africa*, undertaken at the request of the Missionary Society (1815) and his further *Travels in South Africa . . . being a Narrative of a Second Journey, 1820*, 2 vols. (1822), Robert Moffat's *Missionary Labours and Scenes in Southern Africa* (1842), and John Philip's *Researches in South Africa*, 2 vols. (1828). See also Chapter 7 for a fuller missionary bibliography.

For background to early Xhosa Christianity see J. B. Peires, *The House of Phalo* (Johannesburg, 1981), J. Hodgson, *The God of the Xhosa* (Cape Town, 1982), and B. Maclennan, *A Proper Degree of Terror: John Graham and the Cape's Eastern Frontier* (Johannesburg, 1986). For Tshatshu see P. J. Jonas, 'Jan Tshatshu and the Eastern Cape Mission: A Contextual Analysis', *Missionalia* (Pretoria), 18 (1990), 277–92; for Ntsikana see J. B. Peires, 'Nxele, Ntsikana and the Origins of the Xhosa Religious Reaction', *JAH*

20 (1979), 51–61, J. Hodgson, *Ntsikana's Great Hymn: A Xhosa Expression of Christianity in the Early Nineteenth Century* (Cape Town, 1980), and J. Hodgson, 'Ntsikana: History and Symbol. Studies in a Process of Religious Change among Xhosa-Speaking People', Ph.D. thesis (Cape Town, 1985).

CHAPTER 6

THE LION REVIVED: ETHIOPIA IN THE NINETEENTH CENTURY

1. Primary Texts

The principal nineteenth-century Ethiopian sources available in translation for the general history of the country are as follows: *Chronique de Théodoros II, roi des rois d'Éthiopie 1853–1868*, ed. C. Mondon-Vidailhet (Paris, n.d.) (the author, Alaga Walda, was close to Abuna Salama); M. Moreno (ed.), 'La cronaca di re Teodoro attribuita al dabtara "Zaneb"', *RSE* 2 (1942), 143–80; L. Fusella (ed.), 'La cronaca dell'imperatore Teodoro II di Etiopia in un manoscritto amarico', *Annali dell'Istituto Universitario Orientale di Napoli*, NS 6 (1954–6), 61–121; C. Conti Rossini, 'Nuovi documenti per la storia d'Abissinia nel secolo XIX', *Rendiconti della Reale Accademia dei Lincei*, S8, 2 (1947), 357–416, M. Chaine (ed.), 'Histoire du règne de Iohannes IV, roi d'Éthiopie 1868–1889', *Revue sémitique*, 21 (1913), and Guebre Sellasie, *Chronique du règne de Menélik II, Roi des Rois d'Ethiopie*, 2 vols. (Paris, 1930–1).

The most useful non-missionary European published sources for the period up to the fall of Theodore (after which they became far more numerous) are as follows, in roughly chronological order: H. Salt, *A Voyage to Abyssinia . . . in the Years 1809 and 1810* (1814), N. Pearce, *The Life and Adventures of Nathaniel Pearce, Written by himself, during a Residence in Abyssinia from the Years 1810 to 1819*, W. C. Harris, *The Highlands of Ethiopia (being the Account of Eighteen Months of a British Embassy to the Christian Court of Shoa)*, 3 vols. (1844), C. Johnson, *Travels in Southern Ethiopia, through the Country of Adal to the Kingdom of Shoa*, 2 vols. (1844), Antoine d'Abbadie, *Voyage en Abyssinie* (Paris, 1839), and Arnauld d'Abbadie, *Douze ans de séjour dans la Haute-Éthiopie*, 3 vols., ed. J.-M. Allier (Vatican, 1980 and 1983) (in fact eleven years, 1838–48), *Parliamentary Papers, 1867–8*, LXXII, *Accounts and Papers*, 33, *Correspondence respecting Abyssinia 1846–1868* (1868).

2. Emperors and Church

For a helpful review of modern Ethiopian historical writing, see Donald Crummey, 'Society, State and Nationality in the Recent Historiography of

Ethiopia', *JAH* 31 (1990), 103–119, and for a general analysis of Ethiopian society, John Markakis, *Ethiopia: Anatomy of a Traditional Polity* (1974).

Modern studies for the first part of the century include: M. Abir, *Ethiopia: The Era of the Princes, the Challenge of Islam and the Re-unification of the Christian Empire 1769–1855* (1968), Sven Rubenson, *King of Kings: Tewodros of Ethiopia* (1966), D. E Crummey, 'Tewodros as Reformer and Modernizer', *JAH* 10 (1969), 457–69, and D. E. Crummey, 'The Violence of Tewodros', *JES* 9 (1971), 107–25. For the prophecy of Tewodros see René Basset, *Les Apocryphes éthiopiens* (Paris, 1909), sect. 11, 'Fekkare Iyasous', as also J. Bruce, *Travels to Discover the Source of the Nile* (1805), ii. 64.

For the more recent period as a whole, see B. Zewde, *A History of Modern Ethiopia 1855–1974* (1991). For the reigns of Yohannes and Menelik: Bairu Tafla (ed.), *A Chronicle of Emperor Yohannes IV (1872–89)* (Wiesbaden, 1977), Harold Marcus, *The Life and Times of Menelik II* (1975), C. Prouty, *Empress Taytu and Menelik II: Ethiopia 1883–1910* (1986), T. B. Selassie, 'Life and Career of Dajajmach Balca, Aba Näfso', *JES* 9 (1971), 173–89, R. Caulk, 'Religion and the State in Nineteenth-Century Ethiopia', *JES* 10 (1972), 23–41, D. Crummey, 'Sheikh Zäkaryas: An Ethiopian Prophet', *JES* 10 (1972), 55–66, Negaso Gidada and D. Crummcy, 'The Introduction and Expansion of Orthodox Christianity in Qélém Awraja, Western Wälläga, from about 1886 to 1941', *JES* 10 (1972), 103–12, Bairu Tafla, 'Two of the Last Provincial Kings of Ethiopia', *JES* 11 (1973), 29–55, V. Stitz, 'Distribution and Foundation of Churches in Ethiopia', *JES* 13 (1975), 11–36, D. E. Crummey, 'Orthodoxy and Imperial Reconstruction in Ethiopia 1854–87', *Journal of Theological Studies*, NS 29 (1978), 427–42.

3. Catholics and Protestants

For missionary history, both Catholic and Protestant, up to the death of Tewodros, D. E. Crummey, *Priests and Politicians* (1972) is an invaluable guide, including its bibliography. The principal available Protestant sources are S. Gobat, *Journal of a Three Years' Residence in Abyssinia in Furtherance of the Objects of the Church Missionary Society* (1834), C. W. Isenberg and J. L. Krapf, *Travels, Researches and Missionary Labours* (1860; 2nd. edn. with introductory essay by R. C. Bridges, 1968), W. Douglas Veitch (ed.), *Notes from the Journal of F. M. Flad* (1860), Theophilus Waldmeier, *Autobiography* (1886), and H. Gundert, *Biography of the Revd Charles Isenberg* (1885).

On the Catholic side, see I. A. de Villapadierna, 'La Sagrada Congregacion y los problemas de la mision de Etiopia 1838–1922', *PFMR* 3/1, 341–64, but pride of place should be given to the writings of the Ethiopian Catholic priest, Takla Haymanot: *Episodi della vita apostolica di Abuna Jacob* (Asmara, 1915) (unfortunately this is an Italian translation from a French translation of the Ethiopian original), 'Vicende dell'Etiopia e delle missioni cattoliche ai tempi di Ras Ali, Deggiac Ubie e Re Tedoro', ed. C. Conti Rossini, *Rendiconti della Reale Accademia dei Lincei*, 5/25 (1916), 425–550, *Lettere di Abba Tecle Haymanot di Adua*, ed. M. de Leonessa, 4 vols. (Rome, 1939). To these should be added J.-B. Coulbeaux's biography of Ghebra-Michael: *Un martyr abyssin: Ghebra-Michael de la Congregation de la mission* (Paris, 1902), revised and republished as *Vers la Lumière: Le bienheureux abba Ghebre-Michael* (Paris, 1926).

There are several European biographies of de Jacobis including M. Demimuid, *Vie du vénérable Justin de Jacobis* (Paris, 1905), S. Arata, *Abuna Jakob apostolo dell'Abissinia* (Rome, 1934), S. Pane, *Il Beato Giustino de Jacobis* (Naples, 1949) and L. Betta, 'Il B. Giustino de Jacobis, Prefetto Apostolo dell'Ethiopia', *Annali della missione*, 67 (1960), 288–313, 350–73, 68 (1961), 154–206. G. Sapeto, *Viaggio e missione catholica* (Rome, 1857) is a first-hand account by the first of the Lazarists. For Massaja there is a massive published bibliography, A. Dalbesio, *Guglielmo Massaja: Bibliografia-Iconographia* (Turin, 1973). His own twelve volumes, *I miei trentacinque anni di missione nell'Alta Etiopica* (Rome, 1885–95) must be supplemented by G. Farina (ed.), *Le lettere del Cardinal Massaja dal 1846 al 1886* (Turin, 1936) and G. Massaja, *Memorie storiche del Vicariato Apostolico dei Galla*, ed. Antonio Rossi, 6 vols. (Vatican, 1984). See also P. Gimalac, 'Le Vicariat Apostolique d'Abyssinie 1830–1931', *RHM* 9 (1932), 129–90, A. Jarosseau, 'L'Apostolat catholique au Kafa (Éthiopie) de 1862 à 1912', *RHM* 9 (1932), 94–101, G. Bernoville, *Monseigneur Jarosseau et la mission des Gallas 1858–1941* (Paris, 1950), P. Metodio da Nembro, *La missione dei Minori Cappuccini in Eritrea 1894–1952* (Rome, 1953), and Jan de Potter, 'The Role of Ethiopian Officials in the Growth of the Consolata Mission in South-West Ethiopia', *RSE* 26 (1973–7), 5–20. For the most recent history of the Ethiopian Catholic Church see Kevin O'Mahoney, *The Ebullient Phoenix: A History of the Vicariate of Abyssinia*, i (1839–60), ii (1860–81) (Asmara, 1987), and iii (1882–1916) (Addis Ababa, 1992).

CHAPTER 7

THE VICTORIAN MISSIONARY

1. *Introductory*

The wealth of material for the nineteenth-century missionary movement, archival and printed, is overwhelming. For guides to the principal missionary archives, see the General Section, Guides to Archives, above. Most Protestant missionary societies produced annual reports or volumes of official proceedings as well as much else ranging from the heavyweight to the highly ephemeral. Some of it was aimed at the most committed and well-informed readership and could include lengthy accounts of individual missions; some of it was for children or for a popular readership and was distributed free. Thus, to give the single example of the CMS, its annual reports date from 1801. In 1813 the monthly *Missionary Reporter* was begun and continued until 1856. It was not confined to the CMS and published much material relating to other missions but it was for long the principal publication in which CMS activity was reported. A single volume (e.g. that of 1820) might include no fewer than 540 pages. The CMS began to publish its own *Record* from 1830; it had produced the *Quarterly Paper*, distributed free, from 1816; to these it added the *Gleaner* in 1838 and the *Juvenile Instructor* in 1842. In 1849 it began a new, more highbrow, monthly, the *Intelligencer*. While much of this was highly serious, including massive extracts from the letters and reports of individual missionaries, it was all intended to obtain support, emotional and financial, for mission work. Anything likely to discredit the mission was naturally excluded. It was, moreover, put together by people who, in most cases, themselves had no experience of Africa and who could inject an emphasis different from that of the missionaries themselves. Such publications, as also the missionary sermons of numerous clerics who never worked abroad and even the comments of biographers of missionaries, are all good evidence of the way the missionary movement was fuelled at home, but it is not always reliable evidence of the way missionaries were actually behaving or thinking. Such literature tended to idealize missionaries and to degrade Africa both in the nineteenth and the twentieth century. Missionaries themselves at times protested at the way their supporting magazines described their work, but on the whole they may have liked to be depicted as invariably heroic.

2. *The Main Missionary Histories*

There are almost limitless books by missionaries and biographies of missionaries, of unequal value. There are histories of all the more important societies, there are some valuable modern studies of the missions within a particular country or region, and there are a number of more general works, as well as numerous monographs focusing on particular missions, events, or developments. Yet there is no single reliable modern study of either the Protestant or the Catholic missionary movement in the nineteenth century as a whole in relation to Africa, let alone of the two combined. There is not even one of the British missionary movement and its impact on Africa. While much of what was written in the past was uncritically hagiographical, some of what has been written more recently has been unduly dismissive. What is listed here is very much a selection and it leaves out titles judged more appropriate for inclusion under Chapter 5, 9, or 10. C. P. Groves, *The Planting of Christianity in Africa*, i (1948), ii (1954), iii

(1955), all deal in part or entirety with the nineteenth century. This remains by far the best overall survey of missionary activity, Protestant at least. It is very much more patchy for Catholics. K. S. Latourette, *A History of the Expansion of Christianity*, 7 vols. (1937–45), v, fulfils the same role, if in less detail. The principal histories of Protestant societies are as follows: C. F. Pascoe, *Two Hundred Years of the SPG* (1901), C. Hole, *The Early History of the Church Missionary Society* (1896), E. Stock, *A History of the Church Missionary Society*, 3 vols. (1899), R. Lovett, *History of the London Missionary Society*, 3 vols. (1899), E. G. K. Hewat, *Vision and Achievement 1796–1956: A History of the Foreign Missions of the Churches United in the Church of Scotland* (1960), A. Anderson-Morshead, *The History of the Universities' Mission to Central Africa 1859–1909* (1955), H. P. Thompson, *Into All Lands: The History of the Society for the Propagation of the Gospel in Foreign Parts 1701–1950* (1951), G. G. Findlay and W. W. Holdsworth, *The History of the Wesleyan Methodist Missionary Society*, 5 vols. (1922), B. Stanley, *The History of the Baptist Missionary Society 1792–1992* (Edinburgh, 1992), W. Schlatter, *Geschichte der Basler Mission,* 3 vols. (Basle, 1916), E. Strassberger, *The Rhenish Mission Society in South Africa 1830–1950* (Cape Town, 1969), J. Simensen (ed.), *Norwegian Missions in African History*, i, *South Africa 1845–1906* (1986).

3. *Protestant Missionaries: Contemporary Published Accounts*

A selection of the principal writings of or about individual Protestant missionaries who were at work in Africa before 1890, published in their lifetime or shortly after their deaths: John Philip, *Researches in South Africa*, 2 vols. (1828), Robert Moffat, *Missionary Labours and Scenes in Southern Africa* (1842), J. F. Schön and S. A. Crowther, *Journals* (1842), Thomas Birch Freeman, *Journal of Various Visits* (1844), J. W. Colenso, *Ten Weeks in Natal* (1855), David Livingstone, *Missionary Travels and Researches in South Africa* (1857), T. J. Bowen, *Adventures and Mission Labours* (New York, 1857), Johann Krapf, *Travels, Researches and Missionary Labours* (1860), H. M. Waddell, *Twenty-Nine Years in the West Indies and Central Africa* (1863), H. Goodwin, *Memoirs of Bishop Mackenzie* (1864), W. Shaw, *The Story of my Mission in South-Eastern Africa* (1865), John Mackenzie, *Ten Years North of the Orange River* (1871; new edn., ed. Cecil Northcott, 1971), Anna Hinderer, *Seventeen Years in the Yoruba Country* (1872), W. B. Boyce, *Memoir of the Revd William Shaw* (1874), *The Last Journals of David Livingstone*, ed. H. Waller (1874), George Townshend, *Memoirs of Henry Townshend* (1887), E. C. Dawson, *James Hannington* (1887), E. B. Underhill, *Alfred Saker: A Biography* (1884), R. M. Heanley, *A Memoir of Edward Steere* (1888), G. W. Cox, *The Life of John William Colenso* (1888), Eugene Casalis, *My Life in Basutoland* (1889), Mrs H. Grattan Guinness, *The New World of Central Africa* (1890), A. M. Mackay, by his sister (J. W. Harrison) (1890), as also *The Story of*

Mackay of Uganda by his sister (1892)—the matter in the two books is significantly different, M. Benham, *Henry Callaway* (1896), François Coillard, *On the Threshold of Central Africa* (1897), G.W. (Gertrude Ward), *The Life of Charles Alan Smythies* (1898), W. A. Elmslie, *Among the Wild Ngoni* (1899), H. H. Dobinson, *Letters of Henry Hughes Dobinson* (1899), W. Holman Bentley, *Pioneering on the Congo*, 2 vols. (1900), James Wells, *Stewart of Lovedale* (1908), G. Hawker, *The Life of George Grenfell, Congo Missionary and Explorer* (1909), Robert H. Nassau, *My Ogowe* (New York, 1914), W. P. Livingstone, *Mary Slessor of Calabar* (1915), W. P. Livingstone, *Laws of Livingstonia* (1921), W. P. Johnson, *My African Reminiscences 1875–1895* (1924), E. H. Barnes, *Johnson of Nyasaland* (1935). The 800 pages of C. Lewis and C. Edwards (ed.), *Historical Records of the Church of the Province of South Africa* (1934) are a mine of information, even if the choice of documents for publication remains selective. E. Favre, *La Vie d'un missionnaire français: François Coillard, 1834–1904*, 3 vols. (Paris, 1908–13) is the official life of the best-known French Protestant missionary of the period and H. P. Junod, *Henri Alexandre Junod: Missionnaire et savant* (Lausanne, 1934) that of the greatest Swiss one.

4. Journals and Letters

Among more recent scholarly editions of nineteenth-century missionary journals and letters are the following, in roughly chronological order: *The Journals of the Revd T. L. Hodgson, Missionary to the Seleka-Rolong and the Griquas 1821–1831*, ed. R. L. Cope (Johannesburg, 1977), *The Journal of John Ayliff 1821–1830*, ed. P. Hinchliff (Cape Town, 1972), *The Journal of William Shaw*, ed. W. D. Hammond-Tuke (Cape Town, 1972), *Never a Young Man: Extracts from the Letters and Journals of Rev. William Shaw*, ed. C. Sadler (Cape Town, 1967), *The Kitchingman Papers: Missionary Letters and Journals 1817 to 1848*, ed. B. Le Cordeur and C. Saunders (Johannesburg, 1976), including many letters of Philip and Read, *Letters of the American Missionaries 1835–1838*, ed. D. J. Kotze (Cape Town, 1950). See also P. Hinchliff (ed.), *Calendar of Cape Missionary Correspondence 1800–1850* (Grahamstown, 1967). This lists, and summarizes the content of, letters in the British missionary archives of the LMS, SPG, and MMS.

For Robert Moffat we have *Apprenticeship at Kuruman: Being the Journals and Letters of Robert and Mary Moffat 1820–1828*, ed. I. Schapera (1951), and Robert Moffat, *Matebeleland Journals*, ed. J. Wallis, 2 vols. (1945). For Livingstone there is a very great deal. His *Last Journals* were already published by Horace Waller in the year following his death. I. Schapera edited his *Family Letters* in two volumes (1959), the particularly valuable *Missionary Correspondence 1841–1856* (1961), the *Private Journals 1851–1853* (1960), and *South African Papers 1849–1853* (Cape Town, 1974), while J.

Wallis edited *The Zambezi Expedition 1858–1863*, 2 vols. (1956). J. Wallis also edited *The Zambezi Journals of James Stewart* (1952) while N. R. Bennet and M. Ylvisaker have edited *The Central African Journal of Lovell J. Procter 1860–1864* (1971). Procter was a priest colleague of Bishop Mackenzie.

J. Wallis edited *The Matabele Mission: A Selection from the Correspondence of John and Emily Moffat, David Livingstone and Others 1858–1878* (1945). *The Papers of John Mackenzie* were edited by A. J. Dachs (Johannesburg, 1975), and *Gold and the Gospel in Mashonaland 1888*, the first part being the Mashonaland Journal of Bishop Knight-Bruce, was edited by C. Fripp (1949).

5. *Henry Venn*

Henry Venn is treated at length in volumes i and ii of Stock's *History of the CMS*. William Knight published *The Missionary Secretariat of Henry Venn* in 1880 and *Memoir of Henry Venn* in 1882. Max Warren edited a selection of his writings in 1971 entitled *To Apply the Gospel*. The best modern studies are T. E. Yates, *Venn and Victorian Bishops Abroad* (1978), W. B. Shenk, *Henry Venn: Missionary Statesman* (1983) and C. Peter Williams, *The Ideal of the Self-Governing Church* (Leiden, 1990). The last may be the most authoritative.

6. *Livingstone and Other Leading Figures: Recent Monographs*

T. A. Simons (ed.), *A Bibliography of Published Works by and about David Livingstone 1853–1975* (Capetown, 1978) is a basic tool for Livingstone studies, together with G. W. Clendennen, *David Livingstone: A Catalogue of Documents* (Edinburgh, 1979). Modern biographies include G. Seaver, *David Livingstone: His Life and Letters* (1957), T. Jeal, *Livingstone* (1973), and O. Ransford, *David Livingstone: The Dark Interior* (1978), rather psychological. B. Pachai (ed.), *Livingstone: Man of Africa* (1973) is a useful collection of essays.

Other modern biographies of Protestant figures of importance include A. Brooke, *Robert Gray, First Bishop of Cape Town* (1947), Edwin Smith, *The Life and Times of Daniel Lindley* (1949), A. Birtwhistle, *Thomas Birch Freeman* (1950), Owen Chadwick, *Mackenzie's Grave* (1959), C. Northcott, *Robert Moffat: Pioneer in Africa* (1961), J. Buchan, *The Expendable Mary Slessor* (Edinburgh, 1980), Jeff Guy, *The Heretic: A Study of the Life of John William Colenso 1814–1883* (Johannesburg, 1983), A. Ross, *John Philip* (Aberdeen, 1986), and I. H. Enklaar, *Life and Work of Dr J. Th. Van der Kemp* (Cape Town, 1988). For Alexander Mackay, see John Hargreaves, *Aberdeenshire to Africa* (Aberdeen, 1982), 31–8.

7. *Catholic Missionaries*

For Catholic missionaries in this period see, first, the various chapters by T. Filesi, P. Moody, M. Storme, and J. Metzler in *PFMR* 3 /1, 153–340, and A. Picciola, *Missionnaires en Afrique 1840–1940* (Paris, 1987). For the early Upper Nile mission there is D. McEwan, *A Catholic Sudan: Dream, Mission, Reality* (Rome, 1987) as also E. Toniolo and R. Hill (eds.), *The Opening of the Nile Basin* (1974) and Francesco Morland, *Missione in Africa centrale: Diario 1855–1863* (Bologna, 1973). See also E. Schmid, *Alle origini della missione dell'Africa centrale* (Verona, 1987).

The 940 pages of P. Coulon and P. Brasseur, *Libermann 1802–1852: Une pensée et une mystique missionnaires* (1988) provide a magnificent guide to Catholic missionary activity in France and West Africa up to the early 1850s with a massive bibliography, but see also H. Bucher, 'The Village of Glass and Western Intrusion: An Mpongwe Response to the American and French Presence in the Gabon Estuary 1842–1845', *IJA* 6 (1973), 363–40, D. H. Jones, 'The Catholic Mission and Some Aspects of Assimilation in Senegal 1817–1852', *JAH* 21 (1980), 323–40, both good especially for the 1840s. For the later history of the Holy Ghost Fathers see H. Koren, *The Spiritans: A History of the Congregation of the Holy Ghost* (Pittsburg, 1958), and J. A. Kiernan, 'Some Roman Catholic Missionary Attitudes to Africans in Nineteenth Century East Africa', *Race*, 10 (1968–9), 341–59. For the SMA see John Todd, *African Mission* (1962) and Jean Bonfils (ed.), *Marion Brésillac, Founder of the Society of African Missions: Mission and Foundation Documents* (Paris, 1986), Edmund Hogan, 'Sir James Marshall and Catholic Missions to West Africa 1873–1889', *Catholic Historical Review,* 76 (1990), 212–34. For the Verona Fathers, there is Aldo Gilli, *History of the Comboni Missionary Institute* (Rome, 1985), Pietro Chiocchetta, *Daniel Comboni: Papers for the Evangelization of Africa* (Rome, 1982), and P. L. Franchescini, *Mons. Daniel Comboni (1831–1881) Bibliographia* (Rome, 1984). For the most recent interpretation of Comboni see G. Battelli, 'Daniel Comboni et son "image" de l'Afrique', in G. Ruggieri (ed.), *Église et histoire de l'église en Afrique* (Paris, 1988), 63–87.

Lavigerie's *Instructions aux missionnaires* (Namur, 1950) is a text of major importance. There is a valuable commentary by 'Un Père Blanc' (J. Mazé), 'Les Idées principales du Cardinal Lavigerie sur l'évangelisation de l'Afrique', *RHM* 2 (1925), 351–96. François Renault, *Le Cardinal Lavigerie 1825–1892: L'église, l'Afrique et la France* (Paris, 1992), translated into English as *Cardinal Lavigerie, Churchman, Prophet and Missionary* (1994), is now the standard biography, but see also Mgr. Baunard, *Le Cardinal Lavigerie*, 2 vols. (Paris, 1896), while Xavier de Montclos, *Lavigerie: Le Saint-Siège et l'église* (Paris, 1965) and *Le Toast d'Alger* (1966) and F. Renault, *Lavigerie: L'esclavage africain et l'Europe*, 2 vols. (Paris, 1971) are both authoritative and highly detailed. See also J. Dean O'Donnell, *Lavigerie in Tunisia: The Interplay of Imperialist and Missionary* (1979).

Among printed primary sources on Catholic missionary practice in this period note *Spiritana Monumenta Historica: Series Africana, Angola,* ed. A. Brasio (Pittsburgh): the first three volumes (1966–9) cover the period up to 1889; P. P. Augouard, *28 années au Congo: Lettres de Mgr. Augouard,* 2 vols. (Paris, 1905), and *Gubulawayo and Beyond: Letters and Journals of the Early Jesuit Missionaries to Zambezia 1879–1887,* ed. Michael Gelfand (1968).

8. *Wider Studies of the Missionary Presence in Africa*

J. Du Plessis, *A History of Christian Missions in South Africa* (1911), Roland Oliver, *The Missionary Factor in East Africa* (1952), H. A. C. Cairns, *Prelude to Imperialism: British Reactions to Central Africa 1840–1890* (1965), and J. F. A. Ajayi, *Christian Missions in Nigeria 1841–1891: The Making of a New Élite* (1969) remain the best wide-ranging studies of the missionary presence in Africa in this period, though Cairns does not limit himself to missionaries. Oliver is unusual in fully crossing the Protestant–Catholic divide. Max Warren, *The Missionary Movement from Britain in Modern History* (1965) and *Social History and Christian Mission* (1967) are the perceptive reflections of a modern missionary leader of exceptional influence, and J. Boer, *Missionary Messengers of Liberation in a Colonial Context: A Case Study of the Sudan United Mission* (Amsterdam, 1979), a very lengthy review of one influential but less well-known society. For Germany see especially W. Ustorf, *Mission in Kontext: Beiträge zur Sozialgeschichte der Norddeutschen Missionsgesellschaft im 19. Jahrhundert* (Bremen, 1986). J. Van den Berg, *Constrained by Jesus' Love* (Rotterdam, 1956) is an enquiry into the motivation of the missionary awakening in Britain. T. Christensen and W. R. Hutchinson, *Missionary Ideologies in the Imperialist Era 1880–1920* (Åarhus, 1982) looks at attitudes a century later and more internationally. K. Bade (ed.), *Imperialismus und Kolonialmission: Kaiserliches Deutschland und koloniales Imperium* (Wiesbaden, 1982) and Brian Stanley, *The Bible and the Flag: Protestant Missions and British Imperialism in the Nineteenth and Twentieth Centuries* (1990) are reconsiderations of a central theme. J. Bonk, *The Theory and Practice of Missionary Identification 1860–1920* (New York, 1989) is largely concerned with the London Missionary Society in Africa and China and constitutes a major reassessment. J. and J. Comaroff, *Of Revelation and Revolution: Christianity, Colonialism and Consciousness in South Africa,* i (1991) is also, despite its title, largely a study of the LMS among the Southern Tswana. S. M. Jacobs (ed.), *Black Americans and the Missionary Movement in Africa* (1982) and Walter L. Williams, *Black Americans and the Evangelization of Africa 1877–1900* (1982) treat an often overlooked dimension of missionary history.

Among a multitude of articles, the following may be specially recommended: H. A. Gailey, 'John Philip's Role in Hottentot Emancipation', *JAH* 3 (1962), 419–33; P. Ellingworth, 'Christianity and Politics in Dahomey 1843–1867', *JAH* 5 (1964), 209–20; T. Price, 'The Missionary Struggle with Complexity', in C. G. Baëta (ed.), *Christianity in Tropical Africa* (1968), 101–19; I. Tufuoh, 'Relations between Christian Missions, European Administrators and Traders in the Gold Coast 1828–1874', in Baëta (ed.), *Christianity in Tropical Africa*, 34–60; A. F. Walls, 'Missionary Vocation and the Ministry: The First Generation', in M. Glasswell and E. Fasholé-Luke (eds.), *New Testament Christianity for Tropical Africa and for the World* (1974), 141–56; D. Cragg, 'The Role of Wesleyan Missionaries in Relations between the Mpondo and the Colonial Authorities', C. Saunders and R. Derricourt (eds.), *Beyond the Colonial Frontier* (1974); A. F. Walls, 'A Colonial Concordat: Two Views of Christianity and Civilization', in D. Baker (ed.), *Church, Society and Politics*, SCH xii (1975), 293–303; M. Dinnerstein, 'The American Zulu Mission in the Nineteenth Century', *Church History*, 45 (1976), 235–46; A. Porter, 'Cambridge, Keswick and Late Nineteenth-Century Attitudes to Africa', *Journal of Imperial and Commonwealth History*, 5 (1976–7), 5–34; A. Porter, 'Evangelical Enthusiasm, Missionary Motivation and West Africa in the Late Nineteenth Century: The Career of G. W. Brooke', *Journal of Imperial and Commonwealth History*, 6 (1977–8), 23–46; A. F. Walls, 'Black Europeans, White Africans: Some Missionary Motives in West Africa', in D. Baker (ed.), *Religious Motivation: Biographical and Sociological Problems for the Church Historian*, SCH xv (1978), 339–48; A. Porter, 'Late Nineteenth-Century Anglican Missionary Expansion: A Consideration of Some Non-Anglican Sources of Inspiration', in Baker (ed.), *Religious Motivation*, 349–65; C. P. Williams, ' "Not Quite Gentlemen": An Examination of "Middling Class" Protestant Missionaries from Britain, *c.*1850–1900', *Journal of Ecclesiastical History*, 31 (1980), 301–15; A. T. Matson, 'The Instructions Issued in 1876 and 1878 to the Pioneer CMS Parties to Karagwe and Uganda', *JRA* 12 (1981), 191–237, and 13 (1982), 25–46; T. O. Beidelman, 'The Organization and Maintenance of Caravans by the Church Missionary Society in Tanzania in the Nineteenth Century', *IJA* 15 (1982), 601–24; C. P. Williams, 'Healing and Evangelism: The Place of Medicine in Late Victorian Protestant Missionary Thinking', in W. J. Sheils (ed.), *The Church and Healing*, SCH xix (1982), 271–85; J. Hodgson, 'Mission and Empire: A Case Study of Convergent Ideologies in Nineteenth Century Southern Africa', *Journal of Theology of Southern Africa*, 38 (1982), 34–48; A. F. Walls, ' "Such Boastings as the Gentiles use . . .": Some Thoughts on Imperialist Religion', in Roy Bridges (ed.), *An African Miscellany for John Hargreaves* (Aberdeen, 1983), 109–16; B. Stanley, ' "Commerce and Christianity": Providence Theory, the Missionary Movement and the Imperialism of Free

Trade 1842–1860', *Historical Journal*, 26 (1983), 71–94; A. Porter, '"Commerce and Christianity": The Rise and Fall of a Nineteenth-Century Missionary Slogan', *Historical Journal*, 28 (1985), 597–621; P. Hinchliff, 'Voluntary Absolutism: British Missionary Societies in the Nineteenth Century', in W. J. Sheils and D. Wood (eds.), *Voluntary Religion*, SCH xxiii (1986), 363–79; M. Jarrett-Kerr, 'Victorian Certainty and Zulu Doubt', in D. Jasper and T. Wright (eds.), *The Critical Spirit and the Will to Believe* (1986), 145–57; B. Stanley, '"The Miser of Headingley": Robert Arthur and the Baptist Missionary Society 1877–1900', in W. J. Sheils and D. Wood (eds.), *The Church and Wealth*, SCH xxiv (1987), 371–82; N. Etherington, 'Missionary Doctors and African Healers in Mid-Victorian South Africa', *South African Historical Journal*, 19 (1987), 77–92, R. B. Beck, 'Bibles and Beads: Missionaries as Traders in Southern Africa in the Early Nineteenth Century', *JAH* 30 (1989), 211–25; A. F. Walls, 'The Legacy of Thomas Fowell Buxton', *IBMR* 15/2 (Apr. 1991), 74–7; F. Ludwig, 'The Making of a Late Victorian Missionary: John Alfred Robinson, the "Purger" of the Niger Mission', *Neue Zeitschrift für Missionswissenschaft*, 47 (1991), 269–90.

9. *Language and Translation*

It would be pointless to list a selection of the almost innumerable grammars, dictionaries, simple guides to arithmetic, and what have you produced by nineteenth-century missionaries, but see F. Rowling and C. Wilson, *Bibliography of African Christian Literature* (1923), valuable except for its almost complete omission of RC material, and for Scripture translation G. Coldham, *A Bibliography of Scriptures in African Languages* (1966). S. L. Greenslade (ed.), *The Cambridge History of the Bible*, ii (1963), includes 'The Bible and the Missionary' by Eric Fenn, 383–407. See also C. L. Nycmbezi, *A Review of Zulu Literature* (Pietermaritzburg, 1961), C. M. Doke and D. J. Cole, *Contribution to the History of Bantu Linguistics* (Johannesburg, 1961), C. M. Doke, *The Southern Bantu Languages* (1967), and P. E. H. Hair, *The Early Study of Nigerian Languages* (1967), as well as P. Hair, 'Niger Languages and Sierra Leonean Missionary Linguists 1840–1930', *BSACH* 2/2, 127–38.

For the missionary impact on the formation and separation of languages see W. Samarin, 'Protestant Missions and the History of Lingala', *JRA* 16/2 (1986), 138–63, P. Harries, 'The Roots of Ethnicity: Discourse and the Politics of Language Construction in South-East Africa', *AA* 87 (1988), 25–52, and L. Vail (ed.), *The Creation of Tribalism in South Africa* (1989).

CHAPTER 8
KINGS, MARRIAGE, ANCESTORS, AND GOD

Sources for the topics discussed in this chapter are included elsewhere, especially under Chapters 2, 7, 9, 11, and 12.

CHAPTER 9
CHRISTIAN LIFE IN THE AGE OF BISHOP CROWTHER

The principal resources for a knowledge of the life of African Christian communities in the second half of the nineteenth century remain the archives and publications of the main missionary societies, for which see Chapter 7.

1. *West Africa*

The main published writings of black Christians in this period are the following: J. F. Schön and S. A. Crowther, *Journal of an Expedition up the Niger in 1841* (1843), S. Crowther, *Journal of an Expedition up the Niger and the Tshada in 1854* (1855), S. Crowther and J. Taylor, *The Gospel on the Banks of the Niger: Journals of the Niger Expeditions of 1857 and Missionary Notices* (1859), Alexander Crummell, *The Future of Africa* (1862), James Africanus Horton, *West African Countries and Peoples . . . : A Vindication of the Negro Race* (1868; repr. with an introduction by George Shepperson, Edinburgh, 1969), E. W. Blyden, *Christianity, Islam and the Negro Race* (1887; repr. with an introduction by C. Fyfe, Edinburgh, 1967), James Johnson, *Yoruba Heathenism* (1897), and Samuel Johnson, *A History of the Yorubas* (1921, but completed in 1897). H. R. Lynch has edited *Black Spokesman: Selected Published Writings of Edward Wilmot Blyden* (1971).

The principal modern studies remain a group of books published in the 1960s: C. Fyfe, *A History of Sierra Leone* (1962), F. Bartels, *The Roots of Ghana Methodism* (1965), J. H. Kopytoff, *A Preface to Modern Nigeria: The 'Sierra Leoneans' in Yoruba 1830–1890* (1965), J. F. Ajayi, *Christian Missions in Nigeria: The Making of a New Élite* (1965), E. Ayandele, *The Missionary Impact on Modern Nigeria 1842–1914: A Political and Social Analysis* (1966), and R. July, *The Origins of Modern African Thought* (1968). For Liberia there is T. Shiek, *Behold the Promised Land: A History of Afro-American Settlers in Nineteenth Century Liberia* (1980).

For Crowther see the early biography of J. Page, *The Black Bishop* (1908), P. McKenzie, *Inter-Religious Encounter in West Africa: Samuel Ajayi Crowther's Attitude to African Traditional Religion and Islam* (Leicester, 1976), J. F. Ajayi, 'Samuel Ajayi Crowther of Oyo', in P. Curtin (ed.), *Africa Remembered*

(1967), 289–316, and J. Loiello, 'Bishop in Two Worlds: Samuel Ajayi Crowther (1806–1891)', in E. Isichei (ed.), *Varieties of Christian Experience in Nigeria* (1982), 34–61.

Some other biographies: J. Hargreaves, *A Life of Sir Samuel Lewis* (1958), E. Holden, *Blyden of Liberia* (1966), H. R. Lynch, *Edward Wilmot Blyden* (1967), E. Ayandele, *Holy Johnson* (1970), O. Adewoye, 'Sapora Williams: The Lawyer and the Public Servant', *JHN* 6/1 (1971), 47–65, C. Fyfe, *Africanus Horton, 1835–1883* (1972), and J. R. Oldfield, *Alexander Crummell (1819–1898) and the Creation of an African-American Church in Liberia* (1990).

Further studies: S. G. Williamson, 'The Lyric in the Fante Methodist Church', *Africa*, 28 (1958), 126–34, C. Fyfe, 'Peter Nicholls: Old Calabar and Freetown', *JHN* 1 (1960), 105–14, C. Fyfe, 'Four Sierra Leone Recaptives', *JAH* 2 (1961), 77–86, P. Hair, 'CMS "Native Clergy" in West Africa to 1900', *SLB* 4 (1962), 71–2, P. Hair, 'Archdeacon Crowther and the Delta Pastorate 1892–9', *SLB* 5 (1963), 18–27, P. Ellingworth, ' "As Others See Us": Non-Methodist Sources for Methodist History in Ouidah, Dahomey', *BSACH* 1 (1963), 13–17, and ' "As They Saw Themselves": More about the Beginnings of Methodism in Ouidah', *BSACH* 1 (1963), 35–41, H. R. Lynch, 'The Native Pastorate Controversy and Cultural Ethnocentrism in Sierra Leone 1871–1874', *JAH* 5 (1964), 395–413, W. O. Ajayi, 'The Niger Delta Pastorate Church 1892–1902', *BSACH* 2 (1965), 37–54, P. Hair, 'Niger Languages and Sierra Leonean Missionary Linguists 1840–1930', *BSACH* 2 (1966), 127–38, W. O. Ajayi, 'Christian Involvement in the Ijaye War', *BSACH* 2 (1967), 224–38, P. Ellingworth, 'Methodism on the Slave Coast 1842–1870', *BSACH* 2 (1967), 239–48, E. Ayandele, 'The Missionary Factor in Brass 1875–1900: A Study in Advance and Recession', *BSACH* 2 (1967), 249–58, J. Adedeji, 'The Church and the Emergence of the Nigerian Theatre 1866–1914', *JHN* 6/1 (1971), 25–45, G. Tasie, *Christian Missionary Enterprise in the Niger Delta 1864–1918* (Leiden, 1978), A. G. Hopkins, 'Innovation in a Colonial Context: African Origins of the Nigerian Cocoa-Farming Industry 1880–1920', in C. Dewey and A. G. Hopkins (eds.), *Imperial Impact* (1978), 83–96, P. McKenzie, 'Death in Early Nigerian Christianity', *Africana Marburgensia*, 15/2 (1982), 3–16, K. Mann, 'The Dangers of Dependence: Christian Marriage among Élite Women in Lagos Colony 1880–1915', *JAH* 24 (1983), 37–56, J. Iliffe, 'Persecution and Toleration in Pre-Colonial Africa: Nineteenth Century Yorubaland', in W. Shiels (ed.), *Persecution and Toleration, SCH* xxi (1984), 357–78, L. Shyllon, 'Aspects of the Dynamics of Methodism in Sierra Leone: A Reflection', in O. Kalu (ed.), *African Church Historiography: An Ecumenical Perspective* (Berne, 1988), 95–114, J. Peel, 'The Pastor and the Babalawo: The Interaction of Religions in Nineteenth Century Yorubaland', *Africa*, 60 (1990), 338–69, P. F. de Moraes Farias and K. Barber (eds.), *Self-Assertion and Brokerage: Early Cultural Nationalism in West Africa* (Birmingham, 1990), J. Peel, 'Poverty and

Sacrifice in Nineteenth Century Yorubaland: A Critique of Iliffe's Thesis', *JAH* 31 (1990), 465–84, P. McKenzie, 'Dreams and Visions in Nineteenth Century Yoruba Religion', in M. C. Jedrej and R. Shaw (eds.), *Dreaming, Religion and Society in Africa* (Leiden, 1992), 126–34.

2. *Southern Africa*

J. A. Chalmers, *Tiyo Soga: A Page of South African Mission Work* (1887) is an early biography, and D. Williams, *Umfundisi: A Biography of Tiyo Soga 1829–1871* (Lovedale, 1978) a recent one which has been followed up by D. Williams (ed.), *The Journal and Selected Writings of the Reverend Tiyo Soga* (Cape Town, 1983). See also D. D. T. Jabavu, *The Life of John Tengo Jabavu* (Lovedale, 1922), C. Saunders (ed.), *Black Leaders in Southern Africa* (1979) includes D. Williams, 'Tiyo Soga', 127–41, and L. Ngcongco, 'John Tengo Jabavu 1859–1921', 142–56. G. M. Gugelberger (ed.), *Nama/Namibia: Diary and Letters of Nama Chief Hendrik Witbooi 1884–1894* (Boston, Mass., 1984) shows the mind of a Christian chief. Vol. ii of J. Hodgson's Ph.D. thesis 'Ntsikana: History and Symbol. Studies in a Process of Religious Change among Xhosa-Speaking People' (Cape Town, 1985) covers the development of the Ntsikana tradition in the later nineteenth century, while her 'Soga and Dukwana', *JRA* 16 (1986), 187–208, treats of Tiyo's father and Ntsikana's son.

C. Bundy, *The Rise and Fall of the South African Peasantry* (1979), N. Etherington, *Preachers, Peasants and Politics in Southeast Africa 1835–1880: African Christian Communities in Natal, Pondoland and Zululand* (1979), J. B. Pieres, *The Dead Will Arise: Nongqawuse and the Great Cattle-Killing Movement of 1856–1857* (1989) are major recent contributions to the understanding of the African predicament in the later nineteenth century. Among shorter studies, one may begin with B. Hutchinson, 'Some Social Consequences of Nineteenth Century Missionary Activity among the South African Bantu', *Africa*, 27 (1957), 160–75 and Monica Wilson, in M. Wilson and L. Thompson, *The Oxford History of South Africa*, i (1969), 260–71. It may be noted that Professor Wilson was herself one of the white children educated at Lovedale when it was still multiracial—see her memoir, 'Lovedale: Instrument of Peace', in F. Wilson and D. Perrot (eds.), *Outlook on a Century: South Africa 1870–1970* (Lovedale, 1973), 4–12. She continued throughout her life to represent the Lovedale tradition at its most liberal. More recent studies include W. Mills, 'The Taylor Revival of 1866 and the Roots of African Nationalism in the Cape Colony', *JRA* 8 (1976), 105–22, T. Keto, 'Race Relations, Land and the Changing Missionary Role in South Africa: A Case Study of the American Zulu Mission 1850–1910', *IJA* 10 (1977), 600–627 N. Etherington, 'Social Theory and the Study of Christian Missions in Africa: A South African Case Study', *Africa*, 47 (1977),

31–40, J. Hodgson, 'Zonnebloem College and Cape Town 1858–1870', in *Studies in the History of Cape Town*, ed. Christopher Sanders (Cape Town, 1984) 125–52, W. Mills, 'The Roots of African Nationalism in the Cape Colony: Temperance 1866–1898', *IJA* 13 (1980), 193–213, J. Hodgson, *Princess Emma* (1987) and J. Hodgson, 'Kid Gloves and Cricket on the Kei', *Religion in Southern Africa*, 8 (1987), 61–91.

For the Christianity of the Tswana, the Sotho, and their kings there is A. Sillery, *Sechele: The Story of an African Chief* (1954), I. Schapera, 'Christianity and the Tswana', *Journal of the Royal Anthropological Institute*, 88 (1958), A. Dachs, *Khama of Botswana* (1971), J. Chirenje, *Chief Kgama and his Times* (1978), L. Thompson, *Survival in Two Worlds: Moshoeshoe of Lesotho 1786–1870* (1975), P. Saunders, *Moshoeshoe, Chief of the Sotho* (1975) and Ø. Gulbrandsen, 'Missionaries and Northern Tswana Rulers: Who Used Whom?', *JRA* 23 (1983), 44–83.

3. *Buganda*

For the history of Buganda there are available written Luganda sources, both published and unpublished, probably richer than anything comparable for Christian history in any other African language. See J. Rowe, 'Myth, Memoir and Moral Admonition: Luganda Historical Writing 1893–1969', *UJ* 33 (1969), 17–40. There is important material by Apolo Kagwa, Ham Mukasa, Yosefu Ddiba, and others. Four major general studies, all—oddly—published in 1971 are M. Kiwanuka, *A History of Buganda from the Foundation of the Kingdom to 1900*, M. Wright, *Buganda in the Heroic Age*, D. Low, *Buganda in Modern History*, and D. Low, *The Mind of Buganda*. Also important are A. Oded, *Islam in Uganda: Islamization through a Centralized State in Pre-Colonial Africa* (Jerusalem, 1974) and J. Waliggo, 'The Catholic Church in the Buddu Province of Buganda 1879–1925', Ph.D. thesis (Cambridge, 1976).

For Lugard see his *The Rise of our East African Empire* (1893), Margery Perham, *Lugard: The Years of Adventure 1858–1898* (1956) and *The Diaries of Lord Lugard*, ed. M. Perham (1959), but also J. Rowe, *Lugard at Kampala* (Makerere, 1969).

R. P. Ashe, *Two Kings of Uganda* (1889) and *Chronicles of Uganda* (1894) are early published accounts by a CMS missionary, J. Faupel, *African Holocaust* (1965) is based upon the most detailed research into the martyrdoms but should be supplemented by J. Rowe, 'The Purge of Christians at Mwanga's Court', *JAH* 5 (1964), 55–72, D. Low, 'Converts and Martyrs in Buganda', in C. G. Baëta (ed.), *Christianity in Tropical Africa* (1968), 150–63, L. Pirouet, *Strong in the Faith* (Kisubi, 1969), and R. Kassimir, 'Complex Martyrs: Symbols of Catholic Church Formation and Political Differentiation in Uganda', *AA* (1991), 357–82.

Sir John Gray, 'The Year of the Three Kings of Buganda, Mwanga—Kivewa—Kalema, 1888–1889', *UJ* (1950), 15–52, is an important early piece of research on a difficult period, and D. Low, *Religion and Society in Buganda 1875–1900* (Kampala, 1956) a decisive piece of interpretation. See also C. Wrigley, 'The Christian Revolution in Buganda', *Comparative Studies in Society and History*, 2 (1959), 33–48, J. Rowe, 'Mika Sematimba', *UJ* 28 (1964), 179–99, M. Kiwanuka, 'Sir Apolo Kagwa and the Pre-Colonial History of Buganda', *UJ* 30 (1966), 137–52, M. Twaddle, 'The Muslim Revolution in Buganda', *AA* 71 (1972), 54–72, J. Peel, 'Conversion and Tradition in Two African Societies: Ijebu and Buganda', *Past and Present*, 77 (1977), 108–41, N. Bennett, *Arab versus European: Diplomacy and War in Nineteenth Century East Central Africa* (1986), M. Twaddle, 'The Emergence of Politico-Religious Groupings in Late Nineteenth Century Buganda', *JAH* 29 (1988), 81–92, and J. Brierley and T. Spear, 'Mutesa, the Missionaries and Christian Conversion in Buganda', *IJA* 21 (1988), 601–18.

CHAPTER 10
A VARIETY OF SCRAMBLES: 1890–1920

1. *General*

Literature on the scramble is now immense. The best recent guide may be volume vi of the *CHA* and, especially, the contributions of Oliver, Sanderson, and Lonsdale. R. Robinson, J. Gallagher, and A. Denny, *Africa and the Victorians* (1963) remains foundational to the modern debate but its conclusions have been overtaken. For a small selection of later views see H.-U. Wehler, 'Bismarck's Imperialism 1862–1890', *Past and Present*, 48 (1970), 119–55, P. Gifford and W. R. Louis (ed.), *Britain and Germany in Africa* (1967) and *Britain and France in Africa* (1971), Henri Brunschwig, *Le Partage de l'Afrique* (Paris, 1971), C. C. Eldridge, *England's Mission: The Imperial Idea in the Age of Gladstone and Disraeli 1868–1880* (1973), and R. Hyam, *Britain's Imperial Century 1815–1914* (1976). J. Ellis, *The Social History of the Machine Gun* (1976), D. R. Headrick, *The Tools of Empire: Technology and European Imperialism in the Nineteenth Century* (1981), and L. Brockway, *Science and Colonial Expansion: The Role of the British Botanic Gardens* (1979) examine some of the most decisive underlying factors behind the scramble.

Margery Perham's two-volume life of *Lugard* (1956 and 1960), R. Oliver, *Sir Harry Johnston and the Scramble for Africa* (1957), J. Flint, *Sir George Goldie and the Making of Nigeria* (1960), J. S. Galbraith, *Mackinnon and East Africa 1878–1895* (1972), J. Flint, *Cecil Rhodes* (1976), R. Rotberg, *The Founder: Cecil Rhodes and the Pursuit of Power* (1988), and R. E. Nwoye, *The Public*

Image of Pierre Savorgnan de Brazza and the Establishment of French Imperialism in the Congo (Aberdeen, 1981) deal with six of the leading figures of imperialism whose African careers had many connections with the missionary presence.

For the African experience of the scramble in a few of the areas where the colonial–missionary interaction was closest: Igboland, E. Isichei, *The Ibo People and the Europeans* (1973) and *A History of the Igbo People* (1976); the Congo, Ruth Slade, *King Leopold's Congo* (1962), R. T. Anstey, *Britain and the Congo in the Nineteenth Century* (1962), S. J. S. Cookey, *Britain and the Congo Question 1885–1913* (1968), and B. Emmerson, *Leopold II of the Belgians: King of Colonialism* (1979); southern Africa, T. O. Ranger, *Revolt in Southern Rhodesia 1896–1897* (1967), J. Duffy, *A Question of Slavery: Labour Policies in Portuguese Africa and the British Protest 1850–1920* (1967), S. Trapido, 'African Divisional Politics in the Cape Colony 1884–1910', *JAH* 9 (1968), 79–98, Shula Marks, *Reluctant Rebellion: An Assessment of the 1906–1908 Disturbances in Natal* (1970), T. Karis and G. Carter (eds.), *From Protest to Challenge*, four splendid volumes of South African documents 1882–1964 (1973–7), J. Guy, *The Destruction of the Zulu Kingdom* (1979), H. Drechsler, *Let Us Die Fighting: The Struggle of the Herero and Noma against German Imperialism 1884–1915* (1980).

A brief reading-list for Islam in this period will include, besides J. S. Trimingham's *Islam in West Africa* (1959) and *Islam in East Africa* (1964), T. Gbadamosi, *The Growth of Islam among the Yoruba 1841–1908* (1978), N. King, A. Kasozi, and A. Oded, *Islam and the Confluence of Religions in Uganda 1840–1966* (Tallahassee, Fl., 1973), A. Oded, *Islam in Uganda* (1974), A. Kazozi, *The Spread of Islam in Uganda* (1986), E. Alpers, 'Towards a History of the Expansion of Islam in East Africa: The Matrilineal Peoples of the Southern Interior', in T. Ranger and I. Kimambo (eds.), *The Historical Study of African Religion* (1972), E. Alpers, *Ivory and Slaves in East Central Africa* (1975), 'Islam', in J. Iliffe, *A Modern History of Tanganyika* (1979), 208–16, D. Bone, 'Islam in Malawi', *JRA* 12 (1982), 126–38, Donal Cruise O'Brien, *The Mourides of Senegal* (1971), R. Delval, *Les Musulmans au Togo* (Paris, 1980), C. Harrison, *France and Islam in West Africa 1860–1960* (1988), and D. Robinson, 'Beyond Resistance and Collaboration: Amadu Bamba and the Murids of Senegal', *JRA* 21 (1991), 149–71. C. C. Stewart, 'Islam', in *CHA* vii provides an overview and a fuller bibliography.

Volume iii (1955) of C. P. Groves, *The Planting of Christianity in Africa*, remains an invaluable guide to missionary activity in this period within Africa. For Christianity's wider ecclesiastical and missionary development see R. Aubert, *The Church in a Secularised Society* (1978), R. Rouse and S. C. Neill (eds.), *A History of the Ecumenical Movement 1517–1948* (1954), W. H. T. Gairdner, *'Edinburgh 1910': An Account and Interpretation of the World Missionary Conference* (1910), T. Christensen and W. R. Hutchinson (eds.),

Missionary Ideologies in the Imperialist Era 1880–1920 (Åarhus, 1982), G. K. A. Bell, *Randall Davidson, Archbishop of Canterbury,* 2 vols. (1935), S. Koss, 'Wesleyanism and Empire', *Historical Journal* 18 (1975), 105–18, A. C. Ross, 'Scottish Missionary Concern 1874–1914: A Golden Era?', *Scottish Historical Review,* 51 (1972), 52–72, and A. Hodge, 'The Training of Missionaries for Africa: The Church Missionary Society's Training College at Islington 1900–1915', *JRA* 4 (1971), 81–96.

While much listed under Chapters 7 and 9 and some under 12 include sections on this period, the following selection of titles includes what is most important for 1890–1920.

2. West Africa

Books: J. Casely Hayford, *Ethiopia Unbound* (1911; 2nd edn. 1969), J. Jordan, *Bishop Shanahan of Southern Nigeria,* Dublin (1949), F. L. Bartels, *The Roots of Ghana Methodism* (1965), H. W. Debrunner, *A Church between Colonial Powers: A Study of the Church in Togo* (1965), D. Bouche, *Les Villages de liberté en Afrique noire française 1887–1910* (Paris, 1968), K. Müller, *Histoire de l'église catholique au Togo* (Lomé, 1968; the German original, *Geschichte der katholischen Kirche in Togo* was published at Kaldenkirchen in 1958), E. A. Ayandele, *Holy Johnson: Pioneer of African Nationalism 1837–1917* (1970), G. M. Haliburton, *The Prophet Harris* (1971), F. K. Ekechi, *Missionary Enterprise and Rivalry in Igboland 1857–1914* (1972), J. Van Slageren, *Les Origines de l'église évangelique du Cameroun* (Yaoundé, 1972), D. Bouche, *L'Enseignement dans les territoires français de l'Afrique occidentale de 1817 à 1920* (Paris, 1975), Heinrich Berger, *Mission und kolonial Politik: Die katholische Mission in Kamerun während der deutschen Kolonialzeit* (Immersee, 1978), E. S. Akama, 'A Religious History of the Isoko People of the Bendel State of Nigeria', Ph.D. thesis (Aberdeen, 1981), J. Ki-Zerbo, *Alfred Diban: Premier chrétien de Haute-Volta* (Paris, 1983), C. Obi (ed.), *A Hundred Years of the Catholic Church in Eastern Nigeria 1885–1985* (Lagos, 1985), J.-R. de Benoist, *Église et pouvoir colonial au Soudan français 1885–1945* (Paris, 1987), I. Ozigbo, *Roman Catholicism in South Eastern Nigeria 1885–1931* (Onitsha, 1988), G. Johnston, *Of God and Maxim Guns: Presbyterianism in Nigeria 1846–1966* (Waterloo, Ont., 1988), N. I. Omenka, *The School in the Service of Evangelization: The Catholic Educational Impact in Eastern Nigeria 1886–1950* (Leiden, 1989).

Articles: D. Okafor-Omali and P. Hair, 'The First Christian in the Village: A Case-History from Eastern Nigeria', *BSACH* 1/2 (1963), 49–61, W. O. Ajayi, 'The Niger Delta Pastorate Church *1892–1902*', *BSACH* 2/1 (1965), 37–54, E. A. Ayandele, 'The Missionary Factor in Brass 1875–1900: A Study in Advance and Recession', *BSACH* 2/3 (1967), 249–58, E. A. Ayandele, 'The Relations between the Church Missionary Society and the Royal Niger Company 1886–1900', *JHN* 4/3 (1968), 397–49, D. G. Gelzer,

'Missions and Colonialization: Education in Cameroun in the Days of the Germans', *BSACH* 3/1 (1969–70), 1–14, A. E. Afigbo, 'The Calabar Mission and the Aro Expedition of 1901–1902', *JRA* 5 (1973), 94–106, P. B. Clarke, 'The Methods and Ideology of the Holy Ghost Fathers in Eastern Nigeria 1885–1906', *JRA* 6 (1974), 81–108, J. Peel, 'Conversion and Tradition in Two African Societies: Ijebu and Buganda', *Past and Present*, 77 (1977), 108–41, F. K. Ekechi, 'The Missionary Career of the Venerable T. J. Dennis in West Africa 1893–1917', *JRA* 9 (1978), 1–26, O. Kalu, 'The Battle of the Gods: Christianization of Cross River Igboland 1903–1950', *JHN* 10/1 (1979), 1–20, O. Kalu, 'Primitive Methodists on the Railroad Junctions of Igboland 1910–1931', *JRA* 16 (1986), 44–66, N. Omenka, 'The Role of the Catholic Mission in the Development of Vernacular Literature in Eastern Nigeria', *JRA* 16 (1986), 121–37.

3. *Congo (Zaïre)*

Books: L. Denis (ed.), *Les Jésuites belges au Kwango 1893–1943* (Brussels, 1945), Ruth Slade, *English-Speaking Missions in the Congo Independent State 1878–1908* (Brussels, 1959), A. Roeykens, *La Politique religieuse de l'état indépendant du Congo: Documents* (Brussels, 1964), M. Kratz, *La Mission des Rédemptoristes belges au Bas-Congo: La période de semailles* (Brussels, 1968), D. Lagergren, *Mission and State in the Congo 1885–1903* (Uppsala, 1970), S. Axelson, *Culture Confrontation in the Lower Congo* (Uppsala, 1970).

Articles: L. Cuypers, 'La Politique foncière de l'état indépendant du Congo à regard des missions catholiques', *Revue d'histoire ecclésiastique*, 57 (1962), 45–65, 446–69, L. Cuypers, 'La Coopération de l'état indépendant du Congo avec les missions catholiques', *Revue d'histoire ecclésiastique*, 65 (1970), 30–55, L. Greindl, 'Notes sur les sources des Missionnaires d'Afrique (Pères Blancs) pour l'est du Zaïre', *EHA* 7 (1975), 175–202, Jean Stengers, 'King Leopold's Congo 1886–1908', in *CHA* vi. 315–58, D. Northrup, 'A Church in Search of a State: Catholic Missions in Zaïre 1879–1930', *Journal of Church and State*, 30 (1988), 309–20. G. Ciparisse published an extremely detailed study, including massive documentation, of the Jesuit Mission in Kwango and the rise and fall, 1895–1911, of its 'fermes-chapelles' in four parts in the *BIHB*: 'Les Tractations en vue de la création de la "Mission du Kwango": Le dossier de la Compagnie de Jésus 1879–1893', 42 (1972), 453–577; 'Les Origines de la méthode des fermes-chapelles au Bas Congo 1895–1898', 43 (1973), 693–839; 'Les Structures traditionelles de la société mpangu face à l'introduction d'une méthode occidentale de développement: Les fermes chapelles du Bas Congo 1895–1911', 46–7 (1976–7), 368–601, and 52 (1982), 153–270.

4. Eastern Africa

Books: C. Harford-Battersby, *Pilkington of Uganda* (1898), A. Tucker, *Eighteen Years in Uganda and East Africa*, 2 vols. (1908; 2nd edn. 1911), one of the only major published works on Church history by a missionary of this period, E. M. Crawford, *By the Equator's Snowy Peak: A Record of Medical Missionary Work and Travel in British East Africa* (1913), H. Maynard Smith, *Frank Bishop of Zanzibar* (1926), R. Oliver, *The Missionary Factor in East Africa* (1952), D. A. Low, *Religion and Society in Buganda 1875–1900* (Kampala, 1957), J. V. Taylor, *The Growth of the Church in Buganda* (1958), H. P. Gale, *Uganda and the Mill Hill Fathers* (1959), C. H. Hellberg, *Missions on a Colonial Frontier West of Lake Victoria* (Lund, 1963), A. Luck, *African Saint: The Life of Apolo Kivebulaya* (1963), R. Fouquer, *Le Docteur Adrien Atiman, médecin-catéchiste au Tanganyika* (1964), S. von Sicard, *The Lutheran Church on the Coast of Tanzania 1887–1914* (Uppsala, 1970), M. Wright, *German Missions in Tanganyika 1891–1941* (1971), A. J. Temu, *British Protestant Missions* (1972), I. Linden, *Church and Revolution in Rwanda* (1977), R. W. Strayer, *The Making of Mission Communities in East Africa: Anglicans and Africans in Colonial Kenya 1875–1935* (1978), L. Pirouet, *Black Evangelists: The Spread of Christianity in Uganda 1891–1914* (1978), J. Iliffe, *A Modern History of Tanganyika* (1979), particularly good on the impact of the first world war, R. Heremans, *L'Education dans les missions des Pères Blancs en Afrique centrale (1879–1914) (Brussels,* 1983), H. B. Hansen, *Mission, Church and State in a Colonial Setting: Uganda 1890–1925* (1984), J. M. Waliggo, *A History of African Priests* (Masaka, Uganda, 1988), M. Twaddle, *Kakumgulu and the Creation of Uganda* (1993).

Some unpublished doctoral theses: J. Kiernan, 'The Holy Ghost Fathers in East Africa, 1863 to 1911' (London, 1966), B. G. McIntosh, 'The Scottish Mission in Kenya 1891–1923' (Edinburgh, 1969), John Waliggo, 'The Catholic Church in the Buddu Province of Buganda 1879–1925' (Cambridge, 1976)—an outstandingly rich piece of research into a subject of exceptional importance—F. Nolan, 'Christianity in Unyamwezi 1878–1928' (Cambridge, 1976), T. H. Cope, 'The African Inland Mission in Kenya: Aspects of its History 1895–1945' (CNAA, 1979), Renison Githige, 'The Mission–State Relationship in Kenya 1888–1938' (Aberdeen, 1982).

Articles: H. B. Thomas, 'Capax Imperii: The Story of Simei Kakunguru', *UJ* 6 (1939), 125–36, R. Cambier, 'L'Affaire Stokes', *Revue Belge de philologie et d'histoire*, 30 (1952), 109–54, A. D. Roberts, 'The Sub-Imperialism of the Baganda', *JAH* 3 (1962), 435–50, J. M. Gray, 'Kakunguru in Bukedi', *UJ* 27 (1963), 31–60, T. Price, 'The Church as Land-Holder in Eastern Africa', *BSACH* 1/1 (1963), 8–13, T. Williams, 'The Coming of Christianity to Ankole', *BSACH,* 2/2 (1966), 155–73, A. Hastings, 'From Mission to Church in Buganda', *Zeitschrift für Missionwissenschaft und Religionwissenschaft*

(June 1969), reprinted in A. Hastings, *Mission and Ministry* (1971), 144–76, Y. Ssebalijja, 'Memories of Rukiga and Other Places', 179–99, and J. Nicolet, 'The Religious Impact of Yohana Kitagana', 231–40, both in D. Denoon (ed.), *A History of Kigezi* (Kampala, 1972)—there is a longer, unpublished version of Nicolet's memoir of Kitagana entitled 'An Apostle of the Ruwenzori'—L. Pirouet, 'East African Christians and World War I', *JAH* 19 (1978), 117–30, H. B. Hansen, 'European Ideas, Colonial Attitudes and African Realities: The Introduction of a Church Constitution in Uganda 1898–1909', *IJA* 13 (1980), 240–80, R. M. Githige, 'The Issue of Slavery: Relations between the CMS and the State on the East African Coast prior to 1895', *JRA* 16 (1986), 209–25, Paul Rutayisire, 'L'Africanisation du Christianisme et la pratique missionnaire en référence à la Christianisation du Burundi (1897–1937)', in G. Ruggieri (ed.), *Église et histoire de l'église en Afrique* (Paris, 1988).

For Kakunguru's later religious development, besides the two articles in the *Uganda Journal* listed above, see F. B. Welbourn, *East African Rebels* (1961) and A. Oded, 'The Bayudaya of Uganda', *JRA* 6 (1974), 167–86.

5. *Central Africa*

Books: Dan Crawford, *Thinking Black: Twenty-Two Years without a Break in the Long Grass of Central Africa* (1912) is splendidly worth a read (for its background see R. Rotberg, 'Plymouth Brethren and the Occupation of Katanga 1886–1907', *JAH* 5 (1964), 285–97). W. P. Livingstone's two biographies, *Laws of Livingstonia* (1921) and *A Prince of Missionaries: The Rev. Alexander Hetherwick of Blantyre* (1931), as also Agnes Fraser's life of her husband, *Donald Fraser of Livingstonia* (1934) are still worth referring to as accounts of three Scottish missionaries with a high profile of this period. Modern critical writing about the missions begins for Central Africa with a more than usually critical one, R. I. Rotberg, *Christian Missionaries and the Creation of Northern Rhodesia 1880–1924* (1965). J. Farrant, *Mashonaland Martyr: Bernard Mizeki and the Pioneer Church* (1966) and J. C. Weller, *The Priest from the Lakeside: The Story of Leonard Kamungu of Malawi and Zambia 1877–1913* (Blantyre, 1971) provide carefully researched biographies of two African Christian pioneers. I. Linden, *Catholics, Peasants and Chewa Resistance in Nyasaland 1889–1939* (1974), J. McCracken, *Politics and Christianity in Malawi 1875–1940: The Impact of the Livingstonia Mission in the Northern Province* (1977), N. Bhebe, *Christianity and Traditional Religion in Western Zimbabwe 1859–1923* (1979), G. Prins, *The Hidden Hippopotamus* (1980), C. Zvogo, *The Wesleyan Methodist Missions in Zimbabwe 1891–1945* (Harare, 1991), B. Garvey *Bembaland Church* (Leiden, 1993). Some unpublished theses: A. C. Ross, 'The Origins and Development of the Church of Scotland Mission, Blantyre, Nyasaland, 1875–1921' (Edinburgh,

1968), T. J. Thompson, 'Fraser and the Ngoni: A Study of the Growth of Christianity among the Ngoni of Northern Malawi 1879–1933' (Edinburgh, 1980).

Articles: A. Ross, '"The African—a Child or a Man": The Quarrel between the Blantyre Mission of the Church of Scotland and the British Central Africa Administration 1890–1905', E. Stokes and R. Brown (eds.), *The Zambezian Past* (1966), 332–51, M. R. Waldman, 'The Church of Scotland Mission at Blantyre, Nyasaland: Its Political Implications', *BSACH* 2/4 (1968), 299–310, F. Soremekun, 'Religion and Politics in Angola: The American Board Mission and the Portuguese Government 1880–1922', *Cahiers d'études africaines*, 9 (1971), 341–77, W. R. Peaden, 'Nenguwo Training Institution and the First Shona Teachers', in A. J. Dachs (ed.), *Christianity South of the Zambezi*, i (1973) 71–82, R. Peaden, 'The Contribution of the Epworth Mission Settlement to African Development', in T. Ranger and J. Weller (eds.), *Themes in the Christian History of Central Africa* (1975), 135–51, C. Zvogbo, 'Shona and Ndebele Responses to Christianity in Southern Rhodesia 1897–1914', *JRA* 8 (1976), 41–51, B. Garvey, 'Bemba Chiefs and Catholic Missions 1898–1935', *JAH* 18 (1977), 411–26, C. Zvogbo, 'Christian Missionaries and the Establishment of Colonial Rule in Zimbabwe 1888–1918', *Journal of Southern African Affairs*, 2 (1977), 217–34, R. Stuart, 'Anglican Missionaries and a Chewa *Dini*: Conversion and Rejection in Central Malawi', *JRA* 10 (1979), 46–69, H. Langworthy, 'Joseph Booth: Prophet of Radical Change in Central and South Africa 1891–1915', *JRA* 16 (1986), 22–43, E. Yorke, 'The Spectre of a Second Chilembwe: Government, Missions and Social Control in Wartime Northern Rhodesia 1914–1918', *JAH* 31 (1990), 373–91.

The fundamental study of John Chilembwe remains G. A. Shepperson and T. Price, *Independent African: John Chilembwe and the Origins, Setting and Significance of the Nyasaland Native Rising of 1915* (Edinburgh, 1958) but needs to be supplemented by George Mwase, *Strike a Blow and Die*, ed. R. Rotberg (1967), Landeg White, *Magomero: Portrait of an African Village* (1987), and by Jane and Ian Linden, 'John Chilembwe and the New Jerusalem', *JAH* 12 (1971), 629–51. For Charles Domingo see K. Lohrentz, 'Joseph Booth, Charles Domingo and the Seventh Day Baptists in Northern Nyasaland 1910–1912', *JAH* 12 (1971), 461–80, H. Langworthy, 'Charles Domingo, Seventh Day Baptists and Independency', *JRA* 15 (1985), 96–121, the *Letters of Charles Domingo*, ed. H. W. Langworthy (Zomba, Malawi, 1983), and J. Parratt, 'Y. Z. Mwasi and the Origins of the Blackman's Church', *JRA* 9 (1978), 193–206.

6. Southern Africa

Monographs include A. Sillery, *John Mackenzie of Bechuanaland: A Study in Humanitarian Imperialism 1835–1899* (Cape Town, 1971), A. Dachs, 'Missionary Imperialism: The Case of Bechuanaland', *JAH* 13 (1972), 647–58, T. D. Verryn, *A History of the Order of Ethiopia* (Cleveland, Transvaal, 1972), J. L. de Vries, *Mission and Colonialism in Namibia* (Johannesburg, 1978), J. B. Brain, *Catholics in Natal 1886–1925* (Durban, 1982), J. B. Brain, *Christian Indians in Natal 1860–1911* (1983), J. Van Butselaar, *Africains, missionnaires et colonialistes: Les origines de l'église presbytérienne du Mozambique (Mission Suisse) 1880–1896* (Leiden, 1984), J. M. Chirenje, *Ethiopianism and Afro-Americans in Southern Africa 1883–1916* (Baton Rouge, La., 1987), F. Hasselhorn, *Bauernmission in Südafrika: Die Hermannsbriger Mission in Spannungsfeld der Kolonialpolitik 1890–1939* (Erlangen, 1988), and H. H. Hewison, *Hedge of Wild Almonds: South Africa, the 'Pro-Boers' and the Quaker Conscience 1890–1910* (1989).

Articles: S. Marks, 'Hariette Colenso and the Zulus 1874–1913', *JAH* 4 (1963), 403–12, S. Marks, 'Christian African Participation in the 1906 Zulu Rebellion', *BSACH* 2/1 (1965), 55–72, A. J. Dachs, 'Missionary Imperialism: The Case of Bechuanaland', *JAH* 13 (1972), 647–58, G. Cuthbertson, 'James Stewart and the Anglo-Boer War 1899–1902', *South African Historical Journal*, 14 (1982), 68–84, G. Cuthbertson, 'Missionary Imperialism and Colonial Warfare: London Missionary Society Attitudes to the South African War 1899–1902', *South African Historical Journal*, 19 (1987), 93–114, G. Cuthbertson, ' "Cave of Adullam": Missionary Reaction to Ethiopianism at Lovedale 1898–1902', *Missionalia*, 19 (1991), 57–64. Finally, G. Shepperson, 'Ethiopianism: Past and Present', in C. G. Baëta (ed.), *Christianity in Tropical Africa* (1968), 249–68, remains the best introduction to an often misinterpreted phenomenon.

CHAPTER 11

FROM AGBEBI TO DIANGIENDA: INDEPENDENCY AND PROPHETISM

1. General

There is no very satisfactory overall study of prophetism, independency, or—still more vaguely—'new religious movements' in Africa. Two pioneer attempts to provide such a study were published in 1968: D. B. Barrett, *Schism and Renewal in Africa* (Nairobi), an analysis of 6,000 contemporary religious movements, and G. C. Oosthuizen, *Post-Christianity in Africa*. Both were seriously flawed but at least helped reveal the pitfalls of such an enterprise, and R. Mitchell, 'Towards the Sociology of Religious

Independency', *JRA* 3 (1970), 2–21, took the debate a little further. Among more recent general books the following may be noted: N. Ndiokwere, *Prophecy and Revolution* (1981), B. Jules-Rosette (ed.), *The New Religions of Africa* (1979), M. Daneel, *The Quest for Belonging* (Gweru, 1987), as well as the continent-wide survey in A. Hastings, *A History of African Christianity 1950–1975* (1979) of independency in the 1950s, 67–85 and 175–83. H. W. Turner's *Religious Innovation in Africa: Collected Essays on New Religious Movements* (Boston, 1979), remains the most authoritative of wider studies, and the same author's *Bibliography of New Religious Movements in Primal Societies*, i, *Black Africa* (Boston, 1977), the basic, though now somewhat dated, bibliography. Much of the recent literature is too sociological or concerned with movements originating after 1960 to be included here.

2. South Africa

For South Africa, B. Sundkler, *Bantu Prophets in South Africa* (1948, revised 1961), was a work of great influence but both detail and viewpoint are modified in the author's later and more sympathetic *Zulu Zion and some Swazi Zionists* (1976). Other major studies are E. Kamphausen, *Anfänge der kirklichen Unabhängigkeitsbewegung in Südafrika: Geschichte und Theologie der äthiopischen Bewegung 1872–1912* (Berne, 1976), a massive account of the Ethiopian movement, K. Schlosser, *Eingeborenen Kirchen in süd- und südwest Afrika* (1958), M. West, *Bishops and Prophets in a Black City* (1975), G. H. Haliburton, 'Edward Lion of Lesotho', *Journal of Southern African Historical Studies*, 1 (1976), 64–70, and N. Etherington, 'The Historical Sociology of Independent Churches in South East Africa', *JRA* 10 (1979), 108–26, which provides a useful reanalysis of the early period. J. P. Kiernan has written numerous articles on Zionism including 'The Work of Zion: An Analysis of a Zulu Zionist Ritual', *Africa*, 46 (1976), 340–56, ' "Poor and Puritan": An Attempt to View Zionism as a Collective Response to Urban Poverty', *African Studies*, 36 (1977), 31–41, 'The Weapons of Zion', *JRA* 10 (1979), 13–21, and 'The Canticles of Zion', *JRA* 20 (1990), 188–204.

For the Amanazaretha of Isaiah Shembe, besides the two Sundkler volumes noted above, see G. Oosthuizen, *The Theology of a South African Messiah: An Analysis of the Hymnal of the Church of the Nazarites* (Leiden, 1967), H.-J. Becken, 'On the Holy Mountain: A Visit to the New Year's Festival of the Nazaretha Church on Mount Nhlangakazi, January 1967', *JRA* 1 (1967), 138–49, J. Fernandez, 'The Precincts of the Prophet: A Day with Johannes Galilee Shembe', *JRA* 5 (1973), 32–53, and the outstanding study of E. Gunner, 'Power House, Prison House: An Oral Genre and its Use in Isaiah Shembe's Nazareth Baptist Church', *Journal of Southern African Studies*, 14 (1988), 204–27.

3. *Central Africa*

Zimbabwe is fortunate in having the largest single study of any country, the lengthily researched and pondered three volumes of M. Daneel, *Old and New in Southern Shona Independent Churches* (The Hague, 1971, 1974, 1988), but this vast work remains chiefly concerned with Zionism in the Masvingo area and is stronger on description than on history. Zionist origins in Rhodesia are well researched in W. R. Peaden, 'Zionist Churches in Southern Mashonaland 1924–1933', *BSACH* 3 (1969–70), 53–67. For the earliest Shona Independent Church, that of the White Bird founded by Matthew Zwimba, see T. Ranger, *The African Voice in Southern Rhodesia* (1970), 20–5, and for a small and isolated Ndebele Church, that of the Overseer (Madida) near Gwanda, see L. Dube, 'The Spirit of Purity', MA dissertation (University of Zimbabwe, 1984). For the 'apostolic' Churches, A. K. Weinrich, 'The People of the Spirit: An Independent Church in Rhodesia', *Africa*, 37 (1967), 203–19, M. Murphree, *Christianity among the Shona* (1969), B. Jules-Rosette, *African Apostles: Ritual and Conversion in the Church of John Maranke* (1975) and 'Marrapodi: An Independent Religious Community in Transition', *African Studies Review*, 18 (1975), 1–16, C. Dillon-Malone, *The Korsten Basketmakers: A Study of the Masowe Apostles* (1978), and R. Werbner, 'The Argument of Images: From Zion to the Wilderness in African Churches', in W. van Binsbergen and M. Schoffeleers (eds.), *Theoretical Explorations in African Religion* (1985), 253–86. Note an interesting early journalistic account, C. Dunn, 'Black Christians Build an Ark', *The Observer*, 26 June 1955, 13.

˙ Other Churches: P. Chater, *Caught in the Crossfire* (Harare, 1985) for the Church of St Francis, Rusape, C. J. Zvobgo, 'The Rev. E. T. J. Nemapare and the African Methodist Church in Southern Rhodesia 1930–1950', *Rhodesian History*, 6 (1975), 83–7, and C. Gandiya, 'The Guta Rajehova Church', MA dissertation (Zimbabwe, 1984). H. Bucher, *Spirits and Power* (1980) offers a critique of the Christianity of the spirit Churches.

For Malawi, besides the works by G. Shepperson and others listed in the final paragraph of Chapter 10 (section on central Africa), the principal early survey is R. Wishlade, *Sectarianism in Southern Nyasaland* (1965). These can be supplemented by a number of smaller studies such as R. Macdonald, 'Religious Independency as a Means of Social Advance in Northern Nyasaland in the 1930s', *JRA* 3 (1970), 106–29, J. Parratt, 'Y. Z. Mwasi and the Origins of the Blackman's Church', *JRA* 9 (1978), 193–206, O. Kalinga, 'Jordan Msumba, Ben Ngemela and the Last Church of God and his Christ 1924–1935', *JRA* 13 (1982), 207–18. *Sources for the Study of Religion in Malawi*, published by the University of Malawi, include Y. Z. Mwasi, *My Essential and Paramount Reasons for Working Independently*, ed. J. Parratt (1979) and J. C. Chakanza, *An Annotated List of Independent Churches in Malawi*

1900–1981 (1983). J. Chakanza's unpublished Oxford D.Phil. thesis surveys the whole field: 'Continuity and Change: A Study of New Religious Movements in Malawi 1900–1981' (1985).

Independency in Zambia might be said to begin with the tragic history of Tomo Nyirenda, for which see T. Ranger, 'The Mwana Lesa Movement of 1925', in T. Ranger and J. Weller (eds.), *Themes in the Christian History of Central Africa* (1975), 45–75. For Jeremiah Gondwe see S. Cross, 'A Prophet not without Honour', in C. Allen and R. Johnson (eds.), *African Perspectives* (1970), 171–84. There are two early accounts of the Lumpa Church of Alice Lenshina, valuable especially because written prior to its conflict with the State: Dorothea Lehmann's 'Alice Lenshina and the Lumpa Church', in J. Taylor and D. Lehmann, *Christians of the Copperbelt* (1961), 248–68, and L. Oger, WF, *Lumpa Church: The Lenshina Movement in Northern Rhodesia* (Serenje, 1960). The best factual account of its history remains the chapter by A. Roberts in R. Rotberg and A. Mazrui, *Protest and Power in Black Africa* (1970), 513–68, but there is to date no adequate study of this movement despite the valuable interpretative efforts of both W. van Binsbergen, *Religious Change in Zambia* (1981), and H. Hinfelaar, 'Women's Revolt: The Lumpa Church of Lenshina Mulenga in the 1950s', *JRA* 21 (1991), 99–129. For the Bamutima of Emilio Mulolani see chapters in Taylor and Lehmann, *Christians of the Copperbelt*, B. Garvey, *Bembaland Church* (Leiden, 1993), and H. Hinfelaar, *Religious Change among Bemba-Speaking Women of Zambia* (Leiden, 1994).

Watch Tower, Kitawala, and its various ramifications from Kamwana onwards are explored by R. J. Hooker, 'Witnesses and Watch Tower in the Rhodesias and Nyasaland', *JAH* 6 (1965), 91–106, H.-J. Greschat, *Kitawala Ursprung: Ausbreitung und Religion der Watch Tower—Bewegund in zentral Afrika* (Marburg, 1967), J. Gérard, *Les Fondements syncrétiques du Kitawala* (Brussels, 1969), Sholto Cross, 'The Watch Tower Movement in South Central Africa 1908–1945', D.Phil. thesis (Oxford, 1973), J. Chakanza, 'Continuity and Change', 91–157, and K. E. Fields, *Revival and Rebellion in Colonial Central Africa* (1985).

4. *East Africa*

The principal earlier works are F. B. Welbourn, *East African Rebels* (1961) about Ganda and Kikuyu movements, F. B. Welbourn and B. Ogot, *A Place to Feel at Home* (1966), on two west Kenyan bodies, the Church of Christ in Africa, and the African Israel Church Nineveh, and W. Sangree, *Age, Prayer and Politics in Tiriki, Kenya* (1966). C. Rosberg and J. Nottingham, *The Myth of Mau Mau* (1966) should also be consulted. More recently we have J. Murray, 'The Kikuyu Spirit Churches', *JRA* 5 (1973), 198–234, J. Murray, 'The Kikuyu Female Circumcision Controversy, with Special Reference to the Church Missionary Society's Sphere of Influence', Ph.D. thesis (Los Angeles, 1974), A. Wipper, *Rural Rebels: A Study of Two Protest Movements in Kenya* (1977), V. Neckebrouck, *Le Onzième Commandement: Étiologie d'une église indépendante au pied du mont Kenya* (Immensee, 1978) on the African Independent Pentecostal Church, and the mass of information, both statistical and biographical, to be found in D. Barrett and others, *Kenya Churches Handbook* (Kisumu, 1973). For Tanzania's mostly 'negative case' see two discussions by T. Ranger: *The African Churches of Tanzania*, a Historical Association of Tanzania pamphlet (Dar es Salaam, 1970) and 'Christian Independency in Tanzania', in D. Barrett (ed.), *African Initiatives in Religion* (Nairobi, 1971), 122–45.

5. West Africa

The authoritative study of the early African Church movement in Nigeria is J. Webster, *The African Churches among the Yoruba, 1888–1922* (1964), to which should be added J. Webster, 'The Bible and the Plough', *JHN* 2/4 (1963), 418–34, and his chapter 'Attitudes and Policies of the Yoruba African Churches towards Polygamy', in C. Baëta (ed.), *Christianity in Tropical Africa* (1968), 224–48. See also H. King, 'Co-operation in Contextualisation: Two Visionaries of the African Church: Mojola Agbebi and William Hughes of the African Institute, Colwyn Bay', *JRA* 16 (1986), 2–21.

The best early account of Harris is J. Casely Hayford, *William Waddy Harris, the West African Reformer: The Man and his Message* (1915). G. Haliburton, *The Prophet Harris* (1971) provides the most complete published study of Africa's most successful evangelist, but see S. Walker's review in *IJA* 8 (1975), 73–9. For the mind and teaching of Harris, D. Shank, 'A Prophet of Modern Times: The Thought of William Wade Harris', Ph.D. thesis (Aberdeen, 1980) is invaluable and volume iii includes a complete collection of primary sources. See too D. Shank, 'The Prophet Harris: A Historiographical and Bibliographical Survey', *JRA* 14 (1983), 130–60. For post-Harris developments in the Ivory Coast reference may be made to B. Holas, *Le Séparatisme religieux en Afrique noir: L'example de la Côte d'Ivoire* (Paris, 1965), R. Bureau, 'Le Prophète Harris et la religion harriste', *Annales de l'Université d'Abidjan* (Serie F), 3 (1971), 31–196, S. Walker, *The Religious Revolution in the Ivory Coast: The Prophet Harris and the Harrist Church* (1983), D. Shank, 'The Harrist Church in the Ivory Coast', *JRA* 15 (1985), 67–75, a critique of Walker, and J. Krabill, 'Dida Harrist Hymnody (1913–1990)', *JRA* 20 (1990), 118–52.

For Ghana, C. G. Baëta, *Prophetism in Ghana* (1962) remains useful. G. Haliburton devotes an appendix of *The Prophet Harris* to John Swatson (217–27). Among more recent studies are P. Breidenbach, 'Maame Harris

Grace Tasi and Papa Kwesi John Nackenbah', *IJA* 12 (1979), 581–614, K. Opoku, 'Changes within Christianity with Special Reference to the Musama Disco Christo Church', in *CIA* 111–21, J. Fernandez, 'Rededication and Prophetism in Ghana', *Cahiers d'études africaines*, 10 (1970), 228–305, a study of Wovenu, R. Wyllie, 'Pioneers of Ghanaian Pentecostalism: Peter Anim and James McKeown', *JRA* 6 (1974), 102–22, and G. Haliburton, 'Mark Christian Hayford: A Non-Success Story', *JRA* 12 (1981), 20–37.

For Nigeria, the earliest published accounts of Garrick Braide include James Johnson, 'Elijah II', *Church Missionary Review* (Aug. 1916), 455–62, and P. Talbot, 'Some Beliefs of Today and Yesterday', *Journal of the African Society*, 15 (1916), 305–19. Recent accounts include G. Tasie, *Christian Missionary Enterprise in the Niger Delta 1864–1918* (Leiden, 1978), 166–201, and F. Ludwig, 'Elijah II: Radicalisation and Consolidation of the Garrick Braide Movement 1915–1918', *JRA* 23 (1993), 296–317. The literature on Aladura is exceptionally extensive. The principal earlier works were J. Peel, *Aladura* (1968) and H. W. Turner, *African Independent Church*, 2 vols. (1967). The former was a study of Cherubim and Seraphim and of the Christ Apostolic Church, the latter of Oshitelu's Church of the Lord (Aladura). R. C. Mitchell, 'Religious Protest and Social Change: The Origins of the Aladura Movement in West Nigeria', in R. Rotberg and A. Mazrui (eds.), *Protest and Power in Black Africa* (1973), 458–96, was a judicious analysis from the same period. For the Christ Apostolic Church see also the *Ecumenical Review* (1976), 418–28, and for the Celestial Church of Christ, founded in 1947 in Dahomey, the largest of the later Aladura Churches, see R. Hackett, 'Thirty Years of Growth and Change in a West African Independent Church': A Sociological Perspective', *JRA* 11 (1980), 212–24. For two outstandingly creative small Churches see S. Bennett, *The Rise and Fall of an African Utopia: A Wealthy Theocracy in Comparative Perspective* (Waterloo, Ont., 1977), a study of the Holy Apostles' Community at Aiyetoro, and M. Abasiattai, 'The Oberi Okaime Christian Mission: Towards a History of an Ibibio Independent Church', *Africa*, 59 (1989), 496–516. E. Isichei (ed.), *Varieties of Christian Experience in Nigeria* (1982) includes two helpful mini-biographies: A. Ogunranti, 'Pastor and Politician: Isaac Akinyele, Olubadan of Ibadan (1882–1955)', 131–40, and A. Omojayowo, 'Mother in Israel: Christianah Olatunrinle in Ondo (c.1855–1944)', 141–8. For the best recent reassessments of Aladura see J. Omoyajowo, *Cherubim and Seraphim: A History of an African Independent Church* (1982), R. Hackett, *New Religious Movements in Nigeria* (1987), P. Probst, 'The Letter and the Spirit: Literary and Religious Authority in the History of the Aladura Movement in Western Nigeria', *Africa*, 59 (1989), 478–95, and B. Ray, 'Aladura Christianity: A Yoruba Religion', *JRA* 23 (1993), 266–91.

6. *Zaïre, Congo, and Angola*

Two extensive and wide-ranging works for the old Belgian and French Congo are E. Andersson, *Messianic Popular Movements in the Lower Congo* (Uppsala, 1958), and M. Sinda, *Le Messianisme congolaise et ses incidences politiques* (Paris, 1972), to which should be added the very rich collection of primary texts, J. Janzen and W. MacGaffey, *An Anthology of Kongo Religion* (Kansas City, 1974). For a movement in Angola see A. Margarido, 'The Tokoist Church', in R. H. Chilcote (ed.), *Protest and Resistance in Angola and Brazil* (1972), 29–52.

The earliest published account in English of Simon Kimbangu is P. Lerrigo, 'The "Prophet Movement" in the Congo', *International Review of Missions*, 11 (1922), 270–7. The three principal books are M. L. Martin, *Kimbangu: An African Prophet and his Church* (1975), a work which represents the modern Kimbanguist view very closely, W. Ustorf, *Afrikanische Initiative: Das aktive Leiden des Propheten Simon Kimbangu* (Bern, 1975), and S. Asch, *L'Église du prophète Simon Kimbangu de ses origines à son rôle actuel au Zaïre* (Paris, 1983). Among shorter scholarly studies the following are important: J. Chomé, *La Passion de Simon Kimbangu 1921–1951* (Brussels, 1959), P. Raymaekers, 'Histoire de Simon Kimbangu, prophète, d'après les ecrivains Nfinangani et Nzungu (1921)', *Archives de sociologie des religions*, 16 (1971), 15–42, D. Feci, *Vie cachée et vie publique de Simon Kimbangu selon la littérature coloniale et missionaire belge* (Brussels, 1972), E. Libert, 'Les Missionnaires chrétiens face au mouvement kimbanguiste: Documents contemporains (1921)', *EHA* 2 (1971), 121–54, C. Irvine, 'The Birth of the Kimbanguist Movement in the Bas-Zaïre 1921', *JRA* 6 (1974), 23–76, A. Geuns, 'Chronologie des mouvements religieux indépendants au Bas-Zaïre, particulièrement du mouvement fondé par le prophète Simon Kimbangu', *JRA* 6 (1974), 187–222, H. Desroche and P. Raymaekers, 'Départ d'un prophète, arrivée d'une église: Textes et recherches sur la mort de Simon Kimbangu et sur sa survivance', *Archives de sciences sociales des religions*, 42 (1976), 117–62, C. Irvine, 'The Second Baptism of Simon Kimbangu', in J. Thrower (ed.), *Essays in Religious Studies for Andrew Walls* (Aberdeen, 1986), 17–36, and D. Mackay, 'Simon Kimbangu and the BMS Tradition', *JRA* 17 (1987), 113–71. J. Pemberton, 'The History of Simon Kimbangu, Prophet, by the Writers Nfinangani and Nzungu, 1921: An Introduction and Annotated Translation', *JRA* 23 (1993), 194–231, is a translation of P. Raymaekers (above) with a new introduction and notes, while D. Mackay and D. Ntoni-Nzinga, 'Kimbangu's Interlocutor: Nyuvudi's *Nsamu Miangunza*', *JRA* 23 (1993), 232–65, supplements Nfinangani with a second early African text, this time complete with its Kikongo original.

The following articles relate rather to the subsequent life of

Kimbanguism. W. MacGaffey, 'The Beloved City: A Commentary on a Kimbanguist Text', *JRA* 2 (1969), 129–47, M. Muntu-Monji, 'Nzambi wa Malemba: Un mouvement d'inspiration Kimbanguiste au Kasai', *Cahiers des religions africaines*, 8 (1974), 231–55, D. Ndofunsu, 'The Role of Prayer in the Kimbanguist Church', in *CIA* 577–96, A. Droogers, 'Kimbanguism at the Grass Roots: Beliefs in a Local Kimbanguist Church', *JRA* 11 (1980), 188–211, W. MacGaffey, *Modern Kongo Prophets* (1983), G. Molyneux, 'The Place and Function of Hymns in the EJSCK', *JRA* 20 (1990), 153–87, and M. Muntu-Monji, 'Sources imprimées et bibliographie suédoises commentées relatives aux mouvements prophétiques du Zaire', *JRA* 13 (1982), 219–22.

CHAPTER 12

CHURCH, SCHOOL, AND STATE IN THE AGE OF BISHOP
KIWANUKA

Many of the titles included under Chapter 10 also refer to the post-1920 years. They are not repeated here.

1. *General*

Among the more general studies of Christianity in this period C. P. Groves, *The Planting of Christianity in Africa*, iv (1954), remains the most detailed survey of missionary activity throughout the continent. A. Hastings, *A History of African Christianity 1950–1975* (1979) looks at developments in the latter part of our period with special concern for Church-State relations. B. Sundkler, *The Christian Ministry in Africa* (1960), B. A. Pauw, *Religion in a Tswana Chiefdom* (1960), M. Brandel-Syrier, *Black Woman in Search of God* (1962), M. Murphree, *Christianity and the Shona* (1969), H. Mobley, *The Ghanaian's Image of the Missionary: An Analysis of the Published Critiques of Christian Missionaries by Ghanaians 1897–1965* (Leiden, 1970), D. Barrett (ed.), *African Initiatives in Religion* (1971), T. Ranger and J. Weller (eds.), *Themes in the Christian History of Central Africa* (1975), and Gerdien Verstraelen-Gilhuis, *A New Look at Christianity in Africa* (Gweru, 1992), a posthumous collection of essays, all function with a wide frame of reference and a principal focus upon the middle third of this century.

Novels by African writers are rich in depictions of Christian life and the tensions with tradition a Christian commitment involved in this period. While some are more descriptive, others are more ideologically determined. From what is now a very considerable literature any selection to illustrate Christian life between 1920 and 1960 is likely to include Chinua Achebe, *Arrow of God* (1964), and *No Longer at Ease* (1960), Ngugi wa

Thiong'o (formerly James Ngugi), *The River Between* (1965) and *A Grain of Wheat* (1967), Mongo Beti, *Le pauvre Christ de Bomba* (1956; English translation *The Poor Christ of Bomba*, 1971) and *Mission terminée* (1957; English translation *Mission to Kala*, 1958), and Peter Abrahams, *The View from Coyaba* (1985). For further discussion see *JRA* 191 (February) (1989).

Two exceptionally perceptive analyses of African Christianity written in the first part of this period are Norman Leys, *Kenya* (1924), 210–55 'Christian Missions', and Monica Hunter, 'An African Christian Morality', *Africa*, 10 (1937), 265–92. See also Monica Hunter's *Reaction to Conquest* (1936), a study of Pondoland, I. Schapera, *Christianity and the Tswana* (1958), and T. Ranger's delightful 'Taking Hold of the Land: Holy Places and Pilgrimages in Twentieth-Century Zimbabwe', *Past and Present*, 117 (1987), 158–94.

2. *Protestant Missions*

For Protestant missionary approaches in this period, particularly in regard to African culture, one can best start with Edwin Smith, *The Christian Mission in Africa*, a study based on the work of the International Conference at Le Zoute, 1926 (1927), R. Allen, *Le Zoute: A Critical Review of 'The Christian Mission in Africa'* (1927), E. Smith, *The Golden Stool* (1926), Roland Allen, *The Spontaneous Expansion of the Church* (1927), E. R. Morgan (ed.), *Essays Catholic and Missionary* (1928), D. Westermann, *Africa and Christianity* (1935), D. Shropshire, *The Church and Primitive Peoples* (1938), G. Parrinder, *West African Religion* (1949), E. Smith (ed.), *African Ideas of God* (1950), J. V. Taylor, *The Primal Vision* (1963), T. Ranger, 'Missionary Adaptation of African Religious Institutions: The Masasi Case', T. Ranger and I. Kimambo (eds.), *The Historical Study of African Religion* (1972), 221–47, E. Jaeschke, *Bruno Gutmann, his Life, his Thoughts, his Work: An Early Attempt at a Theology in an African Context* (Erlangen, 1985), P. Forster, 'Missionaries and Anthropology: The Case of the Scots of Northern Malawi', *JRA* 16 (1986), 101–20, P. Forster, *T. Cullen Young: Missionary and Anthropologist* (1989), G. Parrinder, 'Dahomey Half a Century Ago', *JRA* 19 (1989), 264–73, N. King and K. Fielder, *Robin Lamburn: From a Missionary's Notebook: The Yao of Tunduru and Other Essays* (Saarbrücken, 1991).

There is as yet no even partially adequate study of J. H. Oldham, but see the memoirs by J. Dougall in *International Review of Mission*, 59 (1970), 8–22, and Kathleen Bliss in *Dictionary of National Biography* (1961–70), 806–8, W. Hogg, *Ecumenical Foundations: A History of the International Missionary Council and its Nineteenth-Century Background* (1952), E. Smith, 'The Story of the Institute', *Africa*, 7 (1934), 1–27, G. Bell, *Randall Davidson, Archbishop of Canterbury* (1935), as well as his own books *Christianity and the Race Problem* (1925) and (with B. D. Gibson) *The Remaking of Man in Africa* (1931), J. Cell,

By Kenya Possessed: The Correspondence of Norman Leys and J. H. Oldham 1918–1926 (1976). Hugh Tinker, *The Ordeal of Love: C. F. Andrews and India* (1979) has much about Kenya and Oldham, as has B. S. Bennett, 'The Archbishop of Canterbury in Politics 1919–1939: Selected Case Studies', Ph.D. thesis (Cambridge, 1992). For someone who was, in a way, Oldham's principal successor, at least as regards African concerns, see A. Porter, 'Margery Perham: Christian Missions and Indirect Rule', *Journal of Imperial and Commonwealth History*, 19/3 (1991), 83–99.

Owen and Arthur have been discussed in a number of studies: J. Lonsdale, 'European Attitudes and African Pressures: Missions and Government in Kenya Between the Wars', *Race*, 10 (1968–9), 141–51, J. Lonsdale, 'Political Associations in Western Kenya', in R. Rotberg (ed.), *Protest and Power in Black Africa* (1970), 589–638, L. Spencer, 'Defence and Protection of Converts: Kenya Missions and the Inheritance of Christian Widows 1912–1931', *JRA* 5 (1973), 107–27, M. Whisson and J. Lonsdale, 'The Case of Jason Gor and Fourteen Others: A Luo Succession Dispute in Historical Perspective', *Africa*, 45 (1975), 50–66, D. Wylie, 'Confrontation over Kenya: The Colonial Office and its Critics 1918–1940', *JAH* (1977), 427–47, N. Murray, 'Archdeacon W. E. Owen: Missionary as Propagandist', *IJA* 15 (1982), 653–70, and L. Spencer, 'Christianity and Colonial Protest: Perceptions of W. E. Owen, Archdeacon of Kavirondo', *JRA* 13 (1982), 47–60. See also R. Githige, 'The Mission–State Relationship in Kenya 1888–1938', Ph.D. thesis (Aberdeen, 1982).

For Cripps see D. V. Steere, *God's Irregular: Arthur Shearly Cripps* (1973), M. Steele, ' "With Hope Unconquered and Unconquerable . . .": Arthur Shearly Cripps, 1869–1952', in T. Ranger and J. Weller (eds.), *Themes in the Christian History of Central Africa* (1975), 152–74, and G. Brown, A. Chennels, and L. Rix (eds.), *Arthur Shearly Cripps: A Selection of his Prose and Verse* (Gweru, 1976). For Schweitzer, another odd man out, see G. Seaver, *Albert Schweitzer: The Man and his Mind* (1947) and N. Griffith and L. Person, *Albert Schweitzer: An International Bibliography* (Boston, Mass., 1981). His own accounts of his missionary work are *On the Edge of the Primeval Forest* (1922) and *More from the Primeval Forest* (1931).

Studies of other missionary figures: C. F. Andrews, *John White of Mashonaland* (1935), J. Weller, 'The Influence on National Affairs of Alston May, Bishop of Northern Rhodesia, 1914–40', in Ranger and Weller (eds.), *Themes in the Christian History of Central Africa*, 195–211, S. Morrow, ' "On the Side of the Robbed": R. J. B. Moore, Missionary on the Copperbelt 1933–1941', *JRA* 19 (1989), 244–63. Max Warren's autobiography is entitled *Crowded Canvas* (1974) and his biography by F. W. Dillistone, *Into All the World* (1980).

3. *Education*

The two Phelps-Stokes Reports (New York, 1920 and 1924), both entitled *Education in Africa* and edited by T. Jesse Jones, are foundational for education in this period. The first deals chiefly with Sierra Leone, Liberia, Gold Coast, Nigeria, South Africa, the Belgian Congo, and Angola, the second with eastern and central Africa. The best subsequent wide-ranging surveys are to be found in the two editions of Lord Hailey's *An African Survey* (1938), 1207–1308, (1956), 1132–1262. Other earlier works to be noted are A. V. Murray's outstanding *The School in the Bush* (1929; 2nd edn. 1938), H. Dumbrell (ed.), *Letters to African Teachers* (1935), and A. Mayhew, *Education in the Colonial Empire* (1938). A. Kerr, *Fort Hare 1915–1948* (1968) and R. H. Shepherd, *Lovedale, South Africa, 1824–1955* (Lovedale, 1971) give the history of two of the most influential missionary educational institutions, and L. B. Greaves, *Carey Francis of Kenya* (1969) a biography of one of the most famous of missionary headmasters. Among recent books the following may be noted: D. G. Scanlon (ed.), *Church, School and Education in Africa* (New York, 1966), J. E. Anderson, *The Struggle for the School: The Interaction of Missionary, Colonial Government and Nationalist Enterprise in the Development of Formal Education in Kenya* (1970), K. King, *Pan-Africanism and Education* (1971), K. Elliott, *An African School: A Record of Experience* (Cambridge, 1970), E. Berman (ed.), *African Reactions to Missionary Education* (New York, 1975), L. and N. Sanderson, *Education, Religion and Politics in Southern Sudan 1899–1964* (1981), and N. Omenka, *The School in the Service of Evangelization: The Catholic Educational Impact in Eastern Nigeria 1886–1950* (Leiden, 1989), together with the following articles: T. Ranger, 'African Attempts to Control Education in East and Central Africa 1900–1939', *Past and Present*, 32 (1965), 57–85, F. Carter, 'Co-operation in Education in Uganda: Mission and Government Relations in the Inter-War Period', *BSACH* 2 (1967), 259–75, K. Ward, 'Evangelism or Education? Mission Priorities and Educational Policy in the African Inland Mission 1900–1950', *Kenya Historical Review*, 3 (1975), 243–60, E. K. Mashingaidze, 'Government–Mission Cooperation in African Education in Southern Rhodesia up to the Late 1920s', *Kenya Historical Review*, 4 (1976), 265–81, A. E. Afigbo, 'The Missions, the State and Education in South-Eastern Nigeria 1956–71', in *CIA* 176–92, C. Cooke, 'Church, State and Education: The Eastern Nigerian Experience 1950–67', in *CIA* 193–206, S. Morrow, ' "No Girl Leaves the School Unmarried": Mabel Shaw and the Education of Girls at Mbereshi, Northern Rhodesia', *IJA* 19 (1986), 601–36, B. Carmody, 'Conversion and Schools at Chikuni 1905–39', *Africa*, 58 (1988), 193–209, and G. Verstraelen-Gilhuis, 'African Education as Seen from Le Zoute, 1926', *A New Look at Christianity in Africa* (Gweru, 1992), 31–61.

4. *Protestant Churches*

For the history of Protestant Churches and their developing life the *International Review of Missions* (1912– , London, then Geneva) is a valuable source throughout this period. J. V. Taylor, *The Growth of the Church in Buganda* (1958), I. Schapera, *Christianity and the Tswana* (1958), E. Braekman, *Histoire du Protestantisme au Congo* (Brussels, 1961), J. V. Taylor and D. Lehmann, *Christians of the Copperbelt* (1961), P. Chater, *Grass Roots: The Story of St Faith's Farm* (1962), N. Smith, *The Presbyterian Church of Ghana 1835–1960* (1966), G. D. Johnston, 'Ohafia 1911–1940: A Study in Church Developments in Eastern Nigeria', *BSACH* 2 (1966), 139–54, M. Nissen, *An African Church is Born: The Story of the Adamawa and Central Sardauna Provinces in Nigeria* (Denmark, 1968), W. V. Stone, 'The Livingstonia Mission and the Bemba', *BSACH* 2 (1968), 311–22, R. Sweeting, 'The Growth of the Church in Buwalasi (Uganda)', *BSACH* 2 (1968), 334–49, and 3 (1969–70), 15–27, F. P. Cotterell, 'An Indigenous Church in Southern Ethiopia', *BSACH* 3 (1969–70), 68–104, R. MacPherson, *The Presbyterian Church in Kenya* (1970), J. Gration, 'The Relationship of the Africa Inland Mission and its National Church in Kenya between 1895 and 1971', Ph.D. thesis (New York University, 1974), O. Saeveras, *On Church–Mission Relations in Ethiopia 1944–1969: With Special Reference to the Evangelical Church Mekane Yesus and the Lutheran Missions* (Oslo, 1974), E. Crampton, *Christianity in Northern Nigeria* (Zaria, 1975), L. Sanderson, 'The Sudan Interior Mission and the Condominium Sudan 1937–1955', *JRA* 8 (1976), 13–40, K. Ward, 'The Development of Protestant Christianity in Kenya 1910–1940', Ph.D. thesis (Cambridge, 1976), W. Johnson, *Worship and Freedom: A Black American Church in Zambia* (1977), R. Strayer, *The Making of Mission Communities in East Africa: Anglicans and Africans in Colonial Kenya 1875–1935* (1978), B. Sundkler, *Bara Bukoba: Church and Community in Tanzania* (1980), W. Omulokoli, 'The Historical Development of the Anglican Church among Abaluyia 1905–1955', Ph.D. thesis (Aberdeen, 1981), G. Verstraelen-Gilhuis, *From Dutch Mission Church to Reformed Church in Zambia* (Franeker, 1982), S. Chimombo, 'Dreams and Ntara's *Man of Africa*', *JRA* 19 (1989), 48–70.

For the East African revival movement see J. E. Church, *Awake Uganda! The Story of Blasio Kigosi and his Vision of Revival* (Kampala, 1937), Max Warren, *Revival: An Enquiry* (1954), E. Wiseman, *Kikuyu Martyrs* (1958), C. Robins, 'Tukutendereza: A Study of Social Change and Sectarian Withdrawal in the Balokole Revival of Uganda', Ph.D. thesis (Columbia, 1975), J. Murray, 'A Bibliography of the East African Revival Movement', *JRA* 8 (1976), 144–7, J. E. Church, *Quest for the Highest* (1981), R. Anker-Petersen, 'A Study of the Spiritual Roots of the East African Revival Movement with Special Reference to its Use of Confession of Sin in

Public', M.Th. thesis (Aberdeen, 1988), K. Ward, ' "Obedient Rebels": The Mukono Crisis of 1941', *JRA* 19 (1989), 194–227.

5. *South Africa*

A. Paton, *Cry, the Beloved Country* (1948), T. Huddleston, *Naught for your Comfort* (1956), M. Scott, *A Time to Speak* (1958), D. Paton (ed.), *Church and Race in South Africa* (1958), including Ambrose Reeves, 'Selections from the Charges to his Diocesan Synod 1952–1957', 9–50, and G. C. Grant, 'The Liquidation of Adams College', 51–93; M. Benson, *Tshekedi Khama* (1960), H. Stanton, *Go Well, Stay Well: South Africa 1956–1960* (1961), C. Hooper, *Brief Authority* (1960), A. Luthuli, *Let my People Go: An Autobiography* (1962), Joost De Blank, *Out of Africa* (1964), P. Walshe, *The Rise of African Nationalism in South Africa: The African National Congress 1912–1952* (1970), F. Wilson and D. Perrot, *Outlook on a Century: South Africa 1870–1970* (Lovedale, 1973), J. Peart-Binns, *Ambrose Reeves* (1973), A. Paton, *Apartheid and the Archbishop: The Life and Times of Geoffrey Clayton* (1973), *Freedom for my People: The Autobiography of Z. K. Matthews*, with a memoir by Monica Wilson (1981), A. Wilkinson, *The Community of the Resurrection: A Centenary History* (1992).

Among more recent analytical studies the following should be noted: T. Sundermeier (ed.), *Church and Nationalism in South Africa* (Johannesburg, 1975), W. A. de Klerk, *The Puritans in Africa* (1975), T. D. Moodie, *The Rise of Afrikanerdom* (1975), J. de Gruchy, *The Church Struggle in South Africa* (1979), E. Regehr, *Perceptions of Apartheid: The Churches and Political Change in South Africa* (1979), I. Hexham, *The Irony of Apartheid* (1980), J. Michener, *The Covenant* (1980), D. J. Bosch, 'The Roots and Fruits of Afrikaner Civil Religion', in J. S. Hofmeyr and W. S. Vorster (eds.), *New Faces of Africa* (Pretoria, 1984), 14–35, A. Du Toit, 'Puritans in South Africa? Afrikaner "Calvinism" and Kuyperian NeoCalvinism in Late Nineteenth Century South Africa', *Comparative Studies in Society and History*, 27 (1985), 209–40, A. Du Toit, 'No Chosen People: The Myth of the Calvinist Origins of Afrikaner Nationalism and Racial Ideology', *American Historical Review*, 88 (1983), 920–52, L. Thompson, *The Political Mythology of Apartheid* (1985), J. R. Cochrane, *Servants of Power: The Role of English-Speaking Churches 1903–1930* (1987), F. England and T. Peterson (eds.), *Bounty in Bondage: The Anglican Church in Southern Africa* (1989), M. Worsnip, *Between Two Fires: The Anglican Church and Apartheid 1948–1957* (Pietermaritzburg, 1991).

For the Catholic Church in South Africa see F. Schimlek, *Against the Stream: The Life of Father Bernard Huss, CMM, the Social Apostle of the Bantu* (Mariannhill, 1949), W. E. Brown, *The Catholic Church in South Africa from its Origin to the Present Day* (1960), A. Prior (ed.), *Catholics in Apartheid Society* (1982), and G. Abraham, *The Catholic Church and Apartheid: The Response of* the Catholic Church in South Africa to the First Decade of National Party Rule 1948–1957 (Johannesburg, 1989).

6. The Catholic Church Elsewhere

F. de Meeus and R. Steenbergher, *Les Missions religieuses au Congo belge* (Antwerp, 1947), *Des Prêtres Noirs s'interrogent* (Paris, 1956), L. Aujoulat, *Aujourd'hui l'Afrique* (Paris, 1958), *The Church to Africa: Pastoral Letters of the African Hierarchies* (1959), G. Mosmans, *L'Église à l'heure de l'Afrique* (Tournai, 1961), P. Francisco Maria Pinheiro, *Anuario Catolico de Moçambique 1961* (first year of publication) (Lourenço Marques, 1961), A. Veloso, *D. Teodosio Clemente de Gouveia*, 2 vols. (Lisbon, 1965), A. Hastings, *Church and Mission in Modern Africa* (1967), J. Fabian, *Jamaa: A Charismatic Movement in Katanga* (1971), A. Shorter and E. Kataza (eds.), *Missionaries to Yourselves: African Catechists Today* (1972), especially F. Nolan, 'History of the Catechist in Eastern Africa', 1–28, F. Lopes, *Missões Franciscanas em Moçambique 1898– 1970* (Braga, 1972), I. Linden, *Catholics, Peasants and Chewa Resistance in Nyasaland 1889–1939* (1974), Mumbanza mwa Bawele, 'La Contribution des Zairois à l'œuvre d'évangelisation et à la prosperité des établissements missionnaires: La mission catholique de Libanda 1933–1960', *EHA* 6 (1974), 225–74, W. de Craemer, *The Jamaa and the Church: A Bantu Catholic Movement in Zaïre* (1977), F. Barr, *Archbishop Aston Chichester 1879–1962* (Gwelo, 1978), C. M. Cooke, 'Church, State and Education: The Eastern Nigerian Experience 1950–67', in *CIA*, 192–206, A. Dachs and W. Rea, *The Catholic Church and Zimbabwe 1879–1979* (Gwelo, 1979), E. Hogan, 'The Motivation of the Modern Irish Missionary Movement 1912–1939', *JRA* 10 (1979), 157–73, A. Okwu, 'The Beginning of the Maynooth Movement in Southern Nigeria and the Rise of the St Patrick's Missionary Society 1920– 1930', *JRA* 10 (1979), 22–45, E. Hogan, *Catholic Missionaries and Liberia 1842–1950* (Cork, 1981), V. Nwosu, *The Catholic Church in Onitsha 1885– 1985* (Onitsha, 1985), N. Omenka, 'The Role of the Catholic Mission in the Development of Vernacular Literature in Eastern Nigeria', *JRA* 16 (1986), 121–37, L. Verbeek, *Ombres et clairières: Histoire de l'implantation de l'église catholique dans le diocèse de Sakania, Zaïre 1910–1970* (Rome, 1987), P. Rutayisire, *La Christianisation du Rwanda: Méthode missionnaire et politique selon Mgr. Léon Classe* (Fribourg, 1987), P. Rutayisire, 'L'Africanisation du christianisme et la pratique missionnaire en référence à la christianisation du Burundi 1897–1937', in G. Ruggieri (ed.), *Église et histoire de l'église en Afrique* (Paris, 1988), 97–118, J. Waliggo, *A History of African Priests* (Masaka, 1988), D. Ogudo, *The Holy Ghost Fathers and Catholic Worship among the Igbo People of Eastern Nigeria* (Paderborn, 1988), O. Okeke, 'Prophetism, Pentecostalism and Conflict in Ikenanzizi', *JRA* 19 (1989), 228–43, V. Nwosu, *The Laity and the Growth of the Catholic Church in Nigeria: The Onitsha Story 1905–1983* (Ibadan, 1990), E. M. Hogan, *The Irish Missionary*

Movement (Dublin, 1990), B. Carmody, 'Secular and Sacred at Chikuni 1905–1940', *JRA* 21 (1991), 130–48, B. Carmody, *Conversion and Jesuit Schooling in Zambia* (Leiden, 1992).

For some accounts of Catholic life of a less historical than descriptive or analytical kind see Mary Douglas, 'The Lele of the Congo', in A. Hastings (ed.), *The Church and the Nations* (1959), 73–89, M. Douglas, *The Lele of the Kasai* (1963), 264–6, J. Asheri, *Promise* (Lagos, 1969), a woman's account of childhood in Cameroon in the 1930s, L. Vambe, *From Rhodesia to Zimbabwe* (1976), the early chapters an account of life in the missions of Chishawasha and Kutama, A. Hastings, 'Ganda Catholic Spirituality', in *African Catholicism* (1989; repr. from *JRA* 8 (1976)), 69–81, a picture of Baganda clergy in the 1950s.

7. Selection of Accounts of Christians Active in this Period

See also the items on Diban, Kivebulaya, Atiman, and Kitagana under Chapter 10.

E. Smith, *Aggrey of Africa* (1929), updated by K. King, 'James K. E. Aggrey: Collaborator, Nationalist, Pan-African', *Canadian Journal of African Studies*, 3 (1969), 511–30, T. B. Adebiyi, *The Beloved Bishop: The Life of Bishop A. B. Akinyele 1875–1968* (Ibadan, 1969), M. Markwei, 'Harry Sawyerr's Patron (Bishop T. S. Johnson)', in N. Glasswell and E. Fasholé-Luke (eds.), *New Testament Christianity for Africa and the World* (1974), 179–97, R. Macdonald, 'Reverend Hanock Msokera Phiri', *African Historical Studies*, 3 (1970), 75–87, A. Hastings, 'John Lester Membe', in T. Ranger and J. Weller (eds.), *Themes in the Christian History of Central Africa* (1975), 175–94, E. N. Wanyoike, *An African Pastor: The Life and Work of the Revd Wanyoike Kamawe 1888–1970* (Nairobi, 1974), E. Isichei, *Entirely for God: The Life of Michael Iwene Tansi* (1980), T. Ranger, 'Thompson Samkange: Tambaram and Beyond', *JRA* 23 (1993), 318–46.

The early chapters of biographies and autobiographies of people influential in the post-1960 period can be of value for a picture of Christian life from the 1930s to the 1950s, such as Abel Muzorewa's autobiography, *Rise Up and Walk* (1978), and C. Du Boulay, *Tutu: Voice of the Voiceless* (1988).

8. Marriage

The *Survey of African Marriage and Family Life*, ed. A. Phillips, published jointly in 1953 by the International Missionary Council and the International African Institute, remains a standard text. Of its three sections that on *Marriage Laws in Africa* by Phillips was republished in 1971 and that by Lucy Mair on *African Marriage and Social Change* in 1969. The third section, 'Christian Marriage in African Society' by Lyndon Harries, has not been republished but could be considered as replaced by A. Hastings, *Christian Marriage in Africa* (1973). I. Schapera, *Married Life in an African Tribe* (1940) remains a little classic. See also B. Kisembo, L. Magesa, and A. Shorter, *African Christian Marriage* (1977), Eugene Hillman, *Polygamy Reconsidered* (New York, 1975), and M. Kirwen, *African Widows* (New York, 1979).

9. *Hymnody*

For the development of African hymnody in the mission Churches, H. Weman, *African Music and the Church in Africa* (Uppsala, 1960) remains the most considerable work together with A. M. Jones, *African Hymnody in Christian Worship* (Gwelo, 1976). See also S. G. Williamson, 'The Lyric in the Fante Methodist Church', *Africa*, 28 (1958), 126–34, K. Carroll, 'African Music', *AFER* (1961), 301–12, S. Mbunga, 'Church Music in Tanzania', *Concilium*, 2 (Feb. 1966), 57–60, and J. Lenherr, 'The Hymnody of the Mission Churches among the Shona and Ndebele', in M. Bourdillon (ed.), *Christianity South of the Zambezi*, ii (Gwelo, 1977), 103–21. *JRA* 20/2 (June 1990) is entirely devoted to hymnody.

10. *Christianity and Politics*

This has come in everywhere. This section simply lists a few significant items which do not fit easily elsewhere.

J. V. Taylor's *Christianity and Politics in Africa* (1957) was an influential Penguin near the end of our period, with which may be compared Robert Delavignette, *Christianisme et colonialisme* (Paris, 1960).

Kenya and Mau Mau: Walter Carey's pamphlet *Crisis in Kenya: Christian Common Sense on Mau Mau and the Colour Bar* (1953) is a fearful example of racialist incomprehension from an elderly, retired bishop, with which may be contrasted another pamphlet published the same year by the CMS, T. F. Bewes, *Kikuyu Conflict: Mau Mau and the Christian Witness* (1953). *Harry Thuku: An Autobiography* (Nairobi, 1970), E. N. Wanyoike's life of the Revd Wanyoike Kamawe, *An African Pastor: The Life and Work of the Rev. Wanyoike Kamawe 1888–1970* (Nairobi, 1974), and J. Murray-Brown, *Kenyatta* (1972), as well as E. Wiseman, *Kikuyu Martyrs* (1958), B. A. Ogot, 'Revolt of the Elders: An Anatomy of the Loyalist Crowd in the Mau Mau Uprising 1952–56', B. A. Ogot (ed.), *Politics and Nationalism in Colonial Kenya* (Nairobi, 1972), 134–48, all provide material for the study of the Mau Mau–Christianity relationship, as do D. Barnett and K. Njama, *Mau Mau from Within* (1966), and C. Rosberg and J. Nottingham, *The Myth of 'Mau Mau': Nationalism in Kenya* (1966). For a subtle recent re-evaluation, see J.

Lonsdale, 'Mau Maus of the Mind: Making Mau Mau and Remaking Kenya', *JAH* 31 (1990), 393–421.

Cameroon: R. Joseph, 'Church, State and Society in Colonial Cameroon', *IJA* 13 (1980), 5–32, A. Ndi, 'The Second World War in Southern Cameroon and its Impact on Mission–State Relations 1939–1950', D. Killingray and R. Rathbone (ed.), *Africa and the Second World War* (1986), 204–31, J. Mfoulou, 'The Catholic Church and Cameroonian Nationalism: From Misunderstanding to Opposition', in *CIA* 216–27.

M. Markovitz, *Cross and Sword: The Political Role of Christian Missions in the Belgian Congo 1908–1960* (Stanford, Calif., 1973), T. Ranger, *Church and State in Southern Rhodesia*, Historical Association of Rhodesia and Nyasaland, Salisbury, local series, 4 (1962). Considerable extracts from the Concordat and Missionary Agreement of 1940 between Portugal and the Vatican are included in A. Hastings, *Wiriyamu* (1974), appendix 1, 135–53.

For Ethiopia and the Italian invasion of Ethiopia see A. del Boca *Gli Italiani in Africa orientale*, 3 vols. (Rome, 1982), C. E. Shenk, 'The Italian Attempt to Reconcile the Ethiopian Orthodox Church: The Use of Religious Celebrations and Assistance to Churches and Monasteries', *JES* 10 (1972), 125–36, G. A. Mikre-Sellassie, 'Church and Missions in Ethiopia in Relation to the Italian War and Occupation and the Second World War', Ph.D. thesis (Aberdeen, 1976), S. Asante, 'West Africa and the Italian Invasion of Ethiopia', *African Affairs*, 73 (1974), 204–16, and V. Norberg, *Swedes in Haile Selassie's Ethiopia 1924–1952* (Uppsala, 1977).

F. MacPherson, *Kenneth Kaunda of Zambia* (1974), W. E. Smith, *Nyerere of Tanzania* (1973), and J. Hymans, *Leopold Sedar Senghor* (Edinburgh, 1971) are biographies of Christian politicians who were approaching power towards the end of our period. For Nyerere see also J. Listowel, *The Making of Tanganyika* (1965). For the interaction of nationalism and Christianity in this period see also T. Mboya, *Freedom and After* (1963), N. Sithole, *African Nationalism* (1959), and N. Sithole, *Obed Mutezo: The Mudzimu Christian Nationalist* (1970).

INDEX

Abeokuta, Nigeria 243, 262, 274, 283, 339, 343–4, 350, 354
Abercorn, Northern Rhodesia 544, 566
Accra, Gold Coast 540
Achebe, Chinua 462
Achimota, Gold Coast 545
Ad Lucem 568
Adams College, Natal 361, 545, 548, 594, 606
Adams, Newton 264–5
Addis Ababa, Ethiopia 236, 547, 577–8
Adel, Muslim Sultanate of 4, 136–7, 150
Adwa, Ethiopia 165, 226, 367
  Battle of (1896) 237–8, 367, 478
Afonso I (Mvemba Nzinga), King of Kongo 76, 79–85, 87, 90–1, 101, 103, 109, 136, 195–6, 367, 478
African Communion of Independent Churches 494
African Congregational Church 522
African Independent Pentecostal Church 519
African Industrial Society 486
African Inland Mission 424, 455
African Israel Church Nineveh 537
African Lakes Company 287–8
African Methodist Church 522
African Methodist Episcopal Church 418, 497, 544, 594
African National Church 594
African National Congress 481, 594, 605–6
African Native Baptist Church 502
African Presbyterian Church 480, 522
African Sabbatarian Church 483
Agbebi, Dr Mojola (David Brown Vincent) 493–7, 518, 537
Agege, Nigeria 496
Aggrey, James 542, 545, 604
Aguleri, Nigeria 313
Ahui, Jean 507, 535
Aitken, J. D. 447
Aiyetoro, Nigeria 522, 533
Ajuoga, Matthew 523
Akan people 332, 402–3
Akinsowon, Abiodun 515
Akinyele, A. B., Bishop of Ibadan 518, 573

Akinyele, Sir Isaac 514, 516–18, 526, 537, 585
Aksum, Ethiopia 4, 9, 21, 36, 134, 137, 139, 142, 149, 160, 163, 536
Aladura 329, 513–18, 526–7, 531, 533, 537–8, 599, 602
Alexandria, Egypt 5–6, 17, 44, 55, 74, 150–1
  Patriarch 66, 68–9, 165, 223
Algiers, Algeria 254–5
Ali II, Ras 223, 229
Aliwaali, Alifonsi 477
All African Conference of Churches 605
Allen, Roland 552, 555, 577–8
Alliance High School, Kenya 545, 553
Alvares, Francisco 40, 44, 46, 69, 73–4, 130, 140, 145, 162
Alvares, Manuel, S. J. 119
Alvaro I (Nimi Lukeni), King of Kongo 82, 84, 86
Alvaro II (Mpanzu Nimi), King of Kongo 81, 87
Alvaro III (Nimi Mpanzu), King of Kongo 89–91
Amanazaretha 502–3, 529, 538
Ambuila, Battle of (1665) 103, 108–10
Amda Masqal 41
Amda Seyon, King of Ethiopia 18–21, 24, 26–7, 40
America 175–6, 178, 182, 245, 248, 360, 419, 436–7, 552, 561
  African Methodist Episcopal 418, 497–8
  Baptists 176, 416, 486, 493
  Congregationalists 256, 361, 362
  Evangelical Movement 183
  Methodists 426
  Presbyterians 262, 416, 436–7
  See also Liberia; Maryknoll Fathers and Sisters; Mendi Mission
American Baptist Missionary Union, see Livingstone Inland Mission
American Board of Missions 243, 264, 414
American Methodist Episcopal Church 414, 480
Amha Seyon, Aqabe-Sa'at of Hayq 41
Amhara, Ethiopia 22, 25, 160–1, 222–3, 240
Amissah, Archbishop Sam 605, 607–8

Ana a Mulungu Church 522
Anderson, Rufus 293
Andrade, Antonio d' 142
Anglican Adam's Preaching Society 600, 602
Anglican Church:
    18th century 173, 178–9
    early–mid 19th century 182–3, 185–7, 210, 242, 245–7, 293–5
    mid–late 19th century 214, 252, 256–7, 260, 277–9, 291, 301, 319, 335, 339–40, 343–9, 352–8, 372, 375–84, 388–93, 410–12, 415, 432–3, 449, 455, 457, 465–8, 494–5, 496–8
    20th century 425, 429, 433–4, 446–7, 449, 454–5, 457, 462, 470, 472, 474, 477, 485–6, 489, 494–9, 507, 513–18, 531–2, 552, 555–9, 567–70, 587, 591–2, 596–600
    See also Church Missionary Society; Universities Mission to Central Africa
Angola 85, 89, 91–2, 95, 100–3, 109, 114, 118, 120, 123, 125–6, 129, 194–6, 248, 250, 372, 397, 416, 433, 455, 472, 478, 549, 563
Ankole, Uganda 335, 381, 383, 460, 466, 469, 471, 597
Antioka, Mozambique 442
Antonio I (Vita Nkanga), King of Kongo 102–3
Antonio Francisco das Necessidades 373
Antonio of Malindi, Dom 128
Antonio Manuel ne Vunda 80–1, 87, 126–7
Antonio, Pa 374
Apena, Benjamin Paul 581–2
Apollonia (or Mattuta), prophetess 104, 107
Apostolic Faith Mission Church 500–1, 522, 537
Apostolic Sabbath Church of God (VaHossana) 521–2
Aqabe-Sa'at, Abbot of Hayq 24, 29, 35, 41, 161, 166
Arab people 54, 56–7, 63, 135, 146, 189, 236, 374–5, 406, 410–11, 429, 431–2
Arathi 519–20, 534, 537
Arthur, J. W. 490, 519, 556–9, 593
Ashanti people 185, 193, 309, 332, 341, 397–8, 405, 447
Asheri, Jedida 581
Askia Al-hajj Mohammad Ture, ruler of Songhay 54, 59–61
Assisi, Luigi-Maria d' 195
Association for the Propagation of the Faith 248–9
Athanasius, Patriarch of Alexandria 5, 8, 10
Augustine of Hippo 63, 65
Augustinians 85, 119, 121, 127–8

Aupiais, Fr 560
Axim, Ghana 444
Azikiwe, Nnamdi 544

Babalola, Joseph 335, 515–17, 530, 537
Bachmann, Traugott 319
Badagry, Nigeria 341, 352, 354
Baëta, C. G. 604–5, 607
Bagamoyo, Tangenyika 211–12, 253, 257, 267
Bagemdir, Ethiopia 222–3, 235, 239
Bagisu people 587
Baida Maryam, King of Ethiopia 42, 44–5, 132, 134
Baillie, John 270
Bakaluba, Matayo 482
Bakhatla people 217
Bakongo people 492, 509
Bakwena people 314, 366
Balikuddembe, Joseph Mukasa 376–8, 381
Balokole 'Revival' 537, 596–602, 608
Bamalaki Church 489, 532
Bamangwato people 366
Bamatope, J. A. 514
Bambara people 191, 402
Bambata Rising 483, 540
Bana ba Mutima 528, 601, 604
Banabakintu, Luke 376–7, 379
Banda, Dr Hastings Kamuzu 594
Banfield, Revd A. W. 445
Bangweolo, Northern Rhodesia 566, 578
Bannabikira, Ganda nuns 473
Baptist Missionary Society 197, 244, 269, 279, 385, 437
Baptists 176, 180, 247, 257, 288, 315, 319, 339, 343, 385–7, 413, 416, 418, 433–4, 462, 508–12, 526–7, 578, 585
Baqt Treaty (652) 67–8
Bari people 266, 304
Barotseland, see Bulozi
Barreto, Francisco 78–9, 87
Barreto, John Nunez, S. J. 140, 142
Barroso, Fr 387, 421
Bartels, F. L. 604–5
Basel Mission 210, 341, 414, 433, 455, 490
Basutoland (Lesotho) 200, 256, 303, 438–9, 492, 501–2, 532, 608
Bathurst, Sierra Leone 187, 339
Baviaanskloof, South Africa 197–8
Bazin, H., Mgr 431
Beatrice (Kimpa Vita) 104–8, 160
Bechuana people 207, 209, 322
Bechuanaland (Botswana) 286, 366, 367, 409, 532, 578
Belgium 406, 416–18, 423, 434–7, 455, 491,

512, 516, 525, 540, 542–3, 547, 550, 561, 563–4, 568, 601
Bella Krestos 153
Beltrame, G. 266
Bemba people 456, 492, 524, 536, 566, 603
Bene, Pietro da 195
Benedict XV, Pope 559
Benedictines 196, 373, 418
    of St Ottilien 414
Benin 50, 53–4, 74–5, 77, 79, 95, 119–20, 402, 447
Benoit, Pierre 479, 507, 535
Bentley, Holman 280, 319, 325, 386, 421, 435
Berber people 54, 56, 63–4
Berlin, Congress of 410, 416, 417
Berlin Missionary Society 414, 438, 576
Bermudez, John 138–40
Bernardo I, King of Kongo 84
Bernardo of São Salvador 196
Berthoud, Henri 442
Berthoud, Paul 441–3
Bessieux, Mgr Jean-Remi 250, 262
Bethelsdorp, South Africa 201–9, 211, 216–17
Bethlehem Fathers 560
Bible Church Missionary Society 577
Bickersteth, Edward 186
Biehler, Edward, S. J. 433–4
Bigirumwami, Bishop Aloysius 573
Birraux, J.-M., W.F. 566
Bismarck, Otto von 399
Blackman's Church 485
Blackman's Church of God 522
Blake, William 299–300
Blantyre Mission, Nyasaland, 210, 212–13, 257, 276, 410–11, 425, 427–9, 432, 455, 484, 487, 557
Bloemfontein, South Africa 569
Blomfield, Charles, Bishop of London 293
Blomjous, Joseph, Bishop of Mwanza 568–9
Blyden, Edward 355–6, 407, 418
Board of Commissioners for Foreign Missions (ABCFM) 244–5, 293
Boer people 236, 251, 267, 286, 409, 411, 429, 436, 569
Boilat, Abbé David 296, 373
Bokwe, John Knox 323, 361, 370–1
Bonny, Nigeria 334–5, 348, 507
Booth, Joseph 433, 483, 486, 504
Borghero, Francesco 249
Borumeda, Council of (1878) 234, 238, 240
Botelho, Estavo 113–14
Botswana, *see* Bechuanaland
Bowen, T. J., missionary 280, 326
Braide, Garrick 445–6, 449, 505, 507, 513

Brancaleone, Nicolas 43, 135
Brandone, Dom Alvaro 116
Brass, Nigeria 346, 348–9, 389–90
Brazil 102, 106, 124–5, 194
Breadfruit, Lagos 356–8, 495, 497, 514–15
Brébeuf, Jean de 88
Bremen Mission, Gold Coast 319, 341, 455
Brésillac, Melchior de Marion 249, 255, 296
Britain 94, 119, 212, 258, 279, 352, 356, 378, 470–1, 481–2, 488, 490, 516, 558
    Catholics 246, 297, 416, 429, 462, 561–2
    'Civilization and Christianity' 285–7
    colonialism and imperial expansion 189, 199, 213, 224, 245–6, 384–5, 392, 397–400, 404, 408–13, 415–16, 429, 436, 468, 538
    Dukwana and 370
    and education 542–3, 553, 561–2
    and Islam 406–8, 462
    Methodists 181, 182, 245–6
    Protestants, Protestantism 177–8, 181–5, 226, 228, 245, 419, 481
    Select Committee on Aborigines 217
    and slave-trade 182–4, 431–2
    and Tewodros 231, 233–4
    and World War I 402, 540
    and World War II 546–8
    Zambezi expedition 252, 274
    See also Anglican Church; Church Missionary Society; London Missionary Society; Universities Mission to Central Africa
British Apostolic Church 514
British East Africa Company 287, 384, 411–12
British and Foreign Bible Society 244, 445
British South Africa Company 412, 426
Broderick, Thomas 418
Brooke, Graham Wilmot 290, 389–92
Brown, Leslie, Bishop of Uganda 556
Brownlee, John 206, 220–1
Bruce, A. Livingstone 487, 489
Bruce Estates 486–7
Bruce, James 165, 175, 230
Brunton, Henry 280
Bücking, Mgr Hermann 434
Buddu, Uganda 465–6, 470, 481, 565, 571–2, 575
Budo, Uganda 545
Buganda 309, 312, 330, 371–85, 392, 402, 441, 450, 452, 460, 461–2, 463, 464–75, 476, 492, 549
    Catholics in 232, 255, 298, 372, 374–7, 379, 381–4, 415, 462, 464–7, 469, 474–5, 565, 572, 580, 603
    civil war 381–2, 415
Buganda (*cont.*):

and evangelization of neighbouring
lands 468–78
government structure 374–5
human sacrifice in 332
Islam in 375, 381–3, 406, 465
martyrdom in 378–9
Protestants in 246, 257, 372, 374–7, 379,
381–4, 415, 429, 464–9, 470, 474–5,
580, 596
transport 268
See also Kivebulaya; Kiwanuka; Mwanga,
King
Buha, Tanganyika 566
Buhaya, Tanganyika 474
Bukalasa, Buganda 572
Bukedi, Uganda 469
Bukoba, Tanganyika 576, 585
Bukumbi Mission, Tanganyika 381, 473
Bulawayo, Rhodesia 256, 412, 414, 521
Bulingugwe Island 382–3
Bulozi, Northern Rhodesia 268, 455, 560
Buningwire, Canon 335
Bunyaruguru, Uganda 471–2
Bunyoro, Uganda 50, 469, 473
Burundi 474, 487, 532, 564, 576, 578
Bushmen 199, 217
Busia, Dr Kofi 605
Butere Mission, Kenya 574
Buwalasi Mission, Uganda 587
Buxton, T. F. 287
Byabacwezi, Regent of Bunyoro 469

Cairo, Egypt 28, 43, 55, 61, 66, 68, 188,
194, 229, 254, 374
Calabar, Nigeria 260, 343, 562, 592
Calata, James 606
Caleb, King of Ethiopia 10, 12
Callaway, Canon Henry 264, 273, 304, 359,
362
Caltanisetta, Luca da 99
Calvinism 246, 256, 560
Cambridge Inter-Collegiate Christian
Union (CICCU) 596
Cameron, Donald 541
Cameron, G. R. 508–9, 511
Cameron, John 319
Cameroon 242, 257, 262, 413, 418, 433,
455, 532, 581, 607–8
Campbell, Revd John 204, 216
Canada 88, 180, 245, 561–2, 565
Cao, Gaspar, Bishop 119
Cape 95, 178–9, 198–9, 206, 245, 248, 248–
9, 292, 338, 341–2, 358, 398, 405, 409,
543
Cape Palmas, Liberia 338, 507
Cape Town, South Africa 175, 193, 197,
199, 202, 207, 216, 221, 247, 256, 549

Cape Verde Islands 118
Capitein, Jacobus 178–9
Capuchins 88–9, 92–105, 107–15, 117–18,
120–1, 124–5, 127–9, 156, 158, 194–6,
227, 237–8, 255, 267, 317, 387, 560–1
Cardoso, Mattheus, S.J. 91–2, 94, 127
Carey, William 197, 244, 259
Carmelites 85, 90, 94, 374
Carneiro, Melchior, S.J. 140
Carthage, Tunisia 62–4, 255
Casalis, Eugene 200, 309, 311
Casement, Roger 436
Castro, Miguel de 93, 104
Catholicism 168
3rd–12th century 62–4
15th–16th century 72, 74, 79, 87, 142,
151, 193
17th century 90, 95, 101, 108, 110–11,
120, 124–5, 127, 142–4, 151–8, 160,
193, 275
18th century 129, 164–5, 177, 193, 194
19th century 194–6, 213, 215, 226–9,
231–2, 235, 237–9, 244, 248–9, 254–7,
260, 262–8, 270–2, 277, 281, 295–8,
300, 304, 331, 343, 372–5, 377–9,
381–5, 392, 406, 411, 413–14, 415–17,
430, 433, 435, 464–6, 481–2
20th century 300, 392, 406–7, 415,
419–20, 422–3, 429, 433–5, 450–2, 460,
462, 469–70, 472–5, 477–8, 490, 504–5,
507–8, 520, 524, 528, 531–2, 538, 553,
559–69, 577–8, 585, 587–92, 594,
603–4, 607–9
See also Capuchins; Holy Ghost Fathers;
Jesuits; White Fathers
Cekwane, Timothy 502, 505
Cela Krestos 152, 155, 158, 160
Cesar, Julio 121
Cetshwayo, king of Zululand 309, 331, 412
Chagga people 403
Chanda, Mother Bernadetta Stuart 601,
604
Cheetham, bishop 355
Chembre Kouré, Battle of (1529) 137
Chewa people 324, 580, 591–2, 600, 603
Chichester, Bishop Aston 573
Chikuni Mission, Rhodesia 590
Chilembwe, John 418, 485–7, 488–9, 491,
505
Chilonga, Northern Rhodesia 561
Chilubula Mission, Northern
Rhodesia 214, 566
China 88, 112, 148, 153, 571, 573
China Inland Mission 290
Chingulia, Dom Jeronimo, King of Malindi
and Mombasa 127–8
Chinula, Charles 522

Chiradzulu, Magomero 486–8
Chishawasha Station, Rhodesia 214, 425, 433
Christ Apostolic Church 514, 517–18, 537
Christ Army Church 446
Christ the King College, Onitsha 562
Christian Catholic Apostolic Church 500
Christian Council of the Gold Coast 604
Christianborg, Gold Coast 178, 334, 341
Christina, Dona, of Mbamba 115
Chumie Mission, South Africa 368
Church of Christ in Africa 523
Church, Dr Joe 596, 598, 602
Church of God 579
Church of Jesus Christ 525
Church of the Light 502
Church of the Lord (Aladura) 517
Church Missionary Society 210, 228, 242, 256, 263, 268, 290–1, 298, 355, 447, 493, 495, 552, 567
  and Balokole 'Revival' 596
  in Buganda 372, 382–3, 429, 468, 475
  in Congo 437
  in Ethiopia 224–5, 232
  foundation 176, 244–5
  home development 246–7, 293, 295
  in Kenya 211, 410, 414, 426, 431, 554
  and medical work 277
  in Mombasa 257
  in Niger delta 389–93, 417, 493, 600
  relations with Bishop Crowther 294–5, 339–40, 343, 346, 349, 389–93
  in Sierra Leone 185–7, 213, 280
  and single woman missionaries 260–1
  in Uganda 267, 279, 392, 411–15, 455, 532, 587
  and Yoruba people 343
  See also Venn, Henry
Church of the Nazarites 502–3
Church of St Francis, Rusape 522, 533, 537
Church of Scotland 210, 212, 257, 277, 291, 343, 411, 413, 426–8, 437, 519, 527, 556–7
Church of the Twelve Apostles 507
Clarkson, John 180
Clarkson, Thomas 180, 183
Classe, Bishop, Leon, W. F. 567
Clayton, Geoffrey, Archbishop of Cape Town 568
Clement XIV, Pope 194
Clifford, Sir Hugh 452, 541
Cochin, India 95
Coillard, François 256, 268, 303, 309–10, 312, 316–17, 420, 439, 455
Coker, R. A. 440
Colenso, Bishop John 264–5, 271–2, 278,

280, 286, 309, 318–19, 331, 333, 362, 412, 424, 496
Comber, Thomas 385
Comboni, Mgr Daniel 253–5, 296, 373–4
Community of the Resurrection 455
Conceiçao, Antonio da 121–2
Congar, Yves 607
Congo 211, 213, 268, 279, 288, 318–19, 325, 403, 406, 410, 416, 418, 423, 434–7, 440, 452, 455, 462, 469–70, 475, 508–12, 526, 532, 535, 547, 550, 560, 563–4, 585, 607
  See also Kongo
Congo Reform Association 436–7
Congregation of the Holy Ghost, see Holy Ghost Fathers
Congregationalism 256, 322, 361–2, 364, 416, 498, 535, 578–9, 594, 606
Consolata Fathers 426
Constantini, Cardinal Celso 565
Cook, Albert 278
Coptic Church 6–8, 12, 18, 65–8
Correa, Bras 90–1, 93–4
Cosgrave, Mother Patrick 414
Countess of Huntingdon's Connection 180–1
Couto, Antonio de 93, 97, 101
Crawford, Dan 422, 440
Crazzolara, J. 560
Creux, Ernest 441
Cripps, Arthur Shearly 425, 433, 552, 556, 558–9
Cristaller, Johannes 280, 341
Crowther, Abigail 340
Crowther, Archdeacon Dandeson 347, 389–93, 445, 574
Crowther, Bishop Samuel (Adjai) 187, 242–3, 278–80, 294–5, 299, 301, 339–41, 344–9, 354, 356, 358, 363–4, 388–93, 420, 493, 496, 518, 555, 572–3
Crummell, Alexander 286, 338
Cugoano, Ottobah (John Stuart) 173–6, 180, 182
Cuvelier, Bishop J. 560
Cyprian, Bishop of Carthage 62, 65, 255
Cyril, of Alexandria 8–10

Dabra Asbo, see Dabra Libanos
Dabra Berhan monastery, Ethiopia 35, 41–2, 161
Dabra Bizan monastery, Ethiopia 3, 29, 31, 36, 131, 163
Dabra Damo monastery, Ethiopia 3–4, 9, 22, 30, 37, 138, 163, 165
Dabra Hayq monastery, Ethiopia 3, 24, 28–31, 223
Dabra Libanos, Ethiopia (formerly Dabra

Asbo) 3, 22, 24–5, 29–30, 33, 35, 44,
  136–7, 145, 147, 163–4, 168–9, 546
Dabra Maryam monastery, Ethiopia 3, 29
Dabra Mitmaq monastery, Ethiopia 3–4, 35
  Council of (1449) 3, 5, 36, 44
Dabra Tabor monastery, Ethiopia 222, 232,
  234, 241
Dagarti people 577
Dagri, Solomon 507
Dahomey 177, 193, 249, 309, 312, 332, 343,
  449, 560, 607, 608
Dakar, Senegal 407, 547
Dambarare, Mutapa 121–2
Dancaz, Ethiopia 161
Daniel of Gar'alta, Abba 28
Danielou, Cardinal, Jean 607
Danquah, J. B. 604–5
Dar es Salaam, Tanganyika 404, 406–7, 562
Daudi Chwa, King of Buganda 312, 429,
  599
Davies, J. H. 355
Davies, William 181
Dawit, King of Ethiopia 29, 32–4, 38
Dazazmac Balca (Makonnen) 240–1
Ddiba, Fr Yozefu 477
de Brazza, Pierre Savorgnan 399
De Lubac, Henri, S. J. 607
Dembea, Ethiopia 162, 164
Denmark 177–8
Dery, Peter, Bishop of Wa 577
Diamper, Synod of (1599) 155, 157
Diangienda, Joseph 525–6, 534, 536–7
Dicomano, Raimondo da 194
Dida people 330, 336, 463, 472, 506
Dimbioni, Nganvan 318–19, 321
Dimieari, Bishop 573
Dinka people 266, 304, 374, 536
Diogo I (Nkumbi Mpudi), King of
  Kongo 84
Dionysius the Great, Bishop of
  Alexandria 8
Divine Word, Fathers of the 418
Dobinson, Henry 277, 389–91
Domingo, Charles 483–6, 505
Domingos, son of Sebastian, Olu of
  Warri 120
Dominicans 120–1, 122–3, 128, 414
Donatists 62–4
Dongola, Nubia 67
dos Santos, Fr Joao 122, 584
Douglas, Arthur 422, 434
Dowie, John Alexander 500
Dubois, Fr, S. J. 554
Dukwana, son of Ntsikana 368–71, 483,
  535
Dunwell, Joseph 342
Dupont, Joseph, W. F., Bishop 456, 536

During, Henry 186, 209
Durrieu, Bishop Louis, W. F. 568
Dutch Reformed Church 198, 414, 438,
  455, 499–500, 569, 584, 591
Dwane, James 393, 480, 497, 499

Ebonou, Ivory Coast 506
Ebrie people 463, 472, 492, 506
Ede people 53–4
Eden, F. N. 389–90
Edmonds, John, L M S missionary 200
Egba people 343, 354
Egypt 46, 55, 61–8, 131, 150, 158, 234–5
Ekukhanyeni, Zululand 502, 536
Ekuphakameni, Zululand 502–3, 536
Ekwendeni, Nyasaland 593
Eleni, Empress of Ethiopia 132, 135–6
Elisabethville (Lubumbashi), Zaïre 525–6
Ellis, William 363
Elmina Castle, Gold Coast 46, 72, 95
Elmslie, William 264, 315, 317
Empandeni Mission, Rhodesia 214, 311,
  414, 425
Enarya, Ethiopia 224
Enbaqom, abbot of Dabra Libanos 69, 136,
  145–7, 240
Enkeldoorn, Rhodesia 425
Equiano, Olaudah (renamed Gustavus
  Vassa) 173–6, 221, 282, 328
Eritrea 36, 237
Eskender, King of Ethiopia 45, 145
Estifanos, monk 38–9, 41
Ethiopia 3–46, 50, 54, 62, 67–70, 73–4,
  100, 130–69, 175, 177, 193, 222–41,
  275, 302, 317, 323, 367, 372, 385,
  397–8, 400, 405, 529, 546–7, 563,
  577–8, 608
Ethiopianism 478–87, 492, 494, 497–9, 501,
  504, 507, 522, 526, 533, 555, 579
Evangelicalism:
  18th century 463
  early–mid 19th century 183, 225–6, 246,
    284
  mid–late 19th century 273–4, 300–1,
    314, 316, 318, 321, 342, 348, 354, 389–
    90, 392, 409, 467, 551
  early 20th century 443, 497, 551–2, 554,
    561–2, 590, 596
  mid-20th century 567, 578
evangelism 232, 244, 255, 259, 283, 290–4,
  323, 346, 359, 408, 415, 425, 438–40,
  446, 448–9, 451–4, 456, 466–7, 469–70,
  476, 530
Evans-Pritchard, Edward 327
Ewe people 334
Ewostatewos, monk 28–30, 32–3, 37, 162,
  168–9

Ewostathians 28–33, 35–8, 44, 131, 144, 163–4, 168
Ezana, King of Ethiopia 4, 13, 19
Ezra the Stefanite 135

Faith Tabernacle 514–17
Falasha 13–16, 35, 37–8, 40, 232–3, 239
Falconbridge, Mrs 181, 199
Fang people 402
Fante people 173, 178–9, 341–2, 463, 492
Fasiladas, Emperor of Ethiopia 139, 156, 158, 160–3
Ferguson, Adam 283, 292
Fernandes, Antonio 154, 157
Filpos, 14th century eccage 24–5, 27
Filpos, abbot of Dabra Bizan 29–33, 37
Filpos, 19th century eccage 224
Flad, Martin 232–3
Flickinger, D. K. 326, 478
Florence, Council of 43, 67
Fon people 402–3
Fort Hare, South Africa 364, 491, 545, 548, 553, 606
Fort Victoria (Masvingo), Rhodesia 520
Foucauld, Charles de 296
Fourah Bay College, Sierra Leone 187, 339, 343, 346, 355–6, 364, 545, 594
France 94–5, 189, 199, 402, 415, 419, 490, 547, 550
  anticlerical campaign (1899) 430
  in Buganda 372
  Calvinists 256
  Capuchins 95, 156
  Catholics 248–9, 254–6, 262, 286, 372, 407, 417, 418, 435, 481, 489, 560–3
  colonialism 399–400, 413, 430, 540
  in Eritrea 224
  and Ethiopia 156, 226, 231, 238
  in Igboland 451
  and Islam 406–8
  and Ivory Coast 445, 489
  in Kongo 109, 117
  and Madagascar 399
  in Natal 249
  in Northern Rhodesia 590
  Revolution, consequences of 194, 248
  in Senegal 397
  in Sierra Leone 181, 183–4, 249
  in West Africa 417, 430
  See also Ad Lucem; Association for the Propagation of the Faith; Coillard; Holy Ghost Fathers; Missionaries of the Holy Heart of Mary; Oblates of Mary Immaculate; Society of African Missions; White Fathers
Francis, Carey 553

Franciscans 85, 110, 119, 164, 194, 253, 271, 289, 560–1, 601
Fraser, A. G. 545
Fraser, Donald 291, 422, 457, 459, 483, 485, 490, 495, 553–4, 584
Free Church of Scotland 257, 288, 440, 480
Free Evangelical Church of Switzerland 441–2
Freeman, Thomas Birch 179, 262, 309, 338, 341, 342
Freetown, Sierra Leone 180, 182–7, 197, 199, 211, 221, 247, 249, 284, 338–43, 346–7, 352, 354–8, 389, 391, 407, 410, 479, 498
Fremona, Ethiopia 142, 148, 152, 158
Frere, Sir Bartle 211
Freretown, Kenya 212, 426, 431–2
Freytag, Prof. Walter 605
Fridoil, Arsene 373
Frumentius, Bishop of Aksum 5, 8–9, 13, 16
Fulani people 189–93, 236
Funchal, Madeira 118–19
Futa Toro, state of 190, 192

Gaba, Burnet and Ntsikana 480
Gabon 262, 286, 416
Gabriel IV, Patriarch of Alexandria 68
Gabri'el, Metropolitan of Egypt 3, 5, 44
Gairdner, Temple 420
Galawdewos, Emperor of Ethiopia 138–44, 147, 149, 156, 164
Galla people (later Oromo) 50, 150, 162, 166–7, 222–4, 227, 230, 233, 235, 239, 242
Gallo, Bernardo da 97, 104–7
Gama, Cristovao da 138–9, 158, 164
Gama, Vasco da 46, 72
Ganda, *see* Buganda
Gantin, Archbishop Bernardin 608–9
Gao, Songhay 54
Garcia I (Mbemba Nkanga), King of Kongo 91
Garcia II (Nkanga Lukeni), King of Kongo 91, 96–7, 102
Garcia V (Nkanga Mbemba), King of Kongo 109, 195–6, 373
Garcia, Dom, secretary to King of Kongo 386
Garrick, J. D. 347–8
Geel, Georges de 99
Geerdes, Joop, W. F. 569
Genadendal, South Africa 198, 201–2, 204, 207, 209–11, 232
George, David 176, 180
George, William 354

Germany 244–5, 279, 414, 418, 419, 431, 434, 455
  Catholics 560–1, 590
  colonialism 399–402, 404, 406–8, 413–14, 540
  and Congo reform 437
  and impact of World War I 487–8, 490–1
  Lutherans 246–7
  and rebellion in South West Africa 483
  See also Benedictines of St Ottilien; Berlin Missionary Society; Church Missionary Society; Krapf; Leipzig Society; Moravians; Schön; Schweitzer; Warneck
Ggoba, W. W. 370
Ghana (medieval kingdom) 54, 56
Ghana (independent state from 1957, formerly Gold Coast) 548, 605, 608
Ghartey, R. J. 342
Ghebra-Mika'el 227, 229, 231, 372
Ghebragzier, Bishop Tobia 164–5
Ghezo, King of Dahomey 309
Girar, Ethiopia 36
Gisu people 323
Giyorgis, Abba 34–5, 37
Gladstone, William 251
Glasgow Missionary Society 206–7
Glele, King of Dahomey 308
Gloucester, Sierra Leone 186, 209, 211
Gnandjoué, Latta 506
Goa, India 118, 141, 148, 158
Gobat, Samuel 224–5, 232, 302
Gobir, kingdom of 190–1
Godinho, Fr 194–5
Gojjam, Ethiopia 24, 135, 137, 142, 152, 161–4, 168, 222–3, 233–5
Gold Coast 46, 185, 262, 418, 485, 604–7
  Catholicism in 577
  educational establishments 545, 547, 604
  farming 289
  Harris in 444, 446, 507
  independence (1957) 548
  Methodists in 341–2, 343, 363, 505, 604–5
  and nationalism 547–9
  Presbyterians in 604–5
  Protestants in 179, 607
  See also Basle Mission; Bremen Mission; Ghana; United Gold Coast Convention
Goldie, Sir George 348, 390, 399
Gomes, Fr Diego 82, 85, 91
Gondar, Ethiopia 159–62, 164–5, 168, 222–4, 227, 229, 232, 233, 236
Gondokoro, Sudan 270, 304
Gorju, Bishop 475
Graham, Billy 598

Gran, Ahmed 137–8, 145–7, 160, 167, 239, 546
Granville, Lord 411
Gray, bishop Robert 278
Graziani, Marshal 546
Grebo people 443
Greek Orthodox Church 532
Gregory VII, Pope 64
Gregory XIV, Pope 248
Gregory XV, Pope 88
Gregory of Nyssa, Saint 30
Grenfell, George 261, 268, 385, 434
Grey, Earl 282
Grey, Sir George 368
Griquatown, South Africa 216
Grout, Alvin 362
Groves, C. P. 426
Gudu, Wilfred 522
Guillemé, bishop 423
Guinea-Bissau 563
Guinness, Mrs H. Grattan 205
Gunde Gunde monastery, Ethiopia 39, 227
Guta ra Jehova 524

Hadrian of Subiaco, Dom Pio Giuseppe 373
Haile Malakot, Emperor of Ethiopia 236
Haile Selassie (Ras Tafari), Emperor of Ethiopia 547, 577–8
al-Hajj Ahmad 59–60
Halifax, Nova Scotia 180
Hallback, Hans Peter 206
Hankey, South Africa 363
Hannington, Bishop James 378
Harar, Ethiopia 193, 239
Harare, Rhodesia 122
Hardinge, Sir Arthur 431
Harris, William Wade 241, 335–6, 443–5, 446, 449–51, 454, 456–8, 462–3, 471–2, 476, 479, 489–90, 505–7, 513, 530, 533, 535, 600
Harrism 506–7, 526, 538
Hart, Joshua 335, 337
Hartmann, Andrew, S. J. 325
Hausa people 54, 57, 60–1, 190–3, 242, 290, 345
Hayford, Joseph Casely 342, 485, 540, 604
Hayford, Joseph DeGrant 342
Hayq, Lake, Ethiopia 22, 239
Heerey, Bishop Charles 589–90
Helm, Charles 412
Henrique II, King of Kongo 109, 373
Henry IV, King of England 43
Henry the Navigator, Prince 71
Henry, Bishop, son of Afonso I 83, 195
Herero people, South West Africa 401, 428, 437, 540, 570

London Missionary Society 175, 185, 199–200, 203–4, 206, 210, 219, 244, 246, 250–2, 256, 259, 270, 286, 293, 295, 363, 366–7, 409, 412, 414–15, 426, 579
Lopes, Duarte 86
Lourdel, Simeon W. F. 309, 372, 375–9, 384, 421
Lourenço, Gregorio 77–8
Lovanium, Congo 547
Lovedale, South Africa 207, 257, 259–60, 288, 322, 361, 368, 371, 439, 479, 481, 483–4, 498, 523, 545, 548, 553, 557, 562, 594
Loyola, Ignatius 140, 151
Lozi people 303, 312, 316, 439, 454, 561
Luapula, Northern Rhodesia 561
Lubwa, Northern Rhodesia 524
Lucas, V., Bishop of Masasi 587
Lucca, Lorenzo da 106–7, 111
Ludolf, Hiob 143n., 158, 242
Lugard, Lord 384, 411, 464–5, 541
Lumpa Church 329, 524–6, 533, 603
Lutherans 198, 243, 246–7, 256, 317–18, 361, 364, 412, 416, 490, 531, 576, 578, 585
Luthuli, Albert 594, 605–6
Luwum, Bishop 598
Luyia people 576, 580
Lwanga, Charles 377, 379–81
Lwangwa, Northern Rhodesia 561, 566

Mabathoana, Archbishop 608
Mabilitsa, Paul 501–2
Macaulay, Herbert 341
Macaulay, Thomas Babington 339–40
MacCarthy, Sir Charles 185–7, 210
MacDonald, Duff 304, 333
Mackay, Alexander 264, 268, 309, 326, 372, 376–7, 384, 392, 421, 432
Mackay, Sembera 301
Mackenzie, Bishop 252, 256, 264, 268, 273, 286, 293, 410, 487
Mackenzie, John 286, 366, 409
Mackinnon, Sir William 427
Madida Moyo 522–3, 537
Madziyire, Salathiel 591–2
Magdala, Ethiopia 233–4
Magila, Tanganyika 257, 459
Magomero, Nyasaland 256, 486–8
Mahdists 234, 407
Mahon, Edgar 500–1
Mai Chaza, Rhodesia 524
Majaliwa, Cecil 455
Maji Maji rebellion 482, 540
Makaba, chief of the Bamangkhetsi 271
Makerere, Uganda 547
Makololo Mission, 261–2

Makoni, Rhodesia 485
Makvria, Nubia 67
Malan, Dr 548
Malawi, see Nyasaland
Mali 54, 56, 59
Manganja people 286
Mangengo, Dom Manuel 386
Mangu, Kenya 426
Manicaland, Rhodesia 452–3, 461
Mansa Musa, King of Mali 54, 59
Mantiziba, Peter 440, 454
Manuel, Dom, Mani Vunda 104, 107, 126
Manuel, King of Portugal 76, 83, 136
Manyano 595–6, 602
Manyika people 463
Maples, Bishop Chauncy 214, 421
Mapula, Rhodesia 561
Maqdala, Ethiopia 236
  Battle of (1868) 234
Marandellas (Marondera), Rhodesia 591
Maranke, Johane 520–2, 533–4, 537
Marha Krestos 26, 44
Mariannhill, Natal 333
Maria Legio 524, 528
Maritain, Jacques 564
Maronites 153, 157
Marqos, Abuna 45, 132, 139, 145, 163
Marshall, T. J. 449
Mary Martin, Mother 561
Maryknoll Fathers and Sisters 560
Masaka, Buganda, 564–5, 571–5, 578
Masasi, Tanganyika 212, 214, 257
Mashona people 301, 325, 414, 433, 531
Mason, Bishop Eduardo 536
Masowe, Johane, see Shoniwa, Peter
Massaja, Guglielmo 227–8
Massawa, Eritrea, 138, 142, 148, 224, 237, 249
Matabeleland 264, 311, 366, 412, 414, 537
Matthews, Z. K. 323, 594, 606
Mau Mau Rebellion 549, 557, 599–600
Mavura (Dom Felipe), Mutapa 121, 123, 127
Mawaggali, Noe 473
Mawokota, Buganda 466, 471
Mbaguta, Chief minister of Ankole 469
Mbala, Northern Rhodesia, see Abercorn
Mbamba, Kongo 90–1, 93, 97, 100, 108, 110–11, 115–16
Mbandila, Baptist deacon 511–12
Mbanza Kongo, Kongo, see São Salvador, Kongo
Mbanza Manteke Station, Congo 318, 387
Mbanza Soyo (Sant Antonio) 81, 96, 105, 110–12
Mbata, Kongo 90–1, 93, 97, 111
Mbelwa, King of Ngoni 315
Mboga, Congo 470

Hetherwick, Alexander 264, 428, 489, 584
Heyling, Peter 163
Hinderer, Anna 261–2, 271, 274, 280, 299–300
Hinderer, David 343, 345, 351, 354, 357–8
Hine, Bishop John 422
Hinsley, Arthur 562, 565
Hirth, Mgr Jean 464, 473, 475
Hlatshwayo, Jonas 500
Holene, Ruti 441–2
Holland 94–5, 97, 103, 109, 119, 129, 177–9, 183, 194, 199, 204, 418, 561, 566, 568–9
Holy Apostles of Aiyetoro 522
Holy Ghost Fathers 211–12, 255, 257, 259–60, 267, 286, 295–6, 414, 416, 418, 421, 430, 451, 561–2, 583
Homatcho, Sidamo 577
Hooper, Douglas 392
Hooper, Handley 554
Hope Fountain, Matabeleland 414
Hope-Waddell Institute, Calabar 562
Horton, James Africanus 339
Hosanna, Ethiopia 577
Hottentots, see Khoikhoi people
Huddleston, Trevor 567–70, 607
Huffman, Ray 327
Hunter, Monica 330
Hutchinson, T. J. 478

Ibadan, Nigeria 261–2, 271, 274, 299, 343, 344, 351, 354, 514, 516–18, 547, 573, 605
Ibanda, Ankole 335–6
Ibiam, Sir Francis 605
Ibn al-Athir 64
Ibn Battuta 59
Ibn Kabar, Abul Barakat 66
Ifa, cult of 352–3
Ife, state of 50, 54, 75
Igbide, Nigeria 447
Igbo people 242, 326, 335, 345–7, 402–3, 417, 450–1, 454, 460, 461–3, 476, 492, 562, 576, 585, 591
Igbudu, Adam Cornelius 600
Ijaye war 354
Ijebu, Yorubaland 50, 440, 449, 452, 461–2, 463
Ijebu-Ode, Nigeria 514
Ijeshaland 449, 460, 472
Ila people 553
Ilesha, Nigeria 516
Ilondola Mission, Northern Rhodesia 566
Ilorin, Nigeria 192–3
India 88, 148, 157, 189, 246, 397, 407, 546, 556–7, 573
Indiryas, Abbot of Dabra Libanos 41

Ingoli, Francesco 89, 112, 127–8, 295
International African Institute 552–3
International Missionary Conference (Jerusalem 1928) 551
International Missionary Council 551
International Missionary Council (Ghana 1958) 605
Inyati, Rhodesia 256, 414
Ireland 174, 249, 301, 415, 418, 451, 560–2, 590
Isabella, Queen of Kongo 195
Isenberg, Charles 225–6, 259, 302
Islam 54–62, 71, 74, 185, 255, 312–13, 345, 415, 462, 496, 550
  advance of, 18th–19th century 188–94
  in Buganda 381–3, 464–5
  Christian–Muslim balance, medieval 64–71
  and colonialism 405–8
  in Ethiopia 135–8, 146, 163, 167, 224, 229, 238–41
  military advance (from 7th century) 55
  Sahara trade 55–8
  and slavery 56–8
  in Tanganyika 490
  in West Africa, 15th–19th century 58–62, 189–92, 339
  and Yoruba people 350, 355–7, 405–6
  See also Fulani people
Isoko people 447–9, 453–4, 476, 581–2, 600
Isokoland 331, 456–7, 461, 463
Italy 194, 196, 226, 301, 399, 413
  Capuchins 95–7, 100, 114, 121, 129, 156, 238
  Catholic Church 418, 560–1, 563
  and Ethiopia 234–8, 289, 478, 546–7, 577–8
Itsekiri people 119–20, 447
Ivory Coast 443–5, 450–1, 456, 463, 476, 489–90, 505, 507–8, 518, 526, 608
Iwe, Agori, Bishop of Benin 600
Iyasu I, the Great, King of Ethiopia 162–3
Iyasus-Mo'a, monk 22, 25, 28, 30–1

Jabavu, D. D. T. 606
Jabavu, John Tengo 361, 491, 499
Jacob, Abuna 227, 238, 241
Jacobis, Justin de 226–9, 231–2, 237–8, 248, 266, 372
Jager Afrikaner, Khoikhoi Chief 216, 218, 221
Jakob, King of Ethiopia 149, 151
Jamaa Movement 585, 601–3
Jamaican Baptist Mission 242, 418
Japan 148, 573
Jariot, Pauline 248

Jarosseau, Bishop 563
Javouhey, Mother Anne-Marie 262, 295, 373
Jennings, R. L. 510, 512
Jerusalem 17, 42–3, 158
Jesuits 214, 225, 255, 420, 433, 453, 554–5
  in the Congo 416, 418
  in Ethiopia 16, 140–4, 147–50, 152–9, 161–2, 164, 275
  expulsion from Kongo (1761) 194
  in Kongo 78, 85, 88–93, 96–7, 101, 103, 110, 112, 119, 123, 127–8
  and land ownership 425
  in Matabeleland 264
  in Mozambique 563–4
  in Northern Rhodesia 590
  in Rhodesia 256, 333, 414, 424
  in Upper Nile region 249, 253
Jews 74, 144
Jirapa, Gold Coast 577
João I (Nzinga Nkuwu), King of Kongo 73, 75–6, 81
João II, King of Portugal 73
Joel, King of Dotawo 68
Johannesburg, South Africa 479
John XXIII, Pope 568–9, 608
John XIII, Patriarch of Alexandria 66
John II, King of Portugal 87
John, William 346–7
Johnson, Henry 347, 348, 364, 389, 391
Johnson, James 'Holy' 323, 339, 355–7, 392, 445, 479–80, 494–8, 507, 518
Johnson, Robert 369
Johnson, Samuel 339
Johnson, William Percival 186–7, 205–6, 209, 214, 265, 274, 280, 291–2, 296, 432
Johnston, Sir Harry 399, 429
Jones, J. C. 596–7
Jones, Jesse 542
Junod, Henri 292, 304–5, 327, 333

Kabula, Buganda 381–3, 571
Kachebere, Nyasaland 573
Kafa, Ethiopia 224, 227
Kaggwa, Andrew 376–7, 380, 466
Kagwa, Apolo 377, 379–82, 464, 467, 469–70, 477, 482
Kaimosi, Kenya 415, 426
Kakunguru, Semei 467–8, 489
Kalema, King of Buganda 381–2, 468
Kalemba, Matthias 376–7, 379–80
Kalilombe, Peter 591–2
Kamawe, Wanyoike 599
Kamba people 403, 426
Kamwana, Elliot Kenan 488, 504–5
Kanedi, Paulus 454
Kariuki, Bishop Obadiah 598–9

Kasagama, King of Toro 469
Kasai, Congo 436, 452
Kat River 220
Katigondo, Buganda 572–3
Kaufmann, Fr Anton 304
Kaunda, Kenneth 594
Kavirondo, Kenya 415, 556–7
  see also Nyanza
Kavirondo Taxpayers Welfare Association 558
Kenya 414, 523, 528, 532, 549, 552, 554, 561, 587, 593
  Baganda evangelists in 469
  and colonialism 403–4, 541
  education (1920s) 543–5
  independency, movements of (1920s) 519–20
  missionary landholding 426–7
  Presbyterians in 591
  settler community in 556–7
  and World War I 487, 490
  See also African Inland Mission; Arathi; Balokole 'Revival'; Maria Legio
Kenyatta, Jomo 599
Kerr, Alexander 545
Kerr, Henry Schomberg, S. J. 264
Khama, kgosi of Bamangwato 301, 309, 311, 366, 367
Khambule, George 537
Khartoum, Sudan 67, 547
Khoikhoi people 197–207, 211, 215–17, 285, 292, 308, 409, 492
Kibanyi, Lui 481–2
Kiburuva, Chief of Ibanda 336
Kibwezi, Kenya 426
Kigezi, Uganda 470–2, 476
Kigozi, Blasio 596
Kikuyu Independent Schools Association 519
Kikuyu people 323, 403, 426–7, 427, 519–20, 537, 544, 549, 557, 586–7, 599
Kiltegan Fathers 560
Kimbangu, Mount 104, 106
Kimbangu, Simon 456, 508–13, 517, 525–7, 530–1, 534–9, 585
Kimbanguism 509, 511–13, 526, 538, 585, 602
Kimpa Vita, see Beatrice
King, Nathaniel 339
Kinjikitile, prophet 482
Kinshasa (Léopoldville), Zaïre 509, 536
Kintu, Gabrieli 382–3, 467, 482
Kipalapala, Tanganyika 573
Kisingiri, Kizito Zakariya 380–1, 468–9, 482
Kisubi Mission, Uganda 471
Kisule, the gunsmith 377, 379, 381

Kisumu, Kenya 415
Kitagana, Yohana 470–2
Kitehimbwa, Mukama of Bunyoro 469
Kivebulaya, Apolo 470–1
Kivengere, Bishop 598
Kivuli, Zakayo 529, 537
Kiwanuka, Joseph, Archbishop of Kampala 565, 572–4, 608–9
Kiwewa, Kabaka 381
Knight, Charles 364
Knight-Bruce, Bishop of Mashonaland 268, 301, 325, 414, 439
Knoblecher, Mgr Ignaz 266, 268
Koelle, S. W. 280
Koko, King Frederick 349
Kolobeng, Matabeleland 242, 251, 275, 321
Kona, Samuel 440
Kongo 50, 71–129, 205, 312–13, 315, 373, 534, 538–9
  Antonian movement 104–8
  Baptists in 385–7
  Capuchins in 94–102, 104, 109–17, 127, 129, 194–6, 317, 387
  Carmelites in 90, 94
  evangelization from 1483 73–7
  Franciscans in 194
  Portugal and 73, 75–7, 81–7, 90, 93–4, 95, 103, 109, 111, 113–15, 143, 387
  slave-trade 125–6
  See also Afonso I; Ambuila, Battle of; Antonio, King; Beatrice; Congo; Garcia, King; Jesuits; São Salvador; Soyo
Korsten Basketmakers 521–2, 533
Koyi, William 439, 457, 483
Krapf, Johann 225–6, 232, 242, 280
Kugler, Christian 224
Kunyiha, Johana 519–20, 523
Kuruman Mission, South Africa 207–9, 211, 217, 242–3, 261, 293, 308, 424
Kuyowa, deacon 511–13
Kwaku Dua, King of Ashanti 309
Kyagwe, Buganda 466, 468

Ladysmith, South Africa 361
Lagos, Nigeria 279, 339, 341, 343, 352, 354–7, 374, 407, 449, 456, 463, 480, 493–5, 513–15, 523, 528
Lalibela, Ethiopia 4, 31, 161, 536
Lamaître, Mgr 423
Lambeth Conference (1888) 319, 496
Lambie, Dr Thomas 577
Lang, Martinus 164
Lavigerie, Cardinal Charles 250, 254–5, 267–8, 273, 276, 281, 289–90, 296–8, 374–6, 410, 416, 475, 565

Law, Augustus, S. J. 264
Laws, Dr Robert 213, 264–5, 291, 421, 439–40, 483, 489, 553, 557, 593
Lazarists 226–7, 232, 237
Le Roux, P. L. 499–501
Le Zoute Conference (1926) 553
League of Nations 491, 540, 546
Lebanon 153, 157
Lebna Dengel, King of Ethiopia 40, 46, 70, 130, 132–6, 138–40, 145, 150
Lefebvre, Marcel, Archbishop of Dakar 607
Legion of Mary 591–2, 603
Legon, Gold Coast 547, 604
Leipzig Society 414
Lejeune, Fr 420
Lekhanyane, Ignatius 501
Lenshina Mulenga, Alice 524–5, 533, 603
Leopold II, King of Belgium 399–400, 406, 410, 416, 431, 434–7
Lesotho, see Basutoland
Lewanika, King of Barotse/Lozi 256, 309–10, 312, 316
Lewis, Samuel 339–40, 346
Leys, Norman 552
Liberia 338, 344, 351, 355–6, 418, 443–4, 455, 507
Libermann, Francis 249, 255, 286, 295–6, 298
Lima, Dom Rodrigo de 46, 130
Limpopo, River 49, 256, 397, 413, 414, 425, 463
Lindley, Daniel 322
Lion, Eduard 501
Livingstone, David 217, 243, 247, 250–3, 255, 257, 259, 263–5, 268–9, 274–5, 277, 286–7, 289–90, 293, 295, 302–3, 308, 314, 320–1, 324, 326, 358, 366, 372–3, 409–10, 487
Livingstone Inland Mission (later American Baptist Missionary Union) 257, 318–19, 321, 385, 387, 435
Livingstone, William Jervis 487, 488–9
Livingstonia Mission, Nyasaland 212–13, 257, 259, 269, 276, 288, 291, 310, 315, 411, 421, 425, 439, 441, 453, 455–6, 458, 463, 483–5, 504–5, 522, 553, 557, 593–4
Livinhac, Mgr Leon W. F. 255, 375, 423, 475, 482
Lloyd, Canon Edgar 422, 433, 486, 559
Loanda, Angola 85, 89, 91–3, 96, 100–4, 112–13, 116, 119, 124, 195–6, 250, [?]
Lobengula, King of Matabeleland 311, [?] 412
Lobo, Jeronimo 124, 275
London 173–6

Mboya, Tom 553
Mbulu, Tanganyika 560
Medeiros, Simao de 93
Medical Missionaries of Mary 561
Meffre, Philip Jose, *babalawo* 353–4, 356
Membe, John 544
Mende people 324, 402
Mendes, Alphonsus, S. J. Patriarch 142, 154–8, 162, 225, 238
Menelik, King of Ethiopia 234–41, 367, 478, 546
Menezes, Aleixo da, Archbishop of Goa 155
Mengo, Buganda 374–5, 378, 382, 421
Battle of (1892) 411–12, 464
Merki, Bishop of Qasr Ibrim 68, 70
Merlaud-Ponty, William 407
Merolla, Girolamo 111
Merrick, Joseph 242
Methodism:
18th–early 19th century 179–82, 187, 206, 245, 283–4, 513
mid–late 19th century 245–7, 256–7, 339, 341, 343, 361, 363–4, 416, 433, 439–40, 449, 498
20th century 426, 447, 452, 454–5, 460, 479, 496, 505–7, 516, 527–8, 582–3, 594–5, 598, 604–5
see also Wesleyan Methodists
Mfantsipim, Gold Coast 545, 594, 604
Mfecane 311
Mhalamhala, Yoseta 441–2
Mhlangu, Elias 456, 501
Mika'el, Metropolitan of Ethiopia 3, 5, 44–5
Mika'el, *Ras* (Muhammed Ali) 165, 239–40
Mill Hill Fathers 415–16, 418
Minas, King of Ethiopia 141, 147
Missionaries of the Holy Heart of Mary 249
Missionaries of Our Lady of Africa, *see* White Fathers
Mityana, Buganda 377
Mizeki, Bernard 439
Mkandawire, Yaphet 522
Moffat, Emily 261, 264, 310
Moffat, John 263, 278, 282
Moffat, Mary 207, 209, 261
Moffat, Robert 205–9, 215–16, 221, 242, 247, 250, 253, 256, 259, 261, 270–1, 275, 279–80, 292–3, 303, 308, 313, 315, 325–6, 408
Mokone, Mangena 479–80, 497
Molele, Molimile 439
Mombasa, Kenya 122, 127–8, 143, 158, 242, 257, 404, 407, 410, 415, 574
Monclaro, Fr 78–9
Monrad, H. C. 334

Monrovia 338–9
Montesarchio, Jerome de 98, 100
Moravians 197–8, 206, 210, 232, 244–5, 263, 319, 414, 499, 576
Moreau, Fr S. J. 590
Morel, E. D. 436–7, 510
Morgenster, Rhodesia 455
Morland, Franz 270
Morrison, William 436
Moshoeshoe, King of Sotho 309, 311–12, 320
Mothibi, King of Thlaping 207–8, 308, 311, 366
Mott, John R. 420
Moussa, Pierre 373
Mozambique 46, 123, 406, 434, 441, 478, 540, 549, 563–4
Mozano, Gold Coast 536
Mpadi, Simon 513, 526
Mpondo people 323
Mqhayi, S. E. K., Xhosa poet 322, 361, 370–1
Msigala, Canon 277
Mtusu, Daniel 584
Mua Mission, Nyasaland 580
Mudeka, Nathaniel 468
Mugwanya, Stanislas 381, 464, 467, 473, 482
Muhammad Ali, *see* Ras Mika'el
Muhammad Bello, Sultan 191, 193
Mukasa, Ham 383–4, 466–7, 468, 477
Mukasa, Katikiro of Buganda 378–9
Mukasa, Victor 473
Mukono College, Uganda 597
Mulago, Vincent 608
Mulenga, Alice Lenshina, *see* Lenshina Mulenga, Alice
Mulolani, Emilio 601
Mumba, Levi 593–4
Murray, Andrew 499
Musajjakawa, Malaki 489
Musinga, King of Rwanda 475
Mussolini, Benito 546
Mutagwanya, Cypriano 466
Mutapa 49–50, 78–9, 120, 122, 478
Mutendi, Bishop Samuel 501–2, 536
Mutesa, King of Buganda 309, 371–2, 374–6, 378–9
Mvemba Nzinga, *see* Afonso I, King of the Kongo
Mvoti, South Africa 360, 362, 364
Mwanga, King of Buganda 312, 376, 378, 381–2, 464, 481–3, 598
Mwasi, Yesaya Z. 484–6, 522–4
Mzilikazi, King of Matabeleland 256, 308, 310, 320, 408
Mzimba, P. J. 480–1, 483, 498

Nagenda, William 597–8
Nairobi, Kenya 522, 553
Nalumansi, Princess of Buganda 379
Namaqualand 207
Namibia 207, 401–2, 578
Namugongo, Buganda 379–80
Nando, Leonardo da 112
Nandom, Gold Coast 577
Natal 243, 248–9, 286, 318, 358, 424, 483, 545, 606
National Congress of British West Africa 540
Native Baptist Church, Lagos 493–5
Naudé, Dr Beyers 560
Ndebele people 256, 300, 311, 329, 367, 412, 433, 438, 456
Ndelengeni, Dom Miguel 386–8
Ndongo, state of 50
Nederduitse Gereformeerde Kerk 569–70
Nemapore, Esau 522
Newton, John 178
Ngala, Ronald 553
Ngombe Lutete Mission, Congo 508, 510, 513
Ngoni people 311, 316, 439, 457, 492, 584
Ngqika, Xhosa King 200–1, 220–1, 271, 307–8, 315
Ngwato people 256, 309, 311, 367
Nicodemus, Abbot of Jerusalem 43
Niger Delta Pastorate 445
Niger, River 54, 191–2, 290, 313, 340–2, 358, 364, 385, 388–93, 417, 445, 449, 451, 498, 507, 573–4, 600
    Expedition (1841) 247, 251, 287, 344–5
    Royal Niger Company 346–9, 390, 417
Nigeria 262, 268, 345, 354, 356, 403, 418, 513, 541, 585, 599
    Baptists in 343
    Catholics in 343, 561–2, 603
    farming 289
    independence 546, 550
    Methodists in 343, 605
    Presbyterians in 605
    role of sultans 407
    secessions 479–80, 493–8, 514–15, 532
    transport 422–3
    See also Aladura; Church Missionary Society; Crowther
Nile, Upper 56, 67–9, 249, 253–4, 266
Nilotic Independent Mission 415
Nine Saints 9, 16, 28
Njonjo, Charles 553
Nkamba, Congo 452, 508–10, 513, 526, 536, 538–9
Nkhata Bay, Nyasaland 504
Nkonyane, Bishop Daniel 500, 502, 505, 526, 537

Nkrumah, Dr Kwame 547, 605
Nlemvo 386–8
Nob, Abba of Dabra Damo 36
Nobili, Roberto de 88, 148
Nogueira, Fr 158
North Nyasaland Association 593
Northern Rhodesia (Zambia) 422, 487, 528, 532–3, 601
    Catholics in 566
    and Central African Federation 549
    settlers in 543
Norway 205, 243, 256, 274, 276, 322, 412
Nova Scotians 176, 180–2, 184, 186–7, 197
Nsibambi, Simeoni 596–7
Nsundi, Kongo 90–1, 93, 97, 99, 106–8, 111, 115–17
Ntara, Samuel 584
Ntsikana 200, 218–21, 368–71, 439, 456, 480–1, 535
Ntsikana Memorial Association 371, 481, 606
Ntsikana Memorial Church 480
Ntsikana, William Kobe 370
Nubia 67–70, 139, 193
Nuer people 325, 327
Numidia 63
Nupe people 345
Nxele, prophet 200, 219, 271
Nyabadza, Francis 522–3, 533, 537
Nyakibanda, Rwanda 573
Nyakyusa people 324, 336
Nyanza, Kenya 574–5, 579
    See also Kavirondo
Nyasa, Lake 205, 252, 256–7, 265, 269, 291, 487
Nyasaland (Malawi) 406, 411, 433, 455, 457, 532, 544, 584
    Catholics in 475, 580
    and Central African Federation 549
    Chewa Nyau societies in 590–1
    impact of World War I 487–80
    missionary landholding 427
    secessions 522, 528
    settler politics 543
    transport 422–3
    welfare associations 593, 603
    See also Blantyre Mission: Chilembwe; Kamwana; Providence Industrial Mission; Seventh-day Baptists
Nyasaland African Congress 594
Nyau, secret society 324, 591–2, 600, 603
Nyeri, Kenya 426
Nyirenda, Tomo 329
Nyländer, Gustav 280
Nyonyintono, Honorat 377, 379, 381–2
Nyundo, Rwanda 573–4

Oblates of Mary Immaculate 248–9
Ockiya, Josiah Constantine 348
Odinga, Oginga 553
Ogbomoso, Yorubaland 578
Ogbonni, secret society 324
Ogere, Nigeria 516–17
Ogot, B. A. 558
Ogunbiyi, Archdeacon 515
O'Hea, Fr Jerome, S. J. 555
Okosi II, Obi of Onitsha 589
Oldham, J. H. 551–2, 555, 557–8
Oliver, Roland 583
Olubi, Daniel 354
Onitsha, Nigeria 277, 346–7, 388, 420, 589
Oppong, Samson 447, 449, 462
Orimolade, Moses 514–15, 518
Oromo, *see* Galla
Oshitelu, Josiah 516–17
Otta, Yorubaland 354
Otuedo, Edda 447
Ouidah, Dahomey 249–50, 275
Oviedo, Fr Andrew, S. J. 140–2, 147, 149, 151
Overtoun Institute, Nyasaland 291, 504, 593
Owen, Walter, Archdeacon of Kavirondo 556–7, 579, 593
Oyebode, R. S. 449, 460, 470
Ozolua, Oba of Benin 53, 77, 79

Pachomius, 4, 6–9
Padroado Real (1514) 72, 90, 95, 114, 118, 127
Paez, Pedro, S. J. 127, 142, 148–58, 161
Pallottines 418, 560
Palmer, Gustav 435
Pamla, Charles 363
Paris 249, 373, 607
Paris Evangelical Missionary Society 207, 256, 455
Parrinder, Geoffrey 567
Paul III, Pope 140
Paul V, Pope 112, 126
Paul, Mother 600
Pavia, Andrea da 111
Pearse, Samuel 352–4
Pedro II (Nkanga Mbemba), King of Kongo 91
Pedro IV (Nsamu Mbemba), King of Kongo 104, 106–8, 113
Pedro V (Elelo), King of Kongo 385–7
Pedro de San Salvador 195–6, 372
Pelly, Douglas 422
Penhalonga Station, Rhodesia 414, 422
Pentecostalism 499–500, 502, 514
Pereira, Pacheco 53
Perkins, Cato 180

Peters, Carl 399
Peters, Thomas 180
Phelps-Stokes Reports (1920, 1924) 491, 541–2, 562, 595
Philip, Durant 363
Philip, John 203, 206, 217, 247, 258–9, 285–6, 302, 304, 363, 365, 409
Pieve, Fr Agostino dalle 114
Pigafetta, Filippo 86–7
Pilkington, George 267, 279–80, 300–1, 422, 457, 481
Pinto, Joao 119
Pitt, William, the Younger 183, 282, 409
Pius VI, Pope 194
Pius VII, Pope 194
Pius IX, Pope 561
Pius XI, Pope 559, 564
Pius XII, Pope 561, 565, 603, 609
Plange, John 342
Platt, W. J. 506
Plowden, W., British Consul in Massawa 229, 231
Pombal, Marquis de 114, 123, 194
Poncet, Charles Jacques 162
Pondoland 330, 358
Port Elizabeth, South Africa 260, 418, 521
Portal, Sir Gerald 466
Porter, Canon 277
Portugal 249, 283, 386, 399, 413, 430
   in Angola 397, 416, 549, 563
   Baptists 387
   Catholics 177
   colonialism 411, 429, 550
   Concordat and Missionary Agreement (1940) 563–4
   in Ethiopia 46, 130, 133, 136–43, 149–50, 152, 156, 158
   Franciscans 194
   and Islam 406
   in Kongo 71–9, 81–91, 93–7, 100, 102–3, 109–11, 114, 118–21, 122–6, 128–9, 194, 196, 387
   in Mozambique 549, 563–4
   and settler politics 543
   and slave-trade 410–11
   in Zambezi region 397, 410
   See also Guinea-Bissau
Precious Stone Society 514
Premonstratensians 418
Presbyterianism 247, 256, 262, 311, 315, 341, 364, 369, 416, 418, 436, 479, 481, 498–9, 505, 524, 527, 584, 587, 591, 594, 598, 604–5
Prestage, Peter, S. J. 310–11
Pretoria, South Africa 497, 501
Price, Roger 261
Principe Island 118

Propaganda Fide, Sacred Congregation
of 88–9, 95–6, 102, 112–13, 123, 125,
127–8, 142, 153, 157–8, 164–5, 194,
248–9, 255–6, 286, 289, 295, 573
Protestantism:
18th century 174–81, 193, 197–8, 283
early–mid 19th century 207, 210, 225–6,
228, 243–7, 249, 270–2, 280, 293–6,
298, 318, 408
mid–late 19th century 232–3, 235, 256,
260–8, 274, 276–7, 286, 290, 293, 298,
304, 360, 367, 372, 374–7, 379–84, 408,
411–18, 441, 498, 503
late 19th-20th century 317, 318, 407,
419–20, 425–6, 429–30, 433–6, 455,
458–9, 464–7, 470, 472, 477–8, 480–1,
486, 489, 527–8, 532, 535, 550–63,
567–9, 572, 574, 577–9, 581–3, 587–8,
593–5, 598, 604–5, 607–8
See also Basel Mission: Church Missionary
Society; Church of Scotland;
Evangelicalism; London Missionary
Society; Methodism; Moravians
Protten, Christian 178
Providence Industrial Mission,
Chiradzulu 418, 486–7
Prutcky, Remedius 164

Quakers 183, 415, 424, 426
Quaque, Philip 178–9, 341
Quelimane, Mozambique 250
Quimulaza, Dom Pedro Manicongo
Ambamba de 115

Rabai, Mombasa 257
Rattray, R. S. 541, 554
Ravenna, Fr Eustachio da 113–14
Read, James 201, 203–7, 216–18, 259, 285,
287, 460
Read, James, Jr 217–18
Rebmann, Johann 242, 257
Redemptorists 418
Reeves, Ambrose 568–9
Regent, Sierra Leone 185–7, 209, 211, 339
Rhenish Mission 207, 428
Rhodes, Alexander de 88
Rhodes, Cecil 311, 366–7, 399, 412–14,
424, 427–9
Rhodesia 127, 268, 412, 414–15, 433, 440,
457, 481, 485, 532, 544
Catholics in 452, 560–1, 573
and Central African Federation 549
Dominicans in 121–2, 414
Jesuits in 333, 414, 424, 426
land grants 427
Methodists in 426, 452–3, 460, 595
settlers in 543, 556

Zionism in 501–2, 520
See also Apostolic Sabbath Church;
Bethlehem Fathers; Cripps
Ricci, Matteo 88, 112, 148, 153
Richards, Henry 315, 321, 387
Richartz, Francis, S.J. 433
Riddell, Alexander 310–11
Rikatla, Mozambique 442–3
Robinson, John Alfred 290, 389–92
Roboredo, Manuel (Francesco
Conghese) 93, 97, 103
Rodrigues, Gonçalo, S. J. 141, 147, 151
Rome 43, 86–9, 125, 126, 140, 147, 158,
253, 565, 572
Roscoe, John 304, 554
Rosebery, Lord 412, 415
Rosettenville, South Africa 455, 545, 548,
606–7
Rudd Concession (1888) 412
Rugambwa, Bishop Laurean 573–4
Rukwadzano 595
Rumfa, Muhammad, ruler of Kano 60–1
Rusape, Rhodesia 422, 522, 533–4
Ruwe, Kolwezi 601
Rwanda 50, 469, 474–5, 487, 532, 537, 564,
567, 576, 596, 607
Ryllo, Maximilian 249
Rzimarz, Giacomo 69

Sabagadis 222, 224
Sabiiti, Archbishop Erica 598, 608–9
Sabla Wangel, Empress of Ethiopia 138,
141, 159
Sabra, Abba, monk 15
Sadare, Joseph 514, 516–17
Sahara desert 49–50, 54–8, 397
Sahela Sellase 222, 224–6, 236
St Anthony, movement of 104–7
St Faith's Mission, Rhodesia 522
St Peter's College, Rosettenville 455, 545,
548, 606–7
St Thomas Christians 155, 157
Sakar, Alfred 242, 262
Salama, Abuna (1348–1388) 19, 29, 33,
Salama, Abuna (1841–1867) 228–9, 229–34,
235
Salazar, Antonio 431
Salomon, Dialungana K. 538
Salt, Henry 224
Salvation Army 414, 424, 513
Sandile, Xhosa Chief 368, 370
São Salvador de Bahia 106
São Salvador, Kongo 73, 76, 81–2, 86–7,
89–94, 96–7, 99–108, 110, 112–13, 116,
119, 194–6, 385–7, 421
São Tomé 72, 77–8, 83, 95, 118–20
bishop of 82, 85, 90

Saraqa-Birhan, Aqabe-Sa'at of Hayq 29, 32–3
Sarsa Dengel, King of Ethiopia 142, 148, 158
Saulmüller, K., missionary 232
Savona, Fr Cherubino da 114–17, 194
Saxony, Duke of 158
Sayfa-Ar'ad, King of Ethiopia 27
Schmidt, Georg 197–8
Schön, J. F. 242, 280
Schreuder, Hans 276, 280
Schweitzer, Albert 419
Scotland 174, 205–8, 217, 257–61, 264, 287, 291, 363
  and London Missionary Society 246–7
  mission landholdings 426–7
  See also Blantyre Mission; Church of Scotland; Elmslie; Fraser; Free Church of Scotland; Hetherwick; Laws; Livingstone; Livingstonia Mission; Moffat; Oldham; Philip, John; Soga, Tiyo; Stewart; World Missionary Conference
Scott, D. Clement 427, 429, 432, 557
Scott, H. E. 427
Scott, Michael 568–70
Sebastian, King of Portugal 78, 119
Sebastian, Mwane Mutapa 119
Sebastian, Olu of Warri 119–20, 127
Sebwato, Nikodemo 380–1, 466–8
Sechele, King of Bakwena 309, 311–12, 314, 320–1, 366
Sechuana people 325–6
Sekhoma, kgosi of Bamangwato 366
Selim I, Sultan of Turkey 46
Sena, Mozambique 78–9, 121, 123
Senegal 190, 295, 373, 397
Sengwayo, Mheke 522
Seraphim Society 515, 518
Seventh-Day Adventists 414–15, 522, 579
Seventh-Day Baptists 483–4
Shaka, King of the Zulus 311
Shanahan, Bishop Joseph 313, 418, 422–3, 450–1, 463, 560
Sharp, Granville 173–5, 179–80, 183, 284
Sharpeville, South Africa 549, 606
Shembe, Isaiah 241, 317, 503–5, 529, 534–6, 538
Shembe, Johannes Galilee 534, 538
Shire, River 252–3, 256, 410–11, 428, 486
Shoa, Ethiopia 3–4, 20, 22, 24–5, 31, 35, 137, 161–2, 164, 168–9, 222–4, 226, 229, 233–6, 239–40, 242
Shoko, Andreas 501
Shona people 301, 325, 438–9, 461, 482, 492
Shoniwa, John 531

Shoniwa, Peter (Johane Masowe) 520–2, 531, 533, 537
Sidamo, Ethiopia 240–1, 577–8
Sierra Leone 95–6, 119, 180–3, 185–7, 209–10, 213, 216, 245, 247, 249, 262, 280, 287, 326, 328, 339–43, 346–7, 350–2, 354–7, 363–4, 405, 418, 444, 454, 492–5, 497
Sierra Leone Company 180–1, 183–4, 284, 287
Silva, Belchior da 142
Silva, Lourenço da 125, 175
Silveira, Gonçalo da 78–9, 88
Sisters of the Infant Jesus 601, 604
Siti Kazurukumusapa (Dom Domingos) 121
Sjöblom, E. V. 435–6
Slessor, Mary 205–6, 260, 288
Smith, Edwin 327, 553–4
Smith, Joseph 179
Smith, Mathilda 202–3
Smith, Sydney 265
Smuts, Jan 548, 560
Smythies, Bishop 214, 291
Soares, Manuel Baptista, Bishop of São Salvador 90
Society of African Missions 240, 255, 275, 374, 418, 561
Society for the Civilization of Africa 251
Society for the Extinction of the Slave Trade 251
Society for the Propagation of the Gospel 178, 244
Society of Saint Patrick 560
Society of Scheut 416
Sofala, Mozambique 46, 50, 78, 122
Soga, Alan Kirkland 370
Soga, councillor to Ngqika 220, 368, 370
Soga, Festiri 368
Soga, Tiyo 260, 361, 363–4, 368–71, 480, 491
Sokoto, Nigeria 190–1, 193, 402
Solomon, John Ahoomah 342
Songhay empire 54, 58, 190
Sontonga, Mankayi Enoch 481
Sophiatown, South Africa 570
Sorur, Fr Daniel Deng Farim 374
Soshong, Botswana 256
Sotho people 207, 311, 438–9, 454, 463
South Africa 197–209, 259, 264, 292, 318, 358–66, 370–1, 401, 409, 438, 441, 537, 544, 556, 568–70, 605–6
  Catholics in 418
  colonialism 306, 398, 529, 540, 542–3
  Congregationalists in 322, 362, 364, 498
  education 360–1, 364, 545
  farming 289, 360, 362

South Africa (*cont.*):
female associations 595–6
impact of World War I 490–1
Methodists in 206, 363–4, 455, 479, 497, 595, 605
missionary landholding 359–60
Moravians in 197–9
Presbyterians in 498, 499
Protestants in 197, 207, 418–19, 499, 528, 553, 568
secessions 493, 497–9, 528–9, 532
transport 267–8
white Afrikaner nationalism 548–9
Zionism in 499–500, 502, 526–7, 533, 602
See also Bethelsdorp; Colenso; Genadendal; Kuruman Mission; Lovedale; Ntsikana; Philip, John; Zionism
South Africa Compounds and Interior Mission 415
South African Native National Congress 481
Soveral, Francisco de, Bishop of São Salvador 92–3
Soyo, Kongo 90–1, 96, 100, 106, 108–17, 127, 194, 217
Spain 71–2, 74–5, 88–90, 94–7, 101, 124, 126, 129, 150, 194
Spelonken, South Africa 441–2
Ssebowa, Alikisi 380–1, 465–7, 481–2
Ssematimba, Daniel 466
Ssemogerere, Timoteo 572
Ssese Islands, Buganda 382, 466
Stanley, Sir Henry Morton 257, 371–2, 374, 385, 399, 434–5
Steere, Edward, Bishop 265, 267, 280
Stefanites 39, 135, 227
Stewart, James 257, 264–5, 288, 361, 365, 439, 479–80, 483, 498, 557
Stoffels, Andries 217–18, 358
Stokes, Charles 263, 382
Storer, Francis 275
Streicher, Bishop Henri, W. F. 466–7, 473, 565–6, 572
Strydom, J. G. 548, 569
Stuart, Bishop 597, 599
Student Volunteer Movement 419
Stuurman, Bootsman 217–18
Sudan 50, 54, 56–8, 60–1, 234, 240, 248, 266, 270, 373, 423, 431, 469, 577, 598
Sudan Interior Mission 552, 577
Sudan United Mission 552
Sufism 189, 192
Sukuma people 403, 468
Sundkler, Bengt 534, 567
Susenyos, King of Ethiopia 127, 142, 149–52, 154–6, 158, 160–1, 230

Susu people 185–6
Svane, Pederson 178
Swatson, John 446–7, 449, 471, 533
Swaziland 501, 526, 532–3
Sweden 205–6, 319–20, 416, 435–6
Switzerland 196, 292, 438, 441–2, 560–1
Sylva, Dom Miguel Castro da 115
Sylva, Dom Pedro Constantino da, the Chibenga 104, 106–7

Tabennisi, Ethiopia 7
Tabora, Tanganyika 404, 406, 423
Takla Giyorgis, King of Ethiopia 165–7, 169, 223
Takla Hawaryat, Saint 41
Takla Haymanot 22, 24, 30, 164, 168
House of 28, 38, 45, 162–3, 227
Takla Haymanot of Adwa 227, 238, 241
Takla Haymanot, Negus (Ras Adal) 235
Takla Haymanot, Negus of Gojjam 240
Takla Iyasus 42
Talbot, P. A. 445, 541
Tambo, Oliver 594, 606–7
Tanganyika 319, 324, 401, 403, 414, 422–3, 455, 459, 469, 482, 487, 490, 532, 541, 543–5, 556, 560, 564, 566, 573, 576, 587, 598
Tansi, Fr Michael 335–7, 585, 591–2
Tasfa Seyon 140, 147
Tavares, Fr 94, 99
Taylor, John 347, 567, 580
Taylor, William 363–4
Tempels, Fr Placide 568, 601–2
Temple, Sir Charles 407
Temqat, feast of, 40–1
Teruel, Antonio de 97–8
Tewodros, King of Ethiopia 34, 229–34, 235, 236, 239
Texeira, Joao 80
Theopolis, South Africa 209, 216–17
Thévenoud, Johanny 567
Third Order of St Francis 601, 604
Thompson, Thomas 178, 326
Thuku, Harry 599
Tigre, Ethiopia 4, 9, 21–2, 25, 29–30, 137, 161–2, 222, 224–6, 229, 232–7
Tijaniyya 189, 191
Timbuktu, Mali 57, 59–61
Timotheos, Nubian bishop 68
Tindall, Joseph 315
Tlhaping people 207–8
Togo 418, 422, 434, 455, 607
Tonga people 504
Toro, Uganda 469–70, 473
Townsend, Henry 243, 262, 309, 343–5, 354

Transkei 256, 481, 600
Transvaal 251, 267, 441–2, 455, 501–2, 521, 543, 570
Trent, Council of (1545–63) 87
Trotha, General von 401
Tshatshu, Jan 217–18, 358, 368–9
Tsonga people 441–2, 454
Tswana people 286, 311–12, 365–7, 409, 438, 492
Tucker, Alfred, Bishop 268, 384, 392, 411, 429, 464–6, 468, 472
Tugwell, Bishop 392–3
Turkana people 325
Turkey 137–8, 141–2, 150, 189
Turner, H. M. 497
Tutu, Desmond, Archbishop of Cape Town 570, 610

Ufipa, Tanganyika 566, 578
Uganda 14, 261, 267, 278–9, 289, 304, 382, 392, 403–4, 411–15, 422, 432, 453, 455, 457, 469, 472, 474–5, 487, 489, 532, 537, 543–7, 556, 560, 564–5, 569, 573, 587, 599, 608
 Agreement (1900) 429, 466
Ujiji, Tanganyika 213, 404, 406
Ukerewe, Tanganyika 474
Umar Tal (al-Hajj Umar bin Said) 191–3
Umtali, Rhodesia 414, 426, 531
United African Methodist Church 496
United Gold Coast Convention 604
United Nations 547, 570
Universities' Mission to Central Africa (UMCA) 212, 214, 246, 252–3, 256–7, 260, 264, 269, 277, 291, 410, 414, 421, 423, 434, 455, 459, 487
Upper Volta 334, 567, 608
Ushirombo, Tanganyika 212–13
Usuman dan Fodio, Shehu 190–2

van der Kemp, Johannes 198–206, 216–19, 221, 273, 280, 285–6, 292, 296, 307–8, 315, 325, 370
van Sambeek, Jan 566, 578
Van Wing, J., S.J. 560
Vapostori Church 521, 522, 534, 537
Vassa, Gustavus, see Equiano, Olaudah
Vatican Council, First (1870) 254
Vatican Council, Second (1962) 607–9
Venn, Henry 279, 290, 293–5, 298, 309, 343, 345, 355, 357, 468
Venn, John 293
Verona Fathers 254–5, 418
Verwoerd, Dr Hendrik 548–9
Victoria, Lake 268–9, 371, 403, 468, 470, 474, 481, 545
Vieira, Fr Antonio 105–6

Vienna, Peace of (1815) 195, 206
Villa Maria, Buddu 466, 565
Villanova, Francisco de, Bishop 85, 119–20
Vives, Juan Baptist, Mgr 87–8, 94, 112, 127
Volker, Leo, W.F. 568–9

Waddilove, Rhodesia 562
Walatta Pietros 159–60
Waldmeier, Th. missionary 232–3
Walker, Archdeacon 304, 383, 429
Wallamo, Ethiopia 577–8
Wallo, Ethiopia 223, 233, 239–40
Walukaga, Nuwa 377, 379–80, 383
Warneck, Gustav 417
Warren, Max 567
Warri, Nigeria 96, 119–20, 127, 447
Wasukuma people 474–5
Watch Tower and Bible Tract Society 488, 504
Waterboer, Andries 216–18, 358
Webe, ruler of Tigre 222–4, 226, 228–9, 229, 231
Weld, Alfred, S. J. 264
Wesleyan Methodists 245, 315, 319, 342, 414, 446, 479, 490, 579
Wesleyan Missionary Society 179
Westermann, Diedrich 327
Westland, Nils 280
Weston, Frank 422
White Fathers 206, 393, 423, 456, 536, 564–9, 583
 in Buganda 257, 372, 374, 376, 381, 415, 467, 474–5, 477, 565, 572, 575
 clothing 206, 254
 in the Congo 416
 foundation 254–5, 418
 in French West Africa 423, 430
 in Gold Coast 577
 linguistic knowledge 267, 281
 and medicine 276
 mission villages 212–14
 in Northern Africa 255
 in Northern Rhodesia 561, 566
 in Nyasaland 422, 573, 580
 in Rwanda 573
 and slavery 410
 in Tanganyika 257, 414, 423, 566, 573
 in Uganda 416, 471, 565
White Fathers (cont.)
 See also Lavigerie
White, James 352, 354
White, John 280, 433, 559
White Sisters 426
Wilberforce, William 183, 245, 287, 410
Wilkinson, Moses 176
Williams, Joseph 206, 219–21
Woguera, Battle of (1543) 138

World Council of Churches 551, 606
World Missionary Conference (Edinburgh 1910) 317–18, 320–1, 324, 419–20, 550–1
World War I 402, 431, 487–92, 540, 552, 559, 561–2, 583, 603
World War II 525, 543, 546–50, 552, 564, 583

Xhosa people 199–201, 205–6, 216–21, 280, 307, 315, 325, 327, 359, 368–71, 438–9, 463, 492, 499, 544
Xintomane, Lois 441–2, 446

Yagbe'a Seyon, King of Ethiopia 42
Ya'iqob, Abuna 18, 25–7
Yao people 286, 406
Yikunno-Amlak, King of Ethiopia 20, 27
Yimrha-Krestos, King of Ethiopia 27
Yohannes I, King of Ethiopia 159, 162–3
Yohannes III, King of Ethiopia 223, 227
Yohannes IV, King of Ethiopia 234–6, 238–40
Yohannes, eccage of Ethiopia 147
Yoruba people, Yorubaland 53–4, 187, 192–3, 279, 307, 324, 326, 332, 334, 340–7, 350–8, 360, 364, 375, 402–3, 405, 440, 449, 492, 495, 497, 514–16, 518–19, 533, 550
Yosab, Abuna 167–9, 223
Young, Cullen 554

Za Dengel, King of Ethiopia 149, 151, 160

za-Krestos, Movement of 160
Zaïre (formerly Congo) 510, 518, 521, 532
Zaïre, River (Congo River) 73, 75, 107, 111, 117, 126, 261, 269, 385
Zakaryas, Sheikh (Newaya Krestos) 240–1
Zambezi Industrial Mission 486
Zambezi, River 49, 78, 120, 123–4, 251–3, 256, 257, 264, 267, 397, 401, 410, 420, 550, 569, 571
Zambia 403, 475, 481, 524–5, 532
See also Northern Rhodesia
Zanzibar 193, 211–12, 242, 256–7, 264, 291, 399, 402, 407, 410, 431–2
Zara Ya'iqob, King of Ethiopia 3–5, 19, 24, 28, 34, 43–4, 68, 134, 144, 150, 161, 166, 168
policies of 34–42
Zigubu, Frank 439
Zimbabwe 522, 532
See also Rhodesia
Zion Christian Church 501
Zionism 499–505, 520–1, 526–7, 533, 537–8, 602
Zionist Apostolic Church 500
Zoa, Jean, Archbishop 608–9
Zoungrana, Paul, Archbishop 608
Zulu Congregational Church 498
Zulu Mbiyana Church 498
Zulu people 205, 271, 274, 286, 309, 311–12, 333, 397–8, 412, 492, 499, 501, 503
Zululand 243, 256, 276, 322, 358, 412, 501, 536